Max Weber's *Economy and Society*

Max Weber's *Economy and Society*

A Critical Companion

Edited by CHARLES CAMIC,
PHILIP S. GORSKI,
and DAVID M. TRUBEK

Stanford University Press
Stanford, California

2005

Stanford University Press
Stanford, California
www.sup.org

Library of Congress Cataloging-in-Publication Data

Max Weber's economy and society : a critical companion / edited by Charles
Camic, Philip S. Gorski, and David M. Trubek.
     p.   cm.
   Includes bibliographical references and index.
   ISBN 0-8047-4716-4 (alk. paper)—ISBN 0-8047-4717-2 (pbk : alk. paper)
     1. Weber, Max, 1864–1920. Wirtschaft und Gesellschaft. English.
2. Sociology.   3. Economics—Sociological aspects.   I. Camic, Charles.
II. Gorski, Philip S.   III. Trubek, David M., 1935–
HM590.M39 2005
306.3—dc22   2004008169

Printed in the United States of America on acid-free, archival-quality
paper.

Original Printing 2005

Last figure below indicates year of this printing:

14   13   12   11   10   09   08   07   06   05

Designed and typeset at Stanford University Press in 10.5 / 12 Bembo.

For Guenther Roth

Contents

Tables and Figures

Tables

Figures

Acknowledgments

This volume has been several years in the making, and we wish to record, with deep appreciation, the many debts we have incurred throughout this period.

The chapters in the volume originated as papers presented in September 2000 at the International Symposium on "*Economy and Society*: Max Weber in 2000," organized by the International Institute at the University of Wisconsin, Madison. The institute provided staff and financial support for the Symposium. The Consulate General of the Federal Republic of Germany also gave valuable assistance for the event. Consul General Michel Engelhard encouraged the project and introduced the symposium, and consulate financial support made possible the substantial participation of German scholars in the Symposium. Additional support came from the Max Kade Foundation, the Anonymous Fund at the University of Wisconsin, Madison, and from several other units of the University: the Center for German and European Studies, the Institute for Legal Studies, the Departments of German, History, and Sociology, and the Religious Studies Program. We gratefully acknowledge the generous help we received from all these sources.

Earlier versions of several chapters have subsequently appeared in print. A previous version of Chapter 3 was published in *History and Theory* 39 (October 2000; volume 39, pp. 364–83) and appears here by permission of the author. A version of Chapter 9 was published in the *American Sociological Review* (December 2002; volume 67, pp. 832–53) and is reprinted here by permission of the author and the American Sociological Association. Portions of Chapter 11 appeared in Philip S. Gorski, *The Disciplinary Revolution: Calvinism and the Rise of the State in Early Modern Europe* (2003), and are published here by permission of the author and the University of Chicago Press. Finally, an earlier version of Chapter 12 was published in the *Journal of Classical Sociology* (September 2001; volume 1, pp. 171–94) and appears here by permission of the author.

This undertaking would not have been possible without the generous help of Guenther Roth, the intellectual force behind the complete English-language edition of Max Weber's *Economy and Society*, which first appeared in 1968. The doyen of Weber scholars and a gracious friend to generations of Weberians, he kindly lent us his wise counsel, in matters large and small, from the time we began planning our symposium until we sent this volume to press, patiently and skillfully diverting our missteps and steering us toward a better course. For this and much else, we are enormously thankful, and we gratefully dedicate this volume to him.

THE EDITORS

CHARLES CAMIC, PHILIP S. GORSKI,
and DAVID M. TRUBEK

Introduction

This volume of essays originates in a paradox. No work in the annals of sociology currently commands as much esteem among sociologists as the unfinished text by Max Weber known to English readers as *Economy and Society*. And yet, thirty-five years after the first full-length translation of the text into English and more than eighty years after its original publication in German, there is still no single volume that has *Economy and Society* as it main subject.

Despite its formidable bulk and density, *Economy and Society* looms as a rarity: a common rallying point in a highly fragmented intellectual discipline, a work from which sociologists of many different persuasions claim to draw intellectual inspiration and sustenance. When, for example, members of the International Sociological Association were asked in 1998 to name the most influential sociological work of the twentieth century, the victor, by a healthy margin, was Max Weber's *Economy and Society*.[1]

But *what is this work* that stands in such a revered place? Confronted with this question, curious students and scholars may feel as if they are attempting to construe the proverbial elephant from the disparate accounts of blind-folded observers, each of whom knows only a part of the animal in question. Some will tell them that *Economy and Society* is a manifesto for a particularizing and interpretive sociology. Others will describe it as a conceptual treasure trove from which to quarry causal generalizations about societal development. And these are only two of the guises that Weber's magnum opus has assumed in the literatures of sociology and the other social sciences.

In size and scope, *Economy and Society* truly is an elephantine work. The English translation consists of 1,372 pages, 356 sections, and 20 chapters, covering topics ranging from the conceptual foundations of sociology, to economic relations and political associations, to the world-historical dynamics of law and religion. Some parts of the book have been well covered by specialists, others less so. There is no work, however, that engages the book as a whole with the goals of providing an up-to-date introduction to its principal parts and of initiating a critical assessment of its form and substance. That is the purpose of the chapters in this volume.

I

We speak of *introducing Economy and Society* and, on this basis, *initiating* the task of critical assessment because the scholarly discussion of *Economy and Society* is still open, multivocal, and fluid, and any attempt to achieve closure on it at this point would be premature. As the chapters in this volume make clear, despite its considerable age, *Economy and Society* is still a living text subject to divergent interpretations and appropriations.

There is one area, however, in which a scholarly consensus seems to be emerging. It concerns the claim, first made by the German editors of Weber's collected works, that *Economy and Society* is in fact not a unified text at all, but a loosely linked assemblage of writings—most of them unfinished and in fragmented forms not intended by the author for publication—that Weber composed in starts and fits during the dramatic second decade of the twentieth century. But even this emerging point of agreement among specialists is scarcely known to non-German readers. What is more, the implications of this conclusion for the understanding and appropriation of Weber's ideas—and for any future rearrangement of the pieces of *Economy and Society*—are only now being discussed. (On both these points, see Chapter 3.)

But the textual integrity of *Economy and Society* is not the only point of critical ferment. Since the mid-1990s, the text has been opened up also by new research into Max Weber's life and ethical stance (see Chapters 1 and 2) and into the substance of his thinking about action, religion, political rulership, and the organization of economic activity (see Chapters 4–7). Meanwhile, other scholars have begun to reconsider the concepts of *Economy and Society* from alternative theoretical stances—pragmatist, feminist, Marxist, critical-legal—and to reassess its arguments in light of contemporary historical scholarship (on these points, see the essays in Part III).

While it is too early to know where these lines of work will lead, it is time that they were moved beyond the province of specialist debate. Through this book, we seek to make them accessible to the wider audience of social scientists, humanists, and their students, who wish to understand this text and to appropriate—or critique—its ideas. The volume is in three parts. Part I consists of three chapters focused on the contextual and textual background of *Economy and Society*; Part II of four chapters devoted to the exposition of the core sections of the text; and Part III of seven chapters that of-fer contemporary critical assessments and applications of various aspects of Weber's analysis. Before turning to a brief description of each chapter, how-ever, we outline Weber's general approach to the social sciences as it is ex-hibited in *Economy and Society*. Understanding this approach is key not only for understanding the text itself but for appreciating its continued relevance as well.

II

There is no single reason why scholars and students far beyond the ranks of Weber specialists continue to turn to *Economy and Society*. Quite apart from its historical significance as one of the intellectual foundation stones of the academic discipline of sociology, the text, even when viewed not as a unified book but as an assemblage of loosely connected pieces, enfolds topics and themes that continue to occupy social-scientific attention: human agency, *Verstehen*, the rationality of action, the division of labor, domination, class and status groups, the relation between religious and economic interests, and the nature of the dynamic processes—bureaucratization, disenchantment, ra-tionalization—that characterize the modern Western world, to give only a partial list. No wonder, then, that this text is recurrently mined, bit by bit.

To these reasons for *Economy and Society*'s continuing vitality we add an-other: the pertinence and fertility of Weber's vision of social science, a vision that seeks to overcome, rather than gloss over, certain fundamental antino-mies that have long structured—and that continue to structure—much so-cial-scientific debate: the individual versus society, the rational versus the nonrational, the material versus the ideal, structure versus agency, stability and order versus conflict and change, nomothetic generalization and expla-nation versus idiographic description and interpretation, and so on.[2] Of course, the relative salience of these antinomies has varied—and still varies—considerably across disciplinary space and scholarly time; each has had its place and its moment in the sun. And the relative independence of the var-ious antinomies from one another, their failure to map neatly onto one an-other, has made way for a large number of intellectual positions, further mul-tiplied by periodic efforts to carve out spaces between some of the polar extremes. Nonetheless, as Andrew Abbott has argued, the broad historical tendency has been for such dichotomies to surface again and again, splitting social-scientific fields, subfields, and sub-subfields into opposed camps, in ways that are not always generative of new empirical and theoretical in-sights.[3]

In the United States, for example, sociologists and political scientists are presently embroiled in heated debates about economic models of explanation, debates that pit proponents of rational-choice explanations, which center on individual interests and beliefs, against: (1) advocates of non- or anti-utilitarian approaches to action that emphasize (inter alia) values, culture, or emotions; and (2) advocates of non- or anti-individualistic forms of theorizing that highlight (inter alia) institutions, relations, and networks.[4] Subject to less open discussion, but even more entrenched, is the divide between those for whom social science is an effort to build robust explanatory generalizations that apply across time and space and those whose primary interest is to understand human actors and social processes by situating them in the context of particular times and places.

If this latter controversy is presently less engrossing and encompassing than it was in Max Weber's own time, this is not because generalizers and particularizers in the social sciences have generally found a satisfactory middle ground where they can coexist peaceably and productively. Rather, it is because the divide has so hardened that the two sides can simply ignore each other if they choose. This hardening can be observed across the contemporary social sciences, where economics now anchors the generalizing pole and cultural anthropology the particularizing pole, with political science (now) closest to economics, history closest to anthropology, and sociology somewhere between history and political science. This same hardening can also be observed within individual social-science disciplines, where subfields tend to be dominated either by generalizers (for example, in microeconomics, economic history, population geography, or physical anthropology) or particularizers (in cultural theory, cultural history, or cultural geography). The tension is especially pronounced in sociology, where it expresses itself in competing approaches to social theory (such as positivist versus antipositivist), as well as in contrasting methodological traditions (statistical analysis versus ethnography), with many subfields gravitating toward one pole or the other. (Thus subfields such as stratification, organizations, and social psychology are weighted more in generalizing directions, while urban sociology, the sociology of science, the sociology of culture, and historical sociology tend in more particularizing directions.)[5]

The distinct achievement of *Economy and Society*, among the classics of sociology, is to provide a means and a model for bridging this divide. Unfinished and fragmentary though it may be, Weber's text self-consciously stakes out a via media, or middle way, between universal law and cultural-historical description, the via media that he first mapped out in his early methodological writings and then reconnoitered in his studies of the world religions. In taking this stance, *Economy and Society* gives expression to the form of theorizing and of generalization appropriate to such a middle course. For this reason, Weber's work in laying this path merits close study, even in those instances where modern scholars, including some of the contributors to this volume, would dispute among themselves the accomplishment of Weber's efforts.

Indeed, while Weber scholars are sometimes at odds about the "success" of particular formulations in *Economy and Society*, they are widely agreed in understanding the book as an attempt to map a third way between the idiographic and nomothetic approaches. Guenther Roth described *Economy and Society* in these terms over three decades ago in his introduction to the full English-language translation,[6] and specialists on Weber's methodological work have often made the point as well.[7] Unfortunately, this point has not been sufficiently appreciated outside of specialist circles, where Weber's methodological writings are less well known. This has allowed social scientists at opposite poles of the idiographic/nomothetic divide to ransack *Economy and Society* for statements that appear to support their views, even when these views run counter to the central thrust of Weber's work.

To bring this aspect of *Economy and Society* squarely into focus, at a time when the split between generalizing and particularizing is deeply ingrained in American social science, is the object of the remainder of this Introduction. In the next section (Section III), we introduce *Economy and Society* to the general reader by briefly outlining some of the distinctive features of Weber's approach: causal explanation, *Verstehen* or interpretation, methodological individualism, and ideal types. In Section IV, we move backward in time and situate Weber's approach in its intellectual and historical context, the so-called *Methodenstreit*, or war of methods, between the German or historical school of economics, on the one hand, and the Austrian or theoretical school, on the other—a debate, in essence, about the merits and limits of generalization and particularization. In Section V we return to Weber to show how his own approach, culminating in *Economy and Society*, can be seen as an attempt to resolve the various issues raised by this debate—and thus to overcome the divide between generalizing and particularizing viewpoints. Finally, against this backdrop, we provide a brief overview of the chapters in this volume (Section VI).

III

An outline of Weber's approach may be found in the discussion "Basic Sociological Terms" that serves as an introduction to the English-language edition of *Economy and Society*. This section of the text was written in 1919, shortly before Weber's death, and was first published in 1921. It is a revision and expansion of an earlier essay that Weber published in 1913 and was one in a long series of essays on the "methodology of the social sciences" that occupied him, on and off, during the final two decades of his life,[8] as he carved out his own position in the intellectual debate that we describe in the next section. As such, "Basic Sociological Terms" is the culmination of nearly twenty years of systematic reflection and, as Weber's final statement on this subject, an effective encapsulation of the position at which he had ultimately arrived.

Weber opens this section of *Economy and Society* with his well-known definition of sociology as "a science concerning itself with the interpretive understanding of social action and thereby with a causal explanation of its course and consequences."[9] Here, we already glimpse two hallmarks of the Weberian approach: the emphasis on "interpretive understanding" and "causal explanation" and the connection between the two. Let us examine each in turn, beginning with the latter, causal explanation. The emphasis on causal explanation is important because it marks off Weber's sociology from two other, closely related endeavors of his time: the exhaustive description of specific events, which was the avowed goal of a certain kind of historical writing that was widespread in this period,[10] and the complete recovery of symbolic meanings, such as those embodied in written texts (e.g., the Bible), which was the goal of hermeneutical disciplines, such as the critical readings of the Bible, which were also immensely influential during Weber's time. While Weber regards the endeavors of "understanding" and "explanation" as distinct in aim, he does not regard them as separate in practice. Quite the contrary. For Weber, descriptive and interpretive accuracy is a key measure of an explanation's "adequacy"; an explanatory account that captures and integrates what we know about the intentions and actions of real individuals, he says, is always preferable to one that does not. For the sociologist, however, interpretive and descriptive accuracy is a means and a metric, rather than an end in itself. The goal of sociological analysis is not to capture all the nuances and complexities of human meaning and intention, but to enter these issues to the degree necessary to render the analyst's account plausible to other observers, who are familiar with the issues and evidence in question.

Weber's definition not only draws a line between sociology and the neighboring hermeneutic disciplines; it also distinguishes his vision of sociology from competing visions. For example, by making causal explanation (of concrete courses of social action) the primary goal of his sociology, Weber distances himself from evolutionary and positivistic versions of sociology, such as Spencer's and Comte's, that sought to discover "universal laws" of social development. This is not to say that Weber denies the existence of social-scientific laws, at least in the loose sense of observable regularities or recurring patterns (such as the "laws of supply and demand," which govern price-setting within capitalist "free markets"). What Weber *does* dispute is the priority given to the search for "universal laws" in these and other sociologies. For Weber, general laws are a means for understanding "concrete reality" (*Wirklichkeit*), rather than ends in themselves. Thus the development of social theory should always be subservient to—and propelled by—the construction of causal explanations.

Weber's sociology is distinguished from other disciplines and other sociologies not only by its *goals*, the priority that it gives to causal explanation, but also by its *means*, its use of interpretive understanding (*Verstehen*). Interpretive understanding, in Weber's usage, is the attempt to reconstruct the intentions behind a particular complex of human actions. To be sure, this is easier said than done because access to, and information about, individual motivations are usually imperfect and incomplete. Weber therefore recommends that the sociologist begin by provisionally treating all action as "rational," that is, as oriented to the conscious pursuit of clear ends, whether material (such as wealth and power) or ideal (salvation or honor).[11] If the actual course of an action cannot be understood in rational terms—as in the case, say, of a panic on the stock market—sociologists should then turn their attention to nonrational forms of action—that is, to types of action driven by habit or emotion, where actors do not have conscious or clear ends in view. But in so doing, says Weber, the sociologist must always be careful to avoid a "rationalistic bias"; that is to say, the sociologist must not assume, prima facie, that the most rational account is necessarily the most accurate one. Generally speaking, in cases where the same action is susceptible of more than one interpretation—which is to say, the overwhelming majority—the analyst should always give preference to the explanation that possesses the highest degree of descriptive accuracy and interpretive plausibility, the one, in other words, that best fits what is known about the actual course of action and the subjective purposes behind it, and *not* simply the one that best fits one's personal intuitions or a priori assumptions about "human nature."

It should be noted that these standards of explanatory adequacy differ from those prevalent in the physical sciences, at least according to certain philosophical renderings of these sciences.[12] On the one hand, Weber's standards are more demanding insofar as they require a plausible account of subjective intentions, something that is neither necessary nor possible in the study of inanimate matter.[13] On the other hand, they are less demanding insofar as they do not involve the invocation of a general law that "predicts" or "covers" the outcome in question—the sine qua non of scientific explanation for some philosophers. In this regard, too, Weber sees the aims and possibilities of social science as related to, but distinct from, those of the humanities and the physical sciences. In his view, the social sciences are united with the humanities (*Geisteswissenschaften*) by their concern with human particularity and subjective meanings, but divided from them by their focus on causal explanation and their use of simplified and generalized interpretations. With the natural sciences, they share the goal of explanation, but are distinguished from them by the structure, standards, and object of explanation. Thus, on the question of whether the social sciences are one with the physical sciences or more closely related to the humanities, Weber adopts an intermediate position.

A third hallmark of Weber's sociology is "methodological individualism."[14] As outlined in *Economy and Society*, methodological individualism means for Weber: (1) that social groups and social institutions (for example, social classes and nation-states) are made up of individual human beings; (2) that the "actions" of such groups and institutions are ultimately the result of individual actions; and (3) that groups and institutions only exist if, and to the degree that, individual action is oriented toward them. The contributors to this volume offer different assessments of this strand in Weber's thinking; in Chapter 4, for example, Donald Levine faults this feature of Weber's work for leading to a neglect of social interaction, while in Chapter 5 Richard Swedberg accents Weber's manner of moving "from single individual actions, to social relationships, to organizations and other complex configurations" (see also Chapter 6). Regardless of these differences, however, the contributors broadly agree that Weber's methodological individualism was not designed to expunge "class," "state," or other relational, organizational, and structural terms from the sociological lexicon. For Weber, methodological individualism serves, rather, as a precaution, a precaution against the intellectual dangers of hypostatizing groups and institutions into thinking and acting subjects. Weber's intention in adopting this principle was to distance himself from other schools of thought (such as Marxism and historicism) that treated groups or institutions (such as social classes and nation-states) as the "real subjects of history," as collective actors with unified interests or values.

The fourth hallmark of Weber's sociology—and one with special relevance to his via media, as we will see—is the use of "ideal types." Weber's ideal types are conceptual constructs that are ideal in the sense that they are abstractions from, and hence simplifications of, concrete social reality, rather than mirrors or full depictions of it. And they are types insofar as they seek to capture what from the analyst's viewpoint are "typical" features of this complex reality—a determination that can only be made in light of extensive historical and comparative knowledge. In Weber's usage, then, ideal types are analytical tools that help the investigator to identify recurring features of the sociohistorical world: action patterns, kinds of social actors, interactional forms, relational configurations, organizational structures, developmental processes, and so on.[15] As such, ideal types constitute benchmarks or yardsticks that enable the researcher to recognize what is general and what is specific in a particular object of investigation. In *Economy and Society*,

Weber explains his thinking here as follows (also making reference to several of the other themes we have discussed):

We have taken for granted that sociology seeks to formulate type concepts and generalized uniformities of empirical process. This distinguishes it from history, which is oriented to the causal analysis and explanation of individual actions, structures, and personalities possessing cultural significance. The empirical material which underlies the concepts of sociology consists to a very large extent, though by no means exclusively, of the same concrete processes of action which are dealt with by historians. An important consideration in the formulation of sociological concepts and generalizations is the contribution that sociology can make toward the causal explanation of some historically and culturally important phenomenon. As is the case of every generalizing science, the abstract character of the concepts of sociology is responsible for the fact that, compared with actual historical reality, they are relatively lacking in fullness of concrete content. To compensate for this disadvantage, sociological analysis can offer a greater precision of concepts. This precision is obtained by striving for the highest possible degree of adequacy on the level of meaning. It has already been repeatedly stressed that this aim can be realized in a particularly high degree in the case of concepts and generalizations which formulate rational processes. But sociological investigation attempts to include in its scope various irrational phenomena, such as prophetic, mystic, and affectual modes of action, formulated in terms of theoretical concepts which are adequate on the level of meaning. In *all* cases, rational or irrational, *sociological analysis abstracts from reality and at the same time helps us to understand it in that it shows with what degree of approximation a concrete historical phenomenon can be subsumed under one or more of these concepts.* For example, the same historical phenomenon may be in one aspect feudal, in another patrimonial, in another bureaucratic, and in still another charismatic.[16]

While, as Weber writes elsewhere, "it is the subsequent task of history to find a causal explanation for these specific traits,"[17] as a contribution to sociology, *Economy and Society* is essentially a multilayered compendium of ideal types, generated by means of historical comparison, that Weber offered to furnish a way out of the fierce methodological controversy that polarized his contemporaries.

IV

The controversy in question was the *Methodenstreit*—the war of methods—that erupted between the historical and neoclassical schools of economics during the 1880s and continued on into the early years of the twentieth century. In this controversy, Weber encountered powerful arguments in favor of both generalizing and particularizing approaches to social scientific knowledge, though in neither case did these arguments stand in isolation. From both sides, they appeared intertwined with other fundamental antinomies of social scientific thinking.

The chief protagonists in this "war," though by no means its only protagonists, were Gustav von Schmoller and Carl Menger.[18] Schmoller was the
doyen of the "historical" or "ethical school" of economics and a major
mover and shaker in the German academic system during the late nineteenth century. Like the founding fathers of the "older" historical school,
Wilhelm Roscher, Bruno Hildebrand, and Karl Knies, Schmoller was highly
critical of the classical school of political economy that emerged in Britain
during the late eighteenth century, with its "atomistic" view of the social
world and its emphasis on self-interest.[19] Menger, by contrast, was a younger
scholar, and a passionate defender of the British tradition. Today he is revered
not only as the founder of the Austrian school of economics, but also as a
leader of the neoclassical revolution that eventually swept to power in that
discipline.[20] In the 1880s, however, Menger's views were still on the margins,
at least on the Continent, and in 1883 he published a defense of them entitled *Untersuchungen über die Methode der Socialwissenschaften und der Politischen
Ökonomie insbesondere (Investigations into the Method of the Social Sciences)*.[21]
The book was at once an attack on the "historical method," as understood
by the German school, and a defense of the "formal theory" of the British
school, as Menger interpreted it. Schmoller responded with a searing review
of Menger's book, which devolved at times into an ad hominem attack.[22]
Menger rejoined with a second, more vitriolic book entitled *Die Irrthuemer
des Historismus in der Deutschen Nationalokonomie (The Errors of Historicism in
the German School of National Economics)*.[23] Schmoller never replied directly
to this second attack, but he continued to defend the historical approach,
and to attack the neoclassical approach, in several of his later works. Although Menger fell silent, he spent many years working on a definitive statement of his methodological position, which he never completed. However,
his followers took up the cudgel, and there were several more skirmishes in
the ensuing decades.

The issues raised by the *Methodenstreit* were multiple. They included problems of method, of course, but also deeper questions about the nature of
social reality and the character of social-scientific knowledge, as well as disciplinary issues about the internal structure of economics and its proper relationship with the other social sciences. The positions taken by the participants were also multiple—and changing. Thus Schmoller's views were
somewhat different from those of the "older" historical school, and they
evolved further in the course of his career. This is not the place to discuss
this debate in its full complexity, since our primary goal here is to contextu-
alize Weber's position. Hence we focus mainly on the writings of Menger
and Schmoller, and especially on those points of contrast that seem most relevant for understanding Weber's vision of sociology and the social sciences.
Specifically, we focus on issues of: (1) methodology and epistemology; (2)

ontology and causality; and (3) priorities and boundaries. Doing so will help to clarify Weber's views on causal explanation, interpretation, methodological individualism, and ideal types, as well as his broader position on the possibilities and limitations of nomothetic and idiographic approaches in the social sciences.

METHODOLOGY AND EPISTEMOLOGY

The historical school espoused what we might call a *comparative-inductive* method.[24] In this vision of the research process, repeated "observations" of economic phenomena would serve as the evidentiary basis for the discovery and confirmation of empirical patterns and regularities and, ultimately, for the formulation of economic "laws." The first step in the process was "classification," understood in quasi-zoological terms as the grouping together of different "species" of economic activity (for example, agriculture, manufacture, finance) and of the various "organs" of an economic system (guilds, merchants, financiers, and others). The results of this enterprise can be seen in the various "handbooks of economic science" produced by the older historical school during the mid-nineteenth century.[25] From the standpoint of the historical school, the next step in the research process consisted of "description," meaning the identification of "equivalences, similarities, correlations, effects, and contexts."[26] The chief yield of this work was narrative histories of particular policies, industries, or national economies (such as mercantilism, or silk production in Germany) of the sort produced by Schmoller and other members of the "younger" historical school.[27] The ultimate goal of such work was a "universal history" of economic life in all times and places, which could serve as the basis for a "general theory" of economics. Not surprisingly, this goal remained—and remains—unfulfilled. While the historical school generated many descriptive works of economic and social history, some of which are still read today, it produced very little in the way of economic or social theory.[28]

Members of the historical school did not devote great reflection to the philosophical underpinnings of their method—they tended to be somewhat disdainful of "philosophical speculation"—but the epistemological assumptions implicit in their approach might best be described as a form of *naïve empiricism*, not unlike that of John Locke. Their view was empiricist in the sense that knowledge about causality is seen as the (relatively unproblematic) product of observation, repeated over time. When the researcher observes a recurring conjunction between two events, he or she infers a causal connection between them. This position was naive insofar as it failed to address two old and important critiques: (1) Hume's critique of Locke, namely, that the observation of a regular conjunction between two events does not necessarily imply the existence of a causal connection between them, at least not from a strictly logical point of view; and (2) Kant's rejoinder to Hume, namely, that causality is not a relationship between things-in-themselves (noumema), but between things as they appear to be (phenomena)—that is, between our perceptions of reality as structured by the pretheoretic categories of our understanding. What the historicists failed to consider, then, was how and if particular observations could be translated into general theories and how particular observations themselves were structured by pretheoretic categories.

Menger fully recognized these problems. He realized that universal laws of economic life could not be generated through historical induction. And he also realized that even the most naively descriptive forms of historical research "cannot dispense with certain abstractions."[29] His solution to these problems was radical: he prescribed a complete divorce between economic theory and economic history. Since universal laws cannot be derived from historical observations, Menger reasoned, they must be based on a priori assumptions. Conversely, since the laws of economics do not obtain in the real world, economic events must be accounted for in purely historical terms. Furthermore, because the ends of economic theory and economic history are fundamentally distinct—universal laws in one case, particular causal explanations in the other—their methods must also be distinct. Economic history must be based on an "empirical-realistic" method, which employs "real types" to identify "empirical laws." By real types, Menger understood "basic forms of real phenomena, within the typical image of which . . . a more or less broad scope is given for particularities." By empirical laws, he meant "theoretical knowledge which makes us aware of the actual regularities (though they are by no means guaranteed to be without exception) in the succession and coexistence of real phenomena."[30] Economic theory, in contrast, must be based, according to Menger, on a methodology of "pure types" and "exact laws." The first step in this kind of theoretical research, argued Menger, is the "purification" of economic reality, the removal of all its noneconomic aspects. Having reduced the economic system to its "simplest elements," the exact theorist can then seek the laws that govern the interaction of these elements. The result, according to Menger, will be laws that are as "exact" as those that obtain in mathematics or geometry. Because they obtain only for the pure entities of economic theory, however, these laws cannot be used to explain or predict the concrete events of economic history. But this does not impugn their validity. "To want to test the pure theory of economy by experience in its full reality," countered Menger, "is a process analogous to that of the mathematician who wants to correct the principles of geometry by measuring real objects. . . . Realism in theoretical research is not something higher than exact orientation, but something different."[31] Nonetheless, Menger believed that the laws of economics could eventually be combined with other laws of social behavior to generate a unified and predictive theory of social life.

Like Schmoller, Menger made little effort to spell out the philosophical assumptions that underlay his method. But modern scholars tend to describe it as an *essentialist-realism* with Aristotelian roots.[32] According to this view, the world consists of various classes of objects. All elements of a class have certain essential properties that allow the researcher to identify these elements *as* members of that class. Individual objects may have also have incidental properties that one must separate out to grasp their essential properties, much as the chemist removes the impurities from a metal sample before trying to determine the general properties of the metal, with the important difference that, in economic science, this purification is achieved *conceptually* rather than physically, by imagining a pure *homo oeconomicus* motivated exclusively by material self-interest. The "exact laws" of theoretical economics obtain only between these underlying essences, not between their actual empirical embodiments. Consequently, these laws cannot be tested or refuted by empirical observations, since these will necessarily be observations of an impure reality, a reality that cannot be purified in practice (in contrast to physical elements, like metals, which can be purified). But while economic theories may not be "realistic" in the sense of capturing the complexity of reality, or explaining real events, asserted Menger, such theories nonetheless capture the *underlying* reality of economic life. Menger's theory is thus a realist theory, in the philosophical, as opposed to commonsensical, meaning of the term, insofar as it claims to describe underlying elements and unobservable properties of reality.

ONTOLOGY AND CAUSALITY

But what are the simplest elements of economic life? For Menger, there were just three: individuals, interests, and goods. The exact theory of economic life, he argued, must begin by assuming an a priori world of self-interested individuals competing for scarce resources. Why? Because the real phenomena of economic life can always be traced back to "the innumerable individual economic efforts in the nation," and because self-interest is "the most original and the most general force and impulse of human nature."[33] Thus Menger is not simply a *methodological* individualist, who views *homo oeconomicus* as a fruitful starting point for economic analysis; he is an *ontological* individualist, who views the rational individual as a historical universal. His argument for formal theory is thus motivated not only by methodological considerations, but by metaphysical ones as well, and it is for this reason that he issued a rhetorical appeal to common sense—common-sense understandings about the reality of individuals and the prevalence of self-interest—for this is the only way he had to ground his purely metaphysical argument. As such, his argument contains at least two crucial assumptions that could be, and have been, called into question. The first is that complex processes can, and should, always be explained in terms of their simplest elements, that is, that valid explanations always proceed by means of reduction. The second is that individuals and interests are the simplest elements of economic life and, as such, incapable of still further reduction—for example, to warring drives, as in a psychodynamic model of the self, for example, or to conflicting roles, as in a sociodynamic model.

Menger himself did not draw out the implications of this ontology for an understanding of causation.[34] But other members of the Austrian school did. They argued that all phenomena of social life must be traced back to individual actions, a position that contemporary philosophers refer to as the *genetic* theory of causality. In this view, any supra-individual entity, such as a group or an institution, can never be the cause of anything in any philosophically meaningful sense because these entities *do not really exist* (any more than do sub-individual entities like drives or roles). Accordingly, the events of economic life can—and *must*—be traced back to the level of individual actions and to the beliefs and interests that drive them because this level is the seat of reality. This position is similar to the one adopted by many contemporary rational-choice theorists, when they insist that all social-scientific explanations can and should be given explicit "micro-foundations."

The position of the historical school on questions of ontology and causality was quite different. Rejecting the reductive "atomism" of the British approach, the historicists argued that the whole is usually greater than the sum of its parts and that the parts are always shaped by the whole. The historicists did not deny the existence of individual economic actors or material self-interest. However, they did argue that:

1. individual economic actors are embedded within particular national economies or other economic communities;

2. the economy itself is embedded within a larger culture or society—the nation-state within modern Europe (this is why the historicists sometimes referred to themselves as "national economists");

3. the economic behavior of individual actors is strongly influenced by (a) nonmaterial motives, such as custom and morality, and by (b) noneconomic institutions, such as law and the state (for which reason historicists also referred to their approach as "ethical").[35]

The position of the historical school could thus be described as *methodological holism*, insofar as it regarded both individual and supra-individual actors as real, but then took the latter as its analytic starting point.

This methodological holism usually went together with an *organic* theory of causality in which the current state of a particular whole (a national economy, for example) is understood as the product of some previous whole (the history of that particular economy), rather than of the past actions of its constituent parts (individual actors). In this sense, the operations of any specific part of the economy can only be understood with reference to the whole. This position is organic both in treating national economies as organisms that grow and evolve and in viewing the constituent parts of national economies as organs that fulfill certain functions within that whole. This perspective is similar, and in some ways nearly identical, to the positions advanced by American institutionalist economics in the early twentieth century and by scholars in comparative political economy in the late twentieth century.

PRIORITIES AND BOUNDARIES

As one might expect, these differences in methodological strategy and philosophical assumption were closely connected with differences in scholarly priorities and disciplinary boundaries. While Schmoller and Menger both saw the empirical study of concrete economic phenomena and the attempt to formulate economic laws as legitimate goals for economic science, they assigned them very different priorities. For Schmoller and the historicists, describing specific economies and explaining particular economic phenomena were methodologically prior—and politically paramount. For Menger and the neoclassicists, in contrast, the development of exact theories and universal laws was philosophically prior—and theoretically superior.

These differences in scholarly priorities were connected with differences of disciplinary vision. The historicists conceived of economics as a substantively broad, theoretically diverse enterprise that would have close relations not only with history, but with work on law, religion, psychology, and politics, to name only a few. Today, the kind of economic research that they envisioned is done mainly *outside* of economics in certain quarters of history, sociology, and political science (for example, by economic historians, historical sociologists, and political economists). Menger and the neoclassicists advanced a narrower and less pluralistic vision of economics, with a clear division of labor both within economics (between the "empiricists" and the "theorists") and between economics and the other social sciences. As is well known, it is their vision that eventually triumphed in economics and, increasingly, at the generalizing end of the social scientific enterprise *tout court*, at least in the United States.

Of course, the lines of intellectual descent are quite tangled and often obscured. Contemporary proponents of generalizing and particularizing do not necessarily see themselves as Menger and Schmoller's offspring; nor do they understand their disagreements as a continuation of the *Methodenstreit*. Indeed, the memory of these men and their battle is alive only within small circles of specialists. Perhaps this is as it should be. Neither, however, do these contemporary proponents typically present or defend their visions with the care, the nuance, and the self-consciousness that Menger and Schmoller brought to the task. From well-formulated and passionately articulated intellectual positions, the generalizing and particularizing alternatives have evolved into unreflectively held academic habitus, no less consequential for all their taken-for-granted character. In this respect Max Weber was dealt a better hand: coming on the scene in the midst of the *Methodenstreit*, he was historically situated to confront the issues head-on and to point a way beyond them. And it is in *Economy and Society* that he puts this via media into practice.

V

Weber was well aware of the players and issues involved in the *Methodenstreit*. As a student, and later a professor, of economics at several German universities, including Humboldt University, where Schmoller reigned supreme, he could not help but be aware of it.[36] But where did he stand on the issues it raised? From a casual inspection of Weber's life and work, one might presume that his sympathies lay with Menger. As a student in Heidelberg, Weber found Knies's lectures on economic history insufferably dull. Later, in middle age, while recovering from his nervous breakdown, he published three essays on the "historical approach," one on Roscher and two on Knies, all highly critical. Then, toward the end of his life, he became engaged in a heated debate with Schmoller and other advocates of the "ethical" approach to economics over the relationship between "facts" and "values" in social science research—the so-called value-judgment debate (*Werturteilsstreit*).[37] Thus it is not entirely surprising that younger members of the Austrian school, like Friedrich von Hayek, would later claim Weber, after his death, as one of their own. After all, did Weber not advocate a theoretical and typological approach similar to Menger's?

But the Austrians were not the only ones to stake a claim to Weber's legacy. Chronicles of the historical school often speak of Weber as a member of the "third generation" (*jüngste Generation*) of historicists, alongside Joseph Schumpeter, Werner Sombart, and Georg Simmel.[38] And not without justification. For the bulk of Weber's scholarly work was comparative and historical, rather than formal and theoretical, and even on the surface *Economy and Society* has more in common with Roscher's and Knies's handbooks on national economics than with Menger's treatise on marginal utility theory. Indeed, it was commissioned as part of just such a handbook! While Weber never devoted an entire essay to Menger or the Austrian school, his methodological works are laced with critical references to the "exact" approach and "formal" theory in economics, as is seen in *The Protestant Ethic and the Spirit of Capitalism*, whose premise is the *historicity* of *homo oeconomicus* and the *cultural specificity* of economic rationalism. The idea that economic rationalism is a cultural universal, Weber once snapped, should be unlearned in the "kindergarten of cultural history."[39]

So what is Max Weber? An early neoclassicist, or a late historicist? The truth, as specialists have long contended, is that he was both—and neither. The distinctiveness of Weber's approach derives precisely from his effort to steer a middle course between—and beyond—the two schools. Hence it is no exaggeration to say that Weber's vision of what social science can and should do emerged out of his critical engagement with the historicists and the neoclassicists and represented an attempt to transcend their opposition by bringing to the project of examining the interaction between economy and society in its multiplicity a typological sociology that combines the substantive breadth of the historical school with the analytical rigor of the neoclassicists.

To see this, let us return to the methodology of ideal types that is the compass for the Weberian via media. The expression "ideal type" recalls Menger's concept of "exact" or "pure types," and indeed, Weber sometime preferred the phrase "pure type" in his later writings.[40] But this does not mean that Weber's position was becoming more similar to Menger's. Far from it. For Weber's types—whether "pure" or "ideal"—are not attempts to distill some underlying universal essence behind the appearances, after the fashion of Menger's. Rather, they are "abstractions" built of repeated (comparative and historical) observation of the particulars found in social reality, a process whose chief goal is to identify crucial historical and cultural *differences*. Hence Weber's types are actually closer to what Menger referred to as "realistic-empirical types" and not entirely unlike the "classifications" espoused by the historical school. Unlike Menger, however, Weber does not see the two kinds of typologization—exact and empirical-realistic—as equally valid and useful. He argues that "abstract economic theory" has "the character of a *utopia*," and that the more universal a theory is, the less it furnishes the kind of generalization that serves to illuminate particulars.[41] Abstract theories may serve a heuristic function in the early stages of research, says Weber, but they should give way once more realistic and nuanced concepts have been developed by means of systematic historical and cross-cultural comparisons. For Weber, Menger's exact types would have formed a useful starting point for social analysis, but certainly not a desirable end point.

The Weberian ideal type may thus be seen as a methodological device for negotiating the conflicting demands of historical accuracy and theoretical precision. That said, it would be wrong to see Weber's method simply as a practical response to the quotidian problems of social research. It was also a philosophically motivated attempt to put social science on firmer epistemological footing. Weber firmly rejected historicist claims that observation is independent of theorization and that (universal) laws can (eventually) be induced from (descriptive) history. Like Menger, he regarded commonsense empiricism of this sort as hopelessly naive. But while he agreed with Menger's statement of the problem, he did not accept his essentialist "solution." Weber is a Kantian.[42] For him, the notion that one can grasp the "essence" of reality reeks of precritical metaphysics, violates the Kantian distinction between phenomena and noumena, and blatantly oversteps the limits and possibilities of human reason. Indeed, Weber goes one step further than Kant, arguing that our observations of social phenomena are affected not only by pretheoretical or logical categories, but also by the investigator's disciplinary and conceptual constructs (such as "economics" or "economic action"). Among other things, ideal types focus attention on one aspect of social reality and thereby help to illuminate one set of causal connections; this is their strength. In so doing, they necessarily leave other sides of reality and other chains of causation in the dark; this is their limitation. Does this mean that Weber believes we will eventually be able to illuminate *all* sides of social reality by combining the perspectives of all the social sciences, and thereby achieve a complete understanding of the social world, as Menger hoped? Absolutely not—and for two reasons. First, Weber believes that there is an inescapable and zero-sum trade-off between empirical completeness and theoretical precision: greater completeness means less precision, and vice versa. Second, he believes that a complete and universal theory of social life is impossible. This is because: (1) sociohistorical reality—human purposes, social relations, organizations, and the like—are in perpetual flux, and (2) the aspect of this reality that constitutes the focus for any given researcher or community of researchers is a function of their historical location, of values rooted in specific times and places, and such values are also constantly changing. For all these reasons, argues Weber, social science will always enjoy the privileges—and the burdens—of "eternal youth."

Consonant with his methodological and epistemological views, Weber's position on ontology and causality was strongly influenced by Kant and at odds with that of both Schmoller and Menger. As we have seen, Weber is highly critical of the holist ontology of the historical school and of the organicist metaphors it employed, and he strongly objects to analyses that treat collectivities or institutions as if they were stable and unitary "subjects." It is for this reason that Weber recommends that the sociologist take individuals, and rational action, as the starting point. But while Weber may have been a *methodological* individualist, he was by no means an *ontological* individualist, like Menger. In Weber's view, groups and institutions are real to the degree that individuals *believe* that they are real and orient their *actions* toward them.[43] Accordingly, in his empirical research, Weber often treats groups and organizations—status groups, communities, nation-states, and so on—as if they are stable and unitary actors (without any effort to make their "micro-foundations" explicit). Indeed, a close reading of Weber's work on religious ethics and worldly rationality reveals that he regarded "economic man," and perhaps even the Kantian subject, as a relatively recent, and specifically West-ern, historical product. Nor is Weber an ontological rationalist. Like Schmoller, Weber denies that material self-interest is the only, or even the principal, wellspring of human action. Unlike Schmoller, however, he seeks to specify the various types of human action systematically in terms of their degree of rationality and their goals, while emphasizing the constructed character of group identity and the potential instability of institutional prac-tices (on this, see Chapter 4). Thus Weber's version of "methodological in-dividualism" can be seen as a synthesis of Schmoller's methodological holism and Menger's ontological individualism, a synthesis grounded in a multidi-mensional theory of human action that allows for both individual and supra-individual levels of analysis.

Weber's rejection of holistic and individualistic ontologies goes hand in hand with a rejection of organicist and genetic understandings of causality. In Weber's view, the chain of real social causation has no single point of ori-gin, whether in the individual or in the whole. Indeed, causation, for Weber, was not a chain at all, with a single, discrete series of links, but an "infinite manifold" with innumerable interconnections, which ideal types can (to a degree) help disentangle, in theory if not in reality. Thus "causal explana-tion" for Weber, means not a tracking of all events back to their "final" or "originating" cause, but a careful tracing of some historically circumscribed set of events (such as the development of capitalism in seventeenth-century Western Europe), the distinctive features of which are cognized by means of some typological construct ("modern capitalism"), to a finite set of earlier events (changes in the relationship between religious values and economic action in Western Europe during the sixteenth century), also understood with the aid of typological constructs ("economic traditionalism" versus "economic rationalism").

From these ideas follows Weber's position on the issues of disciplinary priorities and boundaries. In contrast to both the historicists and the neo-classicists, Weber does not regard the discovery of universal laws as an im-portant or practicable goal for social science. The inexhaustible complexity of social reality and the inexorable flow of historical change render the dis-covery of universal laws well-nigh impossible. And even if such laws were to be discovered, Weber argues, they would be banal formulas with little em-pirical content and therefore of little value for the task of understanding and explaining sociohistorical reality in its particularity—the only proper task that social science can ultimately have. In this regard, Weber's position is closer to that of the historicists than to that of the neoclassicists, though on the question of disciplinary boundaries he moves their debate onto new and reconfigured ground. This he does by reaching beyond the discipline of economics and into the then-emerging field of sociology, a field he conceives as enfolding economic theory and flowing, back and forth, into the field of history (including economic history). From history, sociology acquires the (comparative-historical) base of particulars from which to build its generalizations, its ideal types of action patterns, social types and relations, economic, political, and religious dynamics, and so on; while from sociology, history draws the ideal types without which particularity cannot be recognized, let alone explained. From Weber's standpoint, neither field exists without the other for the reason that there can be no fruitful generalization that is not both formed of particulars and oriented toward their explanation, just as there can be no particularizing without ideal-typical generalizations. For him, particularizing and generalizing are not opposed methods, but complementary strategies.[44]

VI

As the site of Max Weber's "sociology," *Economy and Society* embodies this vision in a dense compendium of ideal types articulated to Weber's ambition to provide a systematic treatment of the relationship between the economy—the modern Western capitalist economy in particular—and other sociocultural spheres, understood against the world-historical backdrop of multiplex developmental processes encapsulated in ideal-typical generalizations about disenchantment, bureaucratization, and various forms of rationalization. Eighty years after its publication, however, virtually all aspects of this project—its origins, its substance, its limitations—remain open areas of scholarly inquiry, too little known outside specialist circles.

This volume is intended as a first step in filling this gap. Part I presents recent research into the contextual and textual background of *Economy and Society*, with special reference to Weber's typological sociology. In Chapter 1, Guenther Roth draws on a decade of archival research to flesh out the biographical and familial context of Weber's work, focusing on Weber's far-flung familial connections to the cosmopolitan bourgeoisie that built the capitalist world economy of the nineteenth century, and examining, in light of these connections, the stance that Weber adopted on questions of economic policy. From this perspective, Roth proceeds to a fresh consideration of the neglected typology of capitalisms that Weber presents in *Economy and Society*—a typology Roth sees as holding greater present-day value than Weber's celebrated generalizations about the development of Western rationality.

This analysis is followed, in Chapter 2, by Harvey Goldman's searching treatment of Weber's own changing ethos and its impact on his methodological views and typological constructs. Goldman argues that the profusion of ideal-types in Weber's mature work was partly the result of his emerging view of modern culture as a battle between warring systems of valuation: that is, that Weber's polytheistic ethical ontology underwrote his pluralistic typologizing. At the same time, Goldman argues that the content of Weber's ideal types was tacitly inflected by Weber's view that the only "manly" response to the contemporary cultural situation was to devote oneself to a particular god—in his case, the god of reason and science.

In Chapter 3, we move from context to text, as the Wolfgang Mommsen unravels the strange tale of *Economy and Society* as text, as the German editors of Weber's collected works have painstakingly reconstructed it. Here, we learn of Weber's ever-changing designs and intentions for the volume during the years when his typological vision of sociology crystallized and of the posthumous decisions of his wife and editors that led to the publication of *Economy and Society* as we know it today. This essay provides the reader with a skeleton key to the enigmatic work. Together with this Introduction, these three chapters provide the broader context—methodological, biographical, ethical, and editorial—for understanding the genesis of Weber's magnum opus.

The four chapters that make up Part II provide a guided tour through the array of ideal types developed in the major topical sections of *Economy and Society*. In Chapter 4, Donald Levine unpacks part I, chapter 1, of *Economy and Society*, the discussion of "Basic Sociological Terms," where Weber presents his taxonomy of action types and views on the rationality of action. Levine shows how these formulation relate not only to fin-de-siècle economics and sociology, but also to German jurisprudence and philosophy. Then, in Chapter 5, Richard Swedberg turns to the next section of *Economy and Society*, part I, chapter 2, the "Sociological Categories of Economic Action," which has long been ignored by Weber scholars and whose centrality has only recently come to be appreciated. Swedberg examines the core concepts that Weber here develops—ideal types of economic action, economic organization, and (as observed in Roth's chapter) capitalism—and then ranges outward from these to Weber's treatment, elsewhere in *Economy and Society*, of the interrelationships among the economy and religion, polity, and law.

Chapter 3 of *Economy and Society* provides the starting point for Regina Titunik's careful analysis, in Chapter 6, of Weber's famous typology of "legitimate domination." Drawing on this and other parts of *Economy and Soci-*

ety as well as on Weber's journalistic writings, Titunik builds a highly original argument both about the hidden role of "democracy" in Weber's analysis of "domination" and about Weber's own views about the desirability and feasibility of democracy in the modern world. Chapter 7 by Hans Kippenberg concludes this section of the volume with an analysis of Weber's long and dense segment of *Economy and Society* that, in the English edition, bears the title "Religious Groups (The Sociology of Religion)," though Kippenberg prefers Weber's own title, "Religious Communities." Kippenberg maps out the forgotten terrain of German religious studies as this field stood in Weber's time and situates Weber's discussions—of religious action, religious communities, types of religious actors, and the developmental processes of disenchantment—within it, providing a sense both of the conventionality and of the originality of Weber's arguments.

Then, in Part III of this volume, the focus turns from dealing with the origins and substance of *Economy and Society* to a critical evaluation and empirical application of Weber's analyses.[45] Although each of the seven chapters in this section represents a different contemporary viewpoint, they are united in their efforts to stay on the Weberian via media, even as they advance beyond the via Weberiana, both conceptually and empirically. In that sense, they are very much in the Weberian spirit, taking sociohistorical inquiry as an open project resistant to closure. Weber himself anticipated that future research would extend and recast his ideal types and engender a multiplicity of others as "the light of great cultural problems moves on," leading social science to change "its standpoint and its analytical apparatus."[46] As befits this forecast, the chapters in this section assess, critically and constructively, some of the pivotal concepts of *Economy and Society* from different contemporary standpoints that issue forth in reformulations—some modest, some radical—of Weber's own types.

In Chapter 8, Mustafa Emirbayer returns to the sections of *Economy and Society* discussed by Donald Levine in Chapter 4 to launch a vigorous critique of Weber's ideal types of action from the combined perspectives of pragmatist, postcolonial, feminist, and race theorists. Emirbayer contends that sociology should abandon the sharp distinction between rational and nonrational action that he sees as anchoring the Weberian taxonomy and its devaluation of habit and affect. Emirbayer argues for a different "schema of categories" that is capable of accommodating "the possibilities in both habit and emotion for growth in discernment, contextual sensitivity, and knowledge." In Chapter 9, Erik Wright interrogates Weber's concept of class from the standpoint of contemporary neo-Marxism. Through a close and nuanced comparison of the inner structure of Weber's and Marx's conceptions of class, Wright shows that Weber's conceptual framework is capable of recognizing capitalist exploitation, but only as an obstacle to economic efficiency, not as an obstacle to human emancipation.

The three chapters that follow rethink the constructs found in the political sociology of *Economy and Society*, as these have recently attracted broad interest among comparative-historical sociologists. In Chapter 10, Julia Adams considers "patrimonialism" an ideal type that figures heavily into Weber's analysis of traditional domination in *Economy and Society*. Arguing for the continuing importance of this type for historical research on early-modern European states, Adams seeks nevertheless "to reshape the concept into a usable tool of analysis" by incorporating into it what Weber omitted: namely, gendered and discursive elements that prove critical for understanding and explaining some of the fundamental political weaknesses of patrimonial states.

In Chapter 11, by contrast, Philip Gorski uses Weber's ideal-typical distinction between "patrimonial" and "bureaucratic" systems of state office-holding as the point of departure for reconsidering the dynamics of early-modern state formation. Gorski critiques standard Weberian explanations of the patrimonial-to-bureaucratic transition, which accent geopolitical competition and fiscal-military mobilization, for their failure to account for the actual distribution of patrimonial and bureaucratic systems of state administration during this period. Gorski suggests an alternative explanation that emphasizes religio-political practices and networks, specifically the impact of the Renaissance papacy, which pioneered venal officeholding, and of the Protestant Reformation, which introduced a separation of (clerical) office from person.

Then, in Chapter 12, Randall Collins turns to "revolution," patiently excavating, from *Economic and Society* and some of Weber's journalistic writings, Weber's view of revolution both as a form of political structure and as a set of dynamic processes. Criticizing Weber's own ideal types for accenting structure over process—thus occluding "the flow of political action in a situation of crisis and conflict"—Collins nonetheless finds Weber's generalizations about the latter consistent with, if inferior to, the analyses furnished by contemporary state-breakdown theory.

Essential to a Weberian analysis of the economy and the polity, as observed in several of the chapters in Part II, is the realm of law. In Chapter 13, Duncan Kennedy provides a critical reinterpretation of the conceptual apparatus of the sociology of law sections of *Economy and Society* and then uses Weberian arguments to propose a new ideal type for the analysis and critique of contemporary legal developments. Contrasting Weber's views on law with those found in the "social" current in the legal theory of his time, Kennedy shows the continuity of Weber's position on law with his approach to history and his distinction between affect and value. Further, by relating Weber's sociology of law to his broader generalizations about rationalization, disenchantment, and bureaucratization, Kennedy puts forth a new interpretation of Weber's views on modern law—an interpretation that stresses Weber's awareness of the errors of the formalist school dominant in his time and his affinity to aspects of the critique of modern law developed subsequently. In addition, Kennedy uses Weberian concepts to construct a hybrid ideal type of "formalized substantive rationality" to describe the mode of mainstream legal thought that has arisen since the demise of both the two ideal-types of legal reasoning that Weber himself recognized—that is, purely formalist and substantive-social approaches. Finally, in Chapter 14, Hans Joas addresses questions that arise at the intersection of Weber's thinking about the economy, the polity, the law, and religion: questions, of pressing contemporary significance, concerning the cultural foundations and historical development of human rights. Joas shows that Weber's scattered remarks, in *Economy and Society* and elsewhere, on these issues derived from the work of his contemporaries, Ernst Troeltsch and Georg Jellinek. Like these two thinkers, Weber believed that the institutionalization of human rights in the modern West emerged from the quest of Protestant dissenters for religious tolerance. Extrapolating from this historical argument, Weber predicted that, with the decline of Christian culture and the spread of capitalist rationality, the cultural foundation of human rights in the West would erode, thereby also preventing their diffusion to the rest of the world—a prediction that has not proven correct. To understand Weber's failure here, Joas suggests the need to develop a more sophisticated understanding of the concept of "individualism," drawing perhaps on Troeltsch's distinction between utilitarian and expressive individualism. Further, Joas urges us to recognize the limitations of Weber's type concepts of "rationalization" and "disenchantment"; only then will we begin to understand the "sacralization of the person" that is at the root of the modern human rights revolution.

Taken together, the chapters in Part III indicate that the core sections of *Economy and Society* are now as open to contemporary reassessment as are the context and the substance of Weber's text itself. Nearly a century after Max Weber first conceived it, the project of *Economy and Society* beckons still.

Notes

1. For the results of the survey, see http://www.ucm.es/info/isa/books/.

2. For a discussion of the history of these divisions, see Donald N. Levine, *Visions of the Sociological Tradition* (Chicago: University of Chicago Press, 1995).

3. Andrew Abbott, *Chaos of Disciplines* (Chicago: University of Chicago Press, 2001).

4. Two works that can be used as portals into the debates are: Donald P. Green and Ian Shapiro, *Pathologies of Rational Choice Theory: A Critique of Applications in Political Science* (New Haven, Conn.: Yale University Press, 1994); and Roger V. Gould, ed., *The Rational Choice Controversy* (Chicago: University of Chicago Press, 2003).

5. The same division does, however, periodically exhibit itself in the latter areas, as shown by the recent debate among historical sociologists about the place of general theory. See, especially, Edgar Kiser and Michael Hechter, "The Role of General Theory in Comparative-Historical Sociology," *American Journal of Sociology* 97 (1991): 1–30, and the reply to this by Margaret R. Somers, "'We're No Angels': Realism, Rational Choice, and Relationality in Social Science," *American Journal of Sociology* 104 (1998): 722–84. See also the contributions to this debate in the resulting symposium in the same journal, *American Journal of Sociology* 104 (1998): 785–871. Note, too, Calhoun's comment at the end of this debate, "Sociologists seem doomed to fight the *methodenstreit* again and again." Craig Calhoun, "Explanation in Historical Sociology: Narrative, General Theory, and Historically Specific Theory," *American Journal of Sociology* 104 (1998): 846. It is to this predicament that we believe that Weber, whose views are a surprising absence in this debate, still speaks powerfully.

6. Guenther Roth, "introduction" to Max Weber, *Economy and Society: An Outline of Interpretive Sociology*, ed. Guenther Roth and Claus Wittich (1921–22; Berkeley: University of California Press, 1978), pp. xxxv–xl, originally published 1968.

7. See, for example, Thomas Burger, *Max Weber's Theory of Concept Formation: History, Laws and Ideal Types* (Durham, N.C.: Duke University Press, 1976); David Zaret, "From Weber to Parsons: The Eclipse of History in Modern Social Theory," *American Journal of Sociology* 85 (1980): 1180–201; Sven Eliaeson, *Max Weber's Methodologies* (Cambridge, England: Polity Press, 2002).

8. The essay in question is "Über einige Kategorien der verstehenden Soziologie," published in *Logos* 4 (1913). It can be found together with Weber's other methodological writings in Max Weber, *Gesammelte Aufsätze zur Wissenschaftslehre* (Tübingen: J. C. B. Mohr, 1968). The essay is translated in full by Edith Graber as "Some Categories of Interpretive Sociology," *Sociological Quarterly* 22 (1981): 151–80. For a partial translation, see appendix I of the English translation of *Economy and Society*.

9. Weber, *Economy and Society*, p. 4.

10. Here one thinks especially of Ranke's goal to describe history "as it actually was" ("wie es eigentlich gewesen").

11. Weber hereby rejects what is known today as the "thick" version of rational-choice theory, which assumes that the ends of action are always material. Neither, however, is his view identical to "thin" versions of rational choice, which make no a priori assumptions about "preferences." This is because, for Weber, "ideal interests" are focused not on the goal of action so much as the process of action; that is, they are not indifferent to the means by which a particular goal is achieved.

12. The contrast, here, is with what is variously referred to as the "nomological," "hypothetico-deductive," or "covering law" model of scientific explanation advocated by Carl Hempel, Karl Popper, and others. It is worth noting that this model enjoys more currency in the social sciences than in the philosophy of science, where "post-Popperian" approaches became dominant in the 1970s.

13. The question of whether it might be possible in the case of animals or other living organisms cannot be considered here, though Weber does offer some thoughts on it in "Basic Sociological Terms."

14. Weber does not use this term himself, but it accurately describes his approach. However, it should be noted that Weber's methodological individualism is not identical to that espoused by economists and economistic theories such as rational choice and game theory. On this, more below.

15. For a more thorough discussion of the various types of types, see Burger, *Max Weber's Theory of Concept Formation*, pp. 130–39.

16. Weber, *Economy and Society*, pp. 19–20 (emphasis added).

17. Weber to Georg von Below, June 14, 1914, as quoted by Roth in *Economy and Society*, p. lxiv.

18. The best historical overview of the debate is provided by Samuel Bostaph, "The Methodological Debate between Carl Menger and the German Historicists," *Atlantic Economic Journal* 1978, no. 3: 3–16. On the debate between formalists and historicists within economic thought more generally, see especially Geoffrey M. Hodgson, *How Economics Forgot History: The Problem of Historical Specificity in Social Science* (London: Routledge, 2001).

19. The best overview of the methodological position of the "older" historical school is Margaret Hüter, *Die Methodologie der Wirtschaftswissenschaft bei Roscher und Knies* (Jena: Gustav Fischer, 1928). For a brief treatment in English, with more recent references, see Hodgson, *How Economics Forgot History*, pp. 56–64.

20. On the Austrian school, see especially Peter J. Boettke, ed., *The Elgar Companion to Austrian Economics* (Aldershot, England: Edward Elgar, 1994).

21. Carl Menger, *Investigations into the Method of the Social Sciences*, trans. Francis J. Nock (Grove City, PA: Libertarian Press, 1996).

22. Gustav Schmoller, "Zur Methodologie der Staats- und Sozialwissenschaften," *Jahrbuch für die Gesetzgebung, Verwaltung und Volkswirtschaft im Deutschen Reich*, vol. 7 (1883).

23. Carl Menger, *Die Irrthuemer des Historismus in der Deutschen Nationaloekonomie* (Vienna: Hölder, 1884).

24. Members of the historical school usually described their method as "inductive." The reason for adding the adjective "comparative" will become clear directly.

25. The most famous was Wilhelm Roscher, *Die Grundlagen der Nationalökonomie: ein Hand- und Lesebuch für Geschäftsmänner und Studierende* (Stuttgart: Gottschen, 1871). Idem, *Principles of Political Economy* (Chicago: Callaghan, 1878).

26. Schmoller, "Zur Methodologie," p. 252.

27. A classic of this genre is Gustav von Schmoller, *Die Entwicklung und die Krisis der deutschen Weberei im 19. Jahrhundert* (Berlin: C. G. Lüderitz'sche Verlagsbuchhandlung Carl Habel, 1873).

28. Some of these scholars, such as Sombart, Schumpeter, Simmel, and Weber himself, will be more familiar to sociologists and political scientists. Others, such as Gierke and Hintze, will be more familiar to historians.

29. Menger, *Investigations*, p. 74.

30. Ibid., p. 57.

31. Ibid., p. 70.

32. See, e.g., Clive Lawson, "Realism, Theory and Individualism in the Work of Carl Menger," *Review of Social Economy* 1996: 445−64.

33. Menger, *Investigations*, pp. 93, 86−87.

34. On this, see Robin Cowan, "Causation and Genetic Causation in Economic Theory," in Boettke, *Companion to Austrian Economics*, pp. 54−62.

35. What was more, historicists believed that correct policies could be derived from scientific study; that is, they denied the distinction between facts and values.

36. For a brief overview of Weber's institutional and intellectual relationship to the economics profession, see Richard Swedberg, *Max Weber and the Idea of Economic Sociology* (Princeton, NJ: Princeton University Press, 1998), appendix.

37. For an overview of this debate, along with key texts, see Hans Albert and Ernst Topitsch, eds., *Werturteilsstreit* (Darmstadt: Wissenschaftliche Buchgesellschaft, 1971).

38. See, e.g., Yuichi Shinoya, "Rational Reconstruction of the German Historical School," in Shinoya, ed., *The German Historical School: The Historical and Ethical Approach to Economics* (London: Routledge, 2001), pp. 6−18, quotation on p. 6.

39. Max Weber, "Introduction" (of 1920), *The Protestant Ethic and the Spirit of Capitalism* (originally published 1904−5), trans. Talcott Parsons (1930; London: Routledge, 1992), p. xxxi.

40. The distinguishing feature of pure types, in Weber's usage, as opposed to ideal types more generally, is that they are empirically exhaustive (within a particular domain of social life) and mutually exclusive (in strictly logical terms). The best example of a pure-type construction in Weber's work is his three types of legitimate domination: charismatic, tradition, and legal-rational. On Weber's use of the term "pure types" and its relationship to his views on method, see especially Wolfgang J. Mommsen, "Ideal Type and Pure Type: Two Variants of Max Weber's Ideal-Typical Method," in Mommsen, *The Political and Social Theory of Max Weber* (Chicago: University of Chicago Press, 1992), pp. 121−32.

41. Max Weber, "'Objectivity' in Social Science and Social Policy," in *Max Weber on the Methodology of the Social Sciences*, trans. and ed. Edward A. Shils and Henry Finch, pp. 49−112 (originally published in German in 1904; Glencoe, IL: Free Press, 1949).

42. On the influence of neo-Kantian philosophy on Weber's methodology, see Burger, *Max Weber's Theory of Concept Formation*; and Guy Oakes, *Weber and Rickert: Concept Formation in the Cultural Sciences* (Cambridge, MA: MIT Press, 1988).

43. Weber, *Economy and Society*, p. 14.

44. In offering this positive assessment of Weber's ideal-type method, we are cognizant that his approach has been much criticized, both by general theorists, running from Parsons to Bourdieu, as well as by historians. General theorists usually insist on the importance of a unified, general theoretical framework of some kind, on the basis of which one can formulate statements of broad regularity; from this standpoint, Weber's ideal-type approach is often found wanting. Contrariwise, historians commonly object that theoretical constructs like ideal types can never capture the full complexity of particular historical cases or phenomena. This is a case where Weber's

critics manage to reproduce the very polarities that he sought to overcome. See Talcott Parsons, *The Structure of Social Action* (1937; New York: Free Press, 1968), pp. 601–10; and Pierre Bourdieu, "Legitimation and Structured Interests in Weber's Sociology of Religion," in *Max Weber, Rationality, and Modernity*, ed. Sam Whimster and Scott Lash (London: Allen & Unwin, 1987), pp. 119–22. See also Alexander von Schelting, *Max Webers Wissenschaftslehre. Das logische Problem der historischen Kulturerkenntnis: die Grenzen der Soziologie des Wissens* (Tübingen: J. C. B. Mohr, 1934).

45. We should, in good Weberian fashion, acknowledge that the distinctions we draw here between this and the previous section of the volume are themselves ideal types that actual chapters only approximate in different degrees. In other words, the boundaries between Parts II and III are not hard and fast; perhaps inevitably, therefore, readers will discover elements of critique in some of the chapters in Part II and elements of explication in some of the chapters in Part III.

46. Weber, "Objectivity," in *Methodology*, p. 112.

PART I

Contextual and Textual Background

Max Weber, Scion of the Cosmopolitan Bourgeoisie

Historical Context and Present-Day Relevance

As American sociology branched out in various directions over the past half-century, it appropriated Max Weber's fragmented oeuvre in a piecemeal fashion. Weber's works have often been compared to a quarry. For decades academic interests have dragged away big boulders or picked out bits and pieces and viewed them in their own light. Over the years, Weber's writings have been used and adapted by the several research and teaching fields that emerged more or less successively after the Second World War: bureaucracy and formal organization; industrial relations and economic development (modernization); stratification; political sociology; sociology of religion; historical sociology; microeconomics (methodological individualism, rational choice); and cultural sociology. Most ambivalent and awkward have been efforts to interpret Weber as a kind of existentialist (even nihilist) philosopher and as a relativist (even decisionist) political theorist, two roles he never claimed for himself. "Weberian" has become a vague label of intellectual orientation, but it has helped many social scientists to define their own identity broadly in relation to other basic approaches. Quite properly, reconstructions and explications have often gone beyond Weber's texts, but for some postmodernists the English translations have become texts in their own right, independent of the author's intent or the inherent meaning of the German originals.[1]

By now the question may be asked whether there is any dimension or component of Weber's "scholarship and partisanship" left that might be relevant to current concerns. My suggestion is that, in an era of renewed global capitalism, Weber's own extended family connections with the world economy, as well as his views on economic policy, warrant closer scrutiny, especially his views on world trade and the role of securities and commodity markets. There are today remarkable parallels to the first global economy that was destroyed by the First World War and seemed to have disappeared forever, and the new world economy that gradually emerged after the Second World War. At a time when even some sociological theorists read and write primarily about macroeconomic issues, a new focus on Weber's economic sociology may be of use, particularly if we shift attention from his developmental history of rationalism to his typology of different kinds of capitalism and examine the ways in which "modern" capitalism is no longer up to date.

I shall first deal with Weber's family connections, then with his economic policies, and finally with the applicability of his typologies of capitalism to the present.

Weber's Cosmopolitan Family Connections

There is a large international literature on Weber as a major spokesman for nationalist power politics and as a "democrat" mainly for reasons of instrumental, not value, rationality.[2] He has been called a liberal imperialist, a social imperialist, or, in his own words, an "economic nationalist." He indeed affirmed the unified Germany created by his father's generation, including the ideal of the culturally homogeneous nation-state. If it is necessary to use a label at all, I prefer to call Weber a "cosmopolitan nationalist" because he was convinced that Germany needed to be, and to remain, integrated in the world economy and on peaceful terms with England, Germany's most important trading partner. In an era of increasing imperialist tensions, he was one of the last anglophile liberals. His nationalism presupposed the "economic community of the world."[3]

I would like to view Weber here as a scion of the cosmopolitan bourgeoisie that created the capitalist world economy of the nineteenth century.[4] His extended family history has been relatively neglected, even though it influenced his worldview and oeuvre in significant respects. The secondary literature has largely followed Marianne Weber's remarkable biography of 1926, although its biases and factual weaknesses have long been recognized.[5] Like most political liberals in Weimar Germany, Marianne considered the Versailles Treaty utterly unjust. This was probably a major reason for her decision to almost completely ignore the Anglo-German family connections. Thus for a long time it was insufficiently recognized that Max descended from Huguenot and Lutheran merchant families that were engaged in worldwide trade. On the maternal side the Frankfurt Souchay clan, based mainly in London and Manchester, was one of the wealthiest Anglo-German families in the middle of the nineteenth century; on the paternal side the Bielefeld Weber clan gained international importance especially through its trading and shipping firms in Hamburg.[6] (The 150-year-old firm of Weber and Schaer is still one of the most important German importers of natural rubber and exporters of machinery.) Again on the maternal side, there was the Fallenstein link with the Bunge family in Antwerp and South America; the Bunge firms are still today among the richest privately held companies in the world, active in the international cereal business. Within Weber's far-flung family both the opposition and the overlapping of cosmopolitan and nationalist attitudes come into sharp focus.

Already at age fifteen, Max was familiar with the details of his family history, including the English and Dutch-Belgian lines. At Christmas 1879, Fritz Baumgarten made "his dear cousin Max Weber" the present of a Goethe calendar, in which the vital dates of many members were listed. But when he also let him read the Fallenstein biography by the famous historian Georg Gottfried Gervinus, father Weber protested, "I was so lacking in pedagogical acumen as to let grandfather's biography fall into little Max's hands—for the big family tree he was busy drawing." At any rate, Max Jr. realized early that his Heidelberg grandmother, Emilie Souchay Fallenstein, was the daughter of the Anglo-German capitalist adventurer (or adventure capitalist), Carl Cornelius Souchay; the sister of the business lawyer, senator, and mayor of Frankfurt, Eduard Souchay, and of the two "patrician merchants" (*Handelsherren*), Charles and John Souchay, cotton traders in Manchester; the sister-in-law of Friedrich Wilhelm Benecke, head of the acceptance house Benecke, Souchay & Co. in London. She was also the mother-in-law of the Baden prime minister, Julius Jolly, formerly an academic expert on securities and exchange law; the political writer and historian, Hermann Baumgarten; the politically active theologian, Adolf Hausrath (also known in England and the United States as the novelist, George Taylor); the Alsatian geologist, Ernst Wilhelm Benecke; the leading Antwerp businessman, Karl Gustav Bunge; and finally of Max's own father, the Berlin city councilor in charge of public construction and member of the Reichstag and Prussian Diet, where he was for many years a key member of the budget committees.

For a number of reasons the young Max could not realize his ambition to pursue a "practical" vocation. He hoped in vain "to learn the practice of the import-export trade for several years."[7] Alternatively, his first choice was an academic career in commercial law, but at the time there was no regular opening in Berlin. At any rate, he chose the academic path with great ambivalence and abandoned teaching after only seven years in the course of his extended illness. Taking the option of living as a capitalist rentier and private scholar (*Privatgelehrter*), he could henceforth afford to be "undisciplined" in both senses of the word: he was free to ignore academic boundary lines and to indulge in a pattern of stop-and-go scholarship. He made the most, however, of his "unstructured" situation and succeeded against great odds in composing his cosmopolitan sociology and developmental history, largely in the Heidelberg family mansion that had been built with profits from world trade accumulated in Manchester and London.

Connections between family background, economic policy views, and scholarly writings have more often been asserted than demonstrated. Marxist writers have singled out Weber as the foremost representative of "bourgeois sociology," but with only superficial knowledge of the family history. Friedrich Engels, partner in a small Manchester firm, reported to Marx several times on the leading firm of Schunck, Souchay & Co., the major source of the Weber fortune, but to my knowledge the secondary literature did not detect the connection. In a nonpolemical manner, Karl-Siegberg Rehberg interpreted the "Basic Categories" of *Economy and Society* as emanating from "a grand-bourgeois worldview," but this was mainly an internal analysis without reference to the wider family history.[8] If we look at the latter, we can recognize that the young Weber's interests in East Elbian agrarian capitalism and in securities and commodity exchanges were to a considerable extent a family matter. In the Reichstag, Max Weber Sr. fought efforts by the conservatives to raise taxes on mobile capital and impede the capital and commodity markets. In the Prussian Diet, he was a member of the commission that drafted the "homesteading act" of 1886, which aimed at reversing the decline of the German population share in the East. On the government's side, responsibility for introducing the legislation rested with the minister of agriculture, Robert Lucius von Ballhausen, with whom Max Sr. often collaborated and competed over three decades and whose English-born wife, Juliet Souchay, was a cousin of his own wife, Helene Fallenstein. While Max Jr. was still synthesizing the survey on East Elbian agrarian labor in 1892, he suddenly developed expertise on the Argentinian economy, which appeared as an unexpected insertion in his 1892 article on the survey and a year later in his article on Argentinian colonists.[9] The source for much of his information was his cousin Julius Fallenstein, who visited him at the same time, one of three Fallensteins who worked in Argentina for Weber's Antwerp cousin Ernest Bunge, who would soon become the biggest wheat exporter to Europe. Weber favored raising protective tariffs but without giving in to the exorbitant self-interested demands of the East Elbian agrarians. When, decades later, in a wartime speech in 1916, he opposed right-wing demands for Belgian annexations, he added: "Antwerp will always remain a non-German city. I know it, I have relatives there." Even though he distanced himself in this speech from cosmopolitan family capitalism in favor of the national interest, he could not resist the temptation to reveal the family nexus. At the time, Eduard Bunge, Weber's other Antwerp cousin, lost control of the biggest natural rubber storage on the continent; plundered by the

German army, it was put at the disposal of the imperial commissioner for caoutchouc, Albert Weber, a Hamburg relative of Max Jr.[10]

Sometimes Weber referred to relatives as cousins who were actually one or two steps removed, but this made it easier for him to remind an audience of his family connections. Thus when he opposed the close cooperation of government and big business cartels at the meetings of the Verein für Sozialpolitik in 1905, he mentioned his "esteemed cousin [Theodor] Möller," the Prussian minister of trade, who was just at the point of moving his aniline factories to England under pressure from the Kirdorf cartel.[11]

When Max was in his teens, his mother, Helene, and her relatives from London to Strasbourg and Heidelberg were avid readers not only of the great English novelists from Walter Scott to George Eliot, but especially of the anti-Calvinist theologians Frederick William Robertson, Charles Kingsley, Theodore Parker, and William Ellery Channing. Thus Weber had an unusual family preparation when he turned later to English sources for the study of the Protestant ethic (in its Calvinist phase). His engagement in the early phase of the Evangelical-social Congress in the early 1890s evolved in large part from his close friendship with a cousin, the theologian Otto Baumgarten, who recruited him as "my policy advisor, who brings along his economic friends" (letter of Aug. 23, 1890) to teach the naïve pastors that the prescriptions of Christian charity could not apply in the autonomous realm of the capitalist economy.[12]

Weber's views on the Anglo-Saxon world were, however, shaped early not only by religious inclinations in the family but also by familial interests in political and economic matters. On Christmas 1875, his paternal mentor Friedrich Kapp, for many years active in Republican politics in New York City, gave the eleven-year-old a German copy of Benjamin Franklin's autobiography. In the introduction Kapp advised: "May every German father put Franklin's autobiography into his son's hands as a textbook. . . . We lag behind the materially more developed peoples, especially the Americans, in appreciating the proper role of money-making and material means in achieving spiritual and moral purposes."[13] But from Kapp the young Max also learned about the darker side of American democracy, from the "predatory wars by the democratic Union against Mexico" to the rule of the bosses and machines in the cities. He did not have to wait for the great works of Hermann von Holst and James Bryce to gain a wider understanding of American history.[14]

Weber's interest in the United States deepened when his father, who represented private railroad interests in parliament, followed an invitation by the German-American railroad tycoon Henry Villard (Heinrich Hilgard, 1835–1900) to attend the opening of the transcontinental line of the Northern Pa-

cific in 1883. Max Sr. traveled for a month in Villard's private train with
Georg Siemens, director of the Deutsche Bank, and also met the former
Heidelberg student James Bryce, who later recounted the trip in his *American Commonwealth*. Max Sr. saw President Chester Arthur, former President
Ulysses Grant, the Sioux chief Sitting Bull, and two thousand Crow Indians,
and attended the laying of the foundation stone of the capitol of the Dakota
Territory near a little railroad depot, which was named Bismarck in order to
attract German immigrants.

Villard, who in the 1880s lived for a time in the Weber family's Berlin circle, financed the travel grants of the imperial government to the Chicago
World's Fair of 1893, which Max Jr. intended to visit (with Paul Göhre). Because of his unexpected engagement to Marianne Schnitger (a second
cousin), Weber postponed his American trip but was determined to undertake it even before the opportunity arose to attend the scholars' congress at
the St. Louis World Fair of 1904. On that occasion he visited Villard's widow,
the daughter of the famous abolitionist William Lloyd Garrison, in New
York.[15]

In the first version of *Economy and Society*, Henry Villard appears in the
charisma fragment (*ES* 1888), an explicit link between family knowledge
and scholarly work:[16]

The antagonism between charisma and everyday life arises also in the capitalist
economy, with the difference that charisma does not confront the household but the
enterprise. An instance of grandiose robber capitalism and of a spoils-oriented following is provided by Henry Villard's exploits. [In 1881] he organized the famous
"blind pool" in order to stage a stock exchange raid on the shares of the Northern
Pacific Railroad; he asked the public for a loan of fifty million pounds without revealing his goal, and received it without security by virtue of his reputation. The
structure and spirit of this robber capitalism differs radically from the rational management of an ordinary capitalist large-scale enterprise and is most similar to some
age-old phenomena.[17]

Weber's judgment may have been influenced by the Northern Pacific's
third bankruptcy in 1893, the second for Villard, when many German professors (including the Heidelberg luminaries Kuno Fischer and Hermann
Helm-holtz) again lost much money from their investments in American
railroad stocks. The Webers themselves held American shares until well into
the First World War. At any rate, the young Weber was well informed about
the connection between railroad expansion and wheat exports to Europe.
His (later) friend Max Sering preceded his father in the spring of 1883 as
Villard's guest and wrote a study for the German government, "The Agrarian Competition of North America in the Present and the Future: Agriculture, Colonisation and Railroad Transport in the United States and British
North America" (1887). The railroad official Alfred von der Leyen, a close

family friend and Friedrich Kapp's son-in-law, wrote two studies about the politics and economics of American railroad expansion between 1885 and 1895. Thus, from early on Weber was familiar with the way in which the world economy linked American economic development and German political reaction.

Weber's Economic Policies and Analyses

In Germany, powerful agrarian pressure groups emerged in response to wheat and meat exports from the Americas, which were facilitated by railroad expansion and advances in shipping technology. Beyond the general goal of raising agricultural tariffs, these agrarian interests demanded legislation to curtail the role of capital and commodity markets, especially the outlawing of trade in grain futures. In the framework of the great policy debate on Germany's economic future (*Industriestaat* or *Agrarstaat?*), Weber defended the need for a strong capital market and efficient commodities exchanges for the sake of strengthening the German economy on the world market.

Whereas Weber's engagement with agrarian capitalism has been treated extensively in the secondary literature, his writings on the functioning and reform of securities and commodities exchanges have been relatively neglected.[18] The latter fall into the realm of commercial law, in which Weber began his teaching career. In the winter of 1891–92 he acquired his academic qualification (*Habilitation*) for Roman public and private law as well as commercial law. He immediately took over for the incapacitated Levin Goldschmidt, his paternalistic dissertation director, who had known him from earliest childhood. His qualification for commercial law had been controversial within the faculty, which also did not propose him for the (associate) professorship for commercial and German law—the latter again something of an irregularity—to which the ministry appointed him in November 1893. Weber taught courses on "money, banking, and exchange," commercial and maritime law, insurance and bottomry, and agrarian law and history. When in the wake of a number of bank failures and exchange scandals government and parliament moved toward regulating and curtailing the exchange, Weber saw a chance to prove his expertise, improve his status in the faculty, and exert some political influence.[19] Similar to the way in which in 1892 he had boiled down the huge survey of the Verein für Sozialpolitik to an 800-page report, "The Conditions of Agricultural Labor in East Elbian Germany" (*MWG*, I/3), he now worked through 5,000 pages issued by a government commission to produce the 350-page "The Results of the Inquiry into the German Exchange" for Goldschmidt's *Zeitschrift für das Gesammte Handelsrecht* (1894–96). This was followed and paralleled by articles in the *Handwörterbuch der Staatswissenschaften* on the proposed reforms (1895) and the passed legislation (1897), "The Technical Functions of Trading in Futures" for the *Deutsche Juristen-Zeitung*, and some other specialized contributions that immediately found recognition among academic experts and government officials. But before Weber could finish his series analyzing the results of the government inquiry, the Reichstag hurried through legislation in June 1896 that was based on moralizing sentiment and vested agrarian interest. This vitiated much of Weber's purpose. His quickly acquired reputation seemed to give him a second chance, however, when he was appointed as one of two academic experts to the Provisional Exchange Commission, an advisory body within the Imperial Ministry of the Interior. There he distinguished himself through a subcommittee report.

In the commission and in his writings, Weber took the position that in principle only persons of means should trade on the exchange—as was true of his own relatives. He was acutely aware that much of his mother's "very large fortune" (*MWG*, II/6: 763), the cause of so much parental tension, was accumulated to a significant extent on the exchanges of Manchester and London, just as the Hamburg family branch operated on the local exchange. The London exchange, an exclusive club, and the Hamburg exchange with its patrician traditions, though open, appeared to him as models. In 1896 he did not hesitate to state a plutocratic position before the commercial and agrarian elite assembled in the exchange commission. Responding to a leader of the agrarians, he said:

If Count Arnim calls the maximum openness of the exchange the most desirable solution, this conflicts to some degree with other tendencies in the discussion of the legislation and also with my personal view which, if you want to put it in unfriendly terms, would bring about a degree of plutocratic closure of the exchange. I would like to introduce less a moral test, as the exchange commission and the legislation envisage it, since it is difficult to achieve, than an economic means test, a proof of a certain level of wealth. But this is an idea that has no chance given the prevailing mood in Germany.[20]

Weber linked his plutocratic proposal with the argument that regulating the exchange should be left as far as possible to exchange traders themselves.[21] This was not acceptable to the agrarians, who wanted their own representatives to supervise the exchange. Since Weber was, in addition, known to be opposed to the outlawing of grain futures, the agrarians successfully prevented his appointment to the permanent board. In a letter to Adolph Wagner (Jan. 1, 1897), Weber had anticipated that "Count Arnim and his minions [may see to it] that professors who are alleged to be as friendly to the exchange as I am will not again be admitted to the Commission" (*MWG*, I/5: 105). The agrarians also tried but failed to push out one of the leading Berlin bankers, Ernst von Mendelssohn-Bartholdy, about whom Weber reported to Marianne (Nov. 22, 1896): "As things have gone until now, I have apparently pleased the millionaires (*Millionen-Knoepfe*). At least Geheimer Kommerzienrat Mendelssohn-Bartholdy always shakes my hand so vigorously that I am surprised not to have found a check for several hundred thousand Marks under my writing pad" (*MWG*, I / 5: 666). Both men knew, of course, that they were not only political allies but also distantly related; Weber's mother was a cousin of Felix Mendelssohn-Bartholdy's wife.[22]

Weber's move to the economics chair in Freiburg in 1894 has usually been understood as a turning away from jurisprudence.[23] It is true that he had to take on the burden of standard courses in theoretical and practical economics and in finance. But his major publications in the Freiburg period concerned exchange matters, and he continued to lecture on money, banking, and exchange and on the history of German law in the law faculty. It appears that he wanted to keep his options between law and economics open longer than has been generally thought (cf. *MWG*, I / 5: 103). The real turning point came after the move to Heidelberg in the spring of 1897, where his existential crisis was quickly building up. His strenuous political and scholarly activities to promote agricultural and commercial reforms in the national interest had come to naught. In 1899 he condemned for a last time the outlawing of grain futures and also resigned from the Pan-German League because of its failure to oppose the big Prussian landowners on the issue of Polish migrant labor. By that time he had also decided against a run for the Reichstag as a National Liberal, holding the party responsible for the moralistic exchange legislation. Weber came to feel totally stymied in politics at the same time that the dramatic conflict with his father and its fatal outcome in the summer of 1897 became the last step in a sequence of mounting inner tensions that precipitated his illness and ended his political and academic careers.

Thereafter Weber was free as a private scholar to pursue a wide range of scholarly interests that ignored academic boundary lines but somewhat paradoxically became important to the disciplinary articulation and differentiation of American sociology. Yet he did not change his basic economic policy views. As a "rather pure bourgeois" (as he liked to call himself), he continued to uphold the imperatives of the capitalist market economy against the right and the left. Although he criticized the older generation for its dogmatic adherence to laissez-faire doctrines, he defended even during the First World War "the so-called anarchy of production—that is, the competition of entrepreneurs with one another" (*MWG*, I / 15: 613). When in the second half of the war the anticapitalist and antidemocratic right publicly attacked "international capital" and "Jewish-led democracy" as the true culprits for the war, he declared: "Before the war we were told that the country has too much capital and industry. That is the outlook of naïve [*weltfremde*] intellectuals. . . . Let us stop the railing against capital and bourgeoisie [*Bürgertum*]! We don't have too much but too little capital and big entrepreneurs"(*MWG*, I / 15: 668). As late as 1917, Weber cautioned that Germany might lose its economic position on the world market "even if the war ends brilliantly" (*MWG*, I / 15: 212). Worried that the spirit of capitalism would lose out to the spirit of the rentier, he was concerned about the impact of the veterans' claims and the middle-class expectations of high returns on their war bonds: "The ideal of the safe rent rises up before an increasing part of the nation, and the stupid outcries of the literati against capitalism pave the way. The decisive problem of the future is how we can get rid again of this spirit of rentiership" (*MWG*, I / 15: 212). Specifically, after the conclusion of peace, Weber expected a return to formally peaceful competition in the world economy.[24] In this crucial respect he differed from virulent Social Darwinist nationalism and Prussian militarism, which treated the use of force not as ultima ratio but as a normal state of affairs. Weber warned of continuing the practices of the war economy into the postwar period and opposed the projects for nationalization and for establishing the *Wirtschaftsstaat* (a once popular term that is forgotten today). In significant respects he remained a liberal critic of the emerging welfare state and its pendant, the militarized state-run economy. In general, the thrust of his rhetoric and polemic was anti-anticapitalist, an attitude of opposition that he also adopted toward the fashionable critics of modernity, whose anti-Semitism, anti-Americanism, and anglophobia he opposed so passionately. Weber's early death in 1920 spared him from experiencing the failure to restore a viable world economy and from facing the triumph of the fascist and communist command economies.

Present-Day Implications of Weber's Politics and Sociology

Weber's economic sociology can be of use particularly if we shift attention from his developmental history of rationalism to his typology of the different kinds of capitalism and examine the ways in which "modern" capitalism is no longer up-to-date. From the typological viewpoint, the revival of the capitalist world economy is characterized by a new combination of old (traditional) and modern forms of capitalism. This means that Weber's typological sociology is more pertinent than his secular developmental history of Occidental rationalism, on which so much of the secondary literature has focused. Whereas the age of the cosmopolitan bourgeoisie has long since passed, new cosmopolitan elites of entrepreneurs, managers, computer technicians, and (sociology) professors are now emerging, repeating the nineteenth-century pattern of sojourners and settlers. At the same time, modern bureaucratic capitalism and the modern bureaucratic welfare state have lost ground. They are no longer the last stage of development. In significant respects "late capitalism" (*Spätkapitalismus*) is followed not only by "postmodern" capitalism but also by "early" forms of capitalism. "Modern" capitalism has been left behind.

When the end of the Cold War was hailed as a triumph of capitalism, capitalism's varieties tended to be overlooked. In the heartland of capitalism, the United States with its peculiar mixture of plutocracy and populism, the principle of private maximization in the marketplace prevails under massive institutional protection. But in many parts of the world, next to new forms of capitalism, ancient ones reemerge: family and clan capitalism, political and adventure capitalism, booty and robber capitalism, and other "varieties of pre-rationalist capitalism known for four millennia" (*MWG*, I / 15: 453; *ES* 1395). They operate, however, at great risk under conditions of institutional instability that reward corruption, extortion, and criminal violence. The breakdown of the Soviet Union and of the other socialist command economies enlarged the territorial opportunities for economic and political liberalism once more, but worldwide political and economic setbacks have demonstrated how difficult it is to create the capitalist and democratic institutions that require one another: without constitutional guarantees and civil society, there could be no "rational" capitalism, and vice versa. If the state socialist countries were ruined by, in Weberian terms, neotraditional and neopatrimonial mindsets and practices, these were bound to make the democratic and capitalist "transformation" all the more difficult.

But the dynamics of capitalism relentlessly transform established ways of doing things and continually put pressure on the institutional framework of the democratic countries. The new "electronic capitalism," which speeds up transactions and permits smaller enterprises, undermines the bureaucratic capitalism that was for Weber a major feature of modernity. The expectations of prominent social scientists in the 1950s and 1960s, from Talcott Parsons to Clark Kerr, that "industrial man" would spend half his life in bureaucratized large enterprises and half in the realm of leisure, have proved utopian. Weber's assertion that "the whole developmental history of modern *Hochkapitalismus* is identical to the increasing bureaucratization of the economic enterprises" is no longer valid.[25] "Full development" (*Vollentwicklung*), which seemed to have been reached, has been followed by devolution. The "most advanced structures of capitalism" (*ES*, p. 956) are today subject to debureaucratization and the decentralization of innovation, production, and service. Finally, as at various points in the nineteenth century, the distance is growing between the "real economy" and the "financial economy," between real output and speculative value. But on this score also Weber fought against entrenched anticapitalist sentiments and tried to promote a balanced judgment, especially on the proper role of speculation in securities and commodity markets. Here too he wanted to instruct an economically unsophisticated public (more of Protestant *Bildungsbürger* than of Social Democratic workers) and indeed offered himself as a teacher to his compatriots, if without the hoped-for success. Perhaps his anti-anticapitalism can still teach some lessons today.

In conclusion, if Weber's nationalism is notorious, his cosmopolitanism also warrants remembering. His economic nationalism presupposed that the capitalist world economy, the "economic community of the nations" (*MWG*, I / 4: 560), was a reality. He remained convinced that Germany's future depended ultimately on its ability to compete on the world market instead of challenging the Anglo-Saxon world powers militarily. Only after two world wars did a majority of Germans learn this lesson in the era of the German *Wirtschaftswunder*. Thus, Weber's basic economic position remains of exemplary interest insofar as it links the presumptive, if contested, national interest with an unsentimental acceptance of the world economy.

Weber's fundamental acceptance of international capitalism was, however, linked with contradictions that remain important today. The young Weber struggled to force together economic internationalism and political and cultural nationalism. His cultural politics (*Kulturpolitik*) maintained an ethnocentric orientation from which he freed himself only slowly and conditionally. Thus the tensions between cosmopolitan and ethnocentric elements remained largely unresolved. The underlying issues have come to the fore again. In this respect Weber is not only a "man of his time" but also a man of our time. He expressed in "classical" fashion hopes and fears that continue to be shared more or less openly by many people today. In principle, international capitalism is multiethnic, but issues of ethnic integration and exclusion remain virulent.[26]

Notes

1. See now Guenther Roth, "Heidelberger kosmopolitische Soziologie," in Gert Albert et al., eds., *Das Weber-Paradigma* (Tübingen: J. C. B. Mohr–Paul Siebeck, 2003), pp. 23–31.

2. Much of this literature has drawn on Wolfgang Mommsen's famous first book, *Max Weber and German Politics*, a political biography first published in 1959. It appeared about the same time as Reinhard Bendix's pathbreaking *Intellectual Portrait*, which synthesized Weber's macrosociology, but is also outdated. See Wolfgang Mommsen, *Max Weber and German Politics 1890–1920*, trans. Michael Steinberg (Chicago: University of Chicago Press, 1984), based on 2nd ed. of 1974; Reinhard Bendix, *Max Weber: An Intellectual Portrait*, 2nd ed. (1960; University of California Press, 1977), with an introduction by myself. Beyond political and intellectual biography there has in recent years been increasing interest in the genre of personal biography and autobiography even in the social sciences, both in Germany and the

United States. There is a felt need for a comprehensive biography of Max Weber at a time when biographies of Alfred Weber, Werner Sombart, Levin Goldschmidt, and the Jellineks have appeared. See Eberhard Demm, *Von der Weimarer Republik zur Bundesrepublik. Der politische Weg Alfred Webers 1920–1958* (Düsseldorf: Droste, 1999); this is the second volume of the biography; the first appeared in 1990 under the title *Ein Liberaler in Kaiserreich und Republik. Der politische Weg Alfred Webers bis 1920*; see also Friedrich Lenger, *Werner Sombart 1863–1941. Eine Biographie* (Munich: Beck, 1994); Lothar Weyhe, *Levin Goldschmidt. Ein Gelehrtenleben in Deutschland* (Berlin: Duncker & Humblot, 1995); Klaus Kempter, *Die Jellineks 1820–1955. Eine familienbiographische Studie zum deutschjüdischen Bildungsbürgertum* (Düsseldorf: Droste, 1998).

3. The phrase is from "Die Börse," in *Max Weber Gesamtausgabe*, ed. H. Baier et al., vol. 5, *Börsenwesen*, ed. Knut Borchardt (2000), p. 155 (Tübingen: J. C. B. Mohr, 1984–), hereafter abbreviated *MWG*, I/5.

4. This chapter draws in part on my German study, *Max Webers deutsch-englische Familiengeschichte 1800–1950* (Tübingen: Mohr–Siebeck, 2001); see also Guenther Roth, "Weber the Would-Be Englishman: Anglophilia and Family History," in Hartmut Lehmann and Guenther Roth, eds., *Weber's Protestant Ethic: Origins, Evidence, Contexts* (Cambridge: Cambridge University Press, 1993), pp. 83–121; and Guenther Roth, "Max Weber: Family History, Economic Policy, Exchange Reform," *International Journal of Politics, Culture and Society* (Spring 2002): 509–20.

5. Marianne Weber, *Max Weber: A Biography*, trans. Harry Zohn (New Brunswick, NJ: Transaction Books, 1988), with my introductory essay, "Marianne Weber and Her Circle."

6. Marianne Weber neglected the most important branch of the Weber family with its Hamburg-based enterprises. In the biography and her own autobiography, *Lebenserinnerungen* (Bremen: Storm, 1948), she focused on her own maternal line, which operated the linen manufacturing firm in Oerlinghausen near Bielefeld. See Guenther Roth, "Zur Geschlechterproblematik in der Weberschen Familiengeschichte," in Bärbel Meurer, ed., *Marianne Weber. Beiträge zu Werk und Person* (Tübingen: Mohr–Siebeck, 2004), pp. 11–27.

7. Letter to Hermann Baumgarten, Jan. 3, 1891, in *Jugendbriefe* (Tübingen: J. C. B. Mohr, 1936), p. 326.

8. Karl-Siegbert Rehberg, "Rationales Handeln als grossbürgerliches Aktionsmodell," *Kölner Zeitschrift für Soziologie* 31 (2) (1979): 199–236; cf. chap. 1 of *Economy and Society: An Outline of Interpretive Sociology*, ed. Guenther Roth and Claus Wittich (1921–22; Berkeley: University of California Press, 1978), hereafter abbreviated *ES*.

9. See *MWG*, I/4: 128ff. and 286–303.

10. The editors of *MWG*, I/4 and I/15, could not yet identify Julius Fallenstein and the Bunges.

11. Ibid., I/8, p. 273. In letters Weber mentioned his family connections with the Mendelssohn-Bartholdys and the Luciuses. Paul Mendelssohn-Bartholdy, who preceded Max in the dueling fraternity Allemannia, founded Agfa (Aktiengesellschaft für Anilinfabrikation) in 1873 and Eugen Lucius founded Meister, Lucius & Brüning in 1863 (later famous as Hoechster Farbwerke and since the 1999 merger with Rhône-Poulenc part of Aventis). The cotton-trading families were vitally interested in chemical advances in dyestuffs.

12. See "The Young Max Weber: Anglo-American Religious Influences and Protestant Social Reform in Germany," *International Journal of Politics, Culture and Society* (Summer 1997): 659–71.

13. See Friedrich Kapp, "Benjamin Franklin," reprinted in *Aus und über Amerika* (Berlin: Springer, 1876), pp. 89 and 46.

14. The quotation is from Dec. 6, 1885, *Jugendbriefe*, p. 192. Long before Bryce wrote his famous account of the bosses and machines, Kapp described the corrupt operations of the New York City administration (1871); see *Aus und über Amerika*, vol. II, pp. 3–43; James Bryce, *The American Commonwealth*, 3 vols. (London: Macmillan, 1888); Hermann von Holst, *Verfassung und Demokratie in den Vereinigten Staaten* (Düsseldorf: Buddeus, 1873); English version: *The Constitutional and Political History of the United States*, 8 vols. (Chicago: Callaghan, 1876–92).

15. In her biography, Marianne Weber did not mention this visit or a meeting with Max's cousin Otto Weber, who worked in the German Wall Street firm Amsinck; she also did not identify their main host, the Columbia University economist Edwin R. A. Seligman, son of the German-born banker and cofounder of the Society for Ethical Culture, Joseph Seligman. Through Edwin Seligman, Weber met Felix Adler as well as David Blaustein of the Educational Alliance. Seligman and Weber corresponded as early as 1897; see Weber's letter, dictated to Marianne, of Mar. 22, 1897 (Columbia U. Libraries, Special Collections). Marianne also never mentioned Max Sr.'s America trip and eliminated a reference to it in the son's *Jugendbriefe* (1936). In line with her own interests, she recalled meeting Florence Kelley in New York and Jane Addams in Chicago. See now Guenther Roth, "Max Weber's Views on Jewish Integration and Zionism: Some American, English, and German Contexts," *Max Weber Studies*, 3: 1 (Nov. 2002): 56–73; idem, "Transatlantic Connections: A Cosmopolitan Context for Max and Marianne Weber's New York Visit 1904," *Max Weber Studies*, 5: 1 (2005).

16. See *ES*, p. 1118. In several other passages of *Economy and Society*, Weber referred to personal knowledge without specific identification. In an early passage on household communism and the rise of capitalist accounting, he suddenly interrupted his impersonal exposition with personal knowledge: "While the household and household authority have outwardly completely disappeared, a communism of risk and profit, that is, sharing of profit and loss of otherwise altogether independent business managements, continues to exist. I know about conditions in international houses with earnings amounting to millions, whose capital belongs for the most part, but not exclusively, to relatives of varying degrees and whose management is predominantly, but not solely, in the hands of the members of the family. The individual establishments operate in very diverse lines of business; they possess highly variable amounts of capital and labor force; and they achieve widely variable profits. In spite of this, after the deduction of the usual interest on capital, the annual returns of all the branches are simply thrown into one hopper, divided into equal portions. . . . The 'calculative' spirit thus does not extend to the distribution of balance-sheet results, but it dominates all the more within the individual enterprise: even a close relative without capital and working as an employee will not be paid more than any other employee. . . . Beyond the balance sheet, those lucky enough to participate

enter the 'realm of equality and brotherhood,'" an ironic reference to the Marxist phrase (*ES*, p. 360). Such usages were not uncommon among families and enterprises in Bremen and Hamburg and their foreign affiliates. Maintaining a common account was also practiced by Weber firms. For instance, Woermann & Weber, established in Bielefeld in 1811, and D. F. Weber & Co., established in Hamburg in 1814, maintained a common account until Gottlieb Christian Woermann withdrew in 1829. The Woermann family, intermarried with the Webers, later established the famous African shipping line. D. F. Weber's son continued the Hamburg firm with a brother and with Otto Weber, a brother of Max Sr.

17. Weber did not check his memory and exaggerated the figures. Only eight million dollars were raised "blindly"; the final pool amounted to fifty million dollars (not pounds). Villard's Oregon Railroad and Navigation Company was efficiently organized and paid good dividends. Investors had reason to trust Villard and could indeed guess the purpose of the pool. Thus Villard straddles Weber's strict dichotomy. If he illustrates some aspects of "grandiose booty capitalism," he was also a rational manager "of an ordinary capitalist large-scale enterprise." Whatever the pertinence of the example, Weber drew on it because it had become part of the family lore. Cf. "Global Capitalism and Multi-Ethnicity: Max Weber Then and Now," in Stephen Turner, ed., *The Cambridge Companion to Weber* (Cambridge: Cambridge University Press, 2000), pp. 121ff.

18. In 1960, Reinhard Bendix, writing in the context of the recently established field of stratification, was the first to call wider attention to Weber's treatment of the exchange (Bendix, *Max Weber*, pp. 47–59; 2nd ed., pp. 23–36). Together with S. M. Lipset, he elaborated the basic dichotomy of class and status. Bendix was particularly interested in how the impersonal exchange could be linked to the emergence of a status group with its own conceptions of probity and honor. Forty-plus years later much of the scholarly interest has shifted away from broad sociological propositions to specific historical contexts as well as their implications for economic policy then and now. In this perspective it is easier to see that Weber's writings on the exchange show him to be not only an "economic nationalist" but also An anglophile member of the *grande bourgeoisie*.

19. For the political and economic context see Knut Borchardt's 100-page introduction to *Börsenwesen: Schriften und Reden 1893–1898*, *MWG*, I / 5 (2000) and the editorial reports to each item; they make indispensable reading for social scientists who are not familiar with the partly highly technical subject matter. Borchardt provides a concise overview of the rise of the securities and commodity exchanges in the nineteenth century and the parallel developments in commercial jurisprudence and legislation. He gives proper attention to Weber's teacher and mentor Levin Goldschmidt, one of the founders of the academic field of commercial law. Goldschmidt, author of a famous *Universalgeschichte des Handelsrechts*, traced the rise of commercial law out of the practices primarily of Italian merchants and actively tried to preserve the "law of merchants for merchants" as long as possible against the increasing intervention of the state—a view that influenced Weber's judgment.

20. *MWG*, I / 5: 714. Weber's insistence that the forms of exchange are not in themselves ethical or unethical, but only the people involved, remains pertinent to-

day. His plutocratic remedy, however, is less feasible than ever before. He would have wanted to exclude the mass of people without substantial means who trade today on their own, especially the day traders, as an inappropriate form of commercial democratization.

21. This was also the conclusion of the first of his popular articles, which he wrote for an untutored audience. In the recent English translation, Weber's argument is put upside down. The two popular essays on the exchange, written for Friedrich Naumann's "Göttinger Arbeiterbibliothek," are now available in a translation by Steven Lestition. See *Theory and Society* 29 (June 2000): Steven Lestition, "Historical Preface," 289–304; Weber "Stock and Commodity Exchanges [Die Börse]," pp. 305–38; Weber, "Commerce on the Stock and Commodity Exchanges [Der Börsenverkehr]," pp. 339–71; and Richard Swedberg, "Afterword: The Role of the Market in Max Weber's Work," pp. 373–84. Apart from some factual slips in Lestition's introduction, the translation regrettably has many errors, which at crucial points reverse the meaning of sentences.

22. The Mendelssohn clan was split between hyphenators and nonhyphenators. Weber spells Ernst von Mendelssohn-Bartholdy without the hyphen in the Felix way.

23. The first to give sustained attention to this issue was Lawrence Scaff, "Weber before Weberian Sociology," *British Journal of Sociology* 35 (1984): 190–215; see also idem, *Fleeing the Iron Cage* (Berkeley: University of California Press, 1989).

24. In the so-called professors' memorandum at the Versailles Peace Conference, Weber, together with Albrecht Mendelssohn-Bartholdy, Hans Delbrück, and Max Graf Montgelas, stated on May 27, 1919: "It is very regrettable that the theory, which is completely erroneous in our view, of the alleged inescapability [*Naturnotwendigkeit*] of trade wars was given strong support by a very accomplished American writer [Veblen, *Theory of Business Enterprise*, 1904]." See "Bemerkungen zum Bericht der alliierten und assoziierten Regierungen über die Verantwortlichkeit der Urheber des Krieges," *MWG*, I / 16: 349.

25. *Gesammelte Aufsätze zur Wissenschaftslehre*, ed. Johannes Winckelmann (Tübingen: J. C. B. Mohr, 1973), p. 477.

26. See "Global Capitalism and Multi-Ethnicity," pp. 117–30.

Economy and Society *and the Revision of Weber's Ethics*

There are many ways that one might periodize Weber's works based on a wide range of possible thematic or methodological concerns. Here I wish to break down the years of Weber's extraordinary creativity into three periods, in order to talk about both his sociology of ethics and the sociology of Weber's own ethics.[1] These periods are 1903–13, 1914–17, and 1918–20. Naturally, it is impossible within the scope of an essay to treat thoroughly the complexity and development of Weber's ethics and the ways in which his studies of religious ethics influenced his own views. In this essay I want to provide the sketch of arguments for three claims.

First, between 1915 and 1917, we can see ways in which Weber maintained certain features of his understanding of ethics, meaning, and the question of how to lead one's life (*Lebensführung*) that he had formulated earlier. We can also see ways in which he revised that understanding through metaphors drawn from war and the ancient world, and then refined and deepened his views in the works of the period 1918–20. This led to an explosive combination of older and newer ethical understandings that Weber then brought very dramatically into the political struggles over the fate of Germany through his enormous effort to influence the current generation of university students, who would be the next generation of leaders. The question I want to raise concerns the *relation* between the changes in the substantive work as evidenced in *Economy and Society*, part I, and Weber's late diagnosis of the "condition of the present" and how to live in it—which involves thinking about the meaning of *Weltanschauungen* and value conflict for the problem of *Lebensführung*. The wartime and postwar writings were to carry this work further, and they greatly influenced Weber's own efforts at an ethical shaping of German youth. Second, neither in 1915–17 nor in 1918–20 did Weber fully analyze sociologically the way he himself conceived of the contemporary situation of the West and its ethical challenges, and this led him to make fundamentally problematic ethical proposals. Finally, while certain basic concepts in *Economy and Society*, part I, were built during 1918–20, quite legitimately, from the personal worldview that Weber propounded in his reflections on ethical matters, we must analyze their construction before we use them, in order to avoid "importing" with them, however unconsciously, the influence of Weber's own personal "values" and diagnosis of his "present" on the posing of sociological questions. Yet Weber's "translation" of some "value" alternatives into sociological concepts in this work provides a link between, on the one hand, the prophetic, personal, and ethical "demands" that Weber made on German youth and, on the other hand, the concepts and tasks of his formal sociology.[2]

The relation between *Economy and Society* and Weber's *Collected Essays on the Sociology of Religion* has been a common subject of debate and reflection.[3] It has an especial significance, given the tremendously diverse, rich, and creative scholarly productivity of the period 1918–20 in Weber's life and work. First, leaving aside his many interventions in political debates and action during that time, Weber wrote the beginnings of his "sociology," *Economy and Society*, part I. Second, at the same time, he was working intensely on his sociology of religion: researching and writing the later parts of his study of ancient Judaism, which appeared from 1917–18 to 1920, and revising all of the studies he intended to include in volume one of his *Collected Essays on the Sociology of Religion*, whose publication, in 1920, Weber himself oversaw. These studies included *The Protestant Ethic and the Spirit of Capitalism* and "The Protestant Sects," and also *Confucianism and Taoism*, the first study to be included under the subheading *The Economic Ethics of the World Religions*. Third, he added at the end of the volume a revised version of an unusual and extremely important essay he first wrote in 1915 as a bridge to his study of Hinduism and Buddhism, entitled "Intermediate Reflection: Theory of the Stages and Directions of Religious Rejection of the World." Finally, he wrote an "Author's Introduction" to the whole collection and greatly revised his "Introduction" to the part entitled *The Economic Ethics*.

However one wishes to view the implications of the complex thinking of this late period, there can be no doubt that Weber's study of the world religions was not, at any period, "only" a study of "economic ethics," but was also a study in the "sociology of ethics" broadly understood. Weber examined the ethical, religious, and "life" orientations of social strata comparatively and throughout the world, orientations whose implications for action in the world he was then able to consider, and whose capacity to produce the impulse and force to revolutionize traditional economic practices he was able to "measure." From the time of *The Protestant Ethic* and the many responses Weber felt obliged to make to the numerous misunderstandings of his work, it was clear that no economic ethic could be grasped without being situated in relation to the material determinations, as well as the beliefs and ethical orientations, of religious intellectuals and believers more concretely. Indeed, the remarkable chapter on the sociology of religion, written from 1910 to 1913, in what we usually think of as *Economy and Society*, part II, shows how far this effort to produce a comparative sociology of ethics had come even before World War I.[4] One key feature of this work from 1910–13, in *The Protestant Ethic* and in *Economy and Society*, part II, was the notion of the ascetic calling and its uniqueness within the ethics of the world religions. The importance of this Calvinist ethic and its continued influence in Western culture are made very plain there, and his already well worked-out analysis of it from that period returns to inform his own later ethical proposals. In addition to his extraordinary analysis of religious ethics, Weber provides, although regrettably only in passing, remarks on aspects of the social foundations of the ethical positions of a number of different, primarily secular, intellectual strata at various periods and in various places, including those of some of his contemporaries in Russia, Germany, and elsewhere. In a number of his late works in particular, he tried to provide at least an outline of what he considered some of the inescapable material and sociological determinants of the ethical concerns of Germany and rationalized society more generally, as well as of his own proposals.

But from about 1914 to 1917, after he had completed the chapter on the sociology of religion in 1913 and before the remarkably creative period of 1918–20, Weber experienced the enormous political, physical, and psychological impact of war. This was to lead him, as it led others, to see a sharpening of ethical, political, and other kinds of conflict that went beyond the bounds of what had seemed containable within the existing political and social world hitherto. The influence of his experiences can be seen in the regular and important presence of metaphors of war, soldiering, battle, and death and their implications, not only for those in the field, but for those at home, in ordinary "callings," as well.[5]

To trace the changes in Weber's understanding of ethics, we need to pay special attention not only to his analysis of certain important religious ethics, but also to the use he made of metaphors drawn from religion in his treatment of values and their conflicts, for through them he set the parameters for what he considered any future understanding of the special conditions and possibilities of ethical action. In "Objectivity in Social Science and Social Policy" from 1904, Weber argued that social policy could not be created by "science," but depended, rather, on the values it was designed to fulfill. In making his point, Weber went so far as to characterize his own epoch as one "that has eaten from the tree of knowledge" and which must realize that "the highest ideals, which move us most powerfully, are worked out in the struggle through all time with other ideals, which are as holy to others as ours are to us." At the same time, there is clearly one "high ideal" that Weber himself appeals to and evidently shares with his audience, namely, the "worth of the 'personality' [which] is contained in the fact that there are values around which it organizes its life," no matter what these values may be.[6] In this early essay, "struggle" is of central importance, yet apart from a relatively minimal use of a Hebrew biblical image and references to faith and the sacred, Weber otherwise deals with the problem of conflicting values with a language of choices, costs, consequences, and internal consistency. This situation of conflict and choice is important not only for the work of social science, but also for the ways in which actors participate in the world.

No later than February 1916, Weber began to use the concept of "polytheism," drawn from John Stuart Mill, to describe his view of the proliferation of, and struggle between, sets of values in the contemporary world, which, he claimed, had become an inescapable fact.[7] Polytheism, as Weber invoked it, appeared in the guise of a diagnosis, now uncovered, of the cultural condition of existence in the present. This characterization of the present in terms of "polytheism" offered interesting possibilities for the conceptualization of ethical action and belief: "In fact, whoever remains in the world (in the Christian sense), can experience nothing other in himself than the struggle between a plurality of series of values, of which one appears as a duty for itself." Here once again the centrality of "struggle" is affirmed, but something new is added: "He has to choose which of these gods he will and should serve, or when he should serve the one and when the other. But at all times he will find himself engaged in a fight against one or other of the gods of this world, and above all far from the God of Christianity—at least from the one proclaimed in the Sermon on the Mount."[8] Thus "God" and "ultimate value" are equated, and there is no evidence yet of the presence of more diabolical forces at work in the world, even though war is raging on the battlefields of France. At the same time, Weber clearly draws on the language of service to a cause in a calling in proposing how we are to manage this condition, what relationship we should have to it, what actions we should undertake in it, no matter what "sphere" we choose, and how we are thus to live a meaningful life. His ethical "prescription" for how one must relate to this multiplicity of values is, first, that one must treat each of them as a "god," and second, that one must "serve" one or more of them. Thus Weber moves the question of "which" god one should "choose," or to which one should make a "commitment," into a proposal that requires that one consider oneself a "servant" of a god, a form of relationship that all are obliged to adopt toward the god they have chosen. The new characterization, combined with the old ethic, provides a foretaste of problems to come.

In 1917, in "The Meaning of 'Value Freedom' in the Social and Economic Sciences," the revision of a discussion paper from 1913, Weber added other elements to his claim that "absolute polytheism" was the "single metaphysic adequate" for describing the conflicting values and "value-spheres" of the present age. We have seen that Weber had already gone beyond Mill's version of how common-sense experience led to polytheism, rather than monotheism, as the most reasonable conclusion of observation and reflection. He now left behind any remnants of Mill's rather restrained language of social coexistence and competition of points of view for a language of much greater polarization: "It is not finally a question everywhere and always of alternatives between values, but of irreconcilable deadly struggle, as that between 'God' and 'Devil.' Between these there are no relativizations and compromises." Of course, in all lives there are real compromises, and value-spheres obviously "cross and intertwine." Yet individuals must still make "the choice between 'God' and 'Devil' and their own ultimate decision about which of the colliding values will be ruled by the one and which by the other." And here, in syncretic fashion, Weber drew a parallel between his claim and the problem of choice in Plato, "through which the soul . . . *chooses* its own fate—this means the meaning of its action and being."[9] Now for the first time we see the mixing of the images of Christian dualisms with ancient Greek images of fate. Yet whatever else the soul may choose in Book X of *The Republic*, Plato does not characterize it as a choice between God and Devil. These words were not spoken by Weber in the less restrictive environment of a public lecture hall, but in a first-rank essay on method, which also pronounced stern lessons about the appropriate understanding of values for social scientists.

In "Science as a Vocation," also from 1917, the significance of the modern situation and its relation to the ancient world is pushed even further.

It is as in the ancient world, still not disenchanted of its gods and demons, only in another sense: as the Hellene sacrificed one time to Aphrodite and then to Apollo, and above all everyone to the gods of his city, so is [the world] still today, disenchanted and stripped of the mythical but inwardly true plasticity of its behavior. And over these gods and in their struggle fate governs, but certainly no "science." It can only be understood *what* the godly is for the one and for the other order or: in the one and the other order.[10]

Speaking from within the most developed form of Occidental rationalization, Weber announces the "return" of ancient gods, gods that had been suppressed, but obviously not "lost," since history has preserved them, despite their having been recast and then expelled in the form of Augustine's defense against the charge that Christianity was responsible for the fall of Rome, because it had supplanted the Roman gods. Indeed, Weber had already noted how typical of the antique world this kind of "rebirth" was: "From time to time phenomena of ancient culture that were completely lost have later emerged in a world strange to them."[11] Thus these "gods" have always been latent and potentially available, though unrecognized as such, but their resurrection is now an inescapable fact of the "everyday" and a "condition of the present," in Weber's view. Wolfgang Mommsen has observed that Weber's "present" confronts the individual with "just that multiplicity of competing forces which people of earlier epochs not infrequently tried to explain in mythological terms." "Humanity," he says, "after a thousand years of emancipation from mythical forms of ontological validation had returned to its initial condition—namely a return to mythological ways of thinking and conversing, although maybe on a higher level." But Weber was ambivalent about this condition. Says Mommsen: "Although in his discussion of the eternal conflict between alternative values and competing worldviews, formulations would always flow from [Weber's] pen which owed something to ancient mythology, he confronted mythological thought and to a certain extent every form of myth in general with skepticism, if not complete rejection." Yet, Mommsen suggests, "one can ask whether Max Weber did not himself hover on the threshold of mythological modes of thought with such a radical conception of the role of the individual as a completely self-dependent mediator between quite separate spheres of reality."[12]

In "Science as a Vocation," the effort of clarification, which can still think of other "orders" in terms of what is godly for them, is reserved for the classroom, and the classroom is limited to this. But outside the university, the struggle over the "problem of *life*" does not stop with the understanding of the other gods: "According to the ultimate standpoint, the one is the devil for the individual and the other is the god, and the individual must choose which, *for him*, is the god and which the devil."[13] Weber's invocation of "god" and "devil" should not be underestimated. Despite his view that the modern world should be grasped in terms of a multiplicity of gods, as in the ancient world, Weber casts the conflict of values in the language of Christianity, which now itself becomes mythic, where a believer chooses to serve the one "God" and do battle with the evil "Devil." Even in this "condition," ethical responsibility dictates that one must relate to these "gods" in the dualism created by Christian faith. Weber has added Christian biblical images of good and evil, god and devil, to the metaphor of polytheism and the return of ancient gods, which, despite his claim about the "opening" of our eyes, have clearly not displaced the dualisms of Western monotheism. And the stakes are, once again, just as serious as they were in Christianity.

Weber argued that ascetic service in a calling should be the form of that relation. This relation, is, as I have indicated, the return of a form of meaning, or at the very least the restoration, or revival, of a form of *Lebensführung* that emerged when Catholic asceticism strode out of the "non-everyday" (*ausseralltäglich*) monastery and into the everyday world of the Calvinist believer. This form had indeed remained alive in Western culture, though shorn of its original meaning in which the believer acted as a tool of God, to obtain some feeling of the certainty of salvation as well. Ironically, Weber is proposing that we recognize and accept the material fact of the "return" of the gods, and that we deal with it through another kind of "return": a "return" of the form of "service to God in a calling," derived strictly from Christian monotheism, and in particular from the Puritans. No discussion of "revisions" or "turns" should obscure the strong continuity of Weber's work, especially in the terms of "service in a calling," for this language, along with the dilemma of the loss of its original god or "object," is present in his work from *The Protestant Ethic* to "Politics as a Vocation" and the 1920 revision of the "Intermediate Reflection." The ascetic calling in service to God has "returned" from the past to cope with the "old" gods of the present, as the one consistent and meaningful way to relate to one's current "gods," the only form of life that can justify itself and meet "the demands of the day," to choose a god and submit oneself to serving it. To Weber, only this can provide the strength and purpose needed to "measure up inwardly" to these demands. Unexpectedly, what remains after Christian monotheism is "overcome" is "Christian polytheism," with its own gods and devils. Thus the problem of service in a calling underlies the intensification of the conceptual resort to gods and devils, while the problem of the conflict of values moves into the concept of polytheism, but always with this link to struggle and to service to one's god.[14]

From the time he wrote the first version of the "Intermediate Reflection" in late 1915, until he delivered the haunting lecture "Science as a Vocation" in 1917, Weber worked the Calvinist calling into the polytheistic metaphysic, based on a Calvinist-like search for rigorous and ineluctable deductions or conclusions from his worldview and his understanding of the present. He demanded inner consistency in all of his own positions and actions, and he demanded the same of others engaged in social or political action, for whom these ethical decisions were significant. At the same time, although he expressly claimed that he was laying out only ethical *problems*, Weber set formal parameters for how one must lead one's life in these conditions that became themselves the foundation of ethical *answers* to these problems, in the same way that the Kantian form of the categorical imperative did. Weber recognized the problem in Kant, but did not recognize it in his own "formal" ethics.[15]

This fusing of two such different, indeed conflicting, worlds, spiritual schemes, and vocabularies raises a serious question about the adequacy of Weber's ethical revisions to cope with what he takes to be an altered world.

The polytheistic interpretation of value-spheres cannot be combined in any consistent way with the Christian language that requires the believer to serve God as a tool and to conquer the Devil, with the goals and form of a *Lebensführung* derived from that same Christian religion that had originally suppressed and put an end to the "first" polytheism, and whose power, Weber claimed, had "blinded" the West for so long. Weber's interpretations and proposals must be understood as an entrant into the world of action, which, in his work, takes on the (unconscious) guise of inevitable facts and conditions of the present, and with the goal of "facing up to the everyday."[16] Though he can relate the vision of "gods" in all other religions also to conditions and experiences, he does not seem to be able to do this here. *He* experiences life as he believes the ancients did, with the modification of impersonality.

This strange mix of metaphors and prescriptions, drawn from both classical antiquity and Christian asceticism, never was, in historical fact, and never could have been, combined together for long in either of the two epochs that "return." As Walter Burkert says,

Polytheism means that many gods are worshiped not only at the same place and at the same time, but by the same community and by the same individual; only the totality of the gods constitutes the divine world. However much a god is intent on his honor, he never disputes the existence of any other god; they are all everlasting ones. There is no jealous god as in the Judeo-Christian faith. What is fatal is if a god is overlooked.[17]

Thus, "we" do not really live as did the ancients, either in the social conditions of their existence, or in the terms of Weber's interpretation of the ancient gods, and Weber's mixing of metaphors shows that he could not quite conceive it either. The mix makes it difficult to recognize that the ancients imagined their "pantheons" of many gods generally in terms of families that returned to forms of harmony and coexistence once conflicts had passed or been resolved by the overlord of the gods. Nor did they have any conception of "radical evil" like the devil, as Weber himself says.[18] In fact, Alexander the Great and later the Romans were able to add or absorb nearly all the gods of the peoples they conquered, with the great exception of the stiff-necked Hebrews, for whom it was monotheism or nothing, and the Christians, who absorbed them and abolished other gods.

Here, Weber's last, most "pure" types in formal sociology can themselves "serve" a moral purpose, by giving people an account of the foundations of their own lives. Weber says that its larger social value is precisely to teach a person who the gods really are that he or she "serves" in actual fact, even if unaware of it, who the devil is, and to argue that we must serve our own gods and causes in this way, because analysis of one's service alone allows one to work out one's own form of what Weber explicitly calls "salvation" through service. Thus, sociology shows everyone his or her gods and how to serve them.[19] The call for the consistent recognition of this need to serve some god or ultimate value lies at the heart of Weber's notions of moral responsibility, honesty, and integrity. Elsewhere, I have argued that Weber assigns such "service" even more significance than before: "service of the gods" provides the solution to the problem of a meaningful death in the modern world, and thus also to the problem of a meaningful life.[20] This is the form in which the question of how to live or direct one's life is answered.

This strong link between the language of ideal or pure types, of polytheism, and of service in a calling is a product of philosophical, historical, and social-scientific elements in a radical conception of the present, its tasks, and how their fulfillment must be accomplished. Ideal types now provide tools for analysis of many forms of service, from many possible standpoints, and thus become useful not only as analytical devices for the arrangement or measurement of reality from particular points of view, but also as means for working out one's own form of what Weber calls "salvation" through ascetic service, no matter whether we think of that service as "value-rational" in essence, or as instrumentally rational for the fulfillment of the "demands" of a cause.

Already by 1913, in the process of dealing with the relationship of religious ethics and politics, Weber had formulated the "ethic" of the calling for the present. Indeed, Weber claims that "only the ethic of the calling of inner-worldly asceticism is truly inwardly adequate to the commitment to impersonal goals characteristic of the coercive structure of domination."[21]

"Without regard for person," "sine ira et studio," without hate and therefore without love, without free will [*Willkür*] and therefore without grace, as objective [*sachliche*] duty in a calling and not on account of a concrete personal relationship, the *homo politicus* as much as the *homo oeconomicus* carries out his task today precisely when he performs it in the most ideal degree in the sense of the rational rules of the modern order of power.[22]

Thus, all action in a rationalized world built on specialization of tasks must have "the character of 'service' vis-à-vis an impersonal *objective purpose* [*sachlichen Zweck*]."[23] This is how the calling is done best, how the ethic is fulfilled, no matter what the ultimate value, goal, or cause.

So many of the efforts made by Karl Jaspers and others to see Weber as a heroic, pessimistic model and inspiration for others confuse him with what Weber himself called the type of the "exemplary prophet," for Weber, in fact, spoke from the point of view of the "ethical" or "emissary prophet"; he was prescribing the one form of "manly" conduct that was consistent in the contemporary situation, using his "ascetic revelation" in "Science as a Vocation" and "Politics as a Vocation" first as a way to upbraid his nation and his time, and second, to reveal to German youth the limiting conditions of, and not the path to, a self-consistent determination of the direction of their own lives. Weber's conviction that he was not prescribing for others a particular path or form of how to live their lives, was, in fact, mistaken. Weber led himself to claim that, no matter toward what "god" or what "sphere" one oriented oneself, the devotion to one's god and opposition to one's devil can only be accomplished through "service in a calling." It was the necessary form through which German youth must "serve" their ultimate values in a way analogous to the way the Puritans had served their God.[24] Once the power of the religious sanctification of moral action has been driven out of a range of "spheres" of human action, which take as their ideal or ideal-typical form a set of "laws" immanent to each sphere, then the only ethic that remains is the ethic of practice for serving the "god" of each sphere, namely, conforming to the god's "laws."[25]

In every task of a *calling*, the *cause* [*Sache*] as such demands its right and wants to be fulfilled according to its own laws. In every task of a calling, he to whom it is set has to limit himself and to exclude that which does not belong strictly to the *cause*, but particularly: his own love and hate. . . . And it is to strip the "calling" of the only sense which today remains still really meaningful, if one does not perform that specific kind of self-limitation that it demands.[26]

Within each sphere, then, there is a set of laws and a cause that prescribe the ethic of how one is to conduct one's life "correctly" in a calling, and which, at the same time, prescribe the ethic of how one is to conduct oneself toward others, with the pressures of the obligation to act "impersonally" to fulfill one's "cause," meeting the injunctions and relationships with the everyday world that demand or need a response. But this is more than an issue of competently following inner laws. It is a matter of conforming to the particular "spirit" of a calling, which demands a particular ethics of practice, of action, indeed, of responsibility. Just like the Calvinist, the modern person in a calling "proves himself exclusively in the work of the calling."[27] This conflict of spheres was already a feature of the earlier sociology of religion in *Economy and Society*, part II: "with the increasing systematization and rationalization of social relationships and of their contents, there emerge the conflicts of the inner autonomous laws of the individual life spheres against the religious postulate, and, the more intense the religious need is, so much the more do they turn the 'world' into a problem."[28] A good leader, one with a "calling for politics," requires not just knowledge, but also an ethos, an ethic that keeps a leader in the "service" of his "ultimate values" in the "calling," with discipline and passion, yet also self-control and responsibility. Without this, a leader does not deserve to be followed. Weber's discussion of this ethos is one of the things that makes his 1919 lecture "Politics as a Vocation" so compelling, because it concerns both politics and how one should lead one's own life more generally, for in most ways, his proposals are alike. But what is also clear is that the tension is not only with the "world" and its compromises: it is with the champions of other causes and values, with the *Gesinnungsethik* of others in the world, and not just against the everyday world, which has the appearance, therefore, more of a war between religions than a struggle with different worldly spheres.

Weber, like Foucault later, had no doubt that the "present" and the "everyday" were the true time and place of human action, and he opposed desires to go beyond or "escape" from the "everydayness" of the present, whether evidenced in elevated philosophical circles or in the pressures of the "street," desires soon to be expressed with philosophical sophistication by Heidegger, who, through the work of Jaspers and the publicity aroused by "Science as a Vocation," knew well and referred to Weber's late lecture. Indeed, in Weber there was a reinvestment in the importance of the everyday world. But there remains the problem of what the relation should be to the everyday. Here there is another interesting convergence of Weber and Foucault. This polytheism, which has "returned" from the dead, does not, in Weber's view, undermine freedom by its proliferation of possible values, causes, or gods to "serve"—a proliferation that, for example, conservative critics of the West usually condemn as a sign of cultural decline, but has in fact enriched it by permitting innumerable forms of "service" in a calling.[29] By mixing a monotheism of God and Devil into his "polytheism," Weber drives up the stakes, forces them, so that the full implications of service become clear, and so that his version of "moral rectitude" will be carried out. It is now possible to become more capable of action, to "choose one's fate," rather than resign oneself to being only the plaything of powers one cannot oppose. Thus, in principle, the present situation offers many paths to meaning, although it also forecloses some for the "mature man," namely, the sacrificing of what one's intellect says in order to join religious communities and faiths. For Weber, as later for Foucault, the tasks of the present, and their difference from the past, must be seen in the context of this new "freedom" within a new condition—for Weber, freedom to "choose" which god to serve, for Foucault, a freedom to shape one's life as a work of art. Both kinds of freedom are now possible precisely because of the weakening of Christianity, which leads Weber to speak of the "blinders" of monotheism and Foucault to speak of "subjectivating" moral rules.

Nietzsche, Weber, and Foucault each spoke of "our" condition, "our" tasks, and the form of life that "we" must pursue.[30] For each of the three, religious faith and practices had become impossible, not only for themselves and other intellectuals who had taken critical positions toward such faith, but also, from the point of view of intellectual credibility, for everyone. Ascetic service of some kind was a necessity for Weber, as *amor fati* (love of one's fate) was for Nietzsche, and as an aesthetics of existence was for Foucault. In speaking always of what "we" must do, they all in effect sentenced everyone to their own solutions, their own "magic."[31] Whether they understood adherence to religion as sublimated resentment, as requiring an "intellectual sacrifice," as the misguided subjection of the self to the fixed identity imposed by moral rules, or as the original prototype of all foundationalisms, all were hard-pressed to imagine in the present anything else that they would consider to be a "mature," intellectually "respectable" set of faiths and practices within a religious community, and not only for themselves. On the one hand, it seems that no Christian of any intellectual bent can "hold his head up" before their critique. On the other hand, each one also articulates a claim that is in genuine *contradiction* with this presumption to speak for "us": from Zarathustra's statement "This now is *my* way; Where is yours?"; to Weber's claim that one cannot tell anyone which "gods" to follow; to Foucault's rejection of subjection to anything that would pin the self to a single imposed identity. Thus, while each seems to insist that there is a single *form* through which the demands of the present must be met, each also seems to renounce the right even to insist on that.

That one side of both Weber and Foucault denies to the present, or better, to the range of empirically diverse people in the present, any really "worthy" position from which traditional faith and practice of any kind could be deserving of respect and even appreciation is a fundamental problem. For Weber as for Foucault, there is a *higher* perspective or "truth" from the point of view of which the others' positions are not simply rejected for oneself, but found to be inadequate for everyone capable of intellectual honesty. Weber calls the Sermon on the Mount and the idea of "Resist not Evil," for example, an ethic that bespeaks "lack of dignity" when seen from within the world, and he opposes it to the "manly dignity" of resisting evil and accepting the consequences.[32] This form of judgment on the "objective" possibilities of the present and the only paths still open is curious, since, in fact, the choices of others, not only for different "gods" but for totally different forms of *relation* to those gods than ascetic service, are of no necessary negative consequence for oneself.

In a sense, both Weber and Foucault work from a highly individualistic perspective, another inescapable aspect of the condition of the present.[33] In Weber's case, this image of the single individual forced to choose between such things was an existential fact, based on the ontological status of values. It is not surprising that Jaspers compared him to Nietzsche and Kierkegaard.[34] As Wolfgang Schluchter has observed, for Weber, "the mod-

ern complex of meaning has institutionalized reflection as an ongoing enterprise, but in a highly individualistic form. It thus possesses a high potential for constructing meaning, but only in an individual and not in a collective sense."[35] Weber saw this reality of the single individual as a consequence
of the unique situation of his time and place, namely, the conditions of rationalization and disenchantment in the West, and it was these conditions,
not he, that put the individual in such a position. Nonetheless, this situation
did not preclude the return of polytheism to form yet another condition of
the present, from a totally different kind of social and religious order, where
alone it had once been possible and meaningful.

We saw earlier how Weber's "ethical revision" and worldview could find
their way even into what is usually the austere presentation of "method."
Economy and Society, part I, shows too how this "revision" had an influence
on the very construction of some of Weber's fundamental sociological concepts. In 1917, Weber, in some sense, already prepared us for it. The "point of
view" from which "ideal types" are constructed does not matter. "For the
purpose of characterizing a specific type of attitude, the investigator may
construct either an ideal-type which is identical with his own personal ethical norms . . . or one which ethically is thoroughly in conflict with his own
normative attitudes; and he may then compare the behavior of the people
being investigated with it."[36] Thus concept construction can take many
forms, and one such form is the legitimate introduction of concepts that are
intended to measure behaviors of particular ethical importance to the investigator. This is not "bias" or the "promotion" of a normative position, but the
formation of concepts to ask very specific kinds of questions.

We can see such formation in some concepts Weber created in *Economy
and Society*, part I, to understand what "determines" (or "decides") social action and what categories one must use to understand ethics: "An 'ethical'
standard [for sociology] is a certain kind of value-rational *belief* which men
treat as a valid norm governing human action, which makes use of the predicate of 'ethically good' in the same way that action which makes use of the
predicate 'beautiful' is measured by aesthetic standards. It is possible for ethically normative beliefs of this kind to have a profound influence on action
in the absence of any sort of guarantee."[37] Much more than in "affectual"
and "traditional" determinations, Weber is most interested in the other two
determinations, one by "instrumental [or goal] rationality" and the other by
"value rationality." The notion of "goal-rational action" emerged early in
Weber's analysis of social orders and powers, in what is now the "Sociology
of Law" in *Economy and Society*, part II, written probably by 1909, and it was
given a more analytical treatment in a methodological essay from 1913.[38]
However, the concept of "value rationality" as a determination of action appears in *Economy and Society* only in part I, as if the particular concerns that

helped form it were of relatively late origin. These two concepts are system- atically characterized as two "pure types" at the opposite ends of a contin- uum, and in opposition to one another in this "pure" form. Weber does not use "orientation" to values as such a determination, but introduces the more concrete and rationally worked-out notion of value rationality as a more us- able conception for his purposes. Here one can see the influence of his mor- alizing "dualist ethics" on what, for Weber, are objective types of determina- tions.[39] At the same time, one can see his attempts to put together these determinations for a newer ethic.

In Part I, Weber says that social action can be determined in four major ways: goal-rationally, value-rationally, affectually, and traditionally: "Value-ra- tionally means conscious belief in the unconditionally unique value—ethi- cal, aesthetic, religious, or some other, however understood—of a specific behavior purely as such and independently of success."

He acts *purely* value-rationally, who acts without regard for the foreseeable conse- quences, in the service of his conviction about what duty, honor, beauty, religious di- rection, piety, or the importance of a "cause," no matter of what kind, seems to him to command. In the sense of our terminology, value-rational action is always action following "commands" or in accordance with "demands," which the actor believes are placed on him. Only in so far as human action orients itself toward such demands do we want to speak of value rationality.

Even Weber expresses some reservation about the utility of this category, when he says: "This is the case in widely varying degrees, but for the most part only to a relatively slight extent."[40]

Opposed to this, Weber argues that social action can be determined "in an instrumental [or goal] rational [*zweckrational*] way: through expectations of the behaviors of objects in the external world, and of other human be- ings, and in the use of these expectations as 'conditions' or as 'means' for the attainment of the actor's own rationally pursued and calculated ends." From the point of view of instrumental rationality, "the more the value to which action is oriented is elevated to the status of an absolute value, the more 'ir- rational'" it is. "The more unconditionally the actor devotes himself to this value for its own sake . . . the less is he influenced by considerations of the consequences of his action."[41] Still, if we include affective and traditional motivations, these determinations are used for understanding which "mix- tures" or degrees of different determinations can be used to interpret a par- ticular social action. From our perspective, the two poles should both be considered "ethical orientations," whether they are oriented toward some kind of "purity" and submission or toward efficacy and mastery.[42] We might say, therefore, that, while a value-rational orientation means an actor has put him- or herself in the position of conforming or submitting to commands or demands, an instrumentally rational orientation means an actor endeavors to be more "in command" of his or her actions, in the sense of weighing consequences in accordance with the laws of efficacy that govern a particular sphere.

These two forms of rationality are Weber's translation into ideal-typical sociological concepts of an ethical distinction he made in several of his "ethical" works, beginning with "The Meaning of 'Value Freedom'" and "Science as a Vocation" in 1917, to "Politics a Vocation" in 1919. Weber argued that there were fundamentally only two "ethics" that guided actors' choices of social action, whether in politics or in the everyday world. They were an "ethic of conviction"—sometimes translated as an ethic of "intention," or of "absolutes," or of "ultimate values"—and an "ethic of responsibility." On the one hand, an ethic of conviction leads to action for its own sake, regardless of consequences or hope of success. The ethic "bears witness" to one's unconditional commitment to the demands of an ideal of whatever kind, and to keeping the ideal or "cause" pure and uncompromised. An ethic of responsibility, on the other hand, pursues the accomplishment of its goals exclusively on the basis of rational planning that anticipates the ways in which humans and objects will act and react. The consideration of consequences, and even of whether the "end" should be pursued at all, given its "costs," is part of its calculation.

There is no question that a "pure" ethic of conviction, of the kind Weber found particularly on the political left—which had no grasp, he thought, of political action or consequences—was the basis for the formation of the concept of value rationality. This fundamental category is an ideal-typical form of an ethic that troubled Weber profoundly and from which he expected grave political, social, and intellectual consequences. Instrumental or goal rationality in some "pure" form, would, of course, stand at the opposite pole—orientation to absolute values versus orientation to purely calculated action. For instrumental rationality, value rationality is always irrational, for whatever the degree of value rationality, there will always be a more limited consideration of consequences than in instrumental rationality. That is why this kind of determination can alone provide the necessary tools for the success of an ethic of responsibility. Interestingly, each of the pure types of rationality seems also to be characteristic of a different type of domination in Weber's schema of the three types of "legitimate domination," which Weber wrote about in the pieces that make up *Economy and Society*, part II. So pure value rationality seems to be a quality associated with the purest "charismatic" leaders, who pronounce new values, while the pure form of instrumental rationality is precisely the quality of bureaucrats and bureaucracies, focused on carrying out orders by rational calculation. Naturally, Weber presumes that the responsible and rational pursuit of high values will be the outcome.

These ethics and forms of rationality were all suffused with the experience of war and political conflict. Still, despite his invocation of "deadly struggles," Weber indicated, at one point, that the modern situation demanded that one "sacrifice" to "now one, now the other God," which shows, of course, that these spheres are not *essentially*, and certainly not always, in the eternal conflict Weber inevitably conjures up with his use of Christian metaphors of god and devil.[43] God and devil certainly dramatize what Weber believes are the stakes of one's choices, by framing "other" gods as enemies of one's own. But "god," "devil," and the notions of "irreconcilable conflict" cannot be mapped onto ancient mythological metaphors, except in the sense of the gods of one city going to war against the gods of another. Of course, the Christian god was still, and had been, called on at times as a "'god of battle' and 'god of our fathers'" like a local god in an ancient *polis.*"[44] Weber imported into his polytheism an understanding of the condition of humankind in the present that is inextricably tied up with Christian dualism and ideas of salvation. And, if I read the New Testament correctly, there can be no peace and no compromise between God and Devil.[45] In the "Intermediate Reflection," he goes further and reminds us that "Christianity makes the Savior triumph over the Devil."[46] Indeed, shortly before his death, Weber wrote: "The politician should and *must* make compromises. But my calling is as a scholar."[47] Ultimately, Weber's late ethical reflections, particularly in "Science as a Vocation" and "Politics as a Vocation," are evidence of foreboding and prediction of battles, without any proposal for a framework within which one might work out a solution within the constraints of the material and social conditions of the existing German social order. The Manichaean distinctions between god and devil, friend and foe, in Weber's late ethics triumph as cultural images and ideals over the development of a language of ideals and struggle joined to negotiation of difference on the basis of some shared understandings.[48]

The problem in Weber's proposals of this kind is their tremendous distance from an analysis of the concrete social conditions, organization, and experience of individuals and groups in Germany. Of course, he does provide historical treatments of the contemporary situation of science and of political leadership. But though Weber is far less teleological than Spengler and never sees things only in terms of fate and necessity, when it comes to prescriptions for that situation, what Weber the hard-headed realist does is to distance himself from those situations and to let concepts of world processes and of epochs, which are fundamentally intellectual constructions, do the ultimate work of setting the conditions and terms for the rescue of individual, society, and nation. Though he had always related the vision of "gods" in all other religions to conditions and experiences, he does not seem to be able to do this here. *He* experiences life as he believes the ancients did, with the modification of impersonality. As a result, while the contemporary situation seems rooted in real history, the solutions that he prescribes are not embedded in any concrete and local sense of what that social situation will actually support or allow. Hence the appeal of Weber's attitudes and solutions primarily to intellectuals of different political persuasions who saw the world through the grand abstractions of epochal change and saw him, as he largely saw himself, as a resigned and thus heroic pessimist fighting against an irreversible "modern" condition that precluded their visions of being brought under control by people like them. And certainly, in terms of the understanding that they shared with him, the renewal they dreamed of could only remain a dream. None of his proposals for the creation of personal meaning and the regeneration of individual and nation had any social foundation outside of a subset of the intellectual stratum. Thus Weber's proposals remained quite out of touch with the concrete conditions and possibilities of his audience and of the German public more generally.

The problem with Weber's ethics is that the material world of many choices—and not just abstract sociological categories—is cast in terms of spiritual oppositions so great that it is hard to imagine what "terms of peace" and mutual recognition of difference could ever resolve such a "battle of each against all" without the total defeat of one side or another. We know how central conflict and struggle were to Weber's whole understanding of society, both in terms of its concrete history and in terms of what Weber considers its "need," if it is to develop and grow strong. In many ways, Weber clearly wanted to provoke forms of channeled conflict, from the strengthening of working-class organizations to the battles of party leaders. The question is whether a language developed during war, and affected by projects of total political conquest and revolution all around him, could lend itself to the struggles of "peacetime" (insofar as the period of the Weimar Republic can be called that). As Weber remarked, "'Peace' means a shifting of the forms of struggle or of the opponents of struggle or of the objects of struggle, and nothing else."[49] It was one thing to analyze Great Britain, where one could find the elements of a background "consensus," and where such language and battles might not threaten to rend society apart. But Germany lacked enough of this shared or negotiated "life-world" to remain for long within an adequate cultural and institutional framework, once military defeat, class conflict, economic crisis, and authoritarian and military factions set massive crises into motion.

Yet Weber had once been able to imagine a solution to what must otherwise have to be unremitting war of each against all in service of different "gods." In a letter of April 2, 1913, to Robert Willbrandt, he says, "I think irreconcilable *conflict*, and therefore the necessity of constant *compromises*, governs the sphere of values; no one knows *how* one should make the compromises, unless a *compelling* 'revealed' *religion* wants to decide."[50] This notion of compromise shows that, still in 1913, Weber had not yet projected the absoluteness of Christian dualisms onto the conflicting value-spheres, and that therefore these conflicts were *not*, to him, so completely "irreconcilable," but between 1915 and 1917, in the midst of war, his late work "turned" away from this possibility. It left behind, first, the possibility of discriminating between *essentially* conflicting values and those that could be "managed," and it left behind, second, the possibility of distinguishing between the absolute demands of those *specific* days and times that force a war of gods, and the demands of those *other* days and times that sustain the terms of peace. The achievements of Weber's late "Sociology" were thus harnessed to his conception of a grim and unremitting struggle, for which his use of Christian dichotomies cannot provide the terms of peace.

Notes

1. Other significant treatments of these problems have been undertaken by Jeffrey Alexander, Wilhelm Hennis, and Wolfgang Schluchter.

2. Wolfgang Mommsen has a different view: "The value aspect comes into play not in the construction of the individual 'pure types' but rather in the manner in which they are related to one another, forming a systematic whole. In the final analysis, these ideal-typical concept constructions are informed by the principle of eternal struggle between different hierarchies of 'ultimate' values and the institutional concretizations they have found in the course of history. . . . The 'pure types' connected with one another to form an integrated system are informed by specific value-attitudes which, in turn, are in constant conflict with one another." Wolfgang Mommsen, "Ideal Type and Pure Type: Two Variants of Max Weber's Ideal-Typical Method," in *The Political and Social Theory of Max Weber: Collected Essays* (Chicago: University of Chicago Press, 1989), pp. 131–32; see also pp. 121–22, 128.

3. For details, see Wolfgang Mommsen, "Max Weber's 'Grand Sociology': The Origins and Composition of *Wirtschaft und Gesellschaft. Soziologie*," *History and Theory* 39 (October 2000): 364–83. After great editorial debate, *Economy and Society* is being issued in related, but separate, volumes. Volume I/22 will be issued in five "subvolumes," I/22-1 through I/22-5, one devoted to each of the sections now known as part II, and which were written generally between 1910 and 1913. Each of these subvolumes will bear the overall title *Economy and Society: The Economy and the Social Orders and Powers. Posthumous Papers*, since its essays were left unpublished and largely unrevised at the time of Weber's death. Part I was written between 1918 and 1920, and is a work whose difference from part II can be seen in the title it has been given as volume I/23: *Economy and Society: Sociology. Unfinished.*

4. This chapter has now been issued as a separate volume of the new edition. See Max Weber, *Gesamtausgabe*, vol. 22: *Wirtschaft und Gesellschaft. Die Wirtschaft und die gesellschaftlichen Ordnungen und Mächte. Nachlass*, Part II: *Religiöse Gemeinschaften*, ed. Hans G. Kippenberg, together with Petra Schilm, and with Jutta Niemeier (Tübingen: J. C. B. Mohr–Paul Siebeck, 2001).

5. From the end of 1915 to August 1916, one sees this influence in several writings of the war period, for example, "Zwischenbetrachtung," "Bismarcks Aussenpolitik und die Gegenwart," "Zwischen zwei Gesetzen," and "An der Schwelle des dritten Kriegsjahres," all in Max Weber, *Zur Politik im Weltkrieg. Schriften und Reden 1914–1918*, in Weber, *Gesamtausgabe*, I / 15, ed.Wolfgang Mommsen and Gangolf Hubinger (Tübingen: Mohr–Siebeck, 1984).

6. Weber, "Die 'Objektivität' sozialwissenschaftlicher und sozialpolitischer Erkenntnis," in Max Weber, *Gesammelte Aufsätze zur Wissenschaftslehre*, 5th ed., ed. Johannes Winckelmann (Tübingen: Mohr–Siebeck, 1982), pp. 154, 152; English in Max Weber, *The Methodology of the Social Sciences*, trans. and ed. Edward A. Shils and Henry A. Finch (New York: Free Press, 1949), pp. 57, 55.

7. John Stuart Mill, *Essays on Ethics, Religion and Society*, in *Collected Works of John Stuart Mill*, vol. 10, ed. J. M. Robson (Toronto: University of Toronto Press, 1969). Mill's name does not appear in the index to volume I / 22, part 2, on religious organizations, in the volume of Max Weber, *Gesamtausgabe*, devoted to *Economy and Society*, nor does it appear in the index to Weber, *Wirtschaft und Gesellschaft. Grundriss der verstehenden Soziologie*, 5th ed., ed. Johannes Winckelmann (Tübingen: Mohr–Siebeck, 1976).

8. Weber, "Zwischen Zwei Gesetzen," in Max Weber, *Zur Politik im Weltkrieg*, in Weber, *Gesamtausgabe*, I / 15, p. 98. English in Weber, "Between Two Laws," in Weber, *Political Writings*, ed. Peter Lassman and Ronald Speirs (Cambridge: Cambridge University Press, 1994), pp. 78–79.

9. Weber, "The Meaning of 'Value Freedom' in the Social and Economic Sciences," in Weber, *Wissenschaftslehre*, pp. 507–8. English in Weber, *Methodology of the Social Sciences*, pp. 17–18. See also the language on the fate of religious ethics in the world, in Weber, *Wirtschaft und Gesellschaft*, p. 353. English in Max Weber, *Economy and Society: An Outline of Interpretive Sociology*, ed. Guenther Roth and Claus Wittich (1921–22; Berkeley: University of California Press, 1978), p. 585. [Here and throughout this chapter, the author uses his own translations, which may differ from the published translations.—Eds.]

10. Max Weber, *Wissenschaftslehre*, p. 604; English in Max Weber, "Science as a Vocation," in *From Max Weber: Essays in Sociology*, trans. and ed. H. H. Gerth and C. Wright Mills (New York: Oxford University Press, 1946), p. 148.

11. Weber, "Agrarverhältnisse im Altertum," *Gesammelte Aufsätze zur Sozial- und Wirtschaftsgeschichte*, ed. Marianne Weber, 2nd ed. (1924; Tübingen: Mohr–Siebeck, 1988), p. 278. This shows the *endurance* or *persistence* or an always available *immanence* of "forms" of personal meaning and orientation in particular, that can either "return" or be "revived" because of historical developments, though they *cannot* evidently be *foreseen*, as, e.g., in the appearance of charisma. Mommsen argues that, in 1919–20, Weber *reversed* the sequence he had seemed to take for granted before: charisma was now the "fount of all creative activity that took its orientation from personal value ideals of non-everyday character." Charisma was thus *the* innovative force, the form in which personality "forces its way" into empirical processes of history. Mommsen, "Personal Conduct and Societal Change: Towards a Reconstruction of Max Weber's Concept of History," in Sam Whimster and Scott Lash, eds., *Max Weber, Rationality and Modernity* (London: Allen & Unwin, 1987), pp. 46–48.

12. Wolfgang Mommsen, "Rationalization and Myth in Weber's Thought," in *The Political and Social Theory of Max Weber*, pp. 144, 140, 135–36. In Mommsen's "Two Dimensions of Social Change," in the same work, p. 146, Mommsen says that, with respect to Weber's analysis of Asiatic creeds of inner-worldly perfection and accepting personal life: "In later years he occasionally toyed with the idea of whether he should not embark upon a similar path, as is indicated in the 'Zwischenbetrachtung' in the *Gesammelte Aufsätze zur Religionssoziologie*, which may be read as a (however sublime) self-confession on the part of Weber, and also in occasional talks with Georg Lukács. . . . However, in principle he still identified with the personal ideal of a rigorous, inner worldly, disciplined life-conduct in the service of ultimate ideals." What is surprising about the first statement is that it is in the *Zwischenbetrachtung* that Weber resolves the "death problem" through the calling as an analogue of war.

13. Weber, "Science as a Vocation," in *Wissenschaftslehre*, p. 604. English in Weber, "Science as a Vocation," in *From Max Weber: Essays in Sociology*, pp. 148–49.

14. As Erich von Kahler notes, in *Der Beruf der Wissenschaft*, translated in *Max Weber's "Science as a Vocation,"* ed. Peter Lassman and Irving Velody, with Herminio Martins (London: Unwin Hyman, 1989), p. 40: "in the ancient world there were struggles between the gods and conflicts of viewpoint, but there could never be a choice in the sense that at this place and time there exist two possibilities of action, each in principle of equal validity, to be chosen according to the fundamental outlook of the individual."

Ernst Robert Curtius goes further in "Max Weber on Science as a Vocation," in *Max Weber's "Science as a Vocation,"* p. 74, regarding conflict of gods: "Max Weber puts forward the view that this conflict has its roots in the ground of reality and therefore must simply be accepted as a fact of life." But: "Is this conflict of values, that is assumed to be of general validity, not perhaps merely the symptom of an anarchy of values that represents a specific manifestation of disturbance in recent West European culture?" That is, could not this problem be situational, in this place and time, rather than a feature of "reality"?

15. Weber, "Value Freedom," in *Wissenschaftslehre*, pp. 505–6. English in Weber, *Methodology of the Social Sciences*, pp. 16–17.

16. Mommsen, "Rationalization and Myth," in *Political and Social Theory of Max Weber*, pp. 144, 140.

17. See Walter Burkert, *Greek Religion*, trans. John Raffan (Cambridge, MA: Harvard University Press, 1985), pp. 216, 182. On Roman gods, see Patrick Atherton, "The City in Ancient Religious Experience," in A. H. Armstrong, ed., *Classical Mediterranean Spirituality: Egyptian, Greek, Roman*, vol. 15, p. 334, of *World Spirituality: An Encyclopedic History of the Religious Quest*, general editor Ewert Cousins (New York: Crossroad, 1986).

18. Weber, *Wirtschaft und Gesellschaft*, p. 268. English in Weber, *Economy and Society*, p. 438. This was also true of Confucianism, and Weber attributes the lack of the conception of radical evil in both cases not just to the lack of an independent priesthood, but to the lack of an ethical prophecy.

19. For Mommsen's view, see note 2, above.

20. Weber, "Zwischenbetrachtung," in *Die Wirtschaftsethik der Weltreligionen. Kon-*

fuzianismus und Taoismus. Schriften 1915–1920, ed. Helwig Schmidt-Glintzer, with Petra Kolonko, vol. I / 19 of Max Weber, *Gesamtausgabe* (Tübingen: Mohr–Siebeck, 1989), p. 493. See also Harvey Goldman, *Politics, Death, and the Devil: Self and Power in Max Weber and Thomas Mann* (Berkeley: University of California Press, 1992).

21. Weber, *Wirtschaft und Gesellschaft,* p. 362. See also p. 357, on how religious inner-worldly asceticism can use impersonal political power for rational ethical ends in the taming of the world. English in *Economy and Society,* pp. 601, 592–93.

22. Weber, *Wirtschaft und Gesellschaft,* p. 361. English in *Economy and Society,* p. 600.

23. Weber, *Wirtschaft und Gesellschaft,* pp. 709. English in *Economy and Society,* p. 1187. Weber addressed the question of personal versus impersonal service in *Wirtschaft und Gesellschaft,* p. 598. English in *Economy and Society,* p. 1031. This was especially important given the existence of "cults" of personal service, to which friends of Weber belonged, and given the widespread longings for personalization even apart from the cults. The most important example of this ideal was the circle around Stefan George. Though they differed a great deal, Weber and George were impressed with each other when they met, and Weber was affected by the seriousness "with which George personally faces his mission."

But, as Weber wrote in 1910, "in decisive points Stefan George and his pupils in the final analysis serve 'other gods' than I." As Marianne wrote of her husband, "Since he believed in the absolute value of intellectual and moral autonomy, he denied the necessity of new forms of *personal* dominion and *personal* service for him and his kind. He acknowledged service and absolute devotion to a *cause,* an ideal, but not to an earthly, finite human being and its limited aims, no matter how outstanding and venerable that person might be." See Marianne Weber, *Max Weber: A Biography,* trans. and ed. Harry Zohn, with a new introduction by Guenther Roth (New Brunswick, NJ: Transaction Books, 1988), pp. 457–62.

24. See Goldman, *Politics, Death, and the Devil;* idem, *Max Weber and Thomas Mann: Calling and the Shaping of the Self* (Berkeley: University of California Press, 1988).

25. Compare Jeffrey Alexander, "The Dialectic of Individuation and Domination: Weber's Rationalization Theory and Beyond," in Whimster and Lash, *Max Weber, Rationality and Modernity,* pp. 185–206, here p. 201.

26. Weber, "Value Freedom," in *Wissenschaftslehre,* p. 494. English in Weber, *Methodology of the Social Sciences,* pp. 5–6.

27. Weber, *Wirtschaft und Gesellschaft,* p. 355. English in Weber, *Economy and Society,* p. 588.

28. Weber, *Wirtschaft und Gesellschaft,* p. 349; compare p. 348. English in Weber, *Economy and Society,* p. 578; compare p. 576.

29. This link lends Mommsen's critique of "developmental history" more strength, I think, for the "return" of polytheism shows at least that any conception of "development" must be construed *very broadly* to accommodate such an element.

30. Weber may be making a mistake in his analysis of the present, speaking of "us" in a way that "we" might not find persuasive, and so may be saying something that applies truly to "him" and to the academics, intellectuals, and middle-class youth to whom he speaks, and for whom he describes this condition. See Wilhelm Hennis, *Max Weber, Essays in Reconstruction,* trans. Keith Tribe (London:

Allen & Unwin, 1988).

31. As Lassman and Velody say, the "individual must be 'forced to be free.' . . . Weber still retains a link with the Enlightenment in his belief in the ability of reason to cast out 'demons,' even if this belief is itself our 'demon.'" *Max Weber's "Science as a Vocation,"* p. 201.

32. Weber, "Science as a Vocation," in *Wissenschaftslehre*, p. 604. English in Weber, *From Max Weber*, p. 148.

33. This is echoed by Wolfgang Schluchter, *Religion und Lebensführung*, vol. 1, *Studien zu Max Webers Kultur- und Werttheorie* (Frankfurt: Suhrkamp, 1988), p. 160.

34. Karl Jaspers, in *Psychologie der Weltanschauungen*, 6th ed. (1919; Munich: Piper Verlag, 1994), p. 14, described Weber's work, which he saw himself as continuing in a *philosophical* form, as "a kind of psychological analysis of *Weltanschauungen*," ("eine Art weltanschauungspsychologischer Analyse"). Jaspers situates the forms of inner and external asceticism, largely borrowed from Weber, within the chapter entitled "Self-reflective Attitudes," and the subchapter entitled "Active Self-reflection." This immediately precedes the subchapter on one of the most important issues of the work, "the Moment." The question here is whether and to what extent Weber's "reborn" asceticism was self-reflective in Jaspers's sense.

35. Schluchter, *Religion und Lebensführung*, vol. 1, p. 160.

36. Weber, "'Value Freedom,'" in *Wissenschaftslehre*, p. 535. English in Weber, *Methodology of the Social Sciences*, p. 43.

37. Weber, *Wirtschaft und Gesellschaft*, pp. 18–19. English in Weber, *Economy and Society*, p. 36.

38. Weber, "Some Categories of Interpretive Sociology," *Sociological Quarterly* 22 (Spring 1981): 151–80, here p. 160. The concept of "value-orientation" appears in the same essay.

39. Weber distinguishes between "formal" and "material" or "substantive" rationality in Weber, *Wirtschaft und Gesellschaft*, pp. 44–45. English in Weber, *Economy and Society*, pp. 85–86. For the importance of this distinction in Weber's work, see Wolfgang Mommsen, "Ideal Type and Pure Type: Two Variants of Max Weber's Idealtypical Method," in *The Political and Social Theory of Max Weber*, pp. 141–42, 121–22, 128; idem, "Max Weber's 'Grand Sociology,'" p. 383; idem, "Personal Conduct and Societal Change," in Whimster and Lash, *Max Weber, Rationality and Modernity*, pp. 46–47. Mommsen says the formal-substantive dichotomy was not "unfolded" before 1915, although I have been hard-pressed to find it even then. The concepts of formal and material or substantive rationality were used, and defined to some extent, in Weber's "Sociology of Law," which, it appears, was one of the only pieces written before 1914 that Weber believed was ready for publication around 1919–20. Other uses of this dichotomy were added in 1920, first, to the revised introduction to *The Economic Ethics*, and, second, to the revised version of "Intermediate Reflection." See Weber, *Die Wirtschaftsethik der Weltreligionen. Konfuzianismus und Taoismus*, pp. 124, 488.

40. Weber, *Wirtschaft und Gesellschaft*, pp. 12–13. English in Weber, *Economy and Society*, pp. 24–25.

41. Weber, *Wirtschaft und Gesellschaft*, pp. 12, 13. English in Weber, *Economy and Society*, pp. 24, 26.

42. It is here that Habermas brings to bear his critique of Weber, by arguing for another type of ethical orientation, namely toward the sphere of communicative action. See Jürgen Habermas, *The Theory of Communicative Action*, vol. 1, *Reason and the Rationalization of Society*, trans. Thomas McCarthy (Boston: Beacon, 1984), pp. 143–271.

43. Compare Schluchter, who speaks of the enormous importance "of how one *understands* the relation of the value spheres that are independent and circumscribed over against one another: whether on the model of value difference or the model of value conflict, of value collision. Weber believed that only the second model was correct. . . . The model of value collision rests on a value absolutism insofar as the independent value spheres, the 'gods,' circumscribed reciprocally, always appear with an absolute validity, which the individual cannot simply evade, toward which he must take a much more positive or negative position. . . . [This is] the experience of the 'struggle of the gods,' of the experience of value conflict. . . . [Weber starts] from the independence and 'absoluteness' of the value spheres and from their reciprocal limitation, therefore from the endemic conflict between them." Schluchter, *Religion und Lebensführung*, vol. 1, pp. 106–7.

44. Weber, *Wirtschaft und Gesellschaft*, pp. 355–56. English in *Economy and Society*, p. 590.

45. See Elaine Pagels, *The Origin of Satan* (New York: Vintage Books, 1996).

46. Weber, "Intermediate Reflection," in *Die Wirtschaftsethik der Weltreligionen. Konfuzianismus and Buddhismus*, p. 521.

47. Letter of Max Weber to Carl Peterson, 1920, in Weber, *Zur Politik im Weltkrieg*, in Weber, *Gesamtausgabe*, I/15, ed. Mommsen and Hubinger, p. 1.

48. Schluchter disagrees. In his view, given the analysis of spheres in the "*Zwischenbetrachtung*," one may grant its "broader perspective, its means of orientation a significant practical use for life alongside the scientific-hermeneutic one. [It] may be valuable in providing practical advice about how to live. The interpretive reconstruction of historically important constellations of conflict and their 'solutions' can in fact help the man of culture to find the demon who 'holds the threads of *his* life.'" Wolfgang Schluchter, *Religion und Lebensführung*, vol. 2, *Studien zu Max Webers Religions- und Herrschaftssoziologie* (Frankfurt: Suhrkamp, 1988), pp. 77–78.

49. Weber, "Value Freedom," in *Wissenschaftslehre*, p. 517. English in Weber, *Methodology of the Social Sciences*, p. 27.

50. Quoted in Wolfgang Mommsen, *Max Weber und die deutsche Politik*, 2nd ed. (Tübingen: Mohr [Siebeck], 1974), p. 47.

Max Weber's "Grand Sociology"

The Origins and Composition of Wirtschaft und Gesellschaft. Soziologie

Max Weber is best known to anglophone readers for *The Protestant Ethic and the Spirit of Capitalism,*[1] but it is his *Economy and Society: Sociology* (*Wirtschaft und Gesellschaft. Soziologie*) that was recently selected by the International Sociological Association as the most important sociological work of the twentieth century. Yet the controversies surrounding *Economy and Society* continue. They began with Friedrich Tenbruck's 1977 review of the fourth edition by Johannes F. Winckelmann.[2] More recently, Wolfgang Schluchter has argued that the work ought to have the title "The Economy and Social Orders and Powers" ("Die Wirtschaft und die gesellschaftlichen Ordnungen und Mächte") rather than *Economy and Society.*[3] Furthermore, he has advanced cogent arguments for a more plausible arrangement of the texts. Hiroshi Orihara has published a welter of detailed philological observations about the composition of *Economy and Society*, with particular attention to internal references within the texts.[4] Earlier studies on the origins and composition of *Economy and Society* were mainly directed against attempts, first by the original editors Marianne Weber and Melchior Palyi and later by the elaborate new editions published by Johannes F. Winckelmann, to present Max Weber's magnum opus essentially as one single work. They saw it as a torso consisting of segments of two and a half unfinished books.[5] Actually the two available German editions by Marianne Weber (hereafter *WuG* 1) and by Winckelmann (hereafter *WuG* 5), as well as the English edition by Guenther Roth (which in a way is the best of them),[6] have to be read from back to front, like a Chinese book, in order to be understood properly. The first four chapters, comprising the so-called "Basic Sociological Categories" ("Soziologische Grundbegriffe"), were written in 1919–20 and brought to publication by Weber himself shortly before his premature death. The other segments, written for the most part between 1909 and 1914, were published posthumously by Marianne Weber on the basis of the manuscripts she found in his desk.

Unfortunately, no manuscripts for *Economy and Society* survived except for the so-called "Sociology of Law" ("Rechtssoziologie") and a small section on the "Sociology of Domination" ("Herrschaftssoziologie"). As Tenbruck had already pointed out long ago, Weber had no intention in 1919 to publish the manuscripts in their 1913–14 version, but rather meant to thoroughly rewrite them. Indeed, it would appear that he subsequently destroyed some of the manuscripts he had used as the basis for the "Sociological Categories of Economic Activity" ("Soziologische Kategorien des Wirtschaftens"). Marianne Weber was obviously mistaken in her assumption that the so-called older section of *Economy and Society*, which she edited from Weber's papers, constituted part of one comprehensive project. In fact, the earlier texts were little more than a heap of manuscripts, many of them incomplete, mostly without definite titles or with no titles at all.

Furthermore, there was no indication of how they ought to have been arranged for publication. Indeed, they represented an earlier version of Weber's sociology. The available correspondence between Marianne Weber and the publishers provides ample proof that the editors rearranged the manuscripts according to a plan that substantially deviated from Weber's original intentions. Her idea was to present Weber's magnum opus as a coherent whole, or rather as one book with two parts, namely a systematic part and a more empirically and historically oriented part.[7] Her motive was obvious: she wished thereby to secure maximum success with the public. Given the circumstances at the time, this procedure was legitimate. However, we now know that the presentation of the texts known as *Economy and Society* does not necessarily reflect Weber's original intentions. The edition in one allegedly coherent volume had two basic consequences: (a) important changes over time in the use and meaning of key concepts in Weber's terminology were rendered less recognizable; and (b) the plastering over of caesuras in Weber's theoretical position made the development of his sociological thought over time more obscure.

This can be demonstrated, for example, in the shift in Weber's usage of the concept "charisma" from the earlier to the later texts. More important, the shift from community (*Gemeinschaft*) and community action (*Gemeinschaftshandeln*) to society (*Gesellschaft*) and social action (*soziales Handeln*), initiated in the famous essay "Some Categories of Interpretative Sociology" ("Einige Kategorien der verstehenden Soziologie"), is also obscured. Written in its final version late in 1912 or early 1913, this essay marked a major step forward in his sociological thought.

Because of the substantial modifications made by Marianne Weber and Palyi in putting together the texts without regard to the chronological sequence of their composition, social scientists have tended to read *Economy and Society* more as a rich quarry of sociological concepts, theories, and observations than as a coherent theory. In this respect, Winckelmann's editions, which followed a different editorial strategy, allow a better view of changes in Weber's sociological method. However, they suffer from the same basic flaw, namely the assumption that *Economy and Society* was one coherent, though incomplete, work that could be made coherent by careful editing. Winckelmann even went out of his way to reconstruct a "Sociology of the State ("Staatssoziologie") from Max Weber's political writings, undoubtedly a rather amateurish undertaking. In addition, in an attempt to improve their readability, he made frequent and extensive emendations of the texts. In many cases his efforts improved the texts, but in others they falsified their meaning. Winckelmann proceeded in a rather arbitrary fashion, applying a "conjectural method." By the fifth edition, Winckelmann ceased to identify the changes he had undertaken, making it impossible for readers to ascertain the original wording.

Consequently, the editors of the new German-language edition of *Economy and Society* were forced to rely on the text of the first edition, in spite of its shortcomings, as the one closest to Max Weber's original intentions.[8] The editorial work on the new German edition of *Economy and Society* has made considerable headway in the meantime. The Editorial Committee, consisting of Horst Baier, Wolfgang Mommsen, Rainer M. Lepsius, and Wolfgang Schluchter, decided to divide the new edition of *Economy and Society* into two volumes, the first (hereafter *MWG* I / 22) comprising the posthumous papers edited by Marianne Weber and Melchior Palyi, and the second (hereafter *MWG* I / 23) comprising the texts that Weber himself prepared for publication in 1919–20 shortly before his death. Largely for pragmatic reasons, vol. 22: *Die Wirtschaft und die gesellschaftlichen Ordnungen und Mächte. Nachlass* (The Economy and Social Orders and Powers: Posthumous Papers) was divided into six subvolumes, of which three have been published in the meantime, namely, vol. 22-1: *Gemeinschaften* (Communities), edited by Wolfgang J. Mommsen; vol. 22-2: *Religiöse Gemeinschaften* (Religious Communities), edited by Hans K. Kippenberg; and vol. 22-5: *Die Stadt* (The City), edited by Wilfrid Nippel. Vol. 22-4: *Herrschaft* (Domination), edited by Edith Hanke, is due to be published in 2005. The decision to divide the editorial work of the older manuscripts into six subvolumes was justified inasmuch as the projected unity of the work, as envisioned by Max Weber in 1914, does not match the respectively incomplete status of the partly fragmentary manuscripts.[9] Weber himself had said in 1919, when he again began to work on the manuscripts for *Economy and Society,* that "the voluminous old manuscript ha[d] to be re-worked altogether."[10] It was planned for publication in

1915, but by the outbreak of the First World War it was by no means ready for publication.

Given the fact that the original manuscripts have been lost, with the exception of most of the so-called "Sociology of Law" and two other fragments, the editors were faced with an arduous task. A sort of philological archaeology was required to find out more about the original texts and their origins.[11] It appears that Marianne Weber and Palyi modified the texts in only a few instances, notably at those points where caesuras required a bridging operation. Moreover, with only a few exceptions, they did not interfere with the text's internal references, allowing us to draw conclusions from these references as to the original arrangement of the manuscripts. This follows from the painstaking reconstruction of the pattern of the references in the texts by Hiroshi Orihara.[12] However, Marianne Weber and Palyi not only substantially rearranged the texts, but also—at times in cooperation with the publisher—invented titles for the newly added sections (*Abteilungen*).[13] They also added titles to most of the individual chapters, some of which were adapted from other texts written by Weber. In the original manuscripts, indications as to headings appear to have been erratic and not entirely consistent. Some of the packages presumably containing the manuscripts (most likely thick, brown, used envelopes) had carried some sort of abbreviated titles. In a reply to Marianne Weber, the publisher confirmed the receipt of manuscripts, listing them as follows: "Sociology of Religion, Sociology of Law, then Forms of Society: (Ethnic Communities, Kinship Groups, Nations, State and Hierocracy, etc.); furthermore, Forms of Domination (Charisma, Patrimonialism, Feudalism)."[14] Yet these headings were clearly not meant to be used for publication (which, as discussed above, was no longer intended anyway). Moreover, it would appear that in some sections, namely the chapter on "communities" ("Gemeinschaften"), the editors inserted subtitles into the manuscript although it presumably had had very few chapter breaks. Only the "Sociology of Law" ("Rechtssoziologie," the title of which is probably also misleading) contained subtitles that Weber himself had inserted into the typewritten manuscript, namely paragraphs and subtitles as well as short summaries of the contents of the individual subsections. This was obviously done at a late stage, presumably late 1913 or early 1914, when Weber was still hoping to forward the manuscript to the publisher by June of 1914.[15] We may safely assume that Marianne Weber and Palyi planned to reorganize all the manuscripts originating from his papers according to this model, a procedure that was in line with their editorial strategy of presenting *Economy and Society* as a single work. However, this was eventually done only in some manuscripts, presumably because Palyi was dismissed from the job before he could see it through to completion (probably because the publisher was unwilling to meet his demand for a larger honorarium). Other sections, notably the "Sociology of Domination," were published without much, if any, interference by the editors, who limited their emendations largely to introducing paragraph differentiations and short content summaries of subsections. In "Basic Sociological Categories," Weber himself had arranged the text in paragraphs, but in a rather different manner. These varied practices further indicate that the edition was put together under rather hectic circumstances.

One may ask: what is the point of this philological analysis of *Economy and Society*? It provides us with an exact reconstruction of the history of the texts as well as establishing an arrangement of the manuscripts in their entirety in line with Weber's original intentions. A careful analysis of the time and circumstances in which the individual texts were first composed allows us to reconstruct *Economy and Society* in a new, more plausible form. The texts ought to be arranged in a chronological order, taking into account all available information as to how Weber intended to compose his "Sociology," while abandoning the pretense that the form in which the texts have survived indicates that they were ever supposed to have formed one coherent work.

As is well known, the history of *Economy and Society* is closely linked with the history of the monumental textbook *Grundriss der Sozialökonomik* (*Outline of Social Economics*)—originally entitled, in consultation with the publisher, "Handbook of Political Economy" ("Handbuch der politischen Ökonomie")—which Weber had agreed in 1908 to edit for his friend and publisher Siebeck as a substitute for the well-established, but by then out-of-date, textbook by Gustav Schönberg (the "Schönberg"). Although Weber first acted only as an adviser to the publisher, steadfastly refusing the formal title of editor (reluctantly accepting only the title "director of writing" [*Schriftleiter*], he became the driving force behind the project). Initially prepared to act only as an intermediary between the publisher and the prospective authors, he soon drew up a new comprehensive plan for the project. In the first half of May 1909, he forwarded to Siebeck the first provisional version of a plan for arranging the materials (*Stoffverteilungsplan*) for the huge project. One year later, a definitive plan and projected table of contents was ready; Weber had already presented this to Karl Bücher, whom Weber considered at this stage to be a key author and whose close cooperation he had sought to secure for the project from the start.[16] This indicates that Weber had assumed that Karl Bücher's theory of the stages of economic development (*Wirtschaftsstufen*), a theory well known at the time, could provide the backbone for the entire project.

There is, to begin with, a contribution entitled "Economy and Race" ("Wirtschaft und Rasse") for the first book of the *Grundriss der Sozial-*

ökonomik: "Economy and Economic Science, Section III: Economy, Nature and Society." As we know, Weber had very strong views about the use of racial theories in the social sciences, and he repeatedly spoke out against them, despite their popularity at the time. Given the lack of serious empirical research on race difference, he regarded any reference to race theories in a scientific context as irresponsible. Nonetheless, this part of the project was eventually assigned to Robert Michels.

Most of Weber's other contributions are to be found in subchapter 4 of the aforesaid section of the *Grundriss* under the title "Economy and Society." These contributions were as follows:

First Book: Economy and Economic Science
(Wirtschaft und Wirtschaftswissenschaft)

> Section III. Economy, Nature, and Society
> (Wirtschaft, Natur und Gesellschaft)
>
> [. . .]
>
> 2. Natural Constraints on the Economy
> (Naturbedingungen der Wirtschaft)
>
> b) Economy and Race (Wirtschaft und Rasse)
>
> [. . .]
>
> 4. Economy and Society (Wirtschaft und Gesellschaft)
>
> a) Economy and Law (Wirtschaft und Recht)
>
> 1. Fundamental Relationship (prinzipielles Verhältnis)
>
> 2. Epochs in the Development of Present Conditions
> (Epochen der Entwicklung des heutigen Zustands)
>
> b) The Economy and Social Groups: Family and Community Association, Orders and Classes, State
> (Wirtschaft und soziale Gruppen: Familien- und Gemeindeverband, Stände und Klassen, Staat)
>
> c) Economy and Culture (Critique of Historical Materialism)
> (Wirtschaft und Kultur [Kritik des historischen Materialismus])
>
> Section IV. Economic Science (Wirtschaftswissenschaft)
>
> 1. Object and Logical Character of Problematics
> (Objekt und logische Natur der Fragestellungen)

Moreover, Max Weber reserved for himself the introductory chapter to section IV of the *Grundriss*: "Economic Sciences," with the title "Object and Logical Character of the Problematics." Apparently this essay was never written. However, since Weber had initially been determined to write it, he demanded that the methodological issues be left out in the projected contributions by Friedrich von Wieser, Wilhelm Lexis, Weber's brother Alfred, and possibly also Joseph Schumpeter, so that he could deal with them himself. He wrote to Paul Siebeck: "The 'methodology' possibly could be written by myself including the relationship to jurisprudence and sociology, etc."[17] Later, however, Weber decided otherwise and justified this decision in a letter to Siebeck, who was apparently not happy that "[t]he essay on the logical issues of the social sciences" could "no longer be accommodated within the *Grundriss* due to reasons of space."[18] For some time this projected essay was confused with another contribution destined to be the lead-in to Weber's section of "Economy and Society." In any case, the essay "Object and Logical Character of Problematics," which was supposed to open the section "Economic Sciences," was presumably to have dealt with another issue. It is likely that it was meant to be a systematic exposition of theoretical economics (largely identical with marginal utility theory) in order to forestall psychological or other interpretations that might put into question the theoretical status of its concepts; such concepts were in his view exclusively tools for the empirical interpretation of the economic behavior of human beings. It should be remembered that in 1908 Weber had strongly criticized a paper by Lujo Brentano, presented to the Bavarian Academy of Sciences, in which marginal utility theory had been described as a sort of psychological interpretation of economic conduct.[19]

The projected table of contents from May 1910 indicates that Weber wished to conduct a comprehensive survey of the complex interrelationships between the economic and the social—what came to be known in Germany as "social economics" (*Sozialökonomik*). Accordingly, the *Grundriss* was supposed to cover the entire range of social-scientific analysis of contemporary society and its historical origins, with special emphasis on the consequences of the rise of capitalism and its corollary, the progressive rationalization of all forms of social activity, and do so in a universal-historical manner. Economics, in the sense in which that term is now understood, was largely left aside, partly for practical reasons, but primarily because Weber wanted the handbook to focus on the interaction of the economy with all spheres of social life, the cultural aspects included, and with the types of communities throughout history, ranging from the household community to the modern state and the capitalist market economy, as well as religious communities and culture.

Of the eighty-one different essays to be assigned to specialists in the field, Max Weber reserved for himself *no fewer than fourteen*, albeit with the proviso that he would relinquish them as soon as competent authors had been found. Even so, the scope of themes that he felt able to cover is impressive. In the projected table of contents of 1910, we find most of the themes that were later elaborated upon in his own contributions to the *Grundriss*—perhaps with the exception of the "Critique of Historical Materialism." Although a section specifically discussing historical materialism was never written, the "Sociology of Religion" may be read as an implicit critique of Marx, an assumption that is indirectly substantiated by the fact that Weber presented parts of the respective text in a lecture course in 1917 at the University of Vienna under the title "Positive Refutation of Historical Materialism." We also encounter here for the first time the title "Economy and Society" (Wirtschaft und Gesellschaft), which, as we shall see, was later given the significant addendum "Sociology" (Soziologie). We have no definitive information to help us ascertain why Max Weber chose the title "Economy and Society" in the first place, given the fact that he only very rarely used the term "society" in his texts. However, it may be assumed that at the time he intended his contributions to complement the largely theoretical treatment of economic issues of the Vienna school by providing a comprehensive account of the social and historical dimensions of human conduct in as much as they affect economic conduct. To put it otherwise, he presumably wished to present the other side of the story altogether neglected by the marginal utility school. This is in line with his views about the deficiencies of the marginal utility school, which he had already put forward in both his *Grundriss zu den Vorlesungen über allgemeine ("theoretische") Nationalökonomie* (*Outline for the Lectures on General ["Theoretical"] National Economics*) from 1898 for his students as well as in his lecture courses on this subject.[20] This perhaps explains the twofold dimension of the title. It was certainly chosen on systematic grounds. Initially, Weber's magnum opus was clearly intended to be merely a part, albeit a substantial one, of the multivolume project *Grundriss der Sozialökonomik*. Indeed, the future handling of the themes enumerated here was closely linked to the development of the *Grundriss* as well as its ups and downs before, during, and after the First World War. Nevertheless, it would be misleading to associate the origins of the texts that later came to be essential parts of his magnum opus exclusively with the history of the *Grundriss*. Indeed, some of the basic ideas of these texts were already present in Weber's earlier work. For example, his studies on the "Agrarian Economy in Antiquity" and on "The Condition of the Rural Working Classes in the East Elbian Provinces of Prussia" had emphasized the revolutionary character and consequences of modern capitalism. Capitalism and bureaucratization had also figured in his monumental work on the "Agrarian History of Antiquity,"[21] as well as in his fascinating little essay on the social causes of the eventual collapse of Ancient Civilization (1896), as did the idea that modern capitalist societies might eventually collapse under the weight of all-powerful bureaucratic structures once the capitalist market economy had lost its dynamism, a prospect that seemed very real in his own time. His famous essay about the *Protestant Ethic and the Spirit of Capitalism* all focused on this same issue, the cultural significance of capitalism and the eventual consequences for mankind of its triumphant march across the globe; namely the gradual emergence of what he called in pathetic terms, reminiscent of Nietzsche's message of doom, the "cage of future serfdom."

However, the idea for Weber's great "Sociology" goes back even further. Already in his early lecture courses in the 1890s, Weber was gradually developing a new approach to the study of social reality that may, roughly speaking, be called a combination of an ideal-typical method, derived from the theory of marginal utility, and a universal-historical analysis, global in scope and comparative in approach. In his lectures on theoretical and practical national economics (theoretische und praktische Nationalökonomie), Weber naturally felt obliged to take his own stand in the famous war of methods (*Methodenstreit*) between Karl Menger and his disciples on the one hand and the followers of Gustav von Schmoller on the other. He discovered that the conceptualizations of the theory of marginal utility had substantial advantages for a rational analysis of economic and social phenomena. However, he tended to emphasize to the utmost extent the purely abstract, unreal quality of the concepts of neoclassical economics.[22] The concept of *homo oeconomicus*, for example, was, as he told his students, a completely theoretical construct totally at odds with everyday reality. He made such claims with far more emphasis than his contemporary fellow economists. "Utility theory," he pointed out:

starts from a theoretically constructed economic subject that—in contrast to an empirically given human being—neglects all motives that are not specifically economic that influence the decisions of an empirical human being, and possesses complete insight as to the means and ways that in view of the respective economic constellation are best suited to achieve his required goal—complete knowledge of the economic situation. This economic subject is thus conceived as possessing complete knowledge of the economic conditions—infallibility in economic respects—applying the most suitable means to secure the desired goal under given conditions and employing his own capabilities to the fullest extent in an uninhibited drive for profit. In other words, neoclassical economics bases its conclusions on a fictitious human being similar to a mathematical model.[23]

Precisely because these concepts are merely theoretical constructs, their heuristic value for a rational understanding of reality was, in Weber's view, unsurpassed. Today this position is widely accepted, proving the modernity of Weber's position at the time. Weber discovered here what he later called "ideal types," an epistemological tool for rationally structuring a great variety of empirical data and, moreover, relating these data to cultural values (*Kulturwerte*) without getting involved with the question of the validity of these values as such. At the same time, he strongly maintained that such concepts, arrived at by purely rational deliberation, had nothing in common with empirical reality. On this point he disagreed sharply with Menger's notion of "real types." Economic behavior and the economic preferences of human beings were the product of long historical developments. Indeed, Weber maintained that humankind had reacted in the past in very different ways to the demands made upon it by the economy. The modern European type of man, which provided the point of departure for the conceptualization of utility theory, was in his view "developed through a process of adaptation lasting thousands of years."[24]

Weber was prepared to concede that under specific historical conditions the theoretical concepts of neoclassical economy might to some degree approximate empirical reality. But this was the exception, not the rule, and it carried no epistemological significance. When Lujo Brentano, in an Academy Lecture in Munich in 1908, broached the idea that the law of marginal utility might be considered as a special application of the so-called "fundamental psycho-physical law," as developed by Ernst Heinrich Weber and Gustav Theodor Fechner, Weber protested violently.[25] He strongly insisted on the exclusively formal character of the laws of theoretical economics as purely theoretical constructs that had nothing whatsoever to do with psychology. However, while emphasizing again the unbridgeable gap between arbitrarily constructed ideal types and social reality investigated through theoretical guidelines, Weber on this occasion made a small concession. He granted that, under the conditions of mature capitalism, the theory of marginal utility was about to become less a merely theoretical construct and more an actual description of empirical reality:

[In the modern capitalist age] the historical distinction of the capitalistic epoch, and thereby also the significance of the theory of marginal utility (as of every economic theory of value) for the understanding of this epoch, rests on the fact that under today's conditions of existence the approximation of reality to the theoretical propositions of economics has been a constantly increasing one. It is an approximation to reality that has been affecting the destiny of ever larger portions [of people] and is going to do so increasingly in the time to come as well, as far as our horizons allow us to see.[26]

"The needs of human beings" (die Bedürfnisse des Menschen), the key concept of marginal utility theory, may, with significant consequences, become more adapted to the economic environment at certain stages of the universal-historical process. In principle, however, these needs are subject to historical change. In other words, according to Weber, they are extremely variable, and are influenced by specific cultural conditions and beliefs, both religious and nonreligious. It goes without saying that in Weber's view there was little point in drawing a rigid distinction between physical and mental needs. "The system of needs" (das System der Bedürfnisse) must, in his view, be understood as encompassing a wide range of factors, rather than merely as narrowly conceived economic needs. It is at this point where history and, for that matter, comparative history of a truly universal nature, in principle encompassing the whole globe, enters the picture. That is to say, an important, or rather the most important, part of economics is the assessment of the cultural conditions and value dispositions of humans in their attitudes toward the economic sphere of life. Broadly speaking, it is history that educates people to develop over long periods of time those mental dispositions that enable them to operate more or less efficiently and more or less rationally in the economic sphere. Here we come across the roots of what later became Weber's grand project of a sociology that concentrates on the interrelationship between cultural dispositions and economic activities in different societies around the globe at different stages of the universal-historical process.

If this aspect is taken into consideration, it becomes understandable why Weber, both in his lecture courses on economics at the University of Freiburg and later at the University of Heidelberg, as well as in his later work, always combined a theoretical with a universal-historical approach to the issues in question. Whatever the particular topic, Weber always undertook a grand sweep through both the ages and geographic regions, looking for the dispositions or patterns of conduct of a wide range of different civilizations (and cultures) vis-à-vis the economic sphere of life and their developmental potentials. This was done with the additional motive of finding out about the specific features of modernity. In a way, these wide-ranging lecture courses form the backbone of what later became *Economy and Society*.

Thus we already find here *in nuce* the ideal-typical method used with comparative intent, which was then later turned into a remarkably sophisticated instrument of sociological analysis. From 1906 to 1908 Weber presented it in theoretical form in several methodological essays. Here he defended the use of ideal types in the social sciences as a means of exact rational assessment of the issues in question, but even more so as a way of establishing the cultural significance of social phenomena from a cultural value vantage point while denying that their validity could be established through scientific reasoning. This was an issue of personal decision, not of scholarly analysis. Scholarship could only help to rationalize the choice between different, and usually competing, alternatives.

It appears that by 1906 Weber had undertaken further ventures in developing what could be called a universal-historical sociology with comparative intent. These activities may have been initiated in Rome in the years 1901 and 1902 when he was recovering from his mental illness. Among his papers are fragments of a project with the heading "Family Unit, Kinship Group, and Neighborhood" (Hausverband, Sippe und Nachbarschaft). This text must have been written in September 1906 or shortly thereafter.[27] Presumably it was a segment of a far larger project, namely an outline of human communities as part of the various forms of associations throughout history, indeed the germ of a comprehensive historical sociology. It can be identified as a blueprint for the respective passages in *Economy and Society*, written about 1909.[28] It is possible that this text survived only because Weber had inserted into it an ideal-typical treatise about the history and development of sexual relations and marriage. It was presumably written to assist his wife, Marianne Weber, who dealt extensively with the same subject in her book *Ehefrau und Mutter in der Rechtsentwicklung* (*Wife and Mother in the Development of Law*) published in 1907.[29] In these notes Weber discussed at length the economic and social positions of women in ancient and modern societies, followed by a discourse on ancient and modern marriage and the economic position of women. Here we come across a precursor to the texts of the older sections of *Economy and Society*.

We may therefore assume that a few of the texts elaborating on types of social and political or cultural institutions throughout universal history, albeit more in the form of extensive notes than continuous texts, were already in existence before Weber was asked to assume the editorship of the *Grundriss*. Among these was presumably an earlier version of the treatise on the "Ancient and Medieval City," a by-product of his "Agrarian Conditions in Antiquity" (Agrarverhältnisse im Altertum).[30] It is likely that Weber had originally intended to bring these texts into this new venture. This is to say that Weber's contributions to the *Grundriss der Sozialökonomik* were from the start far more than a mere by-product of his activities as editor. To be sure, they contained the seeds of his later universal-historical sociology.

Weber envisaged the *Grundriss* becoming a comprehensive presentation of the achievements of the contemporary social sciences with particular emphasis on the impact of the economy upon society, and especially the progressive rationalization of all social relations under the impact of capitalism. The "increasing predominance of established orders" (das zunehmende Eingreifen gesatzter Ordnungen) was merely a part, although a most characteristic part, of the "process of rationalization and socialization" (des Rationalisierungs- und Vergesellschaftungsprozesses). As Weber stated, "it will be our task to pay particular attention to its progressive expansion into social activities in all communal enterprises in all life spheres alike because it is the most important propelling force of [historical] development."[31] However, this ought to be carried out within the context of a universal-historical approach to social reality that outlined the different developmental stages of social and economic institutions. Originally, Karl Bücher's "theory of stages of economic development" had been considered by Weber to be a model for the composition of the *Grundriss*. Significantly, Weber hoped to plan the schema of the project directly with Bücher before letting anybody else know, but the close collaboration with Bücher never materialized. On the contrary, Weber became increasingly disillusioned with Bücher's contributions, which he had initially considered the structuring element of the whole enterprise. Weber complained bitterly that he had to make up for these deficiencies and that he was thereby forced to extend the scope of his own contributions further and further. Moreover, Weber gradually dissociated himself from Bücher's developmental schemes, as he wrote early in 1913 to Johann Plenge: "My personal views are presently undergoing substantial change."[32] His contribution to *Economy and Society* was going to deal with issues altogether different from "economic stages."[33] Indeed, by this time Weber had totally emancipated himself from contemporary economic perspectives on the various developmental reconstructions of world history, such as those of Roscher, Knies, and Lamprecht. He intended to do something different, analyzing the progressive differentiation of various types of communities (Gemeinschaften) in various directions, based upon evidence from all known civilizations. This was to be done with particular attention to the economic sphere and the gradual emergence of rational forms of social interaction. A typical example was the gradual emergence both of the *oikos* and of capitalistic enterprise as offsprings from the household community. In addressing these issues, Weber took up a theme that had already been discussed in 1887 by Ferdinand Tönnies in his famous *Gemeinschaft und Gesellschaft* (*Community and Society*). But he gave it a different twist. In Tönnies's conceptualization, community was ideally constituted by emotional bonds of a personal nature, whereas society was determined by purposive-rational relationships. In Weber's understanding, by contrast, community is the more general concept, encompassing all social relationships of any sort; it could be established just as well by rational, and even purely instrumental, forms of human interaction as by emotional or affective ones. According to Weber, the "market community" (Marktgemeinschaft) established by a rational exchange of goods and services within a market, ideally without interference of any type of personal preference, was just as much a community as the "household community" (Hausgemeinschaft), the oldest and most archaic form of a permanent social relationship established by any group of people. Starting from this premise, Weber developed a wide-ranging and highly differentiated typology of communities, encompassing *in nuce* all ages and known civilizations on the globe.

This ambitious venture upon which Weber embarked around 1909 and 1910, in part relying on older texts like the one dealing with household communities, very soon grew out of proportion and eventually threatened to destroy the original plans for the *Grundriss*. It had become impossible to meet the original publication deadline of January 1912 and then later mid-1912 for the first volume, particularly because he far overstepped the space limit allotted to his own contributions. Furthermore, Weber's excessive engagement in lawsuits against journalists had, among other things, caused a lull in the production of *Economy and Society* in late 1911 and early 1912. However, by late 1912 and early 1913, Weber was feverishly working on his texts. On February 8, 1913, he wrote to the publisher that his great article "Economy, Society, Law, and State" (Wirtschaft, Gesellschaft, Recht und Staat) was going to become "the best systematic piece" (das systematisch Beste) that he had written so far.[34] Half a year later he suggested to Siebeck that he be given more space for his contribution, which he now for the first time called "my 'Sociology'" while adding that he would nonetheless never call it that. By now it had become obvious that Weber's contributions to *Economy and Society* were about to turn into a veritable sociological theory. On December 30, 1913, he wrote to Siebeck that he had now "composed a comprehensive sociological theory and presentation concerning relationships of all major forms of community to the economy, that is: the family, the domestic community, the 'commercial enterprise', the clan, the ethnic community, religion (comprising all great religions on the earth: a sociology of the doctrines of salvation and of the various religious ethics similar to Troeltsch, however now for all religions, only much more concise), finally a comprehensive sociological treatise of the state and the types of domination."[35]

This implied another substantial extension of the original program, inasmuch as the typology of "communities" now grew beyond all previously envisaged limits. The analysis of political communities now became only a prolegomenon for the treatment of various types of political domination, and the treatment of religious communities served merely as a stepping stone to a comprehensive analysis of the impact of religious doctrines on the socioeconomic order.

This new departure also required a rearrangement of the older texts, mostly written in 1910 and 1911. For one, Weber abandoned the plan to open his contributions with the essay "The Economy and the Orders." This text was written fairly early, possibly already in 1909 (as can be surmised by the references to the treatise on Stammler, which was published in the journal *Archiv für Sozialwissenschaft und Sozialpolitik* in 1907). Instead he integrated the text into the "Sociology of Law" that emerged from the section "The Conditions for the Development of Law" (Die Entwicklungsbedingungen des Rechts) planned in the context of the chapter on "Political Communities." Late in 1913 or early in 1914 the manuscripts on the "Sociology of Law," including the text "The Economy and the Orders," were revised by Max Weber apparently in order to be forwarded to the printer (which, however, in the end did not happen since the other sections of "Economy and Society" were not yet finished). The instructions for the printer were written in the identical script and with apparently the same pen used in both manuscripts, leaving no doubt that he now wished to have both texts published jointly.

Max Weber now also abandoned the idea of introducing "Economy and Society" with a theoretical treatise. Instead, as mentioned earlier, he decided to publish his thoughts on the methodology of the social sciences outside the *Grundriss*. Late in 1912 or early 1913 he sent a lengthy treatise entitled "Some Categories of Interpretive Sociology" to the editors of the journal *Logos*.[36] According to a somewhat cryptic annotation, the second part of this text had been written for some time and had been destined to serve as a methodological foundation for several empirical studies, including a contribution to "Economy and Society."[37] This text may have formed a lead-in to "Economy and Society," presumably together with the text "The Economy and the Orders," as has been argued by Wolfgang Schluchter and Hiroshi Orihara.[38] It appears that the terminology of the two texts is closely intertwined, thereby supporting such an interpretation. However, as we know now, the key concepts of "Some Categories of Interpretive Sociology" were inserted only in 1913 or 1914 into the manuscript of "The Economy and the Orders," which was then destined to form part of the "Sociology of Law." Hence the similar terminology in these texts can also be explained otherwise. According to a letter from Max Weber to Heinrich Rickert, the older part of the manuscript, which according to Schluchter and Orihara had been destined to form part of the introductory chapter of "Economy and Society," was written in late 1911 or early 1912, not in 1909–10. By contrast, the final version of "Some Categories of Interpretive Sociology," as published in *Logos*, was sent to the publisher late in 1912 or during the early months of 1913.[39] Presumably Weber wrote this text in 1911 or 1912. This is further corroborated by the fact that the passages on "Linguistic Communities" (Sprachgemeinschaften) found here match the wording of Weber's arguments in the chapter on "Ethnic Communities" written in 1911[40] as well as his contributions to the discussion of "nation" at the 1911 conference of the German Sociological Association (Deutsche Gesellschaft für Soziologie).[41] Given the fact that the older part of the manuscript was amended by Max Weber to some degree before being sent to the editors of *Logos*, the published text no longer represents the original version, which may have been a section of the "lead-in" in its entirety.[42] However, as it stands it can no longer be considered part of the original lead-in to "Economy and Society." Indeed it cannot be said for sure whether it had actually been destined to fulfill this function.[43] However, if it is assumed that this text was to have initially been published in the *Grundriss*, then it could be imagined that, given the fact that the publication of his section on "Economy and Society" in the *Grundriss* was still a long way off, Max Weber no longer wished to wait for its publication in this context and therefore decided to have it published in *Logos*. As such, then the editors were fully justified in not including "Some Categories of Interpretive Sociology" in the new edition of "Wirtschaft und Gesellschaft."[44] By this time Max Weber had conceived, and potentially written, a new chapter, "Categories of the Social Orders" (Kategorien der gesellschaftlichen Ordnungen) to introduce readers to the terminology of "Economy and Society." However, it appears that most of this chapter has been lost.[45]

In general, Max Weber was increasingly worried that the texts designed to be part of the *Grundriss*, not only those of other authors, but also and especially his own, had considerably overshot their allotted length. These texts far exceeded the already fairly liberal space given over to Weber's own contributions to the *Grundriss*. This unbalanced situation was not made any better by Weber's previous strong objections to contributions by other authors that had become too long. These and other factors, notably chronic delays in the delivery of manuscripts by other authors, eventually necessitated a rescheduling of the whole plan for the *Grundriss*. In March 1914, Siebeck presented a thoroughly revised workplan (Werkplan) for the enterprise on the basis of the previous concepts. Weber apparently accepted this new plan with only a few alterations.[46] Weber's contributions were now as follows:[47]

C. Economy and Society (Wirtschaft and Gesellschaft)

    I. The Economy and the Social Orders and Powers[48]
        (Die Wirtschaft und die gesellschaftlichen Ordnungen und Mächte)

        1. Categories of the Various Forms of Social Order
            (Kategorien der gesellschaftlichen Ordnungen)

            The Fundamental Relationships between Economy and Law
            (Wirtschaft und Recht in ihrer prinzipiellen Beziehung)

            The Economic Relationships of Organized Groups
            (Wirtschaftliche Beziehungen der Verbände im allgemeinen)

        2. Household, Oikos and Enterprise
            (Hausgemeinschaft, Oikos und Betrieb)

        3. Neighborhood, Kinship Group and Local Community
            (Nachbarschaftsverband, Sippe, Gemeinde)

        4. Ethnic Group Relationships
            (Ethnische Gemeinschaftsbeziehungen)

        5. Religious Communities (Religiöse Gemeinschaften)

            The Conditioning of Religion by Class Constellations
            (Klassenbedingtheit der Religionen)

            Cultural Religions and Economic Attitudes
            (Kulturreligionen und Wirtschaftsgesinnung)

        6. The Market (Die Marktvergemeinschaftung)

        7. Political Association (Der politische Verband)

            The Social Determinants of Legal Development. Status Groups,
            Classes, Parties, Nation
            (Die Entwicklungsbedingungen des Rechts. Stände, Klassen, Parteien.
            Die Nation)

8. Domination (Die Herrschaft)

(a) The Three Types of Legitimate Domination
(Die drei Typen der legitimen Herrschaft)

(b) Political and Hierocratic Domination
(Politische und hierokratische Herrschaft)

(c) Nonlegitimate Domination: The Typology of Cities
(Die nichtlegitime Herrschaft: Typologie der Städte)

(d) The Development of the Modern State
(Die Entwicklung des modernen Staates)

(e) Modern Political Parties
(Die modernen politischen Parteien)[49]

If we compare this plan with the original proposal, four important innovations become obvious. One is that the title of Weber's contribution was upgraded to the title of a main section and, accordingly, a subtitle was inserted: "I. The Economy and the Social Orders and Powers." In view of this, Wolfgang Schluchter has argued repeatedly that because "Economy and Society" had been made the title for the main section (which included a chapter by Philippovich, "The Economy and the Social Orders and Powers") would be a more correct and suitable title for Weber's magnum opus than *Economy and Society*.[50] However, even though Weber authorized the work plan, including the subtitle "The Economy and the Social Orders and Powers" by writing a preface to it, he continued to refer to his own work for the *Grundriss* either as "Economy and Society" or, especially in the correspondence with Siebeck, as "my Sociology." An advertisement on the cover of the July 1914 issue of the *Archiv für Sozialwissenschaft und Sozialpolitik* announced the forthcoming contribution by Weber to the *Grundriss* as "Sociology."[51] Besides, the introduction of the subtitle probably originated with Siebeck, who had initially suggested the wording "Social Conditioning of the Economy" (Gesellschaftliche Bedingungen der Wirtschaft). It is unknown whether Max Weber modified this passage or just accepted the publisher's suggestion. In any case he never afterward referred to the subtitle himself, nor did the publisher. In fact, he never made the subtitle truly his own.

The second innovation was the addition of a methodological introduction in which the key concepts and categories were to be defined. It was not to be a theoretical treatise on the logic of the social sciences like the one that had been planned during an earlier stage of the project but then subsequently abandoned. Rather it was an attempt to clearly define the key concepts that would be used in the following chapters. We may safely assume that it was also intended to clearly define the concepts used in the following texts, as the heading suggests. However, it would appear that only a short passage of this section has survived, namely the first paragraph of the chapter that in the first edition of *Wirtschaft und Gesellschaft* is called "Economics and Society in General" (Wirtschaftliche Beziehungen der Verbände im Allgemeinen), whereas in the new German-language edition of the posthumous papers (*MWG* I/22−1) the title was amended to "Economic Relations of Communities in General," given the fact that in the text the term "associations" is not used at all.[52] The definition of "economy" in this section does not have a direct continuation in the following text, which deals with societal action (Gesellschaftshandeln). Here we find the passage: "Social action [soziales Handeln] can establish the most diverse relationships to the economy." This is terminology not used by Max Weber at the time, and it is likely that this passage was inserted at a later stage, presumably by Marianne Weber and Melchior Palyi, in order to fill in the gap in the text. It is most likely that the aforesaid paragraph does not belong at all to the chapter "Economic Relations of the Communities in General," but is the remnant of a chapter "Categories of the Social Orders," the remainder of which has been lost.[53] Although we cannot be absolutely sure that this chapter was ever even written, there is good reason to assume that if this text existed, then it was later used by Max Weber in writing the chapter " Sociological Categories of Economic Activity" (Soziologische Grundkategorien des Wirtschaftens).[54] The passages dealing with economic communities that survived were those that had become superfluous and were therefore left aside from the start; presumably the rest were thrown away later. If this conjecture is correct, the new edition in the Complete German Edition ought to have published the aforesaid paragraph under the title "Categories of the Social Orders," making note that the rest of the chapter had been lost. However, as the evidence for this conjecture is scanty, the editors followed the first (German) edition.

Third, there appeared a new subchapter, "Conditions for the Emergence of Law" (Entwicklungsbedingungen des Rechts), an important extension of the chapter on political communities, now aptly rephrased "Political Associations" (Politische Verbände). Last but not least, religion and domination emerge here as new, independent sections.

The so-called workplan has been considered by many scholars to be a definite outline of Weber's plans, as well as a guideline for editing the texts from his papers. However, closer scrutiny reveals that in many ways it was a program for the future rather than the present. Its conceptualization represents a new stage in Weber's own sociological thought that was initiated with his famous essay "Some Categories of Interpretative Sociology," the final version of which was written in late 1912 or early 1913 and not by 1909 or 1910. The majority of the texts (notably those concerning the communities) would have required a revision at least in their terminology, whereas others still had to be written, notably the projected new subsections "The Development of the Modern State" and "Modern Political Parties." Besides, the other chapters were still far from completion. The only texts that may have almost been ready for publication were the chapters "The Economy and the Orders" and the so-called "Sociology of Law." Even here the workplan was ignored almost from the beginning. These two texts should have been published together, rather than in two different sections of *Economy and Society* as the workplan stipulates, as can be gathered from the physical interconnectedness of the manuscripts that were written on the same typewriter and arranged in an identical fashion by Weber himself.

In June 1914, Weber was still hoping for a completion of the manuscripts by the autumn of the same year. At any rate, he permitted his publisher to assume that printing could begin in the autumn. But he increasingly responded to the rather gentle admonitions of Siebeck with outbursts of irritation and despair. Apparently there was still much work to be done, and it is possible that Weber was no longer happy with some of the earlier texts. Besides, the length of the texts far exceeded the limits that had been allotted to them even in the workplan. Weber must have envisaged that the texts on religion and domination would have to be either drastically shortened or totally rewritten in order to be integrated into the *Grundriss* as scheduled in the workplan. It may be that he was reluctant to tell Siebeck anything about this irritating state of affairs. When the First World War broke out, Weber abruptly interrupted his work on the manuscripts for the *Grundriss*, and even the persuasive powers of Siebeck could not bring him to change his mind.[55] In 1917, when Weber took up a professorship at the University of Vienna, he used some of the manuscripts for his lecture course, but it seems that he did not work on them since there are no detectable noteworthy alterations. Instead, he concentrated upon writing the essays on the sociology of world religions, which partly covered the same ground as the section on religious communities for the *Grundriss*, but with an even broader scope. However, by then politics had become his primary concern.

So the manuscripts for *Economy and Society: Sociology* written between 1909 and 1914 remained a torso, albeit a most impressive one. Only some sections dealt with the subject matter in a comprehensive manner, while others were left incomplete or unfinished. We cannot even be sure whether all the texts included in the current editions were, in fact, destined for *Economy and Society*.

Only after Max Weber returned from the Versailles Peace Conference in June 1919, where he participated as a member of the German peace delegation, did he resume work on *Economy and Society*. He did this at the instigation of Siebeck, who employed all psychological tactics at his disposal to make his friend finally finish the grand project. Apparently, Weber worked extremely hard during these months preparing the manuscripts for his *Gesammelte Aufsätze zur Religionssoziologie* (Collected Essays on the Sociology of Religion) for publication at the same time that he was working at his "Sociology." In 1919 he gave widely acclaimed lectures in Munich entitled "The Most General Theories of Social Science" (Die allgemeinsten Theorien der Gesellschaftswissenschaft), which were more or less identical to "Basic Sociological Concepts" (Soziologische Grundbegriffe), the first section of the new version of *Economy and Society*. Furthermore, he began to prepare a new lecture course, "General Theory of the State and Politics" (Allgemeine Staatslehre und Politik [Staatssoziologie]), announced for the summer term of 1920 at the University of Munich. It formed the core of the sociology of domination, which had already been envisaged in 1914.

In the last months of 1919 and the spring and early summer of 1920, Weber was extremely busy bringing his great project to completion. Now Siebeck was hopeful that he would after all receive the manuscript for which he had waited so long. Indeed, the arrival of the first section of the manuscript in September 1919 caused a sensation among staff members at the publishing house J. C. B. Mohr at 22 Wilhelmstraße in Tübingen.[56] They hoped that within a reasonable time the entire manuscript would be in their hands. However, this enthusiasm proved to be premature, for the old manuscripts were by no means "ready for publication," as Weber made the publisher believe; they required almost complete rewriting. The publisher kept asking for manuscripts, even for small bits, in order to spur Weber on and stimulate his working spirit. However, there was very little among the heap of the earlier manuscripts that Weber found good enough to be published without a thorough revision. It was one thing to bring the texts in line with his new, mature sociological terminology, and another to rearrange the vast amount of material according to systematic criteria instead of in historical sequence. Besides, he was constantly widening the scope of his sociological analysis, more determined than ever before to give a comprehensive account based upon his encyclopedic knowledge. He wanted to write a definitive work that would stand the test of time, and he was therefore not inclined to compromise, whatever the publisher might say. The only chapter among the older texts that he appears to have considered ready for publication was "Economy and Law" (Wirtschaft und Recht), the so-called "Sociology of Law" (Rechtssoziologie).[57] It would appear that he let the publisher send it to the printer even though he was still busy rewriting the other sections of the older manuscripts. In any case, in early May 1920 he permitted the publisher to proceed with the production of the final galley proofs of the "Sociology of Law" (at any rate, a section of it) without insisting on a second revision.[58] It appears that for the purposes of publication he then inserted his own handwritten subtitles and content summaries into the typewritten manuscripts. However, this is a somewhat mysterious issue because these proofs must have later gone missing; Marianne Weber seems to have been unaware that the "Sociology of Law" had already been sent to the publisher before Weber's sudden death.[59] It is possible that Palyi lost the galley proofs, together with the proofs of a large part of the manuscripts on communities, as is suggested in the correspondence between Marianne Weber and the publisher.

In any case, work on the manuscripts was proceeding speedily and steadily. In December 1919 a formal publishing contract was signed. Now, after long hesitation, Weber contractually committed himself to writing the section "Economy and Society";[60] the subtitle "The Economy and the Social Orders and Powers" was allowed to lapse without further ado. In April 1920 an advertising leaflet was issued by the publishing house, undoubtedly with Weber's knowledge and connivance, in which his contribution was now formally announced under the title: "*Economy and Society: Sociology*. By Max Weber." This was the title agreed upon by him and his publisher two months before his death. It was in line with the correspondence with Siebeck, in which the publisher had repeatedly referred to the manuscripts as Max Weber's "Sociology." We are therefore justified in conferring on Weber's magnum opus, or at any rate the part of it that he brought to publication in 1920, the title *Economy and Society: Sociology*, whereas the earlier writings must be qualified as posthumous texts edited from his papers, which in 1919–20 had no longer been destined for publication in their present version.

At the time of Max Weber's death on June 20, 1920, only a fraction of his magnum opus had been completed, namely the chapters "Basic Sociological Categories" (Soziologische Grundbegriffe), "Sociological Categories of Economic Activity" (Soziologische Grundkategorien des Wirtschaftens), and "Three Types of Legitimate Domination" (Typen der Herrschaft), and a fragment of the chapter "Status Groups and Classes" (Stände und Klassen). These chapters were already in print before his death. The galley proofs of the revision and the so-called superrevision of parts of these chapters with Weber's handwritten corrections and additions have survived, thanks to Else Jaffé, who collected them as personal memorabilia.

In these manuscripts, we encounter a totally different kind of historical sociology. Though it retained the world-historical perspective and global scope found in the earlier manuscripts, it was no longer governed by an evolutionary model, however vague, but by a systematic presentation of different types of social action extending from purely affective to formal rational conduct. A great variety of alternative types of social action performed by social institutions of various sorts, all of them illustrated by reference to a wide range of historical examples, is presented to readers so that they might draw their own conclusions. With the help of systems of ideal types, a rich and truly impressive panorama of a seemingly unlimited number of different forms of social organization, real or potential, emerges. This is achieved by employing combinations of ideal types, which are often arranged in such a way as to represent diametrically opposed positions. As a rule, the cases define the poles of a spectrum of potentialities, which are taken as a starting point for analysis. The ideal types function throughout as a theoretical guideline for the rational assessment of empirical phenomena, and, at the same time, for measuring the degree of deviation of empirically given cases of social conduct or types of institutions from the ideally constructed rational model. There is little doubt that if Max Weber had been allowed to finish his "Sociology," it would have received a form similar to the sections on sociological categories. However, even though the segments of *Economy and Society: Sociology* come from different periods and represent different stages in the development of his sociological thought, they constitute in their entirety, regardless of their fragmentary character, a magnificent intellectual edifice.

The treatise "The City" appears to have originally been written for another context; it is in substance one of the oldest texts in *Economy and Society: Sociology*. According to Weber, the brotherhoods and urban liberties of medieval Europe represent an important stage in the development of modern liberal society. This issue, however, eventually became marginal within the framework of his "Sociology." The chapters on the emergence and on the various forms of communities represent by and large the oldest version of Weber's "Sociology." They had largely been completed by 1911, although some addenda and modifications were made as late as 1914. Yet by 1913 the notion of community, which originally held a central position in Max Weber's thinking, had been discarded. This commences with the essay "Some Categories of Interpretative Sociology," as published in 1913 in a substantially amended and extended version in *Logos*. It signals a turnabout in Weber's sociological theory. "Community action" (Gemeinschaftshandeln) was supplanted by "social action" (soziales Handeln), and community was progressively replaced by "association" (Verband). The so-called "Sociology of Religion," written about 1912–13, belongs to this new stage in the development of Weber's sociological thought. Here the key theme came to be the interaction of ideal and material ideas in the great world religions. Now the process of rationalization moved to center stage in Weber's sociological analysis, not least because of the great cultural significance that he attributed to it with respect to the future of Western liberal societies. The advance of rationalization was, Weber believed, most noticeable in the field of law. The text "The Economy and the Orders" was written fairly early and may even have originally been intended as one of the opening sections of the whole enterprise. However, by 1912–13 it was amalgamated with the chapter on "Economy and Law," written about this time. The far greater part of the "Sociology of Domination" had also been written in 1912–13, without any further significant amendments. "Basic Sociological Categories," "Sociological Categories of Economic Activity," and "Three Types of Legitimate Domination," which in part overlap with the respective passages in the earlier texts, represent that part of the grand project still completed entirely to his satisfaction. With but a few minor amendments of a mainly technical nature by Marianne Weber and Palyi, these are the only texts that have survived in their original version.

If the development of Max Weber's sociological thought after the turn of the twentieth century is taken into account, his magnum opus will no longer be seen as a more or less opaque work useful only as a rich quarry for concepts and ideas, but as a fascinating sociological analysis of modern societies against the backdrop of world history.

Notes

1. *Die protestantische Ethik und der Geist der Kapitalismus* was originally published in 1904, but was somewhat revised in the 1920 edition. It was this latter edition that served as the basis for the Parsons translation. Max Weber, *The Protestant Ethic and the Spirit of Capitalism*, with a foreword by R. H. Tawney, trans. Talcott Parsons (London: Unwin University Books, 1930).

2. Tenbruck's fascinating and thoughtful essay is "Abschied von *Wirtschaft und Gesellschaft*," *Zeitschrift für die gesamte Staatswissenschaft* 133 (1977): 703–36.

3. Wolfgang Schluchter, "'Kopf' oder 'Doppelkopf'-das ist hier die Frage. Replik auf Hiroshi Orihara," *Kölner Zeitschrift für Soziologie und Sozialpsychologie* 51 (1999): 735–43; Wolfgang Schluchter, "Max Webers Beitrag zum *Grundriss der Sozialökonomik*," *Kölner Zeitschrift für Soziologie und Sozialpsychologie* 50 (1998): 327–43.

4. See Orihara's essays in a series of Working Papers of the University of Tokyo, as well as his contribution, "Max Webers Beitrag zum *Grundriss der Sozialökonomik*: Das Vorkriegsmanuskript als integriertes Ganzes," *Kölner Zeitschrift für Soziologie und Sozialpsychologie* 51 (1999): 724–34, which was published after his essay had been completed, but summarizes his previous arguments. Hiroshi Orihara, "Über den 'Abschied' hinaus zu einer Rekonstruktion von Max Webers Werk 'Wirtschaft und Gesellschaft,'" Working Papers of the University of Tokyo, part 2 (Tokyo: University of Tokyo, Department of Social and International Relations, 1993); Hiroshi Orihara, "Rekonstruktion des Manuskripts 1911–13," Working Papers of the University of Tokyo, part 3 (Tokyo: University of Tokyo, Department of Social and International Relations, 1994–95); Hiroshi Orihara, "Der Kopf des 'Torsos': Zur Rekonstrukion der begrifflichen Einleitung ins alte Manuskript 1911–13 von Max Webers 'Wirtschaft und Gesellschaft,'" Working Papers of the University of Tokyo

(Tokyo: University of Tokyo, Department of Social and International Relations, 1995).

5. Wolfgang J. Mommsen, "Neue Max-Weber-Literatur," *Historische Zeitschrift* 211 (1970): 616–30; Wolfgang J. Mommsen, "Die Siebecks und Max Weber: Ein Beispiel für Wissenschaftsorganisation in Zusammenarbeit von Wissenschaftler und Verlegern," *Geschichte und Gesellschaft* 22 (1996): 30; Hiroshi Orihara, "Eine Grundlegung zur Rekonstruktion von Max Webers 'Wirtschaft und Gesellschaft': Die Authenzität der Verweise im Text des 2. und 3. Teils der 1. Auflage," *Kölner Zeitschrift für Soziologie und Sozialpsychologie* 46 (1994): 103–21; Wolfgang Schluchter, " 'Wirtschaft und Gesellschaft': Das Ende eines Mythos," in Schluchter, *Religion und Lebensführung*, vol.2, *Studien zu Max Webers Religions- und Herrschaftssoziologie* (Frankfurt: Suhrkamp, 1988), pp. 597–634; Tenbruck, "Abschied von *Wirtschaft und Gesellschaft.*" Later J. F. Winckelmann published an elaborate defense of his edition, which, however, cannot rescue his editorial project. Johannes Winckelmann, *Max Webers hinterlassenes Hauptwerk: Die Wirtschaft und die gesellschaftlichen Ordnungen und Mächte. Entstehung und gedanklicher Aufbau* (Tübingen: J.C.B. Mohr [Paul Siebeck], 1986).

6. Max Weber, *Wirtschaft und Gesellschaft: Die Wirtschaft und die gesellschaftlichen Ordnungen und Mächte*, ed. Marianne Weber and Melchior Palyi (Tübingen: J. C. B. Mohr [Paul Siebeck], 1920) (hereafter *WuG* 1); Max Weber, *Wirtschaft und Gesellschaft: Grundriss der verstehenden Soziologie*, ed. Johannes Winckelmann, 5th ed. (Tübingen: J. C. B. Mohr [Paul Siebeck], 1973) (hereafter *WuG* 5); *Economy and Society: An Outline of Interpretive Sociology*, ed. Guenther Roth and Claus Wittich (Berkeley: University of California Press, 1978).

7. Cf. preface to the 2nd edition of *WuG* 1, p. iii.

8. This procedure is, of course, in line with the standards of historical-critical editions, and does not imply a devaluation of Winckelmann's editorial work, as Orihara suggests in a recent sharp critique of the editorial procedures suggested in this chapter. See Hiroshi Orihara, "From 'A Torso with a Wrong Head' to 'Five Disjointed Pieces of Carcass'? Problems of the Editorial Policies for the *Max Weber Gesamtausgabe* I/22," Working Paper No. 8 (Takenoyama, Japan: Sugiyama Jogakuen University, 1996). See also Hiroshi Orihara's lately published essay, "From 'A Torso with a Wrong Head' to 'Five Disjointed Body Parts with a Head': A Critique of the Editorial Policy for Max Weber Gesamtausgabe I/22," *Max Weber Studies* 3, no. 2 (2003).

9. Orihara's recent violent protest against this arrangement seems to be largely unwarranted, inasmuch as it does not prevent the reader from perusing the work in its entirety. This decision was made unanimously by the Editoral Committee (see the editorial introduction to each volume), and not solely by the author of this chapter.

10. "Das dicke alte Manuskript muß ganz gründlich umgestaltet werden." Letter from Max Weber to Paul Siebeck, Oct. 27, 1919, Verlags-Archiv Mohr/Siebeck, Bayerische Staatsbibliothek [hereafter, BSB] München, Deponat Max Weber, Ana 446.

11. For a detailed demonstration of the shortcomings of the first edition, see Wolfgang J. Mommsen, "Zur Entstehung von Max Webers hinterlassenem Werk *Wirtschaft und Gesellschaft. Sociologie,*" Discussion Paper No. 44 (1999), Centre for Comparative Government and Public Policy, Free University of Berlin, 1999.

12. See note 4.

13. Cf. the correspondence between Marianne Weber and the publisher Paul Siebeck between 1919 and 1922. Verlags-Archiv Mohr/Siebeck, BSB München, Deponat Max Weber, Ana 446.

14. "Religionssoziologie, Rechtssoziologie, dann Formen der Gesellschaft: (ethnische Gemeinschaft, Sippen, Nation, Staat und Hierokiatie, etc.) ferner Formen der Herrschaft: (Charismatismus, Patrimonialismus, Feudalismus)." Cf. letter from Marianne Weber to Paul Siebeck, June 30, 1920. See note 13.

15. This point is discussed further later in this chapter.

16. Letter to Karl Bücher, May 16, 1910; cf. Max Weber, *Max Weber Gesamtausgabe* II, vol. 6 (*MWG* II/6), *Briefe 1909–1910*, ed. M. Rainer Lepsius and Wolfgang J. Mommsen (Tübingen: J. C. B. Mohr [Paul Siebeck], 1994), p. 520.

17. Letter to Paul Siebeck, April 20, 1910, *MWG* II/6, p. 103.

18. Letter to Paul Siebeck, May 1, 1910, *MWG* II/6, pp. 484–85.

19. Max Weber, *Gesammelte Aufsätze zur Wissenschaftslehre*, 4th ed. (Tübingen: J. C. B. Mohr [Paul Siebeck], 1973) (hereafter *GAWL*), pp. 360–75.

20. See later discussion.

21. Max Weber, "Agrarverhältnisse im Altertum," *Handwörterbuch der Staatswissenschaften*, ed. J. Conrad et al., 3rd ed. (Jena: Gustav Fischer, 1909), vol. I, pp. 52–188; also Max Weber, *Max Weber Gesamtausgabe* I, vol. 6 (*MWG* I/6), *Zur Sozial- und Wirtschaftsgeschichte des Altertums. Schriften 1893–1909*, ed. Jürgen Deininger (Tübingen: J. C. B. Mohr [Paul Siebeck], forthcoming).

22. A striking example is to be found in his *Grundriss zu den Vorlesungen über Allgemeine ("theoretische") Nationalökonomie (1898)* (Tübingen: J. C. B. Mohr [Paul Siebeck], 1990). In this lecture course on "General (theoretical) Economics," which a research group at the University of Düsseldorf is editing, this argument is constantly repeated (*MWG* III/1; 2005).

23. Ibid., p. 30 (translation by the author).

24. "[. . .] durch einen jahrtausendelangen Anpassungsprozess anerzogen." Ibid., p. 29.

25. Weber, *GAWL*, pp. 384–99; see also Richard Swedberg, *Max Weber and the Idea of Economic Sociology* (Princeton, NJ: Princeton University Press, 1998), pp. 194–95; and also, recently, the book by Zenonas Norkus, *Max Weber und Rational Choice* (Marburg: Metropolis, 2001).

26. Weber, *GAWL*, p. 395. The translation follows Manfred Schön, "Gustav Schmoller and Max Weber," with amendments by the author, *Max Weber and His Contemporaries*, ed. Wolfgang Mommsen and Jürgen Osterhammel (London: Allen & Unwin, 1987), p. 61.

27. A reference to Wynnecken's "freie Schulgemeinde," established on September 1, 1906 (inserted in the original text with the same pen), allows us to date the older segment of this text; it must have been written at the end of 1906 or possibly a few months later. This date is corroborated by a reference to the Youth Movement that had been growing since the late 1890s but was publicly known only from the turn of the century on. There is also an allusion to "ascetic Protestantism" that points to a date close to the *Protestant Ethic*, written in 1904. Weber inserted into this text a lengthy sketch on the emergence and development of marriage and the status of

married women in various ages and cultures, under the heading "Women in Marriage" (Die Frau in der Ehe). This sketch undoubtedly served as a blueprint for much that Marianne Weber had to say on this issue and therefore must also have been written in the fall of 1906. Cf. Marianne Weber, *Ehefrau und Mutter in der Rechtsentwicklung* (Tübingen: J. C. B. Mohr [Paul Siebeck], 1907). Max Weber contributed to Marianne Weber's book a great deal, indirectly and directly, as Marianne Weber herself testifies (cf. ibid., IV, p. 63). Note also the letter from Marianne Weber to Eduard Baumgarten, July 4, 1950, BSB München, Deponat Max Weber, Ana 446. See also the letter from Max Weber to Paul Siebeck, Sept. 11, 1906, in Weber, *MWG* II/5), *Briefe 1906–1908*, ed. M. Rainer Lepsius and Wolfgang J. Mommsen (Tübingen: J. C. B. Mohr [Paul Siebeck], 1990), pp. 158–59. See now *MWG* I/22–1, *Wirtschaft und Gesellschaft: Die Wirtschaft und die gesellschaftlichen Ordnungen und Mächte. Nachlass*, vol. 1: *Gemeinschaften*, ed. Wolfgang J. Mommsen and Michael Meyer (Tübingen: J. C. B. Mohr [Paul Siebeck], 2001), pp. 282–327.

    28. *WuG* 1, pp. 194ff.

    29. It has possibly survived among Marianne Weber's papers for this reason alone.

    30. See the introduction to "Die Stadt," in Max Weber, *MWG* I/22–5, *Wirtschaft und Gesellschaft: Die Wirtschaft und die gesellschaftlichen Ordnungen und Mächte. Nachlass*, vol. 5, *Die Stadt*, ed. Wilfried Nippel (Tübingen: J. C. B. Mohr [Paul Siebeck], 1999).

    31. "[. . .] dessen fortschreitendes Umsichgreifen in allem Gemeinschaftshandeln wir auf allen Gebieten als wesentlichste Triebkraft der Entwicklung zu verfolgen haben werden." *WuG* 1, p. 382.

    32. Letter to Johannes Plenge, Aug. 11, 1913. Published in Weber, *MWG* II/8, *Briefe 1913–1914*, ed. Rainer M. Lepsius and Wolfgang J. Mommsen (Tübingen: J. C. B. Mohr [Paul Siebeck], 2003), p. 305: "Meine persönlichen Ansichten sind z[ur] Z[eit] im starken Wandel begriffen."

    33. Ibid.

    34. Ibid., Max Weber to Paul Siebeck, Feb. 8, 1913, p. 87.

    35. "[. . .] eine geschlossene soziologische Theorie und Darstellung [. . .], welche alle großen Gemeinschaftsformen zur Wirtschaft in Beziehung setzt: von der Familie und Hausgemeinschaft zum 'Betrieb', zur Sippe, zur ethnischen Gemeinschaft, zur Religion (alle großen Religionen der Erde umfassend: Soziologie der Erlösungslehren und der religiösen Ethiken,—was Troeltsch gemacht hat, jetzt für alle Religionen, nur wesentlich knapper), endlich eine umfassende soziologische Staats- und Herrschafts-Lehre." Ibid., Max Weber to Paul Siebeck, Dec. 30, 1913, pp. 449–50.

    36. *GAWL*, 4th ed., pp. 427–74.

    37. Ibid., p. 427 n. 1.

    38. Hiroshi Orihara, "Eine Grundlegung zur Rekonstruktion von Max Webers *Wirtschaft und Gesellschaft*: Die Authenzität der Verweise im Text des 2. und 3. Teils der 1. Auflage," *Kölner Zeitschrift für Soziologie and Sozialpsychoiogie* 46 (1994): 103–21; Wolfgang Schluchter, "*Wirtschaft und Gesellschaft*" in Schluchter, *Religion and Lebensführung*, vol. 2, pp. 597–634.

    39. Letter to Heinrich Rickert, Sept. 5, 1913, *MWG* II/8, p. 318. There it is said that the older section had been finished three quarters of a year earlier ("seit [einem]

dreiviertel Jahr"), not, as the letter had been read previously, three to four years earlier ("seit drei [bis] vier Jahren").

40. *MWG* I/22–1, pp. 185–90.

41. Max Weber, *Gesammelte Aufsätze zur Soziologie und Sozialpolitik* (Tübingen: J.
C. B. Mohr [Paul Siebeck], 1924), p. 485.

42. Weber points out in the letter to Heinrich Rickert just quoted that, because
of the substantial revisions he had made, it was no longer possible to estimate the
precise length of the text.

43. Hiroshi Orihara based his conclusions as to the existence of the "lead-in" on
the argument that some of Weber's own references in other parts of *Economy and Society* can be certified only in respective passages in "Some Categories." However, a
close scrutiny of these references shows that the passages in "Some Categories" that
allegedly correspond to them are so general in nature that this cannot be said to provide conclusive evidence.

44. Hiroshi Orihara's recent violent protest against the decisions of the Editorial
Committee of *MWG* is simply not sustained by the evidence. See above Orihara,
"From 'a Torso with a Wrong Head'," pp. 18–22.

45. See later discussion.

46. Letter from Max Weber to Paul Siebeck, Mar. 18, 1914, *MWG* II/8, 558–
59.

47. The English translations of these titles are in most instances based on terminology used in *Economy and Society: An Outline of Interpretive Sociology*, ed. Guenther
Roth and Claus Wittich (Berkeley: University of California Press, 1978), pp. xxvii–
xxviii.

48. In the English-language version of *Economy and Society*, this phrase is translated as "The Economy and the Arena of De Facto and Normative Powers." Here,
we follow the more literal translation introduced earlier by Mommsen, both for consistency and because we believe it better captures the meaning of the original. *Eds.*

49. *Grundriss der Sozialökonomik*, ed. Max Weber, vol. 1 (Tübingen: J. C. B. Mohr
[Paul Siebeck], 1914), pp. x–xi.

50. Schluchter, "Max Webers Beitrag zum *Grundriss der Sozialökonomik*," pp.
342–44.

51. Cf. *Archiv für Sozialwissenschaft und Sozialpolitik* 38 (July 1914).

52. Cf. *MWG* I/22–1, pp. 74–76.

53. For a detailed presentation of this unsolvable editorial problem, see *MWG* I/
22–1, pp. 78–79.

54. *WuG* 1, pp. 31–121.

55. Mommsen, "Die Siebecks und Max Weber," pp. 28–29.

56. Cf. the letter from Max Weber to Paul Siebeck, Sept. 25, 1919, Verlags-Archiv
Mohr/Siebeck, BSB München, Deponat Max Weber, Ana 446.

57. This is also confirmed by Marianne Weber, *Lebenserinnerungen* (Bremen: J.
Storm, 1948), p. 123.

58. Letter to Paul Siebeck, May 12, 1920, Verlags-Archiv Mohr/Siebeck, BSB
München, Deponat Max Weber, Ana 446.

59. Perhaps we have to envisage the possibility that Max Weber had already sent

the manuscript for the "Sociology of Law" to the publisher during his stay in Munich in the fall of 1917. This would explain why his wife had no knowledge of the matter. It is to be assumed that the publisher returned the original manuscripts to him, because they were found in his desk after his sudden death.

60. In the accompanying general contract, equivalent to the contracts for all the contributors to the *Grundriss,* the term *Abschnitt* ("section" as opposed to "chapter") was used instead.

PART II

The Textual Core

The Continuing Challenge of Weber's Theory of Rational Action

The passage that opens *Wirtschaft und Gesellschaft* is as puzzling as it is famous:

Soziologie . . . soll heissen: eine Wissenschaft, welche soziales Handeln deutend verstehen und dadurch in seinem Ablauf und seinen Wirkungen ursächlich erklären will.

Sociology . . . will be defined here as a discipline that seeks to understand social action interpretively and thereby to explain its course and its consequences causally.[1]

This passage is puzzling on several counts. It stands alone among founding statements of sociology in defining that discipline in terms of *individual* action. The universe of such foundational statements contains nothing comparable. All other originative sociologists define the subject matter of sociology in terms of *supra*individual formations, such as the social organism (Spencer), social facts (Durkheim), social processes (Ross), forms of social interaction (Simmel), reciprocal affirmation (Tönnies), collective behavior (Park and Burgess), and the like.

What is more, Weber seems reluctant to press his definition very far. A few pages after proclaiming sociology as an effort to understand individual actions, he backtracks by acknowledging the continuing relevance of other definitions, noting that sociology "is by no means confined to the study of social action," and that phenomena that lie outside the boundaries of his defined field "may well have a degree of sociological importance at least equal to that of the type which can be called social action in the strict sense."[2]

Further, by confining his sociology to the study of human conduct only insofar as it is imbued by meaning (*Sinn*), Weber seems to make its sphere peculiarly restricted. According to his own repeated testimony, by far the greatest part of human conduct runs its course in states of "inarticulate half-consciousness or actual unconsciousness," that is, as behaviors that border on the meaningless.[3] Consequently, adhering to his definition would confine the subject matter of sociology to a very thin slice of social phenomena.[4]

Finally, note that the concept of social action receives little attention in the opus that follows.[5] In some 1,370 pages of the English translation, the phrase appears only a few dozen times and, apart from the brief definition sections of chapter 1, never as an object of sustained analysis, as it did for contemporaries such as Dewey and Pareto or for later theorists including Mead, Parsons, and Habermas. It figures so minimally in Weber's discourse in *Economy and Society* that standard exegetical works on Weber simply ignore it.[6]

Even so, beginning with Talcott Parsons, who sought to erect a global theory of action on Weberian foundations, Weber's passing attention to the concept of action has stimulated a warehouse of reflection and controversy. Much if not most of this discourse pertains to the concept of rationality, with which Weber's consideration of action was so closely entwined. The continuing importance of this literature, as well as renewed scholarly efforts to clarify the significance of *Economy and Society*, raise three questions that this chapter addresses:

1. Why, given the marginal status of action theory in the discursive field of early sociology and in Weber's own substantive work in comparative historical sociology, did Weber engage the problematic of action in the first place?

2. What is the significance of Weber's focus on rational action?

3. How can his conception of rational action be related to his penetrating substantive analyses of rationalization in world history?

The Context of Weber's Engagement with "Action"

Weber's strictures about sociology as the study of meaningful conduct appear only in the last decade of his life, but the view of action that they embody was scarcely a late afterthought. His engagement with methodological questions about the study of *action* began long before he thought of calling himself a sociologist. During most of his career Weber distanced himself from sociologists, describing them as late as 1905 as "naturalistic dilettantes" marked by "blind enthusiasm."[7] Although by the end of that decade he had come to accept the label of sociologist to cover his comparative historical studies and his general approach to social action, he remained ambivalent about the label for the rest of his life.[8]

It was, after all, the fields of jurisprudence and economics in which Weber received his academic training and his first university appointments,[9] and these fields loaded him with problems, concepts, and methods he would bear throughout his life. Close readers of *Economy and Society* have fingered the chapters on law and economy as representing Weber's scholarship at its most majestically self-confident, and thoughtways current in those fields challenged him early on to engage with issues related to the conceptualization of action. Beyond that, Weber drank deeply from the wells of idealist thought that nourished German thinkers of his generation. Thus it was the traditions of *legal theory, the German historical school of political economy, Austrian marginalist economics, and German idealist philosophy* that gave Max Weber the ideas that informed his distinctive complex of ideas about human action.

In a work subtitled *The Lawyer as Social Thinker*, Stephen Turner and Regis Factor demonstrate the salience of thoughtways Weber acquired from training and experience in law.[10] Conceptualizing human agency, and especially liability based on intention, was and still is important to German legal thought.[11] On this subject the legal philosopher Rudolph Ihering provided the terms of discourse Weber was schooled in. Ihering's magnum opus *Der Zweck im Recht* opens with an account of human action that features problems of causation and intention. In Ihering's analysis, mechanical "causes" are sharply distinguished from psychological "purposes," that is, aims attributed to agents that are intelligible as reasons for their actions.

Ihering's distinctions between mechanical causes and intelligible reasons for action became foundational for Weber's approach to social analysis. So did Ihering's distinction between two types of interests, material interests and ideal interests.[12] Weber early on combined these distinctions with ideas he was deriving from Austrian theoretical economists, most notably Carl Menger and Eugen Böhm-Bawerk. Menger viewed economics as a science that explains complex phenomena like price, commodities, and money as outcomes of discrete efforts to satisfy future wants by employing pertinent means. Menger had recast economic analysis by insisting that economic value is determined not through quantity of labor or quantity of capital expenditure, but by subjective wants. Menger's conception thus foregrounded the assumption that individuals act on the basis of a rational pleasure-pain calculus. Eugen Böhm-Bawerk added a temporal frame, distinguishing short-term from long-run utility-maximizing. These and other agents of the "marginalist revolution" redirected their discipline from macroeconomic issues of productivity and distribution to microeconomic issues of how households and firms set prices, using mathematics to calculate the dynamics of human want-satisfactions.

In Weber's outline of a course on political economy (*Nationalökonomie*), which he planned to teach at Heidelberg in 1898, he placed Menger's 1871 *Grundsötze der Volkswirt-Schaftslehre* and Böhm-Bawerk's *Grundzüge* of 1885 at the head of a list of reading assignments on the conceptual foundation of economic theory. His outline sketched a definition of economic action

(*Wirtschaften*) in Mengerian terms: "conscious, deliberate action toward nature and humans, prompted by needs—of either a 'material' or 'ideal' sort—that require *external means* for their satisfaction and which serve the goal of *providing for the future*."[13]

Weber's main disciplinary commitments thus focused on the *liability* of individuals, on the one hand, and on the performance of actions designed to satisfy *personal wants*, on the other. These commitments brought him into direct conflict with ideas from the social sciences that were becoming increasingly popular in his time. Influenced by Herder's and Hegel's notions of *Volksgeist* and *Zeitgeist*, a number of academic enterprises were striving to overcome individualistic perspectives and, "instead of individual action, were making social forces and collective movements the truly decisive and effective factors" in human life. These included "collective psychology [*Völkerpsychologie*], positivistic sociology, cultural history, milieu theory, moral statistics, historical political economy, ethnology, animal sociology, comparative legal studies, and sociology—disciplines that since the 1860s had emerged as sciences of the supraindividual, as collectivist social theories."[14]

Owing to Weber's focus on personal liability and personal interests, and other supports for an individualistic perspective (discussed below), he developed a strong aversion to notions that represented supraindividual formation as real historic forces. This aversion spilled over into legal theory and political economy insofar as, influenced by historicism, they relied on such entities as supraindividual structures and collective agencies. Thus, while Weber accepted Ihering's distinction between material interests and ideal interests, he refused to associate the latter with the social good, but construed it instead in terms of the ultimate value orientations of individual actors.[15]

In his theoretical and programmatic formulations about human phenomena, Weber's opposition to collectivist concepts was firm, consistent, and unreserved. It extends from his early methodological comments to some of his last utterances on sociology, when he declared that the reason he allowed himself to be appointed as a sociologist at Munich was in order to exorcize that field of the collectivist concepts that continued to haunt it.[16] Thus when the time came to associate himself with sociology—first as an affiliate of the German Sociological Association, then as an author of publications to which he affixed the label of sociology—he did so on the basis of assumptions he had acquired from law and economics, and with an eye to puncturing the social-realist balloons of his adopted profession. Weber repeatedly described his approach as evincing an individualistic method of analysis and maintained this position *despite a long series of brilliant analyses of such supraindividual formations as forms of economic organization, legal systems, religious systems, musical systems, stratification structures, urban structures, administrative forms, political-ecclesiastical relationships, international power relations, and the like.*[17]

Opposition to social realism or methodological holism did not, of course, form the entire basis for Weber's programmatic approach to sociology. One could just as well be a methodological individualist and conceive of individual actors as following universal instincts or psychic drives to maximize utilities—the sort of position that may be glossed as "atomic naturalism."[18] Weber felt impelled to confront atomic naturalist positions from early on. If refuting the notion of real collective formations was a primary objective behind his definition of sociology, the way in which he construed human action reflected other items on Weber's agenda—positions that also served to delimit the kind of sociology he advocated from other disciplines, especially psychology and biology.

It is not uncommon for those who eschew supraindividual entities to advocate reduction to a "psychological" level of explanation. Following the successes of Wilhelm Wundt, and his renowned founding of a psychological laboratory in Leipzig in 1879, many scholars in Germany were inclined to account for human activity by appealing to experimentally grounded general laws about fundamental drives (*Triebe*).[19] In his first programmatic statement about sociology as focused on the intentions of actors, however, Weber was quick to repudiate that sort of approach. "Interpretive sociology . . . is not part of a 'psychology,'" he insisted.[20] Reasons for this assertion had been spelled out in his 1908 paper "Die Grenznutzlehre und das 'psychophysische Grundgesetz,'" a paper occasioned by suggestions made independently by Lujo Brentano and Gustav Fechner that economic value theory could be reduced to experimental psychology. Weber's main objection there was that psychology, with particular reference to the famed Weber-Fechner law of psychophysics, could account only for internal sensations, not for the actor's rational adaptive response to situations manifest in external actions.[21] Consequently, as he wrote in a letter to Brentano that same year, "Marginal utility theory has in my opinion nothing more to do with 'psychology' than with astronomy or I don't know what else."[22] In his programmatic sketch for a *verstehenden* sociology, Weber repeated the point: "The more unambiguously an action is appropriately oriented toward the type of correct rationality, the less the meaningful intelligibility of its course is enhanced by any psychological considerations whatever"[23]—and iterated it once again in the opening pages of *Economy and Society*.[24]

Soon after Weber took steps to differentiate his interpretive sociology from psychology, he began to take a similar stance with regard to biology. The triumph of Darwinian biology had encouraged many scholars to explain human social behavior in terms of biological heredity and evolutionary adaptation. A prominent form of this movement stressed biologically determined categories of race as bases for human behavior and social cohesion. In Weber's milieu, this attitude was represented by second-generation Dar-

winists like Alfred Ploetz and Wilhelm Schallmayer, who adapted such notions to practical programs of social hygiene. Although Weber helped to
bring Ploetz to address the first meeting of the German Sociological Association in 1910, he took strong exception to Ploetz's remarks. Not only did
Ploetz ignore the standards of value-free discourse in advocating his racial
hygienic measures on scientific grounds, he also committed two substantive
sins: in treating society as a living organism he illicitly imported natural scientific categories into sociological discourse, and relatedly, he failed to com-
prehend that society, unlike animal life, required the methods of *Verstehen*.
Hence, although social biology might well contribute to understanding
some piece of the social world, it represented an unacceptable infringement
on the domain of sociology insofar as it attempted to dispense with the
concept of self-consciously meaningful action: "I contest the notion that
there is a single sociologically relevant fact . . . that can be illuminated by
appeal to inborn, hereditary characteristics which are peculiar to a particular race."[25] Again, Weber iterated these thoughts a decade later in *Economy
and Society*.[26]

In sum: Weber's sociology was predicated not just on a plank of methodological individualism, but also on ideas that countered the reduction of individual behavior to biological or psychological causes.[27] His opposition to
using biology or psychology as disciplines to account for human social action stemmed from assumptions that the opening chapter of *Economy and Society* goes on to unpack. In explicating his terse definition of sociology, Weber presents four other points in quick succession: the distinction between
meaningful and nonmeaningful conduct (sec.1, §§2, 4, 6, 8, 9); the process of
interpretive understanding (*Verstehen*) (§§3, 5, 6, 7, 10); the notion of ideal
types (§§3, 6, 11); and the distinction between types of rational and nonrational actions (§§3, 5, 11; sec. 2).

To a certain extent, the assumptions about meaning, interpretation, and
ideal types also reflect Weber's early disciplinary commitments to law and to
theoretical economics. As noted earlier, the legal focus on the liability of actors and the economists' focus on the interests of individuals disposed him to
emphasize elements of conscious choice and intentionality in action, and
thus to discriminate between meaningful and nonmeaningful conduct. What
is more, Weber's early empirical work on East Elbian farm workers emphasized the value-choices of his subjects as a key independent variable. His appropriation of the work of the Austrian marginalists led him to understand
the utilitarian model as a useful scientific construct, *not* as a generic model
of human action.[28] His own Heidelberg course outline in economic theory
emphasized the "*constructed*" (*construiertes*) character of the model of economic actor, "in *contrast* to an empirical human being," which the discipline
of economics employed.[29] However, Weber's self-conscious emphasis on a

methodology of *Verstehen*, on the use of ideal types, and on the analysis of forms of action, which developed with the papers on Roscher and Knies and work on *The Protestant Ethic* in the years between 1903 and 1906, evince an influx of ideas from a broader context as well.

In fact, all the methodological assumptions that Weber employed in the course of articulating his conception of action reflect notions derived from the context of German philosophic idealism, broadly conceived. This complex tradition included strands that I have previously represented in terms of three distinct emphases:

While nearly all authors in the German tradition emphasize ways in which human subjects can and should transcend ordinary natural processes, they do so by construing the subject in different ways. One construction features the subject as *creating meanings* which, in contrast to natural phenomena, ask to be understood. A second emphasizes the ways in which human knowledge about any phenomenon gets organized through *using a priori categories*. A third celebrates the capacity of human subjects for *acting willfully*.[30]

The emphasis on meanings, which involves a focus on what I have called the "expressive subject," developed through a tradition of hermeneutics.[31] Represented among historians by those like Droysen and, preeminently, Dilthey, who contrasted the natural scientific mode of external cognition with a humanistic mode centered on the inner meanings of actions, the hermeneutic tradition was brought vividly to Weber's mind by Simmel's *Probleme der Geschichtsphilosophie* (*Problems of the Philosophy of History*), the second edition of which appeared in 1905. This work, which Weber acknowledged lavishly in the essay on Knies where he first articulated his ideas about *Verstehen*, helped Weber to make *Verstehen* the methodological lynchpin of his approach to theorizing about action—and so, later, of a sociology oriented to the interpretive understanding of human action—thereby supplementing the jural emphasis on intentionality with heavy epistemological reinforcements.[32]

The emphasis on the creative, constitutive work of the knower—the "cognitive subject"[33]—was represented in Weber's time by Windelband and Rickert. Again, this position was set forth forcefully in Simmel's *Probleme der Geschichtsphilosophie*, a work that robustly refuted historical realism and showed the necessity of constructed intellectual forms as preconditions for historical representations. Again, this viewpoint resonated with the lawyer's emphasis on grasping truth in terms of particular angles of juridical interest, a process known technically as "isolation."[34] For Weber, this meant rejecting all assumptions of inductive naturalism in favor of representing historical phenomena through invented ideal types. His formulations about action thus counter any assumption that all human actors are disposed to maximize utilities in an instrumentally rational manner. His Heidelberg course outline of 1898 notes with exquisite clarity that economic theory "postulates an *un-*

realistic person, analogous to a mathematical model."[35] In the writings after 1903, he would phrase this by saying that the model of the instrumentally rational actor represented a constructed ideal type, a heuristic configuration designed to promote unambiguous statements about what in reality were always more complicated phenomena.

If Weber's notions of *Verstehen* and ideal type represent the themes of German idealist thought I have glossed as the "expressive subject" and the "cognitive subject," respectively, his emphasis on the distinction between meaningful action and brute, mindless conduct represents what I have called the "voluntaristic subject."[36] This tradition stressed the capacity of human actors to make conscious choices and determine their own destinies. Its locus classicus was Kant's emphasis on autonomy as a source of human dignity. Kant was uncompromising in his celebration of human autonomy and his denigration of habit per se:

Duty should never be a matter of habit, but should always proceed, fresh and original, from one's mode of thought. . . . The reason for being disgusted with someone's acquired habits lies in the fact that the animal here predominates over the man. . . . Generally all acquired habits are objectionable.[37]

From Kant and Herder through Dilthey and Nietzsche, generations of German writers contrasted conduct that is unthinking, habitual, and animal-like with conduct that is self-conscious and willful. These ideas formed a broad intellectual ambience that reinforced the legal distinction between caused behavior and deliberate action. Its prominence in Weber's thinking reflects an infusion of Nietzsche, who goaded readers to transcend the state of animality through vigorous self-definition and conscious self-assertion.[38]

This Germanic emphasis on the voluntaristic subject found its way inexorably into the very first categories with which Weber sought to establish his sociology of action. In his 1913 essay on *verstehende* sociology, Weber distinguished among associational forms by *the extent to which they involved voluntary agreement*: from groupings whose rules are maintained by a coercive apparatus, to those reflecting constraints of an amorphously imposed consensus, to the voluntary associations wherein all participants have rationally agreed on the principles of their association. His most famous taxonomy in *Economy and Society*, which we shall now consider, ordered the forms of social action in a hierarchy of ascending voluntarism.

Weber's Taxonomy of Types of Action

As we know from Weber himself, typologies regarding human phenomena do not inhere in the nature of those phenomena, but are constructed in accord with the interests we bring to them. When those interests change—

"when the light of the great cultural problems moves on"—then the human sciences change their standpoint and their analytical apparatus.[39] In this section I address two questions: What pressing cultural interests moved Weber to construct his famous typology? How may we assess that typology in the present era?

In Weber's mature typology, as in all his reflections on human action, a central point of reference is what he called *Zweckrationalität*.[40] Why was this concept so central for Weber? I believe there are several reasons.

First, this was the core generative concept of economics, the field to which Weber transferred his allegiance after law and which, in some sense, he never abandoned. The neoclassical economists whom he followed rooted their theory on the heuristic assumption of an economic actor oriented, as we would now say, toward the maximization of utilities.[41]

Second, from his earliest work and with increasing penetration ever after, Weber held in mind the thought that this outlook was spreading. He seemed obsessed by *Zweckrationalität*, not (as Parsons would be) because of needing to find a properly delimited academic location for the conceptual apparatus of economics, but because of the prospect that the economistic outlook was becoming increasingly prominent in the modern world. In 1895, Weber observed that "in every sphere we find that the economic way of looking at things is on the advance"[42] and, a few years later, he noted that this abstraction was based on the "modern occidental type of human being and his economic conduct."[43] Foreshadowed by analyses of the migratory farm workers and participants in the stock exchange, Weber's work on the protestant ethic investigated directly the emergence of the type of orientation appropriate to the modern capitalist market economy. He contrasted it with types of action thought of as deviations from the *zweckrational* ideal type, whether by virtue of customary differences (economic traditionalism, or habitual action), or as types of action of a primarily affectual character (adventure, mysticism). And in the 1908 paper on marginal utility theory he wrote:

The general theorems which economic theory sets up are simply constructions that state what consequences the action of the individual man in its intertwining with the action of all others would *have to* produce, *on the assumption* that everyone were to shape his conduct toward his environment exclusively according to the principles of commercial bookkeeping—and, in *this* sense, "rationally." As we all know, the assumption does not hold. . . . Yet, the historical peculiarity of the capitalist epoch, and thereby also the significance of marginal utility theory (as of every economic theory of value) for the understanding of this epoch, rests on the circumstances that . . . under today's conditions of existence the approximation of reality to the theoretical propositions of economics has been a *constantly increasing* one. It is an approximation to reality that has implicated the destiny of ever-wider layers of humanity. And it will hold more and more broadly, as far as our horizons allow us to see.[44]

When discussing the ideal type of *Zweckrationalität* and of the historic conditions that favor its diffusion, Weber proclaimed repeatedly that his analyses were entirely value-neutral, and that it was important to avoid confusing "the unavoidable tendency of sociological concepts to assume a rationalistic character with a belief in the predominance of rational motives, or even a positive valuation of rationalism."[45] Even so, I believe it is plausible to link his typology with two *contrasting* types of value positions that he ostensibly held. Both of them hinge on his distinction between value-rational and *zweckrational* actions.

One of these reflects Weber's palpable devotion to the strand of the German philosophic tradition we have described as directed to the voluntaristic subject as an ideal value. By temperament a prophet, Weber could never refrain from advocating what was in fact a heroic ethic of self-awareness and self-determination.[46] He scorned the human tendency to submerge decisions about ultimate values under the surface of everyday routines, and urged that "every important decision, indeed life as a whole, *if it is not to slip by like a merely natural process* but to be lived consciously, is a series of ultimate decisions by means of which the soul, as in Plato, chooses its own destiny, in the sense of the meaning of what it does and is."[47] He felt that the calling of scholars and scientists was best justified by the contributions their work makes to enhancing human self-consciousness; as Mommsen aptly remarked, "It was, according to Weber, the most sublime and most essential task of all social science to make people aware of their own values, and to make them face the inevitable conflict of values which occurs in any concrete situation."[48]

The 1905 essay on Knies and the problem of irrationality offered a special occasion for Weber to express himself on this matter. Although Weber aligned himself with efforts by Knies and many others to identify and preserve a domain of freedom of the will as opposed to the deterministic elements of nature and history, he took strong exception to their notion that it was in man's *irrational* actions that such freedom was manifest. On the contrary, Weber argued in a related essay on Eduard Meyer, "we associate the highest measure of an empirical 'feeling of freedom' with those actions which we are conscious of performing rationally—i.e., in the absence of physical and psychic 'compulsions,' vehement 'affects,' and 'accidental' disturbances of the clarity of judgment, in which we pursue a clearly conceived 'end' through 'means' which are the most adequate according to our empirically grounded knowledge."[49] Weber thereby reiterated the classical idealist equation of rationality and freedom.[50] Keeping this position of Weber's in mind, we see that Weber's four types of action form a hierarchy of increasing voluntarism, in which *Zweckrationalität* sits at the apex by virtue of affording a maximum of human freedom. As Weber's exposition of the typology informs us, rationalization can proceed by abandoning ingrained habit-uation for more deliberate kinds of adaptation; by abandoning emotional values for a deliberate formulation of ultimate value standards; and by aban-doning belief in absolute values for a more skeptical kind of rational orien-tation. Of the *zweckrational* type of orientation, Weber writes: "This type, with its clarity of self-consciousness and freedom from subjective scruples, is the polar antithesis of every sort of unthinking acquiescence in customary ways *as well as of devotion to norms consciously accepted as absolute values.*"[51]

Although there are moments where Weber seems to endorse the condi-tion of maximum awareness and maximum freedom as a human ideal, that ideal stands in tension with another ideal that appears to have been closer to Weber's heart. Formulated in the terms of his action typology, this represents the ideal of a synthesis between value-rational and *zweckrational* action ori-entations—which many scholars consider the essential Weberian position. In other Weberian language, it represents the synthesis of an ethics of convic-tion (*Gesinnungsethik*) and an ethics of responsibility.

Whatever its ultimate sources in Weber's own personal makeup, this ideal was resonant with ideas that Weber translated from the German tradition of political economy (*Nationalökonomie*), which, rooted in classical moral phi-losophy, concerned itself with human praxis more broadly. Weber was intro-duced to this tradition through the lectures and writings of Karl Knies. If, in his 1905 essay on Knies, Weber identified the subject matter of *Nation-alökonomie* as "human action" (*menschliches Handeln*),[52] before that declaration he sought to make economics encompass concerns with the formation of character. In his Freiburg inaugural address of 1895, Weber insisted that the ultimate concern of his discipline was not so much the economic well-be-ing of people as "those characteristics that give us the sense that they make up human greatness and the nobility of our nature."[53] This strand of his thought resonates backward to Aristotle's dictum that the primary concern of *oikonomia* is "human excellence rather than the administration of wealth,"[54] and forward to his own apparent lifelong quest for understanding how different kinds of social order affect the formation of character, a quest that Wilhelm Hennis (1988) has illuminated.[55] And just as Aristotle's notion of excellence was rooted in an appreciation of the importance of habit, so it is hard to conceive the kinds of character that Weber admired without asso-ciating some element of ingrained disposition that we commonly describe as habit. First-hand reports as well as cues in Weber's texts tell us that above all he admired actors who maintained a stable commitment to certain artic-ulated values.[56] Thus the ideal of value rationality existed in tension with the idealization of subjective freedom that he associated with pure *Zweckra-tionalität*.

The typology found in the first chapter of *Economy and Society*, and the discourse around it, serves not only to articulate Weber's considered stance among the *Methodenstreiten* (epistemological disputes) of his time—manifesting his opposition to positions that may be glossed as biologism, psychologism, historical materialism, naturalistic economism, sociologism, and cultural emanationism. The typology of action he came to advocate also gave voice to a number of substantive concerns of enduring importance. It distinguished economic action from other types of action; focused on the conditions under which *Zweckrationalität* arose historically; thereby considered types of action classified with respect to the variable of subjective freedom; and attended to the conditions or social orders that fostered what he called genuine "personality." To the extent that these concerns remain alive for us today, the typology continues to be useful.

The valuable typology Weber generates and the assumptions about action from which it departs need not be embraced uncritically. Cutting the pie of human action as Weber does tends to obscure other interests and visions, and tying sociology to a concern with meaningful action precludes attention to other kinds of emphases and issues. Let me broach a large arena of discourse by reviewing some of these omissions schematically.

1. The matter of habitual action. It cannot be said that Weber's general comments underplay the role of habit in human conduct, for he repeatedly noted that the overwhelming part of human conduct is oriented in a habitual manner. As Charles Camic's astute essay on the subject shows, Weber went on to indicate the large role of habit in such domains as the economy, military, and religion, and in the lives of peasants and artisans generally. Even so, he adds, Weber's association of habit with the psychophysical language of stimuli and "automatic reactions" led him to portray this form of action as existing "by nature" and antecedent to culture, so outside the purview of sociology he was prescribing.[57] What is more, Weber's strongly pejorative view of habit, in the tradition of Kant, leads the placement of habit in his typology to obscure some positive consequences of habit—consequences that his contemporaries Emile Durkheim and John Dewey illuminated.

2. The matter of affect. In at least three respects, Weber's conceptualization of action shortchanges the place of sentiment and emotion in human action.

> a. By segregating emotional from rational types of action, Weber's taxonomy obscures the massive fact of the intertwining of rational and affective components of action: both the extent to which rational action rests on an emotional foundation and, conversely, the extent to which feelings are affected by rational processes.
>
> b. By placing emotional action on the borderline of meaningful behavior, Weber obscures the extent to which the great meaning systems are

grounded on nonrational sentiments—the phenomenon to which Pareto devoted so much searching attention.[58]

c. Weber's claim that unconscious behavior was devoid of meaning because it was not subject to interpretive understanding has long since been replaced by the discoveries of Freud, Jung, and others about the way unconscious thoughts can be retrieved and interpreted.

3. The matter of noninstrumental meaning. The point of departure for Weber's conception of meaning, which is the marker for action, is the attainment of goals through appropriate means; other types of action then take their place as so many deviations from this form. The epigraph that Parsons used for *The Structure of Social Action* makes this clear: "Jede denkende Besinnung auf die letzten Elemente sinnvollen menschlichen Handelns ist zunächst gebunden an die Kategorien 'Zweck' und 'Mittel.'"[59] Nevertheless, there are important forms of meaningful action that have no palpable relationship to a calculus of means and ends, a matter to which Hans Joas has resensitized us.[60] I previously listed a number of these, including Kant's notion of acting simply for the sake of duty; Marx's notion of free spontaneous creativity; Simmel's notion of acting without goals (*zwecklos handeln*); Scheler's notion of acting purely from spirit; Buber's notion of engaging in intersubjective dialogue for its own sake; and the religious notion of acting through being attuned to and aligned with a higher power.[61] Except for that of Kant, these modalities are akin to but not quite encompassed by Weber's notion of *Wertrationalität*.

4. The neglect of other variables. Weber's schema derives essentially from two variables, the level of self-conscious deliberation and the selection of ends of action. Although this schema provides a fruitful framework, there are many other conceivable ways of organizing different types of action. One that is of exceptional importance in everyday life, but that has been neglected by social theorists ever since it was first formulated by Auguste Comte was the distinction between constructive and destructive forms of action. It would be interesting to imagine a sociology organized around such a dichotomy.

5. The neglect of interaction. Some theorists reject altogether the construct of individual action as a foundational principle for sociology, claiming—as did Simmel—that sociology's distinctive domain should be phenomena of social *interaction*.[62] Stronger versions of this critique have been voiced by authors who, harking back to early Hegel and Feuerbach, consider the isolation of individual actions to be a problematic abstraction from what is essentially an interactional field. One thinks of G. H. Mead, who finds the human self as originating in and sustained by human interaction; Martin Buber, who finds the human essence to consist of I-Thou dialogue; and Jürgen

Habermas, who rejects the notion of monological rationality in favor of dialogical, communicative action.

6. The limits of typologizing. Whatever range of types might be adduced, one can argue that they inherently obscure certain features of phenomena that relate to systemic complexity. This, of course, was the burden of Parsons's critique of Weber for his "type atomism." In this perspective, the point is not to classify different types of action, but to identify and analyze the different levels and systems of action whose interpenetration constitutes any concrete situation of action. It is only by adopting a perspective of this sort, I argue below, that one can finally theorize in a coherent manner all that Weber says about rationalization in world history.

Rational Action and World Historic Rationalizations

The foregoing argument may be summarized as follows. In proposing his definition of sociology and the types of social action in the opening of *Economy and Society*, Weber was sending a number of messages:

1. that social phenomena have no emergent properties that cannot be accounted for in terms of the properties of individual human agents;

2. that although human conduct may display features that can be represented in the terms of natural science, an important part of human action involves meanings that cannot be reduced to objectively identified genetic dispositions or psychic impulses;

3. that those meanings are variable and complex, and require us to employ constructed typifications if we are to analyze them unambiguously; and

4. that a key point of reference of those meanings consists of a disposition to assess alternative ends and means (*Zweckrationalität*).

In commenting on that typology, I suggested

5. that the *zweckrational* orientation was of special interest to Weber because

a. it formed the model of action assumed in his primary discipline, economics;

b. it appeared to be becoming increasingly dominant in the modern world;

c. it manifests a maximum of freedom of choice;

d. it exists in tension with a different type of rational action, *Wertrationalität*, which orients actors through stable commitments to selected values;

6. that these interests of Weber remain salient today, and so continue to render his typology fruitful; but

7. that their limitations need to be exhibited and other ways of conceptualizing kinds of action need to be encouraged.

All but the first of these points would appear to be fairly noncontroversial. The postulate of methodological individualism, however, is contested not only by a torrent of theoretical argument but by Weber's own substantive work as well. Let us attend to the latter.

Whatever may be debated as a presumptive unifying theme of *Economy and Society*, the work presents us with five bodies of argument that represent what must be glossed as *supraindividual* formations. (1) It includes various typologies of groups that are classified on the basis of such structural variables as size; locus of group authority; mechanisms of recruitment; types of specialization; and monopolistic or expansive tendencies. (2) It presents analyses of different institutional spheres and their varying interrelationships. It offers numerous generalizations about the extent to which structures in one sphere "further or impede or exclude" one another.[63] We read, for example, that the landowning military caste favors an agnatic descent structure; that juridical formalism impedes authoritarian political control; or that public finance from compulsory services in kind is incompatible with a capitalist form of economic system. (3) It identifies structural phenomena that were conducive to the rise of modern capitalism, including legal guarantees of freedom of contract; public finance based on monetary taxes; developed technologies; separation of workers from jural restraints that tie them to land or masters; and cultural systems that favor worldly achievement. (4) It analyzes the structural conditions that favor or disfavor political democracy in industrialized and bureaucratized societies. (5) Finally, it provides accounts of the forms and sources of rationalization in world history.

It is these accounts of rationalization, far more than Weber's scant theorization of rational action, that remain of crucial importance for the proper appropriation of his work and for understanding both the course of world history and the modern world. Our appreciation of that achievement has been impeded by two factors: the limitations of Weber's epistemological position, which afforded him no viable way to integrate the structural phenomena he analyzed so acutely into a theoretic framework consistent with his conceptualization of action; and the simplistic way in which his accounts of rationalization in history have been represented. Some of the most perspicacious readers of Weber represent his conception of rationalization as though it meant one or at most two things—in particular, they equate formal rationality with instrumental rationality.[64] This leads to what I would consider un-Weberian formulations of his position, such as that "reason" is "on the side of capitalism rather than of other economic systems."[65] More than two decades after I registered the complaint about the simplistic appropriation of Weber's concept of rational action,[66] the situation remains little better.

To help remedy this situation, I shall attempt once more to erect a bridge between Weber's programmatic statements about action and his substantive analyses of rationalization processes; to recover the main lines of Weber's arguments about rationalization; and finally to extend them to address certain phenomena of the modern world that Weber was concerned about, the kinds of character and the types of action orientations that are favored by modern conditions.

To begin with: *the notion that the world is becoming increasingly rational and thus increasingly homogeneous must be questioned at the root.* Yes, the world is becoming increasingly rationalized—following Ferdinand Tönnies, Weber focused on the entire Western historical development since the Middle Ages as a progressive enlargement of the sphere of rationalism. In three respects, however, the advancement of rationalization must be seen as generating greater *diversity* in the world. For one thing, rationalization takes place in different spheres of life—religious, scientific, artistic, technological, political, economic, legal, military, and the like—and thereby brings out the distinctive values of each according to its respective inner logic (*Eigengesetzlichkeit*).

Within each of these sectors, moreover, one can "'rationalize' life from extremely varied ultimate standpoints and in very different directions."[67] One can rationalize the economy, for example, in order to raise the standard of living for everyone or to maximize the facilities and rewards for the most aggressive entrepreneurs. Similarly, the law can be rationalized in order to solidify caste or class distinctions, or in order to ensure equality of treatment for all members of the community. Science can be rationalized in order to understand better the working of divine providence and to glorify the Creator, or to provide knowledge that may be used to improve living conditions. As Weber would put it, such modes of rationalization differ according to the "irrational presuppositions" that ground and direct the various ways of leading a rationalized style of life.[68]

Finally, rationalization processes produce different outcomes according to the different *forms* that they take. As I have shown, Weber's terse delineation of four forms of rationalism in the introduction to his *Economic Ethics of the World Religions* affords a plausible sketch of such a typology.[69] According to that sketch, and drawing on other passages throughout the Weberian corpus, one can identify these four forms as

1. conceptual—the "increasing theoretical mastery of reality by means of increasingly precise and abstract concepts";

2. instrumental—the "methodical attainment of a particular given practical end through the increasingly precise calculation of adequate means";

3. substantive—the organization of effort on behalf of normative ideals; and

4. methodical or formal—what Weber terms *Planmässigkeit*, a methodical ordering of activities through the establishment of fixed rules and routines.

How can one adequately theorize all these different rationalization processes? Not very well, if one adheres only to the methodological dicta that Weber propounds. Although the impetus behind rationalization processes can often be traced to certain kinds of individual dispositions—existential frustrations, "abnormal" psychological states, political ambitions, and the like—the processes themselves also depend on supraindividual formations. These include the structure of relationships among different strata and institutional sectors, and their actualization in social and cultural forms that transcend the meanings of individual actors. What Weberian theory requires to theorize these phenomena adequately is something equivalent to what Simmel has described as *objective culture* and Parsons and many others have represented in terms of *institutionalized norms at the social systemic and cultural systemic levels.*

The analysis of objectification has deep roots in the German philosophic tradition. It traces back to Fichte's notion of externalization (*Entäusserung*), a process whereby humans create objects that constrain them from the outside. For Fichte, the knowing subject has to relinquish its attachment to these objects in order to be confronted with itself and eventually to regain itself.[70] The notion reappears in Hegel's account of *Geist*'s creation of an object that opposes it negatively. This occurs on the way to reappropriating the object in a process of self-development, which along the way constitutes such formations as the state, law, and culture.

Post-Hegelians translated this conception into diverse substantive domains. Adapting it to religion, Feuerbach derived all configurations of religious symbols as from the externalization of qualities and yearnings of human subjects. Applying it to the domain of economic productivity, Marx analyzed the creation of commodities as an externalization of creative energies that belonged to their human makers. Considering the domain of culture, Moritz Lazarus translated it into a research program for *Völkerpsychologie*, a cultural anthropology that would investigate the condensation (*Verdichtung*) of thought in history, searching the preconditions for the manifestations of objective Mind (*Geist*).[71] Simmel, whose ideas about culture derived from his studies with Lazarus, used the topos of objectification to account for the creation both of economic value and of the various "worlds" of culture. Simmel also described the hypertrophy of objective culture under conditions of the modern division of labor, and found its production of far more objects than human subjects could absorb to be the source of a chronic crisis in modern experience.[72]

Although something of this tradition finds resonance in Weber's work—especially in his metaphor of the "iron cage" (*stahlhartes Gehäuse*, steel-hard shell), both his commitment to the postulate of methodological individualism and his desire to avoid what he considered value-laden talk of "objective" rationality kept him from theorizing it fully. Had he been able to avail himself of Simmel's language, he could have said that the situation of modern man consists in a enormous degree of objective rationalization, which tended to imperil subjective freedom, coupled with unprecedented resources for the cultivation of subjective rationality, which tended to amplify subjective freedom.[73]

Even so, Simmel's discourse about these matters stands to be refined a good deal further, as I have also argued previously,[74] by incorporating the more differentiated conceptual system available in Parsons's theory of action systems. Following Parsons's division of different aspects of action into the levels of cultural system, social system, personality system, and behavioral system, we can say that objectified rationality manifests itself at the levels of cultural and social systems, whereas subjective rationality manifests itself at the levels of personality and behavioral systems. Simmel's thesis that modernization produces an unprecedented degree of separation between objective structures and personal subjectivity—and therewith the fullest realization of each sphere—would translate, in Parsonian terms, into an argument that modernization involves a progressive specialization of different spheres and dimensions of action. Parsons's framework enables us to represent objectification more precisely by representing the structures of objective rationality as complexes of institutionalized cultural and social norms. It also enables an analytic extension of Simmel's thesis by saying that the behavioral systems and the personality systems of individual subjects come to constitute increasingly autonomous boundary-maintaining systems, just as do the economy, the polity, science, art, and the like in the modern world.

Applying the Parsonian framework to Weber's account of rationalization processes enables us to relate the different forms of rationalization that Weber depicts in a more coherent manner. That is, instrumental, substantive, formal, and conceptual rationality can be seen as more than a random assortment of possibilities, but as forms that fulfill determinate functions in action systems. Retrieving Parsons's schema of systemic functions, it would appear that *Zweckrationalität*, the calculation of the costs and benefits of different means, corresponds to the adaptive function. This is rationality in the sense of identifying and organizing resources so as to facilitate the attainment of whatever goals actors might pursue. Substantive rationality, defined as consistent activity on behalf of stated ends, corresponds to the goal-attainment function. Formal rationality is treated by Weber—in the spheres of economic action, the law, and religion—as establishing rules and procedures that consistently render conduct in a calculable manner. Formal rationality thus performs an integrative function, which is served by the institution of procedures that subordinate diverse inclinations to a common, expectable set of rules. What I have called conceptual rationality signifies the generation of a clear and coherent set of meanings about the world or some part of it. It thus corresponds to the pattern-maintenance function.[75]

Of the many theoretical issues that this reframing of the discourse about rationalization raises, the question of the relationship between instrumental and formal rationality demands immediate attention. The common tendency to equate them does injustice to the subtlety of Weber's treatment and disservice to our sociological understanding. To be sure, Weber sometimes promotes this confusion, as when he describes bureaucracy as the most efficient form of social organization that exists, or when he describes juridical formalism as enabling the legal system to operate like a technically rational machine. Nevertheless, the colloquial view of bureaucracy as monumentally inefficient has roots in Weberian text as well as everyday experience. Thus Weber points up the tension between formal rationality and instrumental rationality when he points out that the rationally debatable reasons that stand behind every act of bureaucratic administration concern "*either* subsumption under norms *or* a weighing of ends and means," or when he notes that the formalization of tenure in bureaucracies "makes it more difficult to staff offices with an eye to technical efficiency."[76]

Finally, how does this reframing of the theory of rationalization affect the Weberian concern with the impact of a rationalized world on human personality? Let us consider three diverse developments.

Recalling Simmel's paradigm of the tragedy in modern culture, we would say that galloping rationalization in all cultural and social spheres, from science and art to law and technology, so far outstrips the individual's ability to assimilate their norms and products that individuals become alienated from a great part of the public universe. Conversely, there are crucial areas where subjective rationality must be cultivated for the sake of survival. In Simmel's terms, the effects of a money economy and of demographic concentrations in large urban centers require enormous amounts of calculation. In Parsons's terms, we might say that the sectors in which individuals participate as employees require high degrees of formally rational and instrumentally rational orientations, while their role as consumers requires an exceptional degree of instrumentally rational orientation. One effect of all this, Simmel maintained, was a diminution of the affective part of experience: adaptation to the modern monetary system produces an extraordinary degree of "intellectual energy . . . in contrast to those energies generally denoted as emotions or sentiments . . . [and] which attach themselves to the turning points of life, to the final purposes."[77]

We can extend Simmel's point by saying that "insofar as modern institutions sanction instrumental or formal rationalities, with their varying patterns and objective consequences, the subjective consequences are likely to include the enhancement of ratiocinative powers at the expense of emotional powers—which can take the form, in more current terms, either of a repression of affect or its dissociation from rational functioning."[78] We might also express this point by suggesting that, in contrast to instrumentally and formally rational dispositions, the orientations involved both in goal-attainment and in pattern-maintenance necessarily involve a higher level of fusion with emotional commitments. It takes little talent as a social observer in our day to detect the further expansion of this syndrome thanks to the newer technologies of cell phones, Palm Pilots, and Internet technologies. What is more, at the symbolic, cultural level, it reflects the heightened prestige of economistic thinking, indeed the extent to which economics continues to expand into and colonize neighboring fields, as a worldview. It was a fundamental insight of Weber, as well as Simmel, that the calculative habits of mind associated with a market economy and its related technology, and with the point of view of his discipline of economics, became inflated in the modern world. This remains a suggestive point of departure for diagnoses of our time.

Notes

1. Max Weber, *Wirtschaft und Gesellschaft*, 5th ed. (Tübingen: J. C. B. Mohr, 1976), p. 1 (translation mine); Max Weber, *Economy and Society: An Outline of Interpretive Sociology* (1921–22; Berkeley: University of California Press, 1978), p. 4.

2. Weber, *Economy and Society*, p. 24.

3. Ibid., p. 21.

4. Weber's "definition of sociology . . . is so restrictive it is difficult to see what sorts of things a sociology limited to this approach *can* explain." Stephen P. Turner and Regis A. Factor, *Max Weber: The Lawyer as Social Thinker* (New York: Routledge, 1994), p. 43.

5. Measured against his comparative studies, writes Alan Sica, "Weber's underdeveloped theory of social action is brittle and artificial." Alan Sica, *Weber, Irrationality, and Social Order* (Berkeley: University of California Press, 1988), p. xii.

6. Reinhard Bendix's acclaimed intellectual biography of Weber contains nary a reference to the concepts of action or social action, nor does Randall Collins's more recent compendium of Weberian sociological theory. Reinhard Bendix, *Max Weber: An Intellectual Portrait* (Berkeley: University of California Press, 1960); Randall Collins, *Weberian Social Theory* (Cambridge: Cambridge University Press, 1986).

7. Max Weber, *Roscher and Knies: The Logical Problems of Historical Economics* (New York: Free Press, 1975), pp. 100, 240.

8. See Donald N. Levine, *The Flight from Ambiguity* (Chicago: University of Chicago Press, 1985), p. 184 n. 6, and Weber's comment referenced in n. 16 below.

9. His first appointments were as "extraordinary professor" in commercial and German law at Berlin in 1893, and professor of political economy at Freiburg in 1894; he occupied what had been Knies's chair in political economy at Heidelberg in 1896.

10. Beyond items noted in this chapter, Weber's work in law provided a fund of ideas that he went on to make famous in social science. These included the notions of objective possibility and adequate causation, from J. von Kries; from Rudolf Ihering, the distinction between living for and off a vocation, and the definition of the state as sole legitimate monopoly of coercive force; from Rudolf Sohm, the notion of asceticism as a source of modern self-regulation as well as the concept of charisma; and with his contemporary Gustav Radbruch, the fundamental notion of the rational irreconcilability of ultimate values (Turner and Factor, *Max Weber*, pp. 4, 53, 103, 110, 58).

11. For an interesting historical sketch of these concepts in German legal thought, see Devin Pendas, "Displaying Justice: Nazis on Trial in Postwar Germany" (Ph.D. diss., Department of History, University of Chicago, 2000), pp. 53–117.

12. Turner and Factor, *Max Weber*, p. 45.

13. Max Weber, *Grundriss zur den Vorlesungen über Allgemeine ("Theoretische") Nationalökonomie* (1898; Tübingen: J. C. B. Mohr, 1990), p. 29.

14. Heinz-Jürgen Dahme, "Georg Simmel und Gustav Schmoller: Berührungen zwischen Katherdersozialismus und Soziologie um 1890," *Simmel Newsletter* 3: 1 (Summer 1993): 40.

15. Turner and Factor, *Max Weber*.

16. Letter to Robert Liefmann of Mar. 9, 1920, cited in H. H. Bruun, *Science, Values and Politics in Max Weber's Methodology* (Copenhagen: Munksgaard, 1972), p. 38 n. 3.

17. This central contradiction in Weber's work has been noted by a number of commentators; it is addressed in the final section of this chapter and forms the focus of a penetrating paper by Mary Fulbrook, "Max Weber's 'Interpretive Sociology': A Comparison of Conception and Practice," *British Journal of Sociology* 29, no. 1 (1978): 71–82.

18. Donald N. Levine, *Visions of the Sociological Tradition* (Chicago: University of Chicago Press, 1995).

19. They did so for diverse reasons, including the ambition of securing psychology a place as an academic discipline. Mitchell Ash, "Academic Politics in the History of Science: Experimental Psychology in Germany, 1870–1941," *Central European History* 13 (3) (1980): 255–86.

20. Max Weber, "Some Categories of Interpretive Sociology," trans. Edith E. Graber, *Sociological Quarterly* 22 ([1913] 1981): 151–80, 154.

21. The Weber-Fechner law of psychophysics states that the intensity of stimulation increases as a logarithm of the stimulus. Marginal utility theory hypothesized that the utility or pleasure deriving from any new increments of wealth would decrease in proportion to total wealth previously accrued. Brentano suggested that this theory was but a particular instance of the Weber-Fechner theory of the constant proportion of the sensation-threshold to the previously existing degree of sensation.

Mark Loeffler, "The Limits to Naturalism: On the Autonomization of German Sociology, 1890–1920" (unpublished paper, Department of History, University of Chicago, 2000), p. 7.

22. Letter from Max Weber to Lujo Brentano, May 28, 1908, trans. from *Max Weber, Gesamtausgabe*, Abt. II: *Briefe*, Bd. 5: *Briefe 1906–1908*, ed. M. Rainer Lepsius and Wolfgang Mommsen (Tübingen: J. C. B. Mohr, 1990), pp. 578–79.

23. Weber, "Some Categories," p. 154.

24. Weber, *Economy and Society*, p. 19.

25. Deutsche Gesellschaft für Soziologie, *Verhandlungen des ersten deutschen Soziologentages* (Tübingen: J. C. B. Mohr, 1911), p. 154.

26. Weber, *Economy and Society*, p. 8. Weber also reiterated this concern at the close of his introduction to the collected essays on the sociology of religion in 1920: "The author confesses that he personally and subjectively is inclined to rate the significance of biological heredity very highly. However . . . it will have to be one of the tasks of sociological and historical work to first do what it can to expose all those influences and causal chains that can be satisfactorily explained by reference to reactions to fate in one's environment. Only then, and when moreover the study of the comparative neurology and psychology of race have progressed beyond their present . . . early stages, shall we *perhaps* be able to hope for satisfactory results relevant to our problem." Max Weber, *Gesammelte Aufsätze zur Religionssoziologie*, vol. 1 (Tübingen: J. C. B. Mohr, 1920), trans. Peter Baehr, *The Protestant Ethic and the "Spirit" of Capitalism* (New York: Penguin, 2002), p. 369.

27. Loeffler makes the suggestive observation that Tönnies was making a similar set of differentiations around the same time (Loeffler, "Limits to Naturalism").

28. Menger actually devoted a whole chapter to *refuting* the allegation of German economic historians that theoretical economists adhere to a utilitarian conception of human action. Of course, he observed, actions manifest a variety of motives, including public spirit, love of fellow humans, custom, feeling for justice, alongside the rational pursuit of self-interest, but economics can function as a theoretical science like physics and chemistry only by abstracting certain aspects of human activity and systematically theorizing their properties and dynamics. Carl Menger, *Problems of Economics and Sociology* (Urbana: University of Illinois Press, [1883] 1963).

29. Weber, *Grundriss*, p. 30.

30. Levine, *Visions*, p. 195.

31. Ibid., pp. 195ff.

32. Weber expressly cited the second edition of Simmel's *Probleme* as containing "by far the most fully developed logical analysis of the elements of a theory of *Verstehen*." The reference in the English translation of the Knies essays misleadingly gives the 1892 first edition as the source Weber refers to. See Levine, *Flight*, pp. 96–98.

33. Levine, *Visions*, pp. 199ff.

34. Turner and Factor, *Max Weber*, chap. 7.

35. Weber, *Grundriss*, p. 30.

36. Levine, *Visions*, pp. 200ff.

37. Immanuel Kant, *Anthropology from a Pragmatic Point of View*, trans. Victor Lyle Dowdell, ed. Hans H. Rudnick (1798; Carbondale: Southern Illinois University Press, 1978), pp. 32, 35.

38. On the Nietzschean strand in Weber's thought, see Robert Eden, *Political Leadership and Nihilism: A Study of Weber and Nietzsche* (Tampa: University Presses of Florida, 1983); Wilhelm Hennis, *Max Weber, Essays in Reconstruction*, trans. Keith Tribe (London: Allen & Unwin, 1988); and Bryan Turner, *Max Weber: From History to Modernity* (New York: Routledge, 1993).

39. Max Weber, *Gesammelte Aufsätze zur Wissenschaftslehre* (Tübingen: J. C. B. Mohr, 1922), p. 214; trans. Edward Shils and Henry Finch, *The Methodology of the Social Sciences* (Glencoe, IL: Free Press, 1949), p. 112.

40. The term *Zweckrationalität* is difficult to translate. Since *Zweck* means "end" or "purpose," it has sometimes been rendered literally as "purpose-rationality." Inasmuch as its primary connotation refers to the *means* to an end, however, it has also been rendered as "means-end rationality." This in turn has led to what is perhaps the most common translation of the term, "instrumental rationality"—a form I have sometimes employed myself. Nevertheless, it is problematic to gloss *Zweckrationalität* as referring simply to actions in which questions of technical expediency alone are considered. Even though some of Weber's passages permit a narrow construction of this sort, his chief discursive exposition of the category presents a broader definition. Action is *zweckrational*, Weber writes, "when the end, the means, and the secondary results are all rationally taken into account and weighed. This involves rational consideration of alternative means to an end, of the relations of the end to the secondary consequences, and finally *of the relative importance of different possible ends" (* Weber, *Economy and Society*, p. 26; emphasis mine). Following Weber's explicit statement on the matter, I shall take means/end rational action in this more inclusive sense, one that includes what he elsewhere calls rational *economic* as well as technically oriented action.

41. Weber's most complete statement about the economic agent appears in his Heidelberg *Grundriss*: this construction

a. *ignores* and treats as *non-existent* all those motives which influence empirical humans that are *not* specifically *economic*, i.e., not concerned with material needs;

b. *imagines* as existent qualities that empirical humans do *not* possess, or possess only *incompletely*, namely,

   complete *insight* into a given *situation*—economic omniscience;

   unfailing choice of the most appropriate means for a given end—absolute "economic rationality" (*Wirtschaflichkeit*);

   complete dedication of one's powers to the purpose of acquiring economic goods—"untiring acquisitional drive." (Weber, *Grundriss*, p. 30; revised trans. from Hennis, *Max Weber*, p. 121).

That the discipline based itself on this conception as a heuristic construct has been obscured by the arguments of Talcott Parsons, *The Structure of Social Action* (New York: McGraw Hill, 1937). However, as an authoritative historian of economic thought sums up the matter:

Most neo-classical writers . . . insisted that their study was restricted to the economic aspects of human action, rather than the whole complex of human aspirations. By the same token they did not wish to be interpreted as saying that all who participated in market transactions were rational calculators. Instead, they sought merely to establish that rationality as a behavioral postulate provided a realistic basis for the study of groups of people. (William J. Barber, *A History of Economic Thought* [New York: Penguin Books, 1967], p. 170.)

J. S. Mill himself insisted that the notion of *homo economicus* was a scientific fiction: "not that any political economist was ever so absurd as to suppose that mankind are really thus constituted, but because this is the mode in which science must necessarily proceed." John Stuart Mill, *The Logic of the Moral Sciences*, book VI of *A System of Logic* (1843; 8th ed. 1872; LaSalle, IL: Open Court Classics, 1987), p. 90.

42. Max Weber, "The Nation State and Economic Policy," in Peter Lassman and Ronald Speirs, eds., *Weber: Political Writings* (Cambridge: Cambridge University Press, [1895] 1994), p. 17.

43. Weber, *Grundriss*, p. 29.

44. Max Weber, "Marginal Utility Theory and 'The Fundamental Law of Psychophysics,'" *Social Science Quarterly* 56, no. 1 ([1908] 1975): 21–36, 32–33.

45. Weber, *Economy and Society*, p. 18.

46. Levine, *Flight*, chap. 8.

47. Max Weber, *Selections in Translation* (Cambridge: Cambridge University Press, 1978), p. 84, ed. W. G. Runciman. [*Gesammelte Aufsätze zur Wissenschaftslehre*, p. 469] (emphasis mine).

48. Wolfgang J. Mommsen, *The Age of Bureaucracy: Perspectives on the Political Sociology of Max Weber* (Oxford: Basil Blackwell & Mott, 1974), p. 110.

49. Weber, *Gesammelte Aufsätze zur Wissenschaftslehre*, p. 226, trans. Shils and Finch, *Methodology*, pp. 124–25 (translation altered). Bothered by what he considers an imbalance in Weber's attention to the rational elements of action, Sica suggests that Weber's violent reaction to Knies's apotheosis of the irrational may have stemmed from his own Herculean efforts to regain control of himself after the neuro-pathological condition from which he was just then recovering (Sica, *Weber*, p. 174).

50. Levine, *Flight*, chap. 7.

51. Weber, *Economy and Society*, p. 30 (emphasis mine).

52. Weber, *Gesammelte Aufsätze zur Wissenschaftslehre*, p. 44; Weber, *Roscher and Knies*, p. 96.

53. Max Weber, "Der Nationalstaat und die Volkswirtschaftspolitik," in Johannes Winckelmann, ed., *Gesammelte Politische Schriften* (1895; Tübingen: J. C. B. Mohr, 1980), p. 13; Weber, "The Nation State," p. 15 (trans. altered). Referring to a text I cannot identify, Hennis claims that this same statement is repeated in altered form in 1913 (Hennis, *Max Weber*, p. 117).

54. Aristotle, *Politics* I, 13, 1059b.

55. Hennis's arguments provide further support for my contention that philosophers and social theorists have long been attempting to restore, albeit piecemeal, the various pieces of the Aristotelian program which were lost following Hobbes's overthrow of the Aristotelian paradigm (Levine, *Visions*, pp. 272–76).

56. Weber's "students report (as did Marianne) that *personally* he always favored historical and contemporary characters whose force of will in the face of coercion

or conformity—the mechanisms for producing calculable behavior—carried them into heroic action" (Sica, *Weber*, p. 175).

57. Charles Camic, "The Matter of Habit," *American Journal of Sociology* 91, no. 55 (1986), 1039–87, quotations on 1066.

58. Sica, *Weber*.

59. "Every thoughtful reflection on the ultimate elements of meaningful human action is bound primarily to the categories of 'means' and 'ends'" (trans. Shils and Finch, *Methodology*, p. 52; translation altered).

60. Hans Joas, *The Creativity of Action*, trans. Jeremy Gaines and Paul Keast (Chicago: University of Chicago Press, 1996).

61. Donald N. Levine, "Putting Voluntarism Back into a Voluntaristic Theory of Action" (paper presented at the 14th World Congress of Sociology, Montreal, July 1998).

62. It is notable that Weber, in his unpublished fragment of a critique of Simmel, rejected this option as being too general. Max Weber, "Georg Simmel as Sociologist," in Donald N. Levine, "Max Weber's 'Georg Simmel as Sociologist,'" translated and with an introduction, *Social Research* 39, no. 1 (1972): 155–63. For a discussion of enduring contrasts between Weber's principle of action and Simmel's principle of interaction, see Donald N. Levine, "Simmel and Parsons Reconsidered," *American Journal of Sociology* 96, no. 5 (1991): 1097–116.

63. Weber, *Economy and Society*, p. 341.

64. Thus, Mommsen holds that "'formal rationality' is identical with the principle of maximizing efficiency" (Mommsen, *Age of Bureaucracy*, p. 64; also pp. 82, 102, and others). Others who fail to differentiate the diverse forms of rationality that Weber identified include Parsons, *Structure*; Jeffrey C. Alexander, *The Classical Attempt at Synthesis: Max Weber* (Berkeley: University of California Press, 1983); and Bryan S. Turner, *For Weber, Essays on the Sociology of Fate* (London: Routledge & Kegan Paul, 1981).

65. Mommsen, *Age of Bureaucracy*, p. 68.

66. I first presented "Rationality and Freedom: Weber and Beyond" at the Max Weber Symposium at the University of Wisconsin-Milwaukee in May 1977. It was published in *Sociological Inquiry* 51, no. 11 (January 1981): 5–25, and, revised, in Levine, *Flight*, chap. 7, as "Rationality and Freedom, Inveterate Multivocals." Others who have sought to promote a more differentiated understanding of the processes of rationalization that Weber depicted include Richard Bendix, "Max Weber's Sociology Today," *International Social Science Journal* 17 (Jan. 1965): 9–22; Wolfgang Schluchter, "The Paradox of Rationalization: On the Relation of Ethics and the World," in Guenther Roth and Wolfgang Schluchter, eds., *Max Weber's Vision of History* (Berkeley: University of California Press, 1979), pp. 11–64; Arnold Eisen, "The Meanings and Confusions of Weberian 'Rationality,'" *British Journal of Sociology* 29, no. 1 (1978): 57–69; and Stephen Kalberg, "Max Weber's Types of Rationality," *American Journal of Sociology* 85 (Mar. 1980): 1145–79.

The chapter on the sociology of law is one of the places where Weber argues most forcefully against equating formal rationality with instrumental and substantive rationality. Each of these forms of rationalization in the sphere of law, he notes, responds to a different interest and points in a different direction. An impulse toward conceptual rationality proceeded from the "intrinsic intellectual needs of the legal theorists and their disciples, the doctors, i.e., of a typical aristocracy of legal literati" and points toward a logical "gapless" systematization of the law (Weber, *Economy and Society*, 855). An impulse toward substantive rationality stems from particular ideologies or social class interest, and informs efforts to fashion law in a way that promotes substantive justice. An interest in formal rationality stems from the need to have calculable rules and regulations, an interest held especially keenly by capitalist entrepreneurs. Emphasizing the divergence between this form of rationalization and the conceptual rationalization of the codifiers, Weber emphasized that the take-off land for bourgeois capitalism, England, was the country that conspicuously maintained an empirically based common law instead of adopting a formally codified legal system as on the Continent. Finally, there is a distinctive interest in turning the law into an efficient technical apparatus based on expediential considerations. This stems from the interests of specialized legal practitioners and, as with the pressures toward substantive rationality, draws the law into "antiformal directions" (pp. 855, 892–95). (Levine, "Rationality and Freedom," pp. 17–18)

67. Weber, *Protestant Ethic*, p. 27.

68. Levine, *Flight*, pp. 156–57.

69. Weber, *Gesammelte Aufsätze zur Religionssoziologie*, pp. 265–66. The full text of that passage, in revised translation, appears as the appendix to Levine, *Flight*.

70. Nicholas Lobkowicz, *Theory and Practice: History of a Concept from Aristotle to Marx* (Notre Dame, IN: University of Notre Dame Press, 1967), pp. 300ff.

71. Klaus Christian Köhnke, *Der junge Simmel in Theoriebeziehungen und sozialen Bewegungen* (Frankfurt: Suhrkamp, 1996), p. 352.

72. The notion would continue to find receptive adherents, especially in Simmel's student Gyorgy Lukacs. See Andrew Arato, "The Search for the Revolutionary Subject: The Philosophy and Social Theory of the Young Lukacs, 1910–23" (Ph.D. diss., Department of History, University of Chicago, 1975); Levine, *Flight*; and Mark Loeffler, "Content as Ontology: Simmel, Lukacs and the Neo-Romantic Critique of Form" (unpublished paper, Department of History, University of Chicago, 1999).

73. Levine, *Flight*, chaps. 7–9; Donald N. Levine, "Simmel as Educator: On Individuality and Modern Culture," *Theory, Culture and Society* 8 (1991): 99–117.

74. Levine, *Flight*, chap. 9.

75. For an illustrative representation of what I mean by objectified rationality at the cultural and social systemic levels, and assignment of different forms of rationalization to their respective systemic functions, see the pertinent figures in Levine, *Flight*, pp. 160–61 and 208.

76. Weber, *Economy and Society*, pp. 979, 962 (emphasis mine).

77. Georg Simmel, *The Philosophy of Money*, trans. Tom Bottomore and David Frisby (London: Routledge & Kegan Paul, 1978), pp. 429, 431.

78. Levine, *Flight*, p. 214.

Max Weber's Economic Sociology
The Centerpiece of Economy and Society?

Economy and Society is often presented as a work in general sociology that begins with a famous chapter in theoretical sociology and then continues with sections on political sociology, sociology of law, sociology of religion, and so on. In my opinion, this is not entirely correct, and to some extent this opinion reflects the fact that *Economy and Society* was translated in a piecemeal fashion in the United States and read mostly by sociologists. *Economy and Society*, however, was not written for American sociologists, but primarily for German economists and students of economics. It was a work that Weber himself wanted to be like a textbook, and more importantly, it was to be part of a large handbook of economics, *Grundriss der Sozialökonomik*. While it would be wrong to present *Economy and Society* as a work in "economics," I do think that this work has a center, and that this center is to be found in its analysis of the economy, carried out with the help of sociology.[1]

Weber's work does indeed contain a first chapter on theoretical sociology, as well as contributions to a general sociology of religion, a general sociology of law, and so on. The main reason why these sections were included, however, may well have been that in order to present his sociological analysis of the economy (including its relationship to politics, to law, to religion, and so on), Weber felt that general sections of this type were needed. And, as was usual for Weber, he got carried away with his task, making excessively large detours in his efforts to lay a proper sociological foundation for his analysis of the economy.

While I hope that the argument I have just presented will be convincing to the reader, a question that immediately needs to be addressed is the following: Does it really matter whether we see *Economy and Society* as a work of general sociology or a work of economic sociology (with large sections on general sociology)? To some extent the answer is no; *Economy and Society* can be profitably read from many perspectives, and in a sense there is no reason to assign a special priority to any of these. We may even argue, for example, that Weber's sociology of law in *Economy and Society* is more innovative than his economic sociology. On a few accounts, however, it *does* matter what Weber's purpose was with *Economy and Society*. First, we need to better understand the structure of *Economy and Society*; and I hope that the alternative I have presented will contribute to this. Second, for those interested in Weber's sociology of law, his sociology of religion, and so on, a realization of Weber's real aim may help to explain why he included certain matters, but not others; and also in other ways throw some new light on his contribution. And third, if economic sociology indeed constitutes the center of *Economy and Society*, this whole work—and not only chapter 2 in part I, which is exclusively devoted to economic sociology—can be read from the perspective of economic sociology and may yield new insights for this field. Since I primarily define myself as an economic sociologist, it is this last aspect that is of most interest to me.

In the rest of this chapter I present the core features of Weber's economic sociology and also try to show its centrality to *Economy and Society* as a whole. I first look at chapter 2, "Sociological Categories of Economic Action," which constitutes the heart of Weber's economic sociology and was included in the only part of *Economy and Society* that Weber himself approved for publication. I then discuss the relationship of the economy to the state (including law) and to religion, primarily as this is to be found in Weber's posthumous writings (*Nachlass*) and then included by Marianne Weber, Melchior Palyi, and other editors in *Economy and Society*. In the concluding remarks I return to the question of the possible centrality of Weber's economic sociology to *Economy and Society*.

The Economy

Chapter 2 of *Economy and Society* ("Sociological Categories of Economic Action") represents the core of Weber's economic sociology in the sense that it contains an analysis of purely economic institutions—what Weber in his 1904 essay on objectivity refers to as economic phenomena, as opposed to economically relevant phenomena and economically conditioned phenomena.[2] This chapter consists, in English translation, of some 150 pages of text, divided into 41 sections, and can be characterized as a small book in its own right. It contains terse definitions as well as terse explications of key economic phenomena from a sociological viewpoint, including economic action, economic relationships, economic organizations, and capitalism.

Chapter 2 was written just before Weber died, probably in 1918–20, and it represents an important intellectual innovation in Weber's work in the sense that he here, for the first time, analyzes purely economic phenomena and not just their relationship to law, politics, and religion, as he had done in the other texts he prepared for *Economy and Society*. Privately Weber referred to chapter 2 as his *Wirtschaftssoziologie*—a term that otherwise only appears in his writings during the last few years of his life.

Although one can describe chapter 2 as a small monograph, one would have difficulty understanding many aspects of this chapter without first reading chapter 1 of *Economy and Society*, "Basic Sociological Terms." A study of these two chapters also shows that they are symmetrically constructed and mirror each other on many points, something that is *not* true of the other chapters in part I (chapter 3, "The Types of Legitimate Domination," and chapter 4, "Status Groups and Classes"). Just as Weber starts out in chapter 1 by defining social action, he begins chapter 2 by defining economic social action. And just as he in chapter 1 goes from single individual actions to social relationships, to organizations, and to other complex configurations, he does the same in chapter 2, albeit with economic social action as his point of departure.

It also deserves to be pointed out that the introductory theoretical chapter in *Economy and Society* contains several items that seem to have been included because this work was to be part of a handbook in economics, as opposed to, say, a general treatise in sociology. Very soon after having defined what constitutes a social action, Weber thus tells the reader what an *economic* social action is. Similarly, Weber is careful to spell out exactly what constitutes the basic unit used in economic theory (exclusively rational economic action), in contrast to economic sociology (economic *social* action). Any reader who works through chapter 1 has a distinct sense of what differentiates economic theory from sociology.

The theoretical point of departure in Weber's economic sociology is, to repeat, his concept of economic social action. This concept is a subcategory of social action, with which it shares the following three traits: (1) the focus is on actions of individuals; (2) for a behavior to become an action, it has to be invested with a meaning; (3) and the action has to be oriented to others (or it does not qualify as social.)[3] Economic action, the key unit in economic theory, is similarly constituted by the action of an individual, to which meaning is attached. Unlike social action, however, economic action can only be rational, and it is always rational; also, its aim is utility. Economic social action, in contrast, is explicitly oriented to others and very rarely, if ever, rational; it also has utility as its aim.

Like many other economists around the turn of the century, Weber saw utility as the goal of economic action. He, however, added a few subtleties of his own that are of interest, mainly that the goal is not so much utility per se as *an opportunity* for utility. The term Weber uses for opportunity is "chance," and several of his concepts in economic sociology have to do with exploiting opportunities or with blocking others from exploiting them. The sociological concept of property, for example, is constructed as a way of blocking other people from certain opportunities and appropriating these for oneself.

While economic theory, as Weber saw it, exclusively analyzes rational economic action, economic sociology has a considerably broader scope through the concept of economic social action, and it especially looks at two types of action that economic theory ignores. These are economic actions that include violence, and economic actions that do not have exclusively economic goals (both are called economically oriented actions by Weber).

After a presentation and discussion of economic social action, Weber proceeds to various combinations of these, such as economic relationships and economic organizations. One relationship that is very common in the economy is that of struggle (*Kampf*). Another is competition, which Weber defines as a peaceful contest over opportunities. Economic relationships, like other social relationships, can also be open or closed. An economic relationship tends to be open or closed depending on what favors the key actors. A profession and a cartel are examples of closed economic relationships; a guild can be open or closed. Weber notes that when you want to close someone out of an economic relationship you seize on whatever excuse is at hand, such as ethnic origin or skin color.

Under certain circumstances, Weber says, a social relationship can turn into an order (*Ordnung*), a concept that has been unduly ignored in Weberian scholarship but which constitutes the second most important theoretical building block in his sociology, complementing social action. A social relationship may turn into an order when the maxims that infuse a social relationship acquire an independence of their own, so that actors may orient their actions to the order. Orders of this type, based on maxims that are either obligatory or exemplary, also exist in economic life, for example, in the form of conventions. They are also at the core of organizations, which Weber in all brevity defines as orders policed by a staff.

Weber has included a typology of economic organizations in chapter 2, which ranges from organizations that deal exclusively with economic matters to those that do so only marginally, say a church. The most important economic organization in modern capitalism is obviously the firm, whose impact on economic life Weber describes as revolutionary.[4] A firm typically consists of an order, maintained by three types of actors: the entrepreneur, the staff (the bureaucracy), and the workers. While much attention has been directed at Weber's concept of bureaucracy, and some at his analysis of industrial workers, very little effort has been made to understand his view of entrepreneurship. Chapter 2 of *Economy and Society* also contains interesting sociological analyses of money and the market. Weber explicitly states that he is not interested in developing a theory of money, and on this point refers the reader to Ludwig von Mises's *The Theory of Money and Credit*. What he feels that economic sociology can accomplish, however, is to analyze the role that money plays in economic reality, as opposed to the role that it plays in economic theory. In empirical reality, there are, for example, always conflicts over economic valuables; and money helps to express these values with precision. Those who argue that Weber thought that the task of economic theory is to state what happens *in theory*, and that economic sociology is a type of analysis that tries to explain what happens *in reality*, can draw on his analysis of money in chapter 2 for support.[5] Weber also has a sociological theory of the market that is well worth exploring. A market, he argues, essentially consists of two types of social actions. First, there is competition between the sellers over who will be the one who sells, as well as competition between the buyers over who will be the one who buys (a struggle between competitors, as Weber puts it). Second, there is the actual deal between one buyer and one seller (a struggle over the price). Weber furthermore argues that in empirical reality the market can be regulated in various ways: through tradition, conventions, laws, and interests. The actors in a market, as touched on earlier, may also try to keep it open or closed, depending on what favors their interests.[6]

A somewhat intriguing, but also exciting analysis of capitalism can finally be found in chapter 2, more precisely in section 31.[7] Weber was very interested in capitalism throughout his career, but I believe that in this section we find his most important theoretical statement on capitalism, at least from the perspective of economic sociology. Particularly two of Weber's points are of much interest: that we should speak not of one but of *several* capitalisms, and that the different types of capitalism should be understood as constellations of social action, not as rigid social structures.

As opposed to Marx, for whom there exists only one type of capitalism, which emerged relatively late in history, Weber argues that there exist three major types of capitalism and that two of these—political capitalism and traditional commercial capitalism—can be traced back very far in history. Political capitalism is defined as the kind of capitalism where profits are closely tied to some connection to the state or to the intervention of the state; while traditional commercial capitalism revolves around small-scale trade in goods and money. The third type of capitalism, rational capitalism, has only existed in the West, and came into its own in the sixteenth century and onward. It typically involves rational firms, capital accounting, and a methodical search for profit. It should finally also be noted that in section 31 Weber prefers to speak of the capitalistic orientation of profit-making rather than of capitalism per se. This is in my mind an important point: it indicates how eager Weber was to avoid collective concepts and replace them with social action terms.

Economy and Politics (Including Law)

By describing the core of Weber's economic sociology as an analysis of purely economic institutions, one might inadvertently give the impression that Weber felt that the economy could operate independently of all political institutions, especially in modern society. This, however, is not true. Indeed, Weber's attempt to work out the relationship between the economy and politics (including law) in his economic sociology *precedes* by many years his attempt to analyze economic institutions. That this is so is clear from Weber's first attempts to outline what *Economy and Society* should contain, something that the plans for *Grundriss der Sozialökonomik* from 1909 and 1914 give an indication of.[8]

In 1909, Weber wanted to deal with the state in one of the three major sections that were to constitute *Economy and Society*, which was entitled "Economy and Social Groups (Family and Community Associations, Status Groups and Classes, State)." A second of the three major sections was to be devoted to law ("Economy and Law [1. Fundamental Relationship, 2. Epochs in the Development of Present Conditions])." Five years later, in 1914, the overall plan for the handbook looked quite a bit different, and the title for Weber's contribution had been changed to "The Economy and the Societal Orders and Powers." The relationship of politics to the economy was to be dealt with in three of the eight major sections of the work. One of these three was termed "Domination," and it was to include a discussion of the development of the modern state. Another of the eight major sections in the plan from 1914 was to contain an analysis entitled "The Fundamental Relationship between Economy and Law." In neither of the two plans can we find sections of *Economy and Society* devoted to the economy itself and which Weber was scheduled to write.

As already mentioned, Weber's efforts to finish his own contribution to *Economy and Society* resulted only in part I being ready before his death, and in a first version of the remaining texts that various editors were to publish as part II.[9] The relationship of politics to economics is discussed in two of the chapters in part I—in chapter 2 on economic sociology and in chapter 3, entitled "The Types of Legitimate Domination." After first presenting what Weber says in part I, I shall say something about his analysis of the relationship between the economy and the state (including the legal system) in part II of *Economy and Society*.

Although chapter 2 on economic sociology may seem to treat economic institutions as if they were independent of political power and the state, one

out of five sections in this chapter deals with the relationship of the economy to the state. Especially three topics are discussed: the financing of political bodies, the monetary policy of the state, and economy and state in socialist society. A few other topics are mentioned as being important, but are
not discussed. One of these—domination and the economy—is, however,
central to chapter 3. It should also be mentioned that even though Weber
does not explicitly introduce the concept of political action in *Economy and
Society*, his mode of analysis is parallel to that of economic action in chapter
2; that is, at the center of the analysis stands political social action or action
directed simultaneously at a political order and at some other actor.

Weber describes financing as the most direct connection between the
economy and political organizations, and he points out that it also influences
the economy as a whole.[10] In particular, two questions about financing are
asked in chapter 2: What is the effect of the many ways that a state can be financed on the different types of capitalism, and in particular on the rise of
modern capitalism (section 39)? And to what extent does the involvement
of the state in the economy, in order to finance its own operations, affect the
different types of capitalism and the rise of modern capitalism (section 38)?[11]
The answer to the second question can be given straightaway: the less involved the state is in the economy, the easier it becomes for rational capitalism to develop. As to the relationship between different types of financing
and the emergence of modern capitalism, Weber's answer is more complicated. There exist, first, several different ways of raising money, which do not
fit any form of capitalism (such as benefices, deliveries in kind, and compulsory services). Then there are measures that go well with political capitalism,
but not with rational capitalism (such as tax farming, monopolistic profit-
making enterprises, and liturgical obligations attached to property). But
there exists only one way to finance a state that is compatible with rational
capitalism, Weber says, and that is taxation.

In analyzing the relationship of politics to economics in socialist society
as well as the monetary policy of the state, Weber makes a number of sociological points. As to socialism, he points out that the strength of the ruling
political elite is enormously increased when power over the economy is
added to power over the state. A second point is similar to the one that von
Mises made around the same time, namely that it will be extremely difficult
to formulate effective prices in a socialist economy since its political system
does not allow for the dispersal of economic power, something that is necessary for prices to emerge. As to the monetary policy of the state, Weber argues that for such a policy to come into being in the first place, the state has
to have a monopoly on the issuance of money and the regulation of the
monetary system. This is something that only exists in the modern rational
state. Weber also emphasizes the limits to the power of the state to regulate

the real value of money, as opposed to its formal value (its substantive validity versus its formal validity in Weber's terminology; section 35).[12]

Weber's most innovative contribution to the analysis of the relationship between the economy and politics is no doubt to be found in the famous chapter 3 on domination. It is commonly known that Weber distinguishes among three forms of domination (legal, charismatic, and traditional domination), and also that a different type of staff answers to each form (bureaucracy to legal domination; disciples and followers to charismatic authority; and a household staff or a staff with ad hoc tasks to traditional domination). What is rarely noted, however, is that Weber's analysis of domination is considerably richer than it may seem because it also has an *economic dimension*. More precisely, Weber discusses how each type of staff is financed, and what effect each type of domination has on the different types of capitalism and especially on the rise of modern capitalism. Indeed, without a link between domination and economic life, there would have been little point in including the analysis of domination in a work on economy and society. Weber, it can be added, used to refer to chapter 3 in *Economy and Society* as "Economy and Domination" in his correspondence with his publisher.[13]

Weber's main findings in chapter 3, insofar as economic sociology is concerned, can be summarized in the following manner. A bureaucracy is financed through taxation, and only legal domination can ensure the kind of predictability that is necessary for modern capitalism. A bureaucrat has a career, a salary, and a pension. A charismatic movement is intensely hostile to all forms of systematic economic activity and finances itself through donations, booty, and the like. The personal economic situation of the followers or disciples is very uncertain at this stage. Once routinized, however, the charismatic movement is transformed in its attitude toward the economy and now favors economic traditionalism. The economic situation of the followers and disciples also becomes more regular at this stage. In patrimonialism, the main form of traditional domination Weber discusses, the staff is paid out of the ruler's pocket. Unpredictable elements dominate patrimonialism, and while these go well with political capitalism, they do not encourage the growth of rational capitalism.

If we now turn to part II of *Economy and Society*, it is clear that it also contains quite a bit of material on the relationship between politics and the economy. We here find, for example, an interesting analysis of the economic policy of the state, such as mercantilism and imperialism. These pages furthermore contain some notable reflections on the relationship between capitalism and the democratic state, where Weber argues that there exists no affinity between capitalism and democracy. Capitalists, he notes, prefer to deal with individual power brokers behind the scenes, rather than get too involved with the cumbersome democratic process. In "The City," Weber also has much to say about the rise of citizenship and economic power, in the *po-lis* of antiquity as well as in the independent cities of later times. The legal system plays a central part in the machinery of the state and, as already mentioned, Weber allotted a central place in *Economy and Society* precisely to the relationship between law and the economy. Nearly all of what Weber wanted to say on this topic, however, was planned to be included in that part (or those parts) of *Economy and Society* that he never had the time to complete. Thus we have a fairly short text entitled "The Economy and Social Norms," and a huge manuscript entitled "Sociology of Law (Economy and Law)."[14] To this can be added a few comments on law and economics in part I of *Economy and Society*.

These few comments, however, are of quite a bit of interest since they allow us fairly well to reconstruct how Weber viewed the relationship between the economy and law from a theoretical viewpoint in his economic sociology. A social action, to recall, consists of meaningful behavior oriented to somebody else or to an order; an economic social action consists of meaningful behavior, similarly oriented, and has utility as its goal. In part I of *Economy and Society*, Weber also says that a social action can be simultaneously oriented toward more than one actor, and he adds that an economic (social) action can be directed at utility, at another actor, *and* at the legal order.[15] We now realize what role the legal order plays in the economy, from the viewpoint of Weber's theoretical sociology. It may impede rational economic actions if it is irrational, but it may also further the probability that an economic action will take place if it is dependable and predictable. What matters is that the actor orients his or her act not only toward some other actor but also toward the legal order, and that this influences his or her actions.

The main theme in Weber's analysis of economy and law has to do with the impact of law on the different types of capitalism, especially on the rise of modern capitalism. Weber works out his arguments from three different angles. First, he emphasizes the importance of certain legal institutions for the rise of Western capitalism, in particular the advanced business contract, the notion of the firm as a legal personality, and a legal machinery that produces a reliable legal order. The advanced business contract has, in all brevity, to be a purposive one, and it should be possible to enforce it in an effective manner. The firm should have a legal personality and be able to act in its own name; its property should also be distinct from the property of individuals. As to the legal machinery—the law itself and the legal personnel—it is essential that the legal decisions be predictable and uniform.

Weber also suggests that law can be substantively or formally either rational or irrational, and that this affects what kind of capitalism is likely to emerge. The term *substantive* here refers to the introduction of nonlegal norms into the law, while *formal* refers to the logical dimension of the law. Formally irrational law—say legal decisions by an oracle—is not compatible with any kind of capitalism. In contrast, substantively irrational law—one example would be khadi justice—goes very well with political capitalism, but not with rational capitalism. This is also true of substantively rational law, Weber notes, such as theocratic law. The only type of law that is truly compatible with rational capitalism, he concludes, is formally rational law, of the type that one can find, for example, in the Code Napoléon.

The third way in which Weber explores the relationship of law to the economy, with special emphasis on the rise of modern capitalism, is by looking at what kinds of commercial law the major legal systems of the world have had. This extremely ambitious undertaking by Weber produced very interesting results. One of Weber's most important findings was that legal systems with high formal rationality do not necessarily have a richly developed commercial legislation, and vice versa. One example is Roman law, which was extremely well developed from a formal-legal perspective, but which also had a primitive commercial legislation. Another example is medieval law of the type that developed in the Italian city-states: it can be characterized as having a low level of formal rationality, but was very advanced in its commercial legislation. Most of the legal institutions that are central to modern capitalism, Weber notes, have their origin in medieval commercial legislation. Many other legal systems—in India, China, and elsewhere—have tended to have a low level of legal rationality, and also a poorly developed commercial legislation.

Economy and Religion

While it would be difficult to deny the high quality of those parts of Weber's economic sociology that deal with economic institutions and the relationship between the economy and politics (including law), it is also true that there is something special about Weber's analysis of the relationship between the economy and religion. Weber's most famous study, *The Protestant Ethic and the Spirit of Capitalism*, is centered on this issue, as is his giant unfinished work *The Economic Ethics of the World Religions*.

Less often mentioned is the fact that Weber also deals with this topic in *Economy and Society*. In the 1909 plan for the handbook in economics there is no mention of any article by Weber on religion and economy, although Weber may have intended to deal with this topic in the section entitled "Economy and Culture (Critique of Historical Materialism)."[16] In the quite different plan from 1914, Weber included a whole section entitled "Religious Communities (The Conditioning of Religion by Class Constellations; Cultural Religions and Economic Attitudes)."[17] In a famous letter to his publisher dated December 8, 1913, Weber describes his finished manuscript for *Economy and Society*, from which it is clear that Weber had high hopes for his manuscript, including the analysis of the economy and religion.[18]

To this must be added that Weber, however, never had the time to rewrite this text and make it more textbook-like and shorter, as he had wanted. In 1915, Weber also said that one important purpose of *The Economic Ethics of the World Religions* was to complement the analysis of religion in *Economy and Society*.[19]

It is not easy to summarize Weber's analysis of economy and religion in *Economy and Society*, which is roughly 300 pages long.[20] Weber starts out with the birth of religion and ends several thousand years later, covering not only key religious actors but also the major religions of the world. To give a sense of the richness of this part of Weber's economic sociology, I here single out what I see as his most significant contributions. These include his analysis of the relationship of the major religious organizations to economic life, the religious inclinations of major social groupings, how the different approaches to salvation may effect economic life, and the relationship to the economy in a few of the major religions. First, however, a few words need to be said about how Weber analyzes religious action as a form of social action, and what this can tell us about the relationship of religious behavior to the economy.

According to Weber, religious social action, like economic social action, consists of a special type of action that is directed at other actors or at an order. While economic action is directed at utility, religious action is directed at what Weber calls *Heilsgüter*, which can be translated as either goods of salvation, or more generally, religious benefits. One reason why Weber chose this term, which has its origin in Lutheran and Calvinist theology from the sixteenth and seventeenth centuries, is that it indicates that what moves the believer is not so much ideas as the concrete and tangible benefits that result from religious behavior. Religious benefits, Weber explains, can be of several different kinds: they can be either material or spiritual, and they can also be this-worldly or other-worldly. Early in history, religions typically promised material benefits in this world, such as a long and healthy life and material riches. As religion evolved, however, the emphasis gradually shifted to spiritual benefits in the afterlife.

In analyzing the relationship between religious organizations and the economy, Weber focuses on four types of organizations: hierocracies, churches, sects, and monastic orders. A hierocracy is defined as an organization that enforces its order through coercion based on the supply or the withdrawal of religious benefits. A church is a hierocratic organization that claims monopoly on the legitimate use of religious benefits. A sect is not as universalistic as a church but carefully screens its members; and a monastic order may perhaps be characterized as a male sect where all the members live together and devote themselves to religiously oriented activities.

A hierocracy often clashes with the existing political power on the issue of landholdings, which both bodies want to accumulate. It is suspicious of economic innovations and deeply traditionalistic in its nature. A hierocracy is consequently anticapitalistic and tends to encourage economic traditionalism. A church typically develops out of a hierocracy, and its influence on the economy is similar: it is suspicious of capitalism and of economic innovations in general. While churches often try to influence and change economic practices—for example through rules about usury and just prices—churches do not have much of an economic program, according to Weber, who also claims that the church did not directly influence basic economic institutions.[21]

Sects affect the economy primarily by influencing the character of their members, according to Weber. A sect can enforce honesty and other character traits among its members much more effectively than a church, and it was two sects—the Baptists and the Quakers—that introduced fixed prices in the West. The monastic order, according to Weber, differs in its attitude toward economic affairs depending on what stage it is in. At first, charismatic elements usually predominate, and the attitude among its members is strongly antieconomic. As time goes by, however, routinization sets in and a more conciliatory attitude toward economic issues develops. But even during these later stages, Weber says, an enormous religious enthusiasm can develop in a monastic order, and this enthusiasm can sometimes be translated into economic energy of a very powerful and strange nature. The fantastic monasteries that Tibetan monks have erected in Lhasa are an example of this, according to Weber.

While Weber was firmly against Marx's proposition that social life and culture, including religion, were directly formed by economic forces (but never the other way around), he fully agreed that most social phenomena are influenced by economic forces to some extent. They are economically conditioned, as he phrased it in his 1904 essay on objectivity; this also includes religious phenomena.[22] The main section on sociology of religion in *Economy and Society* thus includes a discussion of how the mode of work influences the religious beliefs of major social groupings, such as peasants, aristocrats, and artisans.

Aristocracies, in Weber's view, have mainly been prevented from developing a strong religiosity by their fierce sense of honor; and when they have been religious, they have often chosen jealous and warring gods. Peasants tend to be receptive to magic because of their work with nature, and until recently they have rarely been deeply religious. Artisans, who typically work indoors and in cities, vary in the type of religion they adopt—from mysticism to more rational forms of religion. Rich merchants and government officials are typically skeptical of religious fervor and are often indifferent to religious questions. Modern workers, finally, are not very interested in religion at all, except for the poorest strata. Workers typically want what Weber calls just compensation in their lives, while the higher-ups adopt what he terms a theodicy of good fortune or an ideology which states that successful people deserve to be well off (and poor people deserve to be unfortunate).

One of Weber's most innovative contributions to the understanding of the relationship between the economy and religion can be found in his analysis of the economic consequences of the different ways in which one can reach salvation. Some of these ways, Weber argues, have little effect on the character of the person involved, and hence encourage economic traditionalism. This can be exemplified by good deeds, ecstasy, ritualism, and institutional grace. Others, however, may deeply affect the personality of the believer, but the person in question may still not change society and the economy. Mysticism is an example of this. And, finally, there are ways of seeking salvation that may deeply affect the personality of the believer *and* encourage her to want to change social institutions, including economic ones. These are inner-worldly asceticism and predestination, according to Weber. The former typically results in an alert attitude toward social and economic issues as well as an effort to change society in accordance with one's religious ideals. Predestination, as Calvinism attests to, may finally induce a methodical attempt to change one's behavior, including economic behavior.

Weber has also included in *Economy and Society* some of the results from his studies of economic ethics, for example those of Buddhism and Judaism. The former, he notes, typically makes the believer want to withdraw from active life, in order to prepare for the eternal sleep of nirvana. This type of religion, Weber says, does not induce rational behavior or encourage the growth of the capitalist spirit. The same is to a certain extent true for Judaism, and at this point Weber enters into a polemic with Werner Sombart, who claimed that Judaism was the main source of capitalism. In reality, Weber points out, the Jews did not participate at all in industrial capitalism because of their status as a pariah people. Judaism, in Weber's opinion, was a highly traditionalistic religion and did not encourage active behavior or the spirit of capitalism, as Calvinism did.

Since Weber died before he had time to complete his study of the economic ethic of Islam, the section on this topic in *Economy and Society* is of special interest.[23] Islam, in Weber's view, had accommodated itself to the world, but in a different manner than Judaism. It contained, for example, very strong feudal elements: it was positive to slavery and serfdom, and it accepted polygamy. The ideal person according to Islam was not the scholar, as in Judaism, but the warrior; and in many ways the ideals of Islam constituted the sensual paradise of a soldier.[24] The positive attitude in Islam toward booty, as well as its negative attitude toward gambling, contributed, according to Weber, to its antirational character, and also helps to explain why no rational capitalism spontaneously emerged in Islamic countries.

Concluding Remarks

In a 1986 review of *Economy and Society*, Arthur Stinchcombe argues that while Parsons thinks that Weber's work is about values and society, and Reinhard Bendix thinks that it is about domination and society, he himself thinks that *Economy and Society* is about *economy and society*.[25] This argument is in my opinion essentially correct—even though I would like to add that while Weber's work is about economy and society, it can better be characterized as a work centered on economic sociology. Stinchcombe's formulation can also be bettered by explicitly stating that although *Economy and Society* is a work focused on economic sociology, it also contains general sections on theoretical sociology, political sociology, sociology of law, and other topics, and that these are independent contributions to these special fields. Weber's work, in other words, can be profitably read by people with different goals in mind. It also deserves to be pointed out that *Economy and Society* can usefully be read by economists, not only by sociologists. Indeed, Weber's work was written with economists as its primary audience.

That *Economy and Society* contains important contributions to theoretical, political, and other forms of sociology has been known for more than half a century, and it is also an insight that has resulted in a huge amount of secondary literature. But the fact that *Economy and Society* contains an elaborate economic sociology has rarely been realized, and it has resulted in virtually no studies on that topic—something that makes it imperative, as I see it, to devote quite a bit of attention to this aspect of Weber's work today. Apart from getting Weber's general economic sociology in chapter 2 right, which is no easy task, *Economy and Society* also contains analyses of the relationship of the economy to politics, to law, and to religion, all of which need to be thoroughly discussed by sociologists—and economists!—so that they can be better understood. But this is not all; in his work Weber also raises the question of the relationship of the economy, from a sociological viewpoint, to a host of additional phenomena, such as nature (including human nature), population, and technology; these relationships also need to be properly explored. Finally, *Economy and Society* was originally part of *Grundriss der Sozialökonomik*, and we currently know very little about this work. Briefly, a better knowledge of Weber's handbook would allow us to better understand

Weber's economic sociology, since it was conceptually situated in relation to economic studies of various kinds.

This last task—situating *Economy and Society* in relation to *Grundriss der Sozialökonomik*—would also be of interest, as I understand it, to those who are concerned with Weber's work in general. The reason for this is that a number of tasks remain for those whose primary interest is in Weber's types of sociology. In this chapter I have, for example, suggested that we can learn more about chapter 1 by looking at chapter 2. Weber's sociology of domination, as I have tried to show, is also about more than the three forms of domination and their respective staffs; it has a distinct economic dimension—as does Weber's political sociology more generally, his sociology of law, and his sociology of religion in *Economy and Society*.

What all of this adds up to, in my mind, is that quite a bit of research remains to be done on *Economy and Society*, and that this work still holds many secrets. In a well-known statement Weber said, according to his wife, Marianne Weber, that one day his work will be surpassed and it will have played out its role. Well, we are not there yet, and perhaps we never will be. Indeed, is not the definition of a classic that it is never exhausted, but always has something new to teach?

Notes

1. For a different opinion, see Friedrich Tenbruck, "The Problem of Thematic Unity in the Works of Max Weber," *British Journal of Sociology* 31 (1980): 316–51.

2. Max Weber, *The Methodology of the Social Sciences*, trans. and ed. Edward Shils and Henry Finch (New York: Free Press, 1949), pp. 64–65. Economic phenomena are economic institutions, types of banks, money and stock exchanges. Economically relevant phenomena are noneconomic phenomena that have an important impact on economic phenomena. The paradigmatic example is ascetic Protestantism that helped to form the spirit of modern, rational capitalism. Economically conditioned phenomena are noneconomic phenomena that have been partly formed by economic phenomena. One example from Weber's sociology of religion is how the religion of a class is partly formed by the conditions under which its members have to carry out work in their everyday lives. Peasants, for example, work closely with the forces of nature and are therefore likely to believe in magic. Finally, and to make a point that I return to later in this chapter, in speaking exclusively of economic institutions it is *not* implied that political, legal, and cultural factors do not play a role in the economy. On the contrary, according to Weber, all of these are central to the economy, including modern rational capitalism.

3. Cf. Max Weber, *Economy and Society: An Outline of Interpretive Sociology*, ed. Guenther Roth and Claus Wittich (1921–22; Berkeley: University of California Press, 1978), pp. 4–24.

4. Weber, *Economy and Society*, p. 202.

5. Cf. Max Weber, *Grundriss zu den Vorlesungen über Allgemeine ("theoretische") Nationalökonomie (1898)* (Tübingen: J. C. B. Mohr, 1990), p. 6. For a further elaboration

of Weber's view of the market, see Richard Swedberg, "Afterword: The Role of the Market in Max Weber's Work," *Theory and Society* 29 (2000): 373–84.

7. Weber, *Economy and Society*, pp. 164–66.

8. See, e.g., Wolfgang Schluchter, *Rationalism, Religion, and Domination: A Weberian Perspective* (Berkeley: University of California Press, 1989), pp. 466–67; cf. Johannes Winkelmann, *Max Webers hinterlassenes Hauptwerk* (Tübingen: J. C. B. Mohr, 1986), pp. 151–209. The reader may recall that *Economy and Society* was written for the *Grundriss*.

9. See Hiroshi Orihara, "Max Weber's Contribution to *Grundriss der Sozialökonomik*," *Kölner Zeitschrift für Soziologie und Sozialpsychologie* 71 (1999): 724–34; Wolfgang Mommsen, "Max Weber's 'Grand Sociology': The Origins and Composition of *Wirtschaft und Gesellschaft. Soziologie*," *History and Theory* 39 (2001): 364–83.

10. Weber, *Economy and Society*, pp. 194–201.

11. Ibid., pp. 194–99, 199–201.

12. Ibid., pp. 178–80.

13. Winkelmann, *Webers hinterlassenes Hauptwerk*, p. 46.

14. Weber, *Economy and Society*, pp. 311–38, 641–900.

15. Ibid., p. 33.

16. Schluchter, *Rationalism*, p. 415.

17. Ibid., p. 467.

18. Weber wrote: "Since Bücher's treatment of the 'developmental stages' [in his contribution to *Grundriss der Sozialökonomik*] is totally inadequate, I have worked out a complete theory and exposition that relates the major social groups to the economy: from the family and household to the enterprise, the kin group, ethnic community, religion (comprising all religions of the world: a sociology of salvation doctrines and of religious ethics—what Troeltsch did, but now for all religions, if much briefer). I can claim that nothing of the kind has ever been written, not even as a precursor." Cited in Wolfgang Schluchter, *The Rise of Western Rationalism: Max Weber's Developmental History* (Berkeley: University of California Press, 1981), pp. xxv–xxvi.

The reference in this quotation to Bücher's treatment of the "developmental stages" is to his contribution to the handbook in economics that Weber was editing: "Volkswirtschaftliche Entwicklungsstufen," pp. 1–18, in *Wirtschaft und Wirtschaftswissenschaft. Grundriss der Sozialökonomik*. I. Abteilung (1914).

19. Weber, *Economy and Society*, p. 237.

20. Ibid., pp. 399–634, 1156–211.

21. Ibid., p. 1190.

22. On this point the reader is referred to note 2.

23. Weber, *Economy and Society*, pp. 623–27.

24. Ibid., pp. 625.

25. Arthur Stinchcombe, *Stratification and Organization* (Cambridge: Cambridge University Press, 1986), p. 283. Recall that *Economy and Society* was originally written for the *Grundriss*.

*Democracy, Domination, and Legitimacy in
Max Weber's Political Thought*

Democratic forms of governance, which are distinguished by the participation of the governed in directing public business, are not given much attention in Max Weber's sociology of domination. There is a good, though often overlooked, reason for this. Democracy is not, strictly speaking, a form of domination in Weber's view. Democracy entails the minimization of domination or, in its purest and most precarious form, is commensurate with freedom from domination.[1] This mode of conducting public affairs, then, would necessarily find a marginal place in Weber's sociology of domination.[2] Still democracy is one of the main concepts in contrast to which his idea of legitimate domination was delimited and thus, in view of Weber's construction overall, is more significant than appears from the limited consideration given it. This chapter examines the juxtaposition of democracy and domination in *Economy and Society* and links Weber's political thought as it emerges through this consideration with his political commitments as he expressed them in his journalistic political writings.

Legitimized Domination

In his sociology of domination, Weber analyzed power relationships between human beings involving the imposition of one person's or one group's will on others in such a way that the dominated inwardly assent to rule and their obedience can be regularly counted on. The concept of domination, as it was developed and refined through a series of contrasts and examples of transitional forms, excludes the power exercised through the "formally free interplay of interested parties such as occurs especially in the market" and refers more narrowly to the authoritarian power to issue commands that are heeded to a significant extent.[3] Though domination inherently represents a compulsory as opposed to a voluntary relationship,[4] continuous domination involves a significant level of voluntary compliance.[5] The command issuing from the dominating power is accepted by the ruled as a "valid" norm.[6] "Only in the limiting case of the slave," Weber explained, "is subjection to authority absolutely involuntary."[7]

There are a number of motives that induce this compliance, including self-interest, fear, and simple habit.[8] But in addition to these motives the relationship of domination rests on a belief in its legitimacy. The basis on which legitimacy is claimed (and obedience given) significantly shapes the structure of rule.[9] Weber distinguished three pure types of legitimate domination—legal, traditional, and charismatic. In the first case, laws are abstract rules that are intentionally established, and obedience is oriented to the resulting impersonal order and to the right of individuals raised in accordance with that order to exercise authority under it.[10] A bureaucratic administrative staff is typically engendered by this form of legitimacy. Rule is administered by officials who are appointed on the basis of expertise.

In contrast to the idea that rules are intentionally created and rationally enforced, traditional legitimacy views binding norms as emerging out of the immemorial past. Rulers—most often patriarchal authorities and patrimonial princes—are legitimized by lineage, custom, and tradition. Within the limits of tradition, however, the leaders also exercise a large measure of discretionary power and have the opportunity to benefit personal favorites by recruiting members of the ruling apparatus from relatives, friends, allies, and dependents of various sorts.[11] Under the third type of legitimate domination—charismatic domination—binding commands emanate from an individual who inspires personal devotion by virtue of extraordinary individual qualities. These qualities are often seen to have a supernatural source, or at least the individual is believed to transcend the ordinary run of mortals through superhuman heroism, discipline, strength, and the like. The term *charisma* was derived from early Christianity and developed into a sociological concept by Rudolf Sohm.[12] Weber made use of this concept to denote the quality that inspires faith and trust in the followers of this type of leader. The inner circle of the charismatic leader is also composed of individuals distinguished by requisite charismatic endowments (rather than professional qualifications or connections with the chief). These are the three pure types of legitimate domination Weber delineated. He maintained that in empirical reality these types are rarely found in their pure form, but are combined in various ways.[13]

Weber's use of the term *legitimate*, it is necessary to emphasize, does not indicate that these types are objectively or normatively valid. It was not Weber's intention to establish criteria of legitimacy or to distinguish between legitimate and illegitimate rule. Indeed he developed no category of illegitimate rule in the sense of force without right.[14] Virtually all successful domination, for Weber, is "legitimate" domination.[15] Aside from the extreme case of slavery, domination in the sense of brute force without some belief in legitimacy—at least on the part of the staff enforcing the order[16]—is untenable. The "continued exercise of every domination . . . always has the strongest need of self-justification through appealing to the principles of its legitimation."[17]

In order to properly grasp Weber's idea of legitimate domination, it is necessary to clarify his definition of the word *legitimate*, which, consistent with "Weber's penchant for nominalist irony,"[18] contravenes conventional usage. His understanding of legitimacy was connected with his view, expressed in one form or another in most of his writings, of the ultimate "irrationality of the world." Intrinsic to the senselessness of worldly existence—a condition of which human beings, nonetheless, continually endeavor to make sense—is the arbitrary distribution of inequalities, advantages, and privileges. Because advantages are capriciously conferred by an irrational fate, these advantages must be justified or legitimized. Accordingly, individuals and groups that are in a position to issue commands that are regularly obeyed embrace and promulgate meaningful constructs that make their good fortune seem merited.

The fates of human beings are not equal. Men differ in their states of health or wealth or social status or what not. Simple observation shows that in every such situation he who is more favored feels the never ceasing need to look upon his position as in some way "legitimate," upon his advantage as "deserved," and the other's disadvantage as being brought about by the latter's "fault." That the purely accidental differences may be ever so obvious makes no difference.[19]

However, under certain conditions the actual arbitrariness of this position of privilege may become "visible" to the negatively privileged strata, provoking their wrath and inducing them to struggle against this state of affairs.[20]

What is interesting to note is that, for Weber, the opportunity to impose one's will on others requires a legitimizing explanation, while a condition of equal freedom where no one will prevails over others seemingly requires no supporting ideological legitimation. Along the lines of the classical theorists of the liberal tradition, Weber implicitly took the condition of free and equal human beings as the starting point or touchstone for considering relationships of rule. In the liberal view, a condition of equal freedom represented the most genuine human condition—whether such a condition was or ever could be fully realized was irrelevant—and the imposition of will in the form of rule, however necessary, represented a deviation from this fundamental state.[21] Weber also appeared to see the imposition of will in the form of rule as a deviant condition (one that requires a legitimizing explanation).[22]

In contrast to Aristotle's well-known classificatory scheme of political sys-tems,[23] democracy did not find a place as a distinct form of rule in Weber's rival typology. Rather, democracy approximates a condition absent rule, and this condition served, for Weber, as a counterpoint and implied standard against which his ideal types of legitimate domination were delineated.[24] To be sure, he did not think that the purest forms of democracy are possible in human affairs on more than a transitory basis. For Weber, action in concert with other human beings, especially in regard to implementing collective measures, gives rise to a guiding will that is imposed on the rest. Indeed he insisted that "any notion of putting an end to the domination of man over man by whatever sort of socialist system or by however attenuated forms of 'democracy' is utopian."[25] Still, equal freedom appears in his sociology of domination as an elusive and unattainable ideal of self-determination, ap-proximations of which he juxtaposed with the inevitable subordination and superordination that occur through the interaction and struggle of human wills.

Domination and Self-Determination

Manifestations of self-government, in various antidominatory and nonle-gitimized forms, were discussed by Weber intermittently in his sociology of domination. According to Weber's projected outline for the earlier ver-sion of *Economy and Society*, the essay "The Three Types of Legitimate Domination" was to be followed by "Political and Hierocratic Domina-tion." "Non-Legitimate Domination: The Typology of Cities," which was written before his exposition of the types of domination, was to be placed next. Two additional sections were planned—"Development of the Mod-ern State" and "The Modern Political Parties"—that Weber did not live to write.[26] In the earlier version of Weber's typology of legitimate domina-tion, which was to be placed at the beginning of the five essays on domi-nation as indicated, he prefaced his account with the consideration of re-lationships that minimize domination—direct democracy and the rule of notables. In the later version of "The Three Types of Legitimate Domina-tion," this account of direct democracy and rule by notables was included with his most extended consideration of types of democracy in *Economy and Society* in a section on antiauthoritarian (*herrschaftsfremde*) variants of charismatic domination.

Direct (*unmittelbare*) democracy represents the most extreme type of the antiauthoritarian forms of collective rule insofar as, in its most genuine form, its members are "free from domination" (*herrschaftsfreie unmittelbare Demokratie*).[27] In this mode of collective rule-making and administration, a group conducts its common affairs through officials who are thought to be the "servants" of the members.[28] All of the members are regarded as equally fit to discharge public duties, and some system of assuring members a share in governance—such as rotation, lots, or elections—is in place.[29] This form of organization can only take root in conditions where the population is small and the tasks to be accomplished are relatively simple, requiring no special expertise.[30] In *Economy and Society*, Weber provided as examples of direct democracy the "North American 'township' and the smaller Swiss Cantons."[31] This type of direct democracy, Weber noted, easily gives way to "a form of government by notables."[32] The need for most people to direct their energies to making a living fosters the shifting of public responsibilities to individuals and groups that are economically available to play a public role.[33] The rule of notables still tenuously represents a condition in which domination is undeveloped "so long as parties that contend with each other" do not arise.[34] But movement into the channel of parties is a strong tendency once this differentiation among members of the community has occurred. As these parties struggle over the appropriation of offices, a structure of domination comes into being.[35] Both direct democracy and rule by notables become untenable when population increases and public tasks require technical expertise.[36] With the incorporation of large numbers of people under the operations of government and the increasing complexity of these operations, appointed, salaried officials rather than self-governing citizens carry out administrative activities. Although there have been fleeting manifestations of democratic self-rule, the countervailing force of domination renders all achievements on behalf of freedom tenuous.

In addition to these reflections on noncoercive forms of making and implementing collective decisions, consideration of the relationship between domination and free initiative is found in the other sections of Weber's sociology of domination. These examples of organizational forms that maximize self-determination, to which Weber recurred, represent limiting-type cases for contrasting and demarcating legitimate domination.[37] In the section "The City," Weber developed an ideal type of city based on the Occidental city of the Middle Ages and from which all other cities were seen to deviate. Characteristic of the medieval city, most particularly north of the Alps, were the existence of a bourgeoisie estate and the cutting of ties with the rural nobility.[38] In the Occidental city, the agglomeration of individuals assembled in this location was transformed into a communal association of urban citizens. Such an organized vehicle of bourgeoisie social action, Weber showed, was not to be found in the cities of Asia and the Near East.[39] Moreover, the Eastern cities were distinguished from the Occidental type because these settlements usually represented seats of rule rather than independent political units.[40]

The preconditions for the kind of relatively autonomous civic associations that arose in the Occident were the absence of magical, ritual, and clan barriers between groups and classes,[41] the self-equipment of individuals for war, and the reliance on infantry.[42] Very often the origin of these fraternal associations in the Occidental city of the Middle Ages was, Weber suggested, in the revolutionary "defiance of 'legitimate powers'" and the "'spontaneous' usurpation through an act of rational association, a sworn confraternization (*Eidverbrüderung: coniuratio*) of the burghers."[43] In seeking a measure of autonomy and self-government, the urban citizenry "usurped the right to dissolve bonds of seigneurial domination; this was the great—in fact, the *revolutionary*—innovation which differentiated the medieval Occidental cities from all others."[44] Weber associated this kind of revolutionary upheaval with the breakdown of myths sustaining highly privileged groups[45] and referred to this situation where "traditional legitimacy" has been usurped by "consociations of the ruled" as "nonlegitimate domination" (*nichtlegitime Herrschaft*).[46] The deliberate challenging of legitimate authorities in a revolutionary manner by a group constituting themselves as a community of citizens represents, then, a form of human political engagement outside the categories of legitimate domination and in contrast to which the concept of legitimate domination acquires greater distinctness.

Although these autonomous cities were ultimately reabsorbed under the rule of princes or *signorie*, the individuality, citizenship, and self-government manifested in these transitory achievements prepared the ground for the emergence of modern individualism and the notion of the individual citizen as holder of certain political rights. The burgher, Weber observed, joined the citizenry as an individual, and as an individual he swore the oath of citizenship.[47]

The disassociation of the individual from clan and other attachments was also evident in certain religious developments, in particular the "religious association of individual believers"[48] characteristic of the Christian congregations. This tendency was most fully expressed in the phenomenon of religious sects, which represented, for Weber, the antiauthoritarian marginal case of hierocratic domination (a form of domination that "enforces its order through psychic coercion").[49]

In the section of *Economy and Society* entitled "Political and Hierocratic Domination," Weber considered types of religious domination and the complex, contentious, and interdependent relationships between religious and political authorities. Drawing from his earlier writing, "The Protestant Sects and the Spirit of Capitalism,"[50] Weber contrasted the "church" and the "sect" in the final part of this section. The church, he observed, is a compulsory association that dispenses grace and into which the individual member is born. The sect, by contrast, is a voluntary association of fellow believers, admission to which is determined by rigorous examination of the candidate's moral qualifications. In the sect, the individual has to prove his or her worth among peers.[51] The church is universalistic, and hence in this respect democratic, whereas the sect is an aristocracy of merit.[52] Otherwise it is the sect that is akin to direct democracy insofar as "clerical officials" are treated as "servants of the congregation" and the group "insists upon 'direct democratic administration' by the congregation."[53] What is decisive and distinctive about the sect for Weber is that the sects necessarily do not oblige nonmembers to act as part of the group.[54] Insofar as membership is based strictly upon voluntary adherence to the principles of the group—and acceptance of the individual by the group—the sect "rejects any attempt" to compel nonmembers to act as members.[55]

Thus the consistent sect gives rise to an inalienable personal right of the governed as against any power, whether political, hierocratic or patriarchal. Such freedom of conscience may be the oldest Right of Man—as Jellinek has argued convincingly; at any rate, it is the most basic Right of Man because it comprises all ethically conditioned action and guarantees freedom from compulsion, especially from the power of the state.[56]

The sects, in Weber's view, "formed one of the most important historical foundations of modern 'individualism'" and signified a "radical break away from patriarchal and authoritarian bondage."[57]

Weber repeatedly made it clear that the advances in the direction of freedom achieved in the cities and the sects and, ultimately, during the age of the Rights of Man accorded with his own liberal democratic convictions.[58] He saw human dignity as inhering in the ability to be self-directing[59] and encouraged the exercise of this capacity for rational self-direction toward goals and ideals. He feared, however, that these attenuations of the condition of legitimate domination and gains in the direction of individual freedom were, like direct democracy, precarious achievements. These openings for the exercise of individual freedom did not, in his view, portend progressive democratization and the expansion of opportunities for individual freedom. Rather—as suggested by Weber's attention to the constant tension between domination and self-determination—hierarchy, authority, and subordination tend to reassert themselves in the course of human interaction.[60] His melancholy predictions of the rise of new hierarchies in the future evinced his view of a counterswing toward more rigid forms of domination:

The world will see to it, only too certainly, that the trees of democratic individualism will not grow up into the heavens. All our experiences teach us that "history" is unremitting in spawning ever new "aristocracies" and "authorities." . . . We are "individualists" and partisans of "democratic" institutions "against the tide" of material constellations.[61]

Rule and Remnants

In contrast to the tradition of thought, stemming from the Enlightenment and finding perhaps fullest in expression in G. W. F. Hegel's philosophy of history, Weber did not see the advance of reason as realizing freedom. Weber wanted to make clear that the externalization of reason in institutional arrangements could not be counted on to deliver individual freedom and equality. His ideal type of legal domination, in fact, demonstrated that the rational form of rule, based on the creation and implementation of abstract norms, is "most unambiguously a structure of domination."[62] Irrespective of whether laws have been created by agreement, a relationship of command and obedience inheres in the activity through which these laws are administered by bureaucratic officials.[63]

"Bureaucratic administration," Weber maintained, "means fundamentally domination through knowledge."[64] Officials are selected on the basis of technical qualifications acquired through specialized training, offices are hierarchically organized, spheres of competence are clearly delimited, technical rules regulate the conduct of offices, and rules, acts, and information are recorded in writing and preserved in files.[65] Weber regarded pure bureaucratic administration as the most efficient and, consequently, the most inescapable form of rule. As is well known, Weber dreaded the increased bureaucratic regulation of human activity and the concomitant encasing of the individual in a tightening web of efficiently applied rules, which compel and elicit predictable behaviors.

It has often been assumed that Weber's concerns about the advance of bureaucracy—and the diminution of individual freedom it would bring in its wake—represented a critique of modern democracy akin to Alexis de Tocqueville's disparagement of "democratic conformity and tyranny of the majority."[66] To be sure, Weber viewed bureaucratization and mass democratization as parallel and interconnected developments, both of which, in addition, have roots in the Occidental city and sects.[67] Democracy requires the diminution of the role of notables, the leveling of status distinctions, and equality before the law. This social leveling, paradoxically, tends to give rise to the kind of formal and rational administration provided by bureaucracy, which in turn subverts democracy.[68] Democracy, he wrote, is "opposed to the 'rule' of bureaucracy, in spite and perhaps because of its unavoidable yet unintended promotion of bureaucratization."[69]

Weber's dismay about the paradoxical consequences of democratization, however, does not equate with a critique of democratic modes of participatory decision-making or of their potential majoritarian excesses. Rather, his clear concern was the reemergence of *hierarchical* social forms through the dialectical transformation whereby bureaucracy undermines the democratic conditions from which it tends to emerge. It was not rhetorical hyperbole that accounts for Weber's lamentations about new "aristocracies" arising in the future. Weber used the term *aristocracies* deliberately to indicate something essential about the character of future trends connected with the process of bureaucratization.[70] In his view, the officials who occupy the offices of the bureaucracy come to represent a status group with their own sense of social honor and particular interests, which they would advance through control of policy. Although bureaucracy was initially compatible with democracy in their joint struggle against the rule by notables, a status group based on education now takes shape. Again, Weber noted the paradoxical way this development is related to democracy. On the one hand, democracy promotes a system that selects qualified people from all strata by examinations. On the other hand, "democracy fears that examinations and patents of education will create a privileged 'caste,' and for that reason opposes such a system."[71] Speaking with the voice of apprehensive democracy in his political writings, Weber observed:

There is no doubt that educational difference is nowadays the most important difference giving rise to true social *estates* [*Stände*]. . . . However much one may regret the fact, differences of "education" are one of the very strongest social barriers which operate in a purely inward way.[72]

As a result of the bureaucracy's striving for power and creation of new status distinctions, the type of democratization it fosters is only "passive" in the face of the ruling stratum, which now forms a closed status group.[73] The "political concept of democracy, deduced from the 'equal rights' of the governed" aims to minimize the power of the bureaucracy and to prevent "the development of a closed status group of officials."[74]

Weber perceived that the rationalizing tendencies unleashed through modern democracy (and capitalism) would transcend these movements and coalesce with the inevitable reassertion of hierarchy and authority in the human condition. A conservative reaction, he prophesied, was in the offing[75] and a stratified social structure taking shape in the "womb of the future."[76] It was not increased opportunities for mass democratic participation that alarmed Weber, but the diminution of these opportunities in modern conditions where large numbers of people are brought under the sway of a single government and subject to uniform rational regulations. The complexity of tasks connected with governing modern mass states necessitates rule by means of a caste of specially trained officials.

Given the inexorable advance of bureaucracy, Weber asked with a note of urgency: "How is it *at all possible* to salvage any remnants of 'individual' freedom of movement *in any sense?*"[77] A tragic sense that we can realistically aspire only to preserving remnants of freedom was repeated in a well-known letter written by Weber to Roberto Michels. In this letter, Weber reiterated his view of the instability of direct, egalitarian democracy and rejected this as an achievable political goal. Weber confessed to Michels that his reflections on the impossibility of pure egalitarian democracy "stamped [him] as a 'bourgeois' politician, at least for as long as the little that one *can* will does not recede into the endless distance."[78] In the face of the inescapability of domination, and bureaucratic domination in particular, Weber became preoccupied with meaningfully preserving some small measure of human freedom. This aim underlay and directed his program for political reform.

Between Democracy and Domination

In his sociology of domination, Weber explicated a number of transitional forms between democratic and dominatory forms, which he characterized as antiauthoritarian variants of charisma.[79] The reinterpretation of charisma in an antiauthoritarian direction signifies that recognition is no longer "treated as a consequence of legitimacy, it is treated as the basis of legitimacy,"[80] giving rise to the "freely elected leader."[81] The most significant form of this transitional type is the plebiscitary leader who formally derives legitimacy from the affirmation of the ruled.[82] This affirmation, expressed in the plebiscite, does not genuinely express the voluntary will of the subordinates; rather "the plebiscite has been the specific means of deriving the legitimacy of authority from the confidence of the ruled, even though the voluntary nature of such confidence is only formal or fictitious."[83] It was only in reference to this type of leadership that Weber used the expression "democratic legitimacy" (that is, legitimized democratic domination).[84]

It was to this type of plebiscitary leadership that Weber looked to offset the power of the bureaucracy and preserve some measure of freedom. He had witnessed, in Wilhelmian Germany, what he saw as the domination of officialdom and the reduction of the popularly elected Parliament to impotence. The Reichstag, Weber explained, was only in a position to register its displeasure with actions of the administration through budgetary measures or other instances of what he called "negative politics."[85] Although the bureaucracy controlled public business, Weber thought that individuals whose lives are oriented toward obeying and implementing rules make poor leaders.[86] He saw this state of affairs—the powerlessness of Parliament and the dominance of officials without leadership qualities—as responsible for Germany's diplomatic defeats before World War I.[87] In order to counterbalance the power of the bureaucracy and provide leadership, Weber recommended institutional reforms that would induce individuals with power instincts to enter the political fray. During the war he advocated constitutional reforms that would enable Parliament to share meaningfully in the work of government by making leading ministerial posts available to its members. Party leaders in Parliament then would have the opportunity to exercise real power, and this position would represent an object of aspiration for ambitious individuals.[88] Later he lost faith in the potential of Parliament to bring forth leaders and invested his hopes in a directly elected president.[89]

Weber's advocacy of strong leadership has generated considerable controversy and prompted questions about the genuineness of his liberal democratic convictions. How do we reconcile his desire to see the rise of powerful leaders with his professed attachment to the ideals of individual rights and freedoms? One answer is that he simply did not think it was possible to dispense with leadership, as we have noted. He did not think it was feasible for citizens to participate in public life on a continuous basis, especially in large states. Most people are preoccupied with the demands of everyday life; thus involvement in politics and the constant devotion to political business do not involve all people equally. Plebiscitary leadership was the one form of rule that was at least marginally democratic, feasible, and, what is most important, able to provide a countervailing force against the trend most threatening to freedom: increasing bureaucratization. In addition, this kind of individual leadership would foster accountability insofar as the plebiscitary leader could be held personally responsible for the consequences of his or her actions.[90] Weber thought that it is the Caesarist element in mass states alone "which guarantees that responsibility toward the public rests with particular individuals."[91] The people remain judges ready to send leaders "to the gallows"—as Weber expressed it in a famous conversation with General Ludendorff—if they fail in the trust invested in them.[92] In significant respects, then, Weber's preference for plebiscitary leaders was consistent with his liberal democratic ideals.

But this explanation of Weber's predilection for energetic leadership is ultimately unsatisfactory, or at least incomplete. Despite his attachment to the ideal of equal freedom, Weber did not share the hostility to leadership characteristic of the pure forms of democracy he described. Neither did he view leadership as a necessary evil. To the contrary, there is a pronounced admiration for creative, goal-setting leadership in Weber's political thought. Politics, as "independent *leadership*" in action,[93] was regarded by him as a lofty vocation and the exercise of power on behalf of outcomes and ideals to which one is devoted in estimable activity. He spoke grandiloquently of politics as giving its practitioner the opportunity to "rise above everyday existence" and hold "in his hands some vital strand of historically important events."[94]

Self-determining freedom was seen by Weber as the ability to "shape the conditions" of one's own life.[95] He associated the strongest experience of the "feeling of freedom" with rationally pursuing purposes through knowledge of adequate means.[96] This kind of freedom to form circumstances, achieve projects through employment of the most adequate means, and also accept responsibility for the consequences of pursuing goals and ideals would necessarily be manifest most fully in the activity of political leadership.[97] Weber's concept of freedom led to an antinomy whereby he admired both the will to rule and the willfulness in the aspiration not to be ruled.[98]

There is another dimension of Weber's advocacy of plebiscitary leadership that requires consideration, however. It is important to be aware that, in Weber's view, it is not only or even primarily democracy that is hostile to leadership. Recall that, for Weber, collective decision-making and administration based on the equality of the participants is characteristic of aristocratic as well as democratic forms, including the rule of notables and collegiality. Shared decision-making, he explained, is also the product of an aristocratic regime. Every socially privileged class fears the type of leader who seeks support in the emotional devotion of the masses, just as much as the type of democracy without leaders fears the rise of "demagogues."[99]

It was the notables in the German political parties, who, along with party officials, in his view, hindered the rise of leaders and harbored resentment against the "demagogue as a *homo novus.*"[100] Plebiscitary leadership, Weber explained, arises in conditions where the party has transformed itself into a machine for canvassing votes and the notables, as in England under Gladstone, have been subdued.[101] The prevalence of notables in German party politics precluded effective support for leaders who would be able to rally the mass of voters. Under the dominance of notables, party leaders were expected to be puppet-like mouthpieces for the party rather than genuine leaders. The continued dominance of notables in party organizations, he averred, "would mean the end of politically and economically progressive democracy for the foreseeable future."[102] What Germany had, he observed, was "rule by the 'clique'" as opposed to "leadership democracy with a machine."[103] It was with the "vanity of notables" in view that Weber spoke of the necessary "spiritual proletarianization" of the following—that is, the party organization—of a plebiscitary leader.[104]

While his advocacy of plebiscitary leadership evinced an aversion to the rule of notables (as well as to bureaucracy), there is no note of the antipathy to mass democracy of which Weber is so often accused. He did not share the distrust of democracy pervasive in the nineteenth and twentieth centuries. The ostensible problem of the "tyranny of the majority," which was given serious and sustained attention by Alexis de Tocqueville (and John Stuart Mill), is in fact absent from Weber's thought. The rule of the majority, which is both a democratic form and a system of domination—and thus could well be classified under "democratic legitimacy"—was disregarded by Weber. A single, brief reference is made to majority rule in the conceptual exposition at the beginning of *Economy and Society*,[105] but the issue is not raised again in the sociology of domination. He also mentioned the problem of parliamentary majorities running affairs wholly in their own interest, but this meant, he clarified, "the majority in parliament . . . not of the people."[106] The fact that Weber creates no category of "majority rule" as a form "democratic legitimacy" is as significant as it is neglected.

In his political writings, Weber deprecated the fear of democracy—and the conservative literati who promoted this fear. This antagonism toward opponents of democracy was given eloquent and virulent expression in his essay "Suffrage and Democracy in Germany," in which he championed the extension of equal suffrage. In lashing out against the opponents of democratization, Weber derided "all the empty phrases used by vested interests to frighten the philistines. . . . Above all, the fear that 'democracy' will destroy our allegedly 'distinguished' (*vornehm*) and hence culturally productive 'traditions,' as well as the supposedly unfathomable wisdom of the allegedly 'aristocratic' strata who rule the state."[107]

Unlike conservative and many liberal thinkers, Weber did not fear that individual freedom was being undermined by the "crowd," the "herd," or the "mob," that together, as was thought by many during this period, would wield tremendous, spirit-crushing power.[108] For Weber, power is regularly exercised by a small number of people who are politically active: "The 'principle of small number' (that is, the superior political maneuverability of *small* leading groups) always rules political action."[109] Thus there is no danger from the majority or the mob associated with extending the suffrage and giving reign to democracy.

Democratic Participation

I have attempted to show that Weber's sociology of domination and his political writings viewed together reveal a liberal democratic outlook. A condition of equal freedom, where no one is advantaged by the ability to enforce their will against others, represented for Weber a standard, in contrast to which domination appeared as a deviation requiring legitimation. However, in keeping with his methodological strictures, the value of liberal democratic freedom is not validated by his empirical analysis, but is only implicit in the perspective from which the material is organized and the criteria for comparison are selected.[110] In addition, his empirical analysis shows that achievements on behalf of freedom are precarious. Domination, it seems, is an inevitable feature of human collective life; and the imposition of will that arises in the human condition, along with the historical trend toward bureaucracy, necessarily limits opportunities for exercising freedom. Plebiscitary leadership, Weber hoped, might prevail against the expanding power of bureaucracy (and also undermine aristocratic tendencies), thus achieving the best approximation of democracy possible in mass states. But his regard for leadership, as indicated above, stood in an "antinomical relationship" with his moral commitment to the value of equal freedom.[111]

The question that begs consideration at this point is whether, given his analysis of the limitations on self-determination, Weber envisaged any role for ordinary people in the political process other than as "occasional politicians" at the ballot box (which is not insignificant). His advocacy of plebiscitary leadership has given rise to the view that he saw no real role for the mass of people in shaping their political destiny and did not, therefore, explore "participatory options" such as activities that would further "power in the workplace."[112] Raymond Aron has suggested that Weber "believed neither in the general will nor in the right of peoples to self-determination nor in the democratic ideology. If he desired a 'parliamentarization' of the German government, it was, if we are to go by his writings, as a way of improving the recruiting of leaders rather than as a matter of principle."[113]

To be sure, Weber rejected the idea of the "general will." A collectivity is an abstraction, not a real entity, and to impute a will to it is to indulge in myth-making.[114] He did, however, conceive that there are common interests of a people as a whole and hoped precisely that the plebiscitary leader might rise above sectional and special interests to represent wider issues.[115] Indeed the "national interest," with which Weber was so famously concerned, represents the interest of a people as a whole. Still, though he saw the plebiscitary leader as potentially representing broad interests, Weber made no pretense that the quality of dominance does not inhere in the act of legislating and enacting policies, even if these measures reflect the desires of the people and advance the common good. In contrast to the originator of the concept of the "general will," Jean Jacques Rousseau, Weber envisaged no feasible or durable way of reconciling freedom and rule in such a way that authoritative commands reflect the "real" will of each member of the community.[116]

Weber's skepticism about collective agency and the possibility of ending domination did not, however, rule out his considering possibilities for democratic participation. In fact he did explore options for such participation within the limits of the human condition and the historical limitations he perceived. He constantly urged that members of the political community be treated as self-determining agents rather than objects of rule and thus at least share in shaping their collective destiny. "There are only two choices," he asserted,

either the mass of citizens is left without freedom or rights in a bureaucratic, "authoritarian state" which has only the appearance of parliamentary rule, and in which citizens are "administered" like a herd of cattle; or the citizens are integrated into the state by making them its *co-rulers*.[117]

I will briefly consider two possibilities for public involvement that Weber encouraged, both of which evince his desire to see the mass of ordinary human beings afforded some opportunity to participate in the direction of their affairs. First, Weber avidly supported the efforts of working people to strive for self-determination through the trade unions. He admired the trade unions for "taking the education of the masses in hand"[118] and providing a forum for the assertion of the workers' demands. Consistent with his high regard for this vehicle of independent bargaining power, he adamantly opposed legal restrictions on the trade unions. He also denounced Bismarck for having suppressed the unions, which, he maintained, would have enabled the workers to "represent their interests in an objective and confident way."[119] Bismarck, Weber disparagingly observed, made only paternalistic state offerings rather than allowing people the opportunity to secure their own interests.[120]

In a memorandum on issues of policy, Weber expressed his views of the salutary effects of the unions from the standpoint of fostering political participation and active citizenship:

There is no doubt a basic presumption for us in the area of the worker's question: We reject, partly in principle and partly as inadequate, the point of view of master rule or patriarchalism, the bonds of welfare institutions and those who would treat the worker as an object for bureaucratic regulation, and insurance legislation that merely creates dependency. We affirm the equal participation of the workers in the collective determination of working conditions, and to this end we also affirm the strengthening of their organizations, which spearhead this effort; we see the comradeliness and class dignity that develops in this way as a positive cultural value . . . we want to live in a land of citizens, not of subjects.[121]

A second, more indirect, avenue of public involvement Weber envisaged was through the right of parliamentary inquiry. As noted above, he believed that knowledge forms the mainstay of bureaucratic power. Bureaucracy is based on technical knowledge acquired in specialized training. However, this technical know-how "by itself," he suggested, is not "sufficient to ensure [the bureaucracy] a position of extraordinary power."[122] The extension and entrenchment of bureaucratic power rests on additional knowledge gained through the experience of regularly conducting public business and access to official information that is protected from outside control "by means of the infamous concept of the 'official secrecy.'"[123] The establishment of parliamentary commissions of inquiry would, he thought, thwart the bureaucracy's efforts to protect itself from supervision and ensure public access to information, which the administration would otherwise try to monopolize. Such a change would also entail the transformation of the Reichstag into a genuine working Parliament with active committees exercising continuous control over the government. Weber anticipated extending this right of inquiry to minorities in Parliament.[124]

Aside from curtailing the power of bureaucracy, Weber thought that supervising the bureaucracy through commissions of inquiry would exert an educative influence on the public at large. The "high level of political education" in Britain was due, Weber suggested, to "the way in which the proceedings of these committees are followed by the English press and public alike."[125] Weber regretfully observed that under Bismarck his nation had lost the habit of concerning itself with public affairs.[126] He urged measures that would provide a "political education" and enhance "political maturity," enabling citizens to play a more active role in shaping the conditions of their collective life. The publicity resulting from parliamentary commissions of inquiry represented, for him, an important means of engendering popular sophistication about public business and keeping people "well informed about how its officials are conducting their affairs."[127]

The promotion of popular involvement along these two avenues was consistent with Weber's aim of preserving the greatest possible measure of individual freedom and civic participation in the face of reemergent authority. It is vitally important, he exclaimed, "for liberalism to understand that its vocation still lies with the struggle against both bureaucratic and Jacobin *centralism*, and in working to spread the old, fundamental, individualist notion of 'inalienable human rights' amongst the masses."[128]

Notes

1. Max Weber, *Economy and Society: An Outline of Interpretive Sociology*, ed. Guenther Roth and Claus Wittich (1921–22; Berkeley: University of California Press, 1978), p. 292. Two particularly good articles on Weber and democracy bring attention to this point. See J. J. R. Thomas, "Weber and Direct Democracy," *British Journal of Sociology* 35, no. 2 (November 1984): 216–40; and Stefan Breuer, "The Concept of Democracy in Weber's Sociology," in Ralph Schroeder, ed., *Max Weber, Democracy and Modernization* (New York: St. Martin's Press, 1998), pp. 1–13.

2. See Weber, *Economy and Society*, p. 949.

3. Ibid., p. 946.

4. Ibid., pp. 52–53.

5. Ibid., p. 212.

6. Ibid., p. 946.

7. Ibid., p. 214.

8. Ibid., pp. 947 and 212; see also Max Weber, *Political Writings*, ed. Peter Lassman and Ronald Spiers (Cambridge: Cambridge University Press, 1994), p. 312.

9. Weber, *Economy and Society*, pp. 953 and 213; see also Weber, *Political Writings*, p. 312.

10. Weber, *Economy and Society*, pp. 215–17.

11. Ibid., p. 227.

12. Ibid., pp. 216 and 1112.

13. Ibid., p. 216; Weber, *Political Writings*, p. 312.

14. Wolfgang J. Mommsen, *The Political and Social Theory of Max Weber* (Chicago: University of Chicago Press, 1989), p. 21.

15. Weber used the terms *nonlegitimate (nichtlegitime) domination* and *illegitimate (illegitime) domination* in his own restricted sense to refer to conditions where legitimate power has been usurped in a revolutionary manner.

16. See Weber, *Economy and Society*, p. 214; Weber, *Political Writings*, p. 165.

17. Weber, *Economy and Society*, p. 954.

18. Guenther Roth, "Introduction" to Weber, *Economy and Society*, p. xcvi.

19. Weber, *Economy and Society*, p. 953, see also p. 491; and Max Weber, *From Max Weber: Essays in Sociology*, trans. and ed. Hans H. Gerth and C. Wright Mills (New York: Oxford University Press, 1946), p. 271

20. Weber, *Economy and Society*, p. 953.

21. This idea that rule is a created rather than a natural condition was first elaborated by the exponents of what is known as "social contract theory," Thomas Hobbes and John Locke. According to this view, systems of rule are created in order to better secure the natural rights to life and to freely pursue individual desires and goals. For Weber, to be sure, rights are not "natural." In his view, the idea of the free individual with certain rights resulted from historical developments. Still, the condition of equal freedom represented, for Weber, a standard in terms of which other forms of human association were seen as a deviation.

22. Weber's commentators who fault him for not giving fuller consideration to democracy as a "legitimate" form of governance miss this point. Ironically, in view of his implied assumption that democracy is not in need of legitimation, Weber arguably regarded democracy as "legitimate" in the normative sense in which his critics use the word. In his famous essay on Weber, Leo Strauss, another practitioner of nominalist irony whose real meaning is obscured by his unconventional use of words, criticized Weber on just this point. Strauss reproached Weber not for failing to defend "natural right" but for taking for granted that "natural right . . . presupposes the natural equality of all men." Leo Strauss, *Natural Right and History* (Chicago: University of Chicago Press, 1953), p. 58. In the classics, on the other hand, Strauss explained, "natural right" meant the right of those superior by nature to be the ruler of others. Strauss, *Natural Right*, pp. 134–35.

23. This typology includes rule by the one, the few, and the many on behalf of the common interest—kingship, aristocracy, and constitution—and the perversions of these forms of rule—tyranny, oligarchy, and democracy—which represent rule with a view to the private interest of the ruler. Aristotle, *Politics*, book III, chapter 7.

24. See Thomas, "Weber and Direct Democracy," pp. 218 and 225.

25. Max Weber, *Gesamtausgabe*, Vol. II / 5: *Briefe 1906–1908*, ed. Rainer Lepsius and Wolfgang Mommsen (Tübingen: J. C. B. Mohr, 1990), p. 616.

26. Roth, "Introduction" to Weber, *Economy and Society*, lxv–lxvi.

27. Weber, *Economy and Society*, p. 292; Max Weber, *Wirtschaft und Gesellschaft: Grundiss der verstehenden Soziologie*, 4th rev. ed., ed. Johannes Winkelmann (Tübingen: J. C. B. Mohr, 1980), p. 171.

28. Weber, *Economy and Society*, p. 290.

29. Ibid., pp. 289 and 948.

30. Ibid., pp. 290 and 948.

31. Ibid.

32. Ibid., pp. 290–91 and 949–52.

33. Ibid., pp. 290–91; Weber, *Political Writings*, pp. 276, 318–19.

34. Weber, *Economy and Society*, p. 292.

35. Ibid., pp. 292 and 951.

36. Ibid., pp. 291 and 951.

37. Ibid., p. 949.

38. Ibid., pp. 1236–43. The Mediterranean cities of antiquity were regarded by Weber as transitional types since many citizens remained aristocratic rural landholders; see p. 1240.

39. Ibid., pp. 1226–34.

40. Ibid., p. 1228.

41. Ibid., pp. 1241–48, 1249.

42. Ibid., pp. 1260–62.

43. Ibid., p. 1250.

44. Ibid., p. 1239.

45. Ibid., p. 953–54.

46. Ibid, p. 1234 n. 1.

47. Ibid., p. 1246.

48. Ibid., p. 1247.

49. Ibid., p. 54.

50. Max Weber, *From Max Weber: Essays in Sociology*, trans. and ed. Hans H. Gerth and C. Wright Mills (New York: Oxford University Press, 1946), pp. 302–22.

51. Weber, *Economy and Society*, p. 1206.

52. Ibid., p. 1204.

53. Ibid., p. 1208.

54. Ibid., p. 1209.

55. Ibid.

56. Ibid.

57. Ibid., p. 321.

58. Weber, *Political Writings*, p. 159; Max Weber, *The Protestant Ethic and the Spirit of Capitalism*, trans. Talcott Parsons (New York: Charles Scribner's Sons, 1958), p. 245 n. 118.

59. Max Weber, *The Methodology of the Social Sciences*, trans. and ed. Edward Shils and Henry Finch (New York: Free Press, 1949), p. 54.

60. The gravitational pull toward authority is connected with what Weber characterized as a "settled orientation of *man* for observing the accustomed rules and regulations." Weber, *Economy and Society*, p. 988; cf. p. 1108. An interesting comparison in this regard is Dostoyevsky's account of the Grand Inquisitor, an image that Weber alludes to in "Politics as a Vocation" (*Political Writings*, pp. 361–62). The Grand Inquisitor chastises Jesus, who has just returned after fifteen centuries, for burdening humankind with freedom. "We have corrected Thy work," the Grand Inquisitor admonishes, "and have founded it upon *miracle, mystery* and *authority*. And men rejoiced that they were again led like sheep, and that the terrible gift that had brought them

much suffering, was, at last, lifted from their hearts." Fyodor Dostoyevsky, *The Brothers Karamazov*, trans. Constance Garnett (New York: Random House, 1950), p. 305.

61. Weber, *Political Writings*, pp. 68–69.

62. Ibid., p. 219.

63. For example, just because I have agreed to the enactment of a general rule does not mean that an imposition of will does not occur when that rule is applied to me by the bureaucratic staff.

64. Weber, *Economy and Society*, p. 225.

65. Ibid., pp. 218–23.

66. Richard Wolin, "Liberalism as a Vocation: On the Life and Politics of Max Weber," *New Republic*, September 2, 1996, pp. 34–40, which is a review of the book by John Patrick Diggins, *Max Weber: Politics and the Spirit of Tragedy* (New York: Basic Books, 1996).

67. Weber, *Economy and Society*, pp. 226, 998, 1209; Weber, *Political Writings*, p. 322.

68. Weber, *Economy and Society*, pp. 979–80.

69. Ibid., p. 991.

70. Regina F. Titunik, "The Continuation of History: Max Weber on the Advent of a New Aristocracy," *Journal of Politics* 59, no. 3 (1997): 680–700.

71. Weber, *Economy and Society*, p. 999.

72. Weber, *Political Writings*, p. 83; see also Weber, *Economy and Society*, p. 344.

73. Weber, *Economy and Society*, p. 986; see also Weber, *Political Writings*, p. 222.

74. Weber, *Economy and Society*, p. 985.

75. Weber, *Political Writings*, p. 368.

76. Ibid., pp. 158–59.

77. Ibid., p. 159.

78. Weber, *Gesamtausgabe*, Vol. II / 5: *Briefe 1906–1908*, p. 616; see also *Political Writings*, p. 71.

79. Weber, *Economy and Society*, pp. 266–301.

80. Ibid., pp. 266–67.

81. Ibid., p. 267.

82. Ibid., p. 268.

83. Ibid., p. 267.

84. Ibid., p. 267; see Breuer, "The Concept of Democracy," in Schroeder, *Max Weber*, p. 2.

85. Weber, *Political Writings*, pp. 165, 177.

86. Ibid., pp. 160–61, 204, 330–31.

87. Ibid., pp. 204–6.

88. Ibid., pp. 172, 176.

89. Ibid., pp. 304–8, 351; David Beetham, *Max Weber and the Theory of Modern Politics* (Cambridge: Polity Press, 1985), pp. 232–34.

90. Weber, *Political Writings*, p. 331.

91. Ibid., p. 174.

92. Marianne Weber, *A Biography*, trans. Harry Zohn, with a new introduction by Guenther Roth (1926; New Brunswick, NJ: Transaction Books, 1988), p. 653; Weber, *Political Writings*, p. 305.

93. Weber, *Political Writings*, p. 309.

94. Ibid., p. 352.

95. Weber, *Economy and Society*, p. 729.

96. Weber, *Methodology*, p. 124.

97. Edward Portis has convincingly argued that for Weber the activity of politics represented the highest form of a fully human existence. See *Max Weber and Political Commitment*, (Philadelphia: Temple University Press, 1986).

98. In regard to the latter, see Weber, *Political Writings*, p. 69.

99. Weber, *Economy and Society*, p. 279.

100. Weber, *Political Writings*, p. 340.

101. Ibid., p. 342.

102. Ibid., p. 306; see also p. 177.

103. Ibid., p. 351.

104. Ibid.; see also p. 182.

105. Weber, *Economy and Society*, p. 51.

106. Weber, *Political Writings*, p. 307; see also p. 185.

107. Ibid., p. 107.

108. These were common ideas associated most notably with Nietzsche (and also Gustave Le Bon). These ideas would later culminate in Ortega y Gasset's influential *The Revolt of the Masses*. Although Weber mentioned Gustav Le Bon at the beginning of *Economy and Society* (p. 23) and gave intermittent, respectful attention to Nietzsche, he did not pursue this line of thought.

109. Weber, *Political Writings*, p. 174.

110. See Weber, *Methodology*, p. 90.

111. See Mommsen, *Political and Social Theory*, p. 34.

112. Mark Warren, "Max Weber's Liberalism for a Nietzschean World," *American Political Science Review* 82 (1988): 46.

113. Raymond Aron, *Main Current in Sociological Thought*, vol. 2, trans. Richard Howard and Helen Weaver (Garden City, NY: Anchor Books, Doubleday, 1967), p. 247.

114. See Weber, *Gesamtausgabe*, Vol. II / 5: *Briefe 1906–1908*, p. 615. He also, and with greater vigor, assailed the idea of a *Volksgeist*, which was a romanticist variation of the general will, and denounced treating such a concept as "a real, uniform entity which has a metaphysical status." Max Weber, *Roscher and Knies*, trans. Guy Oakes (New York: Free Press, 1975), p. 61.

115. Beetham, *Max Weber*, p. 228.

116. Rule and freedom are reconciled, for Rousseau, through "a form of association which will defend and protect with the whole common force the person and goods of each associate, and in which each, while uniting himself with all, may still obey himself alone, and remain as free as before." It is through the "social contract," which actualizes the "general will," that the individual both obeys rule and remains free. See Jean-Jacques Rousseau, "The Social Contract and Discourses," trans. G. D. H. Cole (London: J. M. Dent and Sons, 1947), pp. 12–13. Weber detected an authoritarian tendency in Rousseau's outlook and contended that "freedom from compulsion" is unknown "to Rousseau's social contract" (*Economy and Society*, p. 1209).

117. Weber, *Political Writings*, p. 129; see also p. 69.

118. Max Weber, *Gesammelte Aufsätze zur Soziologie und Sozialpolitik*, 2nd ed., ed. Marianne Weber (Tübingen: J. C. B. Mohr, 1988), p. 398.

119. Weber, *Political Writings*, p. 143.

120. Ibid.

121. Quoted in Wolfgang Mommsen, *Max Weber and German Politics, 1890–1920*, trans. Michael Steinberg (Chicago: University of Chicago Press, 1984), p. 120.

122. Weber, *Economy and Society*, p. 225.

123. Weber, *Political Writings*, p. 179; Weber, *Economy and Society*, p. 225.

124. Weber, *Political Writings*, p. 185. It was in this connection that he claimed it was necessary to prevent parliamentary majorities from running affairs wholly in their own interest.

125. Ibid., pp. 179–80.

126. Ibid., p. 173.

127. Ibid., p. 180; see also Regina F. Titunik, "Status, Vanity and Equal Dignity in Max Weber's Political Thought," *Economy and Society* 24, no. 1 (1995): 101–21.

128. Weber, *Political Writings*, p. 68.

Religious Communities and the Path to Disenchantment

The Origins, Sources, and Theoretical Core of the Religion Section

Origins of the Section

Economy and Society has a prehistory that has only gradually come to light.[1] In her preface to the second part of the work, Marianne Weber commented that, with the exception of some later additions, Max Weber composed the manuscripts on which *Economy and Society* is based in the years 1911–13.[2] The philological reconstruction of the composition, as described by Wolfgang J. Mommsen in Chapter 3 of this volume, corroborates 1911–13 as the date also for its section on religion. The literature that Weber references in this section supports this dating since it includes no publications after 1913.[3] Indeed, Weber's first outline, from 1910, of the *Handbook of Political Economy*, for which "Economy and Society" was intended as one piece, lacked a separate section on religion. At this early stage, Weber merely planned a section entitled "Economy and Culture (Critique of Historical Materialism)."[4]

Yet this plan was to change in the years ahead. A clear indication of this appears in a letter dated July 3, 1913, in which Weber thanked his longtime friend Heinrich Rickert for an offprint and added that he would soon return the favor by sending him the manuscript of "my systematics of religion." In late November of the same year, Weber repeated this, telling Rickert that he would like to send his "(empirical) casuistry of contemplation and active religion," but the manuscript was only three-quarters typed. Then, on December 30, 1913, Weber informed his publisher, Paul Siebeck, that he had finished an exposition relating all major forms of community to economy: the family, the domestic community, the commercial enterprise, the clan, the ethnic community, and religion. In brackets Weber explained what could be expected from the segment of the manuscript on religion: "comprising all great religions of the earth, a sociology of the doctrines of salvation and of the various religious ethics—similar to Troeltsch, however now for all religions, only much more concise." In an outline of the content of the entire *Handbook* project that appeared in 1914,[5] Weber projected that his own contribution, now called "The Economy and the Social Orders and Powers," would consist of various sections on communities, organized as follows: "Household, Oikos, Enterprise," "Neighborhood, Kinship Group, Local Community," "Ethnic Communities," and finally "Religious Communities." Weber clarified the last item with the further title "The Class Basis of the Religions; Cultural Religions and Economic Orientation."[6] As presented in this announcement, Weber's topics and order of treatment correspond roughly to the manuscript he had described to Siebeck in December 1913 and to the German text of *Economy and Society* published in 1921–22.

The First World War, however, thwarted all plans for rapid publication of the manuscript. So it was not until after the war that Weber resumed these plans, amid many other activities. The latter included the composition of the "first part" of *Economy and Society*, a text in which he twice anticipates a later section on the sociology of religion.[7] But by this point, what Weber had in mind was no longer his 1913 manuscript but a revised version of it. Despite his (unrealized) intention to undertake a revision, however, Marianne Weber later decided that the earlier manuscript was suitable for posthumous publication. With the support of Melchior Palyi, she edited this as the "second part" of Max Weber's *Economy and Society*. In her understanding, while Weber devoted the "first part" of *Economy and Society* to the formation of types and concepts, the earlier manuscript dealt mainly with empirical cases. For this reason, she felt that the earlier manuscript furnished a concrete sociology that would complement the abstract sociology in the "first part" of *Economy and Society*.[8] In combining the two parts in this manner, however, Marianne Weber concealed the circumstance that the "second part" reflected an earlier stage in Weber's thinking. For that reason, the new German critical edition of Weber's work alters the title of this section, replacing "Sociology of Religion" with the title "Religious Communities," as used in Max Weber's outline of 1914.

BRIDGING FROM *The Protestant Ethic and the Spirit of Capitalism* (1904–5) TO *The Economic Ethics of the World Religions* (1915–20)

The changes evident in Weber's 1914 outline, when compared with that of 1910, reflected his growing interest in the history of world religions. In Weber's view, his 1904–5 thesis about the Puritan origins of the methodical pattern of life conduct that encouraged the development of Western capitalism was an argument that had withstood all objections raised in the heated scholarly debate that followed the publication of *The Protestant Ethic and the Spirit of Capitalism.*[9] Nonetheless, after 1910, Weber wanted "to correct the isolation of this study and to place it in relation to the whole of cultural development."[10]

In her biography of her husband, Marianne Weber gives some valuable particulars about this shift in Max Weber's thought.

When around 1911 he resumed his studies on the sociology of religion, he was attracted to the Orient—to China, Japan, and India—then to Judaism and Islam. He now wanted to investigate the relationship of the five great world religions to economic ethics. His study was to come full circle with an analysis of early Christianity. And while in his first treatise on the spirit of capitalism Weber expressly set out to illuminate only one causal sequence, namely, the influence of religious elements of consciousness on everyday economic life, he now undertook the larger task as well—namely, the investigation of the influence of the material, economic, and geographical conditions of the various spheres of culture with a view to their religious and ethical ideas.[11]

The segment of the 1913 manuscript "Religious Communities" was an early outcome of this effort. In composing it, Weber drew (as his direct and indirect quotations reveal) on a profound study of comparative religion: Buddhism, Christianity, Hinduism, Islam, Judaism, Confucianism, Taoism, and Zoroastrianism, as well as tribal, ancient, and Hellenic religions.[12] What is more, although Weber subsequently published separate studies of some of these religions in *The Economic Ethics of the World Religions* (1915–20), he did not see these other studies as standing alone; he conceived of them, rather, as "preliminary studies and annotations to the *systematic* sociology of religions."[13] Thus, in 1915, when the first of these studies, *The Religion of China*, appeared, Weber pointed out that it was designed to be published at the same time as *Economy and Society* and "to interpret and complement the section on the sociology of religion (and, however, to be interpreted by it in many points)."[14] Likewise, in 1919, when Weber reworked the text of *The Protestant Ethic and the Spirit of Capitalism* for inclusion, along with the studies that constituted *The Economic Ethics of the World Religions*, in his *Gesammelte Aufsätze zur Religionssoziologie (Collected Papers on the Sociology of Religions)*, he added that he hoped to treat ethnographic material when systematically revising the sociology of religion.[15] Even at this late date, Weber viewed this section (now in its projected revised form) as a bridge between *The Protestant Ethic* and his subsequent historical studies of the ethic of world religions, emphasizing again how issues of "systematics" were crucial for his purpose.[16]

WEBER'S MAJOR DISCOVERY: THE PROCESS OF DISENCHANTMENT

While pursuing his research on the world religions, Weber had made an exciting discovery, recounted as follows by Marianne Weber:

The process of *rationalization* dissolves magical notions and increasingly "disenchants" the world and renders it godless. Religion changes from magic to doctrine. And now, after the disintegration of the primitive image of the world, there appear two tendencies: a tendency towards the *rational* mastery of the world on the one hand and one towards *mystical* experience on the other. But not only the religions receive their stamp from the increasing development of thought; the process of rationalization moves on several tracks, and its autonomous development encompasses all creations of civilization—the economy, the state, law, science, and art. All forms of *Western* culture in particular are decisively determined by a methodical *way of thinking* that was first developed by the Greeks, and this way of thinking was joined in the Age of Reformation by a methodical *conduct of life* that was oriented to certain purposes. It was this union of a theoretical and a practical rationalism that separated modern culture from ancient culture, and the special character of both separated modern Western culture from Asiatic culture. To be sure, there were processes of rationalization in the Orient as well, but neither the scientific, the political, the economic, nor the artistic kind took the course that is peculiar to the Occident.[17]

For Max Weber, the significance of this discovery was tremendous, as Marianne Weber explained:

Weber regarded this recognition of the special character of occidental *rationalism* and the role it was given to play for Western culture as one of his most important discoveries. As a result, his original inquiry into the relationship between religion and economics expanded into an even more comprehensive inquiry into the *special nature of all of Western culture*.[18]

From this point onward, "disenchantment"—understood as the development *not* (as Marianne Weber implies) of a godless world, but of a world in which the gods lose their former cosmological roots—became a process that figured centrally in Weber's thinking about religion. Indeed, the notion "disenchantment" surfaced for the first time in the same year (1913) in an essay where Weber explained the fundamentals of his theory of action.[19] Thereafter, he constructed the whole "Religious Communities" section of *Economy and Society* around this concept.

Pivotal passages in this section, written to depict the historical process of religious development, including its beginning and its end, effectively encapsulate Weber's view of this course of historical development. According to Weber, at the beginning of the historical process, "only the things or events that actually exist or take place played a role in life"; but this situation did not last. Early on, with the rise of the magician, an important change set in: "Now certain experiences, of a different order in that they only signify something, also play a role. Thus magic is transformed from a direct manipulation of forces into a *symbolic activity*."[20] Likewise, describing the end of the process, Weber writes:"intellectualism suppresses belief in magic, the world's processes become disenchanted, lose their magical significance, and henceforth simply 'are' and 'happen' but no longer signify anything."[21] It was this historical development that, in Weber's judgment, divested the world of inherent meaning and ultimately transformed religion into a separate realm of its own. The same process also profoundly affected the religions of the world in and of themselves.

Intellectual-Historical Sources: Available Paradigms in the Comparative Study of Religions

Behind Weber's claim that the rationality of modern culture emerged as the result of a historical process in which religion was involved lay two new paradigms that had gained acceptance among scholars in religious studies after 1900: in England "pre-animism" replaced the previous scheme of religious evolutionism, while in Germany a new type of historiography focused on the various attitudes toward the world that different religions generated. Both paradigms offered reconstructions of the data of religious history that proved extremely helpful to Max Weber's project.

In terms of the first, Robert Ranulph Marett's paper "Pre-animistic Religion," delivered in 1899 to the British Anthropological Society, dealt a deathblow to Edward Burnett Tylor's evolutionary approach and quickly established a powerful new paradigm in religious studies.[22] According to Tylor, "animism" was an early mode of thought that explained natural events by the activity of spiritual beings;[23] as such, it was a mode of thought that, over the course of history, gave way step-by-step to science—though not entirely, since it survived as the notion of an immaterial personal soul.[24] For Tylor, "survival" was thus the category that accounted for the continuity between primitive culture and fully developed civilized cultures.[25] It was Marett's position, however, that Tylor's concepts of animism as a belief in souls and of primitive religion more generally were "too narrow, because [they were] too intellectualistic." Averring that "religion involves more than thought, namely feeling and will as well,"[26] Marett claimed that an experience of unfathomable powers lay at the root of religions in the past as well as in the present—that is, that a feeling of awe drives human beings into personal relations with the supernatural before they can think or theorize about it.[27] From Marett's perspective, then, the origins of religion derived not from an intellectual need for explanation, but from a primordial experience of uncertainty and dependence, an experience that persists in the modern world. Opening new possibilities for understanding contemporary culture, this perspective had over Tylor's the advantage of facilitating the explanation of modern cultural facts by reference to an ongoing religious history.[28] Max

Weber embraced Marett's approach, as most other scholars of religion did.[29]
The second new scholarly paradigm derived from German scholarship.
This paradigm was the site of an "Orientalist" perspective that differed from
the Orientalism famously described by Edward Said.[30] Said's analysis presents
Orientalist thought as inherently connected to the practices of British colonialism. Significantly, however, this treatment of Orientalism omits the work
of German Orientalists, which Georg Stauth has found to be a body of
thought tied not to colonialism but engaged instead with religious meanings
and their subjective appropriation.[31] In Weber's time, the public forum for
the German Orientalists was a series edited by Paul Hinneberg entitled *Die
Kultur der Gegenwart* (*Contemporary Culture*), which in 1906 issued two important collections, one on Oriental religions, the other on Christianity as
well as Israel and Judaism. Some of the eminent scholars who contributed to
these volumes subsequently became sources for Weber's "Religious Communities": most notably, Julius Wellhausen (1848–1918) on Israel and Judaism; Ignaz Goldziher (1850–1921) on Islam; and Hermann Oldenberg
(1854–1920) on Hinduism and Buddhism.

This group of German Orientalists, whose perspective Weber adopted,
conceived of religions as driving forces that established among their adher-
ents either positive or negative attitudes toward "the world." Wellhausen's
Die israelitisch-jüdische Religion developed this view in conjunction with a
new account of the history of ancient Israel and Judaism.[32] According to
Wellhausen, critical analysis of the Bible revealed that the fifth book of
Moses, Deuteronomy, was the book found in 621 B.C. in the temple in
Jerusalem; this book required the worship of Yahweh exclusively in
Jerusalem and demanded the destruction of all other places of cultic worship
outside of Jerusalem. Before this time, biblical prophets such as Amos had already proclaimed that idolatrous practices were the reason for Yahweh's
anger toward Israel and that pleasing Yahweh required loyalty and obedience
toward his commandments rather than sacrifices. When Judah was threatened with military defeat, however, this message was accepted by the king
and priests since it offered an explanation for Israel's fate. Henceforth, in
Wellhausen's view, ethics defined the true Jew. In this way, Wellhausen in-
verted the biblical sequence of law and prophecy, holding that prophets
came first, then the law, as historical developments in ancient Israel transformed an open religious community into a scrupulously legalistic one. Nor
was this the end of these developments. For, in their aftermath, there existed
righteous believers who obeyed God's laws yet still experienced suffering—
a paradoxical situation that raised for believers new challenges and stimulated
the rise of theodicy and eschatology. These aspects of Wellhausen's account
had an important bearing on Weber's "Religious Communities," in particular with regard to his understanding of the relation between ethics and

prophecy and of the problem of theodicy.

When Weber addressed Islamic history, his major authority was the Hungarian cosmopolitan scholar Ignaz Goldziher, especially his *Vorlesungen über den Islam* (*Lectures on Islam*).[33] In his contribution to Hinneberg's series, Goldziher sketched a series of developments using concepts similar to those of Wellhausen, although the story he narrated was entirely different.[34] It was a story of rivalry, since, according to Goldziher, Islam developed its own characteristics in competition with Judaism and Christianity. During its rise, Islam was surrounded by Christian ideas of asceticism and world-rejection. Subsequently, however, these ideas were discarded as Islam became a religion of war and conquest, aimed at ruling the world.[35] Its one-sided emphasis on conquest, however, provoked opposition from Sufis who resisted a purely legal and political Islam and established asceticism as a highly respected form of voluntary piety.[36] As he had accepted Wellhausen's views of Judaism, Weber accepted Goldziher's reconstruction of the internal dynamics of Islamic history, locating Islam as a religion of warriors as opposed to a religion of world-rejection.[37]

Weber relied as well on the research of Hermann Oldenberg. According to Oldenberg's *Indian Religion* (1906), the gods in early India were simply personified powers of nature.[38] This primordial view ceased, however, when the necessities of social life required gods who would protect law and morals. These later gods were approachable, moreover, not only through sacrifice and prayer, but also through magic—a force that was presumed to intervene directly in the course of events. From cosmological speculation about the efficacy of both sacrifice and magic, there then arose the notion of Brahman, understood as the unchanging essence of the universe, an essence that is also present in the individual (as Atman). Combined with the belief that the transmigration of the soul is dependent upon its karma, these notions formed, according to Oldenberg, the matrix on which Jainism and Buddhism emerged as religions of world-rejection.

These contributions to Hinneberg's series reveal a particularly German point of view for reconstructing religious history. The German Orientalists retrieved from their sources the worldviews and the ethics of various religions and presented these as constitutive of human subjects and their practices. Similar ideas informed the work of contemporary German philosophers. Hermann Siebeck, for example, in an 1893 textbook, divided historical religions into three categories: natural religions, which considered gods saviors from external evil; morality religions, which viewed gods as guarantors of social norms and upheld a positive attitude toward the world; and salvation religions, which postulated a contradiction between the existence of God and the reality of evil in the world and fostered an attitude of world-rejection .[39] Siebeck's schema depended on an understanding of religion in terms of world-rejection, a concept of great use to Weber.

MODERN INSTITUTIONS DERIVED FROM RELIGIOUS HISTORY

Weber was not the only German scholar of his time to link research on religious history to the analysis of modern Western culture. Doing so became a widely appealing undertaking to German scholars in light of their tendency to reject the idea that history was governed by objective natural laws and to prefer, instead, a focus on history's subjective, cultural dimension. From this point of view, not only capitalism but other modern institutions as well demanded explanations that took account of the beliefs of the actors involved. Accordingly, leading German scholars came to incorporate religion in their analyses of the development of modern social institutions, downplaying the role of the Enlightenment in shaping modern culture.[40]

There is no better opportunity to observe this approach in action than to read the minutes of the first official meeting of German social scientists, which was held in Frankfurt in 1910. At this event, Ernst Troeltsch argued that Christianity had generated three social forms: first, the church, an organization administering the means of salvation (for Troeltsch, this was the most powerful type); second, the voluntary sect, a community of committed believers; and third, mysticism, the embodiment of radical individualism.[41] According to Troeltsch, this plurality of social forms was a consequence of the fact that Christianity based its principles on Stoicism, which distinguished the ideal of mankind ruled by reason as the embodiment of perfect natural law from a relative natural law that required ethical control of emotions and passions. Confronted with the challenge of living according to the realities of this world while upholding faith in the coming kingdom of God, the Christian "church" adopted this Stoic distinction between an absolute and a relative natural law.[42] In contrast, "sects" rejected the relative view of natural law and recognized nothing other than the severe ethical requirements of Jesus in his Sermon on the Mount. Finally, "mysticism" denied the inherent validity of the natural order on principle and relied on an interior divine light. By means of this analysis, Troeltsch sought to make sense of the different practical attitudes toward the world that Christianity had generated throughout Western history and which shaped modern culture.

Troeltsch's argument immediately set off a heated debate among Ferdinand Tönnies, Georg Simmel, Eberhard Gothein, Martin Buber, Hermann Kantorowicz, and Max Weber himself. In this debate, Weber clarified issues that would become central in "Religious Communities." First, he opposed Tönnies, who had argued that the various social forms of Christianity derived from their dependence on different economic classes. Weber rejected this idea, holding that religious antagonisms were never caused by economic antagonisms. Second, Weber accepted the three types of religious forms that

Troeltsch outlined, albeit with the qualification that, in reality, these three generally occurred in mixed forms. He also disputed Troeltsch's assertion that the church had been a greater social power than sects in spreading Christianity.[43] Here, Weber cited the example of the United States—the country he considered most religious in terms of numbers of believers and their level of commitment—where Christianity became strong and popular because it was organized by sects and not churches.[44] Finally, Weber reacted to Georg Simmel, who had voiced doubt that Christianity could assume any effective *social* form given its indifference to secular issues and its concern with the intimate relation between the soul and God.[45] Martin Buber urged a similar point, rejecting mysticism as a social form and identifying it as a purely psychological form.[46] Responding to both, Weber observed that even a world-rejecting religion involves practices to prove one's convictions that necessarily infuse religion with a social dimension. This is a point that echoes through Weber's later work in its emphasis on the tremendous impact of world-rejecting religions on modern attitudes toward the world.

The Theoretical Core of the Section

DISSECTING THE CONCEPT OF ACTION

To incorporate the history of religions into his project, Weber felt the necessity to include and to dissect the concept of "action." While working on the text of "Religious Communities" in 1913, he published "Categories of Interpretive Sociology," which (as he explained in a footnote) he hoped would provide "a systematic basis for substantive investigations" (including those in *Economy and Society*).[47] In the same footnote, Weber declared that he intended "to separate sharply subjectively intended meaning from objectively valid meaning (thereby deviating somewhat from Simmel's method)." Years later in the first part of *Economy and Society* he repeated the point: "[t]he present work departs from Simmel's method . . . in drawing a sharp distinction between subjectively intended and objectively valid "meaning," two different things which Simmel not only fails to distinguish but often deliberately treats as belonging together."[48]

Building on this distinction, Weber writes: "Action (including intentional omission and acquiescence) is always intelligible behavior towards objects, behavior whose 'actual' or 'intended' *subjective meaning* may be more or less clear to the actor, whether consciously noted or not."[49] Weber recognized that Simmel, too, had distinguished between the task of understanding the meaning of an action and understanding an actor's motives; but Simmel had not adhered to this distinction. Consequently, like other representatives of vitalism, Simmel assumed that religions have their roots in an irrational dimension of human life[50]—a claim central to what later became known as "phenomenology of religion," one of the master paradigms in twentieth-century religious studies. This was, however, a view Weber rejected. According to him, religions provide actors with categories of meaning. Even if the actor is unable to explicate these meanings, they nonetheless remain part of the actor's social interactions. Weber insisted, therefore, that religious meanings differ from personal motivations and that they are retrievable by scholarly observation.[51] Only when one appreciates this argument can one understand Weber's interest in looking for meanings attached to social interactions. Such meanings emerge in religious communities.

Closely connected to the first distinction is another one that Weber draws between rational and correct action:

Subjectively rational instrumental action and action "correctly" oriented toward objectively valid goals ("correctly rational") are two very different things. An action which the researcher is seeking to explain may appear to him to be instrumentally rational in the highest degree and yet be oriented to assumptions of the actor that are totally invalid to the researcher. Action oriented toward conceptions of magic, for example, is often subjectively of a far more instrumentally rational character than any non-magical "religious" behavior, for precisely in a world increasingly disenchanted [or divested of magic]; religiosity must take on increasingly (subjective) irrational meaning relationships (ethical or mystical, for instance).[52]

This distinction becomes Weber's point of departure for his section "Religious Communities":

Religiously or magically motivated behavior is relatively rational behavior, especially in its earliest manifestations. . . . Only we, judging from our modern views of nature, can distinguish objectively in such behavior those attributions of causality which are "correct" from those which are "fallacious," and then designate the fallacious attributions of causality as irrational, and the corresponding acts as "magic."[53]

In other words, while the "rationality" of life-conduct is independent of falsification or verification by empirical proof, it is dependent on a long course of religious history that culminates in the development both of mysticism and of ethics. From this point of view, "disenchantment," which Weber mentions in his "Categories" essay for the first time, was caused not by an increasing stock of knowledge, but by practices whereby ethics or mysticism became the sole means of endowing meaning to one's life. The primary locus of the process that Weber calls "the disenchantment of the world" is thus not the realm of knowledge but the arena of religious meaning.

RELIGION AS COMMUNAL ACTION

In "Religious Communities," Weber begins by conceiving of "religion" as a "particular type of communal action" (*Gemeinschaftshandeln*).[54] Elsewhere in *Economy and Society*, he elucidates the meaning of this concept, explaining that *communal* actions have a structure and "laws of their own" (*Eigengesetzlichkeit*)[55]—that is, laws other than those followed by the economy. The process of rationalization, one of Weber's main concerns, impinges primarily on the sphere of communal action or community, becoming by this detour an essential factor in supporting or obstructing certain types of social interactions.[56] Although economic factors are, in Weber's account, often of decisive causal importance for communities and communal actions, "conversely the economy is usually also influenced by the autonomous structure of communal action."[57] Weber conceived of this interrelationship as a matter of the "elective affinity" between concrete communal structures and concrete forms of economic organization:"whether they further or impede or exclude one another—whether they are 'adequate' or 'inadequate' in relation to one another."[58] This idea is pivotal to understanding Weber's interest in including a section on religious communities in the design of *Economy and Society*; in his view, religious communities form the matrix for the development of practical attitudes toward the world. The structure of *Economy and Society*, with its cross-references to different topical sections, rests on a model that postulates interrelationships between communal actions and other forms of social interaction.[59]

By conceiving religion in terms of "communal action," Weber avoids the difficult task of defining religion in general. He posits, instead, that "an understanding of [religious] behavior can only be achieved from the viewpoint of the subjective experiences, ideas, and purposes of the individuals concerned, in short from the viewpoint of the religious behavior's 'meaning.' The most elementary forms of behavior motivated by religious or magical factors are oriented to *this* world." Weber illustrates the last point by quoting from Deuteronomy,"that it may go well with thee . . . and that thou mayest prolong thy days upon earth";[60] but he immediately broadens the category of religious meaning to include expectations that transcend the realities of the world. Indeed, his entire exposition depends on this enlarged understanding of "meaning," since the difference between religious and nonreligious behavior lies, for him, solely in the subjective expectations of the actor, not in the type of action itself. One sees here, at the outset of "Religious Communities," that Max Weber parts ways with Emile Durkheim. Where Durkheim's treatment of religion isolates a particular class of actions (rituals, for example) as sacred, Weber conceives any action as religious to the degree that the actors involved nourish a particular type of expectation with regard to that action.

That Weber approaches religion in this manner, rather than providing a general definition of religion, is the first of many indications of the role of "ideal types" in this section of *Economy and Society*. As early as *The Protestant Ethic and the Spirit of Capitalism* (1904–5), Weber warned against establishing historical concepts by way of broad definition, insisting that a historical concept "must be composed from its individual elements taken from historical reality. . . . This is in the nature of 'historical concept-formation,' which for its methodological purposes does not seek to embody historical reality in abstract generic concepts but endeavors to integrate them in concrete configurations which are always and inevitably individual in character."[61] To advance that goal, Weber forged an array of ideal types, some of the most important of which he elaborates in "Religious Communities." From Weber's perspective, the worldview and the ethics of a religious community permeated other social "orders," including law, politics, and, not least, economics, via the "religious" conduct of individuals and classes. This is a clear instance where Weber's use of the ideal-type method—holding concrete historical episodes up to examine the degree to which they approximate the ideal type of religious behavior—enables him to make visible the subjective meanings present in action spheres that otherwise appear dominated by more mundane interests.

TYPES OF RELIGIOUS COMMUNITIES AND SPECIALISTS

To bring the various types of religious communal actions into sharper focus, Weber usefully draws on the idea of "symbolic representation" that Hermann Usener introduced in 1896.[62] Departing from the tendency of scholars such as Rudolph Otto and Wilhelm Dilthey to privilege unmediated human experience over human symbolic expression, Usener sought windows into the human mind by recovering early human conceptions of the world from a study of divine names.[63] Borrowing from this perspective, Weber interprets the earliest human experience of the unfathomable powers of "mana," "orenda," and "maga"—or, Weber's preferred term, "charisma"—as involving conceptual attitudes toward the world. Continuing this historical reconstruction, Weber then observes how these powers crystallized, via a process of symbolic abstraction, into distinct spiritual beings who answered to the human quest to live in a "meaningful world."[64]

In Weber's view, this quest for a meaningful world went hand in hand with the emergence of religious specialists—specialists that "Religious Communities" seeks to differentiate in ideal-type forms. To this end, Weber identifies the magician, the priest, the prophet, and the lay intellectual as divergent types concerned with conceiving and controlling these mysterious powers; he characterizes these types as evoking very different expectations among their followings. While his analysis here speaks continuously of "development," Weber does not present his historical cases as moments of a linear evolution, but as evidence of processes of differentiation.

In this account, Weber's starting point is the magician, a figure whose charisma is represented by ecstasy: "For the laymen this psychological state is accessible only in occasional actions. . . . [It] occurs in a social form, the *orgy*, which is the primordial form of religious community" (*Vergemeinschaftung*).[65] In Weber's understanding, this occasional form of association was usually re-placed by more regular forms, urged on by political necessities. In this con-text, he points to the interdependence of community and society: "There is no concerted communal action [*Gemeinschaftshandeln*], as there is no indi-vidual action, without its special god. Indeed, if a social association [*Verge-sellschaftung*] is to be permanently guaranteed, it must have such a god."[66] By this route, the gods of religious communities became "guardians of the legal order," a transformation accompanied by the emergence of priests and stable cults that, together, ensured the permanence of social association, at the same time that adherents, in their practical lives, began conceiving of the entire world as an "enduringly and meaningfully ordered cosmos" ("dauernd sin-nvoll geordneter Kosmos").[67] Historically, acceptance of this postulate of meaningfulness stimulated the spread of legal orders and ethical require-ments,[68] while simultaneously eliciting an awareness of the rift between the expectation of a meaningfully ordered cosmos and the inevitable experience of a reality devoid of meaning.

In this circumstance, according to Weber, prophets arose to furnish ex-planations for this experience and to address the increasing ethical demands that the gods seemed unable to answer. To differentiate types of prophecy, Weber draws from contemporary religious scholarship the distinction be-tween a strict, transcendent God who demands loyalty and obedience to His commandments and a divine being that is immanent in man and can be ap-proached by contemplation. The former conception dominated Near East-ern religions and was at the origin of Western patterns of rational life-con-duct, while the latter conception prevailed in India and China.[69] The two prophetic types correspond, respectively, to Weber's "ethical" and "emissary" forms of prophecy. Finally, turning to intellectuals, Weber presented this group as driven by "metaphysical needs," by the urge to reflect on ethical and religious questions and to "understand the world as a meaningful cos-mos and to take up a position toward it."[70] Driven by such needs, intellectu-als played a crucial part in suppressing beliefs in magic and promoting the process of world disenchantment.

Insofar as communities arose around these various specialists, their needs called forth answers. The direction of these answers varied, however, accord-ing to "what [a particular] religion . . . provided for the various social strata" with which it was associated.[71] For one thing, different social strata ideal-typically adopted worldviews and ethical doctrines that conformed to their differing economic and political positions.[72] Thus the religious preferences of peasants, a stratum dependent on the unpredictability of nature, were mostly for tradition and magic, while warrior nobles inclined toward a religion of conquest, and bureaucrats toward a manipulation of religion as means to domesticate the masses. The religious preferences of bourgeois strata were less uniform, dependent on the bourgeoisie's economic situation and access to political privileges. Weber introduces ideal-typical categories such as world-rejection, theodicy, and resentment to characterize the directions that religions have taken in relation to the expectations of different social strata.

What is more, the so-called world religions were, in his view, each tied to a "carrier" social stratum—Confucianism to bureaucrats, Hinduism to magicians, Buddhism to mendicant monks, Judaism to wandering traders, Islam to warriors seeking to conquer territories, and Christianity to itinerant journeymen.[73] All told, Weber's analysis identifies a wide range of factors in religious history that shaped how social classes defined their situation and their worldly and otherworldly expectations.

CONGREGATIONS WITH AN ETHIC OF COMMITMENT: THE CENTER OF THE DISENCHANTMENT PROCESS

Historically, according to Weber, most religions have known only occasional associations of their adherents. Only a few developed a full-fledged congregational religiosity: Buddhism, Judaism, Christianity, Islam. Such congregations faced a major challenge, however, when the religion took the direction of world-rejection as the means to salvation. For, in Weber's account, the more a religion of salvation developed and became systematized and internalized as an *ethic of commitment*, in contrast to an ethic of compliance with laws, the more its adherents experienced "tensions" with the world. In their turn, these tensions elicited new forms of religiosity.

Weber sketches this revolutionary analysis for the first time in chapter 11 of "Religious Communities." He later revised and expanded it in the "Zwischenbetrachtung" of 1915.[74] At the core of this argument is Weber's claim that religious congregations that required brotherly love as their ethic of commitment engendered tensions with respect to the spheres of economics, politics, sexuality, and art, spheres that adherents thus came to experience as autonomous and hostile. (Weber adds the sphere of science to the list in the "Zwischenbetrachtung.") In all these spheres, believers resolved these tensions by efforts either to "flee" the world or to "master" it—the former pathway constituting what Weber calls "mysticism," the latter "asceticism." In either case, new practices arose, practices that became integral to religion within the disenchanted rational world. *Contra* Marianne Weber then, "disenchantment" was, for Max Weber, not the development of a godless culture, but quite the opposite. An increasingly rational culture, aware of the unethical character of these other social spheres, stimulated the emergences of varied *new forms of religiosity*. Weber's exposition abounds in examples of this process. Thus, in his view, Calvinism, when it abandoned the prohibition of usury as a result of inherent economic forces, organized charity for orphans and cripples as an undertaking of its own. Historically, mystical religions chose the opposite route and practiced, at least in principle, a loving self-surrender, not for the sake of the poor but for the sake of the surrender itself. Likewise, regarding the sphere of politics, congregational religiosity did not merely oppose state violence, it favored either a world-fleeing pacifism or active measures to fight the powers of sin. Again and again, Weber emphasizes the paradox that the same religious ethic that engendered awareness of a world governed by hostile rational forces simultaneously generated these diverse new forms of religiosity. Regarding the spheres of sexuality and art, he even observes the development of practices that entailed a re-enchantment of the world, practices comparable to those of world-rejection: namely, eroticism and art as means to escape the cold rationality of the modern world.

From the perspective that Weber develops in "Religious Communities," the less inhabitants of the modern world find meaning in nature and history, the more their quest for meaning devolves back onto the individual. Under these circumstances, the religions handed down from the past remain sources for maxims for life conduct, albeit sources whose validity now rests on subjective individual decision alone. In this "disenchanted" context, the gods acquire a peculiar new life, as Weber later declared in "Politics as Vocation": "Today the routines of everyday life challenge religion. Many old gods ascend from their graves; they are disenchanted and hence take the form of impersonal forces. They strive to gain power over our lives and again they resume their eternal struggle with one another."[75]

Notes

1. See Friedrich H. Tenbruck, "Abschied von Wirtschaft und Gesellschaft," *Zeitschrift für die gesamte Staatswissenschaft* 133 (1977): 703–36; Wolfgang Schluchter, "'Wirtschaft und Gesellschaft': Das Ende eines Mythos," in *Religion und Lebensführung*, vol. 2 (Frankfurt: Suhrkamp 1988), pp. 597–634.

2. See Marianne's preface to the posthumous manuscripts in the first edition of *Wirtschaft und Gesellschaft* [hereafter, *WuG* 1], between pp. 180 and 181. Cf. Guenther Roth, introduction to Max Weber, *Economy and Society: An Outline of Interpretive Sociology*, ed. Guenther Roth and Claus Wittich (1921–22; Berkeley: University of California Press, 1978), pp. lxvii–c.

Marianne Weber states in a footnote that an occasional remark made by Weber in reference to a Dr. Frank was "Written about 1912–13." Max Weber, *Wirtschaft und Gesellschaft*, vol. 2, *Religiöse Gemeinschaften*. *MWG* I/22-2, ed. Hans G. Kippenberg in cooperation with Petra Schilm with the help of Jutta Niemeier (Tübingen: J. C. B.

Mohr–Paul Siebeck, 2001), p. 315.

3. Cf. the survey of authors and literature, which Weber quotes directly or indirectly (*Religiöse Gemeinschaften*, pp. 505–7, 75–83).

4. Johannes Winckelmann, *Max Webers Hauptwerk* (Tübingen: Mohr–Paul Siebeck, 1986), p. 151.

5. K. Bücher, J. Schumpeter, Fr. Freiherr von Wieser, *Wirtschaft und Wirtschaftswissenschaft. Grundriß der Sozialökonomik*, I. Abteilung (Tübingen: J. C. B. Mohr–Paul Siebeck, 1914), pp. x–xiii; reprinted in Winckelmann, *Max Webers Hauptwerk*, appendix 3, pp. 168–71.

6. "Religiöse Gemeinschaften. Klassenbedingtheit der Religionen; Kulturreligionen und Wirtschaftsgesinnung." See G. Roth, "Introduction" to Max Weber, *Economy and Society*, pp. lxv–lxvi.

7. Weber, *WuG* 1, pp. 30 and 146; Weber, *Economy and Society*, pp. 56 and 251.

8. See Marianne Weber's preface to the posthumous manuscripts in the first edition between pp. 180 and 181. Cf. G. Roth, "Introduction" to Max Weber, *Economy and Society*, pp. lxvii–c.

9. Max Weber, *The Protestant Ethic and the Spirit of Capitalism and Other Writings*, ed., trans., and with an introduction by Peter Baehr and Gordon Wells (Harmondsworth, Eng.: Penguin, 2002); Max Weber, "Antikritisches zum 'Geist' des Kapitalismus," *Archiv für Sozialwissenschaft und Sozialpolitik* 30 (1910): 176–202; English translation (of the second part only): Max Weber, "Anticritical Last Word on *The Spirit of Capitalism*," trans. and with an introduction by Wallace M. Davis, *American Journal of Sociology* 83 (1978): 1105–31.

10. Max Weber, *The Protestant Ethic and the Spirit of Capitalism*, trans. Talcott Parsons, with a new introduction by Anthony Giddens. (London: Routledge, 1992), p. 284 n. 119.

11. Marianne Weber, *Max Weber. Ein Lebensbild* (Tübingen: Mohr–Siebeck, 1926), p. 346; English translation: Marianne Weber, *Max Weber: A Biography*, trans. and ed. Harry Zohn, with a new introduction by Guenther Roth (New Brunswick, NJ: Transaction Books, 1988), p. 331.

12. Cf. the surveys on authors and literature, which Weber quotes directly and indirectly in *Religiöse Gemeinschaften*, pp. 505–7 and 75–83.

13. Letter to the publisher Paul Siebeck, June 22, 1915. Cf. *Religiöse Gemeinschaften*, p. 91.

14. Max Weber, "Die Wirtschaftsethik der Weltreligionen. Konfuzianismus und Taoismus," (1915–20), in *MWG* I / 19, ed. Helwig Schmidt-Glintzer (Tübingen: Mohr–Siebeck, 1989). p. 236.

15. "I hope to be able to do something about filling it by undertaking a systematic treatment of the sociology of religion." Cf. Weber, Max Weber, *The Protestant Ethic and the Spirit of Capitalism and Other Writings*, p. 369.

16. See Hans G. Kippenberg and Martin Riesebrodt, eds., *Max Webers "Religionssystematik"* (Tübingen: Mohr–Siebeck, 2001).

17. Marianne Weber, *Ein Lebensbild*, p. 348; translation: idem, *A Biography*, p. 333 (translation with emendations of my own).

18. Marianne Weber, *Ein Lebensbild*, p. 349; translation: idem, *A Biography*, p. 333.

19. Max Weber, "Some Categories of Interpretive Sociology," trans. E. E. Graber,

Sociological Quarterly 22 (1981): 154–55; Max Weber, "Über einige Kategorien der verstehenden Soziologie" (1913), in *Gesammelte Aufsätze zur Wissenschaftslehre*, 3rd ed., ed. Johannes Winckelmann (Tübingen: Mohr–Siebeck, 1968), p. 433.

20. Weber, *Economy and Society*, p. 403; Weber, *Religiöse Gemeinschaften*, p. 127.

21. Weber, *Economy and Society*, p. 506; Weber, *Religiöse Gemeinschaften*, p. 273.

22. Robert Ranulph Marett, "Pre-animistic Religion" (1900), in *The Threshold of Religion*, 2nd ed. (London: Methuen, 1914), pp. 1–28.

23. The approach of Edward Burnett Tylor had replaced the comparative mythology of Friedrich Max Müller. In Tylor's view, it was wrong to trace the belief in souls back to a "disease of language," as Müller had done. The change of paradigms is the subject of my book *Discovering Religious History in the Modern Age*, translated from German by Barbara Harshaw (Princeton, NJ: Princeton University Press, 2002), pp. 59–60.

24. Edward Burnett Tylor, "On the Survival of Savage Thought in Modern Civilization," in *Proceedings of the Royal Institution of Great Britain*, vol. 5 (1866–69), pp. 522–35; George W. Stocking Jr., "Animism in Theory and Practice, E. B. Tylor's unpublished 'Notes on Spiritualism,'" *Man* 6 (1971): 88–104.

25. Margaret T. Hodgen, *The Doctrine of Survivals: A Chapter in the History of Scientific Method in the Study of Man* (Folcroft, PA: Folcroft Library Editions [1936] 1977), p. 38; Hans G. Kippenberg, "Survivals: Conceiving of Religious History in an Age of Development," in Arie L. Molendijk and Peter Pels, eds., *Religion in the Making: The Emergence of the Sciences of Religion* (Leiden: Brill, 1998), pp. 297–312.

26. Marett, "Pre-animistic Religion," p. 1.

27. Ibid., p. 15. Cf. Martin Riesebrodt, "Robert Ranulph Marett" (1866–1943), in Axel Michaels, ed., *Klassiker der Religionswissenschaft* (Munich: C. H. Beck, 1997), pp. 171–84.

28. Hans G. Kippenberg, "Explaining Modern Facts by Past Religions: The Study of Religions in Europe around the Year 1900," in Sigurd Hjelde, ed., *Man, Meaning, and Mystery: 100 Years of History of Religions in Norway. The Heritage of W. Brede Kristensen* (Leiden: Brill, 2000), pp. 3–17.

29. Weber, *Economy and Society*, p. 400; Weber, *Religiöse Gemeinschaften*, pp. 122–23.

30. Edward W. Said, *Orientalism* (New York: Vintage, 1979).

31. Georg Stauth, *Islam und westlicher Rationalismus. Der Beitrag des Orientalismus zur Entstehung der Soziologie* (Frankfurt: Campus, 1993), p. 11.

32. Julius Wellhausen, "Die israelitisch-jüdische Religion," in Paul Hinneberg, ed., *Christliche Religion mit Einschluß der israelitisch-jüdischen Religion. Die Kultur der Gegenwart. Ihre Entwicklung und ihre Ziele*, Teil 1, Abt. 4 (Leipzig: B. G. Teubner, 1906), pp. 1–40.

33. Ignaz Goldziher, *Vorlesungen über den Islam* (Heidelberg: Carl Winter's Universitätsbuchhandlung, 1910).

34. Ignaz Goldziher, "Die Religion des Islams," in Paul Hinneberg, ed., *Die orientalischen Religionen. Die Kultur der Gegenwart. Ihre Entwicklung und ihre Ziele*, Teil 1, Abt. 3, 1 (Leipzig: B. G. Teubner, 1906), pp. 87–135.

35. Ibid., p. 112.

36. Ibid., p. 113.

37. Weber, *Economy and Society*, pp. 461, 569, 623–25; Weber, *Religiöse Gemeinschaften*, pp. 209–10, 358, 432–33.

38. Hermann Oldenberg, "Die indische Religion," in Hinneberg, *Die orientalischen Religionen*, Teil 1, Abt. 3, 1, pp. 51–73.

39. Hermann Siebeck, *Lehrbuch der Religionsphilosophie* (Freiburg: Mohr–Siebeck, 1893), p. 49.

40. Cf. Friedrich Lenger, *Werner Sombart 1863–1941. Eine Biographie* (Munich: C. H. Beck, 1994), pp. 128–29; Friedrich Wilhelm Graf, "Rettung der Persönlichkeit. Protestantische Theologie als Kulturwissenschaft des Christentums, in Rüdiger von Bruch, Friedrich Wilhelm Graf, and Gangolf Hübinger, eds., *Kultur und Kulturwissenschaften um 1900* (Stuttgart: Steiner, 1989), pp. 103–31.

41. Ernst Troeltsch, "Das stoisch-christliche Naturrecht und das moderne profane Naturrecht," in *Verhandlungen der Deutschen Soziologentage, I. Band, Verhandlungen des Ersten Deutschen Soziologentages vom 19.–22. Oktober 1910 in Frankfurt am Main. Reden und Vorträge [. . .] und Debatten* (Tübingen: Mohr–Siebeck, 1911), pp. 166–92; the minutes of the debate are on pp. 192–214.

42. Ibid., pp. 175–76.

43. Ibid., p. 175.

44. *Verhandlungen*, pp. 201–2.

45. Ibid., p. 205. Volkhard Krech demonstrates the impact vitalism had on Simmel at that time in *Georg Simmels Religionstheorie* (Tübingen: Mohr–Siebeck, 1998), p. 210.

46. *Verhandlungen*, pp. 206–7.

47. Weber, "Categories," p. 179 n. 1; Weber, "Kategorien," p. 427. The relation between this essay and the earlier parts of *Economy and Society* was the subject of a debate between Hiroshi Orihara and Wolfgang Schluchter; see Hiroshi Orihara, "Max Webers Beitrag zum 'Grundriss der Sozialökonomik,'" in *Kölner Zeitschrift für Soziologie und Sozialpsychologie (KZSS)* 51 (1999): 724–34; and Wolfgang Schluchter, "'Kopf' oder 'Doppelkopf'—das ist hier die Frage. Replik auf Hiroshi Orihara," in *KZSS* 51 (1999): 735–43.

48. Weber, *WuG* 1, p. 1; Weber, *Economy and Society*, p. 4. Cf. Alessandro Cavalli, "Max Weber und Georg Simmel: Sind die Divergenzen wirklich so groß?" in Gerhard Wagner und Heinz Zipprian, *Max Webers Wissenschaftslehre. Interpretation und Kritik* (Frankfurt.: Suhrkamp 1994), pp. 224–38.

49. Weber, "Kategorien," p. 429; Weber, "Categories," p. 152.

50. Krech, *Georg Simmels Religionstheorie*, pp. 184–85.

51. Klaus Lichtblau, "Kausalität oder Wechselwirkung? Max Weber und Georg Simmel im Vergleich," in Gerhard Wagner und Heinz Zipprian, *Max Webers Wissenschaftslehre. Interpretation und Kritik* (Frankfurt: Suhrkamp, 1994), p. 539.

52. Weber, "Categories," pp. 154–55; Weber, "Kategorien," p. 433.

53. Weber, *Economy and Society*, p. 400; Weber, *Religiöse Gemeinschaften*, pp. 121–22.

54. Weber, *Economy and Society*, p. 399 (the translation "social action" is misleading); Weber, *Religiöse Gemeinschaften*, p. 121.

55. Weber, *Economy and Society*, p. 341; Weber, *WuG* 1, p. 183.

56. Weber, *Economy and Society*, p. 333; Weber, *WuG* 1, p. 382.

57. Weber, *Economy and Society*, p. 341 (translation modified).

58. Weber, *Economy and Society*, p. 341; Weber, *WuG* 1, p. 183.

59. Cf. the survey of these cross-references in Weber, *Religiöse Gemeinschaften*, pp. 94–102 and 115–18.

60. Weber, *Economy and Society*, p. 399; Weber, *Religiöse Gemeinschaften*, p. 121.

61. Weber, *The Protestant Ethic and the Spirit of Capitalism and Other Writings*, pp. 8–9.

62. Weber, *Economy and Society*, p. 402; Weber, *Religiöse Gemeinschaften*, p. 126.

63. Hermann Usener, *Götternamen. Versuch einer Lehre von der religiösen Begriffsbildung* (Bonn: Friedrich Cohen, 1896), p. 330; cf. preface, p. v.

64. Weber, *Economy and Society*, p. 400; Weber, *Religiöse Gemeinschaften*, p. 124.

65. Weber, *Economy and Society*, p. 401; Weber, *Religiöse Gemeinschaften*, p. 124. Weber here relied on Erwin Rohdes's *Psyche: The Cult of Souls and Belief in Immortality among the Greeks* (1898), behind whom we discern the shadow of Friedrich Nietzsche.

66. Weber, *Economy and Society*, p. 411; Weber, *Religiöse Gemeinschaften*, p. 140.

67. Weber, *Economy and Society*, p. 430; Weber, *Religiöse Gemeinschaften*, p. 165.

68. Weber, *Economy and Society*, p. 431; Weber, *Religiöse Gemeinschaften*, p. 167.

69. Weber, *Economy and Society*, p. 447–49; Weber, *Religiöse Gemeinschaften*, pp. 189–90.

70. Weber, *Economy and Society*, p. 499; Weber, *Religiöse Gemeinschaften*, p. 265.

71. Weber, *Economy and Society*, p. 491; Weber, *Religiöse Gemeinschaften*, p. 253.

72. Weber, *Economy and Society*, p. 512; Weber, *Religiöse Gemeinschaften*, p. 283.

73. Weber, *Economy and Society*, p.512; Weber, *Religiöse Gemeinschaften*, p. 283.

74. Translated into English as "Religious Rejections of the World and Their Direction," in *From Max Weber: Essays in Sociology*, trans and ed. Hans H. Gerth and C. Wright Mills (Oxford: Oxford University Press, 1946), pp. 323–59.

75. Ibid., p. 149.

PART III

Critical Perspectives

Beyond Weberian Action Theory

What is perhaps most revealing about Max Weber's typology of social action are not the two elements in it that are so widely and incessantly discussed—the two categories of rational action—but rather, *the other two*—affectual and traditional action—and their own theoretical positioning within the broader schema. It is these latter categories, in relation to their far more prominent counterparts, that illuminate most clearly the underlying assumptions of Weber's framework and that shed the greatest light on its fundamental limitations.

In what follows, I shall critically reexamine Weber's fourfold typology from the standpoints first of affectual and then of traditional action, seeking from these perspectives to locate it within a larger tradition of thought whose theoretical inadequacies it clearly shares. I shall also invoke in passing certain of Weber's methodological as well as substantive writings. My aims are partly negative: to expose the faulty preconceptions upon which the edifice is based and thereby to call into question its continuing usefulness for social theorizing and research. But in part as well, my aims here are positive: to contribute to the reconstruction of action theory on a more defensible foundation and to indicate how this task might in turn open up promising new avenues for empirical inquiry. Throughout this endeavor, I shall refer back to a tradition that emerged during Weber's own lifetime and that is deeply at odds with Weber's outlook: that of classical American pragmatism. It is this tradition that points us toward the most satisfactory reconceptualization of action.[1]

I shall also draw upon more recent writings from feminist and race theory and postcolonial studies, whose critiques of reason and of "rational" action as male, white, or Western emblematize and are partially constitutive of the new times in which we live. Together, these perspectives help us to discern the lineaments of a new approach to action that is more appropriate to the problems and challenges of our own era. Weber's action theory was undoubtedly the preeminent such theory of his time; however, today its inadequacies are more apparent than ever, and we need a new theory of action for the new epoch—the new century—that is now upon us.

Rationality and Emotion

Weber's typology of action appears in the opening conceptual exposition of *Economy and Society*. Its crucial passage reads as follows:

Social action, like all action, may be oriented in four ways. It may be:

(1) *instrumentally rational*, that is, determined by expectations as to the behavior of objects in the environment and of other human beings; these expectations are used as "conditions" or "means" for the attainment of the actor's own rationally pursued and calculated ends;

(2) *value-rational*, that is, determined by a conscious belief in the value for its own sake of some ethical, aesthetic, religious, or other forms of behavior, independently of its prospects of success;

(3) *affectual* (especially emotional), that is, determined by the actor's specific affects and feeling states;

(4) *traditional*, that is, determined by ingrained habituation.[2]

In an interesting discussion, Wolfgang Schluchter points out that this typology is "arranged along a [diminishing] scale of rationality." Instrumentally rational action marks the apex of that scale, for it entails a conscious and deliberate selection of means, a methodical weighing of ends, reflection upon the values that guide this choice of ends, and a regard for the secondary consequences of action. "In the case of value-rational action," writes Schluchter, "the consequence is disregarded; in the case of affectual action the consequence and the value; and in the case of traditional action consequence, value, and end."[3] Compelling as this interpretation is, its imagery of a progressive step-by-step falloff from full rationality prevents us from seeing something even more fundamental about Weber's typology: namely, that underlying it is a still more basic distinction between rational and nonrational action. "Insofar as the individual is not the self-conscious and deliberate author of his action," notes one commentator, "insofar as he is carried along by habit (as in purely traditional action) or carried away by feeling (as in purely affectual action)—to this extent, his conduct is non-rational. In so far as the individual acts deliberately and is consciously aware of what he is doing, on the other hand, his action is rational (in the most inclusive sense of this word)."[4] Weber's action categories, of course, are but ideal types, and Weber stresses that most concrete action combines rational and nonrational elements. Moreover, nonrational action can always become more rational over time.[5] But even so, the dichotomy between rational and nonrational remains the key architectural feature of Weber's action theory, and his particular way of rendering it has important implications for all the rest of his sociology. What assumptions, then, are packed into it?

To gain a better perspective on this problem, let us begin by taking a closer look at affectual action. Weber contends that it "stands on the borderline of what can be considered 'meaningfully' oriented, and often it . . . goes over the line. It may, for instance, consist in an uncontrolled reaction to some exceptional stimulus."[6] Emotion-driven conduct, in other words, is often "merely reactive behavior to which no subjective meaning is attached"; it falls short often of even meriting the designation "social action."[7] Emotions themselves entail little or no deliberation or judgment; they are frequently a mere "reaction" or outburst that is lacking in cognition, a spontaneous eruption that one is compelled to undergo. One has a sense of them as disruptive forces that simply happen to a person and over which that person has little or no control. Weber repeatedly characterizes them as "irrational"; he refers, for instance, to "such emotional reactions as anxiety, anger, ambition, envy, jealousy, love, enthusiasm, pride, vengefulness, loyalty, devotion, and appetites of all sorts, and to the 'irrational' conduct which grows out of them,"[8] and he speaks of certain actions as "affectually determined and thus irrational," as "affectually determined and hence derived from irrational motives."[9] At one point, he even classes emotions together with false judgments, as when he speaks of "irrational factors . . . such as affects and errors."[10] Weber's invidious contrast of affectual with rational action (in its value-rational form) is highly revealing of his overall perspective. "The orientation of value-rational action," he writes, "is distinguished from the affectual type by its clearly self-conscious formulation of the ultimate values governing the action and the consistently planned orientation of its detailed course to these values."[11] Affectual action, then, is apparently marked by the very absence or radical deficiency of clarity, self-consciousness, consistency, and control.

We can learn a great deal about Weber's thought, in fact, from examining even more closely the relation that he posits between emotion and reason. Both his methodological and substantive writings can be drawn upon here for illustrative purposes. Central to the former is the proposition that "for the purposes of a typological scientific analysis it is convenient to treat all irrational, affectually determined elements of behavior as factors of deviation from a conceptually pure type of rational action. . . . The construction of a purely rational course of action in such cases serves the sociologist as a type (ideal type) which has the merit of clear understandability and lack of ambiguity."[12] Weber suggests here, once again, that "purely rational action" possesses the quality of perfect transparency, while the presence of emotion makes possible only a "lower degree of certainty."[13] In what cases does one realize the most "certain" form of "rational," as opposed to "emotionally empathic," understanding? Weber suggests that "we have a perfectly clear understanding of what it means when somebody employs the proposition 2 x 2 = 4 or the Pythagorean theorem in reasoning or argument, or when someone correctly carries out a logical train of reasoning. . . . In the same way we also understand what a person is doing when he tries to achieve certain ends by choosing appropriate means on the basis of the facts of the situation."[14] According to Weber, then, rational action is purest and most intelligible when it approaches the ideals of logic and mathematics; emotionally driven action is only second-best by comparison. Although such a bias is described as a "methodological device" only,[15] it clearly reveals Weber's implicit assumption that emotion is a force not only extrinsic to reason, but also disruptive of it, a cause of confusion, opacity, indistinctness, and unreliability.

This animus against the emotions—and against emotion-driven action—is all the more apparent in Weber's more substantive analyses. Perhaps the most striking example here is that of inner-worldly asceticism, especially in its Puritan variety. In describing it, Weber uses language that reveals, despite his own well-known ambivalence, an acceptance of certain of its preconceptions. For instance, in *The Protestant Ethic and the Spirit of Capitalism*, Weber distinguishes Pietism from Calvinism in terms of the former's "greater emphasis on the emotional side of religion." As J. M. Barbalet observes, Weber's "characteristic summary of its consequences, as 'a weakening of the inhibitions which protected the rational personality of the Calvinist from his passions,' accept[s] the flavor of the conventional conceptions of reason and emotion as alternatives in which the possession of one destroys the other."[16] Yet another passage from *The Protestant Ethic* highlights the symbolic link in Christian asceticism—but also in Weber's own thinking—between emotion and nature. Christian asceticism has "the purpose," contends Weber, "of overcoming the *status naturae*, to free man from the power of irrational impulses and his dependence on the world and on nature."[17] What we know already to be a disruptive, disorderly force thus emerges also as a natural one, upon which we are dependent. It is interesting to note, of course—and characteristic of those who work within the terms of this dichotomy—that Weber himself sometimes reverses the valuation of reason and emotion and portrays the latter as the positive liberating force. This is true of his writings on eroticism and, to an extent, of his work on charisma as well.[18] In both of these cases, however—indeed, in all of the distinct areas of analysis across which I am ranging now—the same basic conceptual opposition, the same structure of thought, is retained. We are now in a position to ask, where does this conceptual opposition come from, and what are we to make of it?

An initial response, of course, to the former question would entail exploring systematically the (neo-)Kantian influences on Weber's sociology; these, as is so well known, were pervasive. Kant's understanding of morality "as the antithesis of inclinations and feelings—a transcending of the subjectivity and particularity of passion to enter, as free consciousnesses, the common space of Reason"[19]—reverberated throughout Weber's thought in the form of a generalized suspicion of the affectual.[20] Barbalet makes much as well of the distinctively Cartesian sources of Weber's thought, going back to the division between mind and body, intellect and materiality.[21] What I would like to do here, however, is to invoke John Dewey in tracing the dichotomy between reason and emotion still further back in time, to its first systematic articulation in the thought of the ancient Greeks, as part of an even more fundamental opposition between theory and practice. In *The Quest for Certainty*, Dewey observes that ancient Greek thought—especially the thought of Plato and Aristotle—gave "the depreciation of practice . . . a philosophic, an ontological, justification. . . . Because ultimate Being or reality [was seen as] fixed, permanent, admitting of no change or variation," he notes, "it [could] be grasped by rational intuition and set forth in rational, that is, universal and necessary, demonstration." Change, by contrast—the domain of practical action—was seen as "a realm inferior in value as in Being . . . the source from which comes all our uncertainties and woes."[22] Only belief or opinion—as opposed to rational knowledge—could be cultivated in respect to it. Emotions occupied a distinctly unenviable position within this framework. They were denigrated—seen as irrational—precisely because they accorded too much importance to changing and uncertain things; persons in the grip of emotions were seen as every bit as unstable as the natural, material world itself.

Of course, the metaphysics of the ancient Greeks are no longer with us today, nor were they, for that matter, in Weber's time. And yet the fundamental structure of thought and conceptual oppositions that they presupposed remain encoded still within our everyday discourses and practices: divisions between theoretical and practical; ideal and material; spiritual and natural; intuitive and empirical; immutable and mutable; ordered and chaotic; intentional and spontaneous; certain and uncertain; rational and irrational; intellectual and passional.[23] These divisions also reappear (in various forms and guises) in modern philosophy; we find them at work, for example, in Kantian thought.[24] And certainly, these dichotomies inform Weber's own thinking as well. We have seen in Weber's writings the very same age-old tendency—no less consequential for being so largely unself-conscious—to draw upon and to reinforce the assumption of a mutual exclusivity of reason and emotion. We have found there, too, sharp distinctions between certainty, clarity, and dispassionate reasoning on the one hand, and uncertainty, confusion, and impulsive outbursts on the other. The former are linked to the mental, the latter to the bodily, the former to order, the latter to disorder, the former to freedom, the latter to dependence. And even when these paired concepts are reversed in valuation—with the irrational, for example, elevated above the rational, or the passional above the intellectual (as does happen in aspects of Weber's thought)—the fundamental oppositions to which they refer are nonetheless retained and not overcome. The very polarities that Dewey and other pragmatists were so concerned to transcend reign unchallenged in Weber's sociology and action theory. Is there a better alternative, or must we always work within one version or another of these conceptual dichotomies?

Ironically, a more satisfactory perspective on these problems—in particular, on the relation between reason and emotion—already exists, and the basis for it can be found, in part, in ancient Greek philosophy itself. For despite insisting on the irrationality of the emotions, in the sense discussed above, the Greek tradition was virtually of one voice in maintaining that, in yet another sense, the emotions do at least manifest a complex intentional structure. Most philosophers in this tradition held that the emotions are hardly "blind forces," in classicist Martha Nussbaum's words, "that have nothing (or nothing much) to do with reasoning," like "gusts of wind or the swelling currents of the sea [that] push agents around [and] surd unthinking energies"; on the contrary, they "contain within themselves a directedness toward an object, and within the emotion the object is viewed under an intentional description. . . . Emotions, in short, whatever else they are, are at least in part ways of perceiving" or interpreting the world. Such an insight already marks a clear divergence from Weber's view of the emotions as nearly automatic and reflexive in nature and from his view of emotion-driven action as on the borderline with mere behavior. Ancient Greek thinkers also maintained that the emotions are "connected with certain beliefs about their object."[25] In this respect, emotions entailed, in some deep and constitutive sense, not only perception but also intellectual judgment. (For most philosophers in this tradition, the trouble with the emotions was precisely that the judgments that they do entail, as mentioned above, were prone to be false judgments and hence irrational, on account of their overvaluation of transitory, unstable, and undependable things. It was not a matter of the emotions being somehow irrational in the narrower sense of "noncognitive.")

Even more insightful and illuminating, however, among philosophers concerned with reason and the emotions, were certain thinkers from within the pragmatist tradition. These thinkers—Charles Sanders Peirce, George Herbert Mead, and especially Dewey—sought to overcome altogether the classical dichotomy between theory and practice (and between rationality and irrationality), a dichotomy within which the ancient Greek philosophers, for all of their conceptual subtlety, were ultimately caught up.[26] Pragmatist writers insisted on the possibility of what they termed "intelligence"—"a way of knowing in a world without certainty"[27]—and stressed as well that such intelligence could encompass not only reason but also emotion: they envisioned, in other words, the cultivation of "intelligent emotions" or of "emotionally guided intelligence." For Dewey in particular, it was no longer a matter of denigrating the emotions, but rather one of cultivating the passional dimension in life and of distinguishing among more or less intelligent ways of engaging emotionally with life contexts. "Affections, desires, purposes, choices," wrote Dewey, "are going to endure as long as man is man. . . . But these expressions of our nature need *direction*. . . . When they are informed by knowledge, they . . . constitute, in their directed activity, intelligence in operation."[28] Knowledge, for its own part, was also radically incomplete without the guidance of (intelligent) emotions. The hallmarks of (instrumental) rationality—the methodical weighing of means, ends, values, and consequences—all entailed passional responses on the part of the actor; they, too, required the direction and guidance of the emotions. Dewey pointed out in particular how consideration of the ultimate values that inform action is a profoundly and constitutively emotion-laden process; any attempt to reflect upon ultimate values that was undertaken in abstraction from feeling and passions could only mark a deep perversion of that process.[29]

Much more recently than the classical pragmatists, feminist and race theorists and postcolonial analysts have also elaborated extensively upon such themes, criticizing the reason/emotion dichotomy for both its epistemological and its societal, political, cultural, and economic implications. A vast body of literature has emerged that subverts and rejects this conceptual opposition, often criticizing it in ways that are more socially and historically grounded than anything that is to be found in the pragmatist tradition. Feminist philosophers, for example, repeatedly point out that "[r]eason is a male,"[30] that in its very definition—as well as in what is excluded from that definition—rationality is a deeply gendered concept. While some advocate a simple reversal in valuation, such that an essentialized "feminine" emotionality is to be ranked above "male" intellectuality, others offer ideas more reminiscent of the Deweyan notion of intelligence in emotion, speaking, for example, of embodied passional reasoning and of "appropriate emotions."[31] Much the same can be said of scholars who write on race and whiteness; they demonstrate that rationality has always been associated symbolically with the white race, in contradistinction to the dangerous (but alluring) irrationality that has been assigned to peoples of color. The dominant motif here is to question the very terms of this dichotomy itself and to reveal its (continuing) implication in structures of racism and white hegemony.[32] Finally, postcolonial theorists reveal how the reason/emotion dichotomy is linked as well to that between the West and the non-Western world. For example, Edward Said shows how this division has long figured prominently in the West's discursive construction of the Orient and calls for a dismantling of the very essentialisms around which this discourse revolves.[33] Taken together, such advances now make possible a whole new perspective on action and the emotions. For no longer does action need to be studied through the narrow prism of rationality and irrationality; today it can be investigated in the different and much more revealing light of the qualities of intelligence and emotional appropriateness that it manifests.

Rationality and Habit

But let us recall at this point that Weber not only distinguishes rational action (in its two variants) from emotion-driven action; he also distinguishes it from action oriented by habit. By the latter he seems to mean, as one interpreter has summarized it, "an unreflective, set disposition to engage in actions that have been long practiced."[34] In his gloss on traditional action in *Economy and Society*, Weber suggests that it, too, "lies very close to the borderline of what can justifiably be called meaningfully oriented action, and indeed often on the other side. For it is very often," he adds, "a matter of almost automatic reaction to habitual stimuli which guide behavior in a course which has been repeatedly followed."[35] Elsewhere in *Economy and Society*, Weber also points to the significance of "mechanical and instinctive factors" in "all 'traditional' action and [in] many aspects of charisma. . . . These types of action are very closely related to phenomena which are understandable either only in biological terms or can be interpreted in terms of subjective motives only in fragments."[36] Deviations from custom—a collective phenomenon that is grounded in individual habit[37]—seem, Weber further remarks, "to act on the psyche of the average individual like the disturbance of an organic function."[38] In its roots in human prehistory, the times of "primitive man," custom appears as "organically conditioned regularities which we have to accept as psychophysical reality."[39] Like habit, it can be traced back from culture to nature, from the mental to the bodily, from the deliberative to the merely reactive and automatic. To be sure, habitual action (like emotional action) can sometimes evolve or transmute into something "higher," such as norm-following or value-rational action.[40] But even so, habit (again, like emotion) remains defined by Weber extremely restrictively.

This restrictive understanding of habit and traditional action has important implications for both Weber's methodological and substantive analyses. Methodologically, it renders traditional action just as difficult to interpret "in terms of subjective motives"[41] as affectual action—and for identical reasons:

Weber sees both types of action as highly unreflective, undeliberative, reflex-ive, and virtually unconscious. And substantively, this orientation toward habit and traditional action leaves Weber in a most difficult position. For on the one hand, Weber finds ample stores of subjective meaning in the habit-ual action-patterns that he observes throughout history. Charles Camic has shown us in great detail how different and varied are the social contexts within which such habit, traditionalism, and custom operate.[42] Despite the possibility of "drain[ing] the subjective meaning out of habit," writes Camic, "[Weber's] own researches tended in the opposite direction, not only when examining such great vessels of meaning as the *habitus* of Calvinism and of other salvation religions but also when considering more mundane work habits, military habits, political habits, magical habits, and the like. For at no point did Weber treat such phenomena . . . as nonunderstandable behaviors for which it is impossible to identify any conscious or nonconscious mo-tive."[43] But on the other hand, Weber does affirm that most action is and al-ways has been habitual (or else emotional) in the sense of quasi-automatic or behavioral: "In the great majority of cases actual action goes on in a state of inarticulate half-consciousness or actual unconsciousness of its subjective meaning. . . . The great bulk of all everyday action to which people have become habitually accustomed approaches this type."[44] Such a verdict would hardly seem to render such action-patterns fertile terrain for an interpretive sociology of meaning.

Camic sees the roots of this denigration of the habitual in Weber's thought to lie ultimately in two major intellectual developments of his era: the "rapid growth of the biological sciences" and the "gradual emergence of the science of psychology."[45] Together, these yielded a new biophysiological understanding of habit, and sociologists such as Weber eventually "came un-der the spell" of this novel conceptualization.[46] Now, to be sure, altered def-initions of (and orientations toward) habit did arise during the nineteenth and early twentieth centuries. But it is instructive to note certain continu-ities as well that stretch *back* from that period, continuities in thought, espe-cially, that lead us from Weber back to Kant. In a twist on the classical for-mula, Kant held that both the moral domain (practice) and that of knowledge (theory) are internally bifurcated (not to mention separated from one another); in both, "the quest for certainty is fulfilled; cognitive certainty in the region of phenomena, practical certainty in the realm of moral au-thority."[47] In the practical sphere, he deemed the free legislation of reason far superior to mere habituation; the former produces regularities in conduct based on a firm rational principle, while the latter consists in nothing other than a blind "permanent inclination."[48] Despite his own tendencies toward habitual conduct, Kant claimed that habituation decreases freedom and be-longs to the same realm as nature, mechanism, and heteronomy; in his writings on education he even counseled that children "be prevented from forming any habits."[49] He too, then, like Weber, devalued habit in favor of reason. Of course, Kant was not the founder of such a dualistic cast of mind; similar oppositions prevailed in ancient Greek philosophy between reason, intellect, and freedom on the one hand, and habit, nature, and necessity on the other. Thus, in this sense, Weber represents not so much the rise of a new orientation as he does the culmination of age-old (habitual) ways of thinking.

For a more satisfactory alternative, then, to the approach to habit and traditional action that I have been outlining, where are we to turn? Interestingly, a part of the answer lies once again in the classical tradition—in particular, in Aristotle's philosophy. It was Aristotle who stressed repeatedly that habitual conduct at least potentially involves practical reason, that far from being reducible to mere automatic behavior, it embodies (again, at least potentially) a right perception and evaluation of situations, a sense of what is called for, and a knowledge of what it is best to do under the circumstances at hand. Habits, he argued, could become increasingly rational; they could grow in the discernment and practical wisdom that they entail. Habituation was hardly a mindless process of learning by rote repetition, an unconscious development of patterned reactions to stimuli; rather, it was for Aristotle a critical process of learning that transforms mechanistic behavior into a settled disposition that is informed by proper assessment and judgment of what is most appropriate. One further related point draws us back to our earlier discussion of the emotions. In Aristotle's view, the emotions themselves could become habituated; like other habits, they too could be educated and grow in practical intelligence. "Aristotle's moral theory," writes one philosopher, "must be seen as a theory not only of how to *act* well but also of how to *feel* well. . . . [V]irtues are dispositions toward feeling as well as action."[50] Such habitual tendencies or dispositions could themselves be cultivated and nourished over time. Of course, Aristotle's theory remained true in the end to the broader commitments and framework of classical Greek philosophy; we can see this in the distinctions that it drew, for example, between virtues of character and virtues of the intellect, or more broadly, between practical and theoretical wisdom. But even so, Aristotle provides for us the first systematic account of habitual conduct, the first theoretical perspective that truly highlights the possibility of intelligent or rational habits.

For our purposes, an even more useful conceptualization of habit is to be found closer to home, among Weber's contemporaries, the classical American pragmatists. Peirce, Mead, and Dewey devoted a great deal of attention to the topic of habit, and they developed in considerable detail the idea of educable habits, encompassing both dispositions and intelligence. Peirce made habit an integral element of his philosophy, one intimately linked to his logical category of Thirdness. He saw the passage from a world of Firsts (qualities or mere unactualized possibilities) to a world of Seconds (events or interactions among actualized qualities) to a world of Thirds (laws or uniformities in such interactions) as involving a growth or evolution in "concrete reasonableness." Habits were for Peirce not mere regularities, and the division between reason and habit was a false one; habit was tied intrinsically to beliefs, concepts, and meaning (also Thirds in his categorial schema). In a paper on logic, he wrote: "The whole function of thought is to produce habits of action. . . . To develop its meaning, we have, therefore, simply to determine what habit it produces, for what a thing means is simply what habits it involves."[51] Habits could thus be differentiated on the basis of the thoughts and beliefs that they incorporated.[52] Mead, too, sounded the theme of habit forcefully in his writings on action theory, as well as in his work on democratic reconstruction. Refusing to accept the sharp distinction between reason and habitual conduct, he held that intelligence permeates habit through and through: "Nor is all of human intelligence mental. . . . [O]ur inherited and acquired habits exhibit manners which do not disclose mental operations"; indeed, "a great deal of direct inference lies outside of the processes ordinarily termed 'thinking.'"[53] Such ideas proved crucial for Mead's democratic theory, for he stressed there the possibility to modify "social habits" through the deployment of "scientific method"; much of his work on educational reform, in fact, was aimed at precisely such an end.[54] Mead deemed this application of "organized intelligence" to represent an "evolutionary process grown self-conscious."[55]

It was Dewey, however, who gave us the single most elaborated theory of habit. "'Reason,'" he argued in *Human Nature and Conduct*, "is not an antecedent force. . . . It is a laborious achievement of habit needing continually to be worked over."[56] Heretofore successful habits, when confronted with "untoward circumstance"[57] or with unanticipated events, would give way to the exercise of *creative* intelligence, to a search for new and more appropriate solutions. Such solutions would themselves eventually become embodied in new ways of acting, in new reconstructed habits, whose advent would mark an advance in situated reason or intelligence.[58] Rather than predefine habits, then, as automatic biophysiological behavior (as Weber had done), Dewey allowed for the possibility of meaningful variations in habitual conduct.[59] On the one side were unintelligent habits: "Habits reduce themselves to routine ways of acting or degenerate into ways of action to which we are enslaved just in the degree in which intelligence is disconnected from them. Routine habits are unthinking habits; 'bad' habits are habits so severed from reason that they are opposed to the conclusions of conscious deliberation and decision."[60] On the other side were habits that represented intelligent new solutions to problematic situations. Such ideas had important implications for Dewey's substantive concerns, on matters such as education, citizenship, and democracy. Whenever speaking of social and political reconstruction, he argued that we must redesign our institutions in such a way that intelligent habits can take root there and thrive. Democracy—and education *for* democracy and citizenship—were inconceivable without the cultivation of habits embodying sound judgment and practical wisdom. "Those who wish a monopoly of social power," Dewey wrote, "find desirable the separation of habit and thought . . . so characteristic of history. For this dualism enables them to do the thinking and planning, while others remain the docile, even if awkward, instruments of execution. Until this scheme is changed, democracy is bound to be perverted in realization."[61]

In the present day, it is (once again) feminist and race theorists and writers in the postcolonial tradition who have been the most eloquent in sounding these same themes of situated embodied reason, intelligent habits, and social and political reconstruction. Theorists in these traditions have surpassed even the pragmatists in their specification of the societal, political, cultural, and economic sources of the reason/habit dichotomy and in their delineation of ways beyond this debilitating framework.[62] Feminist theorists, for example, have often stressed the masculinist quality of the reason/habit division and have suggested institutionalized as well as noninstitutionalized ways of enriching and liberating women's routine habitual practices. bell hooks, for example, confronts the problem of how to find more successful solutions to "untoward circumstance" in the lives of black women and of how to convert these solutions into intelligent new modes of habitual conduct,[63] while elsewhere, she articulates a recognizably Deweyan (if radical) vision of the role of reformed institutions of public schooling in the (re-) habituation of young (female) students of color.[64] Race theorists (including hooks herself) further underscore the racialized nature of the reason/habit dichotomy. The whiteness literature, for example, sets the denial of rationality, deliberativeness, and intellect to people of color within a broader genealogical perspective and suggests a range of possible avenues for resistance and critique.[65] Postcolonial theorists extend the analysis still further, exploring how the Eurocentrism of the Western academy has long sustained a vision of "Orientals" as habitually lazy, unthinking, and traditionalist. Said even notes that Weber's work provided "an 'outside' confirmation of many of the canonical theses held by Orientalists, [especially regarding] the Oriental's fundamental incapacity for . . . economic rationality."[66] Such theorists call for an intelligent transformation of traditional modes of life in the non-Western world (as well as of rationalized ones in the West), but always through processes of thoughtful and deliberative self-determination.[67]

The efforts of classical pragmatism and of contemporary theory alike are illuminating certainly in comparison with Weber's sociology, which also, of course, directs attention to the institutional challenges facing modern society and to the special difficulties that these pose for the individual. As has often been noted, Weber lacks a truly satisfactory understanding of education, citizenship, and democracy; he is ill equipped theoretically to conceive of widespread and long-lasting habits of democratic self-governance, or of the educative processes that instill and cultivate such habits in young citizens. Between the cold logic of rationalized bureaucracy, the extraordinarily compelling dynamism of charisma, and the prosaic give-and-take of interest-based politics, there is little room left in Weber's political sociology for the sort of intelligence in habitual conduct that Dewey and later thinkers liked to stress. We do not find in his writings, in fact—in sharp contrast to the likes of Dewey and hooks—much sustained discussion of how institutions or noninstitutional contexts might be (re-)designed with a view to inculcating more successful and appropriate habits.[68] Nor does Weber's ethics accommodate such a possibility very easily, for it offers only the vision of a courageous confrontation with the world on the part of a heroic individual—a virtuoso ethic—which surely cannot be taught in the public schools or be given nourishment in other institutionalized or noninstitutionalized settings. A certain elitism can even be said to permeate Weber's ethical outlook, which prevents it from speaking effectively to the question of how most individuals might actually come to acquire the dispositions and capacities that he so clearly values. This is especially troublesome given that the rationalist tendencies in which he so clearly shares are already, by virtue of their gendered, racialized, and Eurocentric quality, somewhat inhospitable terrain for the development of a democratic ethics in the broadest, most Deweyan sense of that term.[69]

Surely the fundamental reason for all these shortcomings—to begin now to round out our discussion—lies in the severely constraining assumptions that inform and shape Weberian action theory. These assumptions make it difficult for Weber to conceptualize certain phenomena that centrally involve habit—and that involve emotion too—in their subtle and complex relations with cognition, judgment, and intelligence. Such difficulties are by no means insignificant, for Weber himself acknowledges that "[i]n most cases, . . . action is governed by impulse or habit. . . . In prerationalistic periods," he writes, "tradition and charisma between them have almost exhausted the whole of the orientation of action," and even now, when "there is a high degree of rationalization of action, the element of traditional orientation remains considerable," as does that of emotion.[70] Emotion and habit divide much of the world between them, while Weber, who insists on seeing both as irrational, misses much of what is most interesting and important about them. At the very least, a reconstructed theory of action would have to include a significant place for them in its schema of categories and to conceptualize better than Weber does himself the possibilities for variation that they entail—most outstandingly, the possibilities in both habit and emotion for growth in discernment, contextual sensitivity, and knowledge.[71] Such growth is not quite the same thing as a *rationalization* of emotion or habit, as Weber would have it. It points in a different direction altogether, a direction that must be explored if the issues that I have touched upon, substantive as well as methodological, are to be properly addressed and understood. To go beyond Weberian action theory certainly means to come to terms not only with the complications and vexations of its ideas of rational action (in both variants), but also with the fundamental division itself—so simple and yet so deeply problematic—between the rational and the nonrational.

Conclusion

It is possible to imagine that the conceptual oppositions discussed in this essay are matters of common sense only and require no further critical reflection. One of the masters of Weberian scholarship, Reinhard Bendix, seemed to assume just that; after suggesting in his classic work, *Max Weber: An Intellectual Portrait*, that "[t]o indicate the main outline of Weber's framework," he would "substitut[e] common-sense words—'reasoning, emotional, or conventional'—for Weber's complex terminology,"[72] he proceeded to look no further into the matter. Today, some forty years after the publication of that landmark work, we can no longer afford quite so easily to pass over these distinctions and dichotomies. This is especially so not only after classical American pragmatism, but also after the rise of feminist and race theories and of postcolonial studies, which together have alerted us to the deeply unsatisfactory nature of these theoretical divisions. Weber's action theory, intricately interwoven as it is with other aspects of his thought, was surely the foremost such theory of his time and perhaps also the most appropriate such theory for the epoch in which he lived, right up until the final few decades of the twentieth century. Now, however, it is clear that that theory can no longer do much of the work that we need to see done and that a new action theory is required for the new issues and challenges that await us. The shifting light of cultural problems, now so vitally concerned with issues of identity, diversity, and power, directs our attention away from Weber and toward other thinkers such as the pragmatists and the contemporary theorists mentioned above—and toward new perspectives that transcend the age-old division between rationality and nonrationality. It becomes difficult, in fact, even to conceive any longer of how a structure of thought that is so problematic in its very architecture and in its underlying assumptions and associations could serve us well in the times that lie ahead. As we celebrate Weber's considerable achievements, we need also to reflect upon their decreasing relevance for the new century that is dawning.

Notes

1. It is ironic that exciting leads for a reconceptualization of action should come from the pragmatist tradition, for this tradition was experiencing its own moment of effervescence, its heroic moment, precisely during the years in which Weber himself lived and wrote. It might be seen, despite the considerable influence that it has exerted then and since, as the proverbial "road not taken," a perspective whose questioning of dominant assumptions, shared by Weber, are only now being recognized and made use of in constructive theory-building.

2. Max Weber, *Economy and Society: An Outline of Interpretive Sociology*, ed. Guenther Roth and Claus Wittich (1921–22; Berkeley: University of California Press, 1978), pp. 24–25.

3. Wolfgang Schluchter, *The Rise of Western Rationalism*, trans. Guenther Roth (Berkeley: University of California Press, 1981), p. 128. For other interpretations of Weber's typology of action, see Talcott Parsons, *The Structure of Social Action*, 2 vols. (1937; New York: Free Press, 1968); Stephen Kalberg, "Max Weber's Types of Rationality," *American Journal of Sociology* 85 (1980): 1145–79; Donald N. Levine, "Rationality and Freedom," *Sociological Inquiry* 51 (1981): 5–26; Jeffrey C. Alexander, *Theoretical Logic in Sociology*, vol. 3 (Berkeley: University of California Press, 1983); Jürgen Habermas, *The Theory of Communicative Action*, vol. 1, trans. Thomas McCarthy (Boston: Beacon Press, 1984); and Jon Elster, "Rationality, Economy, and Society," in Stephen Turner, ed., *The Cambridge Companion to Weber* (Cambridge: Cambridge University Press, 2000), pp. 21–41.

4. Rogers Brubaker, *The Limits of Rationality* (London: Routledge, 1991), p. 50.

5. Weber, *Economy and Society*, p. 25.

6. Ibid.

7. Ibid., p. 4.

8. Ibid., p. 6.

9. Ibid., p. 9.

10. Ibid., p. 6.

11. Ibid., p. 25.

12. Ibid., p. 6.

13. Ibid., p. 5.

14. Ibid.

15. Ibid., p. 7.

16. J. M. Barbalet, *Emotion, Social Theory, and Social Structure* (Cambridge: Cambridge University Press, 1998), p. 14; quotations from Max Weber, *The Protestant Ethic and the Spirit of Capitalism*, trans. Talcott Parsons (1920–21; New York: Charles Scribner's Sons, 1958), pp. 130, 131. In a later passage in *Economy and Society*, Weber writes that "the person who lives as a worldly ascetic is a rationalist . . . in his rejection of everything that is . . . dependent upon his own emotional reactions" (Weber, *Economy and Society*, p. 544). There is complexity, of course, in the multiple meanings that

Weber attaches to the word "rationalist," but what seems evident, at least, is that rational self-control is attained here (as elsewhere) at the expense of the emotions (and vice versa).

17. Weber, *The Protestant Ethic*, pp. 118–19.

18. On Weber's conceptualization of eroticism, see Roslyn Wallach Bologh, *Love or Greatness: Max Weber and Masculine Thinking—A Feminist Inquiry* (Albany, NY: State University of New York Press, 1990). On his conceptualization of charisma, see Edward Shils, "Charisma, Order, and Status," in *Center and Periphery: Essays in Macrosociology* (Chicago: University of Chicago Press, 1975), pp. 256–75; and S. N. Eisenstadt, "Charisma and Institution Building," in *Power, Trust, and Meaning* (Chicago: University of Chicago Press, 1995), pp. 167–201. Hans Joas, *The Creativity of Action*, trans. Jeremy Gaines and Paul Keast (Chicago: University of Chicago Press, 1996), also provides a useful discussion of the relation between Weber's theory of charisma and a pragmatism-inspired theory of the creativity of action. It is intriguing to ponder the links between Weber's changing valuations of (ir-) rationality—especially in respect to eroticism—and his own biographical trajectory. For a psychoanalytically informed account of Weber's life, see Arthur Mitzman, *The Iron Cage* (New York: Knopf, 1970).

19. Genevieve Lloyd, *The Man of Reason*, 2nd ed. (Minneapolis, MN: University of Minnesota Press, 1993), p. 68.

20. For more on the (neo-)Kantian sources of Weber's thought, see Thomas Burger, *Max Weber's Theory of Concept Formation* (Durham, NC: Duke University Press, 1976); Schluchter, *The Rise of Western Rationalism*; and Martin Albrow, *Max Weber's Construction of Social Theory* (London: Macmillan, 1990).

21. Barbalet, *Emotion*, pp. 25–27.

22. John Dewey, *The Quest for Certainty: The Later Works of John Dewey, 1925–1953*, vol. 4, ed. Jo Ann Boydston (1929; Carbondale: Southern Illinois University Press, 1988), p. 16.

23. See Catherine A. Lutz, *Unnatural Emotions* (Chicago: University of Chicago Press, 1988), for a useful ethnopsychology of "Western discourses on feeling."

24. Dewey, *The Quest for Certainty*, pp. 47–49.

25. Martha C. Nussbaum, *Poetic Justice* (Boston: Beacon Press, 1995), pp. 56, 60–61.

26. William James, the other great pragmatist who wrote extensively on the emotions, held to a somewhat different theory of the emotions that actually retained this dualistic conceptual framework in important respects; see "What Is an Emotion?" in William James, *Collected Essays and Reviews*, ed. Ralph Barton Perry (1884; New York: Longmans, Green, 1920), pp. 244–75.

27. Robert B. Westbrook, *John Dewey and American Democracy* (Ithaca, NY: Cornell University Press), p. 357.

28. Dewey, *The Quest for Certainty*, p. 238.

29. John Dewey, *Theory of Valuation, The Later Works of John Dewey, 1925–1953*, vol. 13, ed. Jo Ann Boydston (1939; Carbondale: Southern Illinois University Press, 1991), pp. 189–251.

30. Lloyd, *The Man of Reason*.

31. Alison M. Jagger, "Love and Knowledge," *Inquiry* 32 (1989): 151–76. See also

Nancy Chodorow, *The Reproduction of Mothering* (Berkeley: University of California Press, 1978); Sandra Harding, *The Science Question in Feminism* (Ithaca, NY: Cornell University Press, 1986); Judith Butler, *Gender Trouble* (New York: Routledge, 1990); Patricia Hill Collins, *Black Feminist Thought* (New York: Routledge, 1990); Donna Haraway, *Simians, Cyborgs, and Women* (New York: Routledge, 1991); Chandra Talpade Mohanty, Ann Russo, and Lourdes Torres, eds., *Third World Women and the Politics of Feminism* (Bloomington: Indiana University Press, 1991); bell hooks, *Black Looks* (Boston: South End Press, 1992); Ruth Frankenberg, *White Women, Race Matters* (Minneapolis: University of Minnesota Press, 1993); Anne McClintock, *Imperial Leather* (New York: Routledge, 1995); and Ann Laura Stoler, *Race and the Education of Desire* (Durham, NC: Duke University Press, 1995).

32. Relevant and important work in race theory and whiteness studies includes Collins, *Black Feminist Thought*; David R. Roediger, *The Wages of Whiteness* (London: Verso, 1991); Frankenberg, *White Women, Race Matters*; and Michael Omi and Howard Winant, *Racial Formation in the United States*, 2nd ed. (New York: Routledge, 1994); see also the references in n. 31.

33. Edward W. Said, *Orientalism* (1978; New York: Vintage, 1994). See also Frantz Fanon, *Black Skin, White Masks*, trans. Charles Lam Markmann (1952; New York: Grove, 1967); Mohanty, Russo, and Torres, *Third World Women*; Homi K. Bhabha, *The Location of Culture* (London: Routledge, 1994); Ella Shohat and Robert Stamm, *Unthinking Eurocentrism* (New York: Routledge, 1994); McClintock, *Imperial Leather*; Stoler, *Race and the Education of Desire*; and Anne McClintock, Aamir Mufti, and Ella Shohat, eds., *Dangerous Liaisons* (Minneapolis: University of Minnesota Press, 1997).

34. Charles Camic, "The Matter of Habit," *American Journal of Sociology* 91 (1986): 1057.

35. Weber, *Economy and Society*, p. 25; see also pp. 4–5.

36. Ibid., p. 17.

37. Ibid., pp. 29–31, 319.

38. Ibid., p. 320.

39. Ibid., p. 321.

40. Ibid., pp. 326, 754.

41. Ibid., p. 17.

42. Camic, "The Matter of Habit." For a contrast, see Parsons, *The Structure of Social Action*, pp. 646–47, on the differences between habit and traditionalism.

43. Camic, "The Matter of Habit," pp. 1065–66.

44. Weber, *Economy and Society*, pp. 21, 25.

45. Camic, "The Matter of Habit," pp. 1048–49.

46. Ibid., p. 1066. Camic claims that many went even further and "discarded" habit altogether "from the language of sociology" in an effort to differentiate it from behaviorist psychology and other disciplines (ibid., p. 1076).

47. Dewey, *The Quest for Certainty*, pp. 47, 49.

48. Immanuel Kant, *The Doctrine of Virtue: Part II of The Metaphysic of Morals*, trans. Mary J. Gregor (1797; New York: Harper and Row, 1964), p. 152.

49. Immanuel Kant, *Education*, trans. Annette Churton (1803; Ann Arbor: University of Michigan Press, 1960), p. 45.

50. L. A. Kosman, "Being Properly Affected," in Amelie Oksenberg Rorty, ed.,

Essays on Aristotle's Ethics (Berkeley: University of California Press, 1980), pp. 105, 106.

51. Charles Sanders Peirce, "How to Make Our Ideas Clear," in Nathan Houser and Christian Kloesel, eds., *The Essential Peirce*, vol. 1 (1878; Bloomington: Indiana University Press, 1992), p. 131.

52. Indeed, belief itself could be conceptualized as "thought at rest," as itself a habit (ibid., p. 129).

53. George Herbert Mead, "Consciousness and the Unquestioned," in Charles W. Morris, ed., *The Philosophy of the Act* (Chicago: University of Chicago Press, 1938), p. 68.

54. For a comprehensive bibliography, which includes many articles and lesser pieces on education reform, see George Herbert Mead, *Selected Writings*, ed. Andrew J. Reck (Indianapolis: Bobbs-Merrill, 1964), pp. lxiii–lxix.

55. George Herbert Mead, *Movements of Thought in the Nineteenth Century*, ed. Merritt H. Moore (Chicago: University of Chicago Press, 1936), p. 364.

56. John Dewey, *Human Nature and Conduct, The Middle Works of John Dewey, 1899–1924*, vol. 14, ed. Jo Ann Boydston (1922; Carbondale: Southern Illinois University Press, 1988), p. 137.

57. Ibid., p. 121.

58. For an especially lucid discussion of the Deweyan (and, more broadly, pragmatist) "model of periodically recurring phases," see Joas, *The Creativity of Action*, pp. 128–29.

59. So intimate was the connection between habit and intelligence in Dewey's eyes that at one point he even suggested that intelligence was itself an ensemble of habits. "Concrete habits," he remarked, "do all the perceiving, recognizing, imagining, recalling, judging, conceiving, and reasoning that is done" (Dewey, *Human Nature and Conduct*, p. 124).

60. John Dewey, *Democracy and Education, The Middle Works of John Dewey, 1899–1924*, vol. 9, ed. Jo Ann Boydston (1916; Carbondale: Southern Illinois University Press, 1985), pp. 53–54. Dewey wrote in *Human Nature and Conduct*: "Consider what happens to thought when habit is merely power to repeat acts without thought. Where does thought exist and operate when it is excluded from habitual activities? Is not such thought of necessity shut out from effective power, from ability to control objects and command events? Habits deprived of thought and thought which is futile are two sides of the same fact" (Dewey, *Human Nature and Conduct*, p. 49).

61. Dewey, *Human Nature and Conduct*, p. 52.

62. From outside these traditions, of course, the most important contributions have come from Pierre Bourdieu (e.g., *The Logic of Practice*, trans. Richard Nice [Stanford, CA: Stanford University Press, 1990]).

63. bell hooks, *Sisters of the Yam* (Boston: South End Press).

64. bell hooks, *Teaching to Transgress* (New York: Routledge). In addition to the two aforementioned works by hooks, see the works cited in n. 31.

65. See the works cited in n. 32.

66. Said, *Orientalism*, p. 259.

67. See the works cited in n. 33.

68. See Anthony Giddens, *Politics and Sociology in the Thought of Max Weber* (London: Macmillan, 1972); Habermas, *The Theory of Communicative Action*; Brubaker, *The Limits of Rationality*; Wolfgang J. Mommsen, *The Political and Social Theory of Max Weber* (Chicago: University of Chicago Press, 1989); Stephen P. Turner and Regis A. Factor, *Max Weber and the Dispute over Reason and Value* (London: Routledge & Kegan Paul, 1984); David Beetham, *Max Weber and the Theory of Modern Politics* (Cambridge: Polity Press, 1985); and Jeffrey C. Alexander, "The Dialectic of Individuation and Domination," in Sam Whimster and Scott Lash, eds., *Max Weber, Rationality, and Modernity* (London: Allen & Unwin, 1987).

69. See, for example, the essays in Whimster and Lash, *Max Weber, Rationality, and Modernity*.

70. Weber, *Economy and Society*, pp. 21, 245, 69; see also pp. 320, 337.

71. One attempt to develop such a theory of action is to be found in Mustafa Emirbayer and Ann Mische, "What Is Agency?" *American Journal of Sociology* 103 (1998): 962–1023. There, action theory is based on a (temporally grounded) tripartite distinction between past-, future-, and present-oriented modalities of agentic engagement with situational contexts. These are termed the iterational, projective, and practical-evaluative moments of agency, respectively. Habitual action is captured by the (past-oriented) category of iteration, while the emotional dimension of action is incorporated into all three of the analytical categories.

72. Reinhard Bendix, *Max Weber* (Berkeley: University of California Press, 1960), p. 477 n. 9.

The Shadow of Exploitation in Weber's Class Analysis

If theoretical frameworks are identified as loudly by their silences as by their proclamations, then one of the defining characteristics of class analysis in the Weberian tradition is the virtual absence of a systematic concept of exploitation. Nothing better captures the central contrast between the Marxist and Weberian traditions of class analysis than the difference between a class concept centered on the problem of life chances in Weber, and a concept rooted in the problem of exploitation in Marx. This is not to say that Weber completely ignores some of the substantive issues connected to the problem of exploitation. For example, Weber, like Marx, sees an intimate connection between the nature of property relations in capitalism and the problem employers face in eliciting high levels of effort from workers. But he does not theorize this issue in terms of a general concept of exploitation, nor does he see the problem of extracting labor effort as a pivotal feature of class relations and a central determinant of class conflict. Instead, Weber treats the problem of eliciting work performance within capitalism as an instance of technical inefficiencies reflecting a tension between formal rationality and substantive rationality within capitalist economic relations.

This chapter has two basic objectives: first, to understand as precisely as possible the inner structure of Weber's concept of class, its similarities and differences from Marx's concept, and its relationship to the problem of exploitation; second, to use this interrogation of Weber's work to defend the importance of the concept of exploitation for sociological theory. The first two sections set the context of the discussion by first briefly situating the problem of class in Weber's larger theoretical project and then examining a number of striking similarities between Weber's and Marx's concepts of class. Although Marxist and Weberian traditions of sociology are often pitted against each other, within the narrower arena of class analysis there is considerable overlap, particularly in their concept of class in capitalist society. The third section then characterizes the pivotal difference in their class concepts through the contrast between "life chances" and "exploitation." A fourth section looks more closely at exploitation, paying particular attention to the way Weber deals with the problem of "extracting" labor effort under conditions that Marxists would describe as "exploitation." Finally, the last section examines the ramifications for the broader contours of a sociological class analysis of Weber's marginalization of exploitation.

Class Analysis in Weber's Work

Unlike Marx, for whom class was a foundational concept in his broad theoretical agenda, the problem of class plays a relatively peripheral role in Weber's work.[1] It appears in his work in three principal ways. First, there are the rare, explicit theoretical discussions of class, most notably in the chapter fragments assembled posthumously in *Economy and Society*.[2] Second, early in Weber's career there are a number of detailed empirical and historical studies in which the analysis of class figures prominently—most notably his studies of East Elbian agricultural workers,[3] his research on the causes of the decline of the Roman Empire,[4] and his more general work on the agrarian sociology of ancient civilizations, first published in the late 1890s and then revised in 1909.[5] Much of this work, especially the work on slavery in ancient civilizations, has a decidedly Marxian inflection and has had almost no impact on the analysis of class within what has come to be known as Weberian sociology.[6] Third, a great deal of Weber's work concerns the analysis of capitalism as a social order—its origins, its internal logic, its dynamics of development, its ramifications, its contrasts with other social orders—and although the problem of class is rarely explicitly foregrounded in these analyses, much of what he says bears on the problem of understanding classes in capitalist societies. For example, Weber's *The Protestant Ethic and the Spirit of Capitalism* is not simply about the creation of the cultural-psychological conditions for modern capitalism to become a dynamic force in the world; it is also about the ways in which this "spirit" is embodied in the distinctive orientations of people located in different class positions within capitalism.[7] Weber writes: "The treatment of labour as a calling became as characteristic of the modern worker as the corresponding attitude towards acquisition of the business man."[8]

Most discussions of Weber's work on class are based on the first of these clusters of writings, especially his brief explicit conceptual analyses of class in *Economy and Society*.[9] What has become the Weber-inspired tradition of class analysis is largely based on these fragmentary expositions.[10] Locating the concept of class within Weber's conceptual menu in these texts generates the

TABLE 9.1

Theoretical Location of the Concept of Class in Weber's Explicit Formulations in Economy and Society

Sphere of Social Interaction[a]	Category That Locates Individuals within the Distribution of Power	Attributes Intrinsic to Categories of the Distribution of Power		
		Objective Properties	Subjective Identity	Collective Action
Economic	Class	Yes	No	No
Communal	Status group	Yes	Yes	No
Political	Party	Yes	Yes	Yes

[a] Weber's terms for these spheres are "economic order," "social order" or "sphere of the distribution of honor," and "sphere of power." Weber, *Economy and Society*, p. 938.

familiar contrast of "class" and "status," the two most important terms in a threefold schema of stratification that also includes "party."[11] Two primary analytical dimensions demarcate these categories: first, the "sphere" or "order" within which social interaction occurs (economic, communal, or political);[12] and second, the degree to which the category intrinsically invokes subjective identity and collective forms of action. The combinations of these criteria differentiate class, status, and party as illustrated in Table 9.1. Within this analytical schema, class is defined within the sphere of economic interaction and involves no necessary subjective identity or collective action. An individual can be in a specific kind of class situation without this generating a specific form of identity or participation in collective action: "In our terminology, 'classes' are not communities; they merely represent possible, and frequent, bases for social action."[13] Status groups are defined within the sphere of communal interaction (or what Weber calls the "social order") and always imply some level of identity in the sense of some recognized "positive or negative social estimation of *honor*."[14] A status group cannot exist without its members being in some way conscious of being members of the group: "In contrast to classes, *Stände* (status groups) are normally groups."[15] Status groups need not, however, imply any kind of collective action. Party, finally, always implies collective action: "As over against the actions of classes and status groups, for which this is not necessarily the case, party-oriented social action always involves association. For it is always directed toward a

TABLE 9.2

The Theoretical Location of Class in Weber's Analysis of Rationalization

Source of Social Power	Degree of Rationalization of Social Relations	
	Rationalized Social Relations	Nonrationalized Social Relations
Social honor	Meritocratic prestige	Ascriptive status groups
Material conditions of life	Class: capital, labor	Ascriptively based consumption groups
Authority	Rational-legal domination: bureaucracy	Patrimonial administration

goal which is striven for in a planned manner."[16] In these terms, members of a class become a status group when they become conscious of sharing a common identity, and they become a party when they *organize* on the basis of that identity.[17]

The conceptual contrast between class and status for Weber is not primarily a question of the *motives* of actors: it is not that status groups are derived from purely symbolic motives and class categories are derived from material interests. Although people care about status categories in part because of their importance for symbolic ideal interests, class positions also entail such symbolic interests, and both status and class are implicated in the pursuit of material interests. As Weber writes, "material monopolies provide the most effective motives for the exclusiveness of a status group."[18] Rather than motives, the central contrast between class and status is the nature of the mechanisms through which class and status shape inequalities of the material and symbolic conditions of people's lives. Class affects material well-being directly through the kinds of economic assets people bring to market exchanges. Status affects material well-being indirectly, through the ways that categories of social honor underwrite various coercive mechanisms that, in Weber's words, "go hand in hand with the monopolization of ideal and material goods or opportunities."[19]

When the wider body of Weber's work is taken into consideration, especially his diverse writings on capitalism, the problem of class becomes embedded in a different conceptual space. Here, the pivotal question is the relationship between the concept of class and the broad theoretical and historical problem of the *rationalization* of social relations. Table 9.2 indicates how class is located with respect to this problem.[20] As in Table 9.1, this conceptual space is defined by two dimensions: first, the *sources of social power* within social interactions, and second, the *degree of rationalization* of social relations. Running throughout Weber's work is a threefold distinction among the sources of power that individuals use to accomplish their goals: social honor, material resources, and authority. Each of these, in turn, can be organized within social interactions in highly rationalized forms or in relatively nonrationalized forms. Class, in these terms, designates highly rationalized social relations that govern the way people get access to and use material resources.[21] It is thus contrasted, on one hand, with nonrationalized ways of governing access to resources, especially ascriptively based consumption groups, and on the other hand, with rationalized forms of social relations involving other sources of social power.

Rationalization, of course, is perhaps the most complex multidimensional concept in Weber's arsenal. Following Levine's decomposition of Weber's conceptual array of rationalizations, the problem of class with Weber is primarily situated within one particular form of rationalization: the *objective instrumental* rationalization of social order.[22] In all societies, the ways people gain access to and use material resources is governed by rules that are objectively embodied in the institutional settings within which they live. When the rules allocate resources to people on the basis of ascriptive characteristics, and when the use of those material resources is given by tradition rather than the result of a calculative weighing of alternatives, then economic interactions take place under nonrationalized conditions. When those rules enable people to make precise calculations about alternative uses of those resources and discipline people to use those resources in more rather than less efficient ways on the basis of those calculations, then those rules can be described as "rationalized." This occurs, in Weber's analysis, when market relations have the most pervasive influence on economic interactions (that is, in fully developed capitalism). His definition of classes in terms of the economic opportunities people face in the market, then, is simultaneously a definition of classes in terms of rationalized economic interactions. Class, in these terms, assumes its central sociological meaning to Weber as a description of the way people are related to the material conditions of life under conditions in which their economic interactions are regulated in a maximally rationalized manner.

Two examples, one a discussion of rural class relations from early in Weber's career and the second a discussion of industrial class relations in *Economy and Society*, illustrate this close link in Weber's thinking between rationalization and class relations. Both Weber and Marx recognized the importance of the destruction of traditional peasant rights in the countryside as a central part of the development of capitalism in agriculture. In Weber's early writings on East Elbian rural labor, he describes the impact of this process on class relations in terms of rationalization. Before the infusion of market relations in the countryside, Weber writes, the rural laborer "found him-self confronted not with an 'employer' but with a small-scale territorial lord. The low level of commercial ambition among estate owners was reinforced by the apathetic resignation of the labourer. . . . "[23] The advance of capital-ism destroyed these traditional labor relations. The resulting impact on class relations, Weber describes, is a process of rationalization:

[I]n place of the landed aristocracy there necessarily enters—with or without a change of person—a class of agricultural entrepreneurs who are in principle no dif-ferent from commercial entrepreneurs in their social characteristics.

This transformation in the general type of rural employer has significant conse-quences for the position of the labourer. . . . [In the patriarchal estate economy,] labour relations were not arranged according to commercial principles and with the objective of profitability, but rather developed historically as a means of affording the landlords a suitable existence. Under these conditions as little deviation as possible was made from the natural and communal economic foundations of this order. Thus a rural working class with *common* economic interests could not and did not exist in the principal regions of the east.

Modern development seeks initially to introduce the principle of *economic ration-ality* into the wage forms within this natural economic order. Accordingly, the communal remnants (plots of land, threshing shares, grazing rates) are initially abol-ished. . . .

With this transformation a necessary condition of the patriarchal relation col-lapses: the connection to *one particular* estate. The differentiation between various categories of labour are reduced and the employer becomes as "fungible" for the ru-ral worker as he already is for the industrial labourer. In other words, this process of development brings the rural labourers steadily closer to the form of a *unified* class of a proletarian type in its material conditions of life, a state already attained by the in-dustrial proletariat.[24]

The emergence of a rural proletariat thus represents the transformation of forms of access to material conditions of life governed by tradition to one governed by calculation and pure economic interests.

The same basic argument appears in Weber's analysis of the industrial working class. For Weber, as for Marx, a central defining characteristic of the "working class" is its complete separation (or "expropriation") from the means of production. For Marx, this is crucial because it enables capitalists to exploit workers; for Weber this expropriation is crucial because it allows for the full realization of economic rationality within production. In his ex-tended discussion of this separation in *Economy and Society*, Weber stresses the relevance of expropriation for economic rationality:

The expropriation of workers *in general*, including clerical personnel and technically trained persons, from possession of the means of production has its *economic* reasons above all in the following factors: . . . [t]he fact that, other things being equal, it is generally possible to achieve a higher level of economic rationality if the management has extensive control over the selection and the modes of use of workers, as compared with the situation created by the appropriation of jobs or the existence of rights to participate in management. These latter conditions produce technically irrational obstacles as well as economic irrationalities. In particular, considerations appropriate to small-scale budgetary administration and the interests of workers in the maintenance of jobs ("livings") are often in conflict with the rationality of the organization.[25]

Similar discussions can be found in Weber's analysis of the relationship between rationalization and free wage labor in *The Protestant Ethic*,[26] and in his discussions of the inefficiencies of slavery.[27] In all of these cases, the central theoretical problem in which the analysis of class and the transformations of class relations is embedded is the problem of the rationalization of the economic order. While class per se may be a relatively secondary theme in Weber's sociology, it is, nevertheless, intimately linked to one of his most pervasive theoretical preoccupations—rationalization.

In the discussion that follows, I draw on both of these theoretical contexts of Weber's thinking about class—the contrast between class and status as two forms of stratification, and the salience of rationalization in defining the theoretical relevance of class. Weber's distilled contrast between class and status is particularly useful in clarifying the substantive criteria embodied in his definition of class relations in terms of market-based life chances; the broader analysis of rationalization will help to illuminate the ways in which Weber deals with the problem of exploitation in capitalist society.

Weber and Marx on Class: Convergences

There is a long history of discussions of the relationship between Marx's and Weber's social theories, beginning with occasional comments by Weber himself, most famously in his discussion of the *Communist Manifesto* in a speech to Austrian officers towards the end of World War I.[28] Although Weber was appreciative of Marx's theoretical formulations, he was highly critical of their excessive materialism and dismissive of the utopianism of Marx's theory of history, with its optimistic deterministic prediction of the transcendence of capitalism and the disappearance of classes and the state. Much of the subsequent discussion of Marx and Weber has also revolved around the sharp differences in the broad contours of their respective, general, theoretical frameworks for understanding the trajectory of historical change—in particular the contrast between Marx's historical materialism as a quasi-teleological theory of history, and Weber's multidimensional theory of historical development and contingency.[29] When the focus of comparison has centered on stratification issues, the central theme in most discussions has also been the contrast between Marx's preoccupation with a single aspect of stratification—class—and Weber's complex multidimensional view, in which the relationship between class and other bases of stratification, especially status, is of central concern.[30] Relatively less attention has been given to the fact that, in spite of the different salience of class within the overall theoretical agendas of Marx and Weber, there are deep similarities between the concepts of class in these two traditions of social theory.[31] To give precision to the specific problem of the location of exploitation within class analysis, I first review these strong similarities.

RELATIONAL RATHER THAN GRADATIONAL CLASS CONCEPTS

Both Marx and Weber adopt relational concepts of class. Neither defines classes simply as nominal levels on some gradational hierarchy. For both, classes are derived from an account of systematic interactions of social actors situated in relation to each other. Classes for both Weber and Marx are thus not primarily identified by quantitative names like upper, upper middle, middle, lower middle, and lower, but by qualitative names like capitalists and workers, debtors and creditors.[32]

THE CENTRALITY OF PROPERTY RELATIONS

Both Marx and Weber see property ownership as the fundamental source of class division in capitalism. For Marx, classes are defined by the "relation to the means of production," where "relation" here means ownership and control over resources used in production. Similarly, Weber writes, "'Property' and 'lack of property' are, therefore, the basic categories of all class situations."[33] What is more, Weber, like Marx, sees propertylessness as an essentially coercive condition: "[Those who are propertyless] have nothing to offer but their labor or the resulting products and . . . are compelled to get rid of these products in order to subsist at all."[34] He even acknowledges, like Marx, that for the working class the apparently freely chosen, voluntary interactions of the market are simply a formal reality, masking an essentially coercive structure of social relations (which he refers to as "heteronomously determined action"):

[Action that is motivated by self-interest can still be] substantively heteronomously determined . . . [in] a market economy, though in a formally voluntary way. This is true whenever the unequal distribution of wealth, and particularly of capital goods, forces the non-owning group to comply with the authority of others in order to obtain any return at all for the utilities they can offer on the market. . . . In a purely capitalist organization of production, this is the fate of the entire working class.[35]

Although this statement may lack the rhetorical force of Marx's account of the essential unfreedom of the worker, the point is fundamentally the same:

being separated from the means of production forces workers to subordinate themselves to capitalists.

CLASSES-AS-PLACES VERSUS CLASSES-AS-COLLECTIVE-ACTORS

Central to the conception of class in both Weber and Marx is a distinction between classes as *objectively defined places* and as *collectively organized social actors*. The language they use to describe this contrast, of course, differs. Weber uses the expression "class situation" to designate objectively defined places within social relations,[36] whereas Marx uses the expression "class-in-itself," and contemporary Marxists have used the expressions "class location" or "class position" or "class structure" depending on the context. Weber uses the expression "class-conscious organization" to designate class as a collectively organized social actor;[37] Marx uses the expression "class-for-itself," and contemporary Marxists use a variety of terms, such as "class formation" or "class organization." But regardless of terminology, the basic idea is similar: Structurally defined classes may have a tendency to generate collectively organized forms of struggle, but the two must be conceptually distinguished.

CLASSES AND MATERIAL INTERESTS

Both Weber and Marx see objectively definable material interests as a central mechanism through which class locations influence social action. By objectively definable material interests I mean that an outside observer can, in principle, specify which courses of action available to an individual by virtue of their location in a social structure would improve that person's material conditions of life. Both Marx and Weber claim that (1) a person's class location, defined by his or her relation to property, systematically affects material interests in this sense; and that (2) material interests so defined do influence actual behavior. These claims are relatively uncontroversial for Marx, even though much debate has been waged over whether "class interests" in Marxism are "objective." Weber, in contrast, is often characterized as a theorist who emphasizes the subjective meanings of actors and who rejects the idea of a determinate relation between objectively specified conditions and subjective states of actors. Nevertheless, in his discussion of class, material interests rooted in individuals' objectively defined class situations are seen as a determinant—albeit a probabilistic determinant—of their behavior. Weber writes:

According to our terminology, the factor that creates "class" is unambiguously economic interest, and indeed, only those interests involved in the existence of the market. Nevertheless the concept of class-interest is an ambiguous one: even as an empirical concept it is ambiguous as soon as one understands by it something other than the *factual direction of interests following with a certain probability from the class situation for a certain average of those people subjected to the class situation.*[38]

Thus, Weber affirms that "for a certain average of those people subjected to the class situation" there is a "certain probability" that the "factual direction of interests" will coincide with class interests. Weber thus allows for deviations between individual behavior and the material interests associated with class situations, but he also argues that there is at least a tendency, on average, for behavior to be in line with those interests.

Of course, the expression "a certain probability" is rather vague and leaves open the possibility that this probability could be extremely low and thus the relationship between objectively defined class interests and the "factual direction of interests" could be very weak. Two earlier passages in *Economy and Society* suggest that Weber in fact believed that purely self-interested economic advantage had a high probability of giving "factual direction" to motivations of most people much of the time. The first passage comes in a discussion of economic motivations within the formation of organizations. Weber writes:

Economic considerations have one very general kind of sociological importance for the formation of organizations if, as is almost always true, the directing authority and the administrative staff are remunerated. If this is the case, *an overwhelmingly strong set of economic interests* become bound up with the continuation of the organization, even though its primary ideological basis may in the meantime have ceased to exist.[39]

Even more starkly, in a discussion of economic activity in a potential socialist society, Weber believes that motivations will be similar to those in a market society, and he thus expresses considerable skepticism about the possibility that ideological commitments will matter very much in socialism. In the long run, Weber argues, most people will be motivated by self-interested material advantage, just as in a market economy:

What is decisive is that in socialism, too, the individual will under these conditions [in which individuals have some capacity to make economically relevant decisions] ask first whether to him, personally, the rations allotted and the work assigned, as compared with other possibilities, appear to conform with his own interests. . . . [It] would be the interests of the individual, possibly organized in terms of the similar interests of many individuals as opposed to those of others, which would underlie all action. The *structure* of interests and the relevant situation would be different [from a market economy], and there would be other means of pursuing interests, but this fundamental factor would remain just as relevant as before. It is of course true that economic action which is oriented on purely ideological grounds to the interests of others does exist. But it is even more certain that the *mass of men do not act in this way and that it is an induction from experience that they cannot do so and never will.*[40]

This is a powerful affirmation of the factual predominance of subjective orientations derived from objectively definable, material interests: although it is theoretically possible that ideological motivations could be important, the mass of people do not act on purely ideological grounds and, furthermore, "they cannot do so and never will." For both Weber and Marx, therefore, the material interests structured by class locations have a strong tendency to shape the actual behavior of people within those locations.

THE CONDITIONS FOR COLLECTIVE CLASS ACTION

If there is one aspect of class analysis where one might expect a sharp difference between Marx and Weber, it is in their understanding of the problem of class struggle. Although both may believe that class situations shape *individual* class behaviors via material interests, Marx believed that capitalism inherently generates *collectively* organized class struggles, eventually culminating in revolutionary challenges to capitalism, whereas Weber rejects this prediction. Yet, even here, there is more similarity in their views than one might initially expect.

In assessing arguments of this sort, it is important to distinguish (1) the *theoretical* analysis of the *conditions under which particular predictions hold*, in this case that class struggles are likely to emerge and intensify, from (2) *the empirical expectations about the likelihood of those conditions actually occurring*. In these terms, Weber shares much with Marx in terms of the first consideration, but disagrees sharply over the second.[41]

In *Economy and Society*, in a section labeled "social action flowing from class interest," Weber lays out some of the conditions that he feels are conducive to collectively organized class struggles:

The degree to which "social action" and possibly associations emerge from the mass behavior of members of a class is linked to general cultural conditions, especially to those of an intellectual sort. It is also linked to the extent of the contrasts that have already evolved, and is especially linked to the transparency of the connections between the causes and the consequences of the class situation. For however different life chances may be, this fact in itself according to all experience, by no means gives birth to "class action" (social action by members of a class). For that, the real conditions and the results of the class situation must be distinctly recognizable. For only then the contrast of life chances can be felt not as an absolutely given fact to be accepted, but as a resultant from either (1) the given distribution of property, or (2) the structure of the concrete economic order. It is only then that people may react against the class structure not only through acts of intermittent and irrational protest, but in the form of rational association. . . . The most important historical example of the second category (2) is the class situation of the modern proletariat.[42]

This complex paragraph involves several very Marx-like theses. First, the emergence of class associations depends on intellectual conditions; it is not simply the result of unmediated spontaneous consciousness of people in disadvantaged class situations. This is congruent with Marx's view of the role of ideological mystification in preventing class organization and the importance of class-conscious intellectual leadership in raising working-class consciousness, a theme stressed in different ways by later Marxists such as Gramsci and Lenin.

Second, where class structures are experienced as natural and inevitable, as "absolutely given facts," class mobilization is impeded. Weber points here to the central issue that Marx, especially in his discussion of commodity fetishism and capital fetishism, also identifies as the most important intellectual obstacle to class consciousness: the belief in the naturalness and permanency of the existing conditions and thus the impossibility of any fundamental change. Much of Marx's work, in fact, can be viewed as an attempt at a scientific challenge to such apparent "naturalness" in the belief that such demystification would contribute to forging revolutionary consciousness.

Third, the transparency of class relations facilitates class mobilization. Marx also believed that class mobilization would be more difficult where there were lots of intermediary classes—petite bourgeois, peasants, professionals—than where class structures were highly polarized, and the causal connection between the class structure and the conditions of people's lives was transparent. This is an important part of Marx's prediction that capitalism's destruction of all precapitalist economic relations and the immiseration of the proletariat would lead to intensified class conflict.

Last, because of the relative transparency of their class situation, the modern proletariat comes to understand that "the contrast of life chances . . . [is the result of] the structure of the concrete economic order." Modern capitalism therefore creates the required kind of transparency for class associations of workers to be likely.

Weber's and Marx's theoretical specification of the conditions for class associations to emerge thus share many elements, and Weber shares with Marx at least the limited expectation that these conditions will be minimally satisfied in the case of the modern proletariat in capitalist economies so that class associations and class struggles are likely to occur. Where they differ—and this is a difference that matters—is in the *empirical prediction* that the inner dynamics of capitalism are such that these conditions will be *progressively strengthened over time*, leading to a systematic tendency for long-term intensification of class struggles within capitalism. *If* Marx's empirical predictions about these conditions had been correct, then Weber would have shared with Marx the prediction that class conflicts would have a tendency to continuously intensify in the course of capitalist development. Where they differ, therefore, is in their predictions about the long-term trajectory of capitalism more than in their views about the conditions under which capitalism would engender a class-conscious organized working class.[43]

CLASS AND STATUS

Finally, Marx and Weber even have some similar things to say theoretically in an area where sociologists generally think they diverge most: in their treatment of the relationship between class and status. A central issue in Weberian sociology is the enduring importance of status groups as a source of identity and privilege. As such, status groups are seen as competing with class as bases of solidarity and collective action. Marx shared with Weber the views that (1) status groups impede the operation of capitalist markets, and further, that (2) they constitute an alternative basis of identity to class formation. And Weber shared with Marx the view that (3) capitalist markets tended to erode the strength of status groups and their effects on the system of stratification.[44] Weber writes:

When the bases of the acquisition and distribution of goods are relatively stable, stratification by status is favored. Every technological repercussion and economic transformation threatens stratification by status and pushes the class situation into the foreground. Epochs and countries in which the naked class situation is of predominant significance are regularly the periods of technical and economic transformations.[45]

Using different rhetoric, Marx and Engels, in *The Communist Manifesto*, made parallel arguments:

Constant revolutionizing of production, uninterrupted disturbances of all social conditions, everlasting uncertainty and agitation distinguish the bourgeois epoch from all earlier ones. All fixed, fast-frozen relations, with their train of ancient and venerable prejudices and opinions, are swept away.[46]

The reference to "all fixed, fast-frozen relations" taps the same kinds of categories that Weber theorized as "stratification by status," and Marx and Engels, like Weber, see these relations threatened by "revolutionizing of production, . . . disturbances of all social conditions," or what Weber termed "periods of technical and economic transformations." So, both Marx and Weber see capitalism as undermining status groups and fostering a predominance of what Weber called "naked class situation." They may have differed in their beliefs about the long-term consequences of this development for class mobilization and struggle—Marx believed it would reinforce tendencies toward polarized class struggle, whereas Weber believed that the development of capitalism was producing a much more complex class structure less vulnerable to polarized struggle[47]—but both saw capitalism as systematically eroding the salience of traditional status groups.

Weber and Marx on Class: Central Differences

If the preceding analysis is correct, then both Weber and Marx deploy varieties of property-centered relational concepts of class in which, among other things, objectively definable, material interests play a central role in explaining class action; class structure and class struggle are distinguished; collective class action is facilitated by class polarization; and the dynamic processes of capitalism create conditions favorable to class playing a pervasive role in systems of stratification. Where they differ most sharply is in their understanding of the causal mechanisms that are linked to such property-relational classes. For Weber, the pivotal issue is how classes determine the *life chances* of people within highly rationalized forms of economic interactions—markets; for Marx, the central issue is how class determines both life chances and *exploitation*.[48]

The basic idea of the determination of life chances by class is laid out in Weber's frequently cited passage:

We may speak of a "class" when (1) a number of people have in common a specific causal component of their life chances, insofar as (2) this component is represented exclusively by economic interests in the possession of goods and opportunities for income, and (3) is represented under the conditions of the commodity or labor markets. This is "class situation."

It is the most elemental economic fact that the way in which the disposition over material property is distributed among a plurality of people, meeting competitively in the market for the purpose of exchange, in itself creates specific life chances. . . .

But always this is the generic connotation of the concept of class: that the kind of chance in the *market* is the decisive moment which presents a common condition for the individual's fate. Class situation is, in this sense, ultimately market situation.[49]

"Opportunity" in this context is a description of the feasible set individuals face, the tradeoffs they encounter in deciding what to do to improve their material conditions. The Weberian claim is that in a market society—a society in which people acquire the wherewithal to live by exchanging things with others in an instrumentally rational way—such opportunities are caused by the quality and quantity of what people have to exchange. When markets are fully and pervasively present, opportunities are not mainly caused by economically irrelevant ascriptive attributes or by individuals' control of violence, but by the resources a person can bring to the market for exchange. Owning the means of production gives a person different alternatives from owning credentials, and both of these differ from simply owning unskilled labor power. Furthermore, in a market economy, access to market-derived income affects a broad array of life experiences and opportunities for oneself and one's children. The study of the life-chances of children based on parents' market capacity—the problem of class mobility—is thus an integral part of the Weberian agenda of class analysis. Within a Weberian perspective, therefore, the salient consequence that flows from people's links to different kinds of economic resources deployed in markets is the way these links confer on them different kinds of economic opportunities and disadvantages, thereby shaping their material interests.

This definition is intimately connected to the problem of rationalization. When people meet to make an exchange in a market, they rationally calculate the costs and benefits of alternatives on the basis of the prices they face. These prices provide people with the kind of information they need to make rational calculations, and the constraints of market interactions force them to make decisions on the basis of these calculations in a more or less rational manner. Weber is fundamentally less interested in the problem of the material deprivations and advantages of different categories of people as such, or in the collective struggles that might spring from those advantages and disadvantages, than he is in the underlying normative order and cognitive practices—instrumental rationality—embodied in the social interactions that generate these life chances.

Marx would agree with Weber that the ownership of different resources used in market exchanges affects life chances. And like Weber, he recognizes that exchanges in the market constitute interactions based on calculation and instrumental rationality.[50] But in Marx's class analysis, the effect of exchange on life chances is only half the story. Of equal significance is how property relations shape the process of exploitation. Both "exploitation" and "life chances" identify inequalities in material well-being that are generated by inequalities in access to resources of various sorts. Thus, both of these concepts point to conflicts of interest over the distribution of the assets. What exploitation adds to this is a claim that conflicts of interest between classes are generated not simply by conflicts over the distribution and value of resources people bring to exchanges in the market, but also by the nature of the interactions and interdependencies generated by the use of those resources in productive activity.

Exploitation, for Marx, identified the process by which labor effort performed by one group of economic actors is extracted and appropriated by another group. That appropriated labor is referred to as "surplus labor," meaning laboring activity above and beyond what is required to reproduce the laborers themselves. In capitalism, for Marx, this appropriation occurs because employers are able to force workers to work longer hours and perform more labor than is embodied in the products that they consume with their wages. Expressed in the classical language of the labor theory of value, the labor value of what they produce is greater than the labor value of what they consume. The difference—surplus value—is appropriated by the capitalist. This appropriation is exploitation.[51]

The concept of exploitation, defined in this way, is used by Marx in two explanatory contexts. First, Marx sees exploitation as the source of profits in capitalism: capitalists appropriate surplus value from workers that, when capitalists sell the commodities embodying that surplus value, is turned into money profits. Profits, in turn, are essential for investment and capital accumulation. In this way, exploitation figures centrally in Marx's account of the dynamics of capitalism. Second, Marx sees exploitation as central to explaining the character of conflict between workers and capitalists. Exploitation constitutes a social relation that simultaneously pits the interests of one class against another, binds the two classes together in ongoing interactions, and confers upon the disadvantaged group a real form of power with which to challenge the interests of exploiters. This is an important point. Exploitation depends on the appropriation of labor effort in ongoing social interactions. Because human beings are conscious agents, they always retain significant levels of control over their expenditure of effort. The extraction of effort within exploitative relations is thus always to a greater or lesser extent problematic and precarious, requiring active institutional devices for its reproduction. Such devices can become expensive to exploiters in the form of the costs of supervision, surveillance, and sanctions, for example. The ability to impose such costs constitutes a form of power among the exploited.

The exchange relations that shape life chances also involve conflicts of interest. Yet, in an idealized competitive market in which direct coercion is absent from the exchange process itself, these conflicts are muted by the apparent voluntariness of the act of exchange. As Weber remarks, "'Exchange' is a compromise of interests on the part of the parties in the course of which goods or other advantages are passed as reciprocal compensation. . . . Every case of rationally oriented exchange is the resolution of a previously open or latent conflict of interests by means of a compromise."[52] Marx, similarly, sees the market exchanges between workers and capitalists as involving reciprocity and a degree of common interest:

[Exchange between labor and capital implies] equality, because each enters into relation with the other, as with a simple owner of commodities, and they exchange equivalent for equivalent. . . . The only force that brings them together and puts them in relation with each other, is the selfishness, the gain and the private interests of each. Each looks to himself only, and no one troubles himself about the rest, and just because they do so, do they all, in accordance with the pre-established harmony of things, or under the auspices of an all-shrewd providence, work together to their mutual advantage, for the common weal and in the interest of all.[53]

Within production, by contrast, the containment of the conflict of interests between the performers of labor effort and the appropriators of that effort requires the ongoing exercise of domination through complex forms of surveillance, discipline, and control of the labor process. The conflict over exploitation is not settled in the reciprocal compromise of a contractual moment; it is continuously present in the interactions through which labor is performed.

The central difference between Marx's and Weber's concepts of class, then, is that the Weberian account revolves exclusively around market transactions, whereas the Marxist account also emphasizes the importance of conflict over the performance and appropriation of labor effort that takes place after market exchanges are contracted. This contrast is illustrated in Figure 9.1. Weber's class analysis revolves around a single causal nexus that works through market exchange; Marxist class analysis includes the Weberian causal processes, but adds to them a causal structure within production itself. The Marxist concept of class directs our attention both theoretically and empirically toward the systematic interaction of exchange and production.

One of the striking implications of this contrast between the Weberian and Marxist concepts of class is that Weber—at least in his most mature work when he is formalizing his concepts—rejects the idea that slaves are a class, whereas for Marxists slavery constitutes one form of precapitalist class relations.[54] Weber writes:

Those men whose fate is not determined by the chance of using goods or services for themselves on the market, e.g. slaves, are not, however, a class in the technical sense of the term. They are, rather, a status group.[55]

For Weber, slaves are a specific instance of a general theoretical category—*status groups*—that also includes ethnic groups, occupational groups, and other categories "that are stratified according to the principles of their *consumption* of goods as represented by special styles of life."[56] These groups differ by the meanings and criteria that accord differential social honor to different "styles of life," and "slavery" is just one way of organizing such status rankings. In contrast, Marxists would see slavery primarily as a special instance of a different general theoretical category—class—that includes capitalists and workers in capitalism, lords and serfs in feudalism, slaves and slave owners in slavery. Although these categories differ in lifestyles and the cultural criteria used to impart symbolic rankings, the crucial difference is their mechanism of exploitation—the ways in which labor effort is appropriated from one category by another. Marx, of course, like Weber, recognized that in precapitalist societies social division was organized around status orders involving personal dependence and extra-economic coercion. But for Marx the most salient feature of such status orders was how they underwrote distinctive forms of exploitation. It is these practices that justify treating slavery as a variety of the abstract category "class relations" within a class concept centered on exploitation.

FIGURE 9.1.   *Core Elements of Weber's and Marx's Class Analysis*

Basic causal structure of Weber's class analysis

Basic causal structure of Marx's class analysis

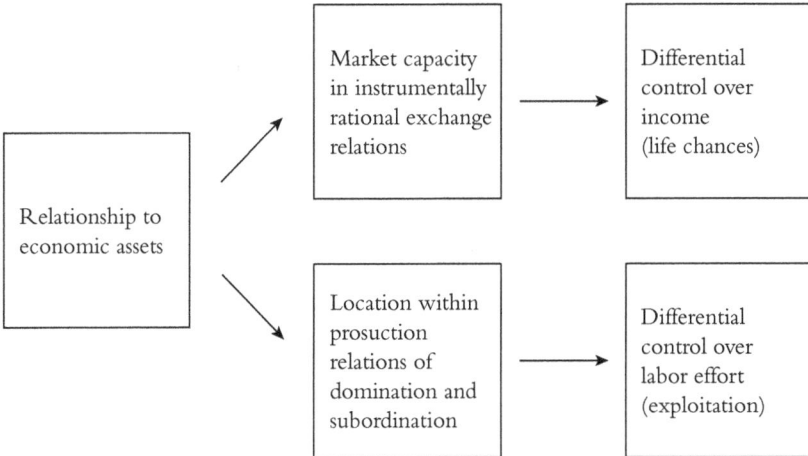

SOURCE: Wright, *Class Counts*, p. 34.

The Shadow of Exploitation in Weber

Although Weber's definition of the concept of class says nothing explicitly about exploitation, in *Economy and Society* and elsewhere Weber touches on the substantive problems that, within Marxist coordinates, would be characterized as involving the exploitation of labor. How Weber deals with these problems is revealing of the inner logic of his approach to class analysis.[57]

Weber engages the problem of the performance and appropriation of labor effort within the system of production primarily as an issue of work discipline, the "incentives to work," and economic efficiency. This identification of the problem of extracting labor effort and technical efficiency is one of the themes in Weber's discussion in *The Protestant Ethic* of the problem of using piece-rates as a strategy for getting workers to work harder. Here is the relevant passage:

One of the technical means which the modern employer uses in order to secure the greatest possible amount of work from his men is the device of piece-rates. In agriculture, for instance, the gathering of the harvest is a case where the greatest possible intensity of labour is called for, since, the weather being uncertain, the difference between high profit and heavy loss may depend on the speed with which the harvesting can be done. Hence a system of piece-rates is almost universal in this case. And since the interest of the employer in a speeding-up of harvesting increases with the increase of the results and the intensity of work, their attempt has again and again been made, by increasing the piece-rates of the workmen, thereby giving them an opportunity to earn what for them is a very high wage, to interest them in increasing their own efficiency. But a peculiar difficulty has been met with surprising frequency: raising piece-rates has often had the result that not more but less has been accomplished in the same time, because the worker reacted to the increase not by increasing but by decreasing the amount of work. . . . The opportunity of working more was less attractive than that of working less. . . . This is an example of what is here meant by traditionalism. A man does not "by nature" wish to earn more and more money, but simply to live as he is accustomed to live and to earn as much as is necessary for that purpose. Whenever modern capitalism has begun its work of increasing the productivity of human labor by increasing its intensity, it has encountered the immensely stubborn resistance of this leading trait of pre-capitalistic labor.[58]

Weber concludes that this technical problem can be effectively solved only when the laborer adopts a set of attitudes toward work—the Protestant work ethic—that generates a moral imperative for him or her to expend a maximum of effort:

Labour must, on the contrary, be performed as if it were an absolute end in itself, a calling. But such an attitude is by no means a product of nature. It cannot be evoked by low wages or high ones alone, but can only be a product of a long and arduous process of education.[59]

Weber discusses at greater length in *Economy and Society* the motivation of workers to expend effort in a discussion of the "conditions affecting the optimization of calculable performance by labor."[60] "Optimization of calculable performance" is a specific problem within the broader discussion of the conditions that foster or impede technical rationality in economic organization. Weber cites three primary conditions for this optimization to occur: "(a) the optimum of aptitude for the function; (b) the optimum of skill acquired through practice; (c) the optimum of inclination for the work."[61] The third of these concerns the performance of labor effort. Weber writes:

> In the specific sense of incentive to execute one's own plans or those of persons supervising one's work [the inclination to work] must be determined either by a strong self-interest in the outcome or by direct or indirect compulsion. The latter is particularly important in relation to work which executes the dispositions of others. This compulsion may consist in the immediate threat of physical force or of other undesirable consequences, or in the probability that unsatisfactory performance will have an adverse effect on earnings.
>
> The second type, which is essential to a market economy, appeals immensely more strongly to the worker's self-interest.[62]

Weber then discusses three necessary conditions for this "indirect compulsion" to be effective: (1) *Employers have a free hand in hiring and firing workers*: "It also necessitates freedom of selection according to performance, both qualitatively and quantitatively, though naturally from the point of view of its bearing on profit." (2) *Workers lack both ownership and control over the means of production*: "It presupposes the expropriation of the workers from the means of production by owners is protected by force."[63] (3) *Workers bear the responsibility for their own reproduction*: "As compared with direct compulsion to work, this systems involves the transferral [of] . . . the responsibility for reproduction (in the family) . . . to the workers themselves."[64] Where these conditions are met, workers will expend the optimum amount of effort from the point of view of profits of the capitalist.

Where the above three conditions do not exist, labor effort will tend to be restricted, resulting in a decline in technical rationality. In particular, Weber discusses situations in which the first condition is violated—conditions in which workers themselves retain some significant degree of control over the deployment of their labor:

> [O]pportunities for disposal of labor services may be appropriated by an organization of workers, either without any appropriation by the individual worker or with important limitations on such appropriation. This may involve absolute or relative closure against outsiders and also prohibition of the dismissal of workers from employment by management without consent of the workers, or at least some kind of limitations on powers of dismissal. . . .
>
> Every form of appropriation of jobs in profit-making enterprises by workers . . . [results in] a limitation on the *formal* rationalization of economic activity.[65]

At the core of this limitation on formal rationalization is the problem of labor effort. If workers appropriate their jobs but owners still appropriate the products of labor, technical rationality is limited "through a tendency to restrict the work effort, either by tradition, or by convention, or by contract; also through the reduction or complete disappearance . . . of the worker's own interest in optimal effort."[66] Weber goes on to argue that the problem of getting a technically rational level of work effort from workers who control their jobs is similar to the problem of getting work effort from slaves:

> The very opposite forms of appropriation—that of jobs by workers and that of workers by owners—nevertheless have in practice very similar results. [When workers are appropriated by owners] it is natural that exploitation of labor services should, to a large extent, be stereotyped; hence that work effort should be restricted and that the workers have little self-interest in the output. . . . Hence, almost universally the work effort of appropriated workers has shown a tendency to restriction. . . . When jobs have been formally appropriated by workers, the same result has come about even more rapidly.[67]

If one wants the technically most efficient performance of labor effort by workers within production, therefore, workers must not only be expropriated from the means of production, but must also lose any real control over their jobs and the labor process.

One situation in which Weber sees that the appropriation of jobs by workers might not lead to restriction of work effort is where the workers are also owners of the means of production: "The appropriation of the means of production and personal control . . . over the process of workers constitute one of the strongest incentives to unlimited willingness to work."[68] But this situation creates other irrationalities, especially because "the interests of workers in the maintenance of jobs ('livings') is often in conflict with the rationality of the organization."[69] Thus, although workers in a worker-owned cooperative might work very hard, they would engage in technically irrational behavior in their allocation of labor and their unwillingness to hire and fire labor as the market required.

Weber's stance toward the problem of work effort in these passages is broadly in line with that of contemporary neoclassical microeconomics. Most neoclassical economists see any restriction by workers of managerial control of labor and the labor process as generating efficiency losses, both because of technically suboptimal allocations of resources and because of restrictions of labor effort by workers. Like Weber, these economists believe that control of the workplace by workers leads to worker opportunism—workers serving their own interests at the expense of efficiency. The only real solution to such opportunism is preventing workers from appropriating their jobs and making the alternative to conscientious performance of work especially unpleasant. Thus, they would endorse Weber's statement that "[f]ree labor and the complete appropriation of the means of production [by the owner] create the most favorable conditions for discipline."[70]

The problem of the performance and appropriation of work effort is thus, for Weber, above all a question of the degree and forms of rationality in economic organization. This does not mean that Weber was unaware that these forms of rationality might impose harms on workers: "The fact that the maximum of *formal* rationality in capital accounting is possible only where the workers are subjected to domination by entrepreneurs is a further specific element of *substantive* irrationality in the modern economic order."[71] Indeed, as Mommsen, Löwith, Schroeter, and others have noted, running throughout Weber's work is the view that rationalization has perverse effects which systematically threaten human dignity and welfare, particularly because of the ways in which it intensifies bureaucratic domination.[72] Weber thus hardly held a benign view of capitalism and the work organization it entailed. Nevertheless, he did not treat this problem of extracting work effort as central to the class relations of capitalism and the conflicts of interests that those relations engendered.

Ramifications

All in all, the formal characteristics of the concept of class in capitalist societies are rather similar in Weber and Marx. They differ primarily in the broader theoretical context in which these definitions are embedded and in their accounts of the central causal mechanisms that are linked to class relations. For Weber, these mechanisms are primarily the ways in which ownership of property affects life chances via instrumentally rational exchanges in the market; for Marx, they are the ways in which ownership of property affects life chances and exploitation through the interplay of markets and production. Although Weber also, if only in passing, touches on issues closely related to exploitation, particularly the problem of labor discipline and domination, he does not integrate these concerns into the general concept of class but treats them primarily as issues in the technical efficiency of systems of production.

One might still ask, so what? Does this really matter? Even if Weber underplayed the importance of extraction of labor effort, there is nothing in his framework that actively blocks attention to this issue. And indeed, class analysts in the Weberian tradition have paid varying degrees of attention to the problem of work discipline, labor effort, and related matters.

Nevertheless, there are consequences of elaborating the concept of class strictly in terms of market relations and life chances without a systematic connection to the problem of exploitation. Conceptual frameworks matter because, among other things, they direct thinking and research in particular ways. Here I would emphasize two issues: first, the ways in which explicitly linking exploitation to the concept of class changes the way class conflict is understood; and second, the ways exploitation infuses class analysis with a specific kind of normative concern.

The concept of exploitation draws attention to the ways in which class conflicts do not simply reflect conflicting interests over the distribution of a pie. Rather, to characterize class relations as exploitative emphasizes the ways in which exploiting classes are *dependent upon* the exploited class for their own economic well-being, and because of this dependency, the ways in which exploited classes have *capacities for resistance* that are organic to the class relation. Because workers always retain some control over the expenditure of effort and diligence, they have a capacity to resist their exploitation; and because capitalists need workers, there are constraints on the strategies available to capitalists to counter this resistance.[73]

Exploitation thus entails a specific kind of duality: conflicting material interests plus a real capacity for resistance. This duality has implications for the way we think about both the individual and collective power of workers: as individuals, the power of workers depends both on the scarcity of the kind of labor power they have to offer in the labor market (and thus their ability to extract individual "skill rents" through the sale of their labor power) and on their ability to control the expenditure of their individual effort within the labor process; as a collectivity, workers' power depends on their ability to collectively regulate the terms of exchange on the labor market (typically through unions) and their ability to control the organization of work, surveillance, and sanctions within production. The concept of exploitation, therefore, suggests a research agenda in which class conflict and the balance of class power must be understood in terms of the systematic interplay of interests and capacities within both exchange and production.

When the appropriation of labor effort is treated not in terms of the basic social relations that bind together workers and capitalists, but in terms of the formal rationality of the "conditions affecting the optimization of calculable performance by labor,"[74] the issue of labor effort becomes analyzed primarily as a technical problem of overcoming the traditionalism or opportunism of workers as individuals. Capitalists face a wide range of problems in enhancing the rational calculability of economic action. One problem is extracting the optimal level of work performance from employees. The fundamental solution to this problem is for workers to develop the right kinds of attitudes, as described in *The Protestant Ethic and the Spirit of Capitalism*. When workers see the performance of labor effort as a calling—when they have the proper work ethic—then the problem of optimizing the calculable performance of labor is greatly reduced, perhaps even eliminated. In the absence of this ethic, even when employees are closely supervised, the extraction of optimal levels of effort is an enduring problem. Instead of understanding the capacity of workers to control their own effort as a fundamental source of class-based power available to workers in their class struggles with capitalists, Weber sees this control as one of the obstacles to forming a fully rationalized economic order.

Beyond the issue of the conceptual mapping of research agendas, Marx's and Weber's conceptual frameworks direct class analysis toward different sets of normative concerns linked to the material interests of different classes. Both theorists ask questions and pursue agendas rooted in their values, although Weber is undoubtedly more self-conscious than Marx about trying to keep his values from shaping his conclusions.[75] The issue here is that the specific way the concept of class is built directs attention toward different kinds of normative agendas.

Weber's treatment of work effort as primarily a problem of economic rationality directs class analysis toward a set of normative concerns centered on the interests of capitalists: efficiency and rationalization. Although Weber is not blindly uncritical of capitalism and recognizes that, from the point of view of workers, the organization of work may be "substantively irrational," nevertheless, throughout his discussion of work effort he emphasizes that arrangements that enhance worker control and autonomy are technically irrational. Whether or not Weber was sympathetic to the conditions of workers, this preoccupation is very much in line with the interests of owners and managers. In contrast, the Marxist tradition of linking the problem of work effort to exploitation directs class analysis toward normative concerns centered on the interests of workers. The issue becomes not simply which arrangements are the most technically efficient from the point of view of profit maximization, but how particular ways of organizing exchange and production impose harms on workers. Marxists recognize that increasing exploitation is "efficient" from the point of view of capitalist economic organization, but the conceptual framework constantly brings to the foreground the ways in which such exploitation imposes harms on workers and poses the question, "under what conditions can such harms be challenged and eliminated?"

Notes

1. Because of the peripheral status of class in the Weberian oeuvre, it is surprising that so much of the literature on class sees Weber as a central source. Sørenson suggests that Weber's prominence in class analysis comes from the accident that his work on class was translated into English:

> The importance of the Weberian class concept in the literature on class analysis is a bit curious. In *Economy and Society* Weber deals with class in two places but both are very short fragments. While Marx can be said to never have given a single explicit development of the class concept, he certainly has class as the central concern of analysis in all of his writings. For Weber, there is neither a discussion

nor an extensive analysis. Class simply seems not to have been an important concept for Weber. . . . Since only Marx and Weber [among the German writers on class] have been translated into English, Weber has become the main justification for developing class concepts that are alternative to Marx's, despite the fragmentary nature of Weber's writings about this and the lack of importance of class concepts in his writings. (Aage Sørenson, "Toward a Sounder Basis for Class Analysis," *American Journal of Sociology* 105, no. 6 [May 2000]: 1527 n. 3.)

2. The chapter in *Economy and Society* in which Weber proposes to define the concept of class (part 1, chapter IV, "Status Groups and Classes") is unfinished. See Max Weber, *Economy and Society: An Outline of Interpretive Sociology*, ed. Guenther Roth and Claus Wittich (1921–22; Berkeley: University of California Press, 1978). In a footnote to the first place in the text in which Weber refers to this chapter, the editors of the English edition of the text comment: "This chapter is . . . a mere fragment which Weber intended to develop on a scale comparable with the others. Hence most of the material to which this note refers was probably never written down" (Weber, *Economy and Society*, p. 210 n. 45).

3. Max Weber, "Developmental Tendencies in the Situation of East Elbian Rural Labourers," in Keith Tribe, *Reading Weber* (1894; New York: Routledge, 1989), pp. 158–87.

4. Max Weber, "The Social Causes of the Decline of Ancient Civilization," in *The Agrarian Sociology of Ancient Civilizations*, trans. R. I. Frank (1909; London: Verso, 1988), pp. 387–411. This study dates from 1896.

5. Max Weber, *The Agrarian Sociology of Ancient Civilizations*. A detailed exegesis of Weber's work on agrarian class relations can be found in Dirk Käsler, *Max Weber: An Introduction to His Life and Work*, trans. Philippa Hurd (Chicago: University of Chicago Press, 1988).

6. The analysis in Weber's 1896 study of the causes of decline of ancient civilizations has a particularly Marxian flavor to it. His central argument is that the contradictions of slavery as a way of organizing production was the fundamental cause of the ultimate collapse of the Roman Empire. Although Weber's later concerns with rationality and calculability in economic relations are already present in this early work, its main preoccupation is with the difficulty of extracting adequate surplus in a slave-based economy once slavery is no longer based on capturing slaves in slave hunts, and the resulting transformations of the political conditions of reproduction of the Roman Empire. If one did not know that this piece was written by Weber, most people would assume it was a fairly sophisticated Marxist analysis of how the development of this particular kind of class system tended to erode the conditions of its own reproduction. For further discussion of this Marxian influence in Weber's early work, see Gerd Schroeter, "Dialogue, Debate, or Dissent: The Difficulties of Assessing Max Weber's Relationship to Marx," in Robert J. Antonio and Ronald M. Glassman, eds., *A Weber-Marx Dialogue* (Lawrence: University of Kansas Press, 1985), pp. 2–19, esp. pp. 6–7. For a contrary view, which denies that this work has a significant Marxian character, see Guenther Roth, "The Historical Relationship to Marxism," in Reinhard Bendix and Guenther Roth, eds., *Scholarship and Partisanship* (Berkeley: University of California Press, 1971), pp. 227–46.

7. Max Weber, *The Protestant Ethic and the Spirit of Capitalism*, trans. Talcott Parsons (1904; New York: Charles Scribner's Sons, 1958).

8. Weber, *The Protestant Ethic*, p. 179. The details of Weber's argument about the psychological ramifications of the ethic of ascetic Protestantism for the spirit of capitalism are familiar. Two more specific citations will suffice. For the Protestant bourgeoisie, wealth, Weber writes, "as a performance of duty in a calling . . . is not only morally permissible, but actually enjoined . . . the providential interpretation of profit-making justified the activities of the businessman" (ibid., p. 163). For the worker, on the other hand, "Labour must . . . be performed as if it were an absolute end in itself, a calling. . . . The ability of mental concentration, as well as the absolutely essential feeling of obligation to one's job, are here most often combined with a strict economy which calculates the possibility of high earnings, and a cool self-control and frugality which enormously increase performance" (ibid., pp. 61, 63).

9. When Weber's work is excerpted in anthologies on stratification, the selections concerning class are almost exclusively from the explicit definitional statement in chapter 11, section 6, of *Economy and Society*, "The Distribution of Power within the Political Community: Class, Status and Party." See, for instance, Reinhard Bendix and Seymour Martin Lipset, *Class, Status, and Power: Social Stratification in Comparative Perspective* (New York: Free Press, 1966); Anthony Giddens and David Held, *Classes, Power and Conflict: Classical and Contemporary Debates* (Berkeley: University of California Press, 1982); David Grusky, ed., *Social Stratification: Class, Race and Gender in Sociological Perspective* (Boulder, CO: Westview Press, 2001). It should be noted that there is a second section of *Economy and Society* that also contains a definitional exposition of the concept of class, the section entitled "Status Groups and Classes" (Weber, *Economy and Society*, pp. 302–7). Although written later than the chapter "Class, Status and Party," the discussion in "Status Groups and Classes" is much more fragmentary, consisting primarily of a series of unelaborated lists of items under general rubrics presented in the form of an outline. It has thus generally been given little attention by scholars interested in class. In any case, nothing in this later statement is at odds with the general interpretation of Weber's approach to class and his treatment of the problem of exploitation discussed here.

10. See, for instance, Anthony Giddens, *The Class Structure of the Advanced Societies* (New York: Harper and Row, 1973); Frank Parkin, *Class Inequality and Political Order* (New York: Praeger, 1971); John Scott, *Stratification and Power: Structures of Class, Status and Command* (Cambridge: Polity Press, 1996).

11. Nearly all of the chapter in *Economy and Society* that has most influenced subsequent discussions of Weber's approach to class—"The Distribution of Power within the Political Community: Class, Status, Party"—is devoted to class and status, with only one page at the end discussing party.

12. The terms Weber uses to differentiate these spheres of social interaction are "economic order," "social order" or "the sphere of the distribution of honor," and "the sphere of power" (Weber, *Economy and Society*, p. 938). This is somewhat confusing terminology because class, status, and party all concern questions of power (and thus power should not simply be identified with "party"), and all also involve

social action (and thus the social should not simply be identified with status). It is for this reason that the terminological distinction between economic, communal, and political seems more useful in the present context.

13. Weber, *Economy and Society*, p. 927.

14. Ibid., p. 932.

15. Ibid.

16. Ibid., p. 938.

17. Bryn Jones argues that because of the inherent qualities of collective action, members of class as defined by Weber could not even in principle act as a collective agent on the basis of their class interests because collective action requires forms of identification and rationality beyond mere instrumental interests. See Bryn Jones, "Max Weber and the Concept of Social Class," *Sociological Review* 23 (1975): 729–59.

18. Weber, *Economy and Society*, p. 935.

19. Ibid.

20. Unlike Table 9.1, which is derived from the relatively explicit, if underdeveloped, theoretical statements by Weber about the properties of the concept of class and its contrast to other concepts, the typology in Table 9.2 is inferred from various arguments dispersed throughout Weber's work.

21. A number of commentators on differences between Weber and Marx have emphasized the centrality of the problem of rationalization in Weber's analysis of capitalism. See, for instance, Karl Löwith, *Max Weber and Karl Marx*, trans. Hans Fantel (1932; London: George Allen & Unwin, 1982); Jones, *Max Weber*; and Derek Sayer, *Capitalism and Modernity: An Excursus on Marx and Weber* (London: Routledge, 1991). Jones and Sayer, in particular, link the problem of rationalization explicitly to Weber's analysis of classes.

22. Levine differentiates eight different forms of rationality in Weber's work. To the standard distinction between *instrumental rationality* (the rationality of adopting the best means for given ends) and *value rationality* or *substantive rationality* (the rationality of choosing actions that are consistent with value commitments), he adds *conceptual rationality* (the formation of increasingly precise and abstract concepts) and *formal rationality* (the creation of methodical, rationally defendable rules). Within each of these four types of rationality, he then distinguishes between *objective rationality* (rationality inscribed in institutionalized norms) and *subjective rationality* (rationality in mental processes). After elaborating these forms of rationalization that occur in Weber's writing, Levine adds one distinction not found so explicitly in Weber's work: within each of the four forms of objective rationalization, Levine differentiates what he terms *symbolic rationalization* and *organizational rationalization*. The final result, then, is a typology of twelve forms of rationalization. Donald Nathan Levine, *The Flight from Ambiguity: Essays in Social and Cultural Theory* (Chicago: University of Chicago Press, 1985), p. 210.

23. Weber, "Developmental Tendencies," p. 161.

24. Ibid., pp. 63, 172.

25. Weber, *Economy and Society*, pp. 137–38.

26. "However all these peculiarities of Western capitalism have derived their sig-

nificance in the last analysis only from their association with the capitalistic organization of labour. . . . Exact calculation—the basis of everything else—is only possible on a basis of free labour" (Weber, *The Protestant Ethic*, p. 22).

27. Weber, *The Agrarian Sociology*, pp. 53–56.

28. Max Weber, "Speech for the General Information of Austrian Officers in Vienna," trans. D. Hÿrch, in J. E. T. Eldridge, ed., *Max Weber: The Interpretation of Social Reality* (1918; London: Michael Joseph, 1971).

29. Although much of the commentary on Weber's and Marx's overall frameworks focuses on the differences in their approaches, some accounts emphasize significant convergences. For example, Löwith's *Max Weber and Karl Marx* discusses the relationship between Weber's concept of rationalization and Marx's concept of alienation in their theories of modern capitalism, and Sayer's *Capitalism and Modernity* analyzes their respective understandings of modernity. For anthologies of comparative analyses of Marx and Weber, see Robert J. Antonio and Ronald M. Glassman, eds., *A Weber-Marx Dialogue* (Lawrence: University of Kansas Press, 1985); and Norbert Wiley, ed., *The Marx-Weber Debate* (Newbury Park, CA: Sage, 1986).

30. For a recent, analytically rigorous discussion of Marx's and Weber's approaches to class that stresses the contrast between the multidimensional character of Weber's approach and Marx's preoccupation with a single dimension, see Scott, *Stratification and Power*.

31. Some writers have noted similarities between Weber's and Marx's class concepts. Bendix sees Weber's analysis of class as departing from a "baseline that Marx had established" (Reinhard Bendix, "Inequality and Social Structure: A Comparison of Marx and Weber," *American Sociological Review*, 39, no 2 [April 1974]: 149–61, p. 152). Holton and Turner observe that "both Marx and Weber are concerned with market relations in the constitution of classes" (Robert Holton and Bryan Turner, *Max Weber on Economy and Society* [London & New York: Routledge, 1989], p. 181). Giddens sees Weber, like Marx, characterizing capitalism as a "class society"—a society within which class is the primary axis of stratification (Giddens, *The Class Structure*). Still, in each of these cases, the observation of similarity is given much less weight than are the differences between Marx's and Weber's class concepts. Sayer is one of the few writers who regards the differences between Marx's and Weber's approaches to both class and status as of secondary importance (Sayer, *Capitalism and Modernity*).

32. For more on relational and gradational concepts of class, see Stanilaw Ossowski, *Class Structure in the Social Consciousness* (London: Routledge & Kegan Paul, 1963); Erik Olin Wright, *Class Structure and Income Determination* (New York: Academic Press, 1979); Erik Olin Wright, *Class Counts* (Cambridge: Cambridge University Press, 1997), pp. 5–8.

33. Weber, *Economy and Society*, p. 927.

34. Ibid. In an earlier statement in the same work, while discussing economic motivations, Weber writes: "[T]he motivation of economic activity under the conditions of a market economy . . . for those without substantial property [includes] the fact that they run the risk of going entirely without provisions. . . . " (Ibid., p. 110). Also see Weber's discussion of the "compulsion of the whip of hunger." Max

Weber, *General Economic History*, trans. Frank H. Knight (1927; New York: Collier Books, 1961), p. 209.

35. Weber, *Economy and Society*, p. 110.

36. Ibid., pp. 302, 927.

37. Ibid., p. 305.

38. Ibid., pp. 928–29 (italics added).

39. Ibid., pp. 201–2 (italics added).

40. Ibid., p. 203 (italics added).

41. Bendix recognizes that Weber shares with Marx many elements of the theory of the conditions under which class mobilization is likely to succeed: " . . . *class organizations* occur only when an immediate economic opponent is involved, organization is technically easy (as in the factory), and clear goals are articulated by an intelligentsia. . . . Weber accepted Marx's reasons for the success of such organizations" (Bendix, "Inequality and Social Structure," p. 152).

42. Weber, *Economy and Society*, pp. 929–30.

43. Another instance in which Weber shares Marx's theoretical analysis of conditions for effective, collective class mobilization, is in their respective analyses of the peasantry. Marx is famous for arguing, in "The Eighteenth Brumaire of Louis Bonaparte," that in spite of their common class interests, peasants had little capacity for collective action because they were so dispersed in the countryside and remained as separate entities with no interdependency—like a "sack of potatoes." See Karl Marx, "The Eighteenth Brumaire of Lous Bonaparte," in Karl Marx and Frederick Engels, *Selected Works in One Volume* (1852; New York: International Publishers 1970). Weber makes a similar point about East Elbian peasants: "For the [agricultural] labourer then the possibility of brutal personal domination that could be only escaped by flight gave way to commercial exploitation which, arising almost unnoticed, was actually much harder to evade and which as a smallholder he was not in a position to do. Formal equality then placed the labourers in a struggle of interests for which, dispersed far over the land as they were, they lacked the means of resistance" (Weber, "Developmental Tendencies," p. 171).

44. Mommsen makes the even stronger claim that, from early in his career, Weber believed that capitalism would not merely erode traditional status orders, but would destroy them: "As early as 1893 Weber predicted that within a few generations, capitalism would destroy all tradition-bound social structures and that this process was irreversible." See Wolfgang Mommsen, "Capitalism and Socialism: Weber's Dialogue with Marx," trans. David Herr, in Robert J. Antonio and Ronald M. Glassman, *A Weber-Marx Dialogue* (Lawrence: University of Kansas Press, 1985), p. 234. Most sociologists drawing on Weber's work assume that status remains a salient dimension of stratification even though capitalism would significantly reduce its weight as a mechanism of identity and exclusion.

45. Weber, *Economy and Society*, p. 938.

46. Karl Marx and Frederick Engels, *The Communist Manifesto*, in Karl Marx and Frederick Engels, *Selected Works in One Volume* (1848; London: Lawrence & Wishart, 1968), p. 38.

47. In Weber's "Speech for the General Information of Austrian Officers in Vi-

enna," in which he puts forth an extended discussion of Marxism and the prospects of socialism in Germany, Weber explains how changes in class structure tie the interests of large numbers of people to the bourgeoisie:

> Parallel to these very complex processes, however, there appears a rapid rise in the number of clerks, i.e., in private *bureaucracy*—its growth rate is statistically much greater than that of the workers—and their interests certainly do not lie with one accord in the direction of a proletarian dictatorship. Then again, the advent of highly diverse and complicated ways of sharing interests means that at the present time it is quite impossible to maintain that the power and number of those directly or indirectly interested in the bourgeois order are on the wane. (Weber, "Speech for the General Information of Austrian Officers in Vienna," p. 207)

48. This is not the only way to characterize the core difference between Marx's and Weber's conceptualizations of class. Other synoptic contrasts include: production versus exchange (Val Burris, "The Neo-Marxist Synthesis of Marx and Weber on Class," in Wiley, *The Marx-Weber Debate*, pp. 43–64; Randall Collins, *Weberian Sociological Theory* [Cambridge: Cambridge University Press, 1986]); unidimensional versus multidimensional (Burris, "The Neo-Marxist Synthesis"; Scott, *Stratification and Power*); and dichotomous versus pluralistic class concepts (Giddens, *Classes, Power and Conflict*). Other authors who discuss the life chances / exploitation contrast include Rosemary Crompton and John Gubbay in *Economy and Class Structure* (London: Macmillan, 1977), esp. pp. 3–20; and Wright, *Class Counts*. Sayer also identifies the problem of exploitation as the central difference between Marx's and Weber's approachs to class, although he is skeptical that this matters very much: "On the question of exploitation there remains an unbridgeable gulf between Marx and Weber, which reflects the very different economic theories—respectively political economy and marginalism—upon which their sociologies of capitalist are predicated. How important this is, I would argue, is debatable . . . altogether too much ink has been wasted over their supposed differences" (Sayer, *Capitalism and Modernity*, pp. 104–5).

49. Weber, *Economy and Society*, pp. 927–28.

50. In *Capital*, Marx describes exchange relations between labor and capital as taking place in a sphere in which "[t]he only force that brings them together and puts them in relation with each other, is the selfishness, the gain and the private interests of each" (Karl Marx, *Capital*, vol. 1 [1867; New York: International Publishers, 1967], p. 176). Although he does not use the language of rational instrumental action, the description here is entirely in line with Weber's view of market exchange.

51. Although Marx elaborated the concept of exploitation in terms of the labor theory of value, as a sociological concept exploitation does not depend on this technical apparatus. As I have argued, class exploitation can be understood as a social relation in which (1) the material well-being of exploiters occurs *at the expense of* the well-being of the exploited, (2) this inverse relation depends upon the *exclusion* of the exploited from access to material resources, and (3) this exclusion from access to resources enables exploiters to *appropriate the labor effort* of the exploited. Taken together, these three criteria imply a relationship in which the advantaged groups depend on the efforts of the disadvantaged groups for the reproduction of their advantages. See Wright, *Class Counts*, pp. 4–17. For a trenchant philosophical discussion of

why the concept of exploitation does not logically depend on the labor theory of value, see G. A. Cohen, "The Labour Theory of Value and the Concept of Exploitation," in *History, Labour and Freedom* (Oxford: Clarendon, 1988), pp. 209–38.

52. Weber, *Economy and Society*, p. 72.

53. Marx, *Capital*, vol. 1, p. 176.

54. For an alternative view of the relationship between class and status in Marx's and Weber's treatment of slavery and feudalism, see Sayer, *Capitalism and Modernity*. Sayer argues that Marx used the word *class* in two quite different ways: in one sense as a generic term covering all systems of exploitation linked to production; in the other sense as a term that is specific to capitalism. This second use of the word, Sayer argues, is the more fundamental to Marx's theory and thus, like Weber, Marx believed that only in capitalism are there fully developed classes.

55. Weber, *Economy and Society*, p. 928. In Weber's early work on agrarian economies in ancient civilizations, which is marked by a much more Marxian kind of analysis than is his later work in *Economy and Society*, slaves were treated as a class, and their relationship to slave owners was treated as involving exploitation.

56. Weber, *Economy and Society*, p. 937.

57. The issue here is not the use of the word *exploitation*. Even in English this term can mean simply taking advantage of some kind of opportunity, as in "exploiting natural resources," and thus the real meaning of the term must be derived from the context of its use. In any case, a variety of different German words can be translated into English as "exploitation." The word does appear in a few places in the English translation of *Economy and Society*, and even more frequently in Weber's earlier work on slavery. In *Economy and Society*, the words in the original German text that are translated as "exploitation" are never the German term used in Marxist technical discussions of exploitation, *Ausbeutung*, or even the relatively morally charged term *Ausnützung* (which suggests taking unfair advantage). Rather, Weber used the much more neutral terms *Benützung* or *Verwertung*, which mean "use." In his earlier work on slavery, however, Weber sometimes uses *Ausnützung* and occasionally the more technical Marxist term *Ausbeutung*, again reflecting the greater Marxian character of that work. In one place, he uses the expression *exploitationsrate*, thus directly invoking the Marxist meaning of exploitation. In his later work, this Marxian usage is completely absent. I thank Phil Gorski for providing me with guidance on these linguistic issues.

58. Weber, *The Protestant Ethic*, pp. 59–60.

59. Ibid., p. 61. In this work, Weber explains that "[l]ow wages are by no means identical with cheap labor" because low wages may lead to a decline in effort and diligence: "Low wages fail even from a purely business point of view wherever it is a question of producing goods which require any sort of skilled labour, or the use of expensive machinery which is easily damaged, or in general wherever any great amount of sharp attention or of initiative is required. Here low wages do not pay, and their effect is the opposite of what was intended" (ibid.). Here Weber lays out the essential arguments of what is now tellingly referred to as "efficiency wage theory." Again, the extraction of labor effort is treated as a problem of instrumental rationality and efficiency rather than as a problem of antagonistic interests.

60. Weber, *Economy and Society*, p. 150.

61. Ibid.

62. Ibid.

63. Ibid.

64. Ibid., p. 151.

65. Ibid., p. 128.

66. Ibid., p. 129.

67. Ibid., pp. 129–30.

68. Ibid., p. 152.

69. Ibid., p. 138.

70. Ibid.

71. Ibid.

72. Mommsen, "Capitalism and Socialism"; Löwith, *Max Weber and Karl Marx*; Schroeter, "Dialogue, Debate, or Dissent"; Mommsen describes Weber's stance toward capitalism this way:

> Although he vigorously defended the capitalist system against its critics from the Left, . . . he did not hesitate to criticize the system's inhuman consequences. . . . His concern for the preservation of human dignity under the societal conditions created by and typical for mature capitalism (particularly the severe discipline of work and exclusion of all principles of personal ethical responsibility from industrial labor) is entirely consistent with Marx's effort to find a way of overcoming the social alienation of the proletariat under industrial capitalism. (Mommsen, "Capitalism and Socialism," p. 235)

Where Weber and Marx differed most deeply is in Weber's belief that socialism, in whatever form, would only intensify this oppression, and thus no viable alternative to capitalism would be possible (unless one were willing to accept a dramatic decline in technical rationality).

73. As I have argued elsewhere, the ways in which exploitation acts as a constraint on the exploiter is revealed in historical situations in which sharp conflicts over exclusion from economic resources occur in the *absence* of exploitation (see Wright, *Class Counts*, pp. 11–12). There is a morally abhorrent nineteenth-century American folk saying: "The only good Indian is a dead Indian." Such a saying has a kind of grotesque "rationality" in the context of the struggles between European settlers and indigenous peoples over control of the land: Although there were sharp and violent conflicts with Native Americans over their expulsion from the land, in general the labor effort of Native Americans was not exploited, and thus the white settlers did not depend on Native Americans for their own prosperity. Native Americans were thus "dispensable" from the settlers' point of view. The parallel aphorisms in the case of slavery or workers in capitalist firms might be something like, "The only good slave is a docile slave," or "The only good worker is an obedient worker" (or in Weber's analysis, "a worker with a Protestant work ethic"), but it would make no sense to say, "The only good slave is a dead slave," or "The only good worker is a dead worker." It is in this sense that exploitation acts as a constraint on the strategies of exploiters: they must seek ways of responding to resistance by the exploited that reproduce, rather than destroy, their interactions with them.

74. Weber, *Economy and Society*, p. 150.

75. Weber, of course, is famous for arguing that social science should attempt to be "objective" in the sense of trying to restrict its moral concerns to the posing of questions rather than to the substance of research and the selection of answers. Marx also believed in scientific objectivity, but was skeptical that in social analysis the analyst could in practice keep the substance of ideas from being influenced by the analyst's own relationship to social forces—especially class interests—in the society.

The Rule of the Father

Patriarchy and Patrimonialism in Early Modern Europe

Patrimony [Latin *patrimonium*]. Paternal estate.

Oxford English Dictionary

The totem is above all a symbol, a tangible expression of something else. But of what? . . . From one point of view, it is the outward and visible form of what I have called the totemic principle or god; and from another, it is also the symbol of a particular society that is called the clan. It is the flag of the clan, the sign by which each clan is distinguished from the others, the visible mark of its distinctiveness, and a mark that is borne by everything that in any way belongs to the clan: men, animals, and things.

Emile Durkheim, *Elementary Forms*

Puzzling over early-modern European political development has become a tradition, even a minor sport, in sociological theory. Critical transitions are supposed to have transpired in the early-modern moment (which conventionally spans the years between 1500 and 1800), and those transitions to have shaped our conceptual and theoretical orientations. So for modernization theorists the early modern signals the shift between tradition and modernity; Marxists locate the transition from the feudal to the capitalist mode of production in this period, along with the transformation of their attendant political forms. For devotees of the world-systems approach, the early-modern era enshrines the end of empire and the big-bang birth of the world system and modern states. Feminist theorists see the end of classical patriarchy and the invention of a new political form, fraternal liberalism. And so on. Grand dichotomies do tell us something, but they have a way of immobilizing history, rendering the past as "a picture or *tableau vivant* of a bygone culture,"[1] and becoming quick and dirty substitutes for more flexible concepts that can register diachronic change in relationships or systems.

On the face of it, Max Weber is as guilty as any other social theorist of joining, or leading, the parade of grand dichotomies. He authored many influential ideal types that are used to divide European and even world history into neat categories signaling an epochal before and after, including the vexed contrast between "traditional" and modern "rational-legal" types of legitimate domination. But he also helped bridge the yawning conceptual gap his own ideal-typical concepts created. The concept of "patrimonialism," which Weber applied inter alia to estatist and absolutist politics of early-modern Europe, is one concept that I for one could not do without, and I hope to convince readers of its broader possibilities. Nevertheless I think it needs to be reconstructed if it is to be useful to today's students of state formation and revolution. This chapter, focused on the high patrimonial politics of early-modern Europe, brings to bear poststructuralist and antifoundationalist thinking to reshape the concept into a usable tool of analysis. I show how there could be simultaneously "no there there" and a sturdy symbolic basis for centuries, even thousands of years of rule.

In Weber's *Economy and Society*, patrimonialism refers mainly to forms of government that are based on rulers' family households. The ruler's authority is personal-familial, and the mechanics of the household are the model for political administration. The concept of patrimonialism captures a distinctive style of regulation and administration that contrasts with Weber's ideal-typical rational-legal bureaucracy, a better-known concept that has made its way into the popular lexicon. Rational-legal bureaucracies are manned by impersonal rulers and substitutable actors; they boast clear-cut spheres of competence, ordered hierarchies of personnel and procedures, and an institutional separation of the "private" and the "official."[2] "Bureaucracy is *the* means of transforming social action into rationally organized action."[3] Technical specialization and rule-governed hierarchical control are its watchwords,[4] and Weber likens it to a "machine," a "precision instrument," a "ceaselessly moving mechanism," an apparatus of cogs and gears.[5] Patrimonialism is more like a manor house with, one would suppose, particularly extensive grounds.[6] Patrimonial rulers cite "age-old rules and powers"—sacred tradition—as the basis of their political authority. Their power is discretionary, and the line between persons and offices notional.[7] This at least is Weber's analytical point of departure, and it's a good first cut at patterns of early-modern European governance.

For Weber, furthermore, patriarchy is at the heart of patrimonialism. Their linguistic connection—"patrimony" derives from the Latin *patrimonium* for paternal estate—is also conceptual and sociological. "Patrimonial domination is thus a special case of patriarchal domination," Weber writes, "domestic authority decentralized through assignment of land and sometimes of equipment to sons of the house or other dependents."[8] And further:

"We shall speak of a *patrimonial state* when the prince organizes his political power over extrapatrimonial areas and political subjects—which is not discretionary and not enforced by physical coercion—just like the exercise of his patriarchal power."[9] Patriarchal domination comes to the fore in Weber's account for two connected reasons. It is the purest logical form of traditional authority, the one in which the conceptual skeleton is most starkly revealed.[10] And patriarchy is the historical seed of patrimonialism, which Weber believes is a genetic extension of the patterns of governance in a ruler's or a chief's family-household. We see this historically when dependents are granted fiefs or other politico-economic privileges and immunities and become clients and agents of their ruler and now patron, separating themselves from his family-household to form their own households.[11] In this defining and reiterated moment, rulers' agents become potential rulers and patriarchal principals themselves.

While the concept of "patrimonialism" has been widely influential, and its tendencies of development spotted in just about everything from ancient Rome to the Chicago mafia to current Middle Eastern and Asian politics, the patriarchal core of Weber's definition tends to drop out of these appropriations. That lapse, if it is a lapse, can in part be laid at Weber's door. Patriarchy tended to be naturalized in *Economy and Society*. In one throwaway line, for example, Weber asserts that "[t]he woman is dependent because of the normal superiority of the physical and intellectual energies of the male. . . . "[12] This is especially interesting because Weber produced an array of nonnaturalized reasons for the relative position of other categories of patriarchal dependents, like grown children and servants.[13] If Weber had wanted to make a sex-based case for the primacy of the biological in patrimonialism, he might have argued that certain features of biological maleness, such as greater capacity to engage in armed single combat—given the sort of weapons prevalent at the time—made men's claim to rule more credible. Such an argument might only apply to brawny, coordinated, and well-schooled men, and it would in any case have limited applicability to the formal structures of rule in early-modern Europe. But it might well pan out for other historical eras and sites.[14] Gender has been an Achilles' heel for all the major classical social theorists, in any case, so it is no surprise that Weber biologizes the relative position of women and men in the context of an explanation that is otherwise social. Today's scholars of *Economy and Society*, who habitually distinguish gender from biological sex, simply ignore these interpretively awkward passages. As Weber's naturalized arguments have fallen by the wayside, however, so has his insight that patriarchy, father-rule, is somehow fundamental to patrimonial politics.[15]

There are a few stray exceptions to this rule. In his comparison of Weber's writings on imperial China and Western Europe, for example, Gary

Hamilton persuasively argues that patriarchalism is fundamental to Weber's concept of patrimonial domination as Weber links it to the organization of the state.[16] In its pure form this meant that " . . . the patriarch—*the person*— in the form of family heads and rulers held discretionary power over rites, over legal judgments, and over the administration of households as well as the state."[17] Hamilton shows that imperial China emphasized roles rather than persons and their personal power.[18] Filial piety (*xiao*) was institutional- ized in Chinese politics, he notes, but did not necessarily empower the con- crete person of the father, as he takes it to have done in Western Europe, in the *ur*-example, ancient Rome: "With *patria potestas*, a person obeys his fa- ther; with *xiao* a person acts like a son."[19] Hamilton builds on this distinction (in the best Weberian manner) to suggest genetic explanations of forms of political order and developmental patterns specific to imperial China. Hamilton draws this stark contrast between China and Western Europe, however, and quarrels with Weber's claim that imperial China can be un- derstood as a patriarchal patrimonial system only because he accepts Weber's vision of the taken-for-granted natural authority of the father in the Euro- pean historical landscape. In this Hamilton is faithful—I think *too* faithful— to Weber's text.

Weber lacked the conceptual equipment that would have enabled him to recognize the constructed basis of all authorizations of political authority: constructed not out of whole cloth, as it were, or of random snippets, but of materials ready to hand. These materials include actors' early childhood ex- periences of historically specific forms of parental, and especially paternal, authority. All this is less a criticism than a comment on the present need to restructure the concepts of patriarchalism and patrimonialism—and by ex- tension all ideal types of domination: traditional; rational-legal; charismatic; and any plausible new ideal types that we might decide to coin. Instead of seeing biological maleness and fatherhood as the politically productive force, as Weber did, we should identify the shifting meanings with which maleness is freighted as the key to understanding how it is deployed in politics. When prevailing assumptions about more or less valued interpretations of mas- culinity—particularly paternity—are italicized as part of the patrimonial ideal type, we can get a better sense of how patrimonial systems work, and why they crumble. I also focus here on the elite, not that elite mechanisms are the only important part of the story, but they are both the piece of the historical narrative on which I am currently working and one of Weber's perennial objects of sociological analysis.

The symbolics of political fatherhood were (and are!) crucial in European monarchies. The court was a major theater of power in medieval and early- modern states, and royal families figured prominently, indeed centrally, in the courtly drama. Monarchs and their pet ideologists were themselves quick to point this out. James I of England, who was also James VI of Scotland, was not the first or last monarch to write on this topic, but he was particularly prolific in print and passionate about his paternal ruling role. Sometimes he held up kings as nurturant fathers: "And as the Father of his fatherly duty is bound to care for the nourishing, education and vertuous gouernment of his children; euen so is the king bound to care for all his subjects." At other moments he stressed the strictures of paternal power: "Now a Father may dispose of his Inheritance to his children, at his pleasure: yea, euen disinherite the eldest vpon iust occasions, and preferre the youngest, according to his liking: make them beggers, or rich at his pleasure; restraine, or banish out of his presence, as hee findes them giue cause of offence, or restore them in fauour againe with the penitent sinner: So may the King deale with Subiects." At times he did both in the space of a single text.[20]

The analogy between father and king has also been a theme of recent feminist political theory. The overthrow of early-modern states and decapitation (or worse!) of monarchs fascinates feminist theorists because of what these events exemplify: the destruction and reconstruction of a patriarchal gender order, and the genesis of a politics of equality and citizenship, including among other things the discourse and practices of feminism itself. As Lynn Hunt observes about the French Revolution, but might as well have said about the English Revolution, or any other thoroughgoing early-modern European political upheaval, "male control of the world never went without saying after the father had been killed."[21] Not just the small-f father, she means, but the king himself. Why should this have made such a difference? In early-modern Europe, the basic argument goes, there was a mimetic or fractal relationship between ruling family and kingdom. The continuity and legitimacy of the royal family formed the bedrock of power relations and underwrote the stability of rule itself. For a monarch, sustaining these images and relations of rule entailed being seen to subsume and control the royal family-household and, by metaphorical extension, the entire kingdom or empire.[22]

Now I would like to press this line of thought further, beginning from the supposition that the category of "patriarch" itself can be seen as an ongoing cultural and social achievement. The people who first soldered together separate signs like "father" and "ruler" had real political imagination.[23] Later propagandists who sought to defend the value of their conjunction—especially in the face of others' efforts to tear them apart—were often astute analysts of the categories of everyday practice and good political tacticians. Some, like Willem I, *Vader Vaderlands* of the Dutch Republic, agitated on behalf of the oppressed by trying to substitute one father-ruler for another (in Willem's case, himself as the representative of the republic against the Spanish overlord).[24] Others fought a rearguard battle against national or international challenges to patriarchy. For example, the opening chapter of Sir Robert Filmer's *Patriarcha*—"That the first kings were fathers of families"— sets the tone for his ringing defense of patriarchal patrimonialism in an England beleaguered by arguments for "liberty" by "usurpers of the right of such fathers."[25] Whatever their politics, and their enthusiasm for patriarchal privilege (which will doubtless displease most of my readers), these early-modern elites were capable of real cultural creativity, of signification as action. The less influential folk who made everyday use of these same homely familial signs and images—whether attracted or repelled by the specific connection between paternity and rule—introduced and embroidered variations of their own. They were all inventors of tradition, paradoxically recreating what Weber called "the sanctity of immemorial traditions and the legitimacy of those exercising authority under them," but *not* by referring them either to capital-N nature or to some rock of "established belief," as Weber supposed.[26] Here I depart both from Weber and Weberianism and from contemporary materialist theorists who see the "father-ruler" as a simple reflection or production of "male power" or dominance. And note that these tropes of father-rule are with us today, trumpeted by the dynastic rulers of Middle Eastern monarchies, now more defiantly than of old. They are certainly not just a thing of the European or American past.[27]

The meanings that these actors invoked and produced rested on other meanings, signs upon signs. By "signs" I mean, following Saussure, arrays of signifiers that get linked to concepts/meanings (signifieds) in more or less stable formations.[28] Signifiers are primarily sounds and written patterns in Saussurean linguistics, but anything can stand in as a signifier and a vehicle for signification. "The soldier who falls defending his flag certainly does not believe he has sacrificed himself to a piece of cloth," as Emile Durkheim succinctly put it.[29] The weightiest signifier in medieval and early-modern European politics was the king's mortal body, which came to represent many connected concepts in political theology—the Crown; the collective assemblage of corporate bodies; the body politic—but only after a long and tortuous historical path.[30] It was not until the early sixteenth century that the English maxim "the king as King never dies" and France's "Le roi est mort! Vive le roi!" made their debut as the defining public aphorisms of royal funerary ceremonies.[31] This relationship of representation was repeatedly dramatized across Europe, most brilliantly at court.[32]

What linked the monarch's own body and the series of bodies it represented, culminating in the whole body politic, was the signifier of the patrilineage, which encoded, in the repeated father-son relationship, heredity, masculinity, and the transcendent promise of immortality.[33] These representations extended far beyond the nodal point of the "collective ruler"—the monarch, the royal family and its agents, and lesser but still privileged

rulers—reaching up to a vision of God-the-Father and down to the lowly
subjects who would be ordered and mobilized as heads of family-households
with authority over their dependents. What interests me here about this representation of the great (patriarchal) chain of being are the patriarchal rulers
and their agents or staffs—the specific network node that is Weber's favorite
point of analytical leverage on systems of legitimate domination. Highlight-
ing the "patriarchy" in patrimonialism means flagging the representation of
two kinds of relations that traverse this nodal point: (1) that between fathers
and sons as dominant and subordinate masculinities ordered around images
of fatherhood and filiality, and (2) that of the political relation among father-
rulers, conducted on the basis of their socially recognized paternal status.[34]
This is the symbolic code of interest. These representations could be folded
into the single, concentrated sign of the king's body, and like an accordion,
unfolded and extended.

Signs are not a part of Weber's sociology of patrimonial domination, or a
broader sociology of domination and freedom, but they should be. Kings,
princes, and lesser rulers in patrimonial politics invoked the vision of patrilineage—a line extending back into the past and forward to the future, and
composed of their ancestors and desired descendants—to appeal for allegiance. Ruling elites purchased property and made investments under the
sign of fatherhood, stood in judgment on their communities, proclaimed
war, schooled their children, and so on. They called upon their children to
act on behalf of the family line, with a modicum of success. Signs of political fatherhood and the vertical genealogies of office that they helped organize created a basis for both the intergenerational continuity in rule and the
stable relationship between princes and lesser rulers in both absolutist
monarchies and estatist republican regimes. The sign of patrilineage knotted
horizontal ties as well, not just among monarchs, but also among ruling elites
of lesser stature. These men directed appeals at others who were seen as
equivalents, opposite numbers in the formation of a ruling group—a set of
elites who could come to recognize themselves as having shared identities,
characteristics, and goals. The formation and cohesion of any ruling group
depends on members' self-recognitions.[35] The lateral recognitions of family
head to family head—both within what we have come to think of as local
and national contexts and apparatuses and over great geographic distances,
via international princely marriages—made possible the pervasive elite pacts
that undergirded early-modern state formation, of which more anon. What
is more, the vertical and horizontal dimensions were interdependent. An individual man could not gain entry to a ruling group without having made
an effective claim to honorable lineal descent. Would the members of that
group let their daughters marry his sons—or their sons marry his daughters?
Conversely, however fictive his family lineage, it would be workable if

backed up by others' willingness to incorporate him into the circuits of exchange.

Did this pervasive masculinism reduce women to ciphers? I don't think so, although this is a complicated issue, worth lingering on for a bit.[36] It is true that women functioned as objects of exchange and signs of relationships among men—particularly among the elite. This was not their sole role, but it was a constitutive one, without which the interlocked systems of marriage and inheritance would have tottered and collapsed. Of course women also pursued independent projects, just as men did, and they were eminently capable of "the mystification of manipulation as disinterested empathy," which Stephen Greenblatt calls the characteristic Renaissance mode of courtly action, elaborated in and definitive of courtly life.[37] For every real-life Iago there was a would-be Marquise de Merteuil.[38] Women were also authorized to perform crucial roles that were defined as both feminine and central in the courtly or manorial theater of power. They gave birth to heirs, and their scripted parts extended to vital supporting performances that dramatized and conferred familial political power. But elite women clearly commanded the largest sphere of action when they operated from the symbolic place of the patriarch. When there was a hiccup in the male line, women were called in as the agents or representatives of men, to act on the behalf of the lineage, the ruling group, and their mimetic extensions, including the nation. In these moments—extraordinary and rule-bound—women assumed the mantle of the patriarchs themselves.

Women rulers in patriarchal patrimonialism were anomalies, and as such likely to be coded as polluting or actively threatening, as sources of unwelcome ambiguity and instability in the categories of rule.[39] Most struggled or foundered in the ensuing contradictions, but a few, a very few, surmounted them with discursive elan. Here is Queen Elizabeth I at Tilbury, famously rallying her troops against the invasion of the Spanish Armada:

I know I have the body but of a weak and feeble woman; but I have the heart and stomach of a king, and of a king of England, too, and think foul scorn that Parma or Spain, or any prince of Europe, should dare to invade the borders of my realm; to which rather than any dishonour shall grow by me, I myself will take up arms, I myself will be your general, judge, and rewarder of every one of your virtues in the field.[40]

Again and again in speeches, letters, and diplomatic encounters on the national and international political stage, Elizabeth proved able to use to her rhetorical and political advantage not simply her symbolic position as a patrilineal patriarch, a king or prince, as she often called herself, but also the signs of femininity, which were systematically subordinated and even derided as the opposite and underside of father-rule.[41] Not the least part of her discursive success—in a patriarchal patrilineal society in which women were defined as the portals through which external pollution might enter—was her insistence on the twin signifiers of Virgin Queen. So there was a price to pay, or at least sustained cultural work to be done: the relentless, delicately balanced public performance of inviolate celibacy, of marriage to a kingdom not a king, especially a foreign one.[42] But perhaps she enjoyed the challenge.

For ruling women, there was always a gap between presentation of self-as-signifier and the totemic body of the absent king, prince, or other ruler for whom they were substituting, a gap widened by worries about the continuity of the patrilineage, and thus the state, itself. But I want to stress that male as well as female rulers felt the bite of this disjunction between totem and flesh; the gap was always there, albeit to varying degrees. There was some ironic amusement to be had from it when kings or other rulers were posthumous babies, and the contrast between magnificent throne and diminutive occupant a wellspring of humor as well as collective anxiety—but rather more symbolic panic when the men whom the bloodline had produced were physically damaged, weak-willed, or crazy. Part of the ruler's role was molding the simulacrum of self into a charismatic signifier, and some family incumbents were simply not up to the job of incarnating the sacred center. Furthermore, the role of agent-in-chief of the ruling patrilineages (and God-the-Father) got harder throughout the early-modern era, I think, as people grew to expect rulers to be responsible for political tasks and to perceive that they had the requisite power to execute them.[43] Perhaps this general tendency is a clue to early-modern rulers' increasing public distance from the ruled, and the greater formality and aristocratic "Frenchification" of the eighteenth-century European elites, of which so many contemporaries bitterly or mockingly complained. As they confronted these difficulties, in any case, ruling families and broader elite groups actively, even consciously, represented themselves to rivals, agents, allies, and subjects, doing culture-work to suture the gap between totem and imperfect mortal representatives.[44] There are interesting variations to be explored: the Habsburgs, for example, may have been particularly adept at manipulating what I would call familial signifiers during their long-term project of dynastic rule.[45] How the familial actors in question would have drawn boundaries around their particular political kin group and regulated the right to signify on its behalf—whether women would have been allowed to stand in as patriarchs in times of need—these things also varied, and with Weber's revised ideal type in hand, we are better equipped for future explorations into how and why they did.[46]

While men made many claims on others, and on themselves, in their guise as father-rulers in early-modern Europe, only a fraction of these claims won practical support, with flows of men, money, and materiel.[47] These

flows or media included streams of daily and generational labor that repro-
duced the bodies and souls slotted into various patrimonial apparatuses; cash;
marriageable women; political and spiritual allegiance; and the mobilization
of military force to back up one's own and allies' family lineage claims to territory and monopoly positions in trading networks, the state, or other institutions. Many flows were transitory, a flash in the pan, but in some situations,
recognized participants made binding agreements as family heads to circu-
late chunks of resource-bearing political privilege and to duly police both
the flow of recognitions and resources. Let me give two brief examples. In
the England of the early seventeenth century, culminating under James I and
his successor Charles I, virtually every office could be bought, whether from
the Crown, Crown favorites who sold Crown patronage, or officeholders
who were entitled to dispose of offices under their jurisdiction. This extrav-
agant handout of politico-economic privilege went to familially linked magnate and gentry groupings in the landed elite[48] and, as Robert Brenner has
shown, to the representatives of merchant dynasties encamped in chartered
companies, the City of London's key political positions, and finally the cus-
toms farm, the most important branch of what was (nominally) the Crown's
revenue administration, and the largest single source of state revenue.[49] Likewise, the "family-state compact" is Sarah Hanley's term for a systematic pattern of regulation that emerged in sixteenth- and early seventeenth-century
France, "designed to bring family formation under parental (that is patriarchal) control in the first instance and under the magisterial control of the
Parlement of Paris in the second."[50] For Hanley, the axis of the deal lay between the king and his household on the one hand—who got perquisites
from selling offices and privileges—and the legists on the other, who were
able to advance their dynastic holdings in state property.[51] There were thus
two key levels to the compact—a set of contractual arrangements between
king and individual elite family heads—and arrangements that collectively
aggregated and bound those family heads one to another.[52]

This basic genre of contract has been discussed by historians and social
scientists, with acumen and learning, but our differentiated modernist theories of social stratification—in fact the modernist map of social life and the
related divisions of labor within and among academic disciplines—continue
to make its specificity hard to grasp. These pacts were not simply family affairs, as some would have it. They were not merely class coalitions or the
fruits of a nascent utilitarian orientation toward property. They were not
only temporal or spiritual power made manifest. They were all of these
things and more, and thus Weber's patriarchal patrimonialism is an appropriate multifocal lens through which to view them. These arrangements projected an entire group's patriarchal property in power into the future, simultaneously broadening and deepening that group as a collective principal

capable of political action. The pacts transcended faction and strengthened elite networks and institutions in a whole series of medieval and early-modern European settings.[53] They set the seal on an enviable degree of political stability—an important foundation for state-building—but also opened up systematic vulnerabilities and developmental possibilities. Yet the extensive scholarly literature on medieval and early-modern European elite pacts is curiously vague. Most works could and should have been much more precise about whether the pacts involved were tacit or explicit, and in describing what difference conscious thematization might have made in the processes and outcomes they examine. This strikes me as crucial for an era in which the actors involved were forging the rules governing contractual arrangements applicable to state office, family, and emergent capitalist enterprise—and reformulating the idea of "contract" itself.

As the elite—or rather elite men and masculinity—was collectively disciplined, state-builders (who included those very men) could put the institutions that they were constructing on an even keel for decades or more.[54] The elite could now plan for a fantasized future, anticipating possible familial rhythms of reproduction that might shift the order of rotation of sons and sons' sons into positions of politico-economic privilege. Demographic pressures could threaten patrimonial political stability in a number of ways, as Jack Goldstone shows in his analysis of elite demography in the early-modern world.[55] Goldstone convincingly argues that the growth of elites in certain periods, and the associated impact of turnover and displacement on elite positions, made for a relative scarcity of offices in some countries, fueling rivalries and competition among elite patronage networks.[56] This was so even in some areas like the Netherlands that do not figure in Goldstone's already lengthy roster of cases. But I also think it is crucial to point out that leading representatives of these elites directly confronted problems of the supply and demand of patrimonial privilege, argued among themselves about what to do about them, and invented explicit intergenerational solutions that worked (more or less) well in different institutional settings. The elite family heads may not always have been collectively successful, but neither were they blind victims of demographic forces. And they knew that demographic disasters (and subtler reproductive unevennesses) were just one contingency that could undermine the emergent institutional nexus of elite families, corporations, and states. Some elite pacts included innovative procedures by which other genuinely unforeseen contingencies could be met—paralleling Kreps's arguments about the role of corporate culture in contemporary capitalism—whereby men tried to contain future shocks, the paradox of the unexpected that could always be expected to erupt into the life of the patriarchal patrimonial system.[57]

An honest Weberian (or a cynic) might point out that rather than doing themselves untold injuries—for men killed each other less frequently where such agreements were in force—they could now take their collective capacities for violence and begin to project them outward, onto other groups, subject populations, and civilizations. That monopoly of force is after all a sine qua non of Weber's definition of a modern state.[58] Here, too, in the projection of power, lay a familial seam along which the family heads composing Weber's collective ruler would stick together or come apart in early-modern Europe. Power tends to diffuse downward in patrimonial arrangements, as rulers hand out bits of monopolistic resource-bearing political privilege, including sovereign rights to make war on foreign powers. Weber gives us some sense of this in *Economy and Society*, when he comments on the agency problems—the difficulties principals had in controlling their agents or representatives—that he took to be typical of patrimonial states.[59] Add to this a host of agency problems peculiar to early-modern state-building and empire, including huge distances and long timelags in communication, intractable problems of oversight, and an unavoidable need to recruit large numbers of indigenous elites as agents and to accommodate at least some of their demands and desires. This was a major way that state formation gained ground in Europe itself, by aggregating such previously autonomous entities, whether peacefully or by force.[60] No wonder that rulers throughout early-modern Europe hoped that the trust, special allegiance, and frankly, obedience that they took to characterize family ties could be used to counteract endemic political segmentation. The ruling patriarchs devoted much time, energy, and argument to figuring out how to dissolve competing family solidarities and nourish what they saw as appropriate family sentiments among their patrimonial agents at home and abroad.[61]

Family ideals and relationships do not always have this palliative effect on far-flung relationships. Weber referred this effect to the mysterious workings of "tradition," as we have seen; he also thought that one's particular father or master merited one's obedience because of the "mere habituation" of a concrete role relationship.[62] This concrete particularism also derived its force, I have argued, from a general system of signification, in which it made sense for a father-ruler to command obedience, " . . . as if the ruled had made the content of the command, the maxim of their conduct for its very own sake."[63] True, the symbolic patriarch might lose this capacity when he had no more resources to give: poverty and powerlessness could make the implicit claims of elite patriarchy seem like so much hot air. Or his agents and subjects might come to resonate to new and competing family ties, a possibility that leaps out in the multiple histories of autonomous family state-building and creole nationalism in the European metropole and colonies. Some men might even abandon family altogether, vibrating to other strings of sentiment. All these things did happen in patrimonial political systems, and in the linked European and colonial revolutions at the end of the eighteenth century—which await their neo-Weberian comparative historical sociology—they can be said to have exploded full force. Meanwhile, the rulers in the metropolitan centers played on the signs and practices of patriarchy as one way of managing their perennial principal/agent woes.

In general, I would expect fathers' family roles and the meaning of fatherhood itself to have been fortified as intergenerationally extended groups of ruling patriarchs became embedded in the familial states of seventeenth- and especially eighteenth-century Europe. Father-rulers increased what they had to distribute to dependents by appropriating political privileges through the pacts, and their threats of withdrawing favor or even of disinheritance became more meaningful. The very image of the father was enlarged. For some social scientists, this would be a perfect example of a self-reinforcing mechanism, or an early-modern version of "lock-in."[64] For the patrimonial patriarchs themselves, this was a reasonably comfortable position to be in as long as the monopoly niches that they had collectively captured and defended continued to relay the resources and recognition they craved. But note that elite men would also experience some paradoxical effects of their collective empowerment. As the stakes go up, the incentives rise for any such group to strengthen its contractual system, in order to make it harder for any one wayward patriarch to disrupt the intergenerational bargain and by extension the state. The position of the individual paternal family head is thus increasingly disciplined and personally disempowered by these brilliant collective inventions. For example, the Contracts of Correspondence in the eighteenth-century Netherlands—which could, without too big a stretch, be termed a cartel of fifty-some cities—formalized the distribution of city offices in written succession rules, laying out systems by which all eligible elite families would take turns getting mayoralties, East Indies Company directorships, and other top corporate privileges. The contracts regulated the membership in and control over corporate bodies, which were the conditions for capital accumulation, political power, and family honor. The settlements, which were ratified by the Stadholder and States-General, protected specific families' stake in an office and guaranteed that regent families' collective office genealogies would continue unbroken.[65] They also tightened the political vise on each family head accordingly, so that he could do nothing without the permission of his fellows. The apotheosis of regulation of the inheritance of landed (and sometimes mercantile) property entailed to the male line was the procedure of strict settlement, invented in seventeenth-century England and widely diffused in the eighteenth century. Like the French Family-State Compact and the Dutch Contracts of Correspondence, strict settlements were half of a two-tier pact, collectively designed and administered, whose ultimate court of appeal was the monarch and the elite patriarchs themselves assembled in Parliament. They were the rock on which patriarchal property in power in eighteenth-century England was centralized and consolidated. But they also disadvantaged daughters, shucked off second and third sons, and decisively converted the elite father and family head into a subsidiary agent and administrator of his lineage and a mere tenant-for-life of his own estates and their political accoutrements.[66]

The heightened centrality of tropes of ruling fatherhood also marked out areas of exceptional macro-political vulnerability. Carole Pateman has argued that chaotic monarchical gender orders destabilized rule in the lead-up to the great revolutions of seventeenth- and eighteenth-century Europe, which eventually unseated various father-kings in favor of fractious fraternal male citizenries.[67] I also suspect that the increased patriarchalism of discourses of rule upped the general expectations of rulers' charisma and performance and was therefore implicated in the perceived "decline" of the French Bourbons, the British Hanoverians, the Dutch House of Orange, and other ruling Houses of eighteenth-century Europe. (This is a hunch, and a topic for future research.)[68] The elite pacts created a distinctive form of institutional rigidity.[69] Here I am emphasizing the neglected dimension of signification, which made for its own vulnerabilities. When a ruling sovereign was female or when a female regency was created to fill a hiatus in the male lineage; when ruling dynasties were founded by "new men" (dynastically speaking, fatherless sons); when a king failed to enforce the gender hierarchies in his own family-household, or was merely thought to have transgressed them in some way: these were situations in which we would expect the foundations of political order to have been shaken. The biggest earthquakes took place when people did away with the king or equivalent symbolic patriarch before there was a viable counterdiscourse of democracy—England during the English Revolution; the Netherlands in the Stadholderless periods—and tried to do without the father-ruler at the apex of the patrimonial state. This was a recipe for anarchy and eventual restoration.

Perhaps the practices of collective contestation and corporate deliberation among elite men helped them redefine their relations as lateral ties among equals. Historians and social scientists have stressed other sources of democratic discourse and practice in eighteenth-century Europe, including novels and philosophy; participation in coffeehouses, salons, and other nascent public spheres; revulsion against European colonialism; religious doctrine; and the dramatic demonstration effect of the French Revolution.[70] As the simpler, sometimes even singular, causal models of second-wave *marxisant* historical sociology have receded, we have been left with multiple genealogies, mechanisms, and other candidate explanations for the emergence of democracy—this is yet one more, as yet rather speculative, possibility. Weber himself distinguished direct democracy, sometimes practiced by notables and other small so-called rational groups, from modern large-scale democracy, which could not subsist without the spread of market economy and status-leveling, bureaucratization, and for the full-fledged version, effective political parties and techniques of mass mobilization and communication.[71] The patriarchal group, he thought, was alien to both forms, since "governing powers are normally appropriated and action is strictly bound to tradition."[72] Nevertheless, suppressed alternatives always haunt political regimes, and in this case, these alternative visions could be expected to cluster around and take their tone from the patriarchal nucleus in patrimonial politics. There was a language of political opposition from below, but it was still predominantly familial in the old regimes, as many writers have pointed out. Those unhappy with the monarch first called upon him to be a better, more benevolent father, and then, more radically, urged their fellow brothers-in-arms to depose him. "Liberty, equality, *fraternity*" were the historic watchwords, and not just in revolutionary France. These potent signifiers also took shape within the discourses of the dynastic elite itself, when some courageous men and women of the ruling classes identified themselves with the cause of the oppressed and made themselves its agents. My working hypothesis is that one key to this revolutionary transformation—ultimately to the emergence of the idea of equality and shared fate—lay in the elite pacts and related interactions that took place under the sign of hierarchical paternity. Once this had happened, it opened the discursive door to the possibility of *anyone's* being considered an equal and a fellow human being—even women, people of other religions, or those who were currently held as slaves.

Not all early-modern elites were infused with a rage for democracy or revolution. There were important countertendencies built into patrimonial systems, including discursive reaffirmations of father-rule and political hierarchy. The elite pacts of eighteenth-century Augustan England, including the patriarchal strict settlements, were evidently compatible with a long period of hegemony and civil peace. But overall, and across Europe and beyond, some bases of elite dissent were likely nourished from *within* hierarchical states organized around ruler-subject relations. What makes this even more probable—although Weber's typological method makes this hard to see—is that the very men who formed part of Weber's collective ruler were contending with some of the other experiences of symbolic leveling and desacralization that Weber discusses in *Economy and Society*. Some of these men were hammering out new kinds of commercial contract progressively shorn of the family nimbus; within patriarchal patrimonial states, others were actually inventing rational-legal bureaucratic practices where patriarchy had no place.[73] The characteristic contradictions of patriarchal patrimonialism pressed down on actors who were the obvious victims of such systems, to be sure, but also those who were the greatest beneficiaries. We may thus look for homegrown roots of discourses of fraternal opposition to patrimonial rule, diffused internationally with particular vigor after the French Revolution, in the heart of relations of patriarchal subjection in both the republican/estatist and monarchical contexts. Precisely where we would expect it to be most secure, paternal rule and gendered order were always already unstable—resting on historically elaborated principles and relations that could under certain conditions call them into radical question. Tracing the confluence of these conditions, discursive and practical, European or not—and how men and women reacted to them—is a fascinating and worthwhile collective project.

In his magisterial and moving "Science as a Vocation," Weber was more than ready to concede that scholars emphasize elements to which our value-orientations direct us. The present essay stands as an example of this interested strategy. It would be reasonable to say that I have a feminist optic, or axe to grind, am intrigued by the explanatory possibilities that present themselves when we highlight the patri/archy in patrimonialism, and hope to broaden academic definitions of the complex of problems surrounding state formation, reproduction, and revolution. All this would be true, and I take tinkering with established ideal types or introducing new ones as one vehicle for enlarging our interpretive and explanatory horizons. But I would not want to say that my version of an ideal type captures any sort of referential "essence" or turns a deliberate spotlight on something called "empirical reality." Here I strongly disagree with Weber's own accounts of what he was about, and with many a Weberian exegete. An ideal type can help us represent what we take to be actors' interpretations, but this is a very different thing than revealing the real and a much more modest claim than Weber was wont to make for his method. All categories are representations, and ideal types are also analytical translations of what we take to be categories of practice. They are subject to all the fundamental indeterminacies of translation, to borrow Quine's phrase.[74] Does this mean that they are wrong, or that we cannot use them? Not at all. Translation is unavoidable in any case.[75] The ideal type is itself an unstable formation of signs. For those who cannot accept the lack of fundamental foundations, we might say: the arms of the old methodological churches are opened widely and compassionately for them.[76] Others can join me in offering a decidedly irreligious homage to the poststructuralist spirit of Elizabeth I and (whether or not they performed gender in an equivalent site of state power) other early moderns like her. Following their sense of the plasticity of gender categories of practice, I hope I have made "patriarchal patrimonialism" even more explicitly insecure—and by the same token more scientific and less ideological—by saying nay to Weber's unreflective effort to ground it in biology at its heart.[77]

My second caveat about ideal types concerns the stuff of history. The elite pacts I have discussed simultaneously marked, made possible, and make sense within the historical flowering of the relationships that Weber named with his ideal type "patriarchal patrimonialism." Certain ideal types, like this one, can be construed as "the end states of a causal process and take on their meaning from that process.[78] When you choose an ideal type, if one wants a very un-early-modern metaphor, you are hitting the "pause" button on your analytical remote and then fiddling with the camera angle on the historical DVD. You might have picked a different "end state" or stopping point, another camera angle—even a different film. At minimum, to the extent that a type concept is identified with a historical process, especially one that tends toward a more or less likely "end state," the process and outcome should be signaled as one that historians and social scientists select theoretically rather than unreflectively or merely conventionally. Ideal types can be put to use in just this way: to capture our interpretation of actors' orientations; suggest likely ways that those actors might come together in social action; lay out plausible tendencies, countertendencies, and points of intersection with other historical processes named, perhaps, by other ideal types.[79] In this chapter I rebuilt the concept of "patriarchal patrimonialism" for these purposes, among other things indicating why elite family heads, including monarchs, might be expected to envision themselves and act in certain ways, and illuminating the interelite pacts that they put together as father-rulers in early-modern Europe. Those pacts intersected with an array of theoretically defined processes and outcomes, some only touched on here, including state-building and breakdown; formations of masculinity and family; European colonialism; the making of ruling classes and elites; and social revolution. This list could—and will—be expanded indefinitely. Scholars influenced by Weber continue to broaden the *marxisant* assumptions about what is historically important that dominated the second-wave historical sociology of the 1970s and 1980s. The future continually recasts our sense of what matters about the past; it recasts the past itself.[80] And any such list is always open to possibilities and formulations that have yet to be imagined.

The newly minted ideal type is now good for further historical comparisons and research questions. We might ask: when was "father" first defined in relation to other signs (like "mother" or "uncle") in a particular political setting, celebrated, and tied to signs of power and rule? How did these signs take shape in practices that dramatized the political authority of the male progenitor and head of household? Were these interrelated signs and practices politically productive, did they get the job done (secure relations of rule), and/or evoke counterpositions and alternative identities? With respect to signification, we are comparing formations of meaning; the processes by which people assemble and reassemble them; how these formations govern action; how they disperse. These questions obviously reach far beyond early-modern Europe, extending over the globe and up to the present moment.[81]

Other Weberian ideal types—all, to my mind, useful materials for sociological bricolage—could benefit from an analogous feminist, poststructuralist overhaul. The definition of "charismatic authority" includes unexamined assumptions about "certain qualities" of individual personality.[82] These mysterious qualities are cultural, theatrically performative, and emphatically gendered, and they demand systematic attention in light of what we now know about signification and audience reception. "Rational-legal authority" is an even bigger can of worms. For Weber, as Alan Sica puts it, "to theorize about social action was to bring it within rational reflection, and through ideal-typification to identify anomalies either as explainable minor deviations from the pure type or as irrationalities and therefore irrelevant."[83] Weber often used the "irrational" as "his own explanation in forswearing examination of certain phenomena, as if to say that the irrational was *ipso facto* impenetrable."[84] Weber went on to link the irrational with the signifier of the feminine—and a whole series of signifiers he took to be associated with the trope of femininity, such as the premodern, the family, the non-Western, the primitive, the sexual—and was therefore flummoxed when what was for him the "irrational" kept surfacing in the core of his neatly opposed categories of rationality, as it was wont to do. Weber was in that sense a man of his time; it is even probable that his particular genius rested on these ordered Apollonian/Dionysian oppositions. But perhaps we who follow after might take disturbing and rearranging them for new uses as part of our calling. In order to understand the things that Weber cared about, including politics and states, and to ask whether, for example, there can be patrimonialism without patriarchy, or a more or less rationalized modernity without a repressed and refused feminine underside, we have first to reexamine—and reject or reconstruct—Weber's and our own naturalized categories. Only then will we have a Weber, and a historical social science, for the twenty-first century.

Notes

An earlier version of this essay was presented as the keynote address at the November 2, 2002, Conference on Law, Family, and State Organization in the Early Modern Atlantic World, sponsored by the Institute for Legal Studies at the University of Wisconsin Law School. I benefited greatly from the comments I received there, especially Richard Ross's, and from the papers of the other conference participants. I would also like to thank Rebecca Emigh, Phil Gorski, Edgar Kiser, Richard Lachmann, Ann Orloff, Steve Pfaff, Mayer Zald, two anonymous reviewers for Stanford University Press, the participants in the NYU Sociology Department's Gender and Inequality Workshop and a Sociology Department colloquium at Rutgers University, and my fellow Russell Sage Scholars for their reactions to various parts of the argument. A series of unresolved argumentative e-mails I had with Art Stinchcombe were especially fun and fruitful. Kari Hodges magically transformed the text into a Sage working paper. Finally, I am grateful to the American Council of Learned Societies, and especially the Russell Sage Foundation, for its marvelous, supportive atmosphere for work on the penultimate draft.

1. Carl E. Schorske, *Thinking with History: Explorations in the Passage to Modernism* (Princeton, NJ: Princeton University Press, 1998).

2. Max Weber, *Economy and Society: An Outline of Interpretive Sociology*, ed. Guenther Roth and Claus Wittich (1921–22; Berkeley: University of California Press, 1978), pp. 1028–31.

3. Ibid., p. 987.

4. Ibid., pp. 956–58.

5. Ibid., pp. 987–90.

6. Ibid., p. 1013.

7. Ibid., p. 225, 1028–29. "Thus there is a double sphere," as Weber says, "(a) that of action which is bound to specific traditions; (b) that of action which is free of specific rules" (ibid., p. 227). There is clearly an endemic conceptual and historical tension encoded in the concept of patrimonialism, right at the point where the notion of personal discretion meets traditional legitimation. Sometimes Weber seems to imagine a utilitarian ruler who is instrumental with respect to tradition as well as his subjects. To wit: "The exercise of power is oriented toward the consideration of how far master and staff can go in view of the subjects' traditional compliance without arousing their resistance" (ibid., p. 227). Few if any patrimonial rulers were so Machiavellian, even where Machiavellianism was traditionally legitimated.

8. Ibid., p. 1011.

9. Ibid., p. 1013.

10. Weber uses the concept of patriarchy in different ways in different parts of his work (is there *any* concept of Weber's of which this could not be said?). In the first part of *Economy and Society* Weber defines patriarchalism as "the situation where, within a group (household) which is usually organized on both an economic and a kinship basis, a particular individual governs who is designated by a definite rule of inheritance" (ibid., p. 231). Elsewhere Weber treats patriarchal domination as "the formally most consistent authority structure that is sanctified by tradition" (ibid., p. 1009), Weber worries more about why this "particular individual" should be male (ibid., p. 1007), and tends to cast patriarchy as a core feature of a wider and more motley apparatus of patrimonial domination, of what he calls, sounding like a systems theorist, "differentiated patriarchal power" (e.g., ibid., pp. 1009–10).

11. Ibid., pp. 1031–32.

12. Ibid., p. 1007.

13. Ibid.

14. Weber himself had dueled while at school, and had the facial scars—and ensuing slap in the face from his horrified mother—to show for it. Arthur Mitzman, *The Iron Cage: An Historical Interpretation of Max Weber* (New York: Transaction

Books, 1969), pp. 23–24. But Weber acquired his scars in an era in which demonstrated prowess in duels, not to mention jousts and other contests, had been decoupled from the right to rule. Note that the issue here is not whether the biological differences between men and women have some sort of relationship to, and even causal role in, the historically varying taxonomies of gender, if we understand gender (as I do) to mean cultural definitions of masculinities and femininities. The problem is rather that Weber persistently elides gender and biological sex as concepts, reducing the former to the latter, and this hampers his analysis of patrimonial politics.

15. This may seem strange, as it has become more accepted in the disciplines of history, anthropology, and Renaissance and early-modern European studies that there is a gendered core of forms of power that I would call patrimonial (I discuss some of this literature later). It is still true, however, that many historians who write on early-modern European rule fail to register the patriarchal patrilineal dimension in their theoretical discussions, even as it pervades their empirical analyses.

16. Gary G. Hamilton "Patriarchy, Patrimonialism, and Filial Piety: A Comparison of China and Western Europe," *British Journal of Sociology* 41, no. 1 (1990): 77–104; "Patriarchalism in Imperial China and Western Europe: A Revision of Weber's Sociology of Domination," *Theory and Society* 13, no. 3 (1984): 393–425. Randall Collins's discussion of Weber's political theory of the family includes an informative section on patriarchy, patrimonialism, and the rise and fall of the household, in which he reminds us that while elite European patriarchal households could be quite large, they did not necessarily include extended kin. Randall Collins, *Weberian Sociological Theory* (New York: Cambridge University Press, 1986), pp. 267–96.

17. Hamilton, "Patriarchy, Patrimonialism, and Filial Piety," p. 402.

18. Ibid., pp. 92–97.

19. Ibid., p. 411.

20. The two citations are drawn from Su Fang Ng's excellent dissertation, "Family Ties, Political Fictions: Metaphorical Communities in Seventeenth-Century England," chapter 1 of which deals with James's writings. Su Fang Ng, "Family Ties, Political Fictions: Metaphorical Communities in Seventeenth-Century England" (Ph.D. diss., English Department, University of Michigan), pp. 1–37. But James's subtle self-presentation availed him not, at least in England. According to Jenny Wormald, James—a dual monarch by dynastic fiat—did better at impersonating the vision of a Scottish "soverane lord" than the more "visually impressive" idea of English "sacred majesty" (Jenny Wormald, "James VI and I: Two Kings or One?" *History* 68 (1983): 204). James' immediate predecessor, Elizabeth I, had the advantage in ceremonial splendor, in spite of her sex (her gender was rather more ambiguous, or perhaps willfully plural, as we shall see below). Contemporaries thought James too "lavish of his presence . . . so common-hackney'd in the eyes of men, so stale and cheap to vulgar company" (Shakespeare, *Henry IV*, 1, scene 2)—though unlike Richard II, he managed to hang onto the crown.

21. Lynn Hunt, *The Family Romance of the French Revolution* (Berkeley: University of California Press, 1993), p. 204.

22. Lynn Hunt's *The Family Romance of the French Revolution* is but one of many versions of this now widely diffused culturalist argument about European kingship.

Other academic versions specific to England and France—and forwarding otherwise quite different analyses—include Gordon J. Schochet, *Patriarchalism in Political Thought: The Authoritarian Family and Political Speculation and Attitudes Especially in Seventeenth-Century England* (Oxford, England: Blackwell, 1975); Joan Landes, *Women and the Public Sphere in the Age of the French Revolution* (Ithaca, NY: Cornell University Press, 1988); Pavla Miller, *Transformations of Patriarchy in the West, 1500–1900* (Bloomington: Indiana University Press, 1998); Carole Pateman, *The Sexual Contract* (Stanford, CA: Stanford University Press, 1988); and J. C. D. Clark, *English Society, 1660–1832: Religion, Ideology, and Politics during the Ancien Regime*, 2nd ed. (New York: Cambridge University Press, 2000). Merrick discusses variations in the ways that the king-as-father discourse was deployed in French politics, particularly in the eighteenth century (Jeffrey Merrick, "Fathers and Kings: Patriarchalism and Absolutism in Eighteenth-Century French Politicism," *Studies on Voltaire and the Eighteenth Century* 308 (1993): 281–303). Desan anatomizes some of the key struggles over what a father might be, discursively and politically, during the French Revolution (Suzanne Desan, "Qu'est-ce qui fait un père? Illegitimité et paternité de l'an II au Code civil," *Annales: Histoire, Sciences Sociales* [2002]: 935–64).

23. The original authors of the father-ruler couplet are lost to us, but traces of their innovation can be found in the world's classic religious texts and practices or in the archaeological footprints of ancient civilizations. See, for example, Gerda Lerner, *The Creation of Patriarchy* (New York: Oxford University Press, 1986). Once joined, the father-ruler signifiers *can* be put asunder. They can also be remarried. The linkage or splitting is contingent, although more or less probable in different historical circumstances.

24. For Willem I, known then and to this day as "Father of the Fatherland," see Herbert Harvey Rowen, *The Princes of Orange: The Stadholders in the Dutch Republic* (Cambridge: Cambridge University Press, 1988).

25. Sir Robert Filmer, *Patriarcha and Other Writings* (New York: Cambridge University Press, 1991), pp. 1–68, esp. 1–2. The 1991 Cambridge edition of Filmer's *Patriarcha*, which includes a helpful introduction by Johann P. Sommerville, should be read up against Gordon Schochet's pioneering analysis of Filmer in *Patriarchalism in Political Thought* (pp. 115–58) and two acute analyses of the specifically gendered content of Filmer's thought: Pateman's *The Sexual Contract* (pp. 82–89) and Rachel Weil's *Political Passions: Gender, the Family and Political Argument in England, 1680–1714* (Manchester, England: Manchester University Press, 2000). Filmer borrowed from patriarchalist predecessors like Aristotle and Jean Bodin, but his tract is more self-consciously engaged in digesting and countering explicit opposition to patriarchal rule; see Jean Bodin, *On Sovereignty* (New York: Cambridge University Press, 1992). *Patriarcha* was probably written before the English Civil War, but was only published posthumously, in 1680.

26. Weber, *Economy and Society*, p. 215. This pleasantly counterintuitive phrase derives from the title of Terence Ranger's 1992 collection; see Terence Ranger, ed., *The Invention of Tradition* (New York: Cambridge University Press, 1992).

27. On the prevalence of familial ideology in the governance of the American colonies and early republic, see, for example, Melvin Yazawa, *From Colonies to Com-*

monwealth: Familial Ideology and the Beginnings of the American Republic, (Baltimore: Johns Hopkins University Press, 1985); Mary Beth Norton, *Founding Mothers and Fathers: Gendered Power and the Forming of American Society* (New York: Vintage, 1997); and Mark Brandon, "Family at the Birth of the American Constitutional Order," 77 *Texas Law Review* 1195 (1999): 1221–26. The broader literature on families and states continues to grow apace. For a sense of the ever-wider field and some emergent approaches, see Lynne Haney and Lisa Pollard's introduction ("In a Family Way: Theorizing State and Familial Relations") to their edited volume, Lynne Haney and Lisa Pollard, eds., *Families of a New World: Gender, Politics, and State Development in a Global Context* (New York: Routledge, 2003), pp. 1–14.

28. Ferdinand de Saussure, *Course in General Linguistics* (New York: McGraw-Hill, 1965).

29. Emile Durkheim, *The Elementary Forms of Religious Life,* trans. Karen Fields (New York: Free Press, 1995), p. 229.

30. But how do we know which signs were "weightier" than others in politics? This chapter does not undertake a formal discourse analysis, so skims over this and other admittedly important issues. Barthes provides an exhilarating literary example of such an analysis, penned at the moment at which structuralism tipped over into poststructuralism, and the proliferation of possible codes and readings threatened to swamp the *analyse de texte;* Roland Barthes, *S/Z* (New York: Hill and Wang, 1974). John Mohr reviews various approaches to "measuring meaning" current in the social sciences (John Mohr, "Measuring Meaning Structures," *Annual Review of Sociology* 24 [1998]: 345–70).

31. Ernst H. Kantorowicz, *The King's Two Bodies: A Study in Medieval Political Theology* (Princeton, NJ: Princeton University Press, 1957), pp. 409–18.

32. Gianfranco Poggi evokes elements of the family-household public theatrics in his delightful description of the seventeenth-century French court:

> The king of France was thoroughly, without residue, a "public" personage. His mother gave birth to him in public, and from that moment on his existence, down to its most trivial moments, was acted out before the eyes of attendants who were holders of dignified offices. He ate in public, went to bed in public, woke up and was clothed and groomed in public, urinated and defecated in public. He did not much bathe in public; but then neither did he do so in private. I know of no evidence that he copulated in public; but he came near enough, considering the circumstances under which he was expected to deflower his august bride. When he died (in public), his body was promptly and messily chopped up in public, and its severed parts ceremoniously handed out to the more exalted among the personages who had been attending him throughout his mortal existence. Gianfranco Poggi, *The Development of The Modern State: A Sociological Introduction* (Stanford, CA: Stanford University Press, 1978), pp. 68–69.

See also Kantorowicz, *The King's Two Bodies,* an early, still influential work that pursues these arguments.

33. This is not to say that the sign of the patrilineage is or was seamless. Eilberg-Schwartz is a good source on some of the cultural contradictions of the patrilineage in ancient Judaism (Howard Eilberg-Schwartz, "The Father, the Phallus, and the

Seminal Word: Dilemmas of Patrilineality in Ancient Judaism," in Mary Jo Maynes, Ann Waltner, Birgitte Soland and Ulrike Strasser, eds., *Gender, Kinship, Power: A Comparative and Interdisciplinary History* (New York: Routledge, 1996). The patriarchal patrilineal family model of rule, "typologised in Scripture," as Jeffrey Merrick reminds us, "did not have just one fixed signification" ("Fathers and Kings, pp. 281–84). Perhaps no signifier has "just one"—better to say that the patrilineage was obsessively marked as a privileged signifier, "with a fundamental immobility and reassuring certitude" (Jacques Derrida, "Structure, Sign and Play in the Discourse of the Human Sciences," in *Writing and Difference*, trans. Alan Bass [Chicago: University of Chicago Press, 1978], p. 279). When it frayed, whether from outside in or inside out (as a result of its internal contradictions), much anxiety followed. Weber actually contributes to the ideological effect of security and seamlessness, alas, when he installs father-rule as an ultimate given and biologically invariant ground at the core of the concept of patrimonialism.

34. This analytical nodal point is not necessarily one empirical site: it can be a singular space like Versailles, or a whole series of geographically dispersed manorial households, or some networked combination. These differences in the geographic organization of rule had consequences for state formation in Europe and for patriarchal relations in family-households, in part because of the distinctive possibilities they offered for the dramatization of masculine power. This is relatively unexplored territory in social science history or historical social science.

35. Two recent, suggestive approaches to the general issue of how symbolics construct groups are provided by Pierre Bourdieu, "What Makes a Social Class? On the Theoretical and Practical Existence of Groups," *Berkeley Journal of Sociology* 32 (1987): 1–17; and Iris Marion Young, "Gender as Seriality: Thinking about Women as a Social Collective," in Barbara Laslett, Johanna Brenner, and Yesim Arat, eds., *Rethinking the Political: Gender, Resistance, and the State* (Chicago: University of Chicago Press, 1994); the original text is Durkheim's *Elementary Forms*. It must be said, however, that none of these texts deals with how *people* use signs to construct groups. People figure as *Träger*, as mute structural supports for ideologies.

36. It's actually worth an article or book in its own right, of course. However eagerly I would like to engage the more general issues of the historical and theoretical relationship between the order of signs of masculinity and femininity, on the one hand, and the biological dichotomy of sexual difference that they comment on and play with, on the other, there is no space to do so here.

37. Stephen Greenblatt, *Renaissance Self-Fashioning: From More to Shakespeare* (Chicago: University of Chicago Press, 1984).

38. Those two characters inhabit Shakespeare's *Othello* and Laclos's *Les Liaisons Dangereuses*, respectively and destructively. Scholars such as Wendy Gibson, who excoriate the elite women of European courts for being too strategic, too much like Laclos's Marquise de Merteuil in their machinations, miss the historical point. See Wendy Gibson, *Women in Seventeenth-Century France* (Basingstoke, England: Macmillan, 1989).

39. Mary Douglas, *Purity and Danger: An Analysis of Concepts of Pollution and Taboo* (New York: Routledge, 1966), pp. 40–41, 122.

40. Elizabeth I of England, "Speech to the Troops at Tilbury," in *The Norton An-thology of English Literature*, 6th ed., vol. 1 (1588; New York: W. W. Norton, 1993), p. 999.

41. The feminine is a not altogether unpromising signifier for male rulers, on the occasions when they want to convey their nurturant care for the ruled. The latter is an ancient trope—the biblical reference is to Isaiah 49: 23—"Kings shall be thy nurs-ing fathers, and their Queens thy nursing mothers"; see, for example, Wildavsky on Moses as "nursing father" and political leader. Aaron B. Wildavsky, *The Nursing Fa-ther: Moses as a Political Leader* (University: University of Alabama Press, 1984). Early-modern patriarchal rulers occasionally tried to signal their own love—authoritative parental love, admittedly—of their subjects. As a practice of patriarchal signification, however, playing the Venus instead of the Mars card is risky, since it may also be taken to signify political weakness, even symbolic castration.

42. See Mary Douglas on women, conveyed in marriage, as doors through which pollution might enter a patriarchal patrilineal system. Mary Douglas, *Purity and Dan-ger: An Analysis of Concepts of Pollution and Taboo* (New York: Routledge, 1966), p. 127. Linda Gregerson gives us a vivid picture of the vulnerability of Elizabeth I to this popular preoccupation with pollution, a vulnerability accentuated by fears of for-eign—especially French and Catholic—influence and invasion (Linda Gregerson, "Native Tongues: Effeminization, Miscegenation, and the Construction of Tudor Nationalism," *Mitteilungen* [Frankfurt: Johann Wolfgang Goethe–Universitat Zen-trum zur Erforschung der Frühen Neuzeit, 1995], pp. 18–38). In one sense, then, Elizabeth I is a representative figure: virtually any female ruler in early-modern Eu-rope could have served as an exemplar of these dynamics. But in another sense not: Elizabeth's responses are particularly adroit, in comparison with those of other Eng-lish rulers and rulers elsewhere: see her 1559 and 1566 Responses to Parliamentary Delegations on Her Marriage and her 1560 Response to Erik of Sweden's Proposal. These dynamics took on an explosive importance in early-modern European sites such as England and the Netherlands, which were being transformed by people's creation of the concepts and discourses of nation and nationalism, entangled, of course, with kingship. See Philip Gorski's analysis of nationalism as a phenomenon of the early modern rather than—as is usually assumed!—modernity. Philip S. Gorski, "The Mosaic Moment: An Early Modernist Critique of the Modernist The-ory of Nationalism," *American Journal of Sociology* 105 (March 2000): 1428–68.

43. Mark Gould offers a politico-economic analysis of the growing functional demands and double binds centered on one early-modern state (particularly its rulers), seventeenth-century England. Mark Gould, *Revolution in the Development of Capitalism* (Berkeley: University of California Press, 1987). I am discussing this ten-dency as part of a broader European—and also culturally mediated—phenomenon.

44. The felt need to close the gap between the totem and the mortal man or woman is always there, but people's responses in one or another historical context differ in content if not in form. In Trotsky's account of mass perceptions of (and de-sires swirling around) the figure of Kerensky during the Russian Revolution, for ex-ample, "Kerensky as a person has to be stripped of many of his characteristics, to be reduced from a whole man who puts on his pants one leg at a time to a public sym-

bol whose few psychologically present characteristics are then compared with a model of what a socialist leader should look like" (Arthur L. Stinchcombe, *Theoretical Methods in Social History* [New York: Academic Press, 1978], p. 73). Indeed, as the expectations of rulers' performances grew over time in Europe, so did the sophistication of ideological operations, invoked especially when chancy bloodlines turned up rulers who—metaphorically speaking, and even with help—couldn't put on their pants at all.

45. Andrew Wheatcroft, *The Habsburgs: Embodying Empire* (New York: Penguin, 1997).

46. Women are unthinkable as public patriarchs in the contemporary Saudi ruling family, for example. The possibility of such a cultural translation is barred, ruled out. Whether a (biological) woman can be a (social) man is obsessively debated in other historical forms of patriarchal patrimonialism—witness the French controversies over Salic Law and female succession to the throne. But in some sites, including early-modern England, female substitutes are deemed not only possible but even preferable to more lineally distant or otherwise problematic males. Why can women's biological femininity be part of a performance of ruling masculinity or fatherhood in only some sites and conjunctures? If specified with care, this question could be as fruitful for present-day world politics as it is for early-modern European states.

47. One might call these flows media, assets, or resources (see, for example, Sewell on schemas and resources and Giddens on rules and resources; William H. Sewell Jr., "A Theory of Structure: Duality, Agency, and Transformation," *American Journal of Sociology* 98, no. 1 (July 1992): 1–29; Anthony Giddens, *The Constitution of Society: Outline of the Theory of Structuration* (Berkeley: University of California Press, 1984). It is true that there are theoretical and empirical stakes involved even here, in the most abstract nomenclature for social practices. But because I am mostly intent in this chapter on installing signs at the center of a Weberian ideal type, and thus reconstructing ways to think about a range of early-modern European political practices and institutions, these conceptual differences matter less for the sociological task at hand.

48. G. E. Aylmer, *The King's Servants: The Civil Service of Charles I, 1625–1642* (New York: Columbia University Press, 1961), p. 279.

49. Robert Brenner, *Merchants and Revolution: Commercial Change, Political Conflict, and London's Overseas Traders, 1550–1653* (Princeton, NJ: Princeton University Press, 1993), pp. 61–73, 89–90.

50. Sarah Hanley, "Engendering the State: Family Formation and State Building in Early Modern France," *French Historical Studies* 16, no. 1 (1989): 8.

51. Ibid., p. 7.

52. Only metaphorically do the two form a *single* "compact," in my view; rather they were functionally interlocked sets of contracts and practices. I have found Ralph Giesey especially helpful in disentangling the complexity of elite lineage property (*propres*) and patrimonial politics in early-modern France (Ralph E. Giesey, "Rules of Inheritance and Strategies of Mobility in Prerevolutionary France," *American Historical Review* 82 (April 1977): 271–89). On medieval and early-modern family strate-

gies and property in land and economic assets in social reproduction, with an eye more to the lower orders than to the elite, see Pierre Bourdieu, "Marriage Strategies as Strategies of Social Reproduction," in Robert Forster and Orest Ranum, eds., *Family and Society: Selections from the Annales*, trans. Elborg Forster and Patricia M. Ranum (Baltimore: Johns Hopkins University Press, 1976); Jack Goody with C. A. Harrison, "Strategies of Heirship," *Comparative Studies in Society and History* 15 (1973): 3–20; and Rebecca Jean Emigh, "Theorizing Strategies: Households and Markets in Fifteenth-Century Tuscany," *History of the Family* 6 (2001): 495–517.

53.   The literature on medieval and early-modern European elite pacts is extensive but curiously vague. Most of these works (including one of my own articles, "The Familial State") could and should have been much more precise about whether the pacts involved were tacit or explicit, and in describing what difference conscious thematization might have made in the processes and outcomes they examine. This strikes me as crucial for an era in which the rules governing contractual arrangements applicable to state office, family, and emergent capitalist enterprise— and the idea of "contract" itself—were under construction. For medieval and early-modern European examples of the operation of elite networks, many of which are rooted in elite pacts, see, inter alia, J. Aalbers and M. Prak, eds., *De Bloem der Natie. Adel en Patriciaat in de Noordelijke Nederlanden* (Amsterdam: Boom Meppel, 1987); Julia Adams, "Culture in Rational-Choice Theories of State-Formation," in George Steinmetz, ed., *State / Culture: State-Formation after the Cultural Turn* (Ithaca, NY: Cornell University Press, 1999); Julia Adams, "The Familial State: Elite Family Practices and State-Making in the Early Modern Netherlands," *Theory and Society* 23, no. 4 (August 1994): 505–39; Peter Bearman, *Relations into Rhetorics: Local Elite Social Structure in Norfolk, England, 1540–1640* (New Brunswick, NJ: Rutgers University Press, 1993); William Beik, *Absolutism and Society in Seventeenth-Century France: State Power and Provincial Aristocracy in Languedoc* (New York: Cambridge University Press, 1985); Richard Bonney, *Political Change in France under Richelieu and Mazarin, 1624–1661* (New York: Oxford University Press, 1978); Robert Brenner, *Merchants and Revolution. Commercial Change, Political Conflict, and London's Overseas Traders, 1550–1653*, (Princeton, NJ: Princeton University Press, 1993); Daniel Dessert, *Argent, pouvoir et société au Grand Siècle* (Paris: Fayard, 1984); Sarah Hanley, "Engendering the State: Family Formation and State Building in Early Modern France," *French Historical Studies* 16, no. 1 (Spring 1989): 4–27; Robert R. Harding, *Anatomy of a Power Elite: The Provincial Governors of Early Modern France* (New Haven, CT: Yale University Press, 1978); Sharon Kettering, *Patrons, Brokers, and Clients in Seventeenth-Century France* (New York: Oxford University Press, 1986); Richard Lachmann, *From Manor to Market: Structural Change in England, 1536–1640* (Madison: University of Wisconsin Press, 1987); Paul D. McLean, "A Frame Analysis of Favor Seeking in the Renaissance: Agency, Networks, and Political Culture," *American Journal of Sociology* 104, no. 1 (July 1988): 51–91; John F. Padgett and Christopher K. Ansell, "Robust Action and the Rise of the Medici, 1400–1434," *American Journal of Sociology* 98 (1993): 1259–1319; David Parker, *The Making of French Absolutism* (London: Edward Arnold, 1983); Linda Levy Peck, *Court Patronage and Corruption in Early Stuart England* (London: Routledge, 1990); Hilton Root, *The Fountain of Privilege: Political Foundations of Mar-*

kets in Old Regime France and England (Berkeley: University of California Press, 1994); Jean-Laurent Rosenthal, "The Political Economy of Absolutism Reconsidered," in Robert H. Bates, Avner Greif, Margaret Levi, Jean-Laurent Rosenthal, and Barry R. Weingast, *Analytic Narratives* (Princeton, NJ: Princeton University Press, 1998); Eleanor Searle, *Predatory Kinship and the Creation of Norman Power, 840–1066* (Berkeley: University of California Press, 1988); Lawrence Stone and Jeanne C. Fawtier Stone, *An Open Elite? England 1540–1880* (New York: Oxford University Press, 1984). Burton and Higley—who give as one of their key examples the England of the 1688–89 Glorious Revolution—discuss the more general processes underlying explicit elite settlements, adopting a modified strategic or soft-utilitarian perspective. See Michael Burton and John Higley, "Political Crises and Elite Settlements," in Mattei Dogan and John Higley, eds., *Elites, Crises, and the Origins of Regimes* (New York: Rowman and Littlefield, 1998).

54. By virtue of their devaluation, ironically, elite women were free from some of the harsher rites prescribed for privileged men, which Norbert Elias limns in his picture of the disciplining of medieval and early-modern European elite men and masculinity on the path to the state's monopolization of the means of violence. Norbert Elias, *The Civilizing Process* (New York: Blackwell, 2000).

55. Jack A. Goldstone, *Revolution and Rebellion in the Early Modern World* (Berkeley: University of California Press, 1991), e.g., pp. 109–25, 228–49, 375–84).

56. Under certain associated conditions, Goldstone argues, revolutions ensued (ibid., pp. xxiii–xxiv). I am rudely truncating a complex argument and extracting one element, but philosophical differences authorize this particular intellectual liberty. Demography comes close to being cast as a primary motor of history for the Goldstone of *Revolution and Rebellion in the Early Modern World*. For me it is but one mechanism among many. That deep disagreement doesn't make Goldstone's rich analysis of the demographic mechanism any the less useful for my and others' neo-Weberian purposes.

57. David M. Kreps, "Corporate Culture and Economic Theory," in James E. Alt and Kenneth A. Shepsle, eds., *Perspectives on Positive Political Economy* (New York: Cambridge University Press, 1990). If I were writing a fully rounded history of elite pacts here, I would say much more about how participants created and demolished them; how they kept competitors and counterfeiters at bay; how they kept track of who was complying and enforced their own collective strictures on one another, and how the implicit and explicit features of contracts were related. On the threat of mimicry, see especially Michael Bacharach and Diego Gambetta on signification and trust games. Michael Bacharach and Diego Gambetta, "Trust in Signs," in Karen Cook, ed., *Trust and Society* (New York, NY: Russell Sage Foundation, 2001). Also important to underline would be women's distinctive roles in forwarding (or at times undermining) the men's pacts, serving as circulating media themselves and, sometimes, playing the parts of male participants. The same dynamics that I outlined above for Elizabeth I and other female rulers also hold here.

58. Weber, *Economy and Society*, p. 56.

59. Kiser does an excellent job of unpacking Weberian agency arguments from a rational-choice perspective. Edgar Kiser, "Comparing Varieties of Agency Theory in

Economics, Political Science and Sociology: An Illustration from State Policy Implementation," *Sociological Theory* 17, no. 2 (July 1999): 146–70.

60. Charles Tilly, "Warmaking and Statemaking as Organized Crime," in P. Evans, D. Rueschemeyer, and T. Skocpol, eds., *Bringing the State Back In* (New York: Cambridge University Press, 1985).

61. By this, those rulers meant a sense of binding obligation tying agents to themselves, the superordinate father-rulers of the respective home state. In his comparative analysis of medieval Maghribi trade, Avner Greif models the way that the trust and accountability characteristic of family relations could be used to counteract tendencies toward parcelization (Avner Greif, "Contract Enforceability and the Economic Institutions in Early Trade: The Maghribi Traders' Coalition," *American Economic Review* 83, no. 3 [June 1993]: 525–48). He is dealing with economic relations, but much of his argument would also hold for the multiplex networks of patrimonial elites. These family systems had their limits (of scale among other things), but they did make agency problems more manageable.

62. Weber, *Economy and Society*, p. 1011.

63. Ibid., p. 946.

64. Brian W. Arthur, "Self-Reinforcing Mechanisms in Economics," in Philip W. Anderson, Kenneth J. Arrow, and David Pines, eds., *The Economy as an Evolving Complex System* (New York: Addison-Wesley, 1988); Paul Pierson, "Increasing Returns, Path Dependence, and the Study of Politics," *American Political Science Review* 94, no. 2 (2000): 251–67.

65. For the Contracts in, for example, the cities of Leiden, Gouda, Haarlem, and Hoorn, see respectively Maarten Roy Prak, *Gezeten Burgers. De Elite in een Hollandse Stad: Leiden 1700–1780* (Dieren, The Netherlands: De Bataafsche Leeuw, 1985); Jacob Johannes de Jong, *Met Goed Fatsoen. De Elite in een Hollandse Stad: Gouda 1700–1780* (Amsterdam: De Bataafsche Leeuw, 1985); J. A. F. de Jongste, *Onrust aan het Spaarne. Haarlem in de jaaren 1747–1751* (Dieren, The Netherlands: De Bataafsche Leeuw, 1984); and L. Kooijmans, *Onder Regenten. De Elite in een Hollandse Stad: Hoorn 1700–1780* (Amsterdam: De Bataafsche Leeuw, 1985).

66. See especially Eileen Spring's work on the development of the English strict settlements, on entailment, and her critical review of historians' debates about their meaning for patriarchy (Eileen Spring, *Law, Land, and Family: Aristocratic Inheritance in England, 1300 and 1800* [Chapel Hill: University of North Carolina Press, 1993], pp. 123–47). Many people who have not broached a single tome of early-modern history will remember Mr. Bennett's predicament in Jane Austen's *Pride and Prejudice*: no sons, too many daughters, not enough family money, and a pompous idiot of an heir imposed by the entail. It was not Mr. Bennett himself who got to say who inherited his estate—for that had been decided before his birth—much to Mrs. Bennett's chagrin and our readerly delight. The disaster of the entail, which threatens to set the daughters of the house adrift upon the world, is absolutely necessary to the plot.

67. Pateman, *The Sexual Contract*.

68. In its codified form, the trope of patriarchal rottenness and dynastic decline is as old as Suetonius; see his *The Lives of the Caesars* (c. 110 C.E.), trans. J. C. Rolfe

(Cambridge, MA: Harvard University Press, 1998). What I am suggesting that we might explore, with a comparative-historical eye, would be the ways in which its specific deployment—including the first stirrings of mass mediation and publicity—affected contemporaries' response to the authority claims of early-modern father-rulers.

69. See Adams, "Culture in Rational-Choice Theories."

70. As a sampling of works that may be taken to nominate specifically familial variables and mechanisms for our consideration as causes of rebellion or revolution, see Goldstone on demographic pressures on early-modern states (Goldstone, *Revolution and Rebellion*); Hunt regarding representations of father-son relationships and brotherhood in eighteenth-century French novels and culture (Hunt, *The Family Romance*); Habermas on the emergent (male) public sphere and the bourgeoisie (Jürgen Habermas, *The Structural Transformation of the Public Sphere: An Inquiry into a Category of Bourgeois Society* [Cambridge, MA: MIT Press, 1989]). There are naturally many other candidate variables and nonfamilial dimensions of change not considered here, and in this deconstructive intellectual moment they are still proliferating.

71. Weber, *Economy and Society*, pp. 289–92.

72. Ibid., p. 290.

73. In this vein, *Economy and Society* has some valuable things to say about the development of the limited-liability company out of the household and the rise of bureaucratic forms within a situation of rule by notables (Weber, *Economy and Society*, pp. 707–29, 951–52).

74. W. V. Quine, *Word and Object* (Cambridge, MA: MIT Press, 1960).

75. "Indeterminacy means not that there is no acceptable translation, but that there are many" (W. V. Quine, "Indeterminacy of Translation Again," *Journal of Philosophy* 84, no. 1: 9). I realize that this settles nothing; it merely opens the possibility of exploring parallels and differences between translation and ideal type.

76. This is Max Weber with a twist. To wit: "To the person who cannot bear the fate of the times like a man, one must say: may he rather return silently, without the usual publicity build-up of renegades, but simply and plainly. The arms of the old churches are opened widely and compassionately for him." Max Weber, "Science as a Vocation," in H. H. Gerth and C. Wright Mills, eds., *From Max Weber: Essays in Sociology* (New York: Oxford University Press), p. 155.

77. No doubt "the biological" (itself a complex, hazy signifier in the disciplines of history and the social sciences) plays a role, or many roles, which remain to be worked out and incorporated into historical sociological descriptions and explanations. People build their castles of signification from the materials that they find around them, and the dichotomous fact of sexual difference is a basic part of that cultural landscape. What that fact comprises or entails is far from obvious, but that people take it to exist is crystal clear. But the variable structure of gender signification and the games of meaning that people play with their perceptions of what it is to be male or female cannot simply be referred to, or analytically exhausted by, the dichotomy of sexual difference. It's what people do with it that counts. That those imaginative practices are subject to further biological selection mechanisms should go without saying.

78. Stinchcombe, *Theoretical Methods in Social History*, p. 62.

79. I have found Fritz Ringer's to be a particularly useful summary discussion of ideal types in Weber's thought. Fritz Ringer, *Max Weber's Methodology: The Unification of the Cultural and Social Sciences* (Cambridge, MA: Harvard University Press, 1997), pp. 110–21. Ringer references Weber's 1904 essay "Objectivity" to define ideal types as "'pure constructs of relationships' that we conceive as 'sufficiently motivated,' 'objectively probable' and thus causally 'adequate' in the light of our 'nomological knowledge.'" He notes further that ideal types are designed with pragmatic purposes in mind: "They are valuable as cognitive means, to the extent that they lead to knowledge of 'concrete cultural phenomena in their interconnections, their causes, and their significance'" (ibid., pp. 111–12).

80. Historical sociologists and sociological historians blithely assume what count as important political outcomes all the time, but it is a more difficult proposition than it seems. For here be methodological monsters. Andrew Abbott's essay on how "outcome" has been understood in American sociology sheds a good deal of light on this murky issue. Andrew Abbott, "The Idea of Outcome in American Sociology," in George Steinmetz, ed., *The Politics of Method in the Human Sciences: Positivism and Its Epistemological Others* (Chapel Hill, NC: Duke University Press, 2004). Also see Adams, Clemens, and Orloff on the limits of second-wave historical sociological definitions of political outcome and the range of third-wave opinion on the topic. Julia Adams, Elisabeth S. Clemens, and Ann Shola Orloff, "Social Theory, Modernity, and the Three Waves of Historical Sociology," in Adams, Clemens, and Orloff, eds., *Remaking Modernity: Politics, History and Sociology* (Durham, NC: Duke University Press, 2004), available at http://www.russellsage.org/publications/working_papers/206adams.pdf.

81. See, e.g., Gillian Feeley-Harnick, "Dying Gods and Queen Mothers: The International Politics of Social Reproduction in Africa and Europe," in Maria Grosz-Ngate and Omari H. Kokole, eds., *Gendered Encounters: Challenging Cultural Boundaries and Social Hierarchies in Africa* (New York: Routledge, 1997).

82. Weber, *Economy and Society*, p. 241.

83. Alan Sica, *Weber, Irrationality, and Social Order* (Berkeley: University of California Press, 1988), p. 229.

84. Ibid., p. 228.

The Protestant Ethic and the Bureaucratic Revolution

Ascetic Protestantism and Administrative Rationalization in Early Modern Europe

Few works of social theory have been more influential than Max Weber's *Economy and Society*; and few parts of *Economy and Society* have been
more influential than Weber's analysis of "bureaucracy." Separation of person
and office, expropriation of the "means of administration," "technical" criteria for recruitment and promotion—these are some of the core characteristics of bureaucratic authority first identified by Weber over eighty years ago.
Even today, Weber's definition still serves as the starting point for most work
on the subject.

But while *Economy and Society* has a good deal to say about the key elements of bureaucratic administration, and about when and where they appeared, it has very little to say about *why* they appeared. It isolates the distinctive features of bureaucracy and identifies the historical systems of rule
that displayed them, but it does not *explain* their presence or absence in particular times and places. Perhaps this is because Weber never drafted the
chapter on the development of the modern state that he had planned to include in *Economy and Society*. But whatever the reason, the fact remains that
the seminal discussion of bureaucracy contains no theory of bureaucratization.

This cannot be said of recent work on European state formation. Early-
modern Europe was one of those times and places where bureaucratic systems of administration arose, and historically oriented sociologists and political scientists have spent a great deal of time trying to account for their
emergence and diffusion. There are two main schools of thought on this
question. The first takes its cues from the great Prussian military and political historian Otto Hintze; it traces administrative rationalization to

geopolitical competition.[1] The other is a neoutilitarian approach inspired by rational-choice theory; it focuses on the material interests of political rulers.[2]

This chapter has two related purposes: (1) to show that these two theories cannot convincingly account for the geographic distribution of a key feature of bureaucratic rule—the separation of person and office—across the states of early-modern Europe; and (2) to sketch out an account that may be able to do so. My central hypothesis is that the geographic distribution of office-holding practices—roughly speaking, patrimonialism in the South, proto-bureaucracy in the North—is best understood as the result of three successive processes: the "papal schism," which routinized venality within the church; the Protestant Reformation, which halted its spread into northern Europe; and the Second Reformation, which touched off bureaucratic revolutions in England, Sweden, and Prussia—the most bureaucratized states in early-modern Europe.

This chapter is in three parts. In the first, I briefly review Weber's typology of bureaucracy in *Economy and Society* and his various remarks on bureaucratization. In the second part, I turn to the theories of bureaucratization contained in recent work on early-modern state formation. Then, in the third and longest part, I present my own account of bureaucratization. And in the conclusion, I reflect on the historical and theoretical implications of this account.

Weber on Bureaucracy and Patrimonialism

While the outlines of Weber's definition are well known, it may be useful to recall the specifics. According to Weber, members of the "administrative staff" in an ideal-typical bureaucracy have ten characteristics. Administrative staff are: (1) "personally free"; (2) "organized in a clearly defined hierarchy"; (3) given "a clearly defined sphere of competence"; (4) employed on the basis of a "free contractual relationship"; (5) "selected on the basis of technical qualifications"; (6) "remunerated by fixed salaries in money"; (7) not engaged in any other major occupation; (8) promoted on the basis of "seniority," "achievement," or both; (9) "separated from ownership of the means of administration and without appropriation of [their] position[s]"; (10) "subject to strict and systematic discipline."[3]

Weber notes that highly bureaucratic systems of state administration may be found in a variety of times and places, including ancient Egypt, imperial Rome, and premodern China.[4] But he argues that the most fully bureaucratized systems are to be found in the territorial states of the modern West.

Weber contrasts bureaucratic systems of administration with "patrimonial" ones that originate in the ruler's household and continue to be modeled after it, even in their most developed forms. Weber distinguishes several different forms of patrimonialism (for a more detailed treatment of this concept, see Chapter 10). These include "primary patriarchalism," "gerontocracy," "sultanism," and the "estates system" (*ständische Herrschaft*). In the history of the West, says Weber, the latter type—the estates system—has been the most important.[5] Its distinguishing feature is private appropriation of offices and of the means of administration by corporate bodies (*Stände* or estates), which are usually conjoined in representative assemblies known variously as parliaments, estates, or states and typically included representatives of the clergy, nobility, and bourgeoisie.[6]

At this point, it is worth digressing briefly to note that the separation of person and office and the expropriation of the means of administration (characteristic 9 in the list above) is probably a historical precondition for the development of several other characteristics of bureaucracy, particularly characteristics 5, 6, 8, and 10. This is because administrators who have appropriated their positions are unlikely to select their successors on the basis of "technical qualifications" or pay themselves "fixed, money salaries"; rather they will tend to select their successors on the basis of blood relationship or material considerations and will remunerate themselves by collecting rents or fees, often *in natura*. Similarly, when administrators have appropriated their positions, rulers may have little control over promotions and will be inclined to base them on loyalty or compensation, rather than "achievement" or "seniority." Rulers will also have a difficult time imposing discipline under these conditions, since they lack effective monitoring mechanisms and possess few sanctions. Hence, separation of person and office would appear to be a crucial turning point along the road to full-blown bureaucracy. It is also interesting to note that the stages in the transition from patrimonialism to bureaucracy identified by Weber are just so many stages in the separation of person from office and the expropriation of the means of administration. Thus, Weber himself gives particular weight to the relation of person and office in the process of bureaucratization.[7]

Returning to the problem at hand, we see that Weber's typology contains an implicit question: What explains the transition from the "estates system" to the "modern state" in the West, and transitions from patrimonialism to bureaucracy more generally? Weber does not address these questions directly. But a close reading of his sociology of domination suggests two possible answers. The first is that bureaucratization is a gradual process that arises out of the ongoing struggles between patrimonial rulers and their administrative staffs. Since Weber clearly sees struggles between rulers and their administrative staffs as the key dynamic in the maintenance and development of systems of domination, and suggests at various points that bureaucratization is an incremental process that advances furthest where patrimonialism persists the longest, one might conclude that he views bureaucracy as the result of a long process of give-and-take between rulers and administrators.[8] The second argument, which Weber develops at some length, is that bureaucracy spreads because of its "technical superiority" over other forms of administration.[9] Here the underlying argument appears to be an evolutionary one: in the struggle for survival, bureaucratic states will prove stronger than patrimonial ones. Thus states must bureaucratize—or die. Though he does not develop this argument at great length, perhaps because it was so commonplace at the time, Weber also suggests that geopolitical competition between states (that is, war) operates as a selection mechanism that eliminates weak systems of state organization.[10] Systematizing these remarks, we arrive at three hypotheses regarding the genesis and spread of bureaucracy:

> (1) *Bureaucracy develops slowly*: it emerges out of the ongoing struggle between rulers and their staffs.
>
> (2) *Bureaucracy diffuses quickly*: once bureaucracy has emerged, its superior efficiency, relative to others forms of administration, creates strong incentives for rulers to adopt it.
>
> (3) *War promotes bureaucratization*: geopolitical competition speeds the emergence and diffusion of bureaucracy insofar as it raises the stakes in rulers' struggles with their staffs and with other rulers by escalating the political costs of administrative inefficiency.

While Weber did not advance these hypotheses himself, they do seem to be implicit within his analysis.

Are they correct? Where early-modern Europe is concerned, there are certainly reasons to question them. In some states, for instance, bureaucracy seems to have developed quickly, rather than incrementally, out of social revolutions or other forms of political contestation.[11] Here, the most famous case is probably the French Revolution, which catalyzed a sweeping process of administrative rationalization and centralization first documented by Alexis de Tocqueville.[12] Similar arguments could be made about the role of the Civil War and the Glorious Revolution in the bureaucratization of the English state, or about the impact of Frederick William I's princely "revolution from above" on the Prussian state.[13] One might also question whether bureaucracy diffuses "quickly." In Europe, at least, one could argue that the diffusion of bureaucracy took decades or even centuries. In addition, the connection between war and bureaucratization is not entirely clear-cut. While it is true that bureaucratic forms of state administration first appeared in Europe following a period of intense military conflict (e.g., the Thirty Years' War, 1618–48) that saw the establishment of standing armies in many states, they did not appear immediately or universally. While the size of state administrations—and state revenues—clearly grew quickly in response to wars, one could argue that the *form* of state administration did not change until at least the late seventeenth century, if at all.

Thus, it is not clear that the above hypotheses obtain in toto or in this general form, at least in the case of Europe—and for three reasons. First, it appears that the emergence of bureaucracy was sometimes a *revolutionary process*, rather than an evolutionary one. Second, it appears that the diffusion of bureaucracy was neither quick nor uniform, but rather *slow and uneven*. Finally, it is quite clear that war was not a *sufficient cause* of bureaucratization; and it is not immediately clear that it was even a *proximate cause* of bureaucratization. In sum, such hypotheses as we can find in Weber's work do not appear to explain the dynamics, diffusion, or genesis of bureaucracy in early-modern Europe. In particular, they offer few clues as to why some early-modern states bureaucratized and others did not. This is one of the central questions that has emerged out of contemporary debates on European state formation, and it is to that literature that we now turn.

Bureaucratization and "State Formation": Neo-Utilitarian and Neo-Hintzian Approaches

The debate on early-modern state formation among Anglo-American historical sociologists has been going on since the 1970s. Surveying the literature on this subject, one can clearly distinguish two waves of scholarship and perhaps also the beginnings of a third.[14] The first was Marxist in origin. As one would expect, it focused on the links between economic and political development.[15] The second wave was inspired largely by the (rediscovered) work of the great Prussian military and political historian Otto Hintze.[16] It argued for the importance of geopolitics.[17] The third wave, if it is one, is more diffuse. It draws on a variety of theoretical perspectives, including feminism, Weberianism, and rational choice, in an effort to challenge and/or deepen first- and second-wave theories.[18]

This is not the place to review all of these theories in detail. Instead, here I focus on the works of two scholars who have addressed the problem of bureaucratization in particularly direct and systematic ways, one from a rational-choice perspective (Edgar Kiser), the other from a neo-Hintzian perspective (Thomas Ertman). This discussion sets the stage for a presentation of my own neo-Weberian account.

Like most rational-choice theorists, Kiser begins with the a priori assumption that the social world consists of utility-maximizing individuals whose preference structures are heavily, if not exclusively, weighted toward material acquisition. For his analysis of bureaucratization, he also assumes that states consist of "rulers," their "agents" (administrators), and the mass of "taxpayers" (subjects), and that:

rulers are interested in maximizing net tax revenues (given the tax rate), officials try to maximize the sum of their legal and corrupt income from tax collection (minus the costs of sanctions for corruption) and taxpayers attemps to minimize the sum of their tax payments and penalties for tax evasion.[19]

In this perspective, the type of administrative system that emerges is a function of the strategic interactions between these three sets of players. In Kiser's model, the optimal strategy for each actor is determined not by their preference sets (which are treated as fixed) or by the expected strategies of other actors (which are treated as exogenous), but rather by the costs of effective "monitoring."[20] Where these costs are high, argues Kiser, rulers will prefer administrative systems that give agents greater autonomy, such as tax-farming, where monitoring is cheap and reliable; by contrast, rulers will opt for bureaucratic systems that afford rulers more control. Of course, rulers will not always be able to impose the system they prefer, owing to resistance from administrators or taxpayers, who may see bureaucracy as contrary to their interests. This, says Kiser, is why social revolutions are often followed by bureaucratic breakthroughs: they smash the distributional coalitions that often stand in the way of reform.

Kiser's analysis improves on Weber's in at least two ways. First, it recognizes the correlation between revolution and bureaucratization and suggests a plausible causal mechanism to account for it. Second, it provides a clear specification of the conditions under which bureaucracy is likely to diffuse within a particular system of state administration.[21] However, Kiser does not say anything about why bureaucracy diffuses across the state system as a whole. Nor does he address the *historical genesis* of bureaucratic practices. Indeed, Kiser treats bureaucracy as a given, as a strategy that is always already available to any prince, rather than as a historical product that emerges at a particular time.

This cannot be said of Ertman's account, which explicitly situates the emergence of bureaucracy in time—around 1450 to be exact. Like other neo-Hintzians, Ertman sees European state formation mainly as a result of intensified geopolitical competition. But while Ertman views the growth of state administration mainly as a product of war—of the need to extract resources and manage materiel—he argues that the *form* this administration took was primarily a function of *timing*—of whether rulers built up their states before or after the year 1450. The year 1450 was important, not because of one particular event, but because of two broad changes. The first was in the available sources of officeholders, and the second was in the models of officeholding available in each period. Before 1450, Ertman claims, rulers had to recruit their administrators from the ranks of the propertied elites: the landed nobility and the urban patriciate. These groups had a great deal of power and autonomy and were able to negotiate highly favorable terms of office. After 1450, by contrast, another source of officeholders became available: university-educated jurists. Their bargaining position was considerably weaker, enabling rulers to impose less favorable terms of office. The year 1450 also marked a change in the available models of officeholding. Before 1450, Ertman argues, the dominant model of officeholding was the ecclesiastical benefice—a proprietary system of officeholding in which there was no legal separation between person and office. But after 1450, he says, a new nonproprietary model of officeholding emerged. Thus, would-be state-builders had very different materials and models at their disposal before and after 1450, and with important results: states that were built before 1450 tended to be "patrimonial" in form—that is, they were characterized by proprietary systems of officeholding; by contrast, states that were built after 1450 tended to be "bureaucratic" in form—that is, they were constructed along nonproprietary lines. And since military conflict was the main impetus behind state-building, Ertman reasons, the crucial variable that explains the administrative system which developed in a particular state is "timing of the onset of sustained geo-political competition." States that became embroiled in long-term wars before 1450 generally developed patrimonial administrations, whereas states that escaped such wars until after 1450 tended to develop bureaucratic ones.

Like Kiser's, Ertman's theory of bureaucratization also goes beyond Weber in several ways. First, it isolates a crucial difference—perhaps *the* crucial difference—between patrimonial and bureaucratic forms of administration: the separation of person and office. Second, it focuses on a crucial weakness—perhaps *the* crucial weakness—in the neo-Hintzian account: the absence of a general or direct correlation between war and bureaucratization. Like Kiser, however, Ertman fails to account for the genesis and diffusion of bureaucracy. While Ertman does trace patrimonialism back to its source—the ecclesiastical benefice—and acknowledges that a new, nonproprietary system of officeholding emerged sometime around 1450, he does not tell us where this system came from. In Ertman's story, then, the nonproprietary model is a deus ex machina of sorts that is rushed onstage to fill a hole in the plot. This is not the only hole in Ertman's analysis; it has empirical gaps as well. Ertman presents no evidence to support his claims about the changing sources of officeholders before and after 1450 and in patrimonial and bureaucratic states, and the evidence that I have uncovered does not suggest any systematic differences between the two periods or the two types of administration.[22] And even if such differences in recruitment could be found, they still would not suffice to explain a number of important cases. For as Ertman himself concedes, there are some states, such as England, that experienced sustained geopolitical competition before 1450 but later became bureaucratic, while there are others, such as Poland, that failed to become bureaucratic, even though they did not experience sustained geopolitical competition until after 1450.

Thus both Kiser and Ertman do not satisfactorily answer two key questions that must figure centrally in any account of bureaucratization: the genesis of nonproprietary systems of officeholding in early-modern Europe and the distribution of patrimonial and bureaucratic systems of officeholding in early-modern Europe. Where does the practice of separating person and office come from? And why was it adopted in some states but not in others?

Patrimonialism and Bureaucracy: Outcomes and Patterns

Before taking up these questions, we must first pose them more concretely, in terms of particular states and regions. Drawing on recent revisionist research by early-modern historians, Ertman argues that Spain, France, Italy, Hungary, and Poland are best seen as "patrimonial," and England, Scandinavia, and "the German states" as "bureaucratic."[23] One could criticize this coding of the cases as too crude. Still, when the cases are listed in this order, a striking pattern emerges: the division between bureaucratic and patrimonial states—states with proprietary and nonproprietary systems of officeholding—coincides almost perfectly with the Protestant/Catholic divide! Of course, it must be emphasized that the coincidence between confessional allegiance and officeholding practices is not complete. Some predominantly Protestant states were not terribly bureaucratic. Take the Dutch Republic.[24] One finds a certain degree of bureaucratization within subaltern posts—in the clerical support staff of the States General or the Amsterdam City Council, for example. But higher-level administrative functions were mostly in the hands of the urban "regents" and their chosen representatives, and the collection of taxes was generally "farmed out." Of course, there was no organized system of venality, such as France or Spain had. But then much the same might be said of the Florentine city-state, which was Catholic.[25] Nor were convergences of this sort specific to the more urbanized areas of Europe; they can also be found in agrarian regions. Take the cases of Saxony and Bavaria, the one Protestant, the other Catholic.[26] In both states, many key administrative posts remained under the control of the territorial diet or *Landtag* and could only be filled with members of the landed nobility—a classic example of the type of patrimonialism Weber referred to as *ständisch* or estates-based. In the case of Bavaria, however, the *Landtag* ceased to meet during the seventeenth century, and the estates were represented through a standing committee that could more easily be controlled by the king. One might therefore argue that Bavaria was less patrimonial, and more bureaucratic, than Saxony. It should also be noted that some of the patrimonial states still had bureaucratic features. This is especially true of Spain, France, and the Papal States, which combined widespread venality with a hierarchical chain of command, and a certain degree of supervision and discipline, usually through royal commissaries, such as the French *intendants*.[27] Similarly, it should be noted that the form of patrimonialism that existed in these states was quite different from that which was found in Hungary or Poland. In the latter countries, offices were appropriated not by private persons, but by social groups, and in particular, by the landed nobility. Hungary and Poland were characterized not by venality, but by an extreme form of estates-based patrimonialism. Similar observations could be made about the Protestant states of northern Europe. There, too, the spread of bureaucratic administration was often limited by the prerogatives of representative assemblies, albeit not to the degree that it was in Hungary or Poland.[28] And even where such barriers had been removed, as in the "absolute" monarchies of Scandinavia and the Empire, patrimonial elements still remained. Prussian and Swedish officials did not have the sort of contractual and legal protections typical of a modern bureaucracy; they could still be fired without warning and at will—and sometimes were.[29] But while the coincidence between confessional allegiance and administrative system is less than perfect, and the initial contrast between patrimonial and bureaucratic states too sharp and simplistic, it is nonetheless true that the most fully bureaucratic states were Protestant (England, Sweden, and Prussia, for example) and that the most deeply patrimonial states were Catholic (Italy, France, Spain, Hungary, and Poland); so there does, in fact, seem to have been a nontrivial degree of correlation between Protestantism and bureaucracy on the one hand, and patrimonialism and Catholicism on the other. The question, of course, is why?

The answer I propose focuses not on utility-maximizing or geopolitics, but on religion. In particular, it focuses on the impact of three events: the papal schism (1378–1417), the Protestant Reformation (ca. 1500–ca. 1550), and the "Further Reformation" movements that began in the late sixteenth century.[30] For it was during the schism that offices were first sold on a grand scale, and it was from the papacy that secular rulers initially borrowed this device. It is for this reason that venality was introduced earliest and spread furthest in precisely those areas where the Roman Church was most influential and most deeply entrenched at this time, namely, France and the Italian and Iberian Peninsulas. Of course, venality did not remain confined to these areas; it eventually spread to northern Europe as well. But its roots were never as deep there, or its growth as lush. Why? The answer to this question, I will argue, has much to do with the Reformation. For it was the reformers who first elaborated and instituted a nonproprietary system of officeholding within the church, and it was through the influence of their followers that venality within the state was nipped in the bud and a protobureaucratic form of administration put in its place.[31]

Patrimonialism and Venality: Types and Degrees

Before tracing out the role of the papacy in the invention and diffusion of venal officeholding, it is important that we distinguish venality from other types of patrimonialism, and identify some of the forms it can take. It is a tedious exercise, but one that will prove useful in the analysis that follows.

The appropriation of political offices in early-modern Europe took a variety of different forms. If we distinguish between individual and collective forms of appropriation on the one hand, and permanent and temporary forms on the other, we arrive at the following fourfold typology (see Figure 11.1): (1) *venal officeholding* (individual and permanent): in this system, functionally and geographically defined offices are treated as the private property of a particular individual and can be legally bought and sold or bequeathed and inherited; (2) *feudal officeholding* (collective and permanent): in this system, geographically defined offices are treated as the private patrimony of a particular lineage; they can be bequeathed and inherited, but not openly or legally bought or sold; (3) *oligarchy* (collective and temporary):[32] in this system, offices of both kinds—functional and territorial—are treated as the corporate patrimony of a particular estate, typically landed nobles or urban patricians, who collectively confer office upon individual members of their estate for some specified time, usually by means of election, rotation, or lottery; such offices cannot be legally bought, sold, bequeathed, or inherited; (4) *farming* (individual and temporary): in this system, offices are sold to the highest bidder for a specified period, but cannot be sold or bequeathed. Obviously, these are ideal types that are rarely found in pure form. As we will see, mixed types are also possible (venal oligarchies and venal farms, for example).

It is important to note that these four systems differ not only in the form of appropriation, but also in the degree. In the venal and feudal systems, particular individuals or lineages obtain a *permanent* claim over an office, and merit and performance can play little if any role in the selection of incumbents. Under the oligarchic and farming systems, by contrast, there is greater room for merit- and performance-based recruitment and promotion—for example, via competitive elections in oligarchies or competitive auctions in farms. For this reason I will assume that oligarchies and farms represent milder forms of patrimonialism, especially when they are competitive.

Since venality is the main focus of this chapter, it will be useful to discuss it in somewhat greater detail. In the broadest sense, venality is simply the sale of public offices. As such, it can assume a variety of different forms and degrees. For example, scholars of venality often distinguish between private and public venality. Private venality involves a transaction between private per-

FIGURE 11.1. *Types of Proprietary Officeholding*

Length of Appropriation

	Temporary	Permanent
Individual	Farming	Venality
Collective	Oligarchy	Feudalism

Mode of Appropriation

sons, typically the holder of an office and a would-be purchaser; the sovereign is not a party to the transaction. By contrast, public venality involves a transaction between a public body and a private person, usually the sale of an office to an individual, typically by the sovereign or his representatives, or, conversely, the repurchase of an office from an individual.[33] One might also draw a second distinction, between de facto and de jure venality. I will speak of de facto venality in two cases: (a) when payment for, or exchange of, an office is expected or tolerated but not required or institutionalized, as when transfer of an office is preceded by a secret payment (a bribe) or a public gift; or (b) when a payment of some kind is required and institutionalized but does not have the *legal* status of a payment for office, as when the incumbent is required to pay certain "fees" upon assuming office. These two types may also be seen as stages or degrees of venality, with the second being the more severe or developed form. To distinguish this latter type in the discussions that follow, I refer to it as "proto-venality." Finally, I will speak of de jure venality as a payment that is not only required and institutionalized, but also officially and legally regarded as a payment for the office. Obviously, the different types of venality distinguished above differ in both form and degree. In its most fully developed form, venality is permanent, public, and de jure. This is the form in which we will be most interested below.

The Development and Diffusion of Venality in Late Medieval and Early-Modern Europe: The Role of the Papacy

The case for papal influence rests mainly on forms of circumstantial evidence. The first is *historical timing*. Most scholars of the subject agree that the popes played a pioneering role in the sale of offices. Strong evidence of de facto public venality, in which gifts to the pope preceded the appointment to benefices, may already be found during the reign of Innocent III (1198–1216).[34] De facto private venality also appeared around this time in the form of the infamous *resignatio in favorem tertii*, in which the holder of an ecclesiastical benefice resigned his post in favor of a third party who then transferred it to the intended recipient in exchange for a consideration paid to the first party and shared with the third. This device allowed the seller and purchaser to evade the charge of simony. Public proto-venality was first instituted during the great schism by the Roman pope Boniface IX (1389–1406). The political and administrative chaos of the schism resulted in a precipitous drop in papal revenues, and Boniface responded by putting many lower-level administrative offices up for sale.[35] By the 1440s, these sales had become de jure: they had a legal status recognized by the courts.[36] Under Sixtus IV (1471–84), clerical offices within the Roman curia were being created and sold,[37] and there is some evidence that higher-level offices within the curia were also for sale.[38] Be that as it may, there can be no doubt that high-level offices within the curia and even the College of Cardinals itself were being openly bought and sold by the first decade of the sixteenth century.[39] In sum, there is evidence of public venality in the Roman Church as early as the twelfth century, and evidence of de jure public venality as early as the mid-fifteenth century.

Among the secular rulers of Europe, the kings of France are generally seen as pioneers in the development of venality. In comparison with the popes, however, they were veritable laggards. Of course, the farming of royal offices was already well established in France by the thirteenth century, and traces of it may even be found three centuries earlier.[40] What is more, private de jure venality seems to have been quite common by the mid-1300s, and there is indirect evidence of its existence a full century earlier.[41] It also appears that members of the king's courts and counsels were involved in this traffic, probably from the late fourteenth century onward.[42] But this traffic was limited to lower-level offices, and it was not until the first two decades of the early sixteenth century that we find clear evidence of public venality—of the permanent sale of offices by the French kings themselves. With the establishment of a special "marketing" agency, the *Bureau des parties casuelles*, Francis I gave official recognition and legal stature to such sales and began the process of creating new offices as a means of generating revenue.

Over the next century and a half, the number and the level of the offices for sale rose fairly steadily. By the time of Richelieu, it is estimated that there were more than 40,000 venal offices in France.

It is sometimes claimed that venality was unknown in Spain.[43] And it is true that the kings of Spain never instituted de jure public venality. But recent research has uncovered clear evidence of venality in all its other forms and degrees. De facto private farming of municipal offices was practiced in the cities of Castile from the late fourteenth century onward, and hints of it can be found more than a century earlier.[44] Evidence of de facto public venality and private proto-venality in the municipal governments may be found in the mid-fifteenth century, when the Castilian Cortes lodged repeated protests against the creation of new municipal offices by the Spanish Crown and against the use of the *resignatio in favorem* for the transfer of offices to third parties.[45] By the 1480s, a system of public proto-venality was clearly in place, with offices in the royal judiciary and financial administration being offered for sale, though only on a modest scale.[46] And in 1494, private traffic in municipal offices was made legal.[47] The kings of early-modern Spain never did legalize the sale of public offices, and they shied away from selling judicial posts. But they did engage in systematic proto-venality, and on a grand scale: thousands of posts were sold during the early-modern period, not only in Castile and Aragon, but also in Spanish America and the Indies, and even in the Spanish Inquisition.[48]

Because of the political fragmentation of the peninsula, the situation in Italy was inevitably more complex and variegated. In the early-modern *mezzogiorno*, venality was both widespread and highly developed. Like their immediate neighbor, the Papal States, the governments of early-modern Sicily and Naples both practiced systematic de jure venality, selling a wide range of offices to the highest bidders from the early sixteenth century onward.[49] Unfortunately, the development of venality in premodern Sicily and Naples has not been systematically studied, so it is not clear how deep the roots of these practices were.[50] But they cannot have extended back as far as they did in France, since thirteenth-century Sicily and Naples both had unusually "rational" administrative systems, with limited-term appointments, money salaries, and other proto-bureaucratic features.[51] In northern Italy, by contrast, venality does not appear to have been as widespread or as fully developed. In Florence, there was no public venality at all, and little if any private venality.[52] In Venice, public venality did not appear until the seventeenth century and only on a limited scale; it was used as a financial expedient during a period of fiscal crisis and was never extended to high-level political and judicial posts.[53] The only major exceptions to this rule were Savoy and Milan, where public venality was introduced from outside, by the French in the one case and the Spanish in the other.

Of course, venality was not limited to the Catholic polities of Latin Europe. It can also be found in the Protestant countries of the North, albeit in milder and less-developed forms. In the Dutch Republic, for example, would-be officeholders sometimes made large "gifts" to influential magistrates in hopes of gaining an appointment.[54] Gifts of this sort also seem to have played a role in the hunt for offices in Stuart England.[55] Brandenburg-Prussia was also not immune. During the late seventeenth and early eighteenth centuries, posts in local government and the royal judiciary were sometimes offered for sale, as were titular posts of various ranks.[56] But the private sale of offices was forbidden.

What the evidence on historical timing shows is that the papacy was the first state to institute a system of full-fledged venal officeholding—public, de jure, and permanent. And it strongly suggests that the papacy also led the way in earlier phases of development, in both private and public venality. What the evidence on historical timing does *not* show is that the development of venality in the secular states was stimulated or influenced by developments in the church and the Papal States. After all, it could be that the genesis of venality was a case of simultaneous invention, of individual rulers responding to similar circumstances in similar ways, without regard to, or knowledge of, one another's actions. But there are at least two bodies of evidence that speak against such a conclusion.

The first has to do with *geographical proximity and institutional ties*. For the areas in which venality seems to have been most pervasive and most highly developed—France, Spain, and certain parts of Italy—were also very close to the papacy, geographically, institutionally, or both. Consider the case of France. The kings of France housed popes in Avignon for most of the fourteenth century and parts of the fifteenth, and their subjects dominated the Roman curia for much of these periods. Their cousins, the dukes of Anjou, had ruled over Naples during the fourteenth century, and the kings themselves conquered Savoy during the early sixteenth century in the course of a long military campaign on the Italian Peninsula. Their chief rivals in this struggle were, of course, the kings of Spain, who gained control over the duchy of Milan in the sixteenth century, and whose forebears had ruled over Naples since the fifteenth century and Sicily since the thirteenth. Given their deep involvement in papal politics, and their long-standing presence on the Italian Peninsula, it is hard to imagine that the kings of France and Spain could have been unaware of the growth of venality in the Roman curia, and in the church more generally. And it is even harder to imagine that the rulers of the Italian states would have been unfamiliar with these practices, since the papacy's personnel were overwhelmingly Italian.

When taken together, these circumstances provide strong evidence of papal *influence* in the development and diffusion of venality. But additional evidence suggests that the link between the papacy and the spread of venality was stronger still, that it involved not only influence but also *imitation*. For the systems of venality instituted in France, Spain, and their dependencies were strikingly similar to those instituted in the Roman church and the Papal States, not only in their broader organization but even in the minutest of details. Consider the rules governing the resignation of proprietary offices. In the Roman curia, the resignation had to occur at least twenty days before the incumbent's death; otherwise the resignation was invalid, and the office reverted to the pope. In France and Spain, the same rule applied to the *resignatio in favorem*. (In France, however, the period was later extended to forty days.) Or consider the types of offices that could be bought and sold. In Rome, the sale of judicial and ecclesiastical offices was frowned upon by many, and though it was widespread, especially during the sixteenth century, it was never legalized. Similar restrictions applied in Spain, where judicial offices were never publicly sold, and in France, where they were not officially put up for sale until the late sixteenth century, long after other categories of office had been made venal. The reasons for these parallels are not hard to find. They have to do with the influence of canon law, which provided the legal foundations for venal officeholding within the Roman curia, and, as it appears, in the secular principalities as well. In this regard, it is striking to note that the countries in which venality took root earliest and most deeply were precisely the countries with the oldest and most prestigious faculties of canon law—Italy, France, and Spain.

Of course, venality was not limited to the Latin countries. As we have seen, rulers throughout Europe experimented with it at one time or another. Thus if we wish to explain variations in the degree of venality, we must understand not only where the seeds came from, but why they took root and grew in some places but not in others. The answer to this question, I argue, has a great deal to do with the influence of the Protestant Reformation, and in particular with the new conception of office that it systematized and propagated, a conception that was explicitly antipatrimonial—and extraordinarily bureaucratic.

The Critique of Simony and the Bureaucratization of the Church

The critique of "simony"—the use of church offices for personal financial gain—is very old, probably as old as the Western church itself. But it seems to have taken on a new urgency during the fifteenth century, especially in Germany. One of the earliest and best-known attacks on the "abuses" of the Roman church was the *Reformatio Sigismundi*, which was originally written during the late 1430s, republished five times in manuscript form by 1476, and eight more times in printed form by 1522.[57] Obviously, the *Reformatio* was an influential document. It contained a wide-ranging critique of abuses within the Western church and the Holy Roman Empire, as well as suggestions for their reform. The critique of the church focused primarily on the problem of simony, but catalogued a variety of "abuses," including the holding of multiple posts (pluralism), the hiring of substitutes and curés (nonresidence), the collection of common services and annates, and of course the sale of indulgences. More interesting from our perspective are the proposals for reform, which centered on the elimination of ecclesiastical benefices in favor of a system of fixed salaries, and included demands that all clergymen have "a diploma from a university," be subject to regular visitations and participate in diocesan synods, be familiar with the statutes governing their appointments, "have the same income and perform the same tasks," and turn over the tasks of financial administration to a "resident curator." Salaries, technical qualifications, discipline, written rules, functional specialization—the *Reformatio* reads like a blueprint for a Weberian-style bureaucracy! The only thing that distinguished the *Reformatio* was its prescience and cogency. The themes and proposals themselves became virtual commonplaces that were echoed in the writings of well-known humanists and reformers such as Erasmus and Luther, as well as in pamphlets and broadsheets by lesser-known authors.

The systems of clerical officeholding that were established in the Protestant polities of Europe during the course of the sixteenth century were remarkably similar to the one proposed in the *Reformatio*.[58] Except in England, benefices were eliminated. And while most clergymen did continue to receive some form of nonmonetary compensation—the use of a field or a house, say—salaries were typically their chief source of income. A certain degree of formal education became a de facto or de jure precondition of office. By the early seventeenth century, the vast majority of Protestant clergymen had spent some time at university, and a sizable minority boasted university degrees. In many countries, aspiring clergymen also had to pass a formal examination, typically an oral examination by their prospective employers or future colleagues. And once in office, most clergymen were also subject to formal oversight of one kind or another—not only by their lay employers and clerical superiors, but often by their peers as well—and those who failed to lead exemplary lives or proved negligent in their duties could be—and often were—subjected to formal admonitions or even expelled from their posts; the expectations were clear, and often codified. Conversely, a man who preached well and avoided scandal might reasonably hope to rise through the ranks to become the head minister of a large church, or perhaps even a member of the clerical hierarchy. And by the eighteenth century he could also reckon with a certain degree of material security even if he did not achieve any great success—a pension if he lived into retirement, or support for his wife and children if he did not. Separation of person and office, fixed money salaries, technical qualifications, formal examinations, written rules, disciplinary oversight, career ladders, and even pensions—it would be no great exaggeration to say that the Protestant clergyman was the first modern bureaucrat.

What impact did these changes in clerical officeholding have on systems of political officeholding in Protestant countries? In the short run—meaning the sixteenth century—the answer would seem to be "very little." Of course, by openly attacking papal officeholding practices, and challenging the authority of canon law, the early reformers probably did help to prevent the spread of venality into northern Europe. But they generally had very little to say about other forms of patrimonialism, such as feudalism or oligarchy, and there is no evidence that they pushed for bureaucratization in the secular sphere. That task fell to the second-generation reformers of the seventeenth century.

The Protestant Ethic and the Bureaucratic Revolution

By the late sixteenth century, the "first" Reformation had run its course: in most of northern Europe, the "lies," "superstitions," and "abuses" of the Roman Church had been removed, and the "true doctrines" and "pure liturgy" of a reformed church had been put in their place. What was needed now was a "second" or "further" reformation, a reformation not just of the church, but of "life" itself, the establishment not only of a godly church, but of a godly society. Or such, at least, was the view of a small but vocal minority within the Protestant churches of northern Europe. These movements went by different names in different places: Puritanism, Pietism, the Further Reformation, and the Second Reformation. They also occupied somewhat different positions within their host societies. Puritanism and the Further Reformation were ascetic reform movements within the Anglican and Reformed Churches of England and the Netherlands, respectively.[59] The Second Reformation was a movement for the introduction of Calvinism into the Lutheran territories of Germany. And Pietism was an ascetic reform movement within the Lutheran Church of Germany. Nonetheless, the agendas of these movements were strikingly similar. They railed against laxity and sloth in the church, indolence and immorality in society, and corruption and decadence in the state. In short, they demanded a stricter application of biblical law and Christian ethics to all classes and all spheres of society—rich as well as poor, the state as well as the church. It is for that reason that some historians group these movements together under the rubric of "puritanism" or "precisionism." As one might expect, there were also numerous interconnections between these movements: the Second Reformation was inspired by the successes of militant Calvinism in the struggles against Catholic resurgence in Western Europe, while Lutheran Pietism and the Second Reformation were both heavily indebted to English Puritanism. Twisted and tangled as they were, the roots of these movements all went back to Geneva in the end.

Generally speaking, precisionist movements seem to have achieved their greatest and most lasting successes where, and to the degree that, they were supported and protected by pious and autocratic rulers, who shared their opposition to "courtly decadence" and "political corruption." Where an antipatrimonial alliance of this sort emerged, linking a precisionist movement with a reformist ruler, the usual result was a rapid transformation of state administration in a strongly bureaucratic direction. The best-known and most influential examples of such transformations are to be found in Brandenburg- Prussia, Sweden, and England. Let us briefly examine each of these cases.

The story of Prussia's bureaucratic revolution begins in 1613, the year in which the elector of Brandenburg, John Sigmund, officially converted to Calvinism. There was nothing unusual about this act; many other German princes had converted as well. What was unusual was the elector's failure to impose a "Second Reformation" on his subjects, who were predominantly Lutheran and vigorously opposed the introduction of Calvinism. The result of this confrontation was confessional bifurcation: the dynasty and the court adopted Calvinism, the nobility and the third estate remained Lutheran. The second chapter of Prussia's bureaucratic revolution begins in 1650, the year in which John Sigmund's grandson, Frederick William, presented the provincial estates (*Landtag*) of Brandenburg with a request for a long-term "contribution" to support a standing army. As was usual in such cases, the estates responded with a list of "grievances," which they wanted the elector to fulfill before granting his request. "*Gravamina in puncto religionis*" topped the list, and became the central sticking point in the negotiations, which dragged on for nearly two years, making this the longest *Landtag* ever. Over the next decade, similar confrontations ensued in other parts of the dynasty. Angered and disgusted at what he perceived as intolerance and intransigence, Frederick William decided to bypass the territorial estates by appointing large numbers of Calvinists and "foreigners" to the royal administration and transferring more and more authority into their hands. By the end of his reign, native-born nobles of the Lutheran persuasion had been almost completely excluded from the upper echelons of the Prussian state. The third and final chapter of Prussia's bureaucratic revolution begins in 1713, the year in which Frederick William's grandson, Frederick William I, ascended the throne. Frederick William I was a severe and autocratic man of deep religious convictions, whom one historian has aptly described as a "Puritan in purple robes." In this, he was the very opposite of his father, Frederick I, a kindly but weak-willed ruler who sought to emulate the grandeur of Louis XIV and be-came the creature of his powerful courtiers. The "laxity" and "decadence" of Frederick's court, and the incompetence and corruption of his administration soon pushed the fledgling monarchy to the brink of financial ruin, and sparked opposition and outcries not only from the crown prince and more pious members of the court and the administration, but also from Pietist lead-ers such as Philipp Jacob Spener, who had a large and growing following within Brandenburg-Prussia. Frederick William I wasted no time in undoing the "abuses" introduced by his father. During the first two years of his reign, he downsized the court to the brink of extinction and transferred all major administrative responsibilities to the War Commissary and the Domains Boards. And in the decades that followed he continued his efforts at admin-istrative centralization and rationalization by creating a single office to over-see all aspects of domestic administration and staffing it with trained and salaried men who were recruited and promoted on the basis of their talent, their "diligence" (*Fleiss*) and, not least, their ability to "cut costs" (*ein Plus machen*). Under his stewardship, Prussia became the most bureaucratic state on the European continent and a model other states sought to imitate.

Prussia's bureaucratic revolution was carried through by an ascetic Protes-tant monarch in alliance with antipatrimonial and anticourt segments of the royal administration and pietistically minded clergymen. The alliance behind Sweden's bureaucratic revolution was similar, if by no means identical, and its progress can also be told as a story in three chapters. It begins with the reigns of Gustav IX (1590–1611) and Gustav II Adolf.[60] Their predecessor, Sigismund, had converted to Catholicism in hopes of securing election to the Polish Crown. In that enterprise he succeeded, but only at the expense of a religious rebellion at home. The rebellion pitted most of the (Lutheran) clergy and nobility—especially the lower clergy and nobility—against a smaller group of prelates and magnates who had remained loyal to the old faith. The rebels triumphed, and their leader, Gustav Vasa, was eventually proclaimed king. Gustav's reign was a tumultuous one. He alienated the magnates early on through his harsh treatment of the Catholic rebels, many of whom were summarily tried and executed. Subsequently, he alienated many of his orthodox Lutheran supporters through his openly Calvinist sympathies. The marriage of his son, Gustav II Adolf, to a Calvinist princess only served to heighten suspicions that the Vasas were preparing a Second Reformation in Sweden. Such suspicions soon proved false, however, as the new king pledged his loyalty to the Lutheran faith, and sought rapproche-ment with the magnates. This rapprochement was symbolized by Gustav Adolf's selection of a prominent magnate (Axel Oxenstierna) as his chancel-lor and closest adviser, and institutionalized in the enhanced powers of the magnate-dominated Royal Council (*hovrätt*). But Gustav Adolf's policies toward the magnates were double-edged. The enhanced powers of the magnates were coupled with the recruitment of commoners and foreigners (a good many of them Calvinists) into the lower ranks of the royal administration and the elevation of career civil servants into the hereditary nobility.[61] In this way, Gustav Adolf was able to build a group of loyal supporters within the lower nobility, men who owed their security and status to the state and the monarchy.[62] Following Gustav Adolf's death on the battlefield in 1634, power devolved to a regency government led by Oxenstierna and the Royal Council. Gustav Adolf and Oxenstierna had made great strides in the field of administrative rationalization and centralization, and many of their reforms were codified in a posthumously published document known as "The Form of Government."[63] But as bureaucratic as it may have looked on paper, the royal administration quickly became the private reserve of powerful magnates, who asserted control over numerous church and state offices and paid themselves with plots from the royal domains, while allowing the salaries of lesser officials to go into arrears for years on end. Not surprisingly, these policies provoked harsh criticism from the lower echelons of the Swedish estates and the royal administration, which insisted that recruitment and promotion to religious and political offices be based on merit, as well as from the peasantry and reform-minded clergy, who decried the devolution of "public" power into "private" hands, and the use of public monies to finance private "decadence."[64] These sentiments were shared by Gustav X, who ascended the throne in 1650. One of his first acts was a partial "reassumption" (*reduktion*) of royal lands alienated to the nobility.[65] But in 1655 the new king fell on the battlefield, his only heir an infant. A new regency government was put into place, and a new period of magnate dominance began. By this time, precisionist views had begun to penetrate into educated circles, including the circle surrounding Gustav XI, who grew to be a stern and autocratic man, and whose rigid personality and ascetic lifestyle strongly resembled those of Frederick William I.[66] Like his Prussian counterpart, Gustav XI wasted little time in tearing down the patrimonial structures of magnate dominance and putting a fully bureaucratic system in its place. By 1686 the leaders of the regency government had been publicly discredited and put on trial, royal lands reclaimed in a massive *reduktion*, and the Swedish bishops stripped of their powers over church liturgy and clerical appointments. The chief beneficiaries of these policies—and the chief supporters of the new regime—were lower-level officials and clergymen, and the groups from whom they were recruited—the lesser nobility, the third estate, and the peasantry. The result of these reforms was one of the most thoroughly bureaucratized systems of state administration in seventeenth-century Europe.[67] And while the era of "Caroline absolutism" eventually ended, when the

Swedish estates reasserted their role as co-rulers of the kingdom in 1718, the legacy of Caroline bureaucracy survived through the "era of liberty" and into the modern era.

England is not often compared to Sweden, and even less frequently to Prussia, except perhaps as a contrasting case. But whatever the differences in its constitutional development, England's administrative development displays some remarkable similarities to these two absolute monarchies. Like Prussia and Sweden, England entered the seventeenth century with a deeply patrimonial system of administration, characterized by a high degree of oligarchy, and unlike them, by a fair amount of private de jure venality as well.[68] As in Prussia and Sweden, these practices evoked widespread criticism and resentment from precisionist reformers and members of the middle strata, who demanded an end to the "spoils system" and the establishment of a salaried civil service that would be "open to talent." Demands of this sort could already be heard during the early decades of the seventeenth century, and eventually wound up on the agenda of the Barebones Parliament and the Cromwellian Protectorate, which largely suppressed the sale of offices, increased the role of salaries in remuneration, and recruited greater numbers of commoners and small gentry into the state administration.[69] Under the Restoration monarchy of Charles II, the three P's of patrimony, patronage, and payment were restored to their old role in the process of administrative appointments.[70] Following the "Glorious Revolution of 1689," however, the throne was once again occupied by an ascetic Protestant monarch (the Dutch stadholder, William III of Orange) with strong connections to precisionist religion, and the assault on "old corruption" was renewed, this time to greater and more lasting effect.[71]

These three cases suggest that there were two basic preconditions for successful bureaucratic revolutions: (1) an ascetic Protestant monarch of severe habit and mind, who regards kingship as an office rather than a patrimony and views the state administration in the same way; and (2) a popular, precisionist movement that opposes "courtly decadence" and upper-class oligarchy as sinful and unjust. In other words, what seems to have been necessary is a coalition between a reformist monarch and reformist segments of the middle and upper strata, linked by a mixture of common interests and worldviews. Where one of these preconditions was absent, no reformist coalition emerged, and no bureaucratic revolution ensued. Where precisionist agitation for political reform was rebuffed by king and court, Pietism was either suppressed, as in Saxony, or took a quietistic turn, as in Württemberg.[72] Conversely, in cases where royal reform lacked religiously founded support, as in Peter the Great's Russia, changes in administrative rules and organization did not lead to deep or lasting changes in administrative practice.[73]

Conclusion

This chapter focuses on a puzzle posed by Weber's sociology of domination: why were some early-modern European states more bureaucratic than others? It is possible to glean some hypotheses from the pages of *Economy and Society*. But they are not entirely convincing. Weber suggests that bureaucracy emerges slowly and diffuses quickly and that war serves as a crucial catalyst of bureaucratization. Specifically, he implies that bureaucratization results from prolonged conflict between patrimonial rulers and their administrative staffs, and that the longer such conflict continues the more likely bureaucratization becomes; but that once it has emerged, its "technical superiority" is so great that other rulers will be forced to adopt it—or be forced out of business. He also suggests that war speeds the genesis and diffusion of bureaucracy by raising the political costs of administrative inefficiency. Unfortunately, these generalizations do not fit the facts terribly well, at least not for the case of early-modern Europe, where some aspects of bureaucratization occurred in a rapid and even revolutionary fashion, but diffused slowly, if at all, even in the context of intense geopolitical competition.

Recent work on European state formation, much of it at least partly inspired by Weber, has generated sharper formulations of the problem and more nuanced responses to it. In this chapter I have examined the work of two prominent scholars in this area: Edgar Kiser and Thomas Ertman. Kiser urges us to look at varying levels of bureaucratization *within* particular states, arguing *pace* Weber that in some contexts patrimonial forms of administration may actually be more efficient than bureaucratic ones. Kiser also draws our attention to the connection between bureaucratization and revolution, suggesting that revolution can catalyze bureaucratization by demolishing distributional coalitions that can stand in the way of reform. Ertman further sharpens the problem by focusing on a single—but crucial—aspect of bureaucratization, the separation of person and office, and by providing a clear picture of where this arrangement prevailed and where it did not. He also advances a more complex account of the relationship between geopolitical competition and administrative development, arguing that war led to bureaucracy only after 1450, when a new model of officeholding and new sources of personnel became available.

While these accounts are both superior to Weber's in some regards, I have contended that they are still deficient in others: *theoretically* deficient in that they fail to account for the *genesis* of bureaucratic officeholding practices, especially the separation of person and office; and *empirically* deficient insofar as they fail to account for the actual *distribution* of proprietary and nonproprietary forms of officeholding across the states of early-modern Europe. Kiser treats bureaucracy as a universally available political strategy that rulers will use whenever and wherever it is cost-effective. But for a strategy to be chosen, it must first be invented and then become known. And to deny this is to take the creativity out of human action, and cultural specificity out of human decision-making. Ertman cannot be accused of this error. He is well aware that the bureaucratic model had to be invented (or rather, *re*invented, since it did arise in other times and places as well). And he even suggests a rough date for its invention: 1450. But he does not tell us *who* invented it. Nor is he entirely successful in explaining why it was implemented in some states but not in others. There are important exceptions to his rule, and key implications of the rule—regarding the social sources of political officehold-ers—do not survive close empirical scrutiny. And while Kiser's model could potentially explain the relative degree of bureaucratization within particular states, it does not explain such variations *across* states, and probably could not do so in its current form.

The goal of this chapter has been to address these two deficiencies, to ex-plain the (re)invention and distribution of bureaucratic officeholding in early-modern Europe. I have argued that the systems of political officehold-ing known today as "venality" and "bureaucracy" had their origins in systems of *clerical* officeholding that emerged during the papal schism and the Protes-tant Reformation, respectively. I have further argued that the Protestant Re-formation largely halted the spread of venal officeholding practices beyond Latin Europe, where they originated and first took hold, and that the Fur-ther Reformation movements helped to diffuse bureaucratic officeholding practices from the churches into the state. If this argument is correct, then it should be possible to account for the degree of bureaucratization that we observe in any given state of this period in terms of the impact that these three events had on that state. More specifically, we would expect to find the most patrimonial systems of administration in those areas that (a) had close cultural and institutional ties with the papacy during the mid- to late fif-teenth century and (b) remained loyal to the Roman Church following the Reformation. Conversely, we would also expect to find the most bureau-cratic systems of administration in those areas that (a) had few ties with the Renaissance papacy, (b) adopted Protestantism during the sixteenth century, and (c) had strong precisionist movements and/or ascetic rulers. Further, we should also find that the absence of one of the factors listed under (1) would typically lead to lower degrees of patrimonialism, while the absence of one or more of the factors listed under (2) would normally lead to lower degrees of bureaucratization. For example, we would expect Poland, Austria, and Bavaria to exhibit lower degrees of patrimonialism than, say, Italy, France, and Spain; and we would expect England, Sweden, and Prussia to exhibit higher degrees of bureaucratization than, say, the Netherlands, Württemberg, and Saxony. I have tried to present enough evidence to render these hypotheses plausible. Obviously, additional research will be necessary to determine if they can be defended in their present form, and whether they can be extended to non-European cases in a more general form.

To say that Kiser and Ertman's accounts are deficient is not to say that they are false and should therefore be discarded. This may be how knowledge advances in certain philosophical renderings of science, but it is not how knowledge advances in the actual practice of science. Concluding from this essay that rulers and administrators are uninterested in maximizing their revenues, or that geopolitics has no effect on state formation, would be a step backward in our understanding, not a step forward, and would be a complete misinterpretation of its intent. Rather, to say that Kiser and Ertman's accounts are deficient is to say that they are *incomplete* and should therefore be *expanded*. What makes Kiser's account incomplete is its singular focus on material interests and rational calculation and the inattention to ideal interests and cultural context that results. Early-modern rulers and administrators were not interested solely, and sometimes not even primarily, in "maximizing revenues." And even when they were, they selected their strategies from a toolbox that was culturally specific and historically constrained. This is why universalizing theories, such as rational choice, can serve only as a heuristic starting point for historical research, as Weber himself well knew. What makes Ertman's account incomplete is its singular focus on political institutions and military competition and the inattention to religious institutions and confessional conflict that results. For the early-modern era was the era not only of the military revolution, but of the Protestant Reformation as well; and the fact that religion and politics are remote from each other in contemporary systems of valuation—at least among intellectuals—should not mislead us into thinking that they were remote from each other in historical chains of causation.

This is an error that Weber warned against in the context of economic history, but seems to have been forgotten in the realm of political history.

Notes

1. The two best examples of this approach are: Brian Downing, *The Military Revolution and Political Change: Origins of Democracy and Autocracy in Early Modern Europe* (Princeton, NJ: Princeton University Press, 1992); and Thomas Ertman, *Birth of the Leviathan: Building States and Regimes in Medieval and Early Modern Europe* (Cambridge: Cambridge University Press, 1997). For an attempt to combine the neo-Hintzian approach with world-systems theory, see also Charles Tilly, *Coercion, Capital and European States, A.D. 990–1990* (Oxford: Basil Blackwell, 1990).

2. Good examples of the rational-choice approach include: Margaret Levi, *Of Rule and Revenue* (Berkeley: University of California Press, 1988); and Edgar Kiser and Joshua Kane, "Revolution and State Structure: The Bureaucratization of Tax

Administration in Early Modern England and France," *American Journal of Sociology* 107, no. 1 (July 2001): 183–223; Edgar Kiser, "Markets and Hierarchies in Early Modern Tax Systems: A Principal-Agent Analysis," *Politics and Society* 22, no. 3 (Sept. 1994): 284–315.

3. Max Weber, *Economy and Society: An Outline of Interpretive Sociology*, ed. Guenther Roth and Claus Wittich (1921–22; Berkeley: University of California Press, 1978), pp. 220–21.

4. Ibid., pp. 1044–51.

5. Ibid., pp. 232–33.

6. A good overview may be found in A. R. Myers, *Parliaments and Estates in Europe to 1789* (London: Thames and Hudson, 1975). For more detailed discussions of the estates systems of particular countries, see especially the volumes *Gouvernés et gouvernants* published in the series entitled "Recueils de la Société Jean Bodin pour l'histoire comparative des institutions."

7. Weber, *Economy and Society*, pp. 231–35.

8. At one point, Weber argues that "patrimonialism moves *imperceptibly* toward a rational bureaucratic administration" (Weber, *Economy and Society*, p. 1014, emphasis mine). Later, he remarks that "the longer patrimonialism lasted, the more it approached pure bureaucratism" (ibid, p. 1087).

9. Ibid., pp. 973–75.

10. Ibid., p. 972. This line of thought is developed at great length in Hendryk Spruyt, *The Sovereign State and Its Competitors* (Princeton, NJ: Princeton University Press, 1994).

11. This argument can be found in well-known works on revolution, such as Theda Skocpol, *States and Social Revolutions* (Cambridge: Cambridge University Press, 1979); and Jack Goldstone, *Revolution and Rebellion in the Early Modern World* (Berkeley: University of California Press, 1991). It can also be found in studies of bureaucratization, such as Clive Church, *Revolution and Red Tape* (Oxford: Clarendon, 1981); and Kiser and Kane, "Revolution and State Structure."

12. Alexis de Tocqueville, *The Old Regime and the Revolution*, trans. Alan Kahan (Chicago: University of Chicago Press, 1998).

13. On England, see G. E. Aylmer, *The State's Servants: The Civil Service of the English Republic, 1649–1660* (London: Routledge & Kegan Paul, 1973); and Craig Rose, *England in the 1690s: Revolution, Religion and War* (Oxford: Blackwell, 1999).

14. A brief overview may be found in Philip S. Gorski, "Beyond Marx and Hintze? Third Wave Theories of Early Modern State Formation," *Contemporary Studies in Society and History* 43, no. 4 (December 2001): 851–61. For a more detailed (if less detached) discussion, see idem, *The Disciplinary Revolution* (Chicago: University of Chicago Press, 2003).

15. The seminal works in this line of inquiry are: Perry Anderson, *Lineages of the Absolutist State* (London: Verso, 1978); Immanuel Wallerstein, *The Modern World System*, 3 vols. (New York: Academic Press, 1974–89).

16. A number of Hintze's most celebrated essays have been translated into English in Otto Hintze, *The Historical Essays of Otto Hintze*, ed. Felix Gilbert (New York: Oxford University Press, 1975). On the topic at hand, see especially the essay entitled "Military Organization and the Organization of the State." The complete collection

is available in German as: Otto Hintze, *Gesammelte Abhandlungen*, 2nd ed., ed. Gerhard Oestreich (Göttingen: Vandenhoeck & Ruprecht, 1962–67).

17. The key works in this tradition are Downing, *The Military Revolution*; and Ertman, *Birth of the Leviathan*. For an attempt to combine the neo-Marxian and neo-Hintzian perspectives, see also Charles Tilly, *Coercion, Capital and European States*.

18. For a feminist perspective, see Julia Adams, *The Familial State* (Ithaca, NY: Cornell University Press, 2005); and also, idem, "The Familial State: Elite Family Practices and State-making in the Early Modern Netherlands," *Theory and Society* 23: 505–39. For a neo-Weberian perspective, see Gorski, *Disciplinary Revolution*. And for a rational-choice perspective, see especially Margaret Levi, *Of Rule and Revenue* (Berkeley: University of California Press, 1988).

19. Edgar Kiser and Joachim Schneider, "Bureaucracy and Efficiency: An Analysis of Taxation in Early Modern Prussia," *American Sociological Review* 59, no. 2 (April 1994): 190.

20. Kiser, "Bureaucratization of Tax Administration."

21. Kiser focuses on the conditions under which bureaucratic administration will be established at various levels in the departments of a particular state, and not on the question of when it will diffuse from one state to another. But it would not be difficult to extend his model to address this question.

22. For a more detailed discussion, along with relevant citations, see Gorski, *Disciplinary Revolution*, chap. 4, part III.

23. The key revisions involve Britain and France. Early-modern Britain has traditionally been seen as highly unbureaucratic, France as the very embodiment of bureaucracy. Recent research has generated a very different interpretation. On England, see esp. John Brewer, *The Sinews of Power: War, Money, and the English State, 1688–1783* (London: Unwin Hyman, 1989). James B. Collins, *The State in Early Modern France* (Cambridge: Cambridge University Press, 1995), provides a good introduction to the voluminous literature on that country.

24. On the Dutch state in general, see especially Marjolein C. 't Hart, *The Making of a Bourgeois State: War, Politics and Finance during the Dutch Revolt* (Manchester: Manchester University Press, 1993). See also the relevant sections of Jonathan I. Israel, *The Dutch Republic: Its Rise, Greatness and Fall, 1477–1806* (Oxford: Clarendon, 1995). On the states of Holland and the city of Amsterdam, see O. Vries, "'Geschappen tot een ieders nut'. Een verkennend onderzoek naar de Noordnederlandse ambtenaar in de tijd van het Ancien Regime," *Tijdschrift voor Geschiedenis* 90 (1977): 328–49

25. See R. Burr Litchfield, *Emergence of a Bureaucracy: The Florentine Patricians, 1530–1790* (Princeton, NJ: Princeton University Press, 1986).

26. On Bavaria, see Niklas Schrenk-Notzing, "Das bayerische Beamtentum, 1430–1740," in Günther Franz, ed., *Beamtentum und Pfarrerstand, 1400–1800* (Limburg an der Lahn: C. A. Starke, 1972); and more generally Max Spindler, *Handbuch der bayerischen Geschichte* (Munich: Beck, 1967–79). On Saxony, see Rudolf Kötzschke and Hellmut Kretzschmar, *Sächsische Geschichte* (Frankfurt: W. Weidlich, 1965). On Germany more generally see Ernst Klein, *Geschichte der öffentlichen Finanzen in Deutschland (1500–1870)* (Wiesbaden: Steiner, 1974).

27. Good introductions may be found in: James B. Collins, *The State in Early Modern France*; Ruth Mackay, *The Limits of Royal Authority. Resistance and Obedience in Seventeenth-Century Castile* (Cambridge: Cambridge University Press, 1999); and on the papacy, see esp. Peter Partner, *The Lands of St. Peter: The Papal State in the Middle Ages and the Early Renaissance* (London: Eyre Methuen, 1972).

28. On Poland, see Michal Kopzynski, "Service or Benefice? Officeholders in Poland and Sweden of the Seventeenth Century," *European Review of History* 1, no. 1 (1994): 19–27, and the chapters in J. K. Fedorowicz, Maria Bogucka, and Henryk Samsonowicz, eds., *A Republic of Nobles: Studies in Polish History to 1864* (Cambridge: Cambridge University Press, 1982). On Hungary, see Heinrich Marczali, *Ungarische Verfassungsgeschichte* (Tübingen: J. C. B. Mohr, 1910).

29. The best overview of the Prussian system is (still) Otto Hintze, *Acta Borussica*, vol. 6, 1: *Die Behördenorganisation und die allgemeine Verwaltung in Preußen um 1740* (Berlin: Paul Parey, 1901). On Sweden, see the relevant sections of Michael Roberts, *Sweden as a Great Power, 1611–1697* (London: Edward Arnold, 1968); and idem, *The Age of Liberty: Sweden 1719–1772* (Cambridge: Cambridge University Press, 1986).

30. By Further Reformation movements, I mean all those movements that sought (what they understood as) a full realization of the Protestant Reformation. These include English Puritanism, the Dutch Further Reformation (*Nadere Reformatie*), and German and Scandinavian Pietism. I have used the Dutch term because it best captures the commonality of these different movements.

31. As the attentive reader will already have noticed, these answers are only partial. They focus on one type of patrimonialism (venality) and one aspect of bureaucratization (separation of person and office), while ignoring other types (such as estates-based) and other aspects (such as legal relations between ruler and official). In the conclusion, I contemplate what impact religious factors might have had on other dimensions of the bureaucratization process.

32. It is perhaps worth noting that Ertman's definition of patrimonialism omits oligarchy, the very type of patrimonialism that Weber regarded as most important in early modern Europe.

33. Some scholars also customarily distinguish between temporary and permanent sales—that is, cases in which the purchaser obtains the office for a specified time, usually of relatively short duration, and cases in which the office becomes the private property of the purchaser and may be resold or bequeathed. The former practice is generally designated as "farming." Some scholars view farming as a form of venality; others regard it as a separate type of officeholding. Insofar as farming occasionally serves as a transitional stage on the road to permanent appropriation of offices, there is some justice in the former view. But it must also be emphasized that farming represents a much less severe form of appropriation than permanent venality because it affords greater scope for the supervision and control of officials from above. Thus if farming is to regarded as a form of venality, it must be considered an especially mild form.

34. Brigide Schwarz, *Die Organisation kurialer Schreiberkollegien von ihrer Entstehung bis zur Mitte des 15. Jahrhunderts* (Tübingen: M. Niemeyer, 1972), pp. 10, 177.

35. Peter Partner, "Papal Financial Policy in the Renaissance and Counter-Reformation," *Past & Present* 88 (1980): 20.

36. W. von Hoffman, *Forschungen zur Geschichte der Kurialen Behörden vom Schisma bis zur Reformation* (Rome: Preußisches historisches Institut, 1914), p. 171.

37. Schwarz, *Organisation kurialer Schreiberkollegien*, pp. 177–80.

38. Hoffmann, *Forschungen*, vol. 2, p. 41; Bernhard Schimmelpfennig, "Der Ämterhandel an der Römischen Kurie von Pius II bis zum Sacco di Roma (1458–1527)," in Ilja Mieck, ed., *Ämterhandel im Spätmittelalter und im 16. Jahrhundert* (Berlin: Colloquium, 1984), p. 12.

39. Barbara Hallman, *Italian Cardinals, Reform, and the Church as Property: 1492–1563* (Berkeley: University of California Press, 1985).

40. Martin Göhring, *Die Ämterkäuflichkeit im Ancien régime* (Berlin: E. Ebering, 1938), p. 13; Paul Viollet, *Histoire des institutions politiques et administratives de la France*, vol. 3 (Paris: L. Larose et Forcel, 1890–1903), vol. 3, pp. 270–74.

41. Kuno Böse, "Die Ämterkäuflichkeit in Frankreich vom 14. bis zum 16. Jahrhundert," in Mieck, *Ämterhandel im Spätmittelalter*, p. 92; Roland Mousnier, *La vénalité des offices sous Henri IV et Louis XIII*, 2nd ed. (Paris: Presses universitaires de France, 1971), p. 17.

42. Mousnier, *Vénalité*, p. 21.

43. Willem Frijhoff, "Patterns," in Hilde de Ridder-Symoens, ed., *Universities in Early Modern Europe, 1500–1800*, vol. 2 of *A History of the University in Europe* (Cambridge: Cambridge University Press, 1983).

44. Joachim Boër, "Ämterhandel in kastilischen Städten," in Mieck, *Ämterhandel im Spätmittelalter*, pp. 148–49.

45. K. W. Swart, *Sale of Offices in the Seventeeenth Century* (The Hague: Nijhoff, 1949), p. 21.

46. Winifried Küchler, "Ämterkäuflichkeit in den Ländern der Krone Aragons," in *Spanische Forschungen der Görresgesellschaft*, vol. 27: *Gesammelte Aufsätze zur Kulturgeschichte Spaniens* (Münster: Aschendorffsche Verlagsbuchhandlung, 1973), pp. 1, 11–13.

47. Swart, *Sale of Offices*, p. 21.

48. Margarita Cuartas Rivera, "La venta de oficios públicos en Castilla-León en el siglo XVI," *Hispania* 44, no. 158 (1984): 495–516; Küchler, "Ämterkäuflichkeit"; Reinhard Liehr, "Ämterkäuflichkeit und Ämterhandel im kolonialen Hispanoamerika," in Mieck, *Ämterhandel im Spätmittelalter*; Luis Navarro Garcia, "Los oficios vendibles en nueva españa durante la guerra de sucesión," *Anuario de Estudios Americanos* 32 (1975): 133–54; Rafael de Lera Garcia, "Venta de oficios en la Inquisicion de Granada (1629–44)," *Hispania* 48, no. 4 (1988): 909–62.

49. Roberto Mantelli, *Il Pubblico impiego nell'economia del Regno di Napoli: Retribuzioni, reclutamento e ricambio sociale nell'epoca spagnuola (secc. XVI–XVII)* (Naples: Istituto italiano per gli studi filosofici, 1986), pp. 217–307; A. Musi, "La Venalità degli uffici in principato Citra," *Rassegna Storica Salernitana* 5 (1986): 71–91.

50. Giuseppe Galasso, *Alla periferia dell'Impero: Il Regno di Napoli nel periodo spagnolo (secoli XVI–XVII)* (Turin: Einaudi, 1994), p. 16.

51. Horst Enzensberger, "La Struttura del potere nel regno: Corte, uffici, cancelleria," in *Potere, società e popolo nell'età sveva (1210–1266)* (Bari: Dedalo, 1985); Jean-Marie Martin, "L'Organisation administrative et militaire du territoire," in *Potere, so-*

cietà e popolo nell'età sveva; Hiroshi Takayama, The Administration of the Norman King-dom of Sicily (Leiden: E. J. Brill, 1993); Pietro Corrao Governare un regno: Potere, società e istituzioni in Sicilia fra trecento e quattrocento (Naples: Liguori Editore Corrao, 1991).

52. Litchfield, Emergence of a Bureaucracy, pp. 157–81.

53. Roland Mousnier, "Le trafic des offices à Venise," Revue historique du droit français et étranger 30 (1952): 552–65; Andrea Zannini, Burocazia e burocrati a Venezia in etá moderna: i cittadini originari (sec. XVI–XVIII) (Venice: Istituto veneto di scienze, lettere ed arti, 1993).

54. Michael Erbe, "Aspekte des Ämterhandels in den Niederlanden im späten Miettelalter und in der frühen Neuzeit," in Mieck, Ämterhandel im Spätmittelalter.

55. Adolf M. Birke, "Zur Kontinuität des Ämterhandels in England," in Mieck, Ämterhandel im Spätmittelalter.

56. Horst Möller, "Ämterkäuflichkeit in Brandenburg-Preussen im 17. und 18. Jahrhundert," in Klaus Malettke, ed., Ämterkäuflichkeit: Aspekte sozialer Mobilität im eu-ropäischen Vergleich (Berlin: Colloquium, 1980).

57. Gerald Strauss, Manifestations of Discontent in Germany on the Eve of the Refor-mation (Bloomington: Indiana University Press, 1971), pp. 3–4.

58. On England, see Rosemary O'Day, The English Clergy: The Emergence and Con-solidation of a Profession, 1558–1642 (Leicester: Leicester University Press, 1979); Peter Heath, The English Parish Clergy on the Eve of the Reformation (London: Routledge & Kegan Paul, 1969); and Viviane Barrie-Curien, "The English Clergy, 1560–1620: Re-cruitment and Social Status," History of European Ideas 9, no. 4 (1988): 451–63. On Germany, see Bernard Vogler, Le clergé protestant rhénan au siècle de la Réforme, 1555–1619 (Paris: Ophrys, 1976); idem, "Rekrutierung, Ausbildung und soziale Verflech-tung: Karrieremuster evangelischer Geistlichkeit," Archiv für Reformationsgeschichte 85 (1994): 225–33; Bruce Tolley, Pastors and Parishioners in Württemberg during the Late Re-formation, 1581–1620 (Stanford, CA: Stanford University Press, 1995); and Luise Schorn-Schütte, Evangelische Geistlichkeit in der Frühneuzeit: Deren Anteil an der Entfal-tung frühmoderner Staatlichkeit und Gesellschaft (Gütersloh: Gütersloher Ver-lagshaus,1995). On Switzerland, see Bruce Gordon, Clerical Discipline and the Rural Reformation: The Synod in Zürich (Bern: Peter Lang, 1992). On the Netherlands, see G. Groenhuis, De Predikanten: De social positie van de Gereformeerde predikanten in de Republiek der Verenigde Nederlanden vóór ± 1700 (Groningen: Wolters-Noordhoff, 1977). On Scandinavia, see Ole Peter Grell, The Scandinavian Reformation: From Evan-gelical Movement to Institutionalisation of Reform (Cambridge: Cambridge University Press, 1995).

59. The literature on English Puritanism is truly vast. A good place to start is Patrick Collinson, The Elizabethan Puritan Movement (New York: Oxford University Press, 1989). The Dutch Further Reformation has only recently become a focus of research, and there is still no survey of the subject. For now, the best introduction is: Stichting Studie der Nadere Reformatie, Figuren en themas van de Nadere Reformatie (Kampen: De Groot Goudriaan, 1987). An excellent survey of developments in Ger-many and many other parts of Europe with an exhaustive bibliographical apparatus may be found in Martin Brecht et al., Geschichte des Pietismus, 2 vols. (Göttingen: Vandenhoek & Ruprecht, 1993–95).

60. Michael Roberts, "The Swedish Church," in Michael Roberts, ed., *Sweden's Age of Greatness* (London: Macmillan, 1973); Nil Ahnlund, *Gustav Adolf the Great*, trans. Michael Roberts (Westport, CT: Greenwood, 1983).

61. Björn Asker, "Aristocracy and Autocracy in Seventeenth-Century Sweden: The Decline of the Aristocracy within the Civil Administration before 1680," *Scandinavian Journal of History* 15, no. 2: 89–95; Johan Holm, "'Skyldig plicht och trohet': Militärstaten och 1634 års regeringsform," *Historisk Tidskrift*, no. 2 (1999): 161–95; and more generally A. F. Upton, *Charles XI and Swedish Absolutism* (Cambridge: Cambridge University Press, 1998).

62. Göran Rystad, "The King, the Nobility and the Growth of the Bureaucracy in 17th Century Sweden," in Göran Rystad, ed., *Europe and Scandinavia: Aspects of the Process of Integration in the 17th Century* (Lund: Wallin & Dalholm Boktr., 1983), p. 64.

63. Roberts, *Sweden as a Great Power*, pp. 18–28.

64. Ibid., pp. 40–48; Rystad, "The King, the Nobility and Growth of the Bureaucracy," p. 67; Kaj Janzon, "Överdåd på kredit: ett rationellt val? Några problem kring högadelns ekonomiska verksamhet i Sverige under 1600-talets första hälft," *Historisk Tidskrift*, no. 2 (1999): 197–226.

65. Stellan Dahlgren, "Charles X and the Constitution," in Roberts, *Sweden's Age of Greatness*.

66. Roberts, "The Swedish Church," pp. 148, 152; A. F. Upton, *Charles XI and Swedish Absolutism* (Cambridge: Cambridge University Press, 1998), pp. 170–71, 216–17.

67. Kopzynski, "Service or Benefice?"

68. G. E. Aylmer, *The King's Servants: The Civil Service of Charles I, 1625–1642* (London: Routledge & Kegan Paul, 1974).

69. G. E. Aylmer, *The State's Servants: The Civil Service of the English Republic, 1649–1660* (London: Routledge & Kegan Paul, 1973).

70. G. E. Aylmer, *The Crown's Servants: Government and Civil Service under Charles II, 1660–1685* (Oxford: Oxford University Press, 2002).

71. For a recent reinterpretation of the Glorious Revolution as Godly Revolution, see Craig Rose, *England in the 1690s: Revolution, Religion and War* (Oxford: Blackwell, 1999); on the postrevolutionary civil service, see John Brewer, *The Sinews of Power: War, Money, and the English State, 1688–1783* (London: Unwin Hyman, 1989).

72. On this, see especially Mary Fulbrook, *Piety and Politics* (Cambridge: Cambridge University Press, 1983).

73. See Paul Dukes, *The Making of Russian Absolutism, 1613–1801* (New York: Longmans, 1982); and Walter Pinter and Don Rowney, eds., *Russian Officialdom* (Chapel Hill: University of North Carolina Press, 1980).

Weber and the Sociology of Revolution

Can studying Weber contribute to current theoretical understanding of a phenomenon like revolution? Revolution is our example, above all others, of social dynamics in contrast to comparative statics, a process of sudden, dramatic social change. Looking for Weber's views on revolution points up, quite clearly, how much of Weber's work concerns the comparison of structures or institutions, including worldviews (which we could just as well call cultural structures). He is a sociologist of social change, but typically at a distance, at telescopic range. His strength is taxonomic description, which is ultimately oriented toward showing what kinds of institutions and beliefs facilitate or impede changes from one structure to another; for the most part these are presented as massive and glacial.

Even when Weber speaks of charisma as a "revolutionary" break from traditional and rational norms his discussion is taxonomic.[1] We see rather little in Weber of the flow of events, of actual struggles, confrontations, turning points. Perhaps all this is merely to say that Weber was not a historian, narrating historical events, but a historical sociologist; but even as such, his focus was on the comparison of structures and not on action per se. To be sure, Weber is often classified in abstract discussions of social theory as an action theorist, but this is on the strength of his methodological writings. When he actually engages in historical sociology, we see relatively little action, but instead comparison and assessment of structures and their potentialities.

What, then, can Weber add to our understanding of revolution, given that today we possess several decades of studies that tell us a great deal about revolutionary dynamics, and about the clashes of social movements generally? Perhaps it is time to admit that scholarship has gone considerably beyond Weber on many points. Where he remains unrivaled is in sheer scope, bringing all the world under one viewpoint (and into single works, like *Economy and Society*, as well as the comparative studies of the world religions treated as a comprehensive project). Subsequent social historians have amassed more information about, and given better analyses of, numerous particular parts of world history; but it is still to Weber that we look for a thematic vision that holds it all together. Weber provides this unity by asking analytical questions that require a comparison of long-term sequences in order to frame an answer. In this sense, we still read Weber because he is our great exemplar of how to go about using history on the largest scale, and the legitimator of our right to do so, too. Thus, one is tempted to say that Weber has become the totem animal for the tribe of comparative, historical sociologists, and *Economy and Society* (hereafter *ES*) the sacred object of our cult.

Nevertheless, Weber helps us to push the boundaries of our theory of revolutions in several ways. His explicit treatment of revolution in *ES* is rather meager, but it serves to remind us that revolution should not be confined to the canonized modern cases (the French Revolution, the Russian, the Chinese), but should consider the medieval Italian city-states, as well as ancient Rome and Greece. In these writings Weber also forces us to consider more deeply what revolution reveals about the character of state power.

The second great resource Weber provides for us is his detailed analysis of revolutions in progress at the time he was writing about them. He became interested in the revolutionary upheavals in Russia in 1905–6, enough to quickly learn Russian and with the help of émigré circles in Heidelberg to follow primary information sources; the result was two long articles published in 1906 in the *Archiv für Sozialwissenschaft*, "Bourgeois Democracy in Russia" and "Russia's Transition to Pseudo-constitutionalism." In 1917, Weber again followed revolutionary events in the aftermath of the downfall of the monarchy and published two newspaper articles, the more extensive of which was entitled "Russia's Transition to Pseudo-Democracy" (April 26, 1917, before, of course, the Bolshevik seizure of power in November). In these writings (especially those on 1905–6) Weber frames his discussion, like the taxonomist he was, around what kinds of political structures are at issue; but he also gives a detailed lineup of the interested parties to the conflict over these structures and comments on their tactics. It is still not quite history of events, but Weber moves us closer to the flow of political action in a situation of crisis and conflict than perhaps anywhere in his oeuvre. Together, these writings give us an opportunity to sharpen our theories of revolutionary dynamics, especially as Weber provides us information situating conflict in an unparalleled understanding of the structures that the conflict was about.

Weber's Analytical Treatment of Revolution

In *ES*, Weber writes about revolution less as an event than as a way of characterizing a particular kind of structural change. Thus he refers to the "administrative revolution" brought about by Athenian democracy;[2] or to bureaucratic rationalization as a "revolutionary force with regard to tradition";[3] and of course to charisma as revolutionary in transforming values.[4] Some of these usages are metaphorical and not entirely consistent with his chief analytical point, which is that revolution is a specifically nonlegitimate form of change and produces illegitimate forms of power. We might wonder why revolution is not a form of charisma, insofar as it breaks with traditional or rational legal domination. But Weber takes the argument in a different direction, one that reveals the distinctive character of the core of state authority.

His discussion occurs in the section "The Plebian City."[5] Writing of the Italian *popolo*, the political associations of entrepreneurs and handicraft workers that struggled against the rule of knightly families, most notably in Milan, Florence, Siena, Verona, Bologna, Perugia, and elsewhere during the thirteenth and fourteenth centuries, Weber describes their organization as "'a state within the state'—the first deliberately nonlegitimate and revolutionary political assocation."[6] At first glance this seems puzzling. In one sense the *popolo*, with its own chief officials, militia, and even statutes and tax system, was a version of what Trotsky called "dual power," the parallel institutions or shadow government that appeared in revolutionary situations as a transition to taking full government power.[7] But although a dual structure might be illegitimate from the point of view of the existing government, it might well become legitimate if it succeeded in becoming the new government. Of course it might never take full power; but Weber himself notes that the *popolo*, and analogous structures in ancient Rome (the tribunes of the people) and Sparta (the ephors) eventually became incorporated into the regular government structure and made up just one more complexity or division of powers within it, by which time they certainly should be considered legitimate. But Weber wants to bring out a different point, even at the cost of some inconsistency in his usage.[8]

Why were the patrician knightly families (in the Italian city-states) and the patrician clans (in ancient Rome and Greece) legitimate in their rule whereas the revolutionary associations of the lower-ranking status groups were not? Weber gives two reasons: (a) "the right to commune with the gods of the city"—that is, to take the lead in religious ceremonies assembling the political community; and (b) "the right to inflict legitimate punishment"; in contrast, the leader of the plebs (here Weber is using the Roman example) had "the power to execute a sort of lynch law against anyone obstructing his official actions: without trial and judgment, he could have such persons arrested and executed by having them thrown off the Tarpeian rock."[9] One point of this colorful example is that there are regular ceremonies (religious and judicial) that enact legitimate political authority. Still, one might wonder why this couldn't change over time, so that the upstarts become surrounded by their own ceremonial (as indeed did occur) and thus acquire their own veneer of legitimacy.

Weber goes on to reveal the key point: the tribune held power only within the city, whereas the legitimate authority named the heads of the army, and their authority on military campaigns was absolute and could not be mitigated by the tribunes. This reminds us that in another context, the key chapter, "Political Communities," where Weber discussed the formation of territorial political associations, he noted that the source of legitimate power was the fact that people who bind themselves together for war put themselves into a community of fate. The state, thus constituted as military community, has life or death power over its members; they are not only obligated to obey commands in combat under pain of death, but this power extends to noncombatants and to members even in peacetime, insofar as their community is permanent and they are subject to a common fate should they be victims of attack by their foreign enemies. The source of judicial power, the legitimate power to punish individuals in the name of the group, comes from the organization of the community for war. Thus both internal domestic authority (which is distinguished from sheer arbitrary power by consent to the very existence of the community) and authority of command in external foreign affairs come from a common root. What is legitimate, then, comes from control of the army on behalf of the community; what is nonlegitimate is any form of political power that is not delegated by this core association of the community, those bound together against other such communities, but arises from some other grouping that disputes this communal/military leadership.

Here, Weber is an ancestor of the contemporary military-centered theory of the modern state, which traces the consequences of the expansion of standing armies for the organization of taxation, administration, and penetration into society by government regulation.[10] The modern state, in Weber's famous phrase, is a claim to the monopolization of legitimate force upon a territory; as I have argued elsewhere, everything in this definition ought to be treated as a historical variable and examined for its causes and consequences.[11] When Weber discusses ancient states such as the Greek cities or Rome, he is dealing with a period when ad hoc alliances among clans were being regularized into a compulsory territorial organization;[12] one consequence is that everyone who lives within the territory becomes subject to the legitimate authority of its rulers (which is to say, those to whom the community looks as its commanders in dealing with foreign communities). Weber goes on to sketch the struggles for political participation that followed from this compulsory territorial structure; for those who lived in the place, whether they belonged to the ruling clans (or other status groups that took the initiative in collective military action) or not, were de facto part of the community of fate, and they became subject to its laws, constituencies for its ceremonies, and potentially subject to military mobilization on its behalf. Thus there was in some sense an inevitable drive toward the mobilization of "illegitimate" movements for a share in political power. For example, in Rome the struggle of the plebs vis-à-vis the patricians eventually became institutionalized in a routine sequence of offices for all political careers; this status group distinction was eclipsed in practice by a new line of class conflict between a newer nobility based on officeholding and wealth and a politically excluded "bourgeois" stratum.[13] In general, Weber notes that the more massive the military mobilization, the more it pulls disenfranchised groups into struggling for inclusion in political power; since they are already within (in regard to liabilities), they struggle to become full members (in regard to honors and procedures as well).

The organization of the state for war thus plays a key role in any revolutionary conflict. In discussing the plebian city, in every instance Weber distinguishes between a legitimate ruling group that are the military commanders in foreign wars (whether they are a military aristocracy, a patrician blend of knightly and mercantile lifestyle, or ancient clans making military alliance) and the "plebian" populace. When the latter put forward their demands, form their own "state within the state," and even engage in violent struggle with the ruling stratum, their actions are illegitimate in the specific sense that they are struggling against the military-centered state. In a sense they can never win; they can be successful, but that means they become incorporated into the military-centered state and lose their revolutionary character, which existed only as long as they formed a rival organization against it. Once they take command (assuming a total revolutionary victory), they represent their community on the field of potential battle against foreign communities; they are revolutionary as they stand against the militarized community, but the very community within which they launch their revolution has this ultimately military character as a community of fate.

In a revealing phrase, Weber notes how the Roman tribune of the people might become "the de facto highest power within the limits of the urban peace district," while the patrician military command still held total authority on campaigns.[14] The city is the "urban peace district"; it is the borders within which affairs are domestic, not foreign. This applies to modern states generally, insofar as they are an expansion of the structure of the city.[15] It is a pacified zone, whose inhabitants are supposed to be allies for military purposes against potential threats from (or for incursions against) similarly organized neighbors. Thus, a revolutionary movement, one that uses the threat of force to dispute power within this pacified zone, is attacking the very bond that makes up the state and constitutes its legitimate authority. I think this is what Weber was getting at in his somewhat tortured use of the concept of "nonlegitimate" associations and their power. One does not have to be sympathetic to the authorities to see that revolutionaries have a formidable task: it is not just the sheer strength of those who command the army that makes them hard to overthrow, but the feeling of most members of a political community that they are bound with this authority as a community of fate.

Contemporary State-Breakdown Theory and Classic Interest-Group Theory of Revolution

In recent decades much research has contributed to a theory of revolution that integrates with what we know about state development, social movements, and the process of conflict. There are three main components: (a) In contrast to the earlier paradigm, which saw revolutions as surging up from below, contemporary theory sees causality as initiated from above, with a state breakdown.[16] This generally occurs through a combination of geopolitical strain (defeat in war, logistical overextension) and financial crisis; states lose their instrument of coercion, their prestige, and their ability to pay their bills and especially their own personnel. (b) The elite splits over how to respond to the crisis; typically this takes the form of reformers willing to undertake major changes in order to restore finances, against a privileged class that resists paying for the cost of the reforms. (c) Social movements take advantage of the state crisis and elite split in order to mobilize around their own grievances. Here, revolution theory meshes with social movement theory, which has documented the importance of resource mobilization (organizational and material conditions for assembling groups for action, publicizing an ideology, keeping the movement going during slack times) and of the "frames" that a series of movements provides for each other in building up a tradition of workable tactics, ideological appeals, and networks of recruitment.[17]

The state-breakdown theory of revolution focuses on the conditions that lead up to the disintegration of state power. It leaves open two further questions: (d) the process of revolution itself, the dynamics of action that happen once the state has broken down and groups struggle to put something else in its place; often there is considerable realignment of factions and the emergence of new groups and factions during this time. Here we have some leads from the general theory of conflict,[18] as well as some discussions of revolutionary process itself.[19] These conflict dynamics involve processes of escalation and polarization, the effects of atrocities, critical mass and bandwagon effects, and factional alliances and splits. (e) The issue of revolutionary outcomes is least specified under the new paradigm, in which revolutions are seen as structural opportunities, a rending of the fabric of the old regime to open the possibilities of putting many different kinds of regimes in its place (including the possibility of putting back something resembling the old regime). In other words, it is no longer assumed that revolutions move inexorably "to the left" or in historical "advance" toward political liberalization or economic egalitarianism.

The new revolution theory paradigm is in pointed contrast to an older paradigm, of which Marx formulated the most famous version. That version saw revolutions as breaking through from below by an accumulation of grievances on the part of a social class that represented the future, as against the outworn social class attached to the existing state. In Marx's paradigm, the key actors are economic classes; the prime mover is change in economic structure, which makes some classes rise and others fall; the crisis condition is an economic crisis, not of the state but of the entire economy; and the outcome is a shift both in the short run, in the class holding political power, and in the long run, in the system of property. Comparing the two paradigms, we can say that the Marxian model puts its emphasis on (c), the mobilization of grievances from below, which it sees as class interests (as compared with the broader and more inclusive set of disgruntled forces in the state-breakdown model); and on (e), where the Marxian model confidently predicts shifts in property relations as the principal revolutionary outcome.

Weber's analysis of revolution, especially in his writings on the Russian revolutions, is explicitly critical of Marxism. Weber both disliked the Bolsheviks and polemically jabbed at the materialist theory. Nevertheless, Weber in many respects is closer to the Marxian paradigm than to the state-breakdown paradigm (not surprisingly, since the latter emerged some sixty years after his death), whereas Weber was born around the time *Das Kapital* came out; and when Marx died in 1883, Weber was nineteen years old and just launching his intellectual career. Moreover, it was during the early part of that career, in German publications by Engels, Bebel, Bernstein, Kautsky, and others, that Marxian ideas first became known in the world of academic research. Weber was in the first generation of the Marx reception. Weber lists at length the various contending interest groups, the actors on the scene, explaining the social bases of their interests; his analysis is broader than Marx's in that Weber goes well beyond class interests (but includes them as well); he discusses the governmental structures favored by these various interests, then tries to assess the strength of the different factions and estimate whose interests were likely to win out. Broadly speaking, Weber stays within the model of contending interests, which struggle to determine structural changes. Over the course of this exposition, Weber jabs away at the Marx-ian/materialist position and thereby adumbrates some of the features of the later paradigm.

In what follows, I list the ways in which Weber builds from this interests-and-structures model into a broader, and implicitly more processual, theory of revolution.

INTEREST GROUPS

Weber lists both economic classes and status groups as having interests pro or contra the political status quo in Russia. Among the classes are: manufac-turers, tied to the state to ensure labor discipline; big landowners, politically conservative to ensure protection of their property from expropriation; workers, struggling over hours and working conditions; peasants, in 1905 united on demands for land redistribution, in 1917 split by intervening re-forms into wealthier peasants and poor landless peasants; the petite bour-geoisie, ambiguous in their leanings but antagonistic to the gentry (on grounds that shade over into status-insults and -interests).

Status groups are based on a different analytical principle, namely lifestyle and thus relations of antagonism among different styles of life and principles of group honor. Among status groups, key divisions are among: the monarchy and its social circles, unwilling to compromise the prestige of autocracy; the aristocracy, split into a conservative faction focused on main-taining its social preeminence, and a liberal faction that stakes its prestige on being at the forefront of movements for modernity, for Western standards, and thus for reform; the bourgeoisie, which as a status group is insulted by the petty intrusions into everyday liberty of action by an autocratic bu-reaucracy (internal passports, arbitrary searches and arrests); the bureaucracy itself, which enjoys the status of being able to harass everyone else; and the peasantry, hostile to bureaucratic regulation. Also among status groups may be counted the various nationalities of the Russian empire (the Poles, Lithuanians, Ukrainians, and others) who feel their national honor insulted by subjugation to Russian authorities, language laws, and the like; these sta-tus interests are complicated, however, by the fact that it is largely the higher classes of each national region that are politically mobilized, and as such have other interests and antagonisms that bind them to conservative positions.

Finally, Weber singles out the intelligentsia, the educated stratum, espe-cially those who work in the world of education, journalism, and as lower employees of the zemstvos providing social services for the peasantry. Weber displays these people as both altruistic and idealistic in one respect, and op-portunistic in another. Sometimes the intellectuals are close to the liberal re-formers of the respectable and even aristocratic classes; sometimes they attach themselves to the peasants or the workers. Thus, the intelligentsia, and more generally the whole altruistic wing of these Russian status groups, have considerable freedom of choice in deciding which direction to go; detaching themselves from their own class interests (or having little in the way of economic concerns of their own, because they will still exist in any modern economic system and in similar base), they formulate programs that play up various solutions to the economic and status problems they see around them. Some formulated a romantic ideal of the peasants as close to the soil, staking everything on an agrarian reform that would return to a peasant communism, and seeking to force the issue by a campaign of assassinations of government officials (these were the Narodniki, most active in the 1870s and 1880s); they routinized in the early 1900s as the Party of Socialist (or Social) Revolutionaries. Others threw themselves into the zemstvos, the institutions of provincial and local self-government developed in 1864 during the reform period following the abolition of serfdom; Weber sees them indulgently as altruists, seeking moderate and gradualist solutions through established channels. We can see, of course, that their moderate stance comes from their standing as institutionalized reformers, having won concessions in previous rounds of struggle that make them a part of the routine organization of Russian government, even if structurally at odds with the central government. Yet others of the intelligentsia associate with the workers and their new trade union organizations; in keeping with ideas circulating in trade union networks in the West, they have socialist beliefs. The socialists exemplify a further principle of the differentiation of interest groups: they split not on the basis of class origins or institutional connections, but on questions of tactics; thus, in 1903 the Social Democratic Workers Party had split into the Bolshevik faction, favoring violent revolution, and the Mensheviks, favoring trade union struggle.

Weber treats all this in passing, but we can pause to underline an analytical point useful for the theory of revolution: interest groups are not merely preexistent, based on location in the occupational and organizational structure. They are also emergent as the process of mobilization takes place. This is a process of creating or activating SMOs (social movement organizations) so that there are new organizational positions for persons to attach themselves to, and from which vantage points they can formulate paths of action. Splits over tactics are, so to speak, splits over which kinds of organization a group of political actors projects into the future; they are splits based not just on past organization but also on imagined prospective organization. Thus, very different kinds of organization will grow from decisions to engage in assassinations, or mass armed uprising, or labor strikes, or protest marches, or parliamentary assemblies.

Another version of emergent interest groups based on prospective orga-

nizational forms are splits over which alliances to make: among persons initially equally radical, in the flux of maneuver some see advantage in allying
with more moderate groups, while others from the same starting point
throw themselves into the opposite stance and seek to maintain their purity
of program and freedom of action. Similarly, among conservatives, some find
themselves shifting in the heat of the occasion to ally with what they perceive as moderate reformers, while others become militant hard-liners.
These splits among adjacent stances are often the most bitter, not so much
because they are adjacent to begin with but because they are identical, and
thus are felt as a betrayal of group solidarity.[20] What I am underlining here is
the fluidity of revolutionary action. But I would not like this message to be
read as saying that anything goes in the heat of conflict, hence it is unpredictable what anyone will do or how things will end up. Quite the contrary;
I am arguing for principles that shape action within conflicts. But these principles are not to be found so much in the acting out of preexisting interests,
as in the patterns of alliances and splits that make up the structure of opportunities in the field of action in any multisided conflict.[21] We will see more
of this in points (2) and (3) below—that is, in the political application of
small numbers theory.

ALLIANCES AND SPLITS, BANDWAGONS AND TURNING POINTS

In a sense, the entire crisis period of a revolution is a matter of who will
ally with whom. The dominant alliance has broken down, or is at least in
question, as different factions of the elite probe for where to place the blame,
and whom to displace from the center of power; and the normal acquiescence of most of the rest of the populace has given way to widespread agitation; each preexisting interest group now seizes the moment to present its
own self-interested diagnosis of the crisis, and what policy should be instituted to rectify it (chief among which is addressing their own grievances); on
top of this, an emergent structure of diverging interests appears, based on
new organizational arenas that grow up, and on the tactical opportunities
that present themselves. This is why, from the canonical case of the French
Revolution onward, there has been a disjunction between the received categories of social division that analysts have tried to impose on the struggle,
and the flux of new factional lines that appear from month to month or
even week to week. The classic instance is Marx's *Eighteenth Brumaire*, where
he scrambled to invent new labels for differentiated class factions in order to
keep intact his vision of struggling interest groups. But this flux is precisely
what the political crisis consists in; the crisis is resolved when it becomes
clear that there is a dominant coalition, around which others will join or ac-
quiesce and against which even the diehards will suffer erosion of support
and end up demobilizing, whether they see what is happening or not. Polit-

ical power is ultimately a matter of bandwagon effects; that is to say, the times of institutional stability are when the critical mass is so large that it is unmistakable, and even its opponents by interest or ideology see that there is no shaking it for the present. A revolutionary crisis begins when this critical mass, breaks apart; it ends when some other coalition establishes a critical mass, and the momentum of the new bandwagon becomes perceived as unstoppable.

In between these beginning and end points, the dynamics of the revolutionary situation consists in factional maneuvers to create alliances, sometimes by offering concessions in return for joint plans of action, sometimes by attempting to scare others into joining with them for fear of worse consequences if they do not.[22] Conversely, a faction loses out by a kind of reverse bandwagon effect, where it becomes perceived as incapable of winning power and no longer a focal point for leading an alliance. This can happen when the faction splits, thereby broadcasting the weakness of its position.[23]

In this light, let us quickly review the progress of the 1905–6 Russian Revolution. In 1904, the war with Japan became disastrous, and confidence in the tsarist regime plummeted. During the fall, liberals began to gather at private banquets and pass resolutions pressing for reform. In November, a congress of the zemstvos met to demand civil liberties and a parliament. In January 1905, demonstrators outside the Winter Palace were fired upon by troops, precipitating a mood of outrage and crisis. In response, the government offered several plans for a parliament (Duma) with limited popular representation, but these failed to quell the labor strikes, peasant rebellions and tax-resistance, military mutinies, and assassinations that swept the country throughout the remainder of the year. The mood darkened yet further in May when the Russian fleet was destroyed by the Japanese at the battle of Tsushima Straits. Zemstvo congresses met repeatedly in May, July, September, and November to present liberal demands. By October, these troubles were compounded by national insurrection in the Ukraine, the Baltic, Poland, and Finland, and by a general strike (October 12–21) set off by railway workers in Moscow and spreading rapidly to industry throughout the country. In the midst of this strike, the prime minister, Count Witte, persuaded the tsar to issue a manifesto conceding civil liberties and promising a legislative parliament with universal suffrage.

The manifesto initiated the turning point; although agitation continued, with a general strike of workers in Petersburg in November, and again in December in Moscow, the liberal reformers split from the Marxists and the agrarian radicals. The December strike in Moscow escalated, under the leadership of radical intellectuals, into full-scale revolutionary insurrection; this was easily put down by troops. Agitation (including widespread assassinations of officials, as well as peasant uprisings, which were put down in serious fighting) continued well into 1906; the mood of the country remained upset by counterrevolutionary lynch mobs promoted by officials (the "Black Hundreds"), by localized anti-Semitic pogroms in this inflammatory atmosphere, and by quarrels between the liberals and the government over the procedures by which the Duma was to be elected and the scope of the powers it was to have. The Duma finally met in April and eventually, having dashed liberal hopes, was prorogued by the tsar. But now the crisis mood of fluid realignment was past, and the center of gravity swung back to the authorities, who eventually stamped out resistance.

During the upward swing of the revolutionary crisis, we see numerous examples of new organizations formed by alliances among smaller organizations. Thus, in May 1905, a Union of Unions was formed, bringing together the liberal professional associations which had been springing up rapidly since the crisis had begun earlier in the year.[24] As the crisis mood intensified, this Union of Unions, which was initially looking for professional dignity and civil liberties, became increasingly radical; acting as a central meeting place and organ for liberal activists, by the fall it was calling for union with the organs of the organized workers and the Peasant League into a "General Union," and by November even endorsing armed revolt to establish a constituent assembly that Weber described as "a monstrous central revolutionary tribunal."[25] In effect, it had taken over as the central organizing point from the zemstvo congresses, which were now being perceived as too moderate, weak, or irresolute to push through reforms against the foot-dragging of the government.

Workers' organizations similarly mushroomed, and for a period, centralized. In Petersburg, a typographers' strike in September 1905 concerning their own labor conditions created a new organizational form, the Petrograd Council of Workers' Deputies. By October, the structure had been imitated by other types of workers, then amalgamated into a pan-workers' organization. When the general strike broke out on October 15, this relatively small organization expanded to represent 113,000 workers within two days.[26] If this isn't example enough of how the crisis situation itself creates and expands organization,[27] there is also the dynamic of polarization that occurs as opposition is mobilized. Thus, as the "Black Hundreds" were stirred up to attack the workers in provincial cities across Russia, Councils of Workers' Deputies sprang up in numerous cities and linked with the Petersburg group by correspondence, thereby conceding its leadership by virtue of its centrality as a node of communication. As Weber commented, the counterrevolutionary attacks had the effect, at first, of "demonstrating for all to see the need for the workers to stick firmly together."[28]

That conflict produces solidarity is a well-known sociological principle.[29] But this will happen only as long as the bandwagon effect is on its upward swing, which is to say, as long as it appears that the coalition is growing and will be victorious. When the weakness of the coalition is publicly demonstrated and it appears that a rival coalition will be the victor, solidarity ebbs. Weber provides materials to illustrate this, too. Thus, the alliance of the various insurgent organizations continued into fall 1905; with the tsar's manifesto in October, the moderates began to pull back from the radicals (although there were several months of uncertainty before it became clear that the Duma would indeed meet and on what terms), while government concession of civil liberties (temporary as it proved to be) allowed even more groups to organize. In November, the peasants made their boldest claim to national organization in the Socialist Revolutionary Peasant Congress meeting in Moscow (they had started with a smaller meeting of the Pan-Peasant Russian League in July). Escalating conflict further polarized the peasants and the government and strengthened alliances among insurgent groups; when the police arrested the board of the Peasant Congress for advocating tax obstruction, the remainder of the Congress allied with the Council of Workers' Deputies. Similarly, arrests of the leaders of the Workers' Councils and of the Union of Unions (who were advocating radical tactics such as bankrupting the government by rejecting all paper money and presenting all banknotes to be cashed) pushed all these organizations into a projected grand alliance, and also into a tactical bid for complete power.[30] The response to the arrests was a general strike, which escalated into a full-scale armed uprising in Moscow.

This now failed. The troops stood firm: the strike failed to spread beyond Moscow. Intended to eclipse the nationwide general strike of October, which finally brought concession of the manifesto from the tsar, this strike fell beneath it, palpably signaling the ebb of the revolutionary tide. The bulk of the liberals began to withdraw support from their own organizations, leaving the radicals in charge of their hulks. Weber acidly remarked: "the present uprising in Moscow will be very beneficial to the discipline of the army."[31] Nothing strengthens solidarity like victory at a showdown moment. Thereafter, military mutinies (which had been concentrated mainly in the navy, the branch most badly defeated in the Japanese war) faded out, giving the government once again a reliable instrument with which to crush the major challenges (the national/regional revolts and the peasant uprisings), although assassinations remained harder to eradicate and continued for some months.

I have sketched the rise and fall of organizational alliances among the insurgents. Let us add one example from the conservative side. The principal weakness of the tsar, Weber forcefully argued, was that the effectiveness of government organization was highest when the tsar had the least power of personal intervention in it.[32] As long as the various government departments were "a multitude of Satrapies" at odds with each other, the tsar could intervene wherever he had the energy to do so; the alternative system, where all government reports are channeled through a council of ministers and passed by a prime minister, centralized power under the prime minister and reduced the monarch's power to vetoing particular policies or removing the PM. In a somewhat Machiavellian vein, Weber goes on to speculate that the tsar would have been better off if he had a constitutional regime, "for then the bureaucracy could be dependent on the Monarch against Parliament and would have a common interest with him. Strange as it may sound, this would be the surest way for the Monarch to remain de facto master of the bureaucracy."[33] The tsar's chief weakness was his "fatal insistence on wanting to rule on his own."[34] Viewed in the light of our theoretical question of alliances and splits, the tsar could control the bureaucracy only if it were internally split; but this weakness made it an ineffective instrument in relation to outside forces. The upshot of Weber's analysis is that, although reformers and revolutionists had weaknesses in keeping their alliance together, due above all to the transitory nature of the opportunity presented by a crisis situation, the autocracy also struggled with a structural weakness. In the long run, he reasoned, the autocracy had to fall because the structural split between personal rulership and an effectively unified administration left it in a condition of ongoing agitation for reform, and vulnerable to any future crisis.

THE SIGNIFICANCE AND VOLATILITY OF IDEAS

In his polemic against Marxism, Weber took frequent occasion to point out the superiority of ideas over material interests as a motive for political action. He refers to the altruism and commitment of upper-class liberal reformers, and indeed of the revolutionary intellectuals themselves (although he viewed the latter as sect-like and dogmatic). Many of Weber's examples of the force of ideas come from the dynamics of alliance-making in the heat of multifactional action. After describing how the December 1905 revolt had brought together a diverse coalition of organizations, he comments: "This example is evidence of what the power of an 'idea' which unites the classes, and the cooperation of broad strata of the bourgeoisie can achieve, and how little [the alleged material indispensability of the workers] can achieve without that uncertainty in the established cadres of the existing social order which is brought about by such cooperation among bourgeois elements."[35] But a close reading shows that "the idea" Weber is talking about is really an emergent mood, not so much an idea about what reforms ought to be carried out as about the uncertainty of where the future of power lies; Weber says as much in this very passage.

Other cases of action in the defense of ideals can be analyzed more deeply by locating them in the dynamics of crisis, the breakdown of authority, and the bandwagon swings of mobilization. A characteristic pattern is the "atrocity": that is, the situation in which the authorities use violence against protestors, which backfires because it mobilizes large numbers of sympathizers and erodes the regime's own supporters. Such was the case after "the slaughter of 9/22 January" [dating by old and new calendrical systems] 1905, when, as Weber notes, the government was thrown on the defensive by its gunning down of petitioners at the Winter Palace and sought to conciliate its outraged opponents by calling for representation by workers' deputies.[36] It thereby took another step down the slippery slope by encouraging its opponents to form organizations, which became vehicles for still more radical actions. One could say there is a general force to the moral ideal not to use violence against good people, and that this constrains the government and mobilizes opponents, even causing conservatives to switch over to the liberal side. This happens regularly in any successful protest movement.

But just what sociological principle does it illustrate? The trouble with invoking the power of the idea or moral principle per se is that its influence is highly situational. On other occasions, there can be even larger slaughter of protesters for a good cause (for example, the large number of casualties and arbitrary executions of lightly armed students and workers in Moscow in December 1905),[37] without a comparable outcry from sympathizers and a guilty offering of concessions by perpetrators. The difference is in the swing of momentum in the making and unmaking of alliances. Where the authorities are visibly falling apart in their response to crisis and thereby encouraging their opponents to organize, atrocities are widely perceived and moral ideals are strongly invoked; but where the authorities have undergone a test of strength and the insurgents are becoming isolated, what happens to them is regarded as their just deserts, or at any rate moral outrage becomes privatized and eventually fades to indifference.

The same is true of procedural "atrocities," when authorities go back on their word or withdraw concessions previously offered. During the upswing of insurgent organization (and its correlate splintering of authority and its supporters), whatever the government does is seen as either outrage or weakness; during the downswing the scope of organization narrows and outrage is felt against the same kinds of government acts (or indeed much worse). At these times, insurgents' outrage does not resonate outward and does not recruit more supporters; although it might still be emotionally very intense within the circles of the committed militants, those circles are becoming isolated. This explains those tragic manifestations of hopeless revolutionary courage when those within these narrow circles mistake their own feelings for those that were once more widely shared in the glory days of protest when the circle was widening.

We can improve on Weber's formulation for the importance of "ideas." Revolutionaries and liberals (and indeed conservatives) are intensely attuned to ideas; ideas, though, are not static, thing-like entities standing outside of situations, but a mode of social action, communication within situations. This has nothing to do with whether the revolutionary orator is sincere; at the moment when s/he is making the impassioned speech, what is significant as a sociological explanation is whether the network of listeners feels that it is expanding and making connections outward, or on the contrary that it is losing contact and becoming isolated. Also significant are various situations between these extremes that comprise the maneuvering for allies during the course of a political crisis. The contents of ideas are important above all as points of reference around which their holders (and listeners) can estimate to what extent these views will be shared in the networks around them. Instead of just seeing ideas per se, as sociologists of revolution we ought to see ideas as rallying points for organizations: both existing organizations and the all-important prospective and emergent organizations that are the vehicles of alliance in a political crisis.

This correspondence between ideas and the social structure (current or projected) of the revolutionary movement is illustrated by Weber himself. In discussing the various factions of populist radicals, he notes: "Where it is a question of 'ideals,' once must centralize, and only where the interests of the mass, which recognizes no ideals, are directly concerned, should the local associations have control. With this Jacobin idea, well-known from the history of the French 'Convention,' . . . [a populist ideologue] makes a pragmatic defense of the all-powerful state: a worrying foretaste of the centralist-bureaucratic path which Russia could all too easily take, under the influence of radical theoreticians."[38] We can reformulate: a radical political movement, arising in circumstances where the entire regime is in crisis and palpably up for reorganization, and living in an organizational milieu that consists of militants, all of whose life activities are devoted to politics, is just the kind of group that would raise its commitment to political ideas to the extreme; and such a group becomes committed to the type of government organization, should it become successful, that enables its members to put their ideas into practice; the more universalistic the ideas, the more uniform their application, and hence the more centralized the authority structure they favor. On the whole, this was an excellent prediction on Weber's part as to the long-term structural possibilities of the Russian revolution.

GEOPOLITICS AND FOREIGN POLICY

Geopolitical strains are a prime mover in the contemporary state-breakdown theory of revolution. Although Weber was an inspiration for this theory, his attention in analyzing the Russian revolutions was concentrated on organizational and constitutional questions, and he brings in the geopolitical side only occasionally. What he does say casts further light on how geopolitical and foreign influences play into the domestic situation.

First, Weber stresses the importance of an intact military in preventing revolution. Writing while events were still up in the air early in 1906, he stated: "If even a tenth of the officer corps and the troops remain at the disposal of the government—and the fraction would be likely to be closer to nine-tenths—then any number of rebels would be powerless against them."[39] In a footnote he went on: "Only in the tragic event of a *European* war would the autocracy finally be destroyed."[40] (By the stress he apparently meant that the primarily naval war against Japan did not qualify as sufficiently debilitating to military discipline.) On the whole, this was one of Weber's better predictions.

Writing in the spring of 1917, as it was becoming true, he saw a more mixed situation. The bourgeoisie would certainly not be strengthened just because of their financial and industrial indispensability, he wrote, since "How this [liberalization] would ever happen if autocracy and bureaucracy had emerged with tremendous prestige from the war, by means of a victory over us, remained mysterious. It would only have been possible as the result of a crushing defeat. . . . For all that, revolution appeared extremely improbable. . . . The fact that the revolution has come after all is due, as well as to the success of our weapons, to the purely personal conduct of the Tsar."[41] Thus, not only does national identification hinge upon the power-prestige of the state in the world arena,[42] but so does the specific prestige of a ruler and a style of rule. But Weber sees these geopolitical conditions as playing into what for him was the more significant domestic situation, above all the issue of the personal intrusions of the monarch upsetting the smooth working of the government, which I have reformulated above as the more general issue of splits and alliances; in this case, the position of the monarch splits his supporters and drives a significant proportion of the conservatives into the camp of reform.

Weber goes on to connect the short-term dynamics of military-logistical strain to the boiling up of a crisis. Since the tsar overrides legal, regularized bureaucracy, his only instrument of rule is violent intervention by the police to check dissent; his reliance on police power even against the liberal administrators of the zemstvo brought about a situation, Weber declared, in which "the economic provision of the country and of the capital was sure to be brought to a complete standstill."[43] This domestic paralysis "added to the failure of the Russian railway system resulting from the demands of [provisioning the Russian army in] the Romanian campaign[44] and led directly to the outbreak of revolt"—that is, it led to the shortage of bread even in Moscow, prompting the women's demonstrations in January 1917 and a crisis of authority resembling January 1905, but this time leading to the abdication of the tsar in the face of overwhelming opposition from all strata of society.

The revolution of 1917 did not end here, with the establishment of a parliamentary regime; Weber, writing in late April, was clear-sighted enough to call it, in his title, a "pseudo-democracy," and he speculated about its fate. As we know in retrospect, the decision of the provisional government to resume fighting, coupled with crushing military defeat in late summer, led to disintegration of the troops and to the swing of support to the Bolshevik-dominated councils (Soviets) promising an end to the war. Weber saw the issue, but put stress on the circumstance that the government was in financial straits and could not keep itself going by paying its own civil servants without bank credit; and this credit depended upon foreign loans from Britain and America, the very allies who insisted on Russia's resuming the war. This contrasted with the situation in 1905, when liberal foreign powers prodded the tsar into issuing the manifesto offering a form of parliamentary representation.[45] Here, Weber adumbrates another piece of the state-breakdown theory, the fiscal crisis of government administration that ushers in the revolutionary situation. But he connects it not so much with the costs of the war itself as with the vulnerability of the government to direction from whatever policy is favored by its foreign bankers: it is a historical accident as to whether those bankers and their associated governments want to encourage reforms (in 1905) or to oppose them (in 1917).

With the wisdom of hindsight, we can draw a lesson that Weber did not: foreign bankers can try to impose their will, but they do not always get what they want. In 1905–6, they hoped to encourage parliamentary democracy, but this did not go very far, and the result was what Weber himself called "pseudo-constitutionalism," leaving the autocratic structures in place, which led to the crisis of 1917. In 1917, Weber noted, the majority of the Russian populace, the peasants, had an objective interest in the cancellation of Russia's foreign debts, since it was their grain that had to be exported to pay the interest, and they were "highly taxed in order to force them to sell."[46] But in Weber's view, this was another reason why neither the foreign bankers nor the landowning interests wanted an end to the war: the political representatives of the peasants could take power only if peace were concluded: "For only then would the peasants even be at home and available. . . . Thus in order to keep the peasants away from their homes, they [bankers and landowners] are absolutely in favour of prolonging the war for its own sake. . . . Only in this way can . . . the mass of the peasants be held in the trenches under the control of the generals. . . . "[47] Weber thus attributes to bankers and conservatives a rather Machiavellian reasoning for continuing the war. What he did not pay sufficient attention to was what has become a key point in the state-breakdown theory: that military defeat, when combined with fiscal crisis and splits among the elites, destroys the structure of the state and opens the way to whomever can organize a sufficiently unified coalition to constitute a new center of authority. The bankers outsmarted themselves (if indeed they were conscious of what they were doing), and the events of Fall, 1917 were the consequence.

WEBER'S PREDICTIONS AND REVOLUTIONARY STRUCTURAL CHANGE

The scorecard of Weber's predictions about Russia is mixed. Obviously, it is not easy to predict in the midst of a volatile revolutionary situation, and Weber often admirably brings his analytical apparatus to bear on what are inevitable points of contention that set the alternatives, and on the organizational structures that will be decisive no matter what. The main structural problems are: first, as we have already seen, the impossibility of long continuing personal rule by an autocrat in a world of bureaucratic administration. This is implied in the evolutionary-sounding terms of Weber's titles: the "Transition to Pseudo-constitutionalism," and its subheading, "Completing the Bureaucratization of the Autocracy" (characterizing the structural changes of 1905–6); and the "Transition to Pseudo-Democracy" (for early 1917). As of April of that year, Weber saw everything still hanging in the balance: "So far, there has been no 'revolution' but merely 'the removal' of an incompetent monarch. . . . At least half of the real power is in the hands of purely monarchist circles, who are only going along with the present 'republican' sham because, to their regret, the monarch has not stayed within the necessary restraints of his power."[48]

Second, a crucial problem of economic class conflict remained. The peasants could not be kept under control, above all if they were allowed full political franchise, which would give them predominant weight in a true parliamentary regime, without expropriation and redistribution of nonpeasant land; and the question of how to pay for this expropriation would lead to "hopeless conflict with the bourgeois landowners."[49] "These difficulties could only be resolved by means of a Socialist Revolutionary dictatorship lasting for years."[50] (Here, Weber uses "Socialist Revolutionary" in a proper sense as the name of the party of agrarian populists.) This is inconsistent with Weber's prediction, some years earlier, that the growth of capitalism in Russia would end populist radicalism and replace it with Marxist radicalism.[51] Weber himself tacitly underlined the latter position by noting that Workers' Councils had become the organizing centers of the insurgencies, both in 1905 and in 1917.[52] So although Weber was still thinking of the agrarian radicals as likely candidates for dictatorship, the Marxists could even more obviously play that role. But as things hung in the balance, he thought yet another possibility most likely: a reactionary dictatorship, probably by the military.[53]

The upshot of these predictions was that Weber expected the course of revolutionary crisis in Russia to tend not toward constitutionalism and bourgeois democracy, but toward dictatorship. This could happen from the right, as an armed suppression of the possibility of carrying out land reforms in the interests of the mass of peasants; it could also happen from the left, both because the radicals would also need dictatorship to overcome the conflict of class interests opposing land reform, and because (as noted earlier) of the affinity of a social movement of militant idealists with centralized bureaucracy to impose their ideals thoroughly upon society.[54]

Against this trend toward undemocratic bureaucracy, Weber saw only unique historical accidents and ideal values "emerging from the concrete historical peculiarity of a certain religious thought world";[55] the hurried list he gives of these historical factors does not add up to a coherent theory of democracy.

For the medium run of history, Weber's predictive analysis is moderately impressive. By underplaying the influence of geopolitical conditions, he missed seeing the short-term shift just ahead of him: that the resumption of the war would bring not just the downfall of the provisional government but also the victory of the Marxian socialists. But he certainly had them on his short list of candidates for dictatorial power, and he accurately predicted the character of their regime. Weber's vision, both in 1906 and in 1917, was like Orwell's *1984*, published some thirty years later (in 1948). Once the bureaucratic dictatorship was in place, it was an iron cage that could never be cracked. As it turned out, both history and sociological theory have gone on in a more complicated direction. The state-breakdown theory that developed around 1980 offered a successful prediction of the scenario that would undermine even this most extreme form of bureaucratic authoritarianism.[56] This theory was in important respects a descendent of certain points of Weber's political sociology. Skocpol called her own state-centered theory of revolution "left Weberian," as a reformulation of Marxian topics within a Weberian emphasis on the centrality of the state and its internal and geopolitical dynamics.[57] My own geopolitically based predictive scheme was put forward under a "neo-Weberian" rubric, since its leading principle is that the legitimacy of rule is a variable affected by the power-prestige of the state in the interstate arena, and thus by the variables of geopolitical strength and weakness.[58]

Weber himself did not analyze the revolutions that he witnessed in these ways. He was too concerned with polemicizing against Marxism, and at the same time still too tied to a frame of analysis he shared with Marxism, which focused on the line-up of preexisting interests battling it out over which structure was to prevail. We are now inclined to see revolution more in terms of situational dynamics that break apart coalitions and put others in their place, creating new interests out of the organizational opportunities that emerge along the way.

But even here Weber had an inkling of what was afoot. In *ES*, noting the similarities between revolutionary conflict in the medieval Italian cities and early Rome, he commented: "It is a fact, after all, that only a limited variety of different administrative techniques is available for effecting compromises between the status groups within a city. Similarities in the forms of political administration can therefore not be interpreted as identical superstructures over identical economic foundations. These things obey their own laws."[59]

Interpreted broadly, "their own laws" are the principles of alliances and splits that make up the structure of opportunities in the field of political action and explain the dynamics of revolution.

Notes

1. Max Weber, *Economy and Society: An Outline of Interpretive Sociology*, ed. Guenther Roth and Claus Wittich (1921–22; Berkeley: University of California Press, 1978), p. 1115.

2. Ibid., p. 1314.

3. Ibid., p. 1116.

4. Ibid., p. 1115.

5. This should remind us that the entire chapter, "The City," is not so much urban sociology, in the sense that the field has become constituted, as it is part of his sociology of political communities and domination.

6. Weber, *Economy and Society*, p. 1302.

7. Leon Trotsky, *History of the Russian Revolution* (New York: Simon and Schuster, 1932), p. 8; Weber, *Economy and Society*, pp. 1307–11.

8. Weber, *Economy and Society*, pp. 1307–11.

9. Ibid., p. 1308.

10. Michael Mann, *The Sources of Social Power*, vol. 1, *A History of Power from the Beginning to A.D. 1760*; vol. 2, *The Rise of Classes and Nation-states, 1760–1914* (Cambridge: Cambridge University Press, 1986–93); Charles Tilly, *Coercion, Capital, and European States, A.D. 990–1990* (Oxford: Blackwell, 1990).

11. Randall Collins, "The Geopolitical Basis of Revolution: The Prediction of the Soviet Collapse," in Randall Collins, *Macro-History: Essays in Sociology of the Long Run* (Stanford, CA: Stanford University Press, 1999).

12. Weber, *Economy and Society*, pp. 1312–13

13. Ibid., p. 1309.

14. Ibid., p. 1308.

15. Guenther Roth, introduction in Weber, *Economy and Society*, p. xciii.

16. Theda Skocpol, *States and Social Revolutions* (New York: Cambridge University Press, 1979); Jack A. Goldstone, *Revolution and Rebellion in the Early Modern World*

(Berkeley: University of California Press, 1991); Charles Tilly, *European Revolutions, 1492–1992* (Oxford: Blackwell, 1993).

17. Charles Tilly, *From Mobilization to Revolution* (Reading, MA: Addison-Wesley, 1978); Charles Tilly, *Popular Contention in Great Britain, 1758–1834* (Cambridge, MA: Harvard University Press, 1995).

18. Summarized in Randall Collins, "What Does Conflict Theory Predict about America's Future?" *Sociological Perspectives* 36 (1993): 289–313.

19. Arthur L. Stinchcombe, "Analogy and Generality in Trotsky and de Tocqueville," in Arthur L. Stinchcombe, *Theoretical Methods in Social History* (New York: Academic Press, 1978); Goldstone, *Revolution and Rebellion*, pp. 421–36; Gerald Marwell and Pamela Oliver, *The Critical Mass in Collective Action: A Micro-Social Theory* (New York: Cambridge University Press, 1993).

20. Lewis Coser, *The Functions of Social Conflict* (Glencoe, IL: Free Press, 1956). Weber gives several examples. Discussing the leftist revolutionaries, he compares their splits and bitter recriminations to persecutions that took place among Dutch Calvinists against their own Arminian heretics, which Weber notes were worse than their persecutions of Catholics or Baptists. He comments scornfully that "sectarians are like men of the cloth" (Max Weber, "Bourgeois Democracy in Russia," in *The Russian Revolutions*, trans. and ed. Gordon C. Wells and Peter Baehr [1906; Ithaca, NY: Cornell University Press, 1995], pp. 132–33). Similarly on the far right: in the 1917 revolution, the tsar preferred not to be rescued even by sharing power with the conservative aristocracy in a parliamentary regime—that is, with monarchists who had decided the only tactical path possible was to take over the movement for reform (Max Weber, "Russia's Transition to Pseudo-democracy," in *The Russian Revolutions*, trans. and ed. Gordon C. Wells and Peter Baehr [1917; Ithaca, NY: Cornell University Press, 1995], p. 247). Likewise, in 1905 "court circles and the civil service would rather do a deal with the devil than with *zemstvo* liberalism" (Weber, "Bourgeois Democracy in Russia," p. 107).

21. I have made an analogous argument in regard to how intellectual life proceeds through emergent or (if you like) "opportunistic" patterns of disputes and alliances among intellectual positions, an ongoing structure of intellectual opportunities opening up and closing off inside a limited attention space. Randall Collins, *The Sociology of Philosophies: A Global Theory of Intellectual Change* (Cambridge, MA: Harvard University Press, 1998).

22. A normal electoral politics version of this dynamic is the "lesser evil" argument: the Greens may not like moderate Democrats, but by staying independent they will take votes from the latter and in effect give votes to conservative Republicans. Virtually all of politics is a version of the "lesser evil" maneuver.

23. Sometimes, however, a faction may split in order to maintain radical tactics; and this may enable it, in a situation down the road, to become the head of a still larger coalition. These are complexities to be examined elsewhere.

24. The Union of Unions consisted of "lawyers, doctors, engineers, journalists, booksellers, primary school teachers, middle school teachers, agriculturalists, statisticians, pharmacists, veterinary surgeons, and also state civil servants. . . . There were also insurance employees, clerks, and actors, as well as representatives of women's and

of Jewish rights organizations. . . . There was even an appeal by police officers from Moscow, calling for the 'comrades' to organize . . . " (Weber, "Bourgeois Democracy in Russia" pp. 70–71).

25. Ibid., p. 73.

26. Max Weber, "Russia's Transition to Pseudo-constitutionalism," in *The Russian Revolutions* (1906), pp. 148–49.

27. It also foreshadows similar mass constituencies springing up overnight, as in the Bolshevik-dominated assemblies of 1917.

28. Weber, "Russia's Transition to Pseudo-constitutionalism," p. 149.

29. Coser, *Functions of Social Conflict.*

30. Weber, "Bourgeois Democracy in Russia," pp. 73, 94; Weber, "Russia's Transition to Pseudo-constitutionalism," p. 150.

31. Weber, "Bourgeois Democracy in Russia," p. 102.

32. Weber, "Russia's Transition to Pseudo-constitutionalism," pp.176–78; Weber, "Russia's Transition to Pseudo-democracy," pp. 244–45.

33. Weber, "Russia's Transition to Pseudo-constitutionalism," p. 178.

34. Weber, "Russia's Transition to Pseudo-democracy," p. 244.

35. Weber, "Russia's Transition to Pseudo-constitutionalism," p. 150.

36. Weber, "Bourgeois Democracy in Russia," p. 69.

37. Weber, "Russia's Transition to Pseudo-constitutionalism," p. 151.

38. Weber, "Bourgeois Democracy in Russia," p. 89.

39. Ibid., p. 103.

40. Ibid., p. 142.

41. Weber, "Russia's Transition to Pseudo-democracy," p. 244.

42. Weber, *Economy and Society*, pp. 922–26.

43. Weber, "Russia's Transition to Pseudo-democracy," p. 247.

44. "The famine occurred simply because the Russian railways were unavailable for civil purposes on account of the demands made on them by the extension of the front due to the Romanian campaign" (Weber, "Russia's Transition to Pseudo-democracy," p. 248).

45. "Without the warning from foreign financiers—not in so many words but by implication—the Manifesto of 17 October would perhaps never have been issued or at least would soon have been revoked. Fear of the rage of the masses and of the mutiny of the troops would have been ineffective had not the autocracy been at the mercy of the cool, hard hand of the banks and stock exchanges" (Weber, "Bourgeois Democracy in Russia," p. 102).

46. Weber, "Russia's Transition to Pseudo-democracy," p. 249.

47. Ibid.

48. Ibid., p. 252.

49. Ibid., p. 249.

50. Ibid.

51. Weber, "Bourgeois Democracy in Russia," pp. 107–8.

52. In the spring of 1917, Weber had already noted that the bourgeois liberals, once the tsar was deposed and not replaced by another more liberal monarchy, were forced "to look to the *proletariat*, whose power was indispensable in the struggle

against the Tsar" (Weber, "Russia's Transition to Pseudo-democracy," p. 247). That is to say, they were indispensable, not because they were anything close to a sizable fraction of the populace, but because they were so obviously central organizationally in the political struggles in Petersburg and Moscow, and because they could exercise a paralyzing influence through their control of the unions of railway, postal, and telegraph workers (ibid., p. 248). Weber refers to the Council of Workers and Soldiers as "a de facto secondary government" alongside the official Provisional Government (Max Weber, "The Russian Revolution and the Peace," in *The Russian Revolutions* [1917], p. 262). This was Trotsky's prime example of "dual power." Kerensky, who in the spring Weber viewed as the leading radical member of the provisional government (as leader of the Socialist Revolutionaries, that is, the agrarian populists), had not yet risen to head of government; at this time he was also connected to the Workers' Soviet, which indeed served him as a counterweight to the monarchists. It was on this play of perceived alliances that Kerensky for a while came to gather all the reigns of administrative power in the provisional government.

53. "It is . . . very unlikely that an open or disguised military dictatorship can be permanently kept at bay, if *the war continues*" (Weber, "Russia's Transition to Pseudo-democracy," p. 248). A few pages later, Weber qualifies this slightly as a dictatorship in the interest of capitalists: "Only a tiny proportion (of money from foreign banks) is used in the struggle against the Central Powers. The great mass of it is used to consolidate the domination of the country by capitalist interests and those representing the propertied Russian intelligentsia. One element in the consolidation is the creation of an army which will be as reliable for the bourgeois regime as the Tsar's Black Gangs were for him. It is designed to be used *primarily* against *internal* enemies. . . . What is also necessary to achieve this is the *arrest* of all those people whom the peasants are capable of influencing in their favour. These are the same means that the Tsar's regime employed. These arrests have already begun" (Weber, "Russia's Transition to Pseudo-democracy," p. 254).

54. In the background of both predictions is Weber's long-standing worry that the world was tending toward subjugation under bureaucracy. In 1906 he wrote:

> "Democracy" and "individualism" would stand little chance today if we were to rely for their "development" on the "automatic" effect of *material* interests. For these point as clearly as they can in the opposite direction. Whether in the shape of American "benevolent feudalism," the German "welfare institutions," or the Russian factory constitution—everywhere the empty shell for new serfdom stands ready; it will be occupied to the degree that the pace of technical-economic "progress" slows down and the victory of "income" over "profit," together with the exhaustion of what remains of "free" lands and the "free" markets, renders the masses "compliant."
>
> At the same time, the growing complexity of the economy, partial nationalization or "municipalization," and the size of national territory, create ever new paperwork, further specialization and administrative training—which means the creation of a caste. Those American workers who were against "Civil Service Reform" knew what they were doing. They would rather be governed by up-

starts of dubious morality than by a class of professional mandarins—but their protest was in vain." (Weber, "Bourgeois Democracy in Russia," p. 108)

55. Ibid., p. 109.

56. Ibid., p. 108. Randall Collins, "The Future Decline of the Russian Empire," chap. 8 in Randall Collins, *Weberian Sociological Theory* (Cambridge: Cambridge University Press, 1986).

57. Skocpol, *States and Social Revolutions.*

58. Collins, "Future Decline of the Russian Empire."

59. Weber, *Economy and Society*, p. 1309.

The Disenchantment of Logically Formal Legal Rationality

Or, Max Weber's Sociology in the Genealogy of the Contemporary Mode of Western Legal Thought

Introduction

Max Weber began his sociology of law with a description of Western legal thought in his time, along with a brief summary of its previous stages. This appreciation begins with a summary description of the Western legal thought of Weber's time, as it looks from our present 100 years later, emphasizing the contrast between the mainstream of his time, now called "classical legal thought," and its critics in the "social current." Part II presents Weber's sociology of law, comparing and contrasting his approach with that of the social current. The most striking thing about Weber's sociology of law, from the perspective of legal theory a century after he wrote, is his ambivalent endorsement of legal formalism. This entailed rejection of the social current's critique, a critique that is close to universally accepted today. In Part III, I explain Weber's attitude toward legal formalism as motivated by the internal requirements of his theory of domination, in which, after the demise of all earlier modes of legitimation, the Iron Cage of modernity is held together by bureaucrats defined by their adherence to that mode of legal reasoning. Part IV argues that Weber's approach was inconsistent with the irrationalist and decisionist strands in his own theory of modernity, a theory that helps in understanding the current situation of legal thought, if we take the un-Weberian step of applying it to legal formalism. Finally, Part V offers an interpretation of the contemporary mode of legal thought as an episode in the sequences of disenchantment and reenchantment suggested by Weber's philosophy of history, and uses Weberian elements to construct a distinct contemporary ideal type of legal thought. The brief conclusion suggests the strong affiliation between Weber (read as above) and one of the sects of modern legal theory, namely critical legal studies.

I. Western Legal Thought in 1900

Weber produced his sociology of law at a moment of dramatic transition in Western legal thought. In 1900 there was a well-defined mainstream mode, which we now customarily call classical legal thought (CLT) and two challengers: what I will call the "social current," or "socially oriented legal thought," and Marxist legal thought. This part presents the classical and social modes. Weber's sociology presents CLT as the mode of the present. His analysis of CLT is heavily indebted to the socially oriented critics who developed a rather elaborate picture of their classical opponents, a picture that remains at least largely plausible to this day. But, as we will see in Part II, Weber had his own distinctive critique of CLT, and also a critique of the social.

CLASSICAL LEGAL THOUGHT

According to its social critics, according to Weber, and according to most (if not all) of today's historians, the late nineteenth-century mainstream saw law as having a strong, internal, structural coherence based on the three traits of exhaustive elaboration of the distinction between private and public law, "individualism," and commitment to legal interpretive formalism. These traits combined in "the will theory."[1]

In the social jurists' version, the will theory was that the private law rules of the "advanced" Western nation-states were well understood as a set of rational derivations from the notion that government should help individuals realize their wills, restrained only as necessary to permit others to do the same. In its more ambitious versions, the will theory made public as well as private law norms follow from this foundational commitment (for example, by generating theories of the separation of powers from the nature of rights).

The will theory was an attempt to identify the rules that should follow from consensus in favor of the goal of individual self-realization. It was not a political or moral philosophy justifying this goal; nor was it a positive historical or sociological theory about how this had come to be the goal. Rather, the theory offered a specific, will-based, and deductive interpretation of the interrelationship of the dozens or hundreds of relatively concrete norms of the extant national legal orders, and of the legislative and adjudicative institutions that generated and applied the norms.

"Outside" or "above" legal theory, there were a variety of rationales for the legal commitment to individualism thus understood. Of these, only natural rights theory was also highly relevant on the "inside," that is, in the development of the technique of legal analysis based on deduction. Natural rights theorists had elaborated the will theory, beginning in the seventeenth century, as a set of implications from their normative premises, and their specific legal technique was the direct ancestor of the legal formalism that the socially oriented reformers were to attack in its positivized form.

In the mid- and late-nineteenth century, the German historical school (Savigny) developed a positivist version of normative formalism. National systems of law reflect as a matter of fact the normative order of the underlying society; such a normative order is coherent or tends toward coherence on the basis of the spirit and history of the people in question; "legal scientists" can and should elaborate the positive legal rules composing the system on the premise of its internal coherence. In the late nineteenth century, the German pandectists (Windschied, Puchta) worked at the analysis of the basic conceptions of the German common-law version of Roman law with the aim of establishing that this particular system could be made internally coherent, and also be made to approach gaplessness. Many Continental legal scholars understood the German Civil Code of 1900 as the legislative adoption of this system.

In France, Britain, and the United States, the historical school was a minor tendency, but the same conception of a will theory combining individualism and deductive form gradually supplanted earlier ways of understanding private and, in the United States, public law. The normative or "outside" force for the theory might come from utilitarianism, or from Lockean or Kantian or French revolutionary natural rights, or from a variant of evolutionism (the movement of the progressive societies has been from contract to status; social Darwinism). But however derived, normative individualism was closely connected with logical method in the constitution of some version of the will theory.

The will theory in turn served a variety of purposes within legal discourse. It guided the scholarly reconceptualization, reorganization, and reform of private law rules, in what the participants understood as an apolitical rationalization project. But it also provided the discursive framework for the decision of hundreds or perhaps thousands of cases, throughout the industrializing West, in which labor confronted capital and small business confronted big business. And it provided an abstract, overarching ideological formulation of the meaning of the rule of law as an essential element in a liberal legal order.

THE "SOCIAL" AS A MODE OF LEGAL THOUGHT

The inventors of the social include Ihering, Ehrlich, Gierke, Geny, Saleilles, Duguit, Lambert, Josserand, Gounod, Gurvitch, Pound, and Cardozo.[2] They had in common with the Marxists that they interpreted the actual regime of the will theory as an epiphenomenon in relation to a "base":

in the case of the Marxists, the capitalist economy; and in the case of the so-cial, "society" conceived as an organism. The idea of both was that the will theory in some sense "suited" the socioeconomic conditions of the first half of the nineteenth century. But the social people were anti-Marxist, just as much as they were anti–laissez faire. Their goal was to save liberalism from itself.

Their basic idea was that the conditions of late nineteenth-century life represented a social transformation, consisting of urbanization, industrializa-tion, organizational society, and globalization of markets, all summarized in the idea of "interdependence." Because the will theory was individualist, it ignored interdependence and endorsed particular legal rules that permitted antisocial behavior of many kinds. The crises of the modern factory (indus-trial accidents) and the urban slum (pauperization), and later the crisis of the financial markets, all derived from the failure of coherently individualist law to respond to the coherently social needs of modern conditions of interde-pendence.

From this "is" analysis, they derived the "ought" of a reform program, one that was astonishingly successful, and globalized even more effectively than classical legal thought, through many of the same mechanisms, but also be-cause the social became the ideology of many third-world nationalist elites. There was labor legislation, the regulation of urban areas through landlord / tenant, sanitary, and zoning regimes, the regulation of financial markets, and the development of new institutions of international law. Just as with CLT's will theory, the abstract idea of the social appealed to a very wide range of legitimating rhetorics. These traversed the left–right spectrum, leaving out only Marxist collectivism at one extreme and pure Manchesterism at the other. Thus the social could be based on socialist or social democratic ideol-ogy (perhaps Durkheimian), on the social Christianity of Protestant sects, on neo-Kantian "situational natural law," on Comtean positivism, on Catholic natural law as enunciated in *Rerum Novarum* and *Quadrigessimo Anno*, on Bismarck / Disraeli social conservatism, or on early fascist ideology.

Regardless of which it was, the slogans included organicism, purpose, function, reproduction, welfare, instrumentalism (law is a means to an end)—and so anti-deduction, because a legal rule is just a means to the ac-complishment of social purposes. A crucial part of their critique of classical legal thought was their claim that it maintained an appearance of objectivity in legal interpretation only through the abuse of deduction. Many advocates of the social argued that various groups within the emerging interdepend-ent society, including, for example, merchant communities and labor unions, were developing new norms to fit the new "social needs." These norms, re-garded as "valid," "living law" (Ehrlich), rather than deduction from individ-ualist postulates, should, and also would, in this "legal pluralist" view, be the basis for legislative, administrative, and judicial elaboration of new rules of state law.

While the social was spectacularly successful as a legislative, reform program, the social as a mode of legal thought underwent the same kind of brutal discrediting that had befallen CLT. We will take up the reasons for this, and Weber's role in it, below.

II. Weber's Sociology of Law

The best way to understand the chapter "The Sociology of Law" in *Economy and Society* is as an analysis of CLT, presented as "just the way we do things now," combined with a historical narrative of how CLT came into existence and a critique of the critique then being leveled against it by the social current.[3] This same sociology of law was an important element in the construction of Weber's broader sociology of domination in modern capitalist society, but this aspect of the story is reserved for Part III.

WEBER'S METHODOLOGY VERSUS THE METHODOLOGY OF THE SOCIAL CURRENT

Weber was substantively in sympathy with a large part of the social, legislative, reform program.[4] But, although he never, as far as I know, stated it explicitly, his methodology is well understood as a root-and-branch attack on, and an alternative to, that of the social people. First, Weber is famous for his insistence on a sharp distinction between the sociological *is* and the ethical or political *ought*. From "The Meaning of 'Ethical Neutrality' in Sociology and Economics"[5] and "Objectivity in Social Science and Social Policy"[6] through to "Science as a Vocation,"[7] Weber argued that the very maneuver that defined the social—that is, the claim that it was possible to go from an analysis of the modern social mode of interdependence, a fact, to the progressive reform agenda, an *ought*—couldn't be done. But this is only the beginning of his divergences from the method of the socially oriented critics of CLT.

Weber is also famous for his opposition to "emanationism," that is, the idea that transpersonal entities like "*Geist*" or "humanity" can figure plausibly in historical or sociological explanation. This is his explicit critique of Hegelianism and of the German historical school.[8] He applied it fully to law.[9] But Turner and Factor have persuasively argued that, in the development of the sociological categories of action and domination presented in the next subsection, Weber was systematically and carefully reworking the superficially similar categorical scheme of Rudolf von Ihering, the German founder of the social approach. The point of the reworking was to purge any suggestion that there are "social purposes" or a telos to social development, or an evolutionary logic that can simultaneously explain and justify legal change.

In this respect, Weber was diametrically opposite Tönnies, Durkheim, and also Talcott Parsons, for each of whom an organicist or functionalist understanding of society allows us to make, if not "objective value judgments," at least judgments about what to do that are the furthest thing imaginable from mere ideological preferences. For Weber, social change is a result of the play of social forces. These include ideals and values as well as diverse material and institutional interests, always in conflict and subject to massive applications of the law of unintended effects. For the socially oriented critics of CLT, on the other hand, there was, at the very least, a logic of social development that law can either facilitate or obstruct.

Finally, it is familiar that Weber was at once an appropriator of, and a strong critic of, Marxist approaches to economic history.[10] What he most strongly criticized was the monocausal approach of the "base / superstructure" distinction, in which legal categories reflect the mode of production and legal rules serve the interests of the ruling class.[11] This kind of criticism applies mutatis mutandis to the social approach, for which law reflects society, albeit sometimes with tragic lags, and ought to serve a depoliticized and universal interest in social development. For Weber, law is, as we might now put it, "relatively autonomous," and also "constitutive," rather than merely reflective.

THE BASIC CATEGORIES OF WEBER'S GENERAL AND
LEGAL SOCIOLOGIES

This section briefly lays out the basic ideal-typical categories Weber used in constructing his sociology of law. Weber's categories for general sociological and legal analysis are the basis for the categories of his sociology of domination as well.

General Sociological Categories

Weber usefully distinguishes between action that is *purpose rational* and action that is *value rational*.

[Social conduct] may be determined rationally and oriented toward an end. In that case it is determined by the expectation that objects in the world outside or other human beings will behave in a certain way, and by the use of such expectations as conditions of, or as means toward, the achievement of the actor's own, rationally desired and considered aims. This will be called purpose-rational conduct.

Or, social conduct may be determined, second, by the conscious faith in the absolute worth of the conduct as such, independent of any aim, and measured by some such standard as ethics, aesthetics, or religion. This case will be called value-rational conduct.[12]

Contrary to what readers sometimes think, purpose rationality is "higher" than value rationality, for Weber, as the order of presentation in *Economy and Society* shows, and as is confirmed by his discussion of the ethics of acts versus the ethics of consequences in "*Politics as a Vocation*." It is important that purpose rationality is oriented toward accomplishing either a single goal in the most effective way, or *some combination of goals through a balancing of costs and benefits*, in each case based on calculating how the situation in which one acts will be modified for good and ill by one's action.

Value rationality means that the actor has identified a rule that applies to the situation and proceeds to obey that rule, experienced as internally binding, based on some mode of legitimation that might be religious, ideological, philosophical, or ethical. The key to the conduct is that the actor obeys without considering the consequences. Once authoritatively established, the rule is the rule, and obedience is the only consideration. Action in obedience, say, to one of the Ten Commandments, or to one's conviction that "the right to control your body is absolute," is value rational.

> The purest type of value-rational validity is represented by natural law. The influence of its logically deduced propositions upon actual conduct may lag far behind their theoretical claims; that they have had some influence cannot be denied, however. Its propositions must be distinguished from those of revealed, of enacted, and of traditional law.[13]

The Legal Mode of Authority (Legitimate Domination)

This is Weber's typology of the modes of legitimate domination:

> The actors can ascribe legitimate validity to an order in a variety of ways:
>
> > The order can be recognized as legitimate, first, by virtue of tradition: valid is that which has always been.
> >
> > Second, the order may be treated as legitimate by virtue of affectual, especially emotional, faith; this situation occurs especially in the case of the newly revealed or the exemplary.
> >
> > Third, the order may be treated as legitimate by virtue of value-rational faith: valid is that which has been deduced as absolutely demanded.
> >
> > Fourth, legitimacy can be ascribed to an order by virtue of positive enactment of recognized legality. Such legality can be recognized as legitimate either (a) because the enactment has been agreed upon by all those who are concerned; or (b) by virtue of imposition by a domination of human beings over human beings which is treated as legitimate and meets with acquiescence.[14]

Orders based on tradition, affect, and value rationality can be reenforced by enacted law. Also, there are other types of law than enacted law, including especially revealed law and natural law. The mode of legitimate domination through enacted law makes a sharp distinction between "lawmaking" and "lawfinding."

According to our contemporary modes of legal thought, the activities of political organizations fall, as regards "law," into two categories, viz., lawmaking and lawfinding, the latter involving "execution" as a technical matter. Today we understand by lawmaking the establishment of general norms, which in the lawyer's thought assume the character of rational rules of law. Lawfinding, as we understand it, is the "application" of such established norms and the legal propositions deduced therefrom by legal thinking, to concrete "facts" which are "subsumed" under these norms. However, this mode of thought has by no means been common to all periods of history. The distinction between lawmaking as creation of general norms and lawfinding as application of these norms to particular cases does not exist where adjudication is "administration" in the sense of free decision from case to case.[15]

In a modern system, lawmaking is open-ended: "any given legal norm may be established by agreement or by imposition, on grounds of expediency or value rationality or both, with a claim to obedience at least on the part of the members of the organization."[16] Once the lawmakers have established the system of legal norms, the modern legal mode of authority (legitimate domination) is defined by the further requirement that lawfinding must be "impersonal":

[E]very single bearer of powers of command is legitimated by that system of rational norms, and his power is legitimate in so far as it corresponds with the norms. Obedience is thus given to the norms rather than to the person.[17]

Again, there is nothing natural or automatic about this conception. It is also possible for lawfinding, like lawmaking power, to be "personal":

Such personal authority can, in turn, be founded upon the sacredness of tradition, i.e., of that which is customary and has always been so and prescribes obedience to some particular person.

Or, personal authority can have its source in the very opposite, viz., the surrender to the extraordinary, the belief in charisma, i.e., actual revelation or grace resting in such a person as a savior, prophet, or a hero.[18]

But in such a case we are not dealing with the ideal type of legal authority.

The Modes of Modern Legal Thought

The different modes of modern legal thought are ideal-typical descriptions of what is done by the specialists in lawfinding (as opposed to lawmaking) when it comes to deciding how to apply enacted law to concrete cases. These can be judges, but they can also be bureaucratic administrators, or professors critiquing judges, or professors deciding hypothetical cases.

Among systems that have gotten beyond supernatural methods (oracles, trial by ordeal), and also beyond ad hoc decision, Weber distinguishes modes of legal thought according to how close they are to his unequivocally most rational mode, which he calls "logically formal rationality" (LFR):

Present-day legal science, at least in those forms which have achieved the highest measure of methodological and logical rationality, i.e., those which have been produced through the legal science of the Pandectists' Civil Law, proceeds from the following five postulates: viz., first, that every concrete legal decision be the "application" of an abstract legal proposition to a concrete "fact situation"; second, that it must be possible in every concrete case to derive the decision from abstract legal propositions by means of legal logic; third, that the law must actually or virtually constitute a "gapless" system of legal propositions, or must at least be treated as if it were such a gapless system; fourth, that whatever cannot be "construed" legally in rational terms is also legally irrelevant; and fifth, that every social action of human beings must always be visualized as either an "application" or "execution" of legal propositions, or as an "infringement" thereof.[19]

An aspect of logically formal legal rationality that Weber reiterated over and over, but that is not found in this definition, is that the lawfinder doing LFR is restricted to the "logical analysis of meaning" performed on a corpus of validly enacted norms that come from the lawmaking institution, whatever it may be. LFR "is found where the legally relevant characteristics of the facts are disclosed through the logical analysis of meaning and where, accordingly, definitely fixed legal concepts in the form of highly abstract rules are formulated and applied."[20]

Logically formal rationality is most definitely not necessary in order for the mode of authority to be ideal-typically legal. All that is needed is that the mode of lawfinding be sufficiently "formal"—that is, rule-bound—so that lawfinding is plausibly impersonal. For example, there are types of formal legal rationality that are not "logical," including particularly the English common law.[21] Formal rationality in general, whether of the higher "logical analysis of meaning type" (LFR), or the more primitive British precedential type, contrasts sharply with the very important, Weberian category of "substantive rationality" as a mode of legal thought.

"[S]ubstantive rationality" . . . means that the decision of legal problems is influenced by norms different from those obtained through logical generalization of abstract interpretations of meaning. The norms to which substantive rationality accords predominance include ethical imperatives, utilitarian and other expediential rules, political maxims, all of which diverge from the formalism . . . which uses logical abstraction.[22]

In LFR, when the lawfinder acts, by deciding the case or making his academic interpretation of what the law "is," his action is always "value rational" in Weber's usage. On the basis of the logical analysis of the meaning of the extant valid norms, he chooses a norm, without regard to the social consequences of his choice, and then applies it to the facts at hand, again without regard to the social consequences. This contrasts sharply with substantively rational legal thought. There, the judge may be, contrary to what some commentators suggest, acting in a value-rational way (say, by applying religious commandments such as "thou shalt not kill" or absolute natural rights such as "respect for private property"). But the legal actor is also substantively rational if what he does is to identify a set of societal goals, or a set of partial political objectives of the ruler, and then craft his rule to maximize their accomplishment through a situation-sensitive balancing test.

In other words, substantive legal rationality can be either value rational or purpose rational (whereas LFR is always value rational).[23] The point about substantive rationality is not its mode of orientation to action, but the extra-juristic or "external" derivation of the criteria of decision—that is, their derivation from the normative practices of society. Weber's emphasis on this distinction is analogous to the preoccupation in contemporary legal theory with the question of the "autonomy" or "relative autonomy" of legal reasoning and legal institutions, and with the problematics of legal "autopoiesis."[24]

The Three Types of Inquiry into Legal Rules

Starting from his three critiques of the social approach (no is-to-ought, no supra-individual social telos, the "relative autonomy" of law), and working from the categorical scheme laid out above, Weber sharply distinguished three types of questions that the socially oriented critics habitually blurred.

Legal validity: A juristic inquiry In a system that is "modern" or of "today," we can ask what, according to legal dogmatics, is the valid legal rule for the legal scientist or the judge interested in deciding how an open legal question or a particular dispute about given facts should be resolved? This is a question of the meaning of the existing system of norms—but only because that is the historically current mode of legal thought, namely LFR. This question has a completely different meaning, or no meaning at all, in other systems and in other periods. While the question of what mode of legal thought will be applied is sociological, the question of the "right answer" within the mode is not. It is a question answered through the application of juristic technique.[25]

Judgments of validity in modern "legal science" (i) are not judgments about a matter of fact, but correct or incorrect interpretations of the logical requirements of the meanings of the system of norms; (ii) they are not ethical judgments, because the logical coherence and gaplessness of the system of norms provides no warrant whatever of the moral desirability or moral (as opposed to legal) validity of the norm system as a whole or of any particular norm; (iii) they are "scientific" judgments because validity is established according to interpretive procedures strictly bound by logic.[26]

Sociological validity: A factual inquiry   What are the norms that actually exist in a society? This is a factual question, requiring first an elaborate differentiation of types of normative systems—all seen as subsets of "regularity"—for example, habit, custom, convention, law, state law. It includes both the question of the substance of the norms (for example, are usurious contracts binding?) and the question of the mode of legal thought.[27]

What causes a particular norm system to come into existence? Like the first sociological question, we can ask this one about both the substance of the norm system and about the mode of legal thought. This is the main topic of Weber's historical sociology of law, discussed in the next subsection.

How does a normative order of the legal type (administered by a specialized staff—for example, of lawfinders) achieve "legitimacy," meaning a probability of obedience higher than what can be explained by the material threat of legal sanctions? This is the question of where legal norms get their intrinsic "oughtness," *in the minds of addressees.* It has nothing to do with our own view of the goodness or badness, rightness or wrongness, of the norm in question. As we have seen above, legal norms can be legitimated by tradition, by charisma (revelation, for example), or "legally," that is, by the mere fact of proper enactment.

What is the impact on the behavior of social actors of factually existing systems of law, in the sense of norms backed by sanctions of various kinds administered by specialized staffs and possessing legitimacy? This is a factual question that requires us to look at what actually influences the practical, particularly the economic behavior of whatever actors we are concerned with. For example, we can ask what norms governed usury in different systems, how effectively they were enforced or evaded, and what the impact of the actual or attempted prohibition of usury was on economic development. We can ask the same kind of question about modes of legal thought: for example, we can ask about the influence of the rationalization of law on the emergence of bureaucracy, or about its influence, through its supposedly superior calculability, on economic development.[28]

Ethical / political judgment: The ethical irrationality of the world   On what should "we" base legal rules when we are choosing consciously among them? For Weber, this is an ethical / political value judgment, and one that we confront in our particular historical circumstance of disenchantment, a process that has affected all the different systems to which we might appeal to ground ethical / political choice by deducing answers from normative postulates or factual regularities, including particularly religion, rationalist natural law, and social science. Weber has a lot to say about this subject, not as a sociologist but as an ethicist in a particular tradition. We will take it up later because it is highly relevant to the contemporary mode of legal thought.

Using the above complex categorical scheme, Weber's sociology of law is a historical account of how the Western European great powers came to have, first, the set of legal concepts that they presently have; second, the set of substantive legal rules through which they regulate economic life; and third, the mode of legal thought through which these rules are administered. His methodology, like that of this chapter with respect to our contemporary mode of legal thought, is "genealogical."[29]

The Origins of Present Legal Categories and Legal Norms of CLT

He starts with the present, in which his contemporaries understand law to be divided into public and private, rights-granting and administrative, tort and crime, and so forth. Moreover, his contemporaries understand LFR to be "the" modern mode of legal thought. Next he takes up the substantive content of a modern system of private law, which consists of what we call property and contract law, commercial law, and corporate law. The system is based on the idea that there is freedom of contract unless the state limits it, which it often does, for a wide variety of reasons, along with a family law system that rejects contractualizaton and commodification of sexual relations through a status conception of marriage, and corporate law regimes that permit economic entities to function legally as self-contained units.

In each case, he shows that the familiar concepts and specific rules of our modern system have a complex legal history, in which the specific economic interests of powerful groups, the agendas of political rulers, and, over and over again, the specifically technical or academic interests of legal specialists drive legal change on the way to the current setup. Just before beginning this summary history, he sums up his conclusion in a famous paragraph:

As we have already pointed out, the mode in which the current basic conceptions of the various fields of law have been differentiated from each other has depended largely upon factors of legal technique and of political organization. Economic factors can therefore be said to have played their part but only to this extent: that certain rationalizations of economic behavior, based upon such phenomena as a market economy or freedom of contract, and the resulting awareness of the underlying and increasingly complex conflicts of interests to be resolved by legal machinery, have influenced the systematization of the law or have intensified the institutionalization of political society. . . . On the other hand, we shall frequently see that those aspects of law which are conditioned by political factors and by the internal structure of legal thought have exercised a strong influence on economic organization.[30]

The odd phrase "certain rationalizations of economic behavior" seems to me to mean the development of modern capitalist enterprise with great economic power; the "resulting awareness" is that law has a large effect on such matters as the distribution of income; and this leads to the development of state institutions designed to control or channel market forces according to the political aims of governments. However, in his actual historical account, Weber often attributes particular legal changes to the needs of particular interest groups or to the needs of a developing economy. The above paragraph exaggerates his opposition to the Marxist approach.

The Development of Lawmaking

Having accounted for the emergence of the specific categories and characteristic rules of a modern legal system (in a manner that is not particularly original or interesting to today's readers, I dare allege), Weber undertakes a fascinating and difficult history of legality. It combines throughout the development of his "universal sociology" (ideal-typical categories, with hypothetical connections among them, for understanding all law in all places throughout history), and his "philosophy of history" (his grand narrative of rationalization and disenchantment).[31]

The universal sociology roams freely around the world, from system to system, showing that such phenomena as oracles, divine revelation, law prophecy, folk assemblies, cadi justice, priestly rationalization of divine law, substantively rational patrimonial administration, and so on, are common to many systems and work in quite similar ways from system to system.[32]

The philosophy of history dimension is about how the West of the European continent, and only the West of the European continent, arrived (a) at the sharp separation of lawmaking and lawfinding, (b) at the view that lawmaking is a secular process through which a state claiming the monopoly of the legitimate exercise of force enacts valid, legal norms as compromises of conflicting interests (legal positivism), and (c) at the practice of elaborating and applying the norms (lawfinding) through logically formal rationality—that is, through the logical elaboration of the meaning of the norm system taken as a whole, excluding all elements of substantive rationality (not to speak of irrational elements). In other words, it turns out that the categorical schemes we presented above simply as a typology were all designed to set up a particular historical narrative progression ending in the Continental present of 1900.

The parts of this Euro-exceptionalist narrative that are most important for our purposes are the latest in time. The peculiar conditions that facilitate the emergence of the notion that law is made by the sovereign and can be elaborated according to LFR include, in chronological order, the peculiarities of Roman law; the peculiarities of canon law administered by the papal bureaucracy; the development of academic law specialists in universities rather than in a powerful guild of legal practitioners; the peculiarities of the revival of Roman law in the late Middle Ages; the need of the seventeenth- and eighteenth-century enlightened despots to consolidate power against feudalism by allying with the bourgeoisie combined with the development of state bureaucracies; the emergence of what Weber calls "revolutionary natural law" (the Rights of Man, particularly to property and freedom of contract, as the only legitimate source of positive law) in the eighteenth century (not to be confused with Catholic natural law); and the creation of the first, modern code by the French in 1804.

Revolutionary Natural Law (the Rights of Man)

We need to pause at Weber's interpretation of the Rights of Man. In the chapter of *Economy and Society* on the sociology of law, Weber introduces revolutionary natural law as a key element in the emergence of the modern conception of lawmaking (we hold positive law to the test of natural rights) and of LFR: "[T]he natural law axioms of legal rationalism . . . alone were able to create norms of a formal type. . . . "[33] Specifically, what happened was the elaboration of the abstract principles of revolutionary natural law, and the fragmentary, not yet "sublimated" provisions of the French Civil Code, into the pyramidally structured, deductive, complete system that I called the will theory: "The purest type of [formal natural law] is that . . . which arose in the seventeenth and eighteenth centuries as a result of the already mentioned influences, especially in the form of the 'contract theory' and more particularly the individualistic aspects of that theory." He goes on to elaborate, and mock, the derivation of the rules of a laissez-faire economy from the individualistic conception. Here Weber simply appropriates the work of the socially oriented critics of classical legal thought (Ihering, Gierke, and Ehrlich). The construct of an individualistic will theory used to deductively elaborate a complete system was their work and not his.

Revolutionary natural law clearly produces "value-rational" orientations to action in the form of rules that are to be observed regardless of the consequences (though it adds elements of substantive rationality in the form of reasonableness tests the minute jurists begin to elaborate it into a normative system.)[34] But how does this type of law fit into Weber's typology of legitimacy? His most basic model of legal development is that tradition is disrupted by charismatic revelation of new norms that are then rationalized (this is one aspect of the famous "routinization of charisma") by the specialized staffs that administer them. Charismatic revelation is at first strictly associated with the divine (oracles; revelation—as in Moses and Mohammed). Religion plays a role here, too, since Weber follows his friend Jellinek in locating the sources of the Rights of Man in "the religious motivation provided by the rationalistic [Protestant] sects. . . . "[35] But natural law is not it-self religious. In fact, "[i]t is the specific and only consistent type of legiti-macy of a legal order which can remain once religious revelation and the authoritarian sacredness of a tradition and its bearers have lost their force."[36]

We have to go elsewhere in *Economy and Society*, to the discussion entitled "Sect, Church and Democracy," for an explanation. The belief in the Rights of Man is the:

charismatic glorification of "Reason," which found a characteristic expression in its apotheosis in Robespierre, [and] is the last form that charisma has adopted in its fate-ful historical course. It is clear that these postulates of formal equality and economic mobility paved the way for the destruction of all patrimonial and feudal law in favor of abstract norms and hence indirectly of bureaucratization. It is also clear that they facilitated the expansion of capitalism. The basic Rights of Man made it possible for the capitalist to use things and men freely, just as this-worldly asceticism—adopted with the same dogmatic variations—and the specific discipline of the sects bred the capitalist spirit and the rational "professional" who was needed by capitalism.[37]

Natural Law Disintegrates into Legal Positivism

Natural law, and the individualistic will theory developed from it, disinte-grated, according to Weber, during the second half of the nineteenth cen-tury. The reasons are the following: first, the rise of socialist substantive nat-ural law theories proclaiming "the right to work," "the right to a minimum standard of living," "the right to the full product of one's labor," and more. Second, "natural law doctrine was destroyed by the evolutionary dogmatism of Marxism, while from the side of 'official' learning it was annihilated partly by the Comtean evolutionary scheme and partly by the historicist theories of organic growth."[38] In other words, classical legal thought, as the will the-ory, was destroyed by its two enemies, namely Marxist theory and the so-cially oriented reform theory (the latter was "official" only in Bismarck's Germany). Weber sums up his diagnosis in a famous passage:

Compared with firm beliefs in the positive religiously revealed character of a legal norm or in the inviolable sacredness of an age old tradition, even the most convinc-ing norms arrived at by abstraction [from natural law axioms] seem to be too subtle to serve as the bases of a legal system. Consequently, legal positivism has, at least for the time being, advanced irresistibly. The disappearance of the old natural law con-ceptions has destroyed all possibility of providing the law with a metaphysical dig-nity by virtue of its immanent qualities. In the great majority of its most important provisions, it has been unmasked all too visibly, indeed, as the technical means of a compromise between conflicting interests.[39]

Weber's Sociology of Law Incompatible with the Socially Oriented View of CLT

There are two further striking traits of Weber's historical sociology of law that we need to note, just because they distinguish his attitude from that of the social critics.

Historicizing the substantive content of CLT   Whereas each of the schools mentioned earlier (the historical school, utilitarians, Kant or Locke natural rights people) had believed that we got to the will theory through the *development of an idea*, he showed that the free contract/property regime was best understood as a historical accident, with many diverse causes, and that many of the causes were "disreputable." This idea was incompatible with the critique developed by the social people because their theory made CLT a highly adequate adaptation to past conditions favorable to individualism (the yeoman theory in the United States; the early-modern, postfeudal situation in Europe).

The freedom/coercion flip   The various schools that agreed on the will theory, and that it was the working out of an idea, also agreed that the idea that got worked out was freedom, or at least autonomy. Weber argued that far from the realization of the will, or of freedom, the modern order of freedom of contract and property was a regime of coercion.[40]

Although the social people had themselves extensively developed the notion that unequal bargaining power rendered formal equality practically meaningless, Weber's stark approach was incompatible with the social approach for two reasons: it presented the choice as between modes of coercion, with different distributive outcomes and different consequences for economic growth, period. For the social, the idea of adaptation to the functions, purposes, or needs of "society" provided an objective basis for good law (from *is* to *ought*), law that would correctly adjust the needs of the individual to the needs of the collective, so a tragic choice between coercions was the last thing they had in mind. Their rhetoric emphasized that their opponents were social scientifically *vieux jeux*, rather than that they were invested in a mode of domination.

WEBER'S AMBIVALENT ATTITUDE TOWARD LOGICALLY FORMAL LEGAL RATIONALITY

The Social Critique of LFR: The Abuse of Deduction

The social critique of CLT was that it failed to develop the rules needed for the new game of interdependence, for two reasons. The first was its ideological commitment to individualism, an outdated philosophy both as description and as norm. Second, according to the social people, CLT people understood themselves to operate as interpreters (judges, administrators, law professors) according to a system of induction and deduction premised on the coherence, or internal logical consistency, of the system of enacted legal norms. One mode was to locate the applicable enacted rule; a second was to develop a rule to fill a gap by a chain of deductions from a more abstract enacted rule or principle; a third, the method of "constructions," was to determine what unenacted principle must be part of "the system," given the various enacted elements in it, if we were to regard it as internally coherent, and then derive a gap-filling rule from the construction.

It is important to recognize that, like his model of the will theory, Weber's ideal type of LFR, which he treats as the "highest" type of legal rationality, is in every way identical to the ideal type developed by the social people, here Ihering, Ehrlich, and especially Geny, to describe CLT. Logically formal rationality, as a descriptive category, is theirs, not his. The difference between him and them was in their respective attitudes toward this mode understood as highly typical of actual late nineteenth-century practice.

In the social analysis, because interpreters must always be logically compelled in one of these ways, they could never legitimately work consciously to adapt the law to the new conditions of the late nineteenth century. Nonetheless those conditions constantly presented them, as interpreters, with gaps. What the CLT people had to do, to stay loyal to their role as they conceived it, was to "abuse deduction." They had to make decisions reached on other grounds look like the operation of deductive work premised on the coherence of the system. And the abuse of deduction permitted the smuggling in, not of the general desiderata of social evolution, but of the partisan ideologies of the parties to the conflicts between labor and capital, large and small business, of the century's end.

In response, the social people had four positive proposals: (a) from the social *is* to the adaptive *ought* for law, (b) from the deductive to the instrumental approach to the formulation of norms, (c) not only by the legislature but also by legal scientists and judges and administrative agencies openly acknowledging gaps in the formally valid order, (d) anchored in the normative practices ("living law") that groups intermediate between the state and the individual were continuously developing in response to the needs of the new interdependent social formation. We know already that Weber had no use for the first point. We now take up his critique of the remaining three.

Weber's Pros and Cons of Logically Formal Rationality

Weber's attitude toward LFR as characteristic of CLT was highly ambivalent. He was aware of the social critique of CLT for the abuse of deduction, and he was careful always to treat logically formal rationality as an ideal type never fully achieved in practice, and maybe even theoretically unachievable. It has its origin, like the substance of modern law, in historical accidents rather than any cunning of history. But the source of his ambivalence had nothing to do with the kind of internal critique of abuse of deduction that the social people leveled against it. Quite the contrary.

The cons of LFR   LFR was a factor in producing the universal bureaucratization of social life, and bureaucracy was equally characteristic of the state apparatus, private capitalist business enterprises, charitable organizations, and churches. Bureaucracy would have to be the characteristic mode of organization of a socialist state and society (state ownership of the means of production would require an increase rather than a decrease in bureaucracy). Moreover, it was bureaucracy rather than either the state or the capitalist market in the abstract that most substantially restrained individual freedom and agency in the modern world. The basic sociopolitical problem of modernity was therefore not the choice between capitalism and socialism but the choice between ever-increasing bureaucratization and whatever alternative might be found.

Together with the argument that the contract/property regime was one mode of coercion among others rather than the realization of human freedom, the argument for universal bureaucratization as the essence of modernity amounted to a radical rejection of the public/private distinction, as it had developed, first in liberal formulae and then in dialectical opposition to the liberal formulae, in socialist thought. The choice was neither between private freedom and public servitude (the liberal version) nor between capitalist servitude and freedom through the collective (the socialist version).

Note just how different this mode of critique is from the abuse-of-deduction idea. Here it is the determinacy, the calculability, of LFR that is the problem, rather than the reverse.

The pros of LFR   But LFR is "how we do it now." It is what we mean by "dogmatic legal analysis" or "legal science," and it would be silly to deny that it exists and is a force in the world. It has many of the good attributes that make bureaucracy, both public and private, the most efficient form of administration, by comparison with which the alternatives are mere dilettantism. In particular, it has an important role in guaranteeing that bureaucracy is calculable and can proceed *sine ira ac studio.*

It is associated as well with the accomplishments of the liberal revolutions, in the way of formal equality, democracy, and due process that, we cannot deny, have transformed our world for the better. LFR, because it operates by the logical analysis of meaning, and then the deductive application of norm to facts, guarantees the "impersonality" of legal administration. That is, it guarantees that only the legislator, who has "the right to make law," makes it in fact.

Many of the same results can be, and indeed have been, achieved by the lower form of formal rationality represented by the common law. Weber, moreover, concedes that while calculability is crucial to capitalism, LFR is not—indeed, capitalism flourished first under the common law, and when the systems compete, the common law tends to win out. But the reasons for this are no credit to the Anglo-Saxons. It is the highly biased irrationality of their system (for example, the cadi justice of justices of the peace to repress the rural masses), that largely explains their success. The common law may have worked, but there is no aspect of it that Weber sees as on the same level of development as Continental LFR.[41]

Closer to home, both the substantive rationality of welfarism (that is, enlightened despotism), and natural law, whether elaborated deductively from individualist premises or as a socially oriented substantive doctrine, have proved failures at the task of providing operative techniques for the development of a legal order adapted to administration of justice in a centralized bureaucratic state. That was the whole point of his narrative of the displacement of natural law by positivism.[42] LFR was, in this view, a big advance, but more importantly, it was all that was left of the ambitions of legal rationalism as a general phenomenon.

Weber's Dismissal of the "Antiformal Tendencies of Modern Law"

The antiformal tendencies of modern law are, according to Weber, multiple. They include the tendency of formal law to adopt subjective rather than objective tests of intention, as well as subjective ethical notions like "good faith," in response to the need of the business community for legal standards that will correspond to the needs of business practice. Other pressures in the same direction included:

the demand for substantive justice by certain social class interests and ideologies; . . . the tendencies inherent in certain forms of political authority of either authoritarian or democratic character concerning the ends of law which are respectively appropriate to them [that is, democracy appeases the masses antiformally, and authoritarianism keeps power antiformally]; and also the demand of the "laity" for a system of justice which would be intelligible to them; finally, . . . antiformal tendencies are being promoted by the ideologically rooted power aspirations of the legal profession itself.[43]

This set of demands, Weber concedes, responds to the fact that "the development of the formal qualities of the law certainly shows some peculiarly antinomian traits,"[44] and has produced a body of "modern sociological and philosophical analyses, many of which are of a high scholarly value." But all of them fly in the face of modern reality.[45] Weber understood himself to be addressing a complex of positions and attitudes, including "demands for a 'social law' to be based upon such emotionally colored ethical postulates as justice or human dignity,"[46] and the "school of 'free law,'" which tried to show that there would be gaps in every statutory scheme, "in view of the irrationality of the facts of life; that, in countless instances the application of the statute 'as interpreted' is a delusion; and that the decision is and ought to be made in the light of concrete evaluations rather than in accordance with formal norms."[47]

In the same direction were theories, here presumably speaking of Ehrlich, according to which the "true foundation of the law is entirely 'sociological,'" meaning that judges should respond to "norms which are factually valid in the course of everyday life and independently of their reaffirmation or declaration in legal procedure."[48] Even further in the same vein, some scholars (Ehrlich again?), first "degrade" statutory enactment to a "mere 'symptom'" of sociological validity, and then argue that "no precedent should be regarded as binding beyond its concrete facts," to reach the conclusion that the judge should engage in "free balancing of values in every case."[49]

In response to these theories, neo-Kantians (Stammler?), Comteans (Duguit?), and Catholic natural lawyers propose rational reconstructions that will "reestablish an objective standard of values."[50] Putting them together, the set of antiformal tendencies "are agreed only in their rejection of the once universally accepted and until recently prevalent *petitio principii* of the consistency and 'gaplessness' of the legal order."[51]

Weber's response remains puzzling. As he lays out the positions, he repeatedly points out that what is proposed is a reversion to substantive justice, a "challenge to legal formalism,"[52] and here is the key charge, that the reformers, "in view of the inevitability of value-compromises, very often [would] have to forget about abstract norms and, at least in cases of conflict, would have to admit concrete evaluations, i.e., not only nonformal but irrational lawfinding."[53] Weber here uses the word *irrational*, according to his categorical scheme, to refer to decision that is oriented to the facts of the particular case rather than to rule application. In context, this means that because of ideological conflict on the one hand, and the vagueness of notions like social justice on the other, the judge will have to decide each case on its facts. The program that he attributes to the antiformal thinkers fits well with this conclusion, since Weber sees them, as noted above, as committed to freeing the judge up for the "balancing of values in every case." At the least, "the juristic precision of judicial opinions will be seriously impaired if sociological, economic, or ethical argument were to take the place of legal concepts."[54]

Although he did not present it in this section, Weber had a sharp critique of the notion that the "living law" developed by intermediary groups, in the mode of Gierke and Ehrlich, should be regarded as having ethical warrant or a claim to being responsive to social needs, just because of its "organic" origin. Although he is happy to "categorically deny that 'law' exists only where legal coercion is guaranteed by the political authority,"[55] there is never the slightest suggestion that customary law is in any way more adaptive or otherwise valuable than state law. The "interests" that drive social development are always those of individuals or competing social groups, and never those of "society."[56] He teasingly points out that, given the way Continental judges are recruited and trained, "it is by no means certain that those classes which are negatively privileged today, especially the working class, may safely expect from an informal administration of justice those results which are claimed for it by the ideology of the jurists [that is, the social people]."[57]

Instead of developing this kind of critique, Weber repeatedly notes that the socially oriented reformers represent the desire of the legal profession to avoid the status degradation associated with the rationalization of a once learned and autonomous occupation.[58] And then, after elaborately summarizing the arguments, he ends abruptly: "At this place we cannot undertake a detailed discussion or a full criticism of these tendencies, which, as our brief sketch has shown, have produced quite contradictory answers."[59] True to his word, he does not make a serious effort to come to grips with the socially oriented critique of LFR, except to reiterate the charge of irrationalism and add an interesting analogy to religion. (Remember that proposals for ad hoc judicial decision or the balancing of values from case to case fall under Weber's definition of methodological irrationality.)

All variants of the developments which have led to the rejection of that purely logical systematization of the law as it had been developed by Pandectist learning, including even the irrational variants, are in their turn products of a self-defeating scientific rationalization of legal thought as well as of its relentless self-criticism. To the extent that they do not themselves have a rationalistic character, they are a flight into the irrational and as such a consequence of the increasing rationalization of legal technique. In that respect they are parallel to the irrationalization of religion.[60]

In the last paragraph of his sociology of law, he has this to say to all the tendencies that want to openly acknowledge judicial discretion and infuse lawfinding with self-conscious concern for substantive justice: "Inevitably the notion must expand that the law is a rational technical apparatus, which is continually transformable in the light of expediential considerations and devoid of all sacredness of content."[61]

III. Logically Formal Rationality in Weber's Sociology of Domination

Weber's attitude toward the social abuse-of-deduction critique of LFR seems strange in light of the developments in legal theory over the past century. Weber's treatment of its inventors seems in retrospect dismissive at best and often tendentious or obtuse. He failed to distinguish the critique of the abuse of deduction from the various kinds of embryonic alternatives being bruited about, and particularly insisted on associating the antiformal critique with cadi justice. To put it bluntly, since he wrote, the socially oriented critique of LFR has won close to universal acceptance, even though the solution of case-by-case adjudication has been equally universally rejected. In modern legal theory, the single most important question is what to do after the demise of LFR, and this is a question Weber resolutely refused to face.

In this section, I offer an explanation for Weber's stance, based on the place of LFR in Weber's sociology of domination in modern society. We have seen already that, in this sociology, the modern system of property and contract law, bureaucratically administered, structuring a market economy also bureaucratically administered, constitutes a pervasively coercive social order, rather than either the realization of human freedom or an invitation to socialist reform. I will argue that in order for this position to make sense, Weber had to defend LFR against the social critique.

RELIGION, RATIONALIZATION, DISENCHANTMENT, MYSTICISM: THE IRON CAGE NARRATIVE

In Weber's sociology, the domains are religion, science, politics, the economy, sexuality, and art.[62] There are complex analogies in the evolution of the domains, established through a basic conceptual vocabulary that includes the concepts of disenchantment, rationalization, bureaucratization, irrationalization, and sectarianism. It is striking that in his "philosophy of history" writings, Weber does not, as far as I know, ever offer an analysis of the legal domain that establishes the analogies with these other ones. This in spite of the fact that he wrote an enormous amount about law, and characterized law in ways that are full of parallels with the others, including the importance of specialists and specialized knowledge, bureaucratization, and above all, rationalization. In fact, Weber treats the development of LFR as of prime importance both to politics and to economics. The rise of the modern bureaucratic state is intimately intertwined with LFR, and LFR makes that state a calculable element in the economy. At the same time, the administration of large corporations comes to resemble more and more closely the administration of the state apparatus.

But law is just as intimately important to the evolution of religion and science. The rationalization of religion is partly a matter of the development of the first bureaucracy by the Catholic Church, and a large part of that bureaucracy's function was the rational development and application of canon law. The modern university, which is the producer of modern science, is a state institution with an internally bureaucratic organization as well. There is the same double relevance of law: organized religions develop religious law and do it bureaucratically; universities develop scientific laws and do it bureaucratically.

The metanarrative: initially, all the domains, and those of sex and art as well, are bound together in religion. Religious thought struggles for a rational answer to the question of theodicy—or of the apparent ethical irrationality of the world (the good suffer, the evil are rewarded). The attempt to find a rational answer sets us down a path of "disenchantment" as it turns out to be possible to explain more and more of what happens in the world without positing miracles, and then without positing the existence of God. This is the work of science. Disenchantment is an existential or phenomenological category. It means loss of belief that humans arrive at birth in a material and social world where events are part of a system of ethical meaning (one that includes supernatural powers) that we have "merely" to discover.

The knowledge of the world as a place of cause and effect goes along with the gradual development of the science of norms—that is, of how to use legal technique to organize people in the state and the economy. Disenchantment here overtakes, first, the divinely revealed laws of social organization, and second, the divine right of kings and other authorities to issue legitimate commands (all the way down the great chain of being to the level of, say, the manor). Together with scientific disenchantment, political disenchantment allows a vast increase of power over the material world, so long as we use the power for secular ends. This is rationalization. Its highest accomplishment is bureaucratization in state and economy.

But religion does not go away. It struggles against science and against legal disenchantment to affirm cosmic meaning accessible to reason, but it also retains and develops "irrational" tendencies, particularly mysticism. It is more and more forced to concede that the world works without direct divine intervention and that reason cannot find the world's ethical meaning simply through the rational interpretation of what we know about it. But it insists more and more strongly that there are other truths, ways of knowing, and experiences than those that are made intelligible through the techniques of disenchantment, or mastered for secular ends through rationalization and bureaucracy.

The organizational correlate of religion's surrender of science and the state to secular forces is religious sectarianism. The process of polarization, so to speak, in which religious meanings are more and more to be found by the individual seeker "beyond" the domains of secular activity undermines, though only slowly, the aspiration to theocratic rule, or even to the religious organization of society through "establishment." The end result is the transition from "church" to "sect," which is a voluntary community of believers existing in the private sphere of civil society without public powers and functioning within the state's regime of civil law. (This strongly resembles Marx's essay "On the Jewish Question.")

When Weber describes the antiformalism of the social people as a disparate set of irrational reactions to the rationalization of legal science, it is to this version of religious development that he refers. It is not a flattering allusion. He clearly regards disenchantment not just as inevitable but as a process whose "truth for us" only "grown-up babies," as he puts it, can deny. He recognizes the fact of mystical otherworldly experience, but does not see it as even a little challenge to disenchantment and rationalization within actual social practices. Antiformal reactions within the actual social practice of law are destined for well-deserved defeat if all we can say for them is that they are the analogue to the flight into mysticism and sectarianism in religion.

In this version of the metanarrative, all the emphasis is on the power of the autonomous "logics" of state and economy, their imperviousness to transformation through religion, and the foolishness of resisting the benefits that come along with acceptance of rationalization. Of course, the situation has the downside that the autonomous logics are logics of domination, and that a disenchanted world has a basic grimness because of our nostalgia for lost meaning, even if we have the refuge of a manly embrace of the partial ethic of our particular calling within one of the domains.

Our modernity is further redeemed, to however limited an extent, by the existence of two other domains, love / eroticism and art, which split from religion through a process closely linked to disenchantment in economy and polity. With the decline of public religious power, they are capable of holding their own and even developing their autonomy as concrete social practices against the perennial hostility of religion. Eroticism and art for art's sake are self-consciously irrational, and self-consciously resistant, as yet, to modern-style social control. Nonetheless, they are in the shadow of rationalization and bureaucratization (sexual science, Foucauldian institutions of sexual discipline, art theory, art markets, museums). We might add (Weber doesn't) that they develop their own intense sectarianism, in the form of the warring art movements and sexual ideologies.

The Disenchantment of Lawmaking (Not of LFR) Fits the Metanarrative

The coherence of this picture of modernity is promoted by a version of the history of modes of legal thought that emphasizes the progressive disappearance of value-rational sources for the legitimation of legal/bureaucratic domination. As Part II explained, Weber offers just such a narrative. Ultimate norms are first legitimated by tradition, with change brought about by charismatic revelation claiming a divine origin. Charismatic revelation is routinized in theocratic regimes into religious law of a more or less formally rational character. Then there is the last gasp of charisma in the form of revolutionary natural law (the Rights of Man) quickly routinized into a deductive legal science, and equally quickly discredited by positivist critique of its fanciful state of nature myths, vagueness, and internal inconsistencies. Another important factor is the rise of the variants of the social ideology, splitting the charismatic camp and reducing its plausibility as pure reason.

All the while, logically formal rationality and state bureaucracy are emerging downstream, so to speak, from the battles at the abstract level of God versus Reason, just as rational economic practices develop in the shadow of medieval and early-modern monarchical absolutist controversies about how to secure the welfare of the populace. Theories of natural law are in fact the last representatives not just of charismatic law-giving but also of premodern enchantment as a general phenomenon. In the words of Colliot-Thélène:

The structure that determines the recent evolution of natural law doctrines [Enthüllung, or the "unveiling" of legal norms as merely compromises of conflicting interests] is closely related to that of disenchantment: the veil is lifted on the reality of law, as the charm is removed that had more generally hidden from prior generations the prosaic character of the here-below. In the brief span of a century, or rather of a few decades, the concept of law repeated, on a smaller scale, the very process of desacralization and elimination of transcendence that at a general level engenders modernity. The "formalist" definition of the legal mode of domination recognizes this twice-over reduction, within which the second in time [the "unveiling" of law as mere compromise] brings the first [general disenchantment] to a close at the same time that it reproduces it. If natural law was the only form of legitimacy that remained after the disappearance of belief in religious revelations or the sacredness of tradition, formal legal rationality was in turn all that remained of the legitimacy of the Rational State once the values on which that legality had originally rested had lost their persuasive power.[63]

Weber's Commitment to the Scientificity of LFR Explained as Necessary in Order for Modernity to Be an Iron Cage

It is at least plausible, it seems to me, that Weber's dismissal of the antiformal social as irrational had one origin in the role of LFR in his theory of modernity as I have just sketched it. Weber is committed to the tragic situation of loss of meaning within a system of domination by the autonomous logics of the spheres—this is the famous "Iron Cage" of modernity—redeemed only by the possibility of stoic pursuit of a vocation and the private pursuit of the erotic and the aesthetic.

The "scientificity" of LFR is essential here because it is the glue that holds the rational/bureaucratic structure of domination together after disenchantment has deprived it of all external traditional or charismatic legitimation. The following seems to me a key to Weber's whole sociology; it is pretty brilliant besides, and so worthy of quotation at length:

> Present-day economic life rests on opportunities acquired through contracts. It is true, the private interests in the obligations of contact, and the common interest of all property holders in the mutual protection of property are still considerable, and individuals are still markedly influenced by convention and custom even today. Yet, the influence of these factors has declined due to the disintegration of tradition, i.e., of the tradition-determined relationships as well as of the belief in their sacredness. Furthermore, class interests have come to diverge more sharply from one another then ever before. The tempo of modern business communication requires a promptly and predictably functioning legal system, i.e., one which is guaranteed by the strongest coercive power. Finally, modern economic life by its very nature has destroyed those other associations which used to be the bearers of law and thus of legal guaranties. This has been the result of the development of the market. The universal predominance of the market consociation requires on the one hand a legal system the functioning of which is *calculable* in accordance with rational rules. On the other hand, the constant expansion of the market, which we shall get to know as an inherent tendency of the market consociation, has favored the monopolization and regulation of all "legitimate" coercive power by *one* universalist coercive institution through the disintegration of all particularist status–determined and other coercive structures which have been resting mainly on economic monopolies.[64]

Given the effacement of traditional and charismatic authority, as well as of the nonstate institutions that once guaranteed order, we couldn't speak of a rationalized, bureaucratized set of domains constituting an iron cage of particular logics if we didn't believe that LFR could function, at least in a gross way, to put the dominant order into effect at the level of application. And the moral picture of tragic loss of meaning would no longer be plausible if within the key domain of legal practice there was the possibility of redemption by the reintroduction, antiformally, of substantive ethical elements. If that were the case, all bureaucrats would have the possibility of agency within their jobs, rather than being condemned to vocational formalism.[65]

IV. The Disenchantment of Logically Formal Rationality

Here begins a second Weberian narrative, in which his sociology works strongly against his own interpretation of modernity in general, and against his defense of LFR in particular.

REHABILITATING THE IRRATIONAL MOMENT WITHIN RATIONALIZED DOMAINS

The Irrational Moment in Economy, Science, and Politics

In the last narrative, religion retreated into mysticism, confronted by the overwhelming theoretical success and practical power of rationalization in science, state, and economy. But there is another Weberian narrative running parallel to this one. In science, state, and economy, under conditions of bureaucratization, there remains an irreducible, irrational element to the activity within each domain. In the Iron Cage discussion, the logics of the domains are both unitary and irresistible, but in conflict with one another. In this second narrative the logics of the domains produce, over and over again, situations of undecidability.

Because this point is more familiar for state and science than for the economy ("Politics as a Vocation" and "Science as a Vocation"), we can begin with the economy. The most developed modern bureaucratic economic systems run partly on the charismatic irrational principle represented by entrepreneurship as risk-taking, by the management of monopolies, and specifically by "robber baronage." Weber's robber barons are individuals who manage to operate outside the constraining logic of competitive price determination, taking advantage of opportunities that are objectively present, but also capitalizing on their own charismatic qualities.

In science, it turns out that "creativity" is not reducible to bureaucratically determinable characteristics that govern the specialized subdomains of the modern university. It involves an agonistic, irrational, intuitive moment without which no amount of learning and technique can accomplish anything of note. In politics, there is a similar split: the state is reduced more and more to a bureaucracy administering a rule system according to LFR, but the politicians are engaged in "fighting" for power, and have to make decisions with big ethical implications using an ethical apparatus that is internally contradictory and so often leaves them just having to "decide." This is the much-commented-on "Schmittian" element in Weber's thought,[66] shared with other post-Nietzschean modes, such as existentialism.[67]

At this point in the analysis, science, economic management, and politics have more in common with love/eroticism and art than at first appeared. Each is a domain split internally between a bureaucratic element operating according to LFR and an irrational but equally essential element within which LFR does not operate, and neither do more mundane techniques for rationally deciding what to do.

The problem is not just that each domain has a logic and that the logics (or Gods, in Weber's terminology) are at war.[68] The situation is much more dramatic, because within the part of each domain where LFR does not operate, there are irreducibly conflicting principles at work, rather than a single logic. Loyalty to one's vocation turns out not to be an answer to the disintegration of the world into antagonistic value-spheres, because antagonism is present within each sphere.

This is where sectarianism comes in. Just as religious irrationalism favors religious sectarianism, the irreducibly irrational in politics favors ideological sectarianism and nationalism. In the economy, it favors national economic rivalry even against the "logic of the market." Only in science, in Weber's view, does the power of the rational grid confine irrationalism to the moment of individual creativity (what would Thomas Kuhn say about that?).

Let me hasten to say that the reading I have just proposed is at least as partial as the previous one, in which science, state, and economy starkly oppose religion, sex, and art. It is moreover an "ideal-typical" rendering of disenchantment as a general phenomenon, and I have embellished Weber's account to give it an internal consistency that will be useful, I hope, in the analysis of the fate of LFR in the contemporary mode of legal thought.

Remember that the puzzle before us is to understand Weber's theory of logically formal rationality, and to trace the fate of his theory into the contemporary mode of legal thought. As a first step, we have already distinguished the question of moral or ethical validity of norms in a system from the question of the mode of legal reasoning once a set of norms is given legislatively. LFR is, in Weber's view, the modern way to do legal interpretation to generate new, legal norms scientifically from the legislative postulates. Keeping to his distinction, the ideal-typical narrative of disenchantment applies without much strain to Weber's account of the enterprise of producing valid legal norms by declaration (rather than by interpretation, as in LFR). His sociology of law elaborates the series of steps that lead us to the modern situation he calls positivism and that we call classical legal thought (see Figure 13.1).

FIGURE 13.1. *Weber's Sociology of Law*

Disenchantment	Law disengaged from religion (oracles, divine revelation)
Rationalization	Legislative codification + logically formal legal rationality
Bureaucratization	Specialized, unitary national legal system
Irrationalization	Natural rights theory (charismatization of reason)
Sectarianism	Proliferation of natural rights theories (e.g., social vs. individual)

The Disenchantment of Lawmaking Merges It into the Political Domain

In the preceding discussion, what is disenchanted is lawmaking understood as such. Weber's theory of the disenchantment of lawmaking ended with its fusion into politics—specifically legislative politics. In other words, once legitimations for lawmaking had reached the point where multiple natural rights theories, Marxism, and the variants of the social ideology contended to define the necessary, ethical substance of the legal order, and none of them were plausibly rationally compelled (they were merely rival charismatic claims), lawmaking was just a branch of politics. This meant that the lawmaking process was subject to the logic of the political sphere—it was about "fighting" between interest groups and ideological sects. Politicians made their decisions about what law to create in the same situation of ethical undecidability (due to contradictory moral imperatives) that applied to all other political questions.

When Weber spoke of the "antiformal tendencies of modern law" he was not referring to the proliferation of schools of thought about what to legislate or declare constitutionally, or about the merger of lawmaking and politics. These had been the topics of the previous sections. They had established for the legal domain the same internal structure—progressive rationalization and bureaucratization in one sector of the domain, combined with irrationalization and sectarianism in another—that existed for religion, politics, economy, sex, and art.

"The Antiformal Tendencies of Modern Law" is rather about an irrationalist assault on the supposedly hard, rational kernel of LFR that remains within the legal domain at the level of interpretation after law-declaration has been politicized. This kernel is important not just to the legal domain, but through its role in the general, social, form of bureaucracy to all the other domains that have undergone the modern form of rationalization.

THE IMPLAUSIBILITY OF LFR AFTER THE POLITICIZATION
OF LAWMAKING

There seems on the face of it to be a serious, indeed invalidatingly serious, problem with Weber's attitude toward LFR. It is implausible that lawmaking, whether by charismatic divine revelation, natural law deductions, or positivist enactment, can lose enchanting power, while LFR grows and even becomes stronger. The problem can be stated simply: Because there are contradictory legislative ideals, we can no longer "presuppose the coherence of the system." As we've seen already, according to Weber, Western legal thought moved from natural law to positivism for two reasons. First, the vagueness, inconsistency, and other problems of natural law makes it inapt as a basis for a modern, legal, bureaucratic order. Second, it was divided from within by the development of new types of charismatic, natural-law thinking, and the variants of the social ideology. These developments undermine both the charismatic and the rational claims of the eighteenth-century "revolutionary" natural law of the bourgeoisie, that is, the "individualist" natural law of absolute property rights and freedom of contract.

Positivism becomes the theory of lawmaking because natural law is implausible in theory, but also because *actual legislation* comes more and more to embody both the program of revolutionary natural law and that of social law. The corpus of codified rules thus no longer plausibly translates a single set of value-rational judgments (say, the rights of man) into the details of legislation. Rather, in Weber's formula already quoted, law "has been unmasked all too visibly, indeed, as the technical means of a compromise between conflicting interests."[69]

This development put LFR in jeopardy. There are two components to the modern legal order: codification and the technique of interpreting the code "as though it were" an internally consistent document each of whose concrete or (in the European phrase) "material" provisions can be understood to be an implication of the meaning of a more abstract provision. In this system, as I explained above, gaps are filled by the analysis of the system, presupposed to be internally coherent, to build a chain downward from some unquestionably valid abstract provision, or upward to, and then downward from, some logically required though unenacted abstract provision.

So in LFR, the statement that the system is "presumed to be gapless" has a particular meaning. It does *not* mean that the code, or the body of legislatively enacted statutes, contains a provision that can be directly applied to every case that comes before the judges. Quite the contrary, LFR presupposes that the judge (or professor) will often find, in the body of legislatively enacted rules, no particular rule that applies to the particular facts of his case.

But the system is indeed gapless in the sense that, by the logical analysis of meaning, the judge or professor can derive deductively a rule that will be the correct one to apply. This, again, involves both finding enacted abstractions from which to derive the subrule and "constructing" new abstractions where they are logically necessary, given the premise of the coherence of the whole code.

The jeopardy created by the recognition of the vagueness of revolutionary natural law combined with the rise of rival forms of natural law was that the method of LFR might no longer be plausible. Why not? If there are rival abstract principles of natural law, representing say the bourgeois property/contract version and the socialist, labor-based version, and each approach has been embodied in legislation, the presumption of internal coherence is false in fact.

This is jeopardy but not yet actual disaster (that is, disenchantment), for the following reason. Weber's modern mode combined LFR with the elaborate "materialization" of law by the legislative adoption of ever more detailed statutory and administrative norms covering more and more particular cases. This meant that there was a kind of race going on, in which the plausible determinacy of the legal order was shored up (by the multiplication of specific enacted norms) at the same time that the plausibility of rational interpretation of the norms was undermined (by the multiplication of flatly incompatible abstract principles, each with a claim to explain a large part of the concrete multitude of enactments).

Already at the time Weber wrote, it seemed obvious to many legal theorists that this race would end in the utter discrediting of logically formal rationality. These are the very theorists he criticizes in the "The Antiformal Tendencies of Modern Law." His dismissive characterization of their position I have already mentioned. But they had good reasons for arguing that LFR was an implausible description of the way legal reasoning worked. Moreover, their experience of the disenchantment of LFR—that is, of its loss of all persuasive power—seems in retrospect a highly plausible consequence, in Weber's own terms, of the dynamic of rationalization. Weber was wrong to see them as irrational in the mode of the religious flight into mysticism. He should have recognized that what was happening was exactly the same movement toward decisionism, this time within the process of legal interpretation, that he had brilliantly traced for the process of formal law declaration, on the model of economy, science, and politics. *Gaps were inevitable, the stakes were high, many valid norms were the product of the abuse of deduction.*

The implausibility of LFR derived, in large part, from two "discoveries" (by which word I mean to endorse them). First, the dynamism of the capitalist economy generated, constantly, increasingly, legal gaps or conflicts involving large economic and political stakes. Second, a large part of the body of norms that applied to economic and political life was judge-made according to LFR, but had involved in its formulation the "abuse of deduction."

While these norms were supposedly derived by the "logical interpretation of meaning" from other norms legitimated by enactment, the derivations were flawed. Because the derivations were flawed, they were open to the charge that they were illegitimate in their resolution of the high stakes issues involved. Worse, they might well represent not random errors in deduction, but "motivated errors" of an ideological kind. The judges were open to the charge that they had settled these high-stakes questions according, as Holmes put it in 1897, to their "economic sympathies."[70]

To the extent that this diagnosis was accurate, the modern judge (or the modern law professor, in systems where professors were understood to have the main task of legal interpretation) confronted a dilemma that Weber never took seriously. The judge was likely to have to decide, as the economy and polity rapidly changed shape, on the choice of a valid, legal rule. Even if the choice seemed to occur at a low level of the system, and therefore not to have major systemic implications, it might have very large economic or political implications (think of modern decisions about intellectual property, or *Bush* v. *Gore*). The massive body of enacted norms is, ex hypothesi, no help. It can't just be "applied"—or there would be no "gap."

The enacted or "constructed" principles from which the concrete norms supposedly derive are contradictory. They embody, for example, radically different attitudes toward freedom of contract according to whether they come from the "revolutionary" or the "social" version of natural law. Moreover, many of the concrete rules that might seem most relevant were chosen through judicial or "scientific" (by professors) "logical interpretations of meaning" that now appear open to the charge that they were abuses of deduction with patent ideological motivations. What's a boy or girl to do under these circumstances?

Contrary to what political philosophers and newspaper editorial writers are likely to think, the one option that is not open is to claim that we must stick to LFR in order to "guarantee certainty" for reasons of economic functionality, or to "guarantee respect for the separation of powers" between judge and legislator for reasons of democratic political legitimacy. The reason for this is that it is LFR itself that has presented us with the choice in question. LFR has proved internally indeterminate. We can't just "stick to LFR" (maybe arguing "what are the alternatives?"). With respect to the particular, high-stakes problem that the judge is asked to decide by choosing among alternative-candidate, valid rules, *there is no LFR to "stick to."* Denying this, and proceeding merrily along in full "fidelity to law," or some other such nonsense, is exactly what we mean by the abuse of deduction.

A jurist who has reached this point can be said to have experienced the disenchantment of LFR in a quite specific Weberian sense. From Savigny's brilliant first volume of *The System of Modern Roman Law*[71] until the 1930s, jurists in Europe were, as has often been noted, obsessed with the idea that the ensemble of valid legal norms constituted a system in the strong sense of an entity whose internal coherence could be presupposed.[72] Given that presupposition, it is plausible to say that "the system determines" the choice of a rule among alternative candidates when there is an apparent gap at the level of materially applicable rules.

The "system" is a "metaphysical" entity because it is the product of, but somehow transcends, a multiplicity of concrete decisions by particular adjudicators, the work of a wide range of jurists, and the enactments of legislators, including the personally clueless legislators of massive codifications. When we say that "the system determined" the choice of a particular materialized rule to resolve a high-stakes dispute, we mean that an entity transcending the above-mentioned individual, social actors determined the choice.

The critique of LFR disenchants it because it deprives the decision-maker of the illusion (for us, it is no longer any more than an illusion) that "the system" in some sense produces the norms that decide cases, rather than some earlier jurist enunciating a particular rule, or we ourselves imposing meaning in the presence of a gap (one we may ourselves have worked hard to open), in the post-Nietzschean mode. Sometimes, there appears before us some earlier jurist's valid norm, and we cannot resist the experience of being bound to apply it. Sometimes—and sometimes as a result of our conscious effort—a space appears in which we can impose meaning. To be disenchanted is to "bracket" the question of what immanences and transcendences (that is, what conception of "the system") might once have rendered this experience of subjective boundness and freedom intelligible.[73]

There are two radically different ways to proceed after acknowledging the bind. The first is the Weberian way, though he refused to take his own way with respect to the issue before us, that of the disenchantment of LFR. The Weberian way is to acknowledge disenchantment and take responsibility, in the antinomian decisionist mode, for making a choice without hoping that it will have a "warrant." The other way, the one pursued by legal theory over the whole course of the last century, is the way of "reconstruction," that is, the attempt to relegitimate legal interpretation according to new ideal-types, after the disenchantment of LFR.

V. The Contemporary Mode of Legal Thought: Policy Analysis

I would distinguish two, historically important, reconstruction projects, one for private, administrative, and substantive criminal law, and the other for constitutional law, with very different content, different origins, and different fates. In constitutional law today, the dominant model is based in a very straightforward way on Unitedstatesean constitutional history and practice, as reinterpreted to some extent by Jellinek and Kelsen. A legitimate order is based on plebiscitary adoption of a written constitution containing a charter or declaration of rights, which judges of a constitutional court are to interpret according to extant juristic technique, with the constitutionally granted power to overrule democratically enacted legislation and executive action, although without direct access to police or military staffs to enforce their judgments against legislature or executive.

It is an interesting question how this ideal-type has gained legitimacy around the world, but it is to my mind less interesting than the one to which I have chosen to devote the remainder of this chapter. That is the question of reconstruction in private law, administrative law, and substantive criminal law, a project that was initially a joint venture of German and French scholars, with the rest of the world looking on, but that became, in the 1930s and 1940s, above all a Unitedstatesean venture, globalized after the Second World War.

WEBER ACCEPTED AND REJECTED WITHIN THE CONTEMPORARY MODE OF LEGAL THOUGHT

In Europe through Kelsen, and in the United States through Llewellyn and the legal realists,[74] Weber's basic critiques of the social—that it illegitimately attempted to generate a legislative *ought* from the *is* of social change, and that it often (not always) tried to bootstrap validity in the juristic sense from the facts of regularity of behavior and normative consensus—were very fully assimilated, and are an important part of the modern mode of legal thought (in its theory part). Moreover, Weber's sociological distinctions are the basis of the methodology of modern legal sociology on both continents.

It is very different with respect to Weber's overall diagnosis of legality and its future. In Europe, the traumas of the middle third of the twentieth century led to a revival of natural law, in a context in which it continued its confrontation with legal positivism à la Kelsen. Legal formalism, though discredited at the level of pure theory, survived and even prospered as part of the mystique of the civil as against the common law, and as part of the liberal post–World War II argument that the antiformalism of the social current was complexly complicit in the rise of fascism and even in Stalinism. (In spite of the intense Marxist critique of the social, you have to be a Hayekian libertarian to believe that the social people are crypto-communists.)

What happened in the United States was no more Weberian, but very different from what happened in Europe. The critique of LFR had been taken seriously and far in the United States during the period between 1900 and 1930. The American critics of classical legal thought used all the European materials, but they were co-inventors of the strategy and actually did it more thoroughly than the Europeans. (Compare, for example, Hohfeld with Josserand.) Moreover, their version was never even slightly enamored of judicial discretion, as was the case briefly in France and Germany.

There was an initial period, the heyday of legal realism, when the critique of the abuse of deduction combined with insistence on a sharp *is/ought* distinction led to two opposite, quite extreme reactions. On one side was a scientific positivist approach aiming to identify the factual regularities of legal behavior, rigorously excluding all reference to the dogmatic materials, influenced by behaviorism in psychology and the Vienna Circle. On the other side was an intuitionist account of judicial behavior in applying law to facts, typified by a famous article called "The Function of the 'Hunch' in Judicial Decision."[75] These tendencies were denounced by the American founder of sociological jurisprudence (Pound) and also by the emigrés from Hitler's Germany, who had recanted their Free Law wildness (Kantorowicz, Kocourek).[76]

This phase was quickly succeeded by the rise of what I have been calling the contemporary mode of legal thought. There was intense development of the "abuse of deduction" strand in the social critique of CLT, decisively discrediting LFR for the legal profession as a whole, in a way that never happened in Europe, and incorporating what Weber called "relentless self-criticism" into the professional training of elite lawyers. A second key trait was the "juridification" of "substantively rational" normative elements—that is, legal "policies"—that for Weber were inconsistent with the highly developed form of LFR.

The best way to understand the Unitedstatesean development would be this: the U.S. post-social scholars accepted, and even greatly intensified, the abuse-of-deduction critique, but recognized Weber's (and others') critique of the social as threatening diffuse judicial usurpation and incalculability. The danger was particularly obvious in the United States, where progressive forces had struggled for several generations against conservative, judge-made, constitutional law restrictive of the very reforms advocated by the social people. Both the rise of policy and the development of human rights judicial review were postrealist responses to these challenges. This means that

Weber's sociology of law was not prophetic: not LFR but a distinctively hybrid contemporary mode of legal thought legitimates contemporary legal/bureaucratic domination.

"FORMALIZING" SUBSTANTIVE RATIONALITY: THE RISE OF POLICY ANALYSIS

In the contemporary mode of legal thought, legal interpretation is based on a combination of deductive argument in the mode of LFR, precedential argument, and what is called "policy argument." Policy argument is sufficiently different from the "traditional" modern modes so that it warrants, I think, an attempt to present it in the form of a new ideal type, rather than as a combination of the modes of legal reasoning typologized by Weber. Weber's typological axes can nonetheless be helpful in this. It is worth noting that Max Rheinstein, in his introduction and footnotes to *Max Weber on Law in Economy and Society*, repeatedly recognizes that Unitedstatesean legal theorists (among whom he includes himself) think they have gone beyond LFR to a method they call policy analysis, and are therefore likely to disagree with Weber's characterization of the modern mode of legal thought.[77]

Ideal-Typical Legal Policy Analysis

Policy analysis presupposes that the interpreter has to decide in the presence of a gap in the system of valid norms, or that he has to apply a norm that in its own terms calls for policy analysis, or that the circumstances for some reason permit application of a norm derived from policy analysis to displace a deductively derived norm. The analysis presupposes that there are many policies or desiderata in rule-making; that they often, though not always conflict; that they are well conceptualized as forces or weights or vectors in a force field; and that they vary in force or weight according to the precise factual circumstances to which they are applied within the field. Policies come in conflicting pairs of different types, including conflicting welfare arguments, conflicting moral maxims, and conflicting subjective rights. There is also an important class of "institutional" policies.

Rational decision-making is defined in policy analysis as choosing a norm to apply to this case and to a class of similar others in the future on the basis of a total-value-maximizing balance of the conflicting policies. It is understood, first, that the rule is no more than a compromise of the policies, rather than a thing valid in and of itself; and second, that the rule will inevitably be more or less adequate across the range of fact situations to which it applies. The ideal type as a whole was the work of Ihering, Holmes, Heck, Demogue, Radbruch, modern Unitedstatesean conflict-of-laws theorists, and the sequence of Hohfeld, W. W. Cook, Llewellyn, Felix Cohen, John

Gardner, Lon Fuller, Myers McDougal, Henry Hart, Albert Sacks, and Stewart Macaulay.[78] Macaulay, interestingly, uses Weber's sociological categories in constructing his catalogue of interests to be balanced.[79]

Policy Analysis as "Formalized Substantive Rationality"

Weberian substantive legal rationality is rational in the sense that it appeals only to rationally calculable factors (no oracles or trials-by-battle). It may also be rational in the sense that it decides according to a rule (derived from one of the extra-juristic normative orders of the society), or it may proceed ad hoc. In the case of policy analysis, the decision-maker has no rule already available that he can just apply because the attempt to do LFR has, by hypothesis, turned up a gap or a conflict. But the goal of the policy analysis is to choose a new rule that will be applied first to this case, and then in the future (except as explained below). Policy analysis is therefore not "irrational" in the sense of refusing to decide according to rule.

Like Weber's substantive rationality, the content of policy analysis is derived from the general political, moral, religious, and expediential goals that drive government in the society as a whole. Nonetheless, modern policy analysis is in several important ways closer to logically formal rationality than it is to Weberian substantive legal rationality. In contemporary policy analysis, the policies (welfarist, moral, rights-based) are understood as strictly legal—fully "inside" the practice of legal interpretation—rather than external, and in this respect policy analysis resembles LFR.[80]

Policies are plausibly "internal" because there is an implicit criterion for their "juridification," namely, universalizability (in Habermas's sense).[81] Only policies, or desiderata, that everyone shares can be included, in order to preserve the legitimacy claim of the procedure. So, for example, efficiency considerations can be included but distributive ones cannot; general moral desiderata are permissible but not moral teachings uniquely associated with a particular church or sect (or for that matter with atheism as a belief system). The only rights that can be consulted are "universal," at least in form.

The self-consciously selective incorporation of substantively rational elements from nonjuristic, normative practice goes along with the typification or ritualization of legal policy argument. The result is a juristic practice that is sharply distinguishable from the general social normative practice from which it derives. However, the commitment to balancing conflicting policies, with an eye to consequences, in a context in which rules represent no more than the means to implement the resulting compromise, sharply distinguishes policy analysis from LFR. It also distinguishes policy analysis from those variants of substantive rationality that are value rational—that is, oriented to rules absolutely valid without regard to consequences.

Policy Analysis Transforms the Will Theory and the Social Theory into Policies to Be Balanced

One of the most striking developments of the 1940s was the transformation of the "formalist" requirements of the will theory, and the equally formal functionalist requirements of the social, into mere policies to be balanced within the larger analysis. The will theory became Lon Fuller's "principle of private autonomy," no longer the fountain of deductions, but rather primus inter pares of a set of principles that included, for example, a potentially conflicting principle of protecting reliance.[82]

In doctrinal writing on modern tort and contract law, both in Europe (for example, by Ghestain, Viney, and Atiyah) and in the United States (by Prosser, Farnsworth, and MacNeil), the principle of private autonomy is often opposed, from case to case or across a doctrinal domain, with varying results, by what is unmistakably the old social principle validating the claims of interdependence. Policy analysis appears to have transcended, in this way, the antinomy of autonomy of the will and social embeddedness.

It is striking that it does this for each type of policy: economic, moral, and rights-based. When rights conflict, it is likely to be an autonomy right conflicting with a right to protection against harm. The autonomy principle of no liability without fault comes up against the counterprinciple of "objective responsibility" (liability based on causation). The efficiency gains from permitting the externalization of costs confront those of internalization of costs. In this way, what seemed to be an insuperable objection to normatively compelling, rational lawmaking, namely the existence of contradictory legal philosophies each claiming to operate according to an absolute (logical or social) necessity, was transformed into something like a technical problem (though the need for value judgments—not political judgments—was not denied).

Policy Analysis Transforms Objections to Its Legitimacy into Additional Policies to Be Balanced

Weber's ideal-type of substantively rational legal thought succumbs, in his theory, to LFR, because LFR is superior both in that it provides calculability for the addressees of the legal order, and because it permits a sharp separation between norm formulation and administration, whether the formulator is an absolute monarch or a parliament. At first blush, it might appear that any legitimacy claims of policy analysis must be defeated on the ground of incalculability and failure to respect the separation of powers.

The true genius of the policy analysis initiative was that it found a way to meet these objections in the mode of confession and avoidance. Because the policy analyst operates within a mode of thought for which LFR has been disenchanted, gaps and conflicts are inevitable, some with high stakes. That means that "value judgments" are also inevitable. All that can be hoped for is to make them as rationally as possible—that is, in a way that poses the least danger (not no danger at all) of incalculability and/or politicization of the adjudicative process. This is accomplished within the contemporary mode of policy analysis *by incorporating the question of the calculability of the chosen rule, and the question of the appropriate division of lawmaking power between judge and legislature, into the policy calculus itself.*

In policy argument, a major question is whether the rule proposed will be adequately calculable (in policy jargon, "adequately administrable") and account taken of the major problem of arbitrary over- and underinclusion that highly calculable rules inevitably generate. In policy argument, a second major question is whether the choice of a rule is consistent with the premise of the separation of powers between judge and legislator, while of course acknowledging that the inevitability of gaps makes this problem insoluble in the old-fashioned terms of LFR ("institutional competence arguments," in policy jargon).[83]

An adjudicative system whose mode of thought corresponded to the ideal type of policy analysis would be "autopoietic" (in the very limited sense that Teubner gave to Luhmann's ideal-type)[84] because its practice includes wholly intrasystem methods (not rules) for the generation of new norms to apply to the data that arrive from "outside," and also methods (not rules) for regulating the boundaries of the legal system vis-à-vis others, namely, the legislative and executive. It is for this reason that it seems right to call it a "formal" (in Weber's sense) version of substantive rationality. It is also purpose rational rather than value rational because it is based on consequence oriented trading-off of values, rather than rule application. But it involves constant value judgments as to what policies should be juridified and how to balance them in any particular case of rule-making.

Of course, policy analysis is never present in pure form in contemporary legal thought, and always operates in uneasy coexistence with at least the following earlier types: cadi justice or lay equity, logically formal rationality, the "social" methodology of deducing a rule from a single social purpose, and the mode of positivized natural rights reasoning characteristic of modern charter-based constitutionalism with judicial review. Moreover, the Weberian category of legitimacy does not capture the subtle psychological attitudes of modern ruler and ruled toward the *ought* claims of law produced in this way. I would prefer to describe them in the register of degrees of "bad faith," in the Sartrean sense.[85]

Conclusion: Irrationality in Adjudication and the Sectarianism of Contemporary Legal Theory

In contemporary legal theory, policy is always a potential Trojan Horse for ideology, just because of the patently weak rationality of choosing policies by universalizability and then merely "balancing" them. The Weberian legitimacy of the legal order rests partly on the claim that "we" use democratic lawmaking procedures—rather than judicial legislation—to deal with ideological conflict. It also rests partly on the claim that constitutional law, with nonideological judicial enforcement, guarantees human rights. As a consequence, the apparent possibility of a moment of a-rational Weberian, or Schmittian decision within the adjudicative process is, at least, "a problem," for apologists for the existing legal and social order.

One way to interpret the proliferation, after about 1970, of "schools" of legal theory is as a Weberian phenomenon of sectarianism in the face of the irreducible ethical irrationality of legal judgment. Thus revived natural law, human rights, law and economics, Habermasian speech act theory, Dworkinian rights theory, libertarian legal theory, feminist legal theory, critical race theory, and, last but by no means least in this list, critical legal studies, would all represent responses to the core dilemma, whether it is called "democracy deficit," "countermajoritarian difficulty," "judicial paternalism," "result orientation," "activism," or anything else.

It is hard to imagine that Weber would have found any of the reconstruction projects of contemporary legal theoretical sects even slightly plausible as a response to his dire decisionist view of political existence. To a degree that has continually surprised me, this inquiry into Weber's sociology of law, viewed in conjunction with his general sociology of disenchantment, seems to lead to the conclusion that much critical legal studies work, in the skeptical vein, has been a reinvention or adaptation, to new non-Weberian purposes, of Weberian wheels.

Notes

1. See generally, Roscoe Pound, "The End of Law as Developed in Juristic Thought II: The Nineteenth Century," 30 *Harvard L. Rev.* 201 (1917); Franz Wieacker, *History of Private Law in Europe with Special Reference to Germany* (1967; Oxford, U.K.: Clarendon, 1995); James Gordley, *The Philosophical Origins of Modern Contract Doctrine* (New York: Oxford University Press, 1991). For the literature on the will theory, see Duncan Kennedy, "From the Will Theory to the Principle of Private Autonomy: Lon Fuller's *Consideration and Form*," 100 *Columbia L. Rev.* 94 (2000). The summary in the text is a slightly modified version of that in Duncan Kennedy, "Legal Formalism," in Neil J. Smelser and Paul B. Baltes, eds., *Encyclopedia of the Social and Behavioral Sciences* (New York: Elsevier, 2001), p. 8634.

2. See generally on the social as legal consciousness, Wieacker, *History*; G. Edward White, "From Sociological Jurisprudence to Realism: Jurisprudence and Social Change in Early Twentieth-Century America," 58 *Virginia. L. Rev.* 999 (1972); Andre-Jean Arnaud, *Les juristes face à la société du XIXième siècle a nos jours* (Paris: Presses Universitaires de France, 1975); Horwitz, *The Transformation of American Law 1870–1960: The Crisis of Legal Orthodoxy* (New York: Oxford University Press, 1992); Nestor DeBuen, *La Decadencia del Contrato* (Mexico City: Porrua, 1965); Duncan Kennedy and Marie-Claire Belleau, "François Gény aux États-Unis," in Claude Thomasset, ed., *François Gény: Mythes et réalités* (Brussels: Dalloz, 2000); Kennedy, "From the Will Theory." The summary in the text is a slightly modified version of that in Duncan Kennedy, "Two Globalizations of Law and Legal Thought: 1850–1968," 36 *Suffolk University L. Rev.* 631 (2003).

3. Max Weber, *Economy and Society: An Outline of Interpretive Sociology*, ed. Guenther Roth and Claus Wittich (1921–22; Berkeley: University of California Press, 1978).

4. See Max Weber, *The Methodology of the Social Sciences* (Glencoe, IL: Free Press, 1949); Max Weber, *Roscher and Knies: The Logical Problems of Historical Economics* (Glencoe, IL: Free Press, 1975).

5. In Weber, *Methodology*.

6. Ibid.

7. In Max Weber, *From Max Weber: Essays in Sociology*, ed. H. H. Gerth and C. Wright Mills (New York: Oxford University Press, 1946).

8. See generally, Weber, *Roscher and Knies*.

9. Weber, *Economy and Society*, p. 754.

10. See, e.g., ibid., p. 334.

11. Ibid., p. 654.

12. Max Weber, *Max Weber on Law in Economy and Society*, ed. Max Rheinstein (New York: Simon & Schuster 1954), p. 1.

13. Ibid., p. 9.

14. Ibid., p. 8.

15. Ibid., p. 59.

16. Weber, *Economy and Society*, p. 217.

17. Weber, *Weber on Law*, p. 336; see also Weber, *Economy and Society*, pp. 217–20.

18. Weber, *Weber on Law*, p. 336.

19. Ibid., p. 64. Weber's point is not historical, but about Weber's present: "According to present modes of thought [systematization] represents an integration of all analytically derived legal propositions in such a way that they constitute a logically clear, internally consistent, and, at least in theory, gapless system of rules, under which it is implied, all conceivable fact situations must be capable of being logically subsumed, lest their order lack an effective guaranty." Ibid., p. 62.

20. Ibid., p. 63.

21. Weber, *Economy and Society*, pp. 787, 889–92.

22. Weber, *Weber on Law*, pp. 63–64.

23. Compare legal rationality, formal and substantive, with economic rationality, in Weber, *Economy and Society*, pp. 85–86. For a better translation, see Max Weber,

The Theory of Social and Economic Organization, ed. Talcott Parsons (Glencoe, IL: Free Press, 1947), pp. 184–85. Economic substantive rationality, like its legal sibling, involves heterogeneous criteria that may be value rational or purpose rational in terms of an indefinite number of value systems.

24. Cf. Gunther Teubner, *Law as an Autopoietic System* (Oxford, U.K.: Blackwell, 1993).

25. Weber, *Economy and Society*, p. 311.

26. It seems to me that Kelsen is indeed the direct descendant of Weber. The major difference between them is that Kelsen accepts the social critique of LFR. For Weber, the framework of powers defined by public law is filled, at the level of adjudication (or academic interpretation) by "doing" LFR on the positively enacted norms of the system. For Kelsen, the "judgment" is a "norm like any other norm," chosen by the judge as lawmaker, albeit within the constraining "frame" (his word) established by the abstract norm to be applied. Norberto Bobbio, "Max Weber e Hans Kelsen," in Renato Treves, ed., *Max Weber e il diritto, Sociologia del diritto* no. 5 (Milan: F. Angeli, 1981).

27. Weber, *Economy and Society*, pp. 319–25.

28. Ibid., pp. 312–37.

29. It is also eminently Nietzschean, as well as poststructuralist. See Michel Foucault, "Nietzsche, Genealogy, History," in Michel Foucault, *Language, Countermemory, Practice: Selected Essays and Interviews*, ed. Donald Bouchard (Ithaca, NY: Cornell University Press, 1977).

30. Weber, *Economy and Society*, pp. 654–55.

31. See Mommsen, this volume.

32. It has been denounced as antihistorical, because it is indifferent to context in its drive for concepts that will apply across contexts. Harold Berman and Charles Reid, "Max Weber as Legal Historian," in Stephen Turner, ed., *The Cambridge Companion to Weber* (Cambridge, U.K.: Cambridge University Press, 2000). But this is to miss its point—which is to find concepts that transcend context, and then use them to describe contexts as parts of larger developments.

33. Weber, *Economy and Society*, p. 867.

34. Ibid., p. 870.

35. Ibid., p. 868.

36. Ibid., p. 867.

37. Ibid., pp. 1209–10.

38. Ibid., p. 874.

39. Ibid., p. 875.

40. Ibid., pp. 729–31.

41. Ibid., pp. 778, 889–92; cf. David Trubek, "Max Weber on Law and the Rise of Capitalism," 3 *Wisconsin L. Rev.* 720–53 (1972); David Trubek, "Reconstructing Max Weber's Sociology of Law," *Stanford L. Rev.* 919–36 (1985); David Trubek, "Max Weber's Tragic Modernism and the Study of Law in Society," 20 *Law & Soc. Rev.* 573–98 (1986); Sally Ewing, "Formal Justice and the Spirit of Capitalism: Max Weber's Sociology of Law," 21 *Law & Society Review* 487–512 (1987).

42. Weber, *Economy and Society*, pp. 873–75.

43. Ibid., p. 894.

44. Ibid.

45. Ibid., p. 895.

46. Ibid., p. 308.

47. Ibid., p. 886.

48. Ibid., p. 887.

49. Ibid., p. 888

50. Ibid.

51. Ibid., p. 889.

52. Ibid., p. 886.

53. Ibid., pp. 886–87.

54. Ibid., p. 894.

55. Ibid., p. 316.

56. Ibid., pp. 753–60.

57. Ibid., p. 893.

58. Ibid., pp. 886, 889, 894.

59. Ibid., p. 889.

60. Ibid.

61. Ibid., p. 895.

62. The discussion that follows is based on "Religious Groups (The Sociology of Religion)," in Weber, *Economy and Society*; "Science as a Vocation," "Politics as a Vocation," "The Social Psychology of the World Religions," and "Religious Rejections of the World and their Direction," all in Weber, *From Max Weber*.

63. Cathérine Colliot-Thélène, *Le désenchantement de l'état, de Hegel à Max Weber* (Paris: Editions de Minuit, 1992), p. 238 (my translation).

64. Weber, *Economy and Society*, pp. 336–37.

65. Cf. Duncan Kennedy, *A Critique of Adjudication [fin de siècle]* (Cambridge, MA: Harvard University Press, 1997), chap. 14.

66. Wolfgang Mommsen, *Max Weber and German Politics: 1890–1920* (Chicago: University of Chicago Press, 1984); Pier Paolo Portinaro, "Max Weber e Carl Schmitt," in Treves, *Max Weber e il diritto*; Colliot-Thélène, *Le désenchantement*; Michel Coutu, *Max Weber et les rationalités du droit* (Quebec City: L. G. D. J., 1995). Anthony Kronman's often useful study, *Max Weber* (Palo Alto, CA: Stanford University Press, 1983), seems to miss this crucial aspect of Weber's thought.

67. Cf. Duncan Kennedy, "A Semiotics of Critique," 22 *Cardozo L. Rev.* 1147 (2001).

68. On this aspect, see Harvey Goldman, *Politics, Death, and the Devil: Self and Power in Max Weber and Thomas Mann* (Berkeley: University of California Press, 1992).

69. Weber, *Economy and Society*, p. 875.

70. Oliver Wendell Holmes, "Privilege, Malice and Intent," 8 *Harvard Law Review* 1 (1897).

71. Friedrich Carl von Savigny, *The System of Modern Roman Law* (1839; Westport, CT: Hyperion, 1980).

72. See, for example, Paolo Grossi, *Scienza giuridica italiana: Un profilo storico 1860–1950* (Milan: Giuffrè, 2000), p. 8.

73. Duncan Kennedy, "Freedom and Constraint in Adjudication: A Critical Phenomenology," 36 *J. Leg. Educ.* 518 (1986); Pierre Schlag, *The Enchantment of Reason* (Durham, NC: Duke University Press, 1997).

74. Hans Kelsen, *Introduction to the Problems of Legal Theory* (1934; Oxford: Clarendon, 1992); Karl Llewellyn, "A Realistic Jurisprudence—The Next Step," 30 *Columbia L. Rev.* 431 (1930).

75. Joseph Hutcheson, "The Judgment Intuitive: The Function of the 'Hunch' in Judicial Decision," 14 *Cornell L. Q.* 274 (1929).

76. See Kennedy and Belleau, "François Gény aux États Unis."

77. E.g., Max Rheinstein, introduction to Weber, *Weber on Law*, p. xliv.

78. See generally, Kennedy, *Critique of Adjudication*, chap. 6; Kennedy, "From the Will Theory."

79. Stewart Macaulay, "Private Legislation and the Duty to Read: Business Run by IBM Machine, the Law of Contracts and Credit Cards, 19 *Vanderbilt Law Rev.* 1061 (1966).

80. This aspect was made explicit by Ronald Dworkin in his famous critique of positivism, "The Model of Rules," in *Taking Rights Seriously* (Cambridge: Harvard University Press, 1978).

81. Jürgen Habermas, *The Theory of Communicative Action: Reason and the Rationalization of Society*, vol. 1, trans. Thomas McCarthy (Boston: Beacon Press, 1984), pp. 16–19.

82. Kennedy, "From the Will Theory."

83. Henry Hart and Albert Sacks, *The Legal Process: Basic Problems in the Making and Application of Law*, ed. William Eskridge and Phillip Frickey (Westbury, NY: Foundation Press, 1994).

84. Teubner, *Law as an Autopoietic System.*

85. Kennedy, *Critique of Adjudication*, chap. 8.

Max Weber and the Origin of Human Rights

A Study of Cultural Innovation

There can be little doubt that a belief in human rights and the dignity of the human person is one of the most important characteristics of our time, at least since the end of the Second World War and to an even greater degree following the collapse of communism in Europe. While this development was anticipated by a few sociological theorists, such as Emile Durkheim, it stands in sharp tension with the gloomy prognoses about the future that Max Weber formulated on various occasions. What is more, since human rights are rarely discussed in Weber's gigantic oeuvre, the question of their origins may at first seem rather marginal for the study of his work. However, it can be shown that the origin of this value complex—so central to the modern age—yields an interesting perspective on several aspects of Weber's sociology.

In his empirical views about the origins of human rights, Max Weber was completely dependent on the research of his friends and colleagues Georg Jellinek and Ernst Troeltsch. So it seems sensible that we begin with them. This detour allows us to pursue three different goals at once. First, it enables us to formulate the problem more clearly. Second, by contrasting Weber's views with those of his contemporaries, we can more precisely specify his position. Third, and finally, this contrast allows us to draw some conclusions regarding the interpretive power of the so-called Weber paradigm.

Our reflections begin with a scene. It takes place on an October evening in 1922 in downtown Berlin, when the German College for Politics (Deutsche Hochschule für Politik) is celebrating its second anniversary in a famous building, Schinkel's Bauakademie. The president of the Reich, Friedrich Ebert, and outstanding figures in Berlin's academic-intellectual life, such as the historians Friedrich Meinecke, Erich Marcks, and Hans Delbrück, had accepted the invitation of this newly created institution, which had set itself the goal of promoting adult education in the spirit of democracy and therefore had a somewhat difficult task in the early years of the Weimar Republic. The keynote address was given by one of the greatest scholars of the old Kaiserreich, the Protestant theologian, historian, and philosopher Ernst Troeltsch; the topic was "The Ideas of Natural Law and Humanity in World Politics."¹ Contemporaries were fascinated by Troeltsch's argument. After reading the text, Thomas Mann responded with a detailed essay that appeared in the *Frankfurter Zeitung*; Friedrich Meinecke dedicated his book *Die Idee der Staatsräson* (*The Idea of Reason of State*) to Troeltsch, and devoted the final chapter of the book to Troeltsch's lecture; and Leo Strauss, the emigrant political philosopher, took it as the starting point for his 1949 lectures at the University of Chicago, in which he warned America against the relativistic influence emanating from defeated Germany, and from which he developed his influential book *Naturrecht und Geschichte* (*Natural Right and History*).² Even today Troeltsch's vision continues to fascinate, and perhaps it can only now be fully understood—by us, some three generations later.

What was so special about this lecture? Its unique contribution lies in a remarkably productive confrontation between the Western human rights tradition and a sophisticated conception of individuality, creativity, and self-realization that was developed primarily in Germany. At the same time, Troeltsch's tone was entirely sober and calm. During the first years of World War I, Troeltsch had stood on the front lines of the heated nationalist output of university professors and the public intellectual debates that took place, and he had mostly emphasized the differences between Germany and the West in his own interventions. Though highly knowledgeable and generally above crude stereotypes, he was mainly interested in marking an impassable cultural and political boundary. The war's events and outcome did not drive him further in the direction of nationalistic radicalism, however, as they did others, such as Oswald Spengler. Neither did Troeltsch simply conform to the new circumstances for external or strategic reasons, by adopting the guise of a "reasonable republican"(Vernunft-Republikaner), or throw himself into the arms of the West, in a complete about-face. Rather, he attempted, by means of a genuine and searching auto-critique, to break open the disastrous alliance that had formed between the German understanding of individuality and the glorification of *raison d'état* and power politics. To reach this goal, he first showed clearly that the ideas of natural law and humanity were not, as was often assumed, "merely modern or merely West European concepts," but rather "ideas of great antiquity . . . and of general European scope; ideas which are the basis of our European philosophy of history and ethics; ideas which have been closely connected, for thousands of years, with theology and humanism."³ He further argued that Catholicism had always remained much closer to this "common tradition of Europe,"[4] the Romantic image of Catholicism notwithstanding. What was really new and modern, according to Troeltsch, were the—typically German—conceptions of the Romantics and historicists that essentially emerged out of a revolt against natural law, which, in its modern form, was perceived as a fusion of utilitarianism and ethics. The Romantics and historicists, for their part, focused "on the particular, the positive: on what is eternally productive of new variety, constructive, spiritually organic, on plastic and super-personal creative forces."[5]

In fact, since Herder and Humboldt, a significant strand of German thought had conceived of the human person neither as a utility-maximizing individual nor as a rational subject following the dictates of morality, but rather as a being that expresses itself, and in this sense realizes itself, in its utterances and acts.[6] In this view, individuals are not just so many identical atoms, whose relationships to each other are subject to universal laws; rather they are highly unique personalities that undergo complex developmental processes as they seek out a path to self-realization through their own actions. This epochal transformation in thought also resulted in a new and different understanding of "community," which is sharply distinguished from contractual relationships; of humanity, which is conceived as the struggle of the national spirits; and of history, which is not interpreted as progress. For Troeltsch—and he believes for us—this transformation cannot simply be undone, any more than this demanding new understanding of all individuality—including our own—can be renounced. His gesture consists not in any such retraction, but rather in the very insistence with which he questions the political realizations of the expressive conception of individuality characteristic of Germany and their opposition to Western universalism. Looking back, Troeltsch tended to see the consequences of the grandiose innovations of the classical period of German thought in terms of a history of decline:

But the conception of a wealth of unique National Minds turns into a feeling of contempt for the idea of Universal Humanity: the old pantheistic deification of the State becomes a blind worship of success and power; the Romantic Revolution sinks into a complacent contentment with things as they are. From the idea of the particular law and right of a given time, men proceed to a merely positive acceptance of the State: morality of the spiritual order, transcending bourgeois convention, passes into moral skepticism, and the urgent movement of the German mind towards a political form and embodiment ends merely in the same cult of imperialism which is rampant everywhere.[7]

Troeltsch very explicitly distances himself from Germany's fatal antipathy toward human rights and the League of Nations. "The theory of the Rights of Man—rights which are not the gift of the State, but the ideal postulates of the State, and indeed of Society itself, in all its forms—is a theory which contains so much of the truth, and satisfies so many of the requirements of a true European attitude, that we cannot afford to neglect it; on the contrary, *we must incorporate it into our own ideas.*"[8] The key point is to be found in the last clause. Troeltsch is not only concerned with conquering the anti-Western mixture of Romantic excess and the militaristic craze for order in Germany; he also wants to draw on the tradition of German thought concerning individuality and history to place the ideal of human rights on a new and possibly superior foundation.

And therein lies the challenge, still unsatisfied, that emanates from the text even today. It might at first appear as if Troeltsch's text simply documents Germany's long and arduous path toward the West. Initially, of course, this path led still deeper into anti-Western resentment, so that during the Third Reich, one historian (Wilhelm Ihde) would actually argue that the idea of human rights derived from a "decadent and pathological type of human."[9] After the step-by-step process of Westernization that occurred in Germany following the catastrophes of the Second World War and the Holocaust, first in the Federal Republic of Germany and then in Germany as a whole, Troeltsch's concerns might seem outdated. But this would be a crude simplification of reality. For the West was never as homogeneous as its critics or the advocates of complete Westernization believed. And the differences among the Western countries and their political camps and cultural traditions can only appear negligible when viewed from a great distance. What is more, the cultural tensions that exist in the West clearly resemble the ones that were employed to construct a cultural boundary between Germany and the West. For example, the French "Declaration of the Rights of Man" from 1789 *simultaneously* proclaims the inviolability of individual freedoms and the sovereignty of a common will, without resolving the tension between the two principles. If one follows Alain Touraine's *Critique de la Modernité*, the tension in the Declaration can be seen as rooted in a tension between two fundamental principles of modernization: a process of progressive rationalization on the one hand, and a process of progressive subjectification on the other.[10] While this tension was indeed contained from time to time, it broke out again and again, most recently during the cultural upheavals of the 1960s experienced by all Western societies. This shows that Troeltsch's search for an alternative to utilitarian and rationalistic justifications of human rights has, in fact, become increasingly relevant, even in the West, in part because of the massive and historically unparalleled diffusion of values of creative self-realization. Troeltsch's question of 1922 can thus be rephrased today as follows: How can belief in human rights and the dignity of the human person be linked to an ethos of self-realization? We can only answer this complex question once we have clarified its two poles. We must first investigate whether it is indeed true that human rights developed out of a desire for "liberty of action in business" (as, for example, Gerhard Ritter has claimed)[11] and the antireligious spirit of the French Enlightenment, as the anti-Western accounts have claimed. This poses the question of the religious roots of human rights. On the other hand, we must determine whether the ethos of self-realization necessarily entails a Promethean self-conceit, or whether it aims instead at a change in the form of religiosity in the direction of individual and expressive forms of spirituality. How, then, can an affective tie to universalistic moral values develop under these new conditions?

First, the question of historical genesis. The point of departure for the discussion that follows is Georg Jellinek's book *Die Erklärung der Menschen-und Bürgerrechte. Ein Beitrag zur modernen Verfassungsgeschichte* (*The Declaration of the Rights of Man and Citizen. A Contribution to Modern Constitutional History*).[12] First published in 1895, this book is widely regarded as the seminal work that initiated study of the subject.[13] It advances four exciting key theses.[14] One of the most important constitutional historians and legal theoreticians of the time, Jellinek begins by arguing that the declaration of human and civil rights in the French Revolution did not mark the point of historical origin for the codification of human rights behind which we cannot go, as had frequently been assumed. Rather, he argues, this declaration was directly influenced by, or even modeled on, the American Declaration of Independence, and the various Bills of Rights proclaimed in Virginia, Pennsylvania, and other newly independent North American states in 1776. Jellinek also contested the claim—dominant in his time—that Rousseau's "*contrat social*" was the model for the French declaration. In addition—and this is the third point—he stressed that we should not overestimate the continuity between natural law and human rights, since the concepts of natural law could never have led to the institutionalization of human rights in or by themselves. A driving force was needed. The driving force behind this development, in Jellinek's fourth thesis, was the struggle of Protestant dissenters for religious freedom in North America. With these theses, Jellinek shifted the credit for the first declarations of human rights away from the French Enlightenment, which was skeptical of, or even hostile toward, religion, and traced them back to their Christian roots. He thereby provided the inspiration for a much more famous book: Max Weber's *Die protestantische Ethik und der Geist des Kapitalismus* (*The Protestant Ethic and the Spirit of Capitalism*). Weber was deeply impressed by Jellinek's argument, and especially by his "demonstration of religious influences in the genesis of 'human rights'" insofar as it contributed to "the investigation of the importance of religious elements in areas where one would not expect to find them."[15] To what extent can Jellinek's theses be maintained given our current state of knowledge?

In answering this question, we must continuously bear in mind three different time periods. The first period is the late eighteenth century, when declarations of human rights were proclaimed in North America and France. The second period is the time around 1900, when the question of the Christian, and specifically Protestant, roots of modernity more generally became a key subject of intellectual debate. And the third period is, of course, the present day, from which we look back over the development of human rights and the effects of their changing historical interpretations (*Wirkungsgeschichte*). The middle period continues to be important because we are concerned here not just with historical details and facts, but also with the interpretation of the historical process that produced human rights. For any such interpretation, controversies over human rights as part of modernity, such as those conducted around 1900, are still of the utmost importance.

Jellinek's book became the subject of a heated national and international debate immediately upon publication. French critics perceived it as a perfidious attempt to deny France's contribution to one of the most significant achievements of modernity.[16] One can still sense a degree of resistance even in Marcel Gauchet's 1989 book on the origin of the French declaration of human rights, where he concedes that "German scholarship" had shown the influence of the American declarations to have been decisive.[17] In Germany, Jellinek's thesis was an important point of reference for all those who wished to separate the question of human rights from the constitutional traditions of France, Germany's "historical enemy"—traditions that were usually looked upon with skepticism and resentment. Here, however, Jellinek's text attracted Catholic critics, who contested vehemently any possible claims of Protestant superiority with respect to the historical development of freedom and tolerance. Jellinek felt that his intentions and his book were misunderstood in many respects. And indeed his intentions are surely missed by such petty, nationalistic, and confessional insinuations. Instead, it seems to me that Jellinek's work must be interpreted as an effort to move beyond the dead-end debate between historicism and the theory of natural law.[18] Like the historicists, Jellinek did not believe that binding metanorms for the regulation of positive law could be derived from any philosophy, even from natural law or Kant. In this sense, he remained a proponent of the unlimited sovereignty of the state. But in contrast to many German historians of his time, especially the antiliberal and nationalistic ones, he did not hold conceptions of natural law to be "idle dreams," but rather sympathized with the notion of a state that limited itself by law and posited individual rights and freedoms.[19] So he had to try to find a place for such rights within his historicist approach. In this sense, his text marks the point where historicism, becoming aware of the dangers of its own relativism, seeks to transcend itself. This point is hardly foreign to us today. If the question of the historical roots of the idea of inalienable individual rights is not conceived of simply as a question of genesis that is completely independent of the question of their grounding and validation, then an essential point is indeed marked here. For then it is a matter of the possibility in principle of advancing universal validity claims, with the awareness that the genesis of values is historically contingent.[20]

Despite all the objections that were and are raised against it, much of Jellinek's argument can now be regarded as confirmed. He was correct not only in his emphasis on the chronological priority of the American declarations of human rights and their influence on the French "Déclaration" (though the latter was certainly no mere imitation of the American declarations). He was also correct when he pointed out that there is a difference between theories of natural law on the one hand, and on the other, the legal codification of specific individual rights that are supposed to hold for all people and be removed from legislative authority. "[T]he assertion of objective moral and legal limits to all worldly powers," writes Hasso Hofmann, agreeing with Jellinek, does not itself devolve into "a theory of subjective rights. The idea of constitutional freedom and security against *illegal* tyranny is not equivalent to the human rights idea of basic, individual freedoms and their protection against *legal* tyranny."[21] We must also agree with Jellinek when he rejects the view that the English legal tradition, with its codification of rights and freedoms, led directly to the declarations of human rights of the late eighteenth century, since these guarantees only applied to the traditional rights of the subjects of the English king, and by no means to all people. It is also true that Rousseau cannot be regarded as the source of inalienable rights to freedom that also apply against the state, since he had argued against any limitations on the legislative power of popular sovereignty. In this political respect, Rousseau is better seen as representing the collectivist pole of the French declaration of human rights, rather than the individualistic one, except if we want to claim that the same unresolved tension is found in his work as in the "Déclaration." If one can thus say today, notwithstanding opposing voices, that there is a widespread consensus in favor of Jellinek on all of these points, then the debate narrows to the last, and in any case the boldest, thesis of the book, namely, the thesis that the American declarations of human rights had religious roots.

Here the utmost caution is necessary. We must first demonstrate that we are not simply dealing with an intellectual background. Of course, Jellinek was aware that the belief in the dignity of all human beings had deep roots in the centuries-old Judeo-Christian tradition—though this tradition cannot be treated as an unbroken process of maturation that gave rise to modern ideas, especially when one considers how often its universalism was violated, when Jews, heretics, or native peoples were denied these selfsame rights. The intellectual roots of human rights in Renaissance humanism, the Reformation, or Spanish late scholasticism are in general less interesting for an understanding of our problem than are the dynamics of their sudden institutionalization. And it is here that Jellinek saw the struggle of American Protestants, especially the (Calvinist) Congregationalists, for religious freedom as decisive. Although religious toleration can be observed in the most varied regimes—the enlightened absolutism of Frederick the Great in Prussia, for example, or colonial Maryland under Catholic leadership—utilitarian calculations usually formed the basis for policies of toleration. Jellinek, however, was interested in the religious roots of the struggle for religious freedom—meaning religious freedom not just for one's own confession but for all believers. This is a highly salient topic today—as the threat from Islamic fundamentalism clearly shows. Accordingly, the hero of Jellinek's story is the Puritan preacher Roger Williams, who left Massachusetts in 1636 for Rhode Island, where he guaranteed religious freedom not only for Christians of all sorts but also "for Jews, heathens, and Turks." Jellinek's central thesis is that "[t]he idea of securing the inalienable, inborn, and sacred rights of the individual in the law is of religious rather than political origin. What has hitherto been viewed as a product of the [French] Revolution is in fact a fruit of the Reformation and its struggles. Its first apostle was not Lafayette but Roger Williams, who, driven by powerful and deep religious enthusiasm, went into the wilderness to found a government of religious freedom, and his name is uttered by Americans even today with the deepest respect."[22] According to Jellinek, all other individual rights, such as freedom of opinion, of the press, and of assembly, stem from this source. The whole idea that individuals not only have rights within a state, but also rights against the state, and that these are not simply conferred by the state, points to a religious origin, at least in the sense of a historical explanation.

Our current state of knowledge necessitates three corrections to Jellinek's fourth and most important thesis. The first of these corrections stems from none other than Ernst Troeltsch. For him, it was not the Calvinists, as for Jellinek, but rather the Baptists, Quakers, and certain types of free spirituality—the "stepchildren of the Reformation" as he famously called them—who helped win acceptance for a religiously founded idea of religious freedom, as he argued in his great work *Die Soziallehren der christlichen Kirchen und Gruppen* (*The Social Teachings of the Christian Churches and Groups*): "Only that spiritualism which individualizes and relativizes all external forms is the father of true tolerance; the only truly Calvinist stance concerns the inviolability of religion by the state."[23] Jellinek himself accepted this correction in the third edition of his book, albeit a little reluctantly.

The second correction relates to the claim—historicist in the negative sense—to have found the germ cell of all human rights in religious freedom. This view cannot be defended. It does not obtain for France in any case. Nor did religious freedom exist in most of the North American colonies or states. Indeed, it was not until the twentieth century that the separation of church and state at the national level was legally secured in the states of the Union as well. The historical codification of human rights was, of course, broadly affected by the opportunistic and strategic considerations of social actors, by constellations of power, and by structures of opportunity. While it is true that the legal recognition of the freedom of religion and of conscience represents the first form of a universal human right, we should not by any means ascribe to it an autonomous causal power or overestimate its significance in the late eighteenth century. To do so would be an injustice to the actual dynamics of institutionalization.

At the same time, however—and this is the third correction—we should not underestimate the role of religious interpretations and motives at this time either. Rather, we must abandon this undialectical opposition of two explanatory hypotheses, one of which gives the responsibility for the origin of human rights to American Protestantism, and the other to the French Enlightenment. Troeltsch, much more than Jellinek, had already recognized the transformative effects that Enlightenment thought exerted on Protestant Christianity in North America. For, in a well-known phrase, Americans in the eighteenth century learned their Enlightenment from the pulpit.[24] Conversely, there were also affinities between forms of Christian spiritualism and Enlightenment rationalism. For Troeltsch, admixtures of this sort were nothing new, since, in his opinion, the entire history of Western culture was characterized by an interplay between the Christian idea of love and conceptions of natural law. Current work on the historical genesis of the American Declaration of Independence vividly shows just how impossible it is to draw any clear boundaries in America's Puritan-Enlightenment synthesis. The primary author of the Declaration, Thomas Jefferson, was of course a deist and only Christian in the broad sense that he accepted the teachings of Jesus, though not his divinity. In his formulations, however, Jefferson strove for a consensus that would be acceptable to the various strains of Christianity as well as to enlightened non-Christians. The claim that the Creator has endowed us with inalienable rights was presented as a self-evident rational truth. The delegates of the Continental Congress later strengthened the references to God in Jefferson's text, partly for strategic reasons no doubt, to increase its acceptance among the citizens, but certainly also out of true conviction. Even if the other human rights thus do not follow from religious freedom in an organic fashion, religious freedom was nevertheless understood in the America of the late eighteenth century "as the 'first freedom,' as the most significant and important of the freedom rights, the one that formed the basis for the entire rest of the constitution."[25] In this modified form, Jellinek's thesis regarding the religious roots of the declaration of human rights can indeed be considered well confirmed for North America.

If this is true, this thesis has important implications for our understanding of modernity, of which human rights are incontestably a part. For it destabilizes the view that the development of human rights is part of a larger process that is sometimes referred to as the sacralization or charismatization of reason. For some authors who build on Max Weber,[26] the origin of human rights plays itself out exclusively in the context of a belief in rationality whose characteristic expression is Robespierre's quasi-religious "cult of reason," but which continued on in Marxism's pretenses toward a "scientific socialism."

Let us consult Max Weber himself at this point. However strongly he may have been influenced by Jellinek (and Troeltsch) in these matters, he nonetheless gave their arguments a particular twist by integrating them into his theory of occidental rationalism and its future. At first glance, Jellinek's thesis seems to fit perfectly into this framework, which is, of course, no coincidence, since Weber's own studies on Puritanism had been strongly inspired by Jellinek's book. The way in which the subject of human rights surfaces in Weber's *Soziologische Grundbegriffe* (*Basic Sociological Terms*) is nonetheless a bit jarring. Though few have noticed it, Weber refers to human rights in this context as "extreme rationalist fanaticism" and as the epitome of those ultimate ends or values, which, like "unusual acts of religious and charitable zeal," are barely understandable, if at all, for one who does not share them or who "radically abhors them."[27] Here Weber was surely thinking of the French Enlightenment version of human rights. But for him there was no contradiction between this emphasis on the rationalistic character of human rights and their religious roots, since he was interested precisely in the religious roots also of such "extremely rationalistic fanaticisms." For Weber, the Enlightenment, as a mere negation of tradition, would have been too weak to effect such an intensification of belief. In this sense, Jellinek's thesis anticipates Weber's views regarding the religious roots of the rational capitalist spirit.

In other contexts Weber relates human rights to the expansion of capitalism and the progress of bureaucratization. For him it is clear that "the demand for formal, legal equality and economic freedom of movement paved the way for the destruction of all specific foundations of patrimonial and feudal legal systems in favor of a cosmos of abstract norms, and thus indirectly of bureaucracy, but, on the other hand, favored the expansion of capitalism in a very specific way."[28] He draws a direct parallel between his own thesis that the "innerworldly asceticism" of the sects engendered the capitalist mindset and the rationally acting "*Berufsmensch*," and the claim that "human rights and basic rights [created] the precondition for the free play of the capitalist drive to valorize goods and persons." It is in this context that we encounter his remark concerning the charismatic transfiguration of reason as the core of the Enlightenment vision, that individual freedom must result in "the relatively best world" for all. This charisma of reason is "the last form that charisma took on in its fateful path." This sentence is of course ambiguous, since we do not know whether Weber was speaking here of the last form that has appeared up until now or the last form that will ever appear.

At this point it may seem as if Weber's understanding of the history of human rights is almost functionalist and materialist. But the opposite is true, as can be seen particularly in his writings on Russia.[29] There Weber is confronted with the direct influence of Jellinek on leading liberal Russian politicians of the time, such as Peter Struve, during a short phase around 1905, when it appeared that the idea of human rights could unite the various wings of a rebellious Russian intelligentsia. The Russian political situation awoke a passionate interest in Weber precisely because it concretely posed the question of whether civic freedoms and constitutionally certified rights could be established afresh under modern conditions, that is, in a world of advanced capitalism and a (more or less) modern bureaucracy. Unlike some optimistic Western liberals and (later) modernization theorists, he did not believe that these elements of modernity bore any particular affinity to democracy and freedom. But he analyzed the political and social forces in Russia in order to determine which side might successfully lead the fight against bureaucratic and Jacobinic centralism, against authoritarianism within the workers' movement, and in favor of the expansion of modern individualism. The Russian situation seemed to him a tragic one insofar as even a success of the liberal forces in the struggle for the right to vote would initially, by strengthening the peasantry, be more likely to hinder than advance the development toward Western individualism.

His pessimism did not apply only to Russia, however. According to Weber, both the ideal and the material preconditions for the belief in human rights have largely vanished throughout the world. Because of the Enlightenment, Weber believed, the religious convictions that Jellinek saw as the source of the political individualism of human rights can no longer arise as a mass phenomenon, at least not in their current form, while the "optimistic faith in the natural harmony of interests among free individuals" has been "destroyed forever by capitalism." This "[s]pecifically bourgeois individualism is now a thing of the past even amongst the classes of 'education and property' and will certainly not now capture the minds of the '*petite bourgeoisie*.'"[30]

Today, in the context of global capitalism, when the future of human rights is itself a question, the question of their origins is posed more sharply still. If Weber could imagine a capitalism of the future absent a belief in human rights, then how exactly should we understand the relationship between capitalist development in the past and the origins of human rights? How did Weber himself understand this relationship, given that he agrees not only with Jellinek's thesis regarding the Protestant origins of human rights but also with the view that freedom of contract was a functional prerequisite of capitalist economies? If one consults Weber's sociology of law in search of an answer, especially the long second section, "Forms of Creation of Rights," one finds astonishingly little about Jellinek, human rights, and rights to freedom, but rather extensive discussions of the freedom of contract, whose history, Weber claims, is much longer than the history of human rights à la Jellinek.[31] Weber emphasizes not only how common contracts were in premodern societies, which allows him to dispense with any simple model of social evolution based on the formula "from status to contract"; he also argues that the degree of freedom of contract is "naturally first of all a function of the expansion of markets."[32] The apparent contradiction in Weber's thought can probably only be resolved in the way suggested in an excellent essay by the French Weber expert Cathérine Colliot-Thélène.[33] According to her interpretation, Weber saw the moral individualism of Protestantism as a historical opportunity for the systematization of all subjective rights; however, the willingness to incorporate the idea of freedom of contract into this system required certain preconditions that were by no means the result of this moral individualism itself. The history of freedom of contract therefore antedates the origin of human rights and would continue even if the epoch of human rights irreversibly approached its end. As Wolfgang Schluchter points out in his essay "Rechtssoziologie als empirische Geltungstheorie" ("The Sociology of Law as an Empirical Theory of Validity"), the law would not be unaffected by this kind of uncoupling from moral universalism; it would certainly change its character, but by no means would those aspects that are necessary for a market-oriented economy completely disappear.[34]

But must we really see the future in such a gloomy light? As salutary as it is that we not simply trust in the stability of Western cultural traditions, neither need we unquestioningly accept the scattered and fragmentary arguments that Weber uses to justify his gloomy perspective.

New forms of religious conviction emerged during the twentieth century. The inherent tendencies of moral judgment promote universalistic moral orientations. The history of violence and human degradation has led in some places to a clearer awareness that the dignity of the person *must* be inviolable. Capitalism has experienced long phases of prosperity, and the construction of welfare states has demonstrated that divergent interests can be reconciled in a peaceful and just manner, even if it has not revived the belief in a natural harmony of interests. The expansion of education has led to the emergence of new milieus in which a belief in human rights is widespread. And Weber surely exaggerated the degree to which the lower-middle-class and the creative entrepreneurial spirit were in retreat. Weber unites his thesis about the religious roots of modern individualism and his diagnosis of the present in the form of a tragedy. In this construal, religious forces bring about a regime that takes the life out of these very forces.

If, however, Weber's historical prognoses—or, better, his sociological assumptions regarding the future—have not proven correct after the close of the twentieth century, then perhaps the relationship between our time and the origin of the belief in human rights and human dignity need not be a tragic one. Treating this relationship as contingent opens up more space for historical complexity and allows for more hope. Indeed, insofar as it has been confirmed, I believe that we should remove Jellinek's thesis from the Weberian framework. Weber assumed that the only alternative to cultural Protestantism, with its sometimes superficial and evolutionistic optimism about the future, was a heroic pessimism that defends liberal individualism against the tendencies threatening its existence together with a stark Kierkegaardian "either-or" in the choice between values. Troeltsch, by contrast, teaches us that another view of Christianity's potential role in the modern period is possible. One must think here of productive reinterpretations and creative continuations of the Judeo-Christian tradition, of new experiential foundations for a belief in individualistic values, and of new religious organizational structures, in which the characteristics of church, sect, and individual spirituality are bound together. This would result in a strengthening of Christianity as a support for the sacrality of each person against the depersonalizing forces of modernity. Here we would no longer be dealing with an overly easy compromise between religion and modernity, of the sort found in cultural Protestantism, or with an antithetic opposition, as in Weber and, with a reversed valuation, in large parts of Catholicism.

Liberating Jellinek's thesis from the Weberian framework also permits us to conceive of the belief in human rights as something other than a sacralization or charismatization of reason. The sacralization of reason touches only one side of human existence and does not affect all people in equal degree. But the belief in human dignity and human rights does affect all of us—and in equal degree. It sacralizes the young and the old, the intelligent and the mentally retarded. When we speak of the "charisma of reason," our attention is misdirected—toward Jacobinism and Bolshevism, two political worldviews whose human rights record is not particularly admirable. The belief in human rights rests in fact on a sacralization of the individual; it is inspired, or so I wish to claim, by a "sacralization" or a "charisma of the person." During the eighteenth century, of course, this charisma of the person was articulated within a framework of rationalistic convictions—in Jefferson and Kant, for example; today, however, we can and must separate these two components more clearly from each other. The historical process of the depersonalization of charisma can lead to a charismatization of the person.

What implications does this discussion have for the existence of a "Weber paradigm"? The considerations presented here display a certain distance from any "Weber orthodoxy." Max Weber should not be treated as a solitary figure, as often happens in sociology, especially outside of German-speaking areas. If we see him in the network of his German and non-German contemporaries, then Weber becomes perceivable as an imposing (perhaps even the most imposing) figure in the transition from German historicism of the nineteenth century to the modern social sciences—social sciences, though, that by no means withdraw from the treatment of normative questions, and that lend historical depth to the analysis of the present and proceed interdisciplinarily in a universal-comparative perspective. If this type of social science is what is signaled with the appeal to Max Weber, then the name "Weber paradigm" can serve well to characterize it.

Notes

1. Ernst Troeltsch, "Naturrecht und Humanität in der Weltpolitik," in Ernst Troeltsch, *Schriften zur Politik und Kulturphilosophie (1918–23)* (1923; Berlin: W. de Gruyter, 2002), pp. 493–512. The "editorial report" (pp. 477–90) and the editor's introduction to this volume (pp. 1–42) contain important information regarding the background of this text. For an English translation see Troeltsch, "The Ideas of Natural Law and Humanity in World Politics," in Otto Gierke, *Natural Law and the Theory of Society 1500–1800*, vol. 1 (Cambridge: Cambridge University Press, 1934), appendix I, pp. 201–22.

2. Thomas Mann, "Naturrecht und Humanität," in Thomas Mann, *Aufsätze, Reden, Essays*, vol. 3 (1923; Berlin: Aufbau Verlag, 1986), pp. 428–31; Friedrich Meinecke, *Die Idee der Staatsräson in der neueren Geschichte* (1924; Munich: Oldenbourg, 1957); Leo Strauss, *Naturrecht und Geschichte* (1956; Frankfurt: Suhrkamp, 1977), p. 1.

3. Troeltsch, *Schriften zur Politik*, p. 495; English translation in Troeltsch, "The Ideas of Natural Law and Humanity in World Politics," p. 203.

4. Troeltsch, *Schriften zur Politik*, p. 497; English: Troeltsch, "The Ideas of Natural Law and Humanity in World Politics," p. 204.

5. Troeltsch, *Schriften zur Politik*, p. 502; English: Troeltsch, "The Ideas of Natural Law and Humanity in World Politics," p. 210.

6. Cf. Hans Joas, *The Creativity of Action* (Chicago: University of Chicago Press, 1996), pp. 75–85.

7. Troeltsch, *Schriften zur Politik*, p. 504; English: Troeltsch, "The Ideas of Natural Law and Humanity in World Politics," p. 214.

8. Troeltsch, *Schriften zur Politik*, p. 510; English: Troeltsch, "The Ideas of Natural Law and Humanity in World Politics," p. 220 (emphasis mine).

9. Wilhelm Ihde, *Wegscheide 1789. Darstellung und Deutung eines Kreuzweges der Eu-*

ropäischen Geschichte (1941), cited in Wolfgang Schmale, *Archäologie der Grund- und Menschenrechte in der Frühen Neuzeit* (Munich: Oldenbourg, 1997), pp. 71ff.

10. Alain Touraine, *Critique de la modernité* (Paris: Fayard, 1992), pp. 70–74.

11. Gerhard Ritter, "Wesen und Wandlungen der Freiheitsidee im politischen Denken der Neuzeit," in Gerhard Ritter, *Das sittliche Problem der Macht* (Bern: Franke, 1948), pp. 105–38, quotation on p. 112.

12. Georg Jellinek, *Die Erklärung der Menschen-und Bürgerrechte. Ein Beitrag zur modernen Verfassungsgeschichte*, 3rd ed. (1895; Leipzig: Duncker & Humblot, 1919); English translation: Georg Jellinek, *The Declaration of the Rights of Man and of Citizens: A Contribution to Modern Constitutional History* (New York: Henry Holt, 1901).

13. Schmale, *Archäologie der Grund- und Menschenrechte*, p. 30.

14. Compare also the foreword by Jellinek's son Walter in ibid, pp. vi–vii.

15. Thus said Max Weber in a commemorative address for his deceased friend on the occasion of the wedding of one of Jellinek's daughters. See Marianne Weber, *Max Weber: A Biography*, trans. Harry Zohn (New Brunswick, NJ: Transaction Books, 1988), p. 476. Guenther Roth has repeatedly pointed to the importance of Jellinek for Weber. See Reinhard Bendix and Guenther Roth, *Scholarship and Partisanship* (Berkeley: University of California Press, 1980), pp. 308–10. The literature on the relationship between Jellinek and Weber (astonishingly) often does not even touch on the question at issue here. See Stefan Breuer, *Georg Jellinek und Max Weber. Von der sozialen zur soziologischen Staatslehre* (Baden-Baden: Nomos, 1999); Gangolf Hübinger, "Staatstheorie und Politik als Wissenschaft im Kaiserreich: Georg Jellinek, Otto Hintze, Max Weber," in Hans Maier et al., eds., *Politik, Philosophie, Praxis. Festschrift für Wilhelm Hennis* (Stuttgart: Klett-Cotta, 1988), pp. 143–61. In spite of its promising title, this also holds for Benjamin Nelson, "Max Weber, Ernst Troeltsch, Georg Jellinek as Comparative Historical Sociologists," in *Sociological Analysis* 36 (1975): 229–40.

16. Best known is the critique of Emile Boutmy, to which Jellinek responded at length. Compare their contributions in the collection by Roman Schnur, ed., *Zur Geschichte der Erklärung der Menschenrechte* (Darmstadt: Wissenschaftliche Buchgesellschaft, 1964): Boutmy, "Die Erklärung der Menschen- und Bürgerrechte und Georg Jellinek;" and Jellinek, "Antwort an Boutmy."

17. Marcel Gauchet, *Die Erklärung der Menschenrechte. Die Debatte um die bürgerlichen Freiheiten 1789* (1989; Reinbek: Rowohlt, 1991), p. 44.

18. In this I follow a suggestion of Ernst Troeltsch. Compare his review of Jellinek's *Ausgewählte Schriften und Reden* in *Zeitschrift für das Privat- und öffentliche Recht in der Gegenwart* 39 (1912): 273–78. For a similar view, see also Friedrich Wilhelm Graf, "Puritanische Sektenfreiheit versus lutherische Volkskirche. Zum Einfluß Georg Jellineks auf religionsdiagnostische Deutungsmuster Max Webers und Ernst Troeltschs," in *Zeitschrift für neuere Theologiegeschichte* 9 (2002): 42–69. Regarding Troeltsch's own position in this respect, the following source is interesting: Jean-Marc Tétaz, "Identité culturelle et réflexion critique. Le problème de l'universalité des droits de l'homme aux prises avec l'affirmation culturaliste. La stratégie argumentative d'Ernst Troeltsch," in *Etudes théologiques et religieuses* 74 (1999): 213–33.

19. These tensions in Jellinek's thought have been particularly intensely pursued in Jens Kersten, *Georg Jellinek und die klassische Staatslehre* (Tübingen: Mohr-Siebeck,

2000). He too sees Jellinek's theory of the state as an attempted "mediation between facticity and normativity" (p. 5) on historical and statist grounds. Compare also p. 410: "The theory of self-commitment wants to answer the question pertaining specifically to German constitutionalism: how a factual national will that is conceived as formally free of any legal commitment can include normativity." He admittedly accuses Jellinek's thought of being visibly anchored in the German tradition of the predemocratic power state, in the primacy of the state over the citizens, and of failing to understand the basic rights in the sense of a charter of a commonwealth of citizens (compare p. 427). In this, Kersten's proximity to contract-theoretical ideas and the French tradition becomes apparent. Because he does not deal with the intrinsic difficulties of these, his judgment concerning Jellinek is somewhat one-sided.

20. This is also the topic of Hans Joas, *Die Entstehung der Werte* (Frankfurt: Suhrkamp, 1997).

21. Hasso Hofmann, "Zur Herkunft der Menschenrechtserklärungen," in *Juristische Schulung* 28 (1988): pp. 841–48, quotation on p. 844.

22. Jellinek, *Die Erklärung der Menschen- und Bürgerrechte*, p. 57. English, Jellinek, *Declaration*, p. 77.

23. Ernst Troeltsch, *Die Soziallehren der christlichen Kirchen und Gruppen* (Tübingen: Mohr, 1912), p. 761.

24. Compare Dieter Grimm, "Europäisches Naturrecht und amerikanische Revolution," in *Ius commune. Veröffentlichungen des Max-Planck-Instituts für Europäische Rechtsgeschichte* 3 (1970), pp. 120–51.

25. Wolfgang Vögele, *Menschenwürde zwischen Recht und Theologie. Begründungen von Menschenrechten in der Perspektive öffentlicher Theologie* (Gütersloh: Kaiser, 2000), p. 103; Max Stackhouse, *Creeds, Society, and Human Rights: A Study in Three Cultures* (Grand Rapids, MI: W. B. Eerdmans, 1984), esp. pp. 70ff., speaks of a "liberal–Puritan synthesis" and its institutionalization in a presentation that, to a large extent, confirms Jellinek's work and—as an exception in American scholarship—also explicitly mentions him. An excellent study on Roger Williams is Timothy L. Hall, *Separating Church and State: Roger Williams and Religious Liberty* (Urbana: University of Illinois Press, 1998).

26. Günther Roth, *Politische Herrschaft und persönliche Freiheit* (Frankfurt: Suhrkamp, 1987), p. 147; Stefan Breuer (1993), "Das Charisma der Vernunft," in Winfried Gebhardt, Arnold Zingerle, and Michael Ebertz, eds., *Charisma. Theorie, Religion, Politik* (Berlin: W. de Gruyter, 1992), pp. 154–84. In his extensive study on Weber's sociology of law, our topic is touched on by Werner Gephardt, *Gesellschaftstheorie und Recht. Das Recht im soziologischen Diskurs der Moderne* (Frankfurt: Suhrkamp, 1993), pp. 565ff. Also worth mentioning: Jean Martin Ouédraogo, "Sociologie religieuse et modernité politique chez Max Weber," in *Revue européenne des sciences sociales* 34 (1996): 24–49. Winfried Brugger has dealt with Max Weber especially thoroughly in the context of the human rights discussion in his works: *Menschenrechtsethos und Verantwortungspolitik. Max Webers Beitrag zur Analyse und Begründung der Menschenrechte* (Freiburg: Alber, 1980); and "Sozialwissenschaftliche Analyse und menschenrechtliches Begründungsdenken. Eine Skizze im Anschluß an Max Webers Werk," in *Rechtstheorie* 11 (1980): 356–77. Brugger's emphasis on the constitutive role of experiences of injustice is particularly interesting. Compare here also:

Matthias König, *Menschenrechte bei Durkheim und Weber* (Frankfurt: Campus, 2002), pp. 78–138.

27. Max Weber, *Economy and Society: An Outline of Interpretive Sociology* (1921–22; Berkeley: University of California Press, 1978), p. 6; German: Max Weber, *Wirtschaft und Gesellschaft* (Tübingen: J. C. B. Mohr, 1922), p. 2.

28. Ibid., p. 1209; German: Weber, *Wirtschaft und Gesellschaft*, p. 817.

29. Max Weber, *Political Writings*, ed. Peter Lassman, trans. Ronald Speirs (Cambridge: Cambridge University Press, 1994), pp. 29–74; German: Max Weber, *Gesammelte politische Schriften* (1921; Tübingen: J. C. B. Mohr, 1980), pp. 33–111. On Weber's Russian writings, compare Richard Pipes, "Max Weber und Rußland," in *Außenpolitik* 6 (1955): 627–39; Gordon Wells and Peter Baehr, editors' introduction in Wells and Baehr, eds., *Max Weber: The Russian Revolution* (Ithaca, NY: Cornell University Press, 1995), pp. 1–39; Wolfgang Mommsen, "Einleitung," in Max Weber, *Zur Russischen Revolution von 1905* (Tübingen: J. C. B. Mohr, 1989), pp. 1–54. On Struve and Jellinek, compare Richard Pipes, *Struve, Liberal on the Left, 1870–1905* (Cambridge, MA: Harvard University Press), esp. pp. 302ff.

30. Weber, *Political Writings*, p. 46; German: Weber, *Politische Schriften*, pp. 42ff.

31. Weber, *Economy and Society*, pp. 666–752; German: Weber, *Wirtschaft und Gesellschaft*, pp. 412–55.

32. [Here, we have preferred our own translation. The corresponding passage may be found in Weber, *Economy and Society*, p. 668—Eds.] German: *Wirtschaft und Gesellschaft*, p. 413.

33. Cathérine Colliot-Thélène, "Les modes de justification des droits subjectifs," in Colliot-Thélène, *Etudes wéberiennes. Rationalités, histoires, droits* (Paris: Presses Universitaires de France, 2001), pp. 259–78. In this, she leans on the thorough thesis by Romain Melot, *La Notion de droit subjectif dans l'oeuvre de Max Weber* (Paris: Mémoire de DEA, Université de Paris I Sorbonne, 2000).

34. Wolfgang Schluchter, "Rechtssoziologie als empirische Geltungstheorie," in Schluchter, *Individualismus, Verantwortungsethik und Vielfalt* (Weilerswist: Velbrück, 2000), pp. 59–85.

About the Contributors

Julia Adams is professor of sociology at Yale University. Her areas of research and teaching interest include historical sociology, gender and family, social theory, and early modern European politics. With Elisabeth S. Clemens and Ann Shola Orloff, she edited *Remaking Modernity: Politics, History, and Sociology* (2004).

Charles Camic is Martindale-Bascom Professor of Sociology in the Department of Sociology and in the Science, Technology, and Society Program at the University of Wisconsin-Madison. From 1999 to 2003, he was co-editor of the *American Sociological Review*. He has published widely on the development of American sociological thought between 1890 and 1940.

Randall Collins is professor of sociology at the University of Pennsylvania. His most recent books include *The Sociology of Philosophies* (1998) and *Interaction Ritual Chains* (2004).

Mustafa Emirbayer teaches sociology at the University of Wisconsin at Madison. He has written extensively on topics in both classical and contemporary social theory, including culture and social networks, relational analysis, agency and action theory, Durkheim and historical sociology, and pragmatism.

Harvey Goldman is professor and chair, Department of Sociology, and adjunct professor, Department of Political Science, at the University of California, San Diego. He is the author of two books on Max Weber and Thomas Mann, and has also published articles on ancient philosophy, contemporary French intellectuals, and problems of reflexivity, all in the area of sociology of knowledge and intellectuals.

Philip S. Gorski is professor of sociology at Yale University. He is the author of *The Disciplinary Revolution: Calvinism and the Rise of the State in Early Modern Europe* (2003).

Hans Joas is director of the Max Weber Center for Advanced Cultural and Social Studies, Erfurt, Germany, and professor of sociology and social thought at the University of Chicago. Among his publications are *G. H. Mead: A Contemporary Re-examination of His Thought* (1985/1997); *Social Action and Human Nature* (with Axel Honneth) (1988); *Pragmatism and Social Theory* (1993); *The Creativity of Action* (1996); *The Genesis of Values* (2000); and *War and Modernity* (2003).

Duncan Kennedy is the Carter Professor of General Jurisprudence at Harvard Law School. He teaches torts, housing law, law and development, and legal theory. He has written extensively on the history of Western legal thought. His most recent book is *A Critique of Adjudication [fin de siècle]* (1997).

Hans G. Kippenberg, chair for Theory and History of Religions at the University of Bremen, Germany, from 1989 to 2004, is a fellow of the Max-Weber-Kolleg, Erfurt, Germany. He is the author of *Discovering Religious History in the Modern Age* (2002). He was in charge of the section "Religion" for the new critical German edition of Max Weber's *Wirtschaft und Gesellschaft*, published under the title *Religiöse Gemeinschaften, MWG* I 22-2 (2001). Together with Martin Riesebrodt, he edited *Webers "Religionssystematik"* (2001).

Donald N. Levine is the Peter B. Ritzma Professor of Sociology at the University of Chicago. He has been editor of the *Heritage of Sociology* series since 1988 and was chair of the ASA Theory Section in 1996–97. His recent publications include *Visions of the Sociological Tradition* (1995); a revised edition of *Greater Ethiopia: The Evolution of a Multiethnic Society* (2000); and *Powers of the Mind: The Reinvention of Liberal Learning* (2005).

Wolfgang J. Mommsen was professor of modern and contemporary history at the University of Düsseldorf, Germany. From 1977 to 1985, he was director of the German Historical Institute in London. His books include *Max Weber and German Politics, 1890–1920* (1959/1974); *The Age of Bureaucracy: Perspectives on the Political Sociology of Max Weber* (1974); and *Max Weber and His Contemporaries* (edited with Jurgen Osterhammel) (1987). He died in August of 2004.

Guenther Roth has published on Max Weber's oeuvre and impact for forty-five years. His publications range from *The Social Democrats in Imperial Germany: A Study in Working-Class Isolation and National Integration* (1963) to *Max Weber's Anglo-German Family History 1800–1950* (2001, in German). He edited, with Claus Wittich, Max Weber's *Economy and Society* (1968/1978), and, with Hartmut Lehmann, *Weber's "Protestant Ethic": Origins, Evidence, Contexts* (1993). He retired from Columbia University in 1997.

Richard Swedberg is professor of sociology at Cornell University. His work is primarily in the field of economic sociology. He is the author of *Max We-*

ber and the Idea of Economic Sociology (1998) and the *Max Weber Dictionary* (2005).

Regina Titunik is associate professor of political science at the University of Hawaii at Hilo. She has written several articles on Max Weber's political thought and made use of Weberian concepts in writings on gender integration in the military.

David M. Trubek is Voss-Bascom Professor of Law and senior fellow of the University of Wisconsin's Center for World Affairs and the Global Economy. He has served as a trustee of the Law and Society Association and of the Research Committee on the Sociology of Law of the International Sociological Association. He has published on such subjects as Max Weber's sociology of law, the role of law in development, the social role of the legal profession, human rights, European integration, the governance of work and welfare in a new economy, civil litigation, social theory, critical legal studies, and new approaches to governance and the emergence of "post-regulatory" law.

Erik Olin Wright is Vilas Distinguished Professor of Sociology at the University of Wisconsin. His academic work has been centrally concerned with reconstructing the Marxist tradition of social theory and research in ways that attempt to make it more relevant to contemporary concerns and more cogent as a scientific framework of analysis. His recent books include *Interrogating Inequality* (1994); *Class Counts: Comparative Studies in Class Analysis* (1997); and *Deepening Democracy: Institutional Innovations in Empowered Participatory Governance* (with Archon Fung) (2003).

Index

Abbott, Andrew, 3, 266n80

action: affectual/emotional action, 7, 60, 90, 109, 111, 112–13, 185–93; caused vs. deliberate, 108; collective class action, 206, 212, 214–16, 217, 230n17, 232n41; communal action, 174–75, 176; communicative action, 114; correct vs. rational, 173; economic action, 21, 112, 128, 129–30, 135; habitual action, 7, 109, 111, 112, 144, 186, 192–98, 203n71, 248; ideal ends of, 7, 14, 25n11, 103–4, 137; material ends of, 7, 14, 19, 25n11, 103–4, 129–30, 137, 208, 212–14, 217; meaningfulness of, 101–2, 106, 113, 114, 125n59, 129, 135, 172–73, 187, 192, 193, 212; nonrational action, 7, 9, 22, 106, 110, 124n49, 173, 186–92, 197–98, 200n18, 254, 322, 341, 342, 345, 347, 348–49, 350, 352; rational action, 3, 4, 7, 14, 18, 19, 21, 22, 25n11, 59–61, 90, 102, 103–4, 105, 106, 107–8, 109–20, 129, 172–73, 185–99, 327–28; rational-choice theory, 4, 14, 25n11, 26n14, 31, 263n59, 268, 271–72, 290; religious action, 137; taxonomy of types of, 21, 108–15; traditional action, 60, 109, 185, 186, 192–96, 197; and the unconscious, 113. *See also* methodological individualism; rationality

Adams, Julia, 266n80

Addams, Jane, 44n15

Adler, Felix, 44n15

"Agrarian Conditions in Antiquity" (Agrarverhältnisse im Altertum), 77, 81, 228n5

Alexander, Jeffrey C., 125n64

alienation, 119, 231n29, 235n72

animism, 168

Antwerp, Bunge family in, 33, 34–35

aristocracies, 138, 151, 154

Aristotle, 13, 124n55, 146, 159n23, 189, 257n25; on emotions, 194; on habit, 111, 194

Aron, Raymond, 156

art, 345, 347, 349, 350

artisans, 138–39

asceticism, 121n10, 139, 170, 177, 199n16; ascetic calling, 49, 52–53, 54–59, 66n12, 67n23, 68n34, 229n8, 345, 347, 349; and bureaucratization, 283–87, 289; and capitalism, 141n2, 188, 229n8, 336, 375; in Protestantism, 49, 52–53, 56, 141n2, 188, 229n8, 283–87, 289

Atiyah, P. S., 359

Augustine, St., 51

Austen, Jane: *Pride and Prejudice,* 264n66

Austria, 289

Baier, Horst, 72

Ballhausen, Robert Lucius von, 34

Baptists, 138, 373

Barbalet, J. M., 188, 189

Barthes, Roland, 258n30

Baumgarten, Fritz, 33

Baumgarten, Hermann, 33

Baumgarten, Otto, 35

Bavaria, 274, 289

Bebel, August, 303

Bendix, Reinhard, 42n2, 45n18, 120n6, 140, 231n31, 232n41; *Max Weber,* 198

Bendix, Richard, 125n66

Benecke, Ernest Wilhelm, 33

Benecke, Friedrich Wilhelm, 33

The authorized representative in the EU for product safety and compliance is:
Mare Nostrum Group
B.V Doelen 72
4831 GR Breda
The Netherlands